I0890001

A SHORT HISTORY OF THE SARACENS

Written by a barrister and Muslim who also authored the well-known book *The Spirit of Islam,* this is an unusual and indispensable history of the Saracens, a people who left behind them a great legacy and incredible intellectual wealth.

The history of the Saracens is also the history of the spread of Islam. The work chronicles the rise and decline of Saracen power and of the economic, social and intellectual development of the Arab nations.

COURT OF LIONS, ALHAMBRA, GRANADA.

A SHORT HISTORY OF THE SARACENS

Ameer Ali

Routledge
Taylor & Francis Group
LONDON AND NEW YORK

First published in 2004 by
Kegan Paul International

This edition first published in 2010 by
Routledge
2 Park Square, Milton Park, Abingdon, Oxfordshire OX14 4RN

Simultaneously published in the USA and Canada
by Routledge
711 Third Avenue, New York, NY 10017

First issued in paperback 2014

Routledge is an imprint of the Taylor & Francis Group, an informa business

British Library Cataloguing in Publication Data
A catalogue record for this book is available from the British Library

ISBN 13: 978-0-7103-0918-1 (hbk)
ISBN 13: 978-0-415-76020-1 (pbk)

Publisher's Note
The publisher has gone to great lengths to ensure the quality of this reprint but points out that some imperfections in the original copies may be apparent. The publisher has made every effort to contact original copyright holders and would welcome correspondence from those they have been unable to trace.

PREFACE TO 1927 EDITION

In the following pages I have attempted to give concisely the story of one of the most interesting periods in the annals of the world. In its extent and its political and cultural influence the expansion of the Arab race can be likened only to that of the Roman. But whilst the Roman took centuries to attain dominance the Arab won his place in as many decades. How an army, almost always overmatched in numbers, collected from a congeries of warring tribes divided by fierce tribal jealousies, who had never before united in common enterprise, shattered the seasoned cohorts of Chosroes and the disciplined and well-armed legions of Caesar is, as Professor Noldeke rightly remarks, a marvel. These unlettered soldiers of the desert re-lit the torch of knowledge and gave an impetus to civilisation which, without exaggeration, has few parallels in the history of mankind. The story of their work and achievements should be an inspiration to their descendants; and not only to them but to all nationalities who follow the Faith of Islâm. For a "History of the Saracens" is a record of the establishment of Islâm as a world-religion.

A brief survey of the present position of the countries which at the period under review in this work formed part of the Islamic Empire may not be without interest. Ibn Saûd, the ruler of Nejd, home of the *Ikhwân*, the Covenanters of Islâm, has expelled from Hijaz the newly created King Husain, and has incorporated it with his dominions.

In Yemen, Imâm Yahya is dominant; Transjordania and Mesopotamia are in the possession of the sons of the ex-King of Hijaz; a new Turkey has arisen from the ashes of the old with a government animated by new ideals. It has signalised its re-entry into the comity of free nations by drastic changes in its institutions.

*

Persia, the heritage of Shah Abbâs the Great, where the Caliphs reigned supreme for centuries, is still on the march to win back her place among the free nations of the world. The Kajârs, after a chequered rule of nearly 200 years, have now made room for a new dynasty. The present sovereign, Shah Rizâ Khan Pahlawi, who has established himself on the throne of Irân, is a man of strong character and liberal ideas, and his reign offers a hopeful augury for the progress and development of the land to which many of the countries of the middle east owed their culture. Afghanistan, where the conqueror Mahmûd of Ghazni, "The Right Hand" of the Caliph, once reigned, under the guidance and rulership of a young, energetic and patriotic sovereign of the Barukzye dynasty, is making gallant efforts to lift the dead weight which Mongol and Uzbeg had left in mid-Asia. Egypt, made famous by the magnificent patronage of the arts and sciences by al-Muiz, has now regained her freedom, and is ruled by a constitutional government under a limited monarchy, which holds out the promise of a prosperous development. Ifrikia and Maghrib-ul-Aksa, the empire of the brilliant Yusuf-ibn-Tashfin, the patron of Averroes, like the Syria of Saladin, are either held or dominated by France. Transoxiana, with the birthplace of Avicenna and of Alfarabi, is under the heel of the Bolshevist.

This work is not a mere chronicle of wars and conquests, or the rise and fall of dynasties. It is a record of the copious contributions made by the Saracenic race under the flag of Islâm, to human knowledge in all departments of science and literature; of their marvellous system of administration; of their economic and cultural development and the remarkable position held by women in the social and legal system of Islâm. The story of the havoc, carnage and savagery wrought by the Crusaders and the Mongols is told from the records of the people who suffered.

AMEER ALI.

December 1926.

PREFACE

Of all the older nations that have carried their arms across vast continents, that have left ineffaceable marks of their achievements on the pages of history, and enriched the world of thought by their discoveries and speculations, the Saracens stand to us the closest in time. Modern Europe is still working with the legacy they left behind, with the intellectual wealth they stored for their successors. It is, therefore, a matter of regret that in the West a knowledge of their history should be more or less confined to specialists; whilst in India, a country which was at one time peculiarly subject to the influence of their civilisation, it should be almost unknown. Much of this no doubt is due to the absence of a proper work on the subject. To arrest attention, to enlist sympathy, to evoke interest, something more is needed than a bare narration of wars and conquests, more especially in the case of a people whose name, unlike the Romans and Greeks, has not been made familiar from childhood. In order to prove attractive and interesting, a history of the Saracens should contain not merely a description of their military successes, but also tell us something of their inner life and their social and economic development. Such a work, by tracing the affinity of modern civilisation to theirs, might serve to remove many prejudices and some of the bitterness engendered by the conflict and quarrels of centuries.

The volume I now offer to the public was undertaken with the object of supplying the want of a history modelled on the above lines. I have endeavoured to describe in these pages the ethical and moral movement that led to the sudden uprise and overflow of the Saracenic race and their extraordinary growth and expansion, to depict the remarkable process of evolution by which a patriarchal rule developed into one of the most civilised systems of government, the machinery of their administration, the state of their culture in all its phases, the condition of the people, the position of their women, their mode of life, and finally the causes which brought about the collapse of their wonderful civilisation. The work was originally designed to be of a more compendious character, but the courtesy of my publishers has enabled me to give effect to the suggestion of competent scholars, some especially interested in University education in India, and thus to enlarge its scope without impairing its general conciseness. Considering that it has been carried through the press in the midst of heavy judicial duties, I can hardly expect it to be free from flaws. Besides, the absence of libraries such as exist in London, Paris, and other great cities in Europe render literary undertakings of every kind in the East peculiarly difficult. I trust, therefore, that allowance will be made for any shortcomings that may be found in the book. I venture, however, to hope that it may be the means of extending among the two great communities of India a knowledge of the civilisation and culture of Western Asia in the Middle Ages. To my mind, such a knowledge is of extreme importance, for whilst it may teach the Moslem the value of the opportunity for social and intellectual regeneration afforded by a liberal and impartial government, it cannot fail to be of profit also to others, in widening their sympathies. The story of the Saracens, like those of many other people, tells us that although each community must work out its regeneration according to its individual genius, yet none can afford to wrap itself in the mantle of a dead Past without the fatal certainty of extinction. It teaches us that moral worth, scholarship, and intellectual attainments, however lightly, owing to factitious causes, they may be thought of for a while, must in time exercise their legitimate influence on society; that self-restraint and steadiness of purpose are qualities which cannot be over-rated.

The racial pride which caused the Saracen to look down on conquered nations, his failure to recognise that mere justice never won the affection of subject peoples, that to achieve this something more was needed—the sympathy of a Mâmûn, the large-heartedness of a Nâsir—that neither nations nor individuals lose by generous, courteous, and liberal dealing—the encouragement in later times of intrigue, sycophancy, and unworthiness with such disastrous results to the Arab's power and greatness—may all be ascribed to one cause. History, which comes down to us "rich with the spoils of time," had no lesson for him. The Saracen's genius for government was intuitive, inborn, self-taught—not acquired. With an overweening sense of pride in his race and creed, for which allowance can easily be made, he stalked through the world feeling, although not proclaiming, that he was an Arab citizen, a member of a great and powerful commonwealth. There was no critical Schopenhauer to laugh him to scorn. Even the tactless treatment of the barbarian tribesmen of Northern Spain must be ascribed to the same cause. The great Hâjib could weep that the lesson of conciliation came too late.

Gibbon's sketch of the rise and progress of the Arab power, in spite of the paucity of the materials at his command, will always remain a grand masterpiece of historical effort. The other works in the English language require no specific notice; each, in its own way, is admirable, and fulfils a purpose in the economy of literature. But there are some in the continental languages which cannot be passed over without a distinct recognition from the students of history. To Caussin de Perceval, Dozy, Des Vergers, de Slane, Fresnel, Sédillot, Berchem, von Hammer, von Kremer, Wustenfeld, Noldeke, Amari, among many others almost equally distinguished, the world of letters owes a special debt of gratitude.

I have dealt very briefly with the pre-Islamite history of the Arabs, and the work and ministry of the Arabian Prophet. More space has been devoted to the Republic. The Ommeyade and Abbasside periods have, I hope, been treated with sufficient fulness to make the account interesting without being wearisome. It was somewhat difficult to compress the story of the eight centuries during which the Saracens held Spain, within about a hundred pages; and yet the reader will, I trust, find that nothing of importance has been omitted. The account of the Saracens in Northern Africa occupies a very small compass, and naturally so, for the glory of the Fatimides expired with them, and their culture sunk into the sands under the misrule of the later Mamelukes. To each period is attached in the shape of a Retrospect a description of the intellectual, social, and economic condition of the people, of their manners and customs, and their system of administration.

AMEER ALI.

Daylesford, Sunningdale,
October 1898.

N.B.—The letter ث (pronounced by the Arab with a lisp like *th* in *thin*), to a non-Arab conveys a sound almost identical with *s* in *sîn*, and he accordingly pronounces it as such. Nor, unless an Arabic scholar, does he perceive any difference between ث, س (*sîn*) or ص (*sâd*). He pronounces them all alike. Similarly ذ (*zâl*), ز (*zay*), ض (*zâd*—pronounced by the Arab something like *dhâd*), and ظ (*zôi*) convey to the non-Arab almost identical sounds; certainly he cannot help pronouncing them identically. He also perceives no difference between ت (soft *t*) and ط (*tôi*), or between the hard aspirate ح (in Ahmed, Mohammed, Mahmûd, etc.) and the softer ه used in Hârûn.

I have therefore not attempted to differentiate these letters by dots or commas, which, however useful for purposes of translation into Arabic, Persian, Turkish or Urdu, is only bewildering to a reader unacquainted with the Arabic alphabet and pronunciation. I have given the words generally as pronounced by non-Arabs. In some instances I have indicated both forms, as in the case of Harsama (with a ث), Hazramaut (with a *zâd*), etc. With regard to Ibn ul-Athîr, which is spelt with a ث, I have adhered to the shape it has assumed in works in the European languages.

The ordinary *fatha* I have represented by *a* (pronounced as *u* in "*cut*" or "*but*"), excepting in such words as are now commonly written in English with an *e*, as Seljûk (pronounced Saljûk), Merwân (pronounced Marwân), etc.; the ordinary *zamma* by *u*, pronounced like *u* in "*pull*," as *Buldân*; the ordinary *kasra* with the letter *i*, as in *Misr*. *Aliph* with the *fatha* is represented by *â*, as in "had"; Aliph with the *zamma*, by *u* as in Abd *ul*-Muttalib; with a *kasra* by *i* as in Ibn Ab*i*'l Jawâri. *Waw* (with a *zamma*) by *o* and sometimes by *ô*. Although, like Kûfa and several other words, the last syllables in Mahmûd, Hârûn and Mamûn are spelt with a *waw*, to have represented them by an *o* or *ô* would have conveyed a wholly wrong notion of the pronunciation, which is like *oo*; I have, therefore, used *û* to represent *waw* in such words. *Waw* with a *fatha* I have represented by *ou*, as in Moudûd. *Yâ* with a *kasra*, when used in the middle of a word, I have represented by *î*, as in Aarîsh. But in Ameer I have kept the classical and time-honoured *ee*. *Yâ* with a *fatha*, similarly situated, by *ai* as in Zaid. *Yâ* with a *fatha* at the beginning of a word is represented by *ye*, as in Yezîd; with a *zamma* by *yu*, as in Yusuf. Excepting such words as are commonly known to be spelt with an *ain* (ع), as *Abd* in Abdul Malik, Abdur

Rahmân, Arab, Abbâs, Azîz, etc., I have tried to convey the slightly prolonged guttural sound of that peculiar letter (when with *fatha*) by *aa* as in *aaskar*. In Mustaîn, however, the *ain* (with the *fatha*) is represented with one *a* in order to avoid the ugliness of *aaî*. I have not attempted, however, to distinguish in any particular way the *ain* with a *zamma*, or *kasra*, but the Arabic scholar knows that Mutasim, Mutazid, Mutamid, Muiz, Muâz, Muâwiyeh, etc., are spelt with an *ain* where the sound is represented by *u*. Similarly Imâd, Ilm, etc., begin with *ain* (with *kasra*); whilst Itibâr, Itimâd, etc., begin with *aliph* and *ain*. With regard to names which have become familiar in certain garbs I have made no alteration, such as Omar, Abdullâh, Basra (spelt with a *sâd*), etc. *Ghain* (غ) is represented by *gh*, but ق I have not attempted to differentiate from *k*. The common *g* (the Persian *gâf*) and *p* have no place in the Arabic alphabet, and therefore the Persian *g* and *p* are transformed in Arabic into *k* and *b* or *ph* (*f*), as in Atâbek and Isphahân. خ is represented by *kh*.

The *Aliph* in certain words, like Târick (spelt with a ط and ق), Wâdi, Wâris (spelt with a ث at the end), etc., is always pronounced by the Hijâzian Arabs, Persians, and other Westerns like *au* in Maurice. The *l* of *al* when occurring before certain letters (technically called *shamsiêh*) is assimilated with them in sound, as *ash-Shams*, *ad-dîn*, *ar-Razâ*, *as-Salât*, etc.

In the accentuation of geographical names I have followed the *Mujam ul-Buldân*. Generally, however, I have adhered to the sound rather than the letter, and therefore I hardly think there is absolute uniformity throughout. Titles and surnames are given in italics.

⁂ In the transliteration of the word "Mutazila" I have followed in this issue the *Lisân-ul-Arab*.

CONTENTS

CHAPTER VI

CHAPTER VII

THE OMMEYADES (THE HARBITE BRANCH)

CHAPTER VIII

CHAPTER IX

CHAPTER X

CHAPTER XI

CHAPTER XII

CHAPTER XIII

CHAPTER XIV

RETROSPECT

CHAPTER XV

THE ABBASSIDES—SAFFÂH AND MANSÛR

CHAPTER XVI

CHAPTER XVII

CHAPTER XVIII

CHAPTER XIX

CHAPTER XX

CHAPTER XXIII

CHAPTER XXIV

RETROSPECT

CHAPTER XXV

RETROSPECT (*continued*)

CHAPTER XXVI

THE SARACENS OF SPAIN—THE OMMEYADES

CHAPTER XXX

CHAPTER XXXI

[illegible]

CHAPTER XXXII

THE SARACENS IN AFRICA

LIST OF ILLUSTRATIONS AND MAPS

ILLUSTRATIONS

MAPS

LIST OF GENEALOGICAL TABLES

A SHORT HISTORY OF

THE SARACENS

CHAPTER I

Arabia—Its Geographical and Physical Condition—The Ancient Arabs.

ARABIA is a large tract of country in the south-west of Asia. It is bounded on the north by the Syrian Desert; on the east by the Persian Gulf; on the south by the Indian Ocean; and on the west by the Red Sea. This vast region, which embraces an area twice the size of France at the height of her greatness, is divided into several parts or provinces, differing more or less from each other in the character of their soil, their climate, and the appearance of the people. Arabia.

To the north, lies the hilly portion, which in olden times was inhabited by the Edomites and the Midianites of the Hebrew Testament. Then comes Hijâz proper, containing the famous city of Medîna, called in ancient times Yathreb; Mecca, the birth-place of the Arabian Prophet, and the port of Jeddah, the landing-place of the pilgrims of Islâm. Hijâz stretches from north to south between the Red Sea and the chain of mountains which runs down from the Isthmus of Suez to the Indian

Ocean. The south-west corner of the Peninsula is named Yemen. The low-lying lands of Hijâz and Yemen are called the Tihâma, which name is sometimes given to the southern part of Hijâz. Hadhramaut lies to the east of Yemen, bordering the Indian Ocean, while far away eastward lies, resting on the Gulf of the same name, Oman. The high table-land which stretches from the mountains of Hijâz eastward to the desert of al-Ahsa and al-Bahrain on the Persian Gulf, is called Nejd, a vast plateau with deserts and mountain gorges interspersed with green plantations which are called oases, forming so many havens of safety in the desert. Hijâz is now held by an independent Arab king. Nejd is ruled by the Abû Saûd family; whilst Oman belongs to the Sultan of Muscat.

This vast tract has no navigable rivers; the rivulets which exist only here and there make the soil fertile. The rainfall is scanty, and the country generally is arid and sterile, except where water is found in any sufficient quantity. But wherever water exists, the fertility is remarkable. The high lands of Yemen, called Jibâl ul-Yemen, rise almost to the height of Mont Blanc, and are split up into numbers of wide and fertile valleys, where the coffee and the indigo plant, the date-palm, and vegetables and fruit trees of all kinds, are grown. The climate is mild, and in the winter frost is by no means uncommon. There are two wet seasons, one in spring and the other in autumn.

Hijâz is a broken country, especially round about Mecca, which is fifty miles from the shores of the Red Sea, and some thirty from the granite heaps of Jabl Kora. Here rugged rocks reflecting the hot sun in all its fierceness, barren valleys with little herbage from which the flocks gather a scanty subsistence, and dry torrent-beds form the chief features of the country. Eastward of this gaunt and arid country there lies a smiling tract covered with vegetation and shady trees, where apples and figs, pomegranates, peaches, and grapes grow in abundance. This is Tâyef.

Arabia has at various times been peopled by various races. The earliest settlers are said to have been of the same stock as the ancient Chaldæans. They attained great civilisation, the remains of which are still observable in Southern Arabia, and are supposed even to have extended their power into Egypt and Mesopotamia. They seem to have built huge palaces and temples; and the famous tanks which still exist near Aden are ascribed to them. The Ancient Arabs

These ancient people were destroyed by a Semitic tribe which, issuing from some country towards the east of the Euphrates, settled in Yemen and parts of Hadhramaut. They are said to have been the descendants of Kahtân, also called Joktan, one of whose sons, YAREB, gave his name to the country and the people. The sovereigns of this dynasty were called Sabæan after Yareb's grandson Abdus Shams ("servant of the sun"), surnamed SABA. The Kahtanite kings were great conquerors and builders of cities, and their dominion in Yemen and other parts of Arabia continued so late as the seventh century of the Christian era. The Kahtanites.

The last of the settlers are called Ishmaelites. Ishmael or Ismâil, as he is called by the Arabs, was a son of Abraham, the great patriarch of the Jews. He settled near Mecca, and his descendants peopled Hijâz and became in fact the founders of Arabian greatness. Ishmael is said to have erected the Kaaba, a place of worship regarded with veneration from the earliest times by the Arabs, and which is now the holiest place in the Moslem world. In it is the famous Black Stone. The Ishmaelites.

The Bedouins.

The people of Arabia have always been divided into two classes, viz. "the dwellers of cities," and "the dwellers of the desert,"—the Bedouins. These latter live in tents, and with their families and flocks roam over the deserts and table-lands in search of pasturage.

Northern and Central Arabia does not appear to have been at any time under foreign rule. In Yemen alone, the Abyssinians exercised a short-lived dominion until expelled by an Arab chief named Saif, son of Zu'l-yezen, with the assistance of the King of Persia. From that time forward, for nearly a century or more, Yemen Proper was ruled by a Persian Viceroy, called a *Marzbân*.

Their Religion.

The Jews and Christians, large numbers of whom were settled in Arabia, followed their own religions. But the Arabs were mostly worshippers of idols and stars. Each city, like each tribe, had its own separate gods and goddesses, its separate temples and forms of worship. In Mecca, which was considered the centre of their national life, a sort of Rome or Benares, there were ranged in the holy temple of the Kaaba 360 idols representing all the gods and goddesses whom the Arabs worshipped. Even human sacrifices were not infrequent.

The people who inhabited this vast region, especially those who wandered in the desert which lay to the west of the Euphrates, were called by the Greeks and Romans, *Saraceni*, and this is the name by which they were known in the West when they issued from their homes to conquer the world.[1]

The word Saraceni is supposed to be derived either from *Sahara* = desert, and *nashîn* = dwellers; or from *Sharkiin*, Eastern,—*Shark*, in Arabic, meaning east.

[1] See Reinaud's *Invasion des Sarrazins* (1836), p. 229.

CHAPTER II

Early History—Kossay—Abdul Muttalib—The Abyssinian Attack—The Birth of Mohammed—His Ministry—The Hegira.

Early History.

OUR knowledge of the ancient history of Arabia is derived chiefly from the Koran, which contains much of the old folk-lore of the country, and from the traditions which the Arabs at all times were in the habit of handing down from father to son. These traditions were collected with great care and industry by the Arab historians of the eighth and succeeding centuries of the Christian era. The inscriptions which have been discovered in the south of Yemen, so far as they have been deciphered, largely verify our knowledge of the past as derived from the Koran and the traditions.

The Koraish.

The people in whose history and fortunes we are chiefly interested are the Arabs of Hijâz and Yemen, who made themselves so famous in the Middle Ages. The principal tribe among the former was that of the Koraish, who were descended from Fihr, surnamed *Koraish*, which in ancient Arabic means a merchant. Fihr lived in the third century of the Christian era. He was descended from Maad, son of Adnân, a descendant of Ishmael. The Koraish have always been proud of their ancestry and their high position among the other tribes, and are considered as the noblest section of the Arabs.

Kossay.

In the fifth century, Kossay, a descendant of Fihr, made himself master of Mecca, and gradually of the whole of Hijâz. Mecca was, until his time, a scattered village, consisting chiefly of huts and tents. Kossay rebuilt the Kaaba, erected for himself a palace in which the principal chamber was used as the Council-hall[1] of the people, for the transaction of public business; and made the Koraish live in houses of stone built round the Temple. He also made rules for the proper government of the people, for raising taxes and supplying food and water to the pilgrims who came from many parts of Arabia to worship at the temple.

Abd ud-Dâr.

Kossay died about the year 480 A.C., and was succeeded by his son Abd ud-Dâr. Upon Abd ud-Dâr's death a dispute broke out among his grandsons and the sons of his brother Abd Manâf about the succession to the rulership of Mecca. This dispute was settled by a division of authority. The administration of the water supply of Mecca and the raising of taxes were entrusted to Abd ush-Shams, a son of Abd Manâf; whilst the guardianship of the Kaaba, of the Council-chamber, and of the Military Standard, was given to the grandsons of Abd ud-Dâr.

Hâshim. Abdul Muttalib.

Abd ush-Shams transferred the authority to his brother HÂSHIM, a leading merchant of Mecca and a man of consequence, noted for his generosity to strangers. Hâshim died about the year 510 A.C., and was succeeded by his brother Muttalib, surnamed "the Generous." Muttalib died towards the end of the year 520 A.C., and was succeeded by his nephew Shayba, better known by his surname of ABDUL MUTTALIB, a son of Hâshim

Ommeya.

The grandsons of Abd ud-Dâr were meanwhile growing rich. Jealous of the position Hâshim's family occupied in the public estimation, they were trying to grasp the entire authority, and to make themselves rulers of Mecca. On their side was ranged OMMEYA, the ambitious son of

[1] Hence called *Dâr-un-nedwa.*

Abd ush-Shams. But in spite of this, the high character of Abdul Muttalib, and the veneration in which he was held by all the Koraish, enabled him to rule Mecca for nearly fifty-nine years. He was assisted in the Government by the Elders, who were the heads of the ten principal families.

The Year of the Elephant.

It was in his time Hijâz was invaded by a large Abyssinian army under the command of Abraha, and as this chief on his march towards Mecca rode on an elephant, an animal the Arabs had never before seen, the year in which the invasion took place (A.C. 570) is called in Arab traditions the "Year of the Elephant." The invading force was destroyed, partly by an epidemic and partly by a terrible storm of rain and hail that swept over the valley where the Abyssinians were encamped.

Mohammed.

Abdul Muttalib had several sons and daughters. Among the sons four are famous in Saracenic history, viz. Abd Manâf, surnamed ABÛ TÂLIB; ABBÂS, the progenitor of the Abbasside Caliphs; HAMZA, and ABDULLÂH. Another son was Abû Lahab, who is referred to in the Koran as a persecutor of Islâm. Abdullâh, the youngest of Abdul Muttalib's sons, was the father of the Arabian Prophet. Abdullâh was married to a lady of Yathreb named ÂM'NA, but he died in the twenty-fifth year of his age, not long after his marriage. A few days after his death Âm'na gave birth [1] to a son, who was named by his grandfather MOHAMMED, or "the Praised One." Mohammed lost his mother when he was only six years old, and was then thrown upon the care of his old grandfather. Abdul Muttalib died about 579 A.C., confiding the infant son of Abdullâh to the charge of Abû Tâlib, who succeeded him in the patriarchate of Mecca. It was in the house of his uncle Abû Tâlib that Mohammed

[1] 29 August, 570 A.C.

passed his early life. Sweet and gentle of disposition, painfully sensitive to human suffering, he was much loved in his small circle. His early life was not free from the burden of labour, for Abû Tâlib was not rich like his ancestors, and the younger members of the family had to take their turn in tending the flocks and herds.

From early youth Mohammed was given to meditation. He travelled twice into Syria with his uncle Abû Tâlib, and there noticed the misery of the people, and their evil ways, their wranglings and strife. In his twenty-fifth year, Mohammed married a lady named Khadîja, who is famous in Arabian history for the nobility of her character. They had several children; all the sons died in infancy, but the daughters lived to see the great events of their father's life. The youngest, Fâtima, surnamed az-Zahra, "the Beautiful," called by Moslems "Our Lady," was married to Ali, the son of Abû Tâlib.

Mohammed lived very quietly for the next fifteen years, appearing only once or twice in public life. He revived the League which had been formed many years before for the protection of widows, orphans, and helpless strangers. He settled by his quick discernment a quarrel which threatened serious consequences; but though these are all we know of his public acts, we know that his gentle disposition and the severe purity of his life, his unflinching faithfulness and stern sense of duty, won for him during this period, from his fellow-citizens, the title of *al-Amîn*, the Trusty. One of his particular characteristics was his fondness for children, who flocked round him whenever he issued from his house; and it is said he never passed them without a kindly smile. He spent a month every year in meditation and spiritual communion in a cave in Mount Hira, not far from Mecca, and one night as he lay in the cave wrapped in his mantle, God spoke to his soul to arise and preach to his people. Henceforth his life is devoted to the task of raising them from their degradation; of making them give up their evil ways, and of teaching them their duty to their fellow-beings.

The first to accept his mission and to abandon idolatry was his wife Khadîja. Then followed Ali and several notable men, Abû Bakr, Omar, Hamza, and Osmân. When Mohammed first began to preach, the Koraish laughed at him, but when they found him earnest in his work their animosity grew into persecution. They began to ill-treat him and his followers, some of whom they tortured to death. Many of his disciples took refuge with a good Christian king in Abyssinia, whilst others remained to suffer ill-treatment and persecution by the side of their Teacher. On the death of Abû Tâlib and Khadîja, which happened shortly after, the Koraish redoubled their persecutions. Hopeless now of success among the Meccans, Mohammed bethought himself of some other field for the exercise of his ministry. He accordingly proceeded to Tâyef, but the people there drove him from their city, pelting him with stones. Mohammed returned to his native town sorely stricken in heart. He lived there for some time, retired from his people, preaching occasionally and confining his efforts mainly to the strangers who came to Mecca during the season of pilgrimage, hoping that some among them might listen to his words and give up their evil and inhuman ways.

His Ministry.

Thus he obtained a few disciples among some Yathrebites who had come to Mecca. They accepted his mission, and took a pledge that they would not worship idols, would not steal, nor commit any wicked act, or kill their children,[1] or slander people. These Yathrebites,

[1] Infanticide was frequent among the pre-Islamite Arabs.

on their return to their homes, spread the news that a Prophet had arisen among the Arabs to wean them from evil ways, and accordingly a number of them came the following year and repeated their pledge. In the year 622 A.C., the Yathrebites sent a deputation to invite Mohammed to their city. As Yathreb was a rival city to Mecca, the news of this invitation and of the pledge roused the fury of the Koraish against the Prophet and his disciples. Many of the latter succeeded in escaping to Yathreb, where they were received with much kindness. However, when the Koraish came to know this, they planned to murder the Prophet, who had remained at his post with Abû Bakr and Ali. Warned of the danger, he took refuge with Abû Bakr in a cave, not far from Mecca, leaving Ali behind. When the Koraish found their intended victims had escaped, they severely maltreated Ali, and started in pursuit of Mohammed. They could not, however, find the cave where the fugitives were concealed. For two days the Prophet and his companion remained in the cave. In the evening of the third day they left the place, and procuring two camels journeyed swiftly to Yathreb, where they arrived on Friday, the 2nd of July 622. Here they were subsequently joined by Ali.

The Hegira.

This is called the *Hijrat* (Exile); in European annals, "the Hegira," "the Flight of Mohammed," from which dates the Mohammedan Calendar.[1]

[1] The "Hegira," or the era of the Hijrat, was instituted seventeen years later by the Second Caliph. The commencement, however, is not laid at the real time of the departure from Mecca, which happened on the 4th of Rabî I., but on the 1st day of the first lunar month of the year—viz. Moharram—which day, in the year when the era was established, fell on the 15th of July.

CHAPTER III

Mohammed at Medîna—Factions in Medîna—The Charter.
1—10 A.H., 622—632 A.C.

THE people of Yathreb received the Prophet and his Meccan disciples, who had abandoned home for the sake of their faith, with great enthusiasm; and the ancient name of the city was changed to *Medînat un-Nabi*, "the City of the Prophet," or shortly, Medîna, which name it has borne ever since. A mosque was built, made of bricks and earth covered with palm-leaves. Mohammed himself assisted in the building of this humble place of worship; and there he preached his simple religion, telling the people not only of the glory and beneficence of God, but inculcating strong moral principles. He preached brotherly love, kindness to children, widows and orphans, and gentleness to animals. Medîna.

The Prophet's Charter.

At this time Medîna was inhabited by two tribes which had long been at feud with each other. The Arabian Prophet abolished all tribal distinctions, and grouped the inhabitants of Medîna under one generic name, *Ansâr*, or Helpers. The people who had followed him from Mecca were called "The Exiles."[1] In the days of which we are speaking, there was no law or order in any city in Arabia. Different factions were at strife with each other, and general lawlessness and confusion prevailed in the Peninsula. Mohammed applied himself first to the task of introducing order in

[1] Muhajjarîn.

622—632 A.C. Medîna, and organising the commonwealth upon a proper basis. With this object he issued a Charter, by which all blood-feud was abolished and lawlessness repressed. Equal rights were granted to the Jews, who lived in large numbers in and about Medîna, whilst they on their side bound themselves to help the Moslems in defending the city.

Mohammed was now not only a Teacher, but the Chief Magistrate of a people, who had invited him and his disciples into their midst, and had entrusted him with the safety of their city; his duty was to be ever on the watch to suppress sedition and to guard against treachery. The Meccans were much angered with the Medinites for sheltering Mohammed and his disciples, whom they considered as revolutionaries, and a conflict between them and the people of Medîna was unavoidable. The first fight took place in the valley of Badr, a few miles from Medîna, where the Meccans were defeated, leaving many prisoners in the hands of the Moslems. These were treated with great kindness in their captivity.

Battle of Badr.

3 A.H. 26 April, 624—15 April, 625 A.C.

The second year of the Hegira would have passed quietly in Medîna but for occasional raids by the Meccans. In the third year, Abû Sufiân, son of Harb, son of Ommeya, the great rival of the Hâshimides, with a large army of the Meccans and their allies, entered the Medinite territories. The Moslem force, which proceeded to repel the attack, was smaller in number. A battle took place at the foot of a hill called Ohod, which resulted in the defeat of the Medinites. The loss of the Meccans, however, was too great to allow them to attack the city, and they retreated to Mecca. The Jews, who were settled in and around Medîna in strongly fortified villages, now began to give trouble. From their position they were a source of constant danger to the little State. Those who lived in the city acted as

Battle of Ohod.

spies to the Meccans, and, frequently, by their turbulent and unruly conduct, led to brawls and bloodshed. Two of these Jewish tribes, the Banû Kainukâ and the Banû Nadhîr, who lived in the suburbs, were therefore expelled. 1—10 A.H.

In the fifth year of the Hegira, the Meccans again invaded Medîna with a large army of 10,000 men. To oppose this formidable host the Moslems could muster only 3000 men. So they dug a trench, under the Prophet's direction, round the unprotected quarter of the city, and relied for the safety of the other parts on the Banû Koraizha, a tribe of Jews who possessed several strong fortresses in the vicinity of Medîna towards the south, and with whom they were allied by treaty.

The treachery of the Jews.

These Jews, however, broke their pledged faith and joined the Meccans in their attack on Medîna. The siege lasted a long time, but every effort to storm the city was warded off by the vigilance of the Prophet. At last the elements seemed to combine against the besieging force; rain and storm killed their horses, provisions became scanty, and the Meccan army dissolved as it had gathered.

The Banû Koraizha.

It was considered unsafe to leave the traitorous Banû-Koraizha so near the city, as their treachery might at any moment lead to the destruction of Medîna. So they were called upon to leave the place; on refusal they were besieged and compelled to surrender at discretion. They made only one condition, that their punishment should be left to the judgment of the Ausite chief, Saad bin Muâz, whose clients they were. This man, a fierce soldier who had been wounded in the attack, and indeed died from his wounds the next day, infuriated by their treacherous conduct, gave sentence that the fighting men should be put to death and that the

622—632 A.C. women and children should become the slaves of the Moslems, and this sentence was carried into execution.

This was a severe punishment according to our ideas, but it was customary according to the rules of war then prevalent.

After this Meccan failure, the new Religion began to make rapid progress in the Peninsula, and tribe after tribe gave up their old evil ways and adopted Islâm.[1]

The Charter to the Christians.

In the sixth year of the Hegira, the Prophet granted to the monks of the Monastery of St. Catherine, near Mount Sinai, and to all Christians, a Charter, which is a monument of enlightened tolerance. By it the Prophet secured to the Christians important privileges and immunities, and the Moslems were prohibited under severe penalties from violating and abusing what was therein ordered. In this charter the Prophet undertook himself, and enjoined on his followers, to protect the Christians, to guard them from all injuries, and to defend their churches, and the residences of their priests. They were not to be unfairly taxed; no bishop was to be driven out of his bishopric; no Christian was to be forced to reject his religion; no monk was to be expelled from his monastery; no pilgrim was to be detained from his pilgrimage; nor were the Christian churches to be pulled down for the sake of building mosques or houses for the Moslems. Christian women married to Moslems were to enjoy their own religion, and not to be subjected to compulsion or annoyance of any kind on that account. If the Christians should stand in need of assistance for the repair of their churches

[1] The religion of Mohammed is called Islâm. It means peace, safety, salvation: derived from *salm* (*salama* in the first conjugation), "to be at perfect peace."

or monasteries, or any other matter pertaining to their religion, the Moslems were to assist them. 1—10 A.H.

Embassies sent abroad.

Mohammed also despatched embassies to the King of Persia and the Byzantine Emperor, to invite them to accept Islâm. The latter received the ambassador with courtesy, whilst the former drove the envoy from his presence with contumely. Another messenger sent to a Christian prince subject to Byzantium, who lived near Damascus, was cruelly murdered.

In the seventh year, the Jews of Khaibar revolted, but were soon reduced to subjection. Their lands and property were guaranteed to them, with the free practice of their religion, upon payment of a fixed land-tax.

In accordance with a truce, concluded with the Meccans, the Moslems visited the Kaaba, the inhabitants vacating their city so as not to come in contact with Mohammed and his followers. After three days the Moslems retired to Medîna and the Meccans returned to their homes.

Soon after, the Meccans and some of their allies treacherously attacked a tribe in alliance with the Moslems, and killed a large number of them. The injured people applied to the Prophet for redress. The reign of iniquity and oppression had lasted long enough at Mecca. In response to the appeal he marched ten thousand men against the idolaters; with the exception of a slight resistance from the heads of two clans, they entered Mecca almost unopposed. Thus Mohammed entered the city which had so cruelly ill-treated him. It lay now completely at his mercy. But in the hour of triumph every evil suffered was forgotten, every injury inflicted was forgiven, and a general amnesty was extended to the population of Mecca. Only four criminals, whom justice condemned, made up Mohammed's pro-

622—632 A.C. scription list when as a conqueror he entered the city of his bitterest enemies. The army followed his example, and entered quietly and peaceably; no house was robbed, no woman was insulted. Most truly has it been said, that "through all the annals of conquest, there has been no triumphant entry like unto this one." But the idols of the nation were unrelentingly destroyed. Sorrowfully the idolaters stood round and watched the downfall of the images they worshipped. And then dawned upon them the truth,—when they heard the old voice at which they were wont to scoff and jeer, cry as he struck down the idols, "Truth has come and falsehood vanisheth; verily falsehood is evanescent,"—how utterly powerless were their gods!

The Year of Deputations.

The ninth year of the Hegira is known in Moslem history as the *Year of Deputations*, in consequence of the large number of embassies which came from all quarters to accept Islâm. The principal companions of the Prophet, and the leading citizens of Medîna, at his request, received these envoys in their houses, and entertained them with the time-honoured hospitality of the Arabs. On departure, they always received an ample sum for the expenses of the road, with some additional presents corresponding to their rank. A written treaty, guaranteeing the privileges of the tribe, was often granted, and a teacher invariably accompanied the departing guests to instruct the newly-converted people in the duties of Islâm, and to see that every evil practice was obliterated from their midst. To the teachers, whom Mohammed sent into the different provinces, he always gave the following injunctions :—" Deal gently with the people, and be not harsh; cheer them, and contemn them not. And ye will meet with many people of the Book who will question thee, what is the key to heaven?

Reply to them, [the key to heaven is] 'to testify to the truth of God, and to do good work.'" 1–10 A.H.

When the hosts of Arabia came flocking to join his faith, Mohammed felt that his work was accomplished; and under the impression of his approaching end, he determined to make a farewell pilgrimage to Mecca. On the 25th of Zu'l-Kaada (23rd February, 632) the Prophet left Medîna with an immense concourse of Moslems. On his arrival at Mecca, on the 8th of Zu'l-Hijja, 7th March, and before completing all the rites of the pilgrimage, he addressed the assembled multitude from the top of the Jabal ul-Arafât in words which yet live in the hearts of all Moslems.

The Sermon on the Mount of Arafât.

"Ye people! listen to my words, for I know not whether another year will be vouchsafed to me after this year to find myself amongst you.

"Your lives and property are sacred and inviolable amongst one another until ye appear before the Lord, as this day and this month is sacred for all, and remember ye shall have to appear before your Lord, who shall demand from you an account of all your actions. Ye people, ye have rights over your wives, and your wives have rights over you. . . . Treat your wives with kindness. . . . Verily ye have taken them on the security of God, and made them lawful unto you by the words of God.

"And your slaves! See that ye feed them with such food as ye eat yourselves, and clothe them with the stuff ye wear; and if they commit a fault which ye are not inclined to forgive, then part from them, for they are the servants of the Lord, and are not to be harshly treated.

"Ye people! listen to my words, and understand the same. Know that all Moslems are brothers unto one another. Ye are one brotherhood. Nothing which

622—632 A.C. belongs to another is lawful unto his brother, unless freely given out of good-will. Guard yourselves from committing injustice.

"Let him that is present tell it unto him that is absent. Haply he that shall be told may remember better than he who hath heard it."

On his return to Medîna he settled the organisation of the provinces and tribal communities.

Officers were sent to the provinces and to the various tribes for the purpose of teaching the people the duties of Islâm, administering justice, and collecting the tithes or *zakât*.

The last days of the Prophet were remarkable for the calmness and serenity of his mind, which enabled him, though weak and feeble, to preside at the public prayers until within three days of his death. One midnight he went to the place where his old companions were lying in the slumber of death, and prayed and wept by their tombs, invoking God's blessings for his "companions resting in peace." He chose Âyesha's house,[1] close to the mosque, for his stay during his illness, and, so long as his strength lasted, took part in the public prayers. The last time he appeared in the mosque he was supported by his two cousins, Ali and Fazl the son of Abbâs.

After the usual praises and hymns to God, he addressed the multitude thus: "Moslems, if I have wronged any

[1] After the death of Khadîja, Mohammed, in accordance with Arab customs and the old patriarchal ways, married several wives, partly with the object of uniting hostile tribes, and partly to provide means of subsistence to helpless women. Âyesha was the daughter of Mohammed's old friend Abû Bakr, who was anxious to cement their friendship by the union of his daughter with one whom he recognised as his teacher.

one of you, here I am to answer for it; if I owe ought to any one, all I may happen to possess belongs to you." The Prophet then prayed and implored heaven's mercy for those present, and for those who had fallen in the persecution of their enemies, and recommended to all his people the observance of religious duties, and the practice of a life of peace and good-will, and concluded with the following words of the Koran. "The dwelling of the other life we will give unto them who do not seek to exalt themselves on earth or to do wrong; for the happy issue shall attend the pious." 1—10 A.H.

After this, Mohammed's strength rapidly failed. At noon on Monday (12th of Rabî I., 11 A.H.—8th June, 632 A.C.), whilst praying earnestly in whisper, the spirit of the great Prophet took flight to the "blessed companionship on high."

During the ten years Mohammed presided over the commonwealth of Islâm, a great change had come over the character of the Arab people. By the appointment of delegates to the different tribes and cities, with powers to decide internal as well as tribal disputes, the ancient system of private vendetta was put an end to, and an impetus was given to trade and commerce. The style of living and mode of dress underwent a great change, especially among women. The reckless freedom of heathenism was abandoned, and manners became decorous, almost austere; gambling and drunkenness were forbidden. Before this there had been no privacy in houses; from this time, it became customary to have special apartments for women.

CHAPTER IV

THE REPUBLIC

11—23 A.H., 632—644 A.C.

Abû Bakr—Insurrections—War with Persia and the Romans—Abû Bakr's death—Omar—Conquest of Chaldæa and Mesopotamia—Persia—Defeat of the Romans—Conquest of Syria, Palestine, and Egypt—Death of Omar.

Abû Bakr. THE hold which the personality of the Arabian Prophet had acquired over the minds of his followers is shown by the fact that none of them would at first believe that he was dead. They could hardly realise that the man who in the course of a few years had changed the whole aspect of Arabia was subject to the same laws as other human beings. Had he lived in a less historical age, or had his words with reference to himself been less rationalistic, like other great men, he too, probably, would have received divine honours. The commotion among the people was allayed by the venerable Abû Bakr, who, having ascertained that their Teacher was really dead and not in a swoon, as some had asserted, addressed the crowd thus: "Mussulmans, if you adored Mohammed, know that Mohammed is dead; if it is God that you adore, know that He liveth, He never dies. Forget not this verse of the Koran, 'Mohammed is only a man charged with a mission; before him there have been men who received the heavenly mission and died;'—nor this verse, 'Thou too, Mohammed, shalt die as others have died before thee.'" It was then that a wail went up from the assembled multitude that their great Master was gone from among them. 11—23 A.H.

And now arose the question as to who was to succeed in the government of the Commonwealth. Mohammed had often indicated Ali as his successor, but had laid down no definite rule. This gave scope to individual ambitions, to the detriment of Islâm, and in later times became the fruitful cause of dynastic wars and religious schisms. Had Ali been accepted to the Headship of Islâm, the birth of those disastrous pretensions that led to so much bloodshed in the Moslem world would have been averted.

Among the Arabs, the chieftaincy of a tribe is not hereditary, but elective; the principle of universal suffrage is recognised in its extremest form, and all the members of the tribe have a voice in the election of their chief. The election is made on the basis of seniority among the surviving male members of the deceased chieftain's family. This old tribal custom was followed in the choice of a successor to the Prophet, for the urgency of the times admitted of no delay. Abû Bakr, who by virtue of his age and the position he had held at Mecca occupied a high place in the estimation of the Arabs, was hastily elected to the office of Khalîfa (Caliph) or Vicegerent of the Prophet. He was recognised as a man of wisdom and moderation, and his election was accepted with their usual devotion to the Faith by Ali and the chief members of Mohammed's family.

Abû Bakr is elected Caliph.

"Behold me," said the Patriarch, after the multitude had sworn allegiance to him, "behold me charged with the cares of Government. I am not the best among you; I need all your advice and all your help. If I do well, support me; if I mistake, counsel me. To tell

632—644 A.C. truth to a person commissioned to rule is faithful allegiance ; to conceal it is treason. In my sight, the powerful and the weak are alike ; and to both I wish to render justice. As I obey God and His Prophet, obey me : if I neglect the laws of God and the Prophet, I have no more right to your obedience."

The Rising of the Tribes. No sooner had it become noised abroad that the Prophet was dead than the unruly spirit of the Arab broke forth ; whilst a great fear fell upon the earnest followers of the new Faith. Some of the tribes who had only recently abandoned idolatry, reverted at once to their evil ways, and several impostors who had appeared in distant provinces in the lifetime of the Prophet began harrying the Moslems. Within a little time the Faith had become almost confined to the city of Medîna, and again a single town had to contend against the idolatrous hordes of the Peninsula.

Osâma's Expedition. The rising of the tribes was due, firstly, to the strict rules of morality enforced by Islâm, and, secondly, to their unwillingness to pay the poor-tax. Though hemmed in on all sides, the Moslems did not lose heart ; and faith and enthusiasm again led them to victory. The first care of the Caliph, after the funeral ceremonies of the Prophet, was to organise the administration and stand on guard against the rebels. Mohammed had shortly before his death issued orders for the despatch of an expedition into Syria to seek reparation for the murder of the Moslem envoy. With that object troops had been collected in the neighbourhood of Medîna. The expedition now became doubly necessary by the defection of the northern tribes, who had fallen away after the disaster at Mûta, where the faithful Zaid had lost his life. To give effect to his Master's last wishes, and to restore order on the northern frontier, Abû Bakr, though hard pressed himself, sent forward the troops. When the Moslems were departing, the aged Caliph addressed them as follows—"See," said he, addressing Osâma, the son of Zaid, who was placed at the head of the expedition, "see that thou avoidest treachery. Depart not in any wise from the right. Thou shalt mutilate none, neither shalt thou kill child or aged man, nor any woman. Injure not the date-palm, neither burn it with fire, and cut not down any tree wherein is food for man or beast. Slay not the flocks or herds or camels, saving for needful sustenance. Ye may eat of the meat which the men of the land shall bring unto you in their vessels, making mention thereon of the name of the Lord. And the monks with shaven heads, if they submit, leave them unmolested. Now march forward in the name of the Lord, and may He protect you from sword and pestilence!" 11—23 A.H.

Pacification of the Peninsula.

Whilst Osâma was away in the north, Medîna was attacked by the rebels, but they were beaten back. Osâma also gained a victory over the Syrians, and shortly after returned to the help of Abû Bakr, who was now able to send out troops to reduce the insurgent tribes to order. The principal work of subjection was entrusted to Khâlid, son of Walîd, a ferocious soldier but a skilled general. Some of the tribes gave in their adhesion without fighting; others were unyielding, and with them were fought great battles, in which both sides suffered severely. At the battle of Yemâma the formidable tribe of the Banû Hanîfa were thoroughly defeated, and their leader, the impostor Mosailima, was killed. After this the insurgents gradually submitted, and were received back into Islâm.

War with Persia.

The work of pacification in the north-east of Arabia

632—644 A.C. brought the Moslems into collision with the wandering tribes subject to Hîra, a semi-Arab kingdom which at that time acknowledged the suzerainty of Persia. A glance at the map will show how the conflict, which afterwards widened into a struggle for empire, originally arose. From Hajar, the north-east corner of Arabia which borders on Chaldæa, then held by the Persians, and westward of the lower branch of the Euphrates, lies that waterless tract, a continuation of the Arabian Nafûd, far away to the Dead Sea, and the high lands of Haurân and ancient Tadmor towards the north. Over this vast tract roamed then, as now, the nomadic hordes, whose names alone have changed, but whose manners and habits have remained the same. They were chiefly Christians. Those on the Syrian side, like the Ghassân, were subject to the Byzantines; those on the east, like the Banû Taghlib, owed allegiance to Persia. All these were connected by ties of blood and friendship with the neighbouring Arabian tribes. The delta of the Euphrates itself was inhabited by settled Arabs, who had abandoned the pastoral life of their kinsmen of the Desert and taken to the cultivation of the soil. Naturally, the conflict between the Moslems and the insurgents on the western shores of the Persian Gulf re-acted on the neighbouring tribes subject to Persia. Raids from the north were followed by reprisals, with the same result that we now see in the advance of the British in India, and of the Russians in Central Asia. The region watered by the two great rivers, the Tigris and the Euphrates, has from time immemorial formed the prize of monarchs struggling for empire. On one side the Tigris (Dajla) issuing from the mountains of Armenia, on the other the Euphrates (Furât) taking its rise in the heights of Taurus, roll down towards the Persian

Its causes.

Gulf, joining their waters a few hundred miles before they reach the sea. Here they lose their names as well as their identity, and receive the designation of the Shatt ul-Arab. The upper portion of the region enclosed by the two rivers was in ancient times known as Mesopotamia.[1] The lower part, a flat alluvial country, was called Babylonia and Chaldæa; to the Arabs, it was known as Irâk Arab.[2] Many flourishing cities have existed by the side of these famous rivers. Ancient Nineveh (not far from modern Mosul), the seat of the mighty Assyrian monarchs, was situated on the Tigris; so was Madâin, the capital of the Persian sovereigns; so is Bagdad, the metropolis of the Caliphs in the Middle Ages, and now the seat of King Faisal, the new ruler of Irâk. On the Euphrates were situated ancient Babylon, Hîra, Kûfa, built by the Arabs, Kirkessia (ancient Circesium) and Rakka. To the east of the Zagros mountains, beyond the Tigris, lies the country called by the Arabs Irâk Ajam, the centre of Persia. The pacification of the Peninsula having been completed, Khâlid and Mosanna (Mothanna),[3] the generals operating in Hejr, took in hand the repression of the raids from the Hirite side. The Persian governor of Chaldæa offered battle on the frontier, and was defeated with heavy loss, and Hîra, after a short resistance, capitulated to the Moslems.

11—23 A.H.

The Capitulation of Hîra.

Following the example of the people of Hîra, the *dehkâns* or great landed proprietors of Chaldæa gave in

Rabî I. 12 A.H. May-June 633 A.C.

[1] Sometimes Mesopotamia also included Assyria, the country which stretched from the Tigris to the Zagrus or Zagros mountains.

[2] Both Mesopotamia and Irâk Arab are now included in the Kingdom of Irâk.

[3] Mothanna, son of Hâris (Shaybâni), of the tribe of the Banû Bakr, was a general of consummate ability and a kind-hearted man, different from the ferocious Khâlid.

632—644 A.C. their adhesion, and were guaranteed in their possessions, subject to a fixed land-tax. The peasantry were not interfered with, and were left in the safe enjoyment of their fields and lands.

The conquest of Hîra opened the eyes of the Persian Government to the gravity of the danger. A young and rising power, animated with a national sentiment in the shape of religious enthusiasm, was now seated at their door. Had they been wise, they would have strengthened their internal defences, and re-organised their empire, which was rent by domestic quarrels. They might even have come to terms with the Saracens. Still, the Persian Empire was rich and powerful. It comprised within its dominions the whole of Modern Persia, Bactria, and all the inferior provinces of Central Asia to the confines of Tartary and India, besides Irâk and Mesopotamia. A large army was sent to drive the Saracens out of Chaldæa.

Death of Abû Bakr. 23rd of August, 634 A.C.

About this time the Caliph was obliged to send Khâlid into Syria with half of the troops. The other general, Mothanna, was thus left alone with a small force to make head against the Persian host. Withdrawing his advanced posts, he proceeded in haste to Medîna to ask for reinforcements, but found the aged Caliph dying.

Abû Bakr died after a reign of only two years and a half, on the 22nd of Jamâdi II., 13 A.H. He is described as "a man of a very fair complexion, thin countenance, of slender build, and with a stoop." Before he became a disciple of the Prophet, he wielded great authority over the Koraish as one of their chief magistrates, and his wealth as a merchant, and his sagacity as a chief, gave him great consequence among the Meccans. Like his Master, Abû Bakr was extremely simple in his habits; gentle but firm, he devoted all his energies to the administration of the new-born State and to the good of the people. He would sally forth by night to help the distressed and relieve the destitute. For a time, after his election, he continued to maintain himself with his own private income, but finding that in looking after his property and business he was not able to pay sufficient attention to the affairs of the State, he consented to receive 6000 dirhems annually from the Treasury. On his death-bed, however, he was so troubled at having taken public money that he directed one of his properties to be sold, in order to refund to the State the sum he had received. 11—23 A.H.

Such were the simple, honest ways of the immediate disciples of Mohammed.

Before his death, Abû Bakr nominated Omar as his successor in the Caliphate, and his appointment was accepted by the people. Omar.

Omar's accession to the Caliphate was of immense value to Islâm. He was a man of strong moral fibre and a keen sense of justice, possessed of great energy and force of character. His first act, after re-organising the internal administration of Arabia, was to hurry on reinforcements to the help of Mothanna. These troops were under Abû Obaid, who, on arrival on the scene of action, assumed the chief command. Without listening to the prudent advice of Mothanna, he gave battle to the Persians at a place where he was unable to manœuvre, and incurred a heavy defeat, in which he was killed. The Persians, however, did not press their advantage, and were ultimately out-generalled and defeated with great loss by Mothanna, at a place called Buwaib, on the western branch of the Euphrates. Mothanna again re-occupied the country and re-entered Hîra.

About this time a new sovereign had been raised to Yezdjard.

632—644 A.C. the throne of Persia. Young, energetic, and ambitious, Yezdjard was bent not only on driving the Saracens from Hîra, but also on conquering their country. With this object he sent forward into Chaldæa an army consisting of 100,000 men, which marching southward was to overwhelm the Moslems, and oust them from their possessions. The Saracens under Mothanna, wholly unable to cope with this enormous force, again abandoned Chaldæa, and retired to the borders of the desert, where they awaited reinforcements from Medîna.

Whilst the Moslems were thus waiting for the Persian attack, they lost their great general, who was stricken down by the Chaldæan fever. Saad, son of Wakkâs, who brought the additional troops sent forward by the Caliph, assumed chief command over the whole Saracenic army, which now amounted to 30,000. The battle that followed was hotly contested. It lasted for three days, and was distinguished by heroic feats on both sides. On the third day the Persian host broke. Defeated with terrible loss, their general killed, they fled towards the north. The battle of Kâdessia practically decided the fate of both Chaldæa and Mesopotamia: Chaldæa was re-occupied without opposition, and the Hirites, who had torn up the treaties made with Mothanna, were punished for their defection by the imposition of a higher tax.

Battle of Kâdessia.

Moharram 15 A.H. February–March 636 A.C.

After receiving the submission of the towns and villages in the neighbourhood of Hîra, Saad turned towards Bâbil (Babylon), where the broken remnants of the Persian host had re-assembled under Firuzân, Hurmuzân, and Mihrân. They were beaten and dispersed. Mihrân escaped to Madâin, the Persian capital; Hurmuzân fled to his government of Ahwâz, beyond the Persian range; and Firuzân betook himself to Nehâwand, where were the treasures of the Persian king. A permanent hold over Chaldæa was, however, impossible, so long as it was dominated by Madâin, where Mihrân lay encamped with a large Persian army. Saad was therefore compelled to march upon the royal city. Like the Bagdad of Mansûr, fifteen miles higher up the river, it was built on both sides of the Tigris. The western portion, called Seleucia, was founded by the Seleucidæ, the descendants of Alexander's great general; the eastern part, called Ctesiphon, was built by the Persian monarchs. The two conjointly were called Madâin (or the Two Cities). The palaces of the kings and nobles were luxurious and beautiful, and the first sight of them considerably impressed the simple Saracens. After a siege of some duration, Madâin opened its gate, and its capitulation was followed by the submission of the entire country lying to the west of the Tigris. A Service of Thanksgiving,[1] at which the whole army assisted, was held in the palace of the Chosroes.

11—23 A.H.

Capture of Madâin.

Safar 16 A.H. March 673 A.C.

Saad, as the civil and military head of Irâk (which now included Mesopotamia), made Madâin his head-quarters. He established himself in the royal palace, where the offices were located, and "cathedral service" was held every Friday in the Grand Hall. From here he conducted the administration of the province. But it was not long before another conflict was forced upon the Moslems. The Persian king, who was stationed at Holwân on the western side of the mountains, sent forward a large force to recapture Madâin. This army was met at Jalula, about fifty miles to the north-east of the capital, and defeated with terrible loss. Holwân itself was captured and strongly garrisoned. When the spoils of Jalula and Madâin arrived at Medîna, the Caliph was found weeping. Asked his reason, he replied that he saw in those spoils the future ruin of his

December 673 A.C. Battle of Jalula.

[1] Called in the original *Salât-uz-Zafar*, "Prayer of Victory."

632—644 A.C. people, and he was not wrong; for the unprecedented success of the Saracens led eventually to the loss of those qualities of frugality, austerity, and self-sacrifice that in the beginning so materially contributed to their victories.

After the capture of Holwân, a treaty of peace was concluded with the Persian king, by which the Persian Range was made the boundary between the two empires; and the Caliph now issued peremptory injunctions that the Saracens were under no circumstance to go beyond that limit. The country at the head of the Persian Gulf, as far as the range of hills on the eastern side, had been already reduced to order, and the sea-port of Obolla had fallen into the hands of the Moslems. Nothing attests so clearly the capacity of Omar as a wise and just ruler, or the ability of the council with which he was assisted, as the energy with which the Moslems applied themselves to the regeneration of this province, and the development of its resources. A great cadastral survey was set on foot under the advice of Ali, a new system of assessment was introduced, the burdens of the peasantry were lightened and they were secured in the possession of their lands. The tax imposed on the large land-holders by the Persian monarchs was revised, a complete network of canals was made for purposes of irrigation, and an order was issued for giving advances to the cultivators when needed. The sale of land was strictly prohibited, to safeguard against the eviction of the native peasantry. The Crown domains of the Persian kings, the royal hunting forests, the abandoned possessions of fugitive princes and land-holders, and property appertaining to the fire-temples whence the priests had fled, became State property, and were administered by agents appointed from Medîna. The army had clamoured for the distribution, as spoils of war, of these lands as well as of the plains of Chaldæa, called the *Sawâd*, but the Caliph, guided by Ali and Ibn Abbâs, firmly rejected the demand. The income from the State domains, after defraying the public charges, was distributed among the Arab settlers. 11—23 A.H.

Breach of treaty by the Persians.

But neither the prudence of the Caliph nor the moderation of his generals was of avail in preventing a fresh conflict with the Persians. Yezdjard was chafing under the loss of his capital and two of his best provinces. His governors were out of hand, and his army was clamorous for a fresh advance against the Saracens. Hurmuzân, the governor of Ahwâz, repeatedly attacked the Arab settlements; as often as he was beaten back, he sued for peace, but always broke it at the first opportunity.

About this time two new cities were built in Irâk. 17 A.H. 638 A.C.
Basra (Bussorah), on the Shatt ul-Arab, peopled chiefly by the northern Arabs, took the place of Obolla, and became the sea-port of Irâk. Kûfa on the western bank of the Euphrates, three miles south of Hîra, was peopled 18 A.H. 638 A.C.
by Arabs of the Yemenite stock, and took the place of Madâin, which was abandoned as unhealthy. Both cities were laid out on regular lines. A square was made, with the principal mosque in the centre, and the governor's mansion close by. The streets were straight, wide, and spacious; the bazaars commodious, and the public gardens numerous.

At last, wearied beyond endurance by the incessant raids of the Persians, and apprehending a serious attack from their king, who had collected a large army towards the north, the Saracens in Mesopotamia sent a deputation to the Caliph for permission to repel the threatened danger. Omar inquired of the deputation the

632—644 A.C. cause of the frequent risings on the part of the Persians. "Maybe," said he, "the Moslems treat the *Zimmis*[1] badly, that they break their faith persistently and rebel against us." "Not so," they answered, "we do not deal with them otherwise than with honesty and good faith." "How can that be?" naturally asked the Caliph. "Is there not one honest man among them?" Then answered the leader of the deputation, "Thou hast forbidden us, Commander of the Faithful, to enlarge our boundaries; and their king is in their midst to stir them up. Two kings can in no wise exist together, until the one expel the other. It is not that we have treated them harshly, but that their king has incited them to rise against us after having made submission. And so it will go on, until thou shalt remove the barrier and leave us to go forward and expel their king. Not till then will their hopes and machinations cease."[2]

These views were also enforced by Hurmuzân, who had been brought as a prisoner to Medîna, and had adopted Islâm. It now became clear to Omar that the ban against an advance towards the east must be withdrawn. In self-defence, nothing was left but to crush the Chosroes, and take entire possession of his realm.[3]

The Persians had responded with alacrity to the call of their sovereign for a final and desperate blow at the intruders of the Desert, who had ousted him from his capital and wrested from him some of his fairest provinces. The army raised by Yezdjard for this last struggle far exceeded any he had had before. The news of the Persian preparations caused great excitement in Medîna, and the Caliph at once hurried off reinforce-

[1] Non-Moslem subjects, see p. 33. [2] Ibn ul-Athîr, vol. ii. p. 429.

[3] Muir admits the justice and necessity of the withdrawal of the ban.

ments towards the frontier. A general of the name of Nomân, who was then engaged with the Persian raiders in the south, was placed in command of the Saracenic forces. The battle, which took place at Nehâwand, at the foot of the Elburz, decided the fate of Asia, and is called the *Victory of Victories*.[1] The Persians, who outnumbered the Saracens by six to one, were defeated with terrible loss. Their king fled from place to place, until he was killed some years later by one of his own men, like Darius the *Short-handed*, at a distant village on the confines of Turkestan. Persia thus passed under Moslem domination. As in Mesopotamia, the Caliph took immediate measures to settle the peasantry securely in their possessions. They were released from the galling oppression of the large land-holders; their assessments were revised and placed on a stable basis; the broken aqueducts were restored and new ones built. The land-holders or *dehkâns* kept their estates, subject to the payment of a fixed tax. Liberty of conscience was allowed to every one, and the Moslems were ordered not to interfere with the religion of the people. Those who adhered to their old faith received the designation of *Zimmis* (the protected people or liege-men). The sole inducement to proselytism, if inducement it can be called, consisted in the fact that whereas Moslems, who were liable at any time to be called to serve in the army, contributed only a tithe to the State, the *Zimmis* paid a higher tax in consideration of being exempted from military service.[2] The bulk of the people, without any such compulsion as is used by some

11—23 A.H.

Battle of Nehâwand 21 A.H. 642 A.C.

Subjugation of Persia.

The *Zimmis*

[1] The Saracen general was killed in this battle, just as the victory was won.

[2] Such distinctions are common in the history of all dominant nations, and are to be found even now.

632—644 A.C. modern nations for the conversion of unorthodox communities, adopted Islâm. Among these converts and the Arab settlers intermarriages became frequent, numbers of Persians were introduced into the tribal brotherhood of the Arabs as *Mawâlis* (friends or clients), and many of those who had rendered eminent services, or were otherwise distinguished, were inscribed in the State Register as recipients of allowances. For a long time, however, as under Alexander of Macedon, the priests were a source of trouble and danger. Often they incited to rebellion the people who still conformed to the old faith. In the repression of these outbreaks cruelties were committed on both sides. The wise and conciliatory policy, however, of the Abbasside Caliphs, and the general diffusion of Islâm, removed in time all causes of disaffection.

War with the Romans. Its causes. Very soon after the accession of Abû Bakr to the Caliphate the Saracens came into conflict with the Romans. The entire country to the west of Mesopotamia and Chaldæa belonged then to the Eastern Roman Empire. Palestine and Syria were, like Irâk, inhabited by people of the Arab race; and the Syrian *Nafûd*, or Desert, was roamed over by Arabs; they thus came within the legitimate sphere of the Islâmic Commonwealth. The punitive expedition of Osâma had set ablaze the Syrian tribes, and naturally led to retaliatory raids. The Romans at the same time massed a large army at Balca, not far from the frontier. Like the British Government in India, when threatened by the Sikhs in 1848, the Caliph had no choice but to repel the Romans, and reduce the tribes to subjection. It was a measure necessary in the interests of his empire. His appeal for levies was answered with enthusiasm, and as the troops arrived at Medîna he hurried them towards the north. The theatre of the new war requires a slight notice. Palestine, according to the Arab geographers, is the country south of a line drawn from Mount Carmel to the northern extremity of the Sea of Galilee (Lake Tiberias), and extending from the Jordan as far as the Mediterranean Sea. Here the Romans held some strongly garrisoned places, such as Cæsarea on the sea, Jericho, Jerusalem, Ascalon, Gaza, and Jaffa. The township of Zoghar (Seger), or ancient Pentapolis, and all the region which stretched from the southern extremity of the Dead Sea to the Arabian Gulf, was a dependency of Palestine. North of the line mentioned above was the Province of Jordan (*Ordûn*,) which comprised the garrisoned towns of Acre (ancient Ptolemais) and Sûr (Tyre). To the north of Palestine lay that beautiful and interesting country called Syria[1] by the Romans, and *Barr ush-Shâm* (the land to the left), or simply Shâm by the Arabs, with the historical cities of Damascus, Hems (Emessa), Aleppo (Chalybon), Antioch, etc., all held by strong Roman garrisons. East of the valley of the Jordan, and south of the Lake of Tiberias, were the high-lands of Haurân. The first army sent into Syria by Abû Bakr met with a disastrous repulse. The old Patriarch, instead of being dispirited, threw fresh energy into the organisation of the levies; and the new army that was hurried to the theatre of war was divided into four corps, which were directed to operate under the command of four generals, in different parts of the country. The gentle and kind-hearted Abû Obaidah was in command of the division of Hems, with head-quarters at Jâbia, and was accompanied by a large number of Medinites and the Companions of the Prophet. The Palestine division was under the command of Amr, the

11—23 A.H.

[1] The Syria of the Romans included a portion of Palestine.

632—644 A.C. son of al-Aâs, famous for his conquest of Egypt, and infamous for his treachery to Ali. The division intended for Damascus was under the command of Yezîd, son of Abû Sufiân, the old enemy of Islâm, and now fighting under its banners. The army of Yezîd was composed principally of the Meccans and of the Arabs of the Tehâma, and included several notables of Mecca, most of whom had fought against the Prophet before the fall of the city. Tempted now by the rich spoils of Syria, they had joined as volunteers the army under Yezîd. Between the Meccans and the Arabs of the Tehâma on one side, and the Medinites on the other, there existed bitter hostility, the consequences of which were perceptible in later times. The fourth division, under Shorâbhîl, operated in the valley of the Jordan. Another corps, under Muâwiyah, the second son of Abû Sufiân, who afterwards usurped the Caliphate, formed a reserve. Whilst Amr, the son of al-Aâs, advancing upon Lower Palestine, threatened Gaza and Jerusalem, the three armies under Abû Obaidah, Shorâbhîl, and Yezîd, echeloned as above, and mutually supporting each other, menaced Basra, Damascus, and the Tiberiade. But the forces at their disposal barely exceeded 35,000, and, considering the power and resources of the Empire against which they were directing the attack, seemed hardly adequate to the task. The Roman Empire of Constantinople, even after it had been shorn of several of its European dependencies, was colossal. Its resources, its wealth, and its supply of fighting material were unlimited. It included the spacious Peninsula of Lesser Asia, encompassed by three seas and studded with rich maritime cities; Syria, Phœnicia, and Palestine; Egypt, the granary of the surrounding nations; together with "the long sleeve of the Mantle," the vast strip of territory extending from the Egyptian coast to the Atlantic, and including the once renowned dominions of Cyrene and Carthage. 11—23 A. H.

In order to repel the invaders Heraclius came in person to Hems, and from there sent forward four separate armies to crush the Arab generals. At the first news of this move on the part of the Romans, the Moslem Ameers, having consulted with each other by a rapid exchange of messengers, decided to concentrate all their forces on one point, and accordingly all the four divisions united in the month of April 634 at Jaulân, near the river Yermuk (ancient Hieromax). Upon this the Romans on their side drew together all their corps. The Yermuk is an obscure river, which, rising in the high-lands of Haurân, falls into the Jordan a few miles south of the Lake of Tiberias. About thirty miles above its junction with the Jordan, it forms on the northern side a semi-circular loop, which encloses a vast plain suited for the encampment of a large army. The banks of the Yermuk are rugged and steep; at the neck of the loop there is a ravine, which forms the entrance to the flat space inside. This spot is called Wakusa, famous in the annals of Islâm. The Romans considered this, protected, as it appeared to them, on all sides, as a natural camping-ground; and their forces marched into it without any thought of the Saracens. These quickly perceived the enemy's mistake, and crossing towards the northern side of the river, a little higher up, took up their position immediately by the side of the ravine, ready to strike the moment the Romans issued from within. The two armies watched each other for two months, until the Caliph, getting tired of the waiting game, sent Khâlid, the son of Walîd, from Chaldæa into Syria. Marching across the desert, Khâlid joined the Moslems

Battle of Yermuk. 30 August 634 A.C.

632—644 A.C. before the Romans knew of his approach. The army of Heraclius numbered 240,000, whilst the Saracens were only 40,000 all told. But the Romans had already lost heart, having been beaten in several attempts to issue from the trap in which they had been caught. At last, on the morning of the last day of Jamâdi II. (30th August 634), inspirited by the priests, the Roman army issued from its camp to give battle to the Saracens. That eventful fight is now known as the battle of Yermuk. The Romans were defeated with fearful slaughter, a part of their army was driven into the river and drowned, and the whole of Southern Syria lay at the feet of the Saracens.[1]

Death of Abû Bakr. Abû Bakr died about this time—in fact, the news of his death was brought to the camp before the battle began, but was not published by Khâlid until the fight was won. Omar, who never approved of Khâlid's ferocity, deposed him from the chief command, and made the wise and far-seeing Abû Obaidah the General-in-Chief. Khâlid worked under Abû Obaidah, and the Syrian cities one by one capitulated to the Moslems. Damascus, Hems, Hama (Epiphania), Kinnisrîn (Chalcis), Aleppo, and other important towns, opened their gates to Abû Obaidah. At last this general presented himself before Antioch, the rival of Constantinople and the capital of the Roman East. It was held by a large garrison, augmented by the fragments of those that had fled from other places. The population was considerable, though enervated by luxury and pleasure. One slight battle outside the city, in which the Moslems were victors, so disheartened the citizens that after a siege of a few days they proffered their subjection. Whilst Abû Obaidah had thus subjugated the

[1] The Roman loss is said to have been 140,000, whilst the Saracens lost only 3000 ;—Caussin de Perceval.

11—23 A.H.

greater part of Northern Syria, the operations of Amr, the son of al-Aâs, were no less successful in Palestine. The Roman governor, named Artabîn, had assembled a large army for the defence of the Province, and had placed bodies of troops at Jerusalem, Gaza, and Ramleh, whilst he himself, with the mass of his forces, was installed at Ajnadîn, a village situated to the east of Jerusalem, between Ramleh and Bait(u)-Jibrin. The Saracen generals, after detaching troops to hold in check Jerusalem, Gaza, Ramleh, and Cæsarea, now advanced upon Artabîn.

Battle of Ajnadîn.

The battle that followed was as disastrous to the Romans as the day of Yermuk. Their army was entirely destroyed; only a few escaped with their chief, and found a refuge within the walls of Jerusalem. As the fruit of this victory, the Saracens obtained without difficulty the submission of the towns of Jaffa and Nablûs (Neapolis). Ascalon, Gaza, Ramleh, and Acre (Ptolemais), Berytus, Sidon, Laodicea, Apamea, and Gobula opened their gates without a fight. Jerusalem alone, garrisoned by a heavy force, resisted for a time. After a siege of some duration, the Patriarch sued for peace, but refused to surrender the place to any but the Caliph in person. Omar acceded to the request, and travelling with a single attendant, without escort and without any pomp or ceremony, arrived at Jâbia, where he was met by a deputation from Jerusalem. To them he accorded the free exercise of their religion, and the possession of their churches, subject to a light tax. He then proceeded with the deputation towards Jerusalem, where he was received by Sophronius the Patriarch.

Capitulation of Jerusalem.

The chief of Islâm and the head of the Christians entered the sacred city together, conversing on its antiquities. Omar declined to perform his devotions in the Church of the Resurrection, in

632—644 A.C. which he chanced to be at the hour of prayer, but prayed on the steps of the Church of Constantine; "for," said he to the Patriarch, "had I done so, the Mussulmans in a future age might have infringed the treaty, under colour of imitating my example." A deputation from Ramleh received the same considerate terms; whilst the Samaritan Jews, who had assisted the Moslems, were guaranteed in their possessions without the payment of any tax.[1]

The depredations of the Armenian and the Kurdish tribes in Mesopotamia led to punitive expeditions, which ended in the subjugation of Kurdistan and Armenia. The Romans, however, again assumed the offensive. Hardly had the spring of 638 begun, than Heraclius, joining hands with the still unconquered people in the east, poured a large army into Syria.

17 A.H. 23 January 638 to 12 January 639 A.C. The cities, which had capitulated to the Moslems, now opened their gates to him, and the Christian Arab tribes also gave in their adhesion. An army from Egypt, landed on the sea-board, re-occupied Northern Palestine. The position of the Saracens was thus threatened in all directions. But daring, dash and generalship, combined with enthusiasm and trust in their cause, were on their side. Though outnumbered in some places as twenty to one, they broke the coalition with heavy loss. The son of Heraclius was defeated, and barely escaped with a few troops. The country once more submitted to Moslem rule. Only one place in Northern Syria remained in the Roman hands. Cæsarea on the coast, assisted from Egypt by the sea, defied the Moslems for a time, but the flight of Constantine, the son of Heraclius, broke the spirit of its defenders, and

[1] This privilege was withdrawn from them by Yezîd, the son of Muâwiyah.

Cæsarea surrendered under the guarantee of protection. 11—23 A.H.
The subjugation of the country was now complete, and "Syria bowed under the sceptre of the Caliphs seven hundred years after Pompey had deposed the last of the Macedonian kings." After their last defeat, the Romans recognised themselves hopelessly beaten, though they still continued to raid into the Moslem territories. In order to erect an impassable barrier between themselves and the Saracens, they converted into a veritable desert a vast tract on the frontiers of their remaining Asiatic possessions. All the cities in this doomed tract were razed to the ground, fortresses were dismantled, and the population carried away further north. And what has been deemed to be the work of Saracenic hordes, was really the outcome of Byzantine barbarism. This short-sighted measure, however, was of no avail, for Iyâz, who now commanded in Northern Syria, passed the mountains of Taurus, and reduced under Moslem rule the province of Cilicia, with its capital Tarsus, the ancient monument of the Assyrian kings. He even carried the Saracenic arms as far as the Black Sea. His name became one of terror to the Romans in Asia Minor. About this time the Saracens, with their usual energy, turned their attention to the creation of a fleet; and it was not long before they rode masters of the sea. The Roman navy fled before them to the Hellespont, and the islands of the Greek Archipelago were successively invaded and reduced. The frequent incursions into Syria from the Egyptian side, and the harassment to which the sea-board was subjected by the Romans, led the Caliph, after some hesitation, to authorise an expedition into the land of the Pharaohs. Amr, the son of al-Aâs, started with only 4000 men, and in the course of three weeks cleared the country of the Byzantines. The Romans, flying from other parts of Egypt, took refuge

632—644 A.C. in Alexandria, which was well fortified. After a siege of some duration, the city capitulated on favourable terms. 19-20 A.H. 640-641 A.C. The whole of Egypt, up to the borders of Abyssinia on the south and Libya on the west, became subject to Moslem domination. As in other countries, immediately it was conquered, measures were taken to improve the condition of the peasantry. The soil was left in the hands of the cultivators; the old irrigation works, which had been neglected or which had fallen into ruin, were restored; and the ancient canal connecting the Mediterranean with the Red Sea was cleared out. The Egyptian Christians, who were called Copts and belonged to the Melchite sect, were treated with marked favour, in consequence of their goodwill towards the Moslems. Taxation was regulated upon a fixed and moderate scale, and trade was fostered by light customs dues. In 645 A.C. Alexandria was recaptured by the Romans. It was, however, finally reduced by the Saracens a year later. The story about the burning of the Alexandrian Library under the orders of the Caliph Omar is without any foundation. Such an act of vandalism was totally opposed to the tolerant and liberal spirit of that great ruler. As a matter of fact, a large part of this library was destroyed in the siege which Julius Cæsar underwent in that city; and the remainder was lost in the reign of the Emperor Theodosius, in the fourth century of the Christian era. This Emperor, who was a devout Christian and hated works written by pagans, had ordered the destruction and dispersion of the splendid remnant of the Philadelphian Library, which order was so zealously carried out that little or nothing remained of it in the seventh century for the Moslems to destroy.[1] After the conquest of Egypt, Amr became involved in a war with the tribes

[1] Compare Sédillot, vol. i. p. 439. The books are said to have been used to heat the baths with. There were no public *hammams* then in existence. They came into vogue years later.

towards the west, which ended in the reduction of the coast as far as Barca. 11—23 A.H.

In the eighteenth year of the Hegira, Northern Arabia and Syria were visited by a severe famine and pestilence, in which 25,000 people are said to have perished. Some of the best and most prominent men among the Moslems, including Abû Obaidah, Yezîd, and Shorâbhîl, fell victims to the epidemic. The wail which went up from the land called the Caliph forth again from Medîna. He was then nearly seventy years of age, but he bravely undertook the journey to Syria, as before, with a single attendant. He visited the Bishop of Ayla, guaranteed afresh the privileges of the Christians, and by his presence and speeches revived the spirit of the people.

On his return to Medîna, the Caliph devoted himself to organising the administration of the new Empire, and planning the development of its resources. But the hand of an assassin put an end to all his plans. A foreigner,[1] who bore the Caliph some grudge, inflicted on him a fatal wound from which he never recovered. Before his death he appointed an electorate, consisting of six men, to choose his successor.

The Death of Omar.

The death of Omar was a real calamity to Islâm. Stern but just, far-sighted, thoroughly versed in the character of his people, he was especially fitted for the leadership of the unruly Arabs. He had held the helm with a strong hand, and severely repressed the natural tendency to demoralisation among nomadic tribes and semi-civilised people when coming in contact with the luxury and vices of cities. He had established the *Diwân*, or department of finance, to which was entrusted the administration of the revenues; and had introduced

[1] Some say he was a Magian; others, like Dozy, state he was a Christian artisan of Kûfa.

632—644 A.C. fixed rules for the government of the provinces. He was a man of towering height, strong build, and fair complexion. Of simple habits, austere and frugal, always accessible to the meanest of his subjects, wandering about at night to inquire into the condition of the people without any guard or court—such was the greatest and most powerful ruler of the time.

CHAPTER V

THE REPUBLIC (*continued*)

24—40 A.H., 644—661 A.C.

Osmân—His favouritism—Osmân's death—Ali—Rebellion of Muâwiyah—Battle of Siffîn—The Khârijis—Assassination of Ali—End of the Republic.

Osmân.

OMAR could easily have nominated Ali or his own son, the virtuous Abdullâh, surnamed Ibn Omar, as his successor to the Caliphate; but with the conscientiousness which characterised him he entrusted the election to six notables of Medîna. In deviating, however, from the example of his predecessor he made a mistake which paved the way to Ommeyade intrigue. The Ommeyades now formed a strong party in Medîna; they had long been the rivals of the Hâshimides, the family of the Prophet, and hated them fiercely; they had pursued Mohammed with bitter ferocity; and it was only after the fall of Mecca that they had adopted Islâm from motives of self-interest. They had seen in the progress of Islâm the means of personal aggrandisement. Their hatred of the simple austere companions of the Prophet who ruled over Islâm was burning and implacable. They viewed with ill-concealed jealousy the old Moslems who formed the Council of State, and held the chief offices of government. The pure and simple lives of these saints were a standing reproach to them for their laxity and selfishness. And

644—661 A.C. they easily found allies among the chiefs of the Bedouin tribes attached to them by kinship. By their intrigues they succeeded in keeping Ali out of the Caliphate. After considerable debate and discussion, lasting over several days, the choice of the electorate fell upon Osmân, son of Affân, a member of the Ommeyade family. His election proved in the end the ruin of Islâm. Osmân, though virtuous and honest, was very old and feeble in character, and quite unequal to the task of government. He fell at once, as they had anticipated, under the influence of his family. He was guided entirely by his secretary, Merwân, one of the most unprincipled of the Ommeyades, who had once been expelled by the Prophet for breach of trust. With his usual patriotism and devotion to the Faith, Ali gave his adhesion to Osmân as soon as he was elected. Under Osmân commenced that bitter feud between the Hâshimides and the Ommeyades which lasted for over a century. But this was not the only evil which came into existence under him. The general body of the Arabs, always refractory and impatient of control, had been brought to order by the personality of the Prophet. The firmness of Abû Bakr and Omar had kept them under discipline. They now began to chafe under Koraishite predominance, and to sow the seeds of sedition in distant parts, and the old racial jealousy between the Modharites and Himyarites, which had nearly died out, began to smoulder afresh, with the most disastrous consequences to Islâm. Osmân displaced most of the lieutenants employed by Omar, and appointed in their stead incompetent and worthless members of his own family. During the first six years of his rule, the people, though grievously oppressed by the new governors, remained quiet. And in the out-

Elected Caliph. 1st Moharram, 24 A.H. 7th November 644 A.C.

lying provinces, the dangers to which the Saracens were exposed from the common enemies, kept the armies employed. The incursions of the Turks in Transoxiana led to the conquest of Balkh. Similarly were Herat, Kabul, and Ghazni captured. The risings in Southern Persia led to the subjugation of Kermân and Sistân. In the settlement of the new acquisitions, the policy of Omar was followed. No sooner were these countries conquered, than effective measures were set on foot for the development of their material resources. Watercourses were dug, roads made, fruit trees planted, and security given to trade by the establishment of a regular police organisation. Byzantine inroads from the north led to an advance on the country now called Asia Minor, towards the Black Sea. In Africa, Tripoli and Barca, and in the Mediterranean Cyprus, were conquered. A large fleet sent by the Romans to re-conquer Egypt was destroyed off Alexandria.

24—40 A.H.

31 A.H. 652 A.C.

Whilst Islâm was thus extending its sway in distant parts, Ali was endeavouring in Medîna to give an intellectual turn to the newly-developed energy of the Saracenic race. In the public mosque at Medîna, Ali and his cousin, Abdullah the son of Abbâs,[1] delivered weekly lectures on philosophy and logic, the traditions (history), rhetoric and law, whilst others dealt with other subjects. Thus was formed the nucleus of that intellectual movement which displayed itself in such great force in later times at Bagdad.

In the meantime, the weakness of the Caliph and the wickedness of his favourites were creating a great ferment among the people. Loud complaints of exaction and oppression by his governors began pouring into

[1] Better known as *Ibn Abbâs*, the son of Abbâs, born 619 A.C., died 687 A.C.

644—661 A.C. the capital. Ali expostulated several times with the Caliph on the manner in which he allowed the government to fall into the hands of his unworthy favourites. But Osmân, under the influence of his evil genius, Merwân, paid no heed to these counsels. At last deputations from the provinces arrived at Medîna, to demand redress. They were sent back with promises. On their way home they intercepted a letter of Merwân, purporting to bear the seal of the Caliph, containing directions to the local governors to behead the leaders of the deputations on their arrival at their destinations. Furious at this treachery, they returned to Medîna, and demanded the surrender of Merwân. And this demand was enforced even by members of the house of Ommeya.[1] The ill-fated Osmân met this demand with a stern refusal. Enraged at what they believed the complicity of the Caliph, they beseiged him in his house. At this hour of peril, the Ommeyades deserted the old Chief, and fled towards Syria, where their kinsman Muâwiyah was governor. But Osmân was bravely defended by Ali and his sons and dependents, and the insurgents had great difficulty in making any impression on the defenders. At last two of the besiegers scaled the wall, entered the house, and there killed the aged Caliph. Osmân was at the time of his assassination eighty-two, some say eighty-six, years of age; a man of medium size, bearded and large of limb, and without any strength of character. His chief merit lay in his piety. He habitually bestowed large gifts upon his relatives, and on several occasions presented his evil genius Merwân with the income of the State in the public Treasury, which naturally made him extremely unpopular among the people.

Osmân's Death.

18th Zu'l Hijja 34 A.H. 17th June 656 A.C.

[1] Masûdi, *Murûj uz-Zahab*.

On the tragical death of Osmân, Ali was proclaimed Caliph without opposition. During the three preceding administrations he had been a prominent member of the Council of State, ever ready to assist his predecessors with advice and guidance. And many of the great administrative works undertaken in the time of Omar were due to his counsel. In fact, that chief placed great reliance upon him and left him as his deputy at Medîna during his journey abroad. But throughout he had maintained a noble independence of character, and had devoted himself to the pursuit of learning and the education of his sons. Upon his election he walked with his usual simplicity to the public Mosque, and there, leaning on his long-bow, received the oath of fealty from the people, declaring himself at the same time ready to resign the office to any one more worthy.

24—40 A.H. 24th Moharram 35 A.H. 23rd June 656 A.C.

The husband of Fâtima united in his person the hereditary right with that of election. "One would have thought," says a French historian, "that all would have bowed before this glory so pure and grand; but it was not to be."[1] From the beginning he was beset with the hostility of the Ommeyades. With the honesty of purpose which always distinguished him, and disregarding all advice for temporising, immediately on his accession he gave orders for the dismissal of the corrupt governors appointed by Osmân, the resumption of the fiefs and estates that had been bestowed, at public loss, by the aged Caliph upon his principal favourites, and the distribution of the revenues in accordance with the rules laid down by Omar.[2] These orders gave great offence to those who had enriched themselves under the last administration. Some of Osmân's nominees gave up

[1] Sédillot. [2] Masûdi.

644—661 A.C.

The Revolt of Muâwiyah.

their posts without resistance, others revolted. Among the latter was Muâwiyah, the son of Abû Sufiân, who held the government of Syria, and who had, with the wealth of the Province, collected a large force of mercenaries, bound to him by love of pay. Thus supported Muâwiyah raised the standard of rebellion.

But this was not the only difficulty Ali had to contend with. His refusal to give to Talha and Zubair, two prominent members of the Koraish, the governments of Kûfa and Basra had converted their uncertain friendship into implacable hatred; and Âyesha, the daughter of Abû Bakr, who entertained an inconceivable dislike to Ali, fanned the flame. Talha and Zubair, forgetting their oath of fealty, escaped first to Mecca and then towards Irâk, where they were joined by Âyesha. The insurgents were able to collect here a large army with the object of attacking the Caliph. Ali, who had pursued them closely, besought them several times to desist

The Battle of the Camel.

from fratricidal war; but to no avail. The unavoidable fight took place at Khoraiba, where Talha and Zubair were killed[1]; and Âyesha was taken prisoner. She was sent back with every mark of consideration and respect to Medîna. After settling Chaldæa and Mesopotamia,

The Battle of Siffîn.

the Caliph proceeded towards Syria. He met the rebels at a place called Siffîn, to the west of Rakka. With his usual humanity, Ali endeavoured to bring about a peaceful settlement. But Muâwiyah was inflated by pride, and wanted impossible conditions. To avoid unnecessary shedding of blood, Ali offered to end the quarrel by personal combat, but the Ommeyade declined the challenge. In spite of every exasperation, the Caliph commanded his troops to await the enemy's attack, to

[1] The place where the fight actually took place, and where these men were killed, is called *Wâdi-us-Sabâa*, "Valley of the Lion."

spare the fugitives, and to respect the captives. The rebels were defeated in three successive battles, and Muâwiyah was ready to fly from the field, when a trick of his accomplice Amr, son of al-Aâs, saved them from destruction. He made his mercenaries tie copies of the Koran to their lances and flags, and shout for quarter. The soldiers of the Caliph at once desisted from pursuit, and called upon him to refer the dispute to arbitration. The Caliph saw through the ruse practised by the rebels, but the clamour of the army led him to consent to the course suggested. The choice of an arbitrator on his side fell unfortunately on a weak old man named Abû Mûsa Ashaari, who was also secretly hostile to Ali. Nor was he any match for the astute Amr, the son of al-Aâs, who represented Muâwiyah. The Caliph, deprived thus of the fruit of his victories by his own soldiers, retired in disgust with his army towards Kûfa. Here, the men who had been most clamorous at Siffin for the reference to arbitration, now repudiated it, and denounced it as sinful. They openly mutinied,[1] and withdrawing to Nahrwân on the borders of the Desert assumed a threatening attitude. They refused either to return to duty or quietly to disperse to their homes. Their conduct became at last so serious as to compel the Caliph to attack them. The majority fell fighting; a few escaped to al-Bahrain and al-Ahsa, where they formed the nucleus of the fanatical horde which time after time harassed the empire by their sanguinary attacks. Whilst these events were happening in the east, the Caliph's representative had either proved a traitor, or been completely duped at Daumat ul-jandâl. Amr had advised him that for the peace of Islâm, both Ali and Muâwiyah should be put aside, that Abû Mûsa should

24—40 A.H.

The Khâriji Revolt.

[1] Hence called *Khârijis.*

644—661 A.C. pronounce the deposition of Ali, and that he should then depose Muâwiyah, and that being done they should elect a new Caliph. The simple Abû Mûsa fell into the trap, and mounting the pulpit pronounced, "I depose Ali from the Caliphate;" Amr, mounting after him, said, "I accept the deposition of Ali, and appoint Muâwiyah in his place." This audacious announcement infuriated the followers of the Caliph. The two parties separated, vowing undying vengeance; and Abû Mûsa retired to Medîna, where in subsequent years he received a pension from the Ommeyade court. After this, the war against Muâwiyah proceeded in a desultory manner. The Caliph was hampered by difficulties on the eastern frontier, and was unable to direct a large force against him. He thus found himself able not only to secure Syria and proclaim himself Caliph, but also to conquer Egypt. Poison and the dagger helped to remove the most notable followers of the Caliph, who himself was struck down by the hand of an assassin, on the 27th of January, 661 A.C., whilst offering his devotions at the public mosque at Kûfa. Thus died, in the prime of his life, "the best-hearted Moslem," to use Colonel Osborn's words, "that ever lived." Mild, beneficent, and humane, ready to help the weak and distressed, his life had been devoted to the cause of Islâm. Had he possessed the sternness of Omar's character he would have been more successful in governing an unruly race like the Arabs. But his forbearance and magnanimity were misunderstood, and his humanity and love of truth was turned by his enemies to their own advantage.

Assassination of Ali.

17th Ramzan, 40 A.H.

Ali is described as a man of ruddy complexion, not very tall, but extremely strong, inclined to stoutness, with a flowing beard, soft grey eyes, and a look of great amiability and kindness. His bravery had won him the title of the "Lion of God"; his learning, that of the "Gate of Knowledge." Chivalrous, humane, and forbearing to the verge of weakness, as a ruler he came before his time. Most of the grand undertakings initiated by Omar for the welfare of the people were due to his counsel. Ever ready to succour the weak and to redress the wrongs of the injured, the accounts of his valorous deeds are still recited with enthusiasm from the bazaars of Cairo to those of Delhi. How the mail-clad knight rescued a stranger beset by lions in the desert; how the poor woman, captured by brigands with her wounded and dying husband, wailed for the succour which never failed, and how the "Lion of God" appeared and saved them. Such stories bring back to life the chivalry of the Arabs—personified in their greatest hero. With his dying breath, he inculcated lessons of charity, love, humility, and self-abnegation to his sons. He expressly ordered that no harshness should be used towards his murderer, who should be executed with one blow. In summing up his worth, Masûdi says—"If the glorious name of being the first Moslem, a comrade of the Prophet in exile, his faithful companion in the struggle for the Faith, his intimate associate in life, and his kinsman; if a true knowledge of the spirit of his teachings and of the Book; if self-abnegation and practice of justice; if honesty, purity, and love of truth; if a knowledge of law and science, constitute a claim to pre-eminence, then all must regard Ali as the foremost Moslem. We shall search in vain to find, either among his precedessors (save one) or among his successors, those virtues with which God had endowed him." 24—40 A.H.

By Fâtima, Ali had three sons and four daughters. Fâtima had survived the Prophet, her father, only a few months. Whilst she lived, Ali never married another, though the custom of the Arabs permitted his so doing. She was a remarkable woman for the age in which she lived, clever, accomplished and witty; her sermons, songs and aphorisms, serve as an index to her strength of character and nobility of mind. Her virtues gained her the title of "Our Lady of Light," by which name she is known among the Moslems. She was tall, slender, and endowed with great beauty, which caused her to be called *az-Zahra*, "the Beautiful."

With Ali ended the Republic of Islâm.

"Thus vanished," says a philosophical writer, "the popular *régime*, which had for its basis a patriarchal simplicity, never again to appear among any Mussulman nation; only the jurisprudence and the rules which depended on the Koran, survived the fall of the elective Government. Some of the republican passion, however, which gave to the small States a certain grandeur, and to the grand an excess of force, maintained itself in the nation in spite of the armies of the usurpers."[1]

[1] Oelsner, *Des Effets de la Religion de Mahomet.*

CHAPTER VI

Retrospect—Government—Policy—Administration—The Army—Social Life.

Retro-spect.

DURING the ten years of the Prophet's life at Medîna, a congeries of warring tribes and clans were rapidly consolidated into a nation under the influence of one great Idea. The work done within that short period will always remain as one of the most wonderful achievements recorded in history.

Under Abû Bakr the tribes thus brought into subjection made a wild but ineffectual attempt to revert to the old condition. After this we see what can only be likened to the overflow of the Nile. There is much misery and disruption at first, but wherever the flood has passed, it has fertilised the soil. The on-rush of the Saracens, chiefly induced by the hostility of the neighbouring nations, had this effect over people and countries. During the thirty years the Republic lasted, a wonderful change had come over the Arabs. Society was still archaic, but a taste for those accessories which first lead to its development and then to its deterioration was growing up. The chief cities were embellished with beautiful buildings, and life became luxurious. The system of clientage in vogue in the Peninsula was introduced in the conquered countries; the Persians, Turks, and Greeks who adopted Islâm becoming the clients or *Moulas*[1] of some Arab family or clan, thus increasing the strength of the latter and gaining for themselves prestige. Though all the Saracens were dominated by the centralised religious Idea, their fusion was never complete. And hence at the close of the Republic, we see the dominion of Islâm rent into two factions, just as Mecca was before Mohammed, one owning allegiance to his family (the Banû Hâshim), the other to their bitter enemies—the family of Ommeya. Though the treachery of Amr, the son of al-Aâs, caused an irreparable breach in Islâm, and led eventually to bitter feuds between the Himyarites and the Modarites, as yet there were no religious sects. Even the Khârijis (the Covenanters of Islâm) differed chiefly on the question of allegiance, refusing to recognise any Caliph after Omar.

Government.

The Caliph, who was the supreme head of the Government, was assisted by a Council of Elders composed of the principal Companions of the Prophet, who held their sittings in the principal Mosque, often assisted by the city notables and Bedouin chiefs present in Medîna. Several of the Companions were entrusted with special duties. For instance, during Abû Bakr's Caliphate, Omar had charge of the administration of justice and the distribution of the poor-tax. Ali, as a scholar, was entrusted with the work of correspondence, the supervision of the captives of war and their treatment and ransom. Another Companion presided over the equip-

[1] European authors, generally speaking, have made a mistake in supposing that the *Moulas* were all freedmen. There were two kinds of clientage among the Arabs, one arising from emancipation and the other from alliance (called *Wala ul-Mawâlât*). Some *Moulas* were freedmen no doubt, but the bulk were clients or allies.

ment of the troops. Every detail of the administration was thus looked after, but nothing was decided without consultation.

Policy.

During the thirty years that the Republic lasted, the policy derived its character chiefly from Omar, both during his lifetime and after his death. His policy was to consolidate Arabia and to fuse the Arab tribes into a nation. Forced by circumstances to moderate foreign conquests, he was anxious that the Saracens should not, in their foreign settlements, lose their nationality or merge with the people of other lands. Had Omar lived longer, his force of character would have enabled him to make the Arabs more homogeneous, and thus prevented the disastrous civil wars that led to the ruin of Islâm.[1]

Several features in his policy deserve special attention. The first was to exclude all hostile or alien element from Arabia, and to keep it exclusively for the Saracens;[2] the second was to avoid an excessive extension of the Republic.

With a far-sightedness often wanting in rulers of later times, he perceived that the stability of the empire and its material development depended upon the prosperity of the agricultural classes. To secure that object he forbade the sale of holdings and agricultural lands in the conquered countries.[3] As a further protection against encroachment on the part of the Arabs, he ordained that no Saracen should acquire land from the natives of the soil. The peasantry and land-owners were

[1] A European writer considers these civil wars and bitter tribal feuds as the salvation of Europe.

[2] A similar policy was in force in Czarist Russia.

[3] The district of Hîra, where free sale existed from before, was exempted from this rule.

thus doubly protected from eviction. In making these rules he was probably also actuated with a motive to keep the Arab race distinct from, and predominant among, the people and communities among whom they settled—a motive which is by no means infrequent in history, either ancient or modern. But the predominance which he gave to the Saracens, and the privileges he conferred, were not of an exclusive character; nor was a difference of colour, race and nationality considered as a bar to equality. Under Omar, the adoption of Islâm, or the introduction by clientage of a non-Arab into a Saracenic tribe, raised him to the status of a born Arab; and this policy at least was continued under all the succeeding rulers. Thus many Persian families, without changing their Faith, became *Moulas* of Arab families. Similarly were many Christian clans of Syria and Egypt, and the Berbers of Africa affiliated to Arabian tribes. Of course there were privileges attached to the dominant Faith, as has always been the practice in other countries and among other communities, which acted equally with conviction in inducing a rapid abandonment of the older cults. The tendency of the rules and principles of Islâm is towards democracy with a strong tinge of socialism. All men, rich and poor, are equal in the sight of God, and the rulers are only His lieutenants to protect them from anarchy. The revenues of the State were not for the benefit or enrichment of the Caliph, but for the good of the people. The poor-tax was ordained from the rich for the relief of the poor, and charity was embodied into a law. Consequently in the early days of the Republic, the Treasury required neither guard nor account-books. The tithes were distributed among the poor directly they were received, or were applied in the equipment of the troops who defended the State. The spoils of war were similarly distributed, but in these all shared alike, young and old, male and female, bond and free. Afterwards these distributions, being found unwieldy in practice, were commuted into fixed allowances. The entire nation became entitled to stipends out of the public revenue which were according to a graduated scale. And the benefit was not confined to the Moslems; *the people of the Zimmah* (the non-Moslem subjects), if distinguished for loyalty or faithful service, received similar consideration. The Caliphs had no civil list or any extraordinary allowance. The subdivision of landed property was never within the contemplation of the Prophet or his great lieutenant Omar, for it involved the eventual pauperisation of families. As a safeguard against this eventuality, the lands of the Medinites were protected from subdivision and alienation by entailment (*Wakf*); and with this same object, the public lands in the conquered countries, instead of being parcelled among the soldiers, were held by the State, and the income only, after defraying the charges, was distributed among the people entitled to it.

Unfortunately, under Osmân, there was a complete reversal of the main features of his great predecessor's policy. He not only removed the efficient and capable governors whom Omar had placed in charge of the Provinces, but, in order to gratify the grasping demands of his kinsmen, made a new distribution of the appointments. The State domains, which were public property, were granted by this ill-advised Caliph to his relatives. In this way Muâwiyah obtained all the public lands in Syria, and in part of Mesopotamia. The Sawâd, which was sacredly reserved by Omar for the purposes of the State, was given to another kinsman. The State Treasury, which was a public Trust under Abû Bakr and Omar, was emptied time after time for these unworthy favourites and the wealth of the Provinces went to enrich the Ommeyades, and to help them in preparing for the struggle for power. Osmân withdrew the privileges which had been granted to non-Moslems, and introduced various harsh rules in direct opposition to those of his predecessors. He allowed the sale of land, and was the first to create military fiefs. Ali's administration was too disturbed by civil war to remedy the evils of the previous administration; but he removed most of the corrupt governors and restored the policy of Omar where he had the power; established a State archive for the safe custody and preservation of the records of the Caliphate; created the office of *Hâjib* or Chamberlain, and of the *Sâhib ush-Shurta* or Captain of the Guard; and re-organised the police and regulated their duties.

Administration.

After the fall of Mecca and the subjugation of the Peninsula, the Prophet had appointed governors, under the designation of *Ameers*, for all the chief cities and provinces. The title was continued by Omar, who may be regarded as the practical founder of the political administration of Islâm. He divided the conquered lands into compact governorships, so as to enable his lieutenants to develop the resources of the countries in their charge. Ahwâz and Bahrain formed thus one Province; Sijistân, Mekran and Kermân, another; whilst Tabaristân and Khorâsân remained separate. Southern Persia was placed under three governors, whilst Irâk was under two, one stationed at Kûfa, the other at Basra. Similarly with Syria. The governor of the northern Provinces had his head-quarters at Hems, whilst the *wâli* of the southern part resided at Damascus. Palestine was under another governor. In Africa there were three governorships, one consisting of Upper Egypt, the other of Egypt Proper, and the third of the Provinces beyond the Libyan Desert. Arabia was divided into five Provinces. In the smaller Provinces the governors were called *wâlis* or *nâibs*[1] (deputies). In most places the governor, by virtue of his office, led the public or cathedral service and prayers, and delivered the Friday oration (*Khutba*), which was often a political manifesto. For Palestine, Damascus, Hems and Kinnisrin, Omar appointed special judges to lead the prayers as well as to administer justice. To regulate the receipt and disbursement of the revenue, he established the department of finance under the name of the *Diwân.* The expense of the fiscal and civil administration of each Province constituted the first charge upon its revenues; the next was for military requirements; the surplus was applied to the support of the nation. In this all persons of the Arab race and their *Mawâlis* (clients) were entitled according to well-defined and strictly regulated shares. A register was kept in the *Diwân* of all persons, Arab and non-Arab, men, women and children, entitled to a stipend. Whilst the governor was the military and civil head of the Province, the fiscal and administrative functions were actually discharged by subordinate officers, specially appointed for the particular duty. In the administration of the acquired countries, the improvement of the peasantry and the development of trade were particularly insisted upon. With that object, Egypt, Syria, Irâk and Southern Persia were measured field by field, and the assessment was fixed on an uniform basis. The record of this magnificent cadastral survey forms a veritable "catalogue," which, besides giving the area of the lands, describes in detail the quality of the soil, the

[1] The word *nawwâb* or *nawâb* is derived from nâib.

nature of the produce, the character of the holdings, and so forth. A network of canals was constructed in Babylonia, and the embankments of the Tigris and Euphrates, culpably neglected by the Chosroes,[1] were placed under the supervision of special officers. Omar reduced the tax on cereals and fostered trade. In order to facilitate direct communication between Egypt and Arabia, he had the old disused canal between the Nile and the Red Sea re-excavated. The Arabs named it "the Canal of the Commander of the Faithful." It was completed in less than a year, and when the Nile boats sailed up to Yembo and Jedda with the produce of Egypt, the price of grain fell in the markets of Mecca and Medîna, and hardly realised more than it did in its original home.

Justice. Justice was administered by civil judges, who were appointed by the Caliph and were independent of the governors. Omar was the first ruler in Islâm to fix salaries for his judges, and to make their offices distinct from those of executive officers.[2] The title of *Hâkim*, *i. e.* ruler, was reserved for the *Kâzis*[3] (judges). "The judge was named and is still named," says Von Hammer, "the *hâkim ush-sharaa*, *i. e.* ruler through the law, for law rules through the utterance of justice, and the power of the governor carries out the utterance of it. Thus the Islâmite administration, even in its infancy, proclaims in word and in deed the necessary separation between judicial and executive power." The administration of justice was perfectly equal, and the Caliphs set the example of equality by holding themselves amenable to the orders of the legally-constituted

[1] The same expression might apply to some of the later rulers.

[2] Zaid, the son of Sâbit, was the first salaried judge of Medîna.

[3] Lit., watcher of duties.

judge. In the beginning, the police duties were performed by the public generally. Omar introduced night-watches and patrols; but a regularly organised police was not established until the time of Ali, who formed a municipal guard called *Shurta*, whose chief was styled the *Sahib ush-Shurta*.[1] Under the advice of Ali, Omar also established the era of the Hegira, and founded and endowed schools and mosques in every part of the empire.

The revenue of the Commonwealth was derived from three sources:—(1) From the tithes or poor-tax payable on a graduated scale by all Moslems possessed of means. This was devoted to the defence of the State, the payment of the salaries of the officials employed in its collection, and the support of indigent Moslems. (2) From the land-tax levied from the *Zimmis* (non-Moslem subjects) under the name of *Kharâj* (*tributum soli*); and (3) from the capitation-tax, *jazia* (*tributum capitis*). Both these imposts were in existence in the Roman Empire under the very same designations, and it is a well-established fact that the capitation-tax was universally in force under the Sassanides in the Persian Empire. So that in introducing these taxes in Egypt, Syria, Irâk and Persia, the Moslems followed the old precedents. Both were fixed on a mild and equitable basis. But special cities, provinces and tribes were exempt from these burdens; and even where payment was obligatory, it was laid down that the tax should be levied so as to cause the least possible hardship. Jews, Christians, Samaritans, and Magians, who were styled "people of the Book," were treated with justice and humanity.

[1] Suyûti says it was under Osmân that the Shurta were formed; but see Ibn Khaldûn and von Hammer.

The Army. The army was comprised of tribal levies, and volunteers drawn chiefly from Medîna, Tâyef, and other cities. They were paid at first from the tithes; afterwards from the tithes and taxes. In the beginning the Caliph appointed the commander-in-chief only, upon whom devolved the choice of the officers. As the commander-in-chief represented the Caliph, he presided at the daily prayers. Where several army corps were united, it was always clearly stated which of the generals should preside at prayers, as that indicated his position as general-in-chief. Towards the end of his administration, Omar began to nominate subordinate officers also, such as the *Aârif*[1] and others. Breach of discipline and cowardice in the field were punished by pillory and tearing off the turban from the culprit's head—punishments regarded so degrading in those days as to be completely efficacious. The army was composed of cavalry and infantry; the former were armed with shields, swords, and long lances; the latter with shields, lances, and swords, or shields and bows and arrows. Among the infantry the archers formed the most important element. The formation of the infantry was in lines generally three deep, with the lancers in front to repel cavalry attacks, and the archers behind. The cavalry were usually posted on the flanks; and the battles commenced with challenges and single combats. The great superiority of the Saracenic armies consisted in their extreme mobility, their perseverance, and their powers of endurance—qualities which, joined to enthusiasm, made them invincible. They were always well-provisioned, and long marches were made on camels. At first the troops erected for encampments, huts made of palm-leaves; but afterwards Omar directed the con-

[1] Analogous to the Roman decurion.

struction of permanent stations or cantonments; and this was the origin of the military stations of Basra and Kûfa in Irâk, Fostât in Egypt, Kairowan in Africa, Mansurah in Sind, etc. In other places, like Hems, Gaza, Edessa, Isphahân, and Alexandria, heavy garrisons were kept up to repel sudden attacks. The cavalry wore chain-armour, with steel helmets often adorned with eagles' feathers. The foot soldiers were clad in tight-fitting tunics descending below the knees, shalwârs (trousers), and boots or shoes like those still in use among the Afghans and Punjabis. They marched to battle chanting verses from the Koran, like the Covenanters of Scotland, or the Protestants in the Thirty Years' War; and delivered their attacks with shouts of "*Allaho-Akbar*," "God is great."[1] Drums and kettle-drums were in use. The tribal levies were often accompanied by their families, and in the garrison towns and military stations special quarters were allotted to them. Impropriety of conduct was strictly prohibited, and drunkenness was punished by eighty stripes. Soldiers on foreign service away from their families were not required to serve for more than four months at a time. The Caliph Omar also introduced the system of muster-rolls, established frontier fortresses, and appointed commanders of the marches.

Social Life.

In the beginning, there was no system of architecture. Mecca possessed a few buildings like the Kaaba, with architectural pretensions; and the houses of the rich citizens were built either of stone or brick. In Medîna, the houses were chiefly made of the latter material, and even the principal Mosque was a humble structure made of sun-dried bricks covered with plastered earth. The houses were mostly one-storied, with court-yards and

[1] This is called the Takbîr.

a well in the centre. But towards the end of the second Caliph's rule, the influx of foreign architects into the capital of Islâm gave an impetus to architectural undertakings. All the chief men both at Mecca and Medîna erected mansions of stone and marble. The palace built for Osmân is said to have been immense, and of beautiful and imposing appearance. The principal Mosque was pulled down, and a fine structure of stone and marble erected on its site. Masûdi states that during the Caliphate of Osmân the Companions of the Prophet built for themselves magnificent mansions. The house built by Zubair, son of Awwâm, was in existence in the year 352 of the Hegira when Masûdi wrote, and was used by merchants and bankers for business purposes. Zubair also built several mansions at Kûfa, Fostât and Alexandria; and these houses, with their gardens, existed in good order in Masûdi's time. After mentioning these and many other signs of magnificence, the historian remarks with a sigh, "how different all this was from the simple and austere manners, and the life in the grand days of Omar." While Mecca was devoted to commerce, the citizens of Medîna depended for their prosperity on their fields and lands. And this circumstance added bitterness to the long-standing rivalry between the two cities. It was the old story of Athens and Sparta. The Meccans were addicted to gambling, wine and luxury. The Medinites, especially under the Islâmic *régime*, and with the example of their leaders, were austere in their manners and sincerely devout in their lives. After the fall of Mecca, the inhabitants of that gay and frivolous city were obliged to conform to the rules of morality inculcated by Islâm, and this continued under the first two Caliphs. With the accession of Osmân, the old gay and reckless life was resumed by many of the patrician youths, belonging chiefly to the Ommeyade family. His own nephew started a gambling club, and the serenading of ladies again became the fashion. The frivolity of Mecca was reproduced in a worse form at Damascus under the Ommeyades. In Medîna, the people took their lives more seriously. The lecture-rooms were filled with enthusiastic students, and members of either sex attended the sermons of the Caliphs. Music had not been yet placed under the ban, and the chief recreation of the people, after their day's work, consisted in singing and playing on the flute and the guitar. The women of the northern city were good singers, and according to the chroniclers, the austere Omar often stopped in his rounds to listen to their music.

In the houses of the well-to-do the floors were covered with carpets. There were no chairs or tables, but over the carpets and round the room were spread felt rugs, and on these sat the master and his guests. The ladies' apartments, as in England under the Anglo-Saxons and the early Normans, were separate, and were similarly furnished. The meals were laid over a *floor* cloth, which was spread over a sheet of leather in front of the rugs. Hands were washed both before and after dinner, just as among the ancients and in the Middle Ages in Europe. As yet there were no knives and forks, and the people ate with their fingers as in Europe until very recent times. But it was the height of ill-breeding to put more than three fingers into the plate.

The dress of the Bedouins under the rank of a Sheikh consisted then, as it does now, of a simple long shirt, its loose folds descending to the ankles, confined by a leathern girdle. This was and still is the common dress of both men and women. Over the shirt was thrown loosely a cloak, generally of camel's hair. When fighting and on horseback, trousers were worn with the shirt. Their head-dress was a long and broad kerchief, embroidered with tassels thrown over the head and neck, and tied round the head with a cord of camel's hair.

Among the settled inhabitants, the dress of the men of the better class and of the tribal Sheikhs generally, consisted of a shirt which reached down to the knees and was worn under the *Shalwâr*[1] or trousers. The next garment was a loose-fitting tunic reaching to the ankles, with a girdle of silk or shawl round the waist. Over this was worn a robe or *Jubbah*,[2] or a cloak called *Aba*. The well-fitting *Kaba*,[3] borrowed from the Byzantines, or as some say from the Persians, did not come into vogue until towards the end of the Republic. The *Kaba* was of two kinds, one with wide sleeves like the outer long coats of the Anglo-Saxon nobles; the other with tight closely-buttoned sleeves, often worn by Persian noblemen of the present day. On the head they wore turbans, which varied in size according to age, position, and learning. Over the turban, often was thrown the *Tailasân*, a kerchief which hung over the shoulders and shielded the neck from the sun. The covering for the feet were either sandals or boots.

The women's dress consisted of the loose *Shalwâr*, the shirt open at the neck, over which was worn, especially in cool weather, a close-fitting jacket. But the main

[1] Sometimes called Sirwal. The Spaniards corrupted this into Zaraguelles (or Çaraguelles).

[2] See Dozy's *Dictionnaire Détaillé des noms des vêtements chez les Arabes*, p. 107.

[3] *Ibid.* p. 352. Ibn ul-Athîr says Nomân, the Saracen general at the battle of Nehâwand, wore a *Kaba*.

dress was a long robe something like those worn by Anglo-Saxon dames. Over this, for out-door purposes, a loose robe which could be drawn round to hide the figure or to protect the clothes from dust or mud. The head was covered with a kerchief tied round the forehead. In pre-Islâmic times the women's shirt and jacket were worn open over the chest; the Prophet recommended for out-door use the long robe. And hence arose under the later Abbassides the custom of that complete envelopment of the body which we see now-a-days in Egypt and some other Moslem countries.

Among the Arabs, women were and still are perfectly free. The system of seclusion in vogue in many Moslem countries did not come into practice until long after. Among the Republican Moslems, the women moved freely in public, attended the sermons of the Caliphs, and the lectures delivered by Ali, Ibn Abbâs, and others. Nor among the men had the old Arab chivalry been killed by contact with the Byzantines and the Persians. The pre-Islâmite Arabs were like the ancient Hebrews, accustomed to marry many wives. This was the natural consequence of the decimation of men in the tribal wars; for the women would otherwise have starved. The Arabian Prophet, by imposing a limit to the custom, indirectly forbade polygamy, but made it conformable to all stages of society. Thus, under the Republic, the home-life was patriarchal. The buying and selling of slaves was strictly forbidden; in fact, human chattelhood was denounced in the strongest terms. Only persons made captives in lawful warfare were permitted to be held in "bond" until ransomed; and the bondsmen and bondswomen were regarded as members of the family.

CHAPTER VII

THE OMMEYADES (THE HARBITE BRANCH)

40—64 A.H., 661—683 A.C.

Hassan—His Abdication—Muâwiyah—The Usurpation—Tribal Dissensions—The Modharites—The Himyarites or Yemenites—Effect of Tribal Discord on Islâm—The Extension of the Empire—The Death of Muâwiyah—Yezîd I.—Hussain—The Massacre of Kerbela—The Rising in Hijâz—Syrian Victory at Harra—The Sack of Medîna—Death of Yezîd I.—Muâwiyah II.—Abdullâh the son of Zubair—Oath of Fealty to him in Hijâz.

Hassan.
40 A.H.
661 A.C.

HASSAN, the eldest son of Ali, was elected to the vacant Caliphate by the unanimous suffrage of Kûfa and its dependencies, but the inconstancy of the volatile people that had wrecked the hopes of the father soon drove the son to abdication. Hardly had the new Caliph been seated on the pontifical throne when Muâwiyah invaded Irâk. Hassan was thus compelled to take the field before he had either strengthened himself in his position or organised the administration thrown into confusion by the death of his father. Sending forward a general of the name of Kais to hold the Syrians at bay, he proceeded with his main force to Madâin. Here a false report of the defeat and death of Kais excited a mutiny among the young Caliph's troops; they broke into his camp, plundered his effects, and even thought of seizing his person and making him over to the enemy. Thoroughly disheartened, Hassan retraced his steps towards Kûfa, firmly resolved to resign the Pontificate. Mistrust of his Irakian supporters, so lavish of promise, so faithless in performance, led him to lend a willing ear to the proposals of Muâwiyah. The negotiations resulted in a treaty by which the Caliphate was assigned to Muâwiyah for life; upon his death it was to devolve on Hussain, the younger son of Ali. After his abdication Hassan retired with his family to Medîna, but did not long enjoy the pension secured to him under the compact, as many years did not pass before he was poisoned at the instigation of Yezîd the son of Muâwiyah.

40—64 A.H.

Abdicates the Caliphate.

Upon the abdication of Hassan, Muâwiyah became the *de facto* ruler of Islâm. Thus, by one of the strangest freaks of fortune recorded in history, "did the persecutors of Mohammed usurp the inheritance of his children, and the champions of idolatry become the supreme heads of his religion and empire." The seat of government, which Ali had fixed at Kûfa, was now removed to Damascus, where Muâwiyah surrounded himself with the pomp and pageantry of the Persian and Byzantine monarchs. Like the Borgias and the Medicis in later times, he frequently resorted to poison and the dagger to remove an inconvenient enemy or an impossible friend. Neither claims of kinship nor services to Islâm formed any protection. Among those thus sacrificed to ambition or policy, was Abdur Rahmân the son of the great conqueror of Syria. Abdur Rahmân's popularity among the Syrians, and the esteem in which he was held by thoughtful Moslems, formed the cause of his assassination. Muâwiyah's character and the circumstances which ensured his success are thus summed up by an English writer, whose views on this point at least are free from prejudice. "Astute, unscrupulous, and pitiless, the first Caliph of the

MUÂWIYAH.

30 July 661 A.C. Shawwâl 41 A.H.

661—683 A.C. Ommayas shrank from no crime necessary to secure his position. Murder was his accustomed mode of removing a formidable opponent. The grandson of the Prophet he caused to be poisoned; Malek al-Ashtar, the heroic lieutenant of Ali, was destroyed in a like way. To secure the succession of his son Yezîd, Muâwiyah hesitated not to break the word he had pledged to Hussain, the surviving son of Ali. And yet this cool, calculating, atheistic Arab ruled over the regions of Islâm, and the sceptre remained in his family for the space of nearly ninety years. The explanation of this anomaly is to be found in two circumstances to which I have more than once adverted. The one is, that 'the truly devout and earnest Mohammedan conceived that he manifested his religion most effectually by withdrawing himself from the affairs of the world. The other is the tribal spirit of the Arabs. Conquerors of Asia, of Northern Africa, of Spain, the Arabs never rose to the level of their position. Greatness had been thrust upon them, but in the midst of their grandeur they retained in all their previous force and intensity the passions, the rivalries, the petty jealousies of the desert. They merely fought again on a wider field 'the battle of the Arabs before Islâm.'"[1]

The Accession of the Ommeyades: its effects on Islâm.

The accession of the Ommeyades did not simply imply a change of dynasty; it meant the reversal of a principle and the birth of new factors which, as we shall see, exercised the most potent influence on the fortunes of the Empire and the development of the nation. To apprehend these circumstances and to note the current of history, it is necessary to review briefly the position of the various Arabian tribes in their settlements and of their relations to each other.

[1] Osborn's *Islam under the Arabs.*

If we exclude from our consideration the wars that owe their origin to religious hatred, or to difference in fundamental principles, such as the struggle of democracy with autocracy, of personal liberty with feudal tyranny, there is no cause more enduring or more persistent, either in Asia or in Europe, among Christians or among Moslems, in keeping asunder people and nationalities and in involving them in disastrous and sanguinary warfare, as antipathy of race—a sentiment which casts its lurid shadow over centuries, and survives all political, social, and religious revolutions. At the time of Mohammed's advent, as already mentioned, Arabia was inhabited by people claiming origin from two different stocks—the one from Kahtân, the other from Ishmael, the son of the Patriarch Abraham. The cradle of the former was Yemen; of the latter Hijâz. From Himyar, one of the sons of Abd us-Shams,[1] their ancient king, the Kahtanites came to be called in later times Himyarites, though by the Arabian writers they are spoken of, from their original habitat, as Yemenites. In the following pages I shall speak of them indifferently as Himyarites or Yemenites. The tribe which dwelt in and round Mareb or Saba, the capital of Yemen under the Himyarite kings (the *Tobbas*),[2] were the Banû Azd, the children of Azd, a descendant of Kahtân. In the second century of the Christian era, there seems to have been a movement of the Azdites towards the north, which led to the displacement of other tribes. Eventually, a portion of the Azdites settled themselves at Batn Marr near Mecca, under the name of *Khuzaa* (*separated*), where they still

40—64 A.H.

The Himyarites.

[1] See *ante*, p. 3. Himyar succeeded Abd us-Shams. He is said to have received the title of *Himyar* (*red*) as he always wore a red mantle.

[2] This is a generic title, like Cæsar, etc.

D 2

661—683 A.C. resided at the time of the Prophet; another branch found its way into Yathreb (Medîna), where, in the course of ages, it developed into the two tribes of Aus and Khazraj, of whom we have spoken before.[1] Others wandered into Syria and Irâk; those who settled on the Syrian side were called the Banû Ghassân (the Ghassanides); those on the Irakian side were called the Banû Kalb (the Kalbites). Another detachment settled at Hamadan; whilst a large number, turning eastward, found a home in the province of Oman on the shores of the Persian Gulf. This in brief was the position occupied by the Himyarite Arabs about the time of the ministry of Mohammed.

The Modharites. The Ishmaelite tribes of Arabia are sometimes called Banû Maad,[2] but oftener Banû Modhar, or Modharites, from Modhar, a grandson of Maad. I shall call them in these pages by this latter name, though in Arabian histories this general designation often gives place to sub-tribal names, such as the Banû Koraish, the Banû Kais, the Banû Bakr, the Banû Taghlib, and the Banû Tamîm. The Koraish, as we have already seen, inhabited Mecca and its environs; the others were spread over Hijâz (with the exception of Yathreb or Medîna) and Central Arabia.

Antagonism between Himyar and Modhar. Between these two races, the Himyarites and Modharites, there had existed a keen and constant antagonism, verging on hatred, which would be unintelligible to any one looking at the subject from the point of view of European history. The hatred of the Celt towards the Saxon, of the Irish towards the English, of the Pole against the Russ, is explained by centuries of tyranny and

[1] See *ante*, p. 11.

[2] Maad was the son of Adnân, a descendant of Ishmael; Modhar was the grandson of Maad.

misrule under which the weaker nation has groaned. 40—64 A.H.
Political rivalry is the key to the burning rancour of the Guelf and the Ghibeline. In Europe, diversity of idioms and customs, often of faith, forms a barrier against the fusion of two people violently brought under the same rule; but generally speaking a few centuries of hacking and harrying fuse them together.

With the Arabs before Mohammed it was different. Long before the appearance of the Prophet, the Himyarite tongue, born of the mixture of Semitic and indigenous idioms, had given place to pure Arabic, the language spoken by the Banû Modhar, which had acquired a certain intellectual preponderance; and the Arabs all over the Peninsula talked, with slight differences of dialect, one common language. Their customs and manners, their ideas and tastes, were similar. And yet the division between the two races was sharp and well-defined. We must search deeper to arrive at the cause. Its causes.
The Himyarites had attained a high state of civilisation several centuries before the birth of Islâm; wherever settled, they possessed an organised government, no doubt archaic, but still sufficiently regular for the ordinary purposes of civil life. They knew the art of writing, and were chiefly addicted to agriculture. The Modharites, on the other hand, with the exception of the Koraish since the time of Kossay, were nomadic and pastoral. Each tribe was separate from the other, divided in interest and sympathies, and electing its own chief by a sort of popular suffrage. This divided condition had naturally led to their subjugation by the Himyarite kings, to whom, in spite of frequent wars, they paid tribute until late into the fifth century of the Christian era. The incessant struggle between Himyar and Modhar, for preponderance on one side, for independence on the

661—683 A.C. other, had created a bitter feeling of jealousy, and a burning antagonism on the part of both, which were kept alive by their bards, who sang of the "Days" when Kinda harried Tamîm, or Kais swooped down upon Azd. The preachings of Mohammed began to efface this racial hatred and to nullify the influence of the bards. Had the Prophet lived longer, in all human probability his teachings and his wonderful personality would have moulded the tribes into a homogeneous nation. Ten years of ministry, however earnest, were much too short to eradicate the poison of race-antagonism which had worked for centuries in the Arab blood. In Medîna alone, where his influence was persistent and continuous, was the fusion complete.

The wave of conquest under Abû Bakr and Omar carried the Saracenic tribes into different parts of the world. The Modhar settled at Basra, whilst Kûfa was occupied chiefly by the Himyar. In Palestine and in the province of Damascus, the Modhar were preponderant; whilst the northern part of Syria like Northern Arabia was held by the Himyar. In the Eastern Provinces, as also in Egypt and in Africa, the two tribes were more or less equally dispersed. But wherever they went they carried with them the old feeling of discord. Under the stern rule of the great Omar, it was kept down with a strong hand; nor would the work in which the nation was then engaged—the work of self-preservation, and the necessity of self-expansion—allow much room for any sentiment other than generous emulation. Had Ali been allowed peaceably to succeed Omar, probably the two tribes would have imperceptibly merged into one nation. But under Osmân, the Ommeyades, for their own ends, fanned the smouldering ashes of dying hatred until they had worked it into a flame which burnt as furiously in Spain and Sicily as in the deserts of Africa, the plains of Khorâsân, and the wilds of Kabul. This lamentable discord proved most disastrous to its fomentors, and exercised a far-reaching effect on the fortunes of the Saracenic nation, and on the destinies of the Roman and Germanic races with whom the Arabs soon became involved in contest. It stopped them on their road to conquest just at the moment when the west lay at their feet, and eventually led to the loss of a great portion of their Empire.

40—64 A.H.

Muâwiyah's Policy.

Muâwiyah, whilst leaning for support on the Modhar, was astute enough to hold the balance fairly between them and the Himyar; and not to allow the one unduly to oppress the other. Under his successors whichever party became preponderant for the time fiercely and cruelly persecuted its rival. But the Ommeyade clan, knit together by ties of kinship and self-interest, never wavered in its allegiance to its chief; and the Syrian mercenaries always formed a bulwark of strength for Muâwiyah and his family. The more thoughtful and religious-minded people now withdrew from all interest in public affairs; they devoted themselves to the cultivation of literature, to the pursuit of Islâmic jurisprudence,—the first foundations of which were laid at this period,—or to the quiet observance of the rules of their religion. They helped in the propagation of the Faith, but took no part in the government of the Empire. The bigots who had rebelled against the Caliph Ali and been crushed at Nahrwân, had taken refuge in the inaccessible province of al-Ahsa and other parts of Central Arabia. Here they had spread their dark, gloomy, and fanatical doctrines.[1] Their number, their recklessness, and their

[1] They acknowledged the authority of the first two Caliphs only. They denounced both Osmân and Ali, and reprobated the Omme-

661–683 A.C. devotion to what they considered right made them a formidable enemy to the Damascus government. They rose against Muâwiyah, invaded Chaldæa, and threatened Irâk, but were ultimately beaten and forced to take refuge in their strongholds in the desert.

Conquests in Africa. Muâwiyah, now firmly seated on the throne of Damascus, turned his attention towards Africa. It must be noted that among the Arabs the term "Ifrîkia" was applied only to the northern parts of Africa beyond Egypt. This vast tract was divided into three parts—(1) the Remote West (*Maghrib ul-Aksâ*), which stretched from the shores of the Atlantic to Tlemsen southward towards the Sahara; (2) the Lower West (*Maghrib ul-Adnâ*), which included the country lying between Oran and the district of Bugia; and (3) *Ifrîkia* proper, which extended from the eastern limits of modern Algeria to the frontiers of Egypt. Northern Africa west of the Libyan Desert and north of the *Black Country* (Soudan) was inhabited by people belonging to the Semitic stock; and many of the tribes who dwelt in the plains and on the hills of this region claimed descent from the two principal Arab branches.[1] Hardy and brave, they were animated by the same fierce love of independence as the Arabs. The first invasion of this province had taken place in the

yades as profligate pagans. They claimed the right of electing an Imâm (religious leader) from among the universality of the people irrespective of clan or family, and sought to enforce the kingdom of God. They considered every one but themselves as doomed to perdition. All amusements, however innocent, were forbidden on pain of death. These fanatics have had and still have their analogues in other creeds.

[1] One of the Himyarite kings is said to have penetrated into Northern Africa and established there Kahtanite colonies. He is thus called Ifrîkius or Africanus from his African conquests.

reign of Omar;[1] under Osmân the Saracenic forces had advanced as far as Barca. After the defeat of Gregorius the Byzantine Prefect, at the memorable battle fought not far from ancient Carthage, the Romans undertook to pay an annual tribute to the Saracens, who then withdrew from the country, leaving small garrisons at Zawîlah and Barca. The Roman governors re-occupied the abandoned territories; but their rapacity and exactions were so intolerable that before long the natives themselves invited the Saracens to liberate them from the Byzantine yoke. Muâwiyah responded to their call, and an army under the celebrated Okba, son of Nâfè, marched into Ifrîkia, beat down all opposition, and reduced the country into a Saracenic dependency. 40—64 A.H.

In 50 A.H. Okba built the famous military city of Kairowân to the south of Tunis to keep in check the fierce unruly Berbers, and also to guard against the Roman ravages from the sea. The forest, hitherto infested by wild beasts and reptiles, was levelled, and the magnificent town, the remains of which may still be seen, was erected on the spot. The Romans, who held *Maghrib* (modern Morocco), assisted by Berber auxiliaries, frequently raided into Ifrîkia. In 55 A.H. Okba determined upon an advance into the west. The open towns surrendered as he approached; the Romans and Greeks hung about his flanks, cut off the stragglers, and tried to obstruct his passage towards the west; but Okba forced his way through until he reached the Atlantic. Disappointed at the sight of the vast expanse of water which checked any further advance, he spurred his horse chest-deep into the waves, and raising his hands towards heaven exclaimed, "Almighty Lord! but for this sea I 670 A.D. Building of Kairowân.

[1] See p. 42.

661—683 A.C. would have gone into still remoter regions, spreading the glory of Thy name and smiting Thine enemies."

The brilliant march of Okba and the crushing blows he inflicted on the Romans and the Berbers had the effect of keeping the country quiet for several years. With a slight intermission owing to his recall to Damascus, he ruled Ifrîkia and its western dependency until his death in 65 A.H. In this year the wild hordes of the Berbers, a countless host issuing from the mountains and valleys of the Atlas, poured down upon the handful of Saracens that held Kairowân. It was like the gathering of the clans in Scotland; the same methods were used for summoning the tribes, and the same tactics were employed against the conquerors. No nation or race has shown more dauntless courage or more indomitable energy than the Saracens in their wars with the wild and warlike races of Northern Africa. With a comparatively small army the Arabs essayed the conquest of a vast country, inhabited, not like India, by an essentially peaceful population, but by fierce and turbulent tribes accustomed to warfare. The Berbers surrounded the capital; but Okba was not the man to die like a mouse in a trap. He broke the scabbard of his sword, the usual mode of showing a resolution to conquer or to die, charged into the midst of the beleaguering host, and was killed fighting. Most of his soldiers fell with him. A few cut their way into Egypt. Kairowân fell into the hands of the Berbers, and Arab domination in Africa and the west seemed at an end.

Death of Okba.

Conquests in the East.

Whilst Okba was thus employed in the west, Sind and the lower valley of the Indus was conquered by Muhallib, the son of Abu Sufra. Eastern Afghanistan was also brought under subjection about the same time. The Romans, who had taken advantage of the civil wars to make encroachments on the Moslem territories, were defeated in several battles, and the Saracenic army wintered in Cappadocia. The Roman fleet fled before that of the Saracens; and many of the islands of the Grecian Archipelago were conquered and annexed to the Empire. 40—64 A.H.

Under the instigation of Mughîra, the governor of Basra, Muâwiyah conceived the design of nominating his son Yezîd as his successor to the throne. This was in direct breach of his covenant with Hassan, but he was supported in his design by the Bastard[1] who then ruled as his lieutenant over Irâk and Khorâsân. The Irakians were bribed, cajoled, or coerced to take the oath of fealty to Yezîd; the Syrians, of course, followed Muâwiyah's lead. Muâwiyah instals his son Yezîd as his successor.

In the year 51 A.H. Muâwiyah proceeded to Medîna and Mecca to secure the covenant of the people of Hijâz. Here, too, his menaces or his arts were partially successful. Four men, then foremost among the Moslems—Hussain the son of Ali, Abdullâh the son of Omar (the Caliph), Abdur Rahmân the son of Abû Bakr, and Abdullâh the son of Zubair, refused to take the oath on any condition, and their example gave heart to the Hijâzians. Abdullâh the son of Zubair, whom Muâwiyah called "the crafty fox of the Koraish," had himself an eye to the Caliphate; the others were actuated by abhorrence of Yezîd, whose wickedness was notorious.

Muâwiyah died in the month of Rajab 60 A.C. (April 680). He is said to have been of fair complexion, tall and unwieldy. The annalists say, "he was the first who preached seated to the people, the first who appointed MUÂWIYAH'S DEATH. April 680 A.C.

[1] Ziâd was an illegitimate son of Abû Sufiân, the father of Muâwiyah, and was therefore simply called "Ibn Abîh," "the son of his father," without the mention of any name.

661—683 A.C. eunuchs for his personal service, and the first with whom his courtiers jested familiarly." Astute, unscrupulous, clear-headed, miserly, but lavishly liberal when necessary, outwardly observant of all religious duties, but never permitting any human or divine ordinances to interfere with the prosecution of his plans or ambitions—such was Muâwiyah. But once firmly seated on the throne and his path clear of all enemies, he applied himself with assiduity to the good government of the Empire. The historian Masûdi gives an account of his daily life, which is curious and interesting. After the early morning prayers, he received the town-commandant's report. His ministers and privy councillors then came to him for the transaction of public business. During breakfast he listened to the correspondence from the provinces read to him by one of the secretaries. At midday he issued for the public prayers, and in the Mosque seated within an enclosure received the complaints of all who desired to approach him. On his return to the Palace he gave audience to the grandees. When that was over the principal meal of the day was served, which was followed by a short rest. After the afternoon prayers another audience was given to the ministers for the transaction of business. In the evening he dined in state, and afterwards held another reception which closed the day. On the whole Muâwiyah's rule was prosperous and peaceful at home and successful abroad.

His daily life.

Muâwiyah's contemporaries at Constantinople.

Constans II., who murdered his brother Theodosius, ruled the Roman Empire at the beginning of Muâwiyah's reign, and on his expulsion his son Constantine IV., surnamed Pogonatus, was invested with the purple. This descendant of the Cæsars distinguished himself by amputating the noses of his brothers Heraclius and Tiberius, and crucifying numbers of the dignitaries of the Church.

On Muâwiyah's death, Yezîd ascended the throne according to his father's testament. The accession of Yezîd gave the death-stroke to the republican principle that "the Commander of the Faithful" should be elected by the plebiscite of the people,—a principle to which the Arabs were so devoted, and which had led them to ignore the right of the Prophet's family to the spiritual and temporal headship of Islâm. Henceforth the ruling sovereign nominated his successor, whose reversion he endeavoured to assure during his lifetime by the oath of fealty of his soldiers and grandees. The celebrated doctor (Imâm) Hassan of Basra, who lived towards the close of the century, declared that "two men threw into confusion the affairs of the Moslems—Amr the son of al-Aâs, when he suggested to Muâwiyah the lifting of the Koran on the lances, and it was so uplifted,[1] and Mughîrah, who advised Muâwiyah to take the covenant of allegiance for Yezîd. Were it not for that, there would have been a Council of Election till the day of resurrection, for those who succeeded Muâwiyah followed his example in taking the covenant for their sons."

40—64 A.H.

Yezîd I. Shabân 61 A.H. April 680 A.C.

Yezîd was both cruel and treacherous; his depraved nature knew no pity or justice. His pleasures were as degrading as his companions were low and vicious. He insulted the ministers of religion by dressing up a monkey as a learned divine and carrying the animal mounted on a beautifully caparisoned Syrian donkey wherever he went. Drunken riotousness prevailed at court, and was naturally imitated in the streets of the capital. Hussain, the second son of Ali, had inherited his father's virtues and chivalrous disposition. "The

[1] See *ante*, p. 51.

661—683 A.C. only quality," says Sédillot, "that he lacked was the spirit of intrigue which characterised the descendants of Ommeya." He had served with honour against the Christians in the siege of Constantinople, and combined in his person the right of descent both from the Prophet and Ali. In the terms of peace signed between Muâwiyah and Hassan, his right to the Caliphate had been expressly reserved. Hussain had never deigned to acknowledge the title of the tyrant of Damascus, whose vices he despised, and whose character he regarded with abhorrence, and when the Moslems of Kûfa besought his help to release them from the curse of the Ommeyade rule, he felt it his duty to respond to the appeal for deliverance. With the exception of Abdullâh the son of Zubair, who wanted Hussain out of his way, and therefore encouraged him in his enterprise, all Hussain's friends tried to persuade him not to trust to the Kûfan promises. They knew the Irâkian character. Eager, fierce, and impetuous, the people of Kûfa were utterly wanting in perseverance and steadiness. "They knew not their own minds from day to day. One moment ardent as fire for some cause or person, the next they were as cold as ice and as indifferent as the dead." But the assurances that all Irâk was ready to spring to its feet the moment he appeared on the scene, decided him to start for Kûfa. He traversed the desert of Arabia unmolested, accompanied by several of his kinsmen, his two grown-up sons, a few devoted followers, and a timorous retinue of women and children; but as he approached the confines of Irâk he saw no signs of the Kûfan army, which had promised to meet him; he was alarmed by the solitary and hostile face of the country, and suspecting treachery, the Ommeyade's weapon, he encamped his small band at a place called Kerbela near the western bank of the Euphrates. Hussain's apprehensions of betrayal proved only too true. He was overtaken by an Ommeyade army sent by the brutal and ferocious son of the Bastard.[1] For days their tents were surrounded; and as the murderous ruffians dared not come within the reach of Hussain's sword, they cut the victims off from the waters of the Euphrates, causing terrible suffering to the small band of martyrs. In a conference with the chief of the enemy, Hussain proposed the option of three honourable conditions: that he should be allowed to return to Medîna, or be stationed in a frontier garrison against the Turks, or safely conducted to the presence of Yezîd. But the commands of the Ommeyade tyrant were stern and inexorable,—that no mercy should be shown to Hussain or his party, and that they must be brought as criminals before the "Caliph" to be dealt with according to the Ommeyade sense of justice. As a last resource, Hussain besought these monsters not to war upon the helpless women and children, but to take his life and end the unequal contest. But they knew no pity. He pressed his friends to consult their safety by timely flight; they unanimously refused to desert or survive their beloved master. One of the enemy's chiefs, struck with horror at the sacrilege of warring against the grandson of the Prophet, deserted with thirty followers "to claim the partnership of inevitable death." In every single combat and close fight the valour of the Fatimides was invincible. But the enemy's archers picked them off from a safe distance. One by one the defenders fell, until at last there remained but the grandson of the Prophet. Wounded and dying he dragged himself to the riverside for a last drink; they turned

40—64 A.H.

Massacre of Kerbela.

[1] Obaidullâh the son of Ziâd, surnamed the Butcher, who was acting as the lieutenant of Yezîd.

661—683 A.C. him off from there with arrows. Re-entering his tent he took his infant child in his arms; they transfixed him with a dart. And his sons and his nephews were killed in his arms. Able no more to stand up against his pitiless foes, alone and weary, he seated himself at the entrance of his tent. One of the women handed him water to assuage his burning thirst; as he raised it to his lips he was pierced in the mouth with a dart. He lifted his hands to heaven, and uttered a funeral prayer for the living and the dead. Raising himself for one desperate charge, he threw himself among the Ommeyades, who fell back on every side. But faint with loss of blood he soon sank to the ground, and then the murderous crew rushed upon the dying hero. They cut off his head, trampled on his body, and with savage ferocity subjected it to every ignominy. They carried his head to the castle of Kûfa, and the inhuman Obaidullâh struck it on the mouth with a cane. "Alas!" exclaimed an aged Moslem, "on these lips have I seen the lips of the Apostle of God." "In a distant age and climate," says Gibbon, "the tragic scene of the death of Hussain will awaken the sympathy of the coldest reader." It will be now easy to understand, perhaps to sympathise with, the frenzy of sorrow and indignation to which the adherents of Ali and of his children give vent on the recurrence of the anniversary of Hussain's martyrdom.

Thus fell one of the noblest spirits of the age, and with him perished all the male members of his family—old and young—with the solitary exception of a sickly child, whom Hussain's sister, Zainab (Zenobia), saved from the general massacre. He, too, bore the name of Ali, and in after life received the designation of Zain-ul-Aâbidîn, "the ornament of the Pious." He was the son of Hussain by the daughter of Yezdjard, the last

Sassanide king of Persia, and in him was perpetuated the house of the Prophet. He represented also, in his mother's right, the claims of the Sassanians to the throne of Irân. When the young lad was brought before Obaidullâh, he thought of murdering him also, to put an end to the progeny of Mohammed; but something in the look of Zainab, her determination to die with her young nephew, struck fear into the tyrant's heart. The women of Hussain's family with young Ali were sent to Damascus; the soldiers of their escort carrying on their lances the heads of the martyrs. On their arrival at Damascus, the granddaughters of the Prophet, in their tattered and travel-worn garments, sat themselves down under the walls of Yezîd's Palace and wailed as only Arab women can wail. Their sorrowful cry frightened Yezîd, and, afraid of some outburst in his capital in favour of the Prophet's family, he hurriedly sent them back to their homes. 40—64 A.H.

The butchery of Kerbela caused a thrill of horror throughout Islâm, and gave birth in Persia to a national sentiment which afterwards helped the descendants of Abbâs to destroy the Ommeyades. In Medîna the feeling was so strong that Yezîd sent in haste a special governor to calm the people. At his advice the notables despatched a deputation to Damascus to seek redress for Hussain's family. The deputation, however, returned disgusted with Yezîd's abominable life and his conduct towards them. Enraged at the unsatisfactory result of their endeavours, the Medinites proclaimed Yezîd's deposition and drove his governor from their city. This news threw Yezîd into a fury, and he immediately hurried off a large army, consisting of his Syrian mercenaries and Ommeyade partisans, under Muslim the son of Okba, known in Arabian history as

661—683 A.C.

The Battle of Harrah.

"the accursed murderer." The Medinites met the Syrians at a place called Harrah, where a desperate battle took place. The Moslems were overmatched, and in spite of heroic valour, were defeated with terrible loss. The flower of the Medinite chivalry and the noblest Companions of the Prophet, both Ansâr and Muhajerîn, perished in that disastrous fight,—disastrous to Islâm in more ways than one. The city which had sheltered the Prophet, and which was sanctified by his life and ministry, was foully desecrated; and the people who had stood by him in the hour of his need were subjected to revolting atrocities, which find a parallel only in those committed by the soldiers of the Constable of France, and the equally ferocious Lutherans of Georges Frundsberg at the sack of Rome. The public Mosque was turned into a stable, and the shrines were demolished for the sake of their ornaments. Paganism was once more triumphant, and "its reaction," says a European historian, "against Islâm was cruel, terrible, and revolting." The Ommeyades thus repaid the clemency and forbearance shown to them in the hour of Islâm's triumph. Its best men were either killed or fled for safety into distant countries. The few who were spared had to acknowledge themselves the slaves of Yezîd; such as refused were branded on their necks. From this ignominy only two persons were spared, Ali II. the son of Hussain, and Ali the grandson of Abbâs. The colleges, hospitals, and other public edifices built under the Caliphs were closed or demolished, and Arabia relapsed into a wilderness! In later years a grandson of Ali II., whose name was Jaafar, surnamed the True (*as-Sâdik*), revived, in Medîna, the school of learning which had flourished under his ancestor, the Caliph Ali; but it was a veritable oasis in the desert; all around lay in gloom and darkness. Medîna never recovered her prosperity. It seems under the Ommeyades to have become a city of the unknown Past, for when Mansûr, the second Abbasside Caliph, visited the place, he needed a guide to point out where the early heroes and heroines had lived and worked. 40—64 A.H.

After wreaking their vengeance on the Medinites, the Syrians marched upon Mecca, where Abdullâh the son of Zubair had installed himself as Caliph. On arrival in the neighbourhood of Mecca the Syrians surrounded the city, and in course of the fights that followed great damage was done to the Kaaba and other sacred edifices. The timely death of Yezîd, however, made the Syrians raise the siege and hurry back to Damascus. The first siege of Mecca. Rabi I. 64 A.H. November 683 A.C.

Yezîd was succeeded by his son Muâwiyah, a youth of mild disposition, who, it is said, abhorred the crimes of his family. He retired into private life after a reign of a few months, and died shortly after, supposed to have been poisoned. With Muâwiyah II. ended the rule of Abû Sufiân's branch. This dynasty is called the *Harbite*, from the name of Abû Sufiân's father, Harb, in contradistinction to the Hakamites,[1] who derived their name from Hakam, the father of Merwân, who, as we shall presently see, managed to oust the first Muâwiyah's young grandson from the succession to the throne. End of the Harbite Dynasty.

Immediately on the death of Yezîd, Abdullâh bin Zubair had been acknowledged as Caliph all over Hijâz, Irâk, and Khorâsân. Had he now issued from Mecca, and with his old audacity struck for Syria, there is little doubt the Ommeyade domination would have ended for ever. But he lay supinely at Mecca, and gave time to the Ommeyades to join their forces.

[1] Often also called the Merwanian branch, from the name of its founder.

CHAPTER VIII

THE OMMEYADES (THE HAKAMITE BRANCH)

64–86 A.H., 683–705 A.C.

Merwân, son of Hakam—Accepted as the Chief of the Ommeyades—Battle of Marj Râhat—Destruction of the Syrian Modhar—Merwân's Treachery—The Penitents—The Death of Merwân—Abdul Malik, the Ruler of Syria—The Rise of Mukhtâr—The Destruction of the Murderers of Hussain—The Death of Mukhtâr—Musaab—Invasion of Irâk by Abdul Malik—Death of Musaab—Invasion of Hijâz by Abdul Malik's Army—Siege of Mecca—Death of Abdullâh, the son of Zubair (the Meccan Caliph)—Abdul Malik, Chief of Islâm—The Tyrant Hajjâj—Progress in Africa—War with the Romans—The Khârijis—Abdul Malik's Death.

Merwân. ON the death of Muâwiyah II. the succession devolved on his brother Khâlid, but as he was a mere lad at the time, the Ommeyades refused to acknowledge him as their ruler, and demanded the elevation of an elder (*kabîr*) in accordance with the tribal practice. The Ommeyades at this juncture were in a state of paralysis. Merwân, the oldest member of the clan, was ready to take the oath of fealty to Abdullâh bin Zubair. He was a cousin of Muâwiyah I., and wielded considerable influence among the Ommeyades; and his adhesion would have secured the submission of the family. But the over-cautious son of Zubair, content with the possession of Arabia, Egypt, Irâk, and Khorâsân, declined to move upon Syria. Whilst Abdullâh lay thus 64—86 A.H. supinely at Mecca, the notorious Obaidullâh bin Ziâd tried to instal himself as Caliph at Basra, the seat of his government; failing in his endeavours, he fled to Merwân and instigated him to make a bid for the Empire on his own account. The task before Merwân was not free from difficulty; the Ommeyades were suspicious and divided; and the Himyarites of Syria were jealous of Modharite ascendency. But age had not dimmed Merwân's genius for intrigue. He won the support of Khâlid's[1] partisans by promising him the succession to the throne; he secured the adhesion of Amr,[2] his own cousin, who had a considerable following in the clan, by a similar promise. He bribed the Syrian Himyarites by lavish concessions to their chiefs. Thus did Merwân obtain the power for which he was bidding. Masûdi says, "he was the first to seize the throne with the help of his sword." The adhesion of these Syrian Himyarites enabled Merwân to march against the Modharite chief Zahhâk, who had espoused the cause of Abdullâh the son of Zubair. A battle took place at Marj Râhat, a The Battle of Marj Râhat. few miles to the north-east of Damascus. In spite of the numerical superiority of the Himyarites, the first fights were indecisive, but a device of Merwân led to

[1] The younger son of Yezîd.

[2] The relationship between Amr and Merwân will appear from the following table :—

Ommeya.
|
Abu'l Aâs.
|
Hakam. — Saîd.
| |
Merwân. — Amr.

683—705 A.C. the death of the opposing chief Zahhâk, and then followed a conflict in which the Modharites were literally annihilated. The whole of Syria now passed under the rule of Merwân, and Egypt soon after fell into his hands. Finding his position thus sufficiently secured, Merwân withdrew his promise to Khâlid, and forced Amr, whom he had also nominated as his successor, to resign the right to the throne in favour of his own sons, Abdul Malik and Abdul Azîz.

With the battle of Marj Râhat the disastrous feud between Himyar and Modhar, which had slept for so many years, rekindled in all its fury. The Himyarites were now in the ascendant, and cruelly oppressed their rivals. This continued, more or less, under Merwân's son and successor, Abdul Malik.

The Penitents. About this time, a large body of Irâkians, struck with remorse at their desertion of Hussain and his family on the fatal field of Kerbela, rose in arms, vowing vengeance upon his murderers. One night they prayed and wept by his tomb, and next morning they issued against the Syrians. They called themselves "the Penitents," and under their leader Sulaimân[1] carried at first everything before them, but they were ultimately defeated by an overwhelming force sent against them by Merwân. Sulaimân and his lieutenants were killed, and the shattered remnants of "the Penitents" retreated upon Kûfa. Here they were subsequently rallied by Mukhtâr, another of the "Avengers."

Merwân's Death, 65 A.H. Merwân's death at the hands of Yezîd's widow was a fitting end to a life of intrigue and violence. He had married this lady with the object of reconciling the partisans of her son Khâlid. One day he grossly

[1] Sulaimân, the son of Surrâd, was held in great veneration as a Companion of the Prophet.

insulted the boy whom he had ousted from the throne; that same night he was smothered by the enraged mother. Merwân is not recognised by the Sunnis as a Caliph (Commander of the Faithful). Their foremost writers count him as a rebel against Abdullâh the son of Zubair, "whose authority was acknowledged from all the pulpits of Islâm," save and except in Syria. Nor do they "hold his covenant for his sons legal," though they regard the Caliphate of Abdul Malik as rightful from the time the son of Zubair was killed. 64—86 A.H.

On the death of Merwân, Abdul Malik was accepted as their ruler by the majority of the clan. Abdul Malik was a typical Ommeyade; energetic, intriguing and unscrupulous, he applied himself with extraordinary ability to strengthen his position. Whilst he was thus employed, Mukhtâr established himself in Irâk, and from there hunted the murderers of Hussain. They were systematically pursued and killed like vermin. An army sent by Abdul Malik under the "Butcher" [1] was destroyed; he himself was killed and his head was taken to Mukhtâr. Having achieved the object for which they had taken up arms, the "Avengers" became rent into factions, and were one after another subdued by Musaab, Abdullâh's brother and deputy in Irâk. The struggle with Mukhtâr was protracted and sanguinary, but in the end the "Avenger" was killed, his adherents were put to the sword, and Musaab was left complete master of the field. The authority of the son of Zubair was now unquestioned both in Irâk and Mesopotamia. Khorâsân also was under his sway. But his power rested on precarious foundations. The Irâkians were faithless, and entered into secret negotiations with Abdul Malik to accept him as their ruler in return for certain rewards. Abdul Malik. Mukhtâr.

[1] Obaidullâh bin Ziâd.

683—705 A.C. In the meantime, Abdullâh's forces were weakened by incessant fights with the Khârijis, who issuing from their desert fastnesses were committing depredations and atrocities upon the unoffending inhabitants of Chaldæa and Southern Persia. These ruthless fanatics, in their religious fury, perpetrated revolting cruelties to avenge themselves on organised society.

An incident connected with the Hajj[1] of 71 A.H. is mentioned by the Arab historians as showing the divided condition of Islâm at this period. On this occasion four standards, representing four different factions, were displayed at Arafât.[2] One belonged to Abdullâh, the son of Zubair; the second to Abdul Malik, the son of Merwân; the third to Mohammed al-Hanafia;[3] and the fourth to the rebel Khârijis. Round each flag were gathered its partisans, but in spite of their mutual animosity, during the sacred season of truce none molested the other.

Amr bin Saîd killed, 70 A.H. By the unsparing use of the sword, Abdul Malik in a few years cleared Syria of his enemies. Amr, the son of Saîd, had attempted a rising. He was inveigled into the Palace, and killed by Abdul Malik with his own hands. Firmly established in Damascus, he turned his attention towards Mesopotamia and Chaldæa, held by Musaab on behalf of Abdullâh bin Zubair. The defection of the Irâkians encouraged him to move upon Kûfa. Musaab, his son Yahya, and his heroic lieutenant Ibrâ-

[1] The annual pilgrimage to Mecca.

[2] The hill near Mecca where the final ceremony takes place.

[3] The son of the Caliph Ali by a lady of the Hanîfa tribe, whom he married after the death of Fâtima. Mohammed (called al-Hanafia after the tribe of his mother) was not present with Hussain on the fatal field of Kerbela, and thus escaped the slaughter of his family. From him the Abbassides claim their title to the Caliphate; see *post*.

64—86 A.H.

him, the son of Al-Ashtar,[1] were slain in battle, and Irâk passed once more under the rule of the Ommeyades. After crushing Musaab, Abdul Malik despatched his troops against Abdullâh. An overwhelming force under Hajjâj the son of Yusuf marched into Hijâz. Medîna was captured without much difficulty, and Mecca was again surrounded; and massive missiles, hurled from battering engines placed on the hills which encircled the devoted city, spread havoc and ruin all round. But Abdullâh, by repeated sorties, long held the Syrians at bay. The siege was then turned into a blockade; the inhabitants, suffering from the rigours of famine, deserted in large numbers, until Abdullâh was left with only a few defenders. Before making his last sortie, he consulted his mother Asma, the daughter of Abû Bakr, whether he should submit to the yoke of the hated Ommeyade or die fighting. The aged lady, in the heroic spirit of the Arab matron, answered that if he believed in the justness of his cause, it was his duty to fight to the last, but if he thought he was in the wrong, he should submit. She allayed his fear that the enemy would desecrate his body after his death by the answer, that it mattered little what became of the body when the soul had returned to its Creator. Bidding her farewell, he kissed her tenderly on the forehead, and then issued, sword in hand, determined to conquer or to die. The Ommeyades were driven back on all sides, but in the end the brave warrior fell, overpowered by numbers. A soldier's death is generally respected by a brave enemy. But the Syrians possessed no sense of chivalry, and ignored the command of the Prophet, "to respect the dead." They refused the prayer of Abdullâh's

The Second Siege of Mecca. 72 A.H. 691 A.C.

Death of Abdullâh Jamâdi II., 73 A.H. October 692 A.C.

[1] The commander of the Caliph Ali's cavalry at Siffîn. He has been called the Marshal Ney of the Arabs.

683—705 A.C. mother to give up her son's body for burial, and, in the ferocious spirit of the times, they impaled his corpse on a gibbet. The heads of Abdullâh and of two of his leaders were exhibited at Medîna and thence sent to Damascus.

There was much to admire in Abdullâh's character; crafty and ambitious, he was yet cast in a heroic mould, and a strong sense of justice distinguished him from most of his compeers. The one great defect in his character, which probably led to his fall, was his niggardliness. Even when Hajjâj was battering at his gate, he refused to bring out his hoards to pay his men or buy materials of war. Abdullâh is recognised by the Sunnis as one of the legitimate Caliphs of Islâm, as he was in possession of the Holy Cities (*Haramain-Sharîfain*), and prayers were offered for him from the pulpits of Medîna and Mecca.

Abdul Malik undisputed master of the Empire.

Abdul Malik was now the undisputed master of the Islâmic Empire. Muhallib, son of Abû Sufra, the lieutenant of Abdullâh bin Zubair in Southern Persia, perceiving the futility of further opposition, took the oath of fealty to Abdul Malik. The viceroy of Khorâsân, less tractable than Muhallib, replied to Abdul Malik's demand for submission by making the messenger swallow his master's missive and then return to Damascus.

The Khârijis.

During the struggle between Abdullâh and Abdul Malik, the Khârijis had acquired strength and spread themselves over Southern Persia and Chaldæa. Goaded into fury by the insensate persecution of the Ommeyade governors, they fought wildly, reckless of their lives. Mere handfuls defeated time after time the legions of Abdul Malik. But they possessed no cohesion or unity. Some desired to return to the days of Omar, under a

Caliph elected by the people; others, among them the Theocrats, rejected all personal government and demanded the Lord's Rule under a Council of Elders. They were at last defeated and suppressed. In Persia, they met their match in Muhallib, whose military talents were appreciated by Abdul Malik. After a protracted and sanguinary struggle, he destroyed their strongholds and put them to the sword. The remnant again took refuge in the deserts of al-Ahsa. Like the Khârijis, the Romans had taken advantage of the civil war to make encroachments upon the dominions of Islâm. Abdul Malik now forced them back, and after a series of successful operations, obtained a large cession of territory from the Byzantine emperor. In the east, the districts in the neighbourhood of modern Cabul, ruled by a Hindoo prince of the name of Ratbil, were brought into subjection. Similarly, a large part of Northern Africa was either subjugated or reconquered.

64—86 A.H.

War with the Romans.

The conquest of Africa by the Saracens is full of romance. In 693 A.H. (69 A.C.) Abdul Malik despatched an army for the reconquest of Barbary (*Ifrîkia*). The command was entrusted to Zuhair, an able lieutenant of Okba, who had, since the death of his chief, maintained himself against tremendous odds at Barca. The first operations were eminently successful; the rebel chief Koseila and the united forces of the Berbers and Romans were destroyed, and the whole province cleared of the enemy. Zuhair now committed a fatal mistake; keeping a small detachment with him at a place near Barca, which formed his head-quarters, he sent out expeditions for the subjugation of the outlying parts. In this perilous situation, the danger of which was enhanced by the absence of all scouting, he was sud-

Reconquest of Barbary.

683—705 A.C. denly attacked by a large Roman army landed in the rear. The fight was desperate; the Saracen general was killed and his soldiers cut to pieces. Barbary again slipped out of the hands of the Moslems. But the tenacity of purpose that had led to Abdul Malik's
74 A.H. 698 A.C. success over his rivals did not fail him on this occasion. He despatched a third army under Hassân, the son of Nomân, which for a time swept all opposition before it; Kairowân was recaptured; the city of Carthage was stormed, and the Romans and Berbers were defeated in open field. The remnant of the Roman army hastily abandoned the country, and the Saracen was once more supreme from the walls of Barca to the shores of the Atlantic. At this period the Berbers and the wild tribes of the Atlas acknowledged the authority of a woman, who is called by Arab historians the *Kâhina* (Divineress). This Berber Pythoness was supposed to be gifted with supernatural attributes, and at her call a host of Numidians and other savages swept down upon the con-
The *Kâhina*. querors. The Saracens were simply overwhelmed; several detachments were cut to pieces, and the main army was once more forced back upon Barca. For five years the *Kâhina* remained the queen of Africa. In 79 A.H., Abdul Malik despatched another army to the assistance of Hassân. In those days one side was not possessed of quick-firing machine-guns and rifles whilst the other was armed with ancient muskets or the still more primitive matchlocks. So far as actual weapons went, the Berbers and Saracens were equally matched, though the latter excelled their rebellious foes in equipment, organisation, and discipline. Their great superiority lay in those qualities of courage, energy and perseverance, and boundless trust in their prowess and their Faith, of which there are few parallels in history, ancient

or modern. Abdul Malik's army cut its way through the Numidian hosts like a ship passing through the swirling waves. To bar the progress of the pertinacious Saracen, and to deprive him once for all of his chief temptation in the wealth of the cities, the Berber Pythoness formed the desperate resolution of turning the country into a desert. She gave orders that the entire tract under her sway should be laid waste. Mansions and palaces were pulled down; whatever valuables could not be carried away to the mountains were destroyed; cities and villages were laid in ruin; groves and gardens were cut down, and the once prosperous country was turned into a howling wilderness. The Arab historian calls this "the first devastation of Africa," not thinking of the havoc and waste created by the Romans or by Genseric the Vandal. The savagery of the Pythoness, however, proved of no avail. Hassân was hailed by the inhabitants as a deliverer, the dismantled and ruined cities hastened once more to make their submission, and the people readily took the oath of allegiance. The *Kâhina* was defeated and slain in a great battle at the foot of the Atlas. The Berbers, exhausted by the indomitable perseverance of the Saracens, sued for peace, which was granted upon condition of their supplying to the Saracen general an auxiliary contingent of 25,000 cavalry. Islâm now spread rapidly among the Berbers. But unfortunately the Khârijis, driven from Persia and Arabia, began at this time to pour into Africa. Their narrow and bigoted conceptions, their exclusive and reactionary doctrines, their hatred of the government of Damascus, chimed in with Berber feelings and ideas. The Theocrats and Separatists, who had been hunted by Abdul Malik and his lieutenants, now found themselves the leaders of

64—86 A.H.

Her defeat and death.

683—705 A.C.

hosts.[1] Henceforth the frequent and sanguinary revolts of the Berbers were due to their teachings.

Hajjâj bin Yusuf.

Hajjâj, at one time governor of Hijâz, was Abdul Malik's viceroy over Irâk, Sejistân, Kermân, and Khorâsân, which included Cabul and parts of Transoxiana. Western Arabia was under a separate governor named Hishâm, son of Ismâil, whilst Egypt was ruled by Abdul Malik's brother, Abdul Azîz. The intolerable and ferocious cruelty of Hajjâj gave rise to several furious revolts, one of which under Abdur Rahmân, the son of al-Ashas, nearly cost Abdul Malik his throne. But numbers and perseverance bore down all opposition, and the insurgents were driven to take refuge in distant parts. Whilst governor of Hijâz, Hajjâj had cruelly oppressed the inhabitants of Medîna and ill-treated the surviving companions of the Prophet. At one time he thought of rasing the city to the ground. In the course of his long government over Irâk, he put to death nearly 150,000 men, many on false charges, some of them the best of the Arab race. At the time of his death, 50,000 people of both sexes were found rotting in his prisons and cursing the tyrant. The effect of these wholesale massacres was "to attenuate," as M. Sédillot observes, "the Saracenic nation by depriving it of its noblest and most capable leaders."

Muhallib, the conqueror of the Khârijis, who was acting as the deputy of Hajjâj in Khorâsân, died in 703 A.C., and "with him died," says the Arab poet, "generosity and friendship." He was succeeded in his office by his son Yezîd, to whom for a time Hajjâj showed the same favour.

Abdul Malik's death. 705 A.C.

Abdul Malik died at the age of 62 in 86 A.H. He

[1] The latter-day Mahdists of Africa seem to be the descendants of the old Khârijis.

loved poetry, especially when in praise of himself. 64—86 A.H. Avarice and cruelty dominated his character; and his lieutenants, says Masûdi, followed in his footsteps in the reckless shedding of blood. Of Abdul Malik it is stated, that in his young days he was much given to piety and devotional exercises; but the moment it was announced to him that he had succeeded his father, he put aside the Koran which he had been studying, with the remark, "This is my last time with thee." He was the first, says the annalist, who acted treacherously in Islâm, the first who forbade speaking in the presence of the Caliphs, and the first who prohibited exhortations to justice, saying, "Let no one enjoin upon me the fear of God or love of equity, but I will smite his neck." In character he resembled Charlemagne. Just, when justice was not opposed to dynastic interest; daring and energetic, resolute and ambitious, he never faltered in the pursuit of his designs. But he was certainly less cruel than Charlemagne. No such cruel deed as the promiscuous massacre of the Frisians or Saxons can be laid at his door. Compared to Charlemagne or Peter the Great of Russia, he might even be regarded as humane. Before engaging in battle with Musaab and the insurgents under Abdur Rahmân, he repeatedly offered them terms. His cruelty, like his frequent breaches of faith, was due to an anxiety to safeguard and promote the interests of his dynasty. But nothing can relieve him of responsibility for the cruelties of the ferocious Hajjâj, although he sometimes interfered to protect the victims. Abdul Malik was the first to open a mint in Islâm. After him the Saracen rulers were extremely careful in maintaining the value of their coinage and in preventing counterfeit. Tampering with coins was punished with great severity. Until Abdul Malik's time, all public

683—705 A.C. registers and the records of taxes were kept either in Greek or in Persian. Owing to the abuses resulting from this practice, he directed that thenceforth all records were to be kept in Arabic.

Some time before his death, he tried to induce his brother Abdul Azîz to resign the succession in favour of his son Walîd. Abdul Azîz, however, firmly declined to do so, but dying soon after, Walîd quietly succeeded to the throne.

Abdul Malik's contemporary at Byzantium.

Abdul Malik's contemporary on the throne of Constantinople was the tyrant Justinian II.,[1] the son of Pogonatus, who when returning from exile, and advised to show forgiveness to his enemies, declared—"Speak of forgiveness? May I perish this instant—may the Almighty whelm me in the waves, if I consent to spare a single head of my enemies."

[1] Called by the Arabs *al-Akhram*, "the Slit-nosed." This tyrant was once deposed when his nose was amputated (695 A.C.). He was recalled to the throne a few years after, and reigned until 711 A.C., when he was put to death. Masûdi mentions Lawi, the son of Falanat, and Jurjîs, as the contemporaries of Abdul Malik, Walîd, Sulaimân, and Omar II.

CHAPTER IX

THE OMMEYADES (THE HAKAMITE BRANCH) (*continued*)

86—96 A.H., 705—715 A.C.

Walîd I.—Conquests in the East—Progress in Africa—Mûsa bin Nusair, Viceroy of the West—Condition of Spain—The Oppression of Roderick—Târick bin Ziâd lands at Gibraltar—The battle of Medina Sidonia—Death of Roderick—Conquest of Spain—Advance into France—Recall of Mûsa and Târick—Character of the Saracenic Administration in Spain—The Provinces—The effect of the tribal jealousies—Death of Walîd I. —His Character.

SOON after the accession of Walîd Hajjâj, who still held the viceroyalty of the Eastern Provinces, removed Yezîd, the son and successor of Muhallib, from the lieutenancy of Khorâsân. He appointed in his place a Modharite chief, Kotaiba, an able strategist and a consummate general, but hard and relentless, like many we read of in European history. The Sogdians, who inhabited the countries in Central Asia to the north of the river Oxus,[1] had undertaken to live in peace with the Moslems, and not to molest their colonists. They had also agreed to receive Residents or *Aâmils* in their chief cities to watch over Moslem interests. But Yezîd's removal seemed to them a favourable opportunity to regain their independence. All of a sudden they rose against the Saracens, expelled the Residents, and massacred the

Accession of Walîd I.

Koteiba.

Conquest of Transoxiana.

[1] Hence called "Mâ-warâ-aan-Nahr"—the land on the other side of the river.

705—715 A.C. colonists. Similar acts have led within recent times to similar results both in Asia and Africa; and after ten years of incessant warfare, in which many cruelties were perpetrated on both sides, Kotaiba achieved the subjugation of the whole of Central Asia to the confines of Kashgar.

Conquests in India. 89—96 A.H. 708—715 A.C. About the same time, Mohammed the son of Kâsim, governor of Mekrân, harassed by the predatory tribes who inhabited the country between Sind and Beluchistan, led an expedition into India, which ended in the annexation of Sind, Multan, and part of the Punjab as far as the Beas.

Maslamah Captain-General in Asia Minor. During the whole of Walîd's reign, Maslamah his brother, who seems to have been the warrior of the family, was Captain-General of the Moslem forces in Asia Minor. He was supported by an army under Abbâs, Walîd's own son. Their combined operations led to the conquest of several important places. A large part of Asia Minor was now held by the Saracens.

Omar the son of Abdul Azîz, governor of Hijâz. In the year 87 A.H. Walîd appointed his cousin Omar, the son of Abdul Azîz, governor over Hijâz. Immediately on his arrival at Medîna, Omar formed a council composed of the jurists and notables of the city, and no administrative or executive act was done without consultation with them. He tried to erase the signs of the ravages committed in the holy cities of Islâm under Yezîd and Abdul Malik. He beautified Medîna and Mecca with numerous public structures, made new aqueducts, and improved the roads connecting the cities of Hijâz with the capital. Moderate, yet firm, anxious to promote the welfare of the people whom he governed, Omar's rule proved beneficent to all classes.

The mild, just, and generous government of Omar attracted a number of refugees from Irâk, who, fleeing from the terrible oppression of the sanguinary tyrant who ruled over the Eastern Provinces, found shelter and peace in Hijâz. Hajjâj was extremely wroth at this, and complained bitterly to his master Walîd, who was as much under his influence as old Abdul Malik. The intrigues of Hajjâj were at length successful, and in 92 A.H. Omar was removed from his viceroyalty amidst universal mourning. His successor signalised his entry into office by expelling from Medîna and Mecca all the Irâkian refugees. 86—96 A.H.

About this time, Yezîd the son of Muhallib along with his brothers was thrown into prison by Hajjâj, and subjected to the cruellest torture. His victims however succeeded in effecting their escape from the hands of the tyrant, and took refuge with Sulaimân, the brother and successor of Walîd.

We must now turn our attention to the West. Africa had been held by Hassân with comparative peace and safety after the death of the Pythoness. In 89 A.H. he was removed from the governorship, and the famous Mûsa, the son of Nusair, was made Viceroy of Ifrîkia. Mûsa's father was the chief of the police (*Sâhib-us-Shurta*) under Muâwiyah, but had refused to serve against Ali in the battle of Siffîn, and the son of Abû Sufiân, who knew the man's worth, had respected his scruples. Hassân's withdrawal was the signal for an insurrection of the Berbers, but they had miscalculated the energy and vigour of the new Viceroy. By a series of daring operations conducted by himself and his sons, Mûsa overthrew the Berber combination, drove out the Greek conspirators and pacified the entire country. By his conciliatory attitude towards the chiefs, he inspired them with unbounded confidence and won their attachment. Instructors were appointed to teach the people Conquests in Africa. 89 A.H.

705–715 A.C. the principles of Islâm, and in a short time the whole of the Berber nation was converted to the religion of Mohammed. As the Saracenic settlements were harassed by the Byzantines from the islands of the Mediterranean, Mûsa sent out expeditions for their reduction; Majorca, Minorca and Ivica were conquered and incorporated with the empire of Islâm. Under the Moslem rule these islands soon became extremely flourishing. As in other places, the Saracens erected beautiful buildings, introduced various kinds of handicraft, and otherwise materially improved the country. Mûsa's viceroyalty was now almost equal to that of Hajjâj in extent; but its importance in the demand for administrative ability and generalship, was far greater. It extended from the western confines of Egypt to the shores of the Atlantic, with the exception of Ceuta, which was held by Count Julian under the Gothic King of Spain on behalf of the Roman Emperor; and included the western islands of the Mediterranean. It was soon to receive a magnificent addition in a country which was an empire in itself.

Spain. Whilst Africa was enjoying the blessings of toleration and justice, and was advancing with rapid strides in the path of material prosperity under the Moslem rule, the neighbouring peninsula of Spain groaned under the iron heel of the Goth. Never was the condition of the country or of the people so bad or so miserable as under the grinding yoke of the Gothic kings. As in the Roman times, the rich, the noble and the privileged classes in general were exempt from taxation; the middle classes, upon whom alone fell the public burdens, were reduced to ruin and misery. Industrial activity was killed by heavy imposts; there was no manufacture or commerce; and a terrible sterility, almost equal to that which has fallen on the land since the expulsion of the Moslems, prevailed all over the Peninsula. The country was split up into immense domains whose owners, lay and cleric, lived in palatial mansions where they spent their days in riotous and wicked indulgence. Cultivation was in the hands of either serfs tied to the soil, or of miserable herds of slaves who worked under the pitiless lashes of cruel overseers. Serfs or slaves, for them there was no hope of freedom or gleam of sunshine on this side of the grave. Neither serf nor slave might possess anything that he could call his own; they could not marry without the consent of the master; and if the serfs of two neighbouring estates intermarried, their children were divided equally between the two owners. Sunk in the grossest superstitions, their moral state was as depraved and degraded as their material condition was wretched. 86—96 A.H.

The Jews in Spain.

The Jews, who had settled in large numbers in the Peninsula, had suffered terribly from the persecutions of the kings, the clergy and the nobles. Goaded by their sufferings, they had attempted a rising, which, badly conceived and hastily executed, proved abortive with the direst results. Their goods and chattels, in fact all they possessed, were confiscated; such of the nation as survived the massacre were condemned to wholesale slavery. Old and young, male and female, were made over as slaves to the Christians. The old, as a matter of grace, were allowed to retain their religion; but the young were to be brought up in the Christian faith. All marriage within the community was forbidden, and a Jewish slave was henceforth to marry a Christian slave. Such was the punishment meted out to the Jews by the bishops, who held all the power in the land. The impoverished and ruined citizen, the wretched slave, the miserable serf, the persecuted and hunted Jew, all waited for the relief which was so long in coming. It was in the

705—715 A.C. moment of their acutest agony that the deliverance arrived from an unexpected quarter. The Saracenic Province on the other side of the straits was regarded as a haven of safety by the victims of Gothic and ecclesiastical oppression, and many Spaniards had found refuge in Moslem Africa from the grinding tyranny of their kings and bishops. At this time when Mûsa ruled over Africa, the Iberian throne was occupied by Roderick, who had deposed and murdered the former king Witiza. Julian, the Governor of Ceuta, smarting under a cruel wrong inflicted on him by Roderick in the person of his daughter Florinda, joined in the appeal of the Spanish refugees to Mûsa to liberate the country from the usurper's yoke. In answer to their prayers, with the sanction of Walîd, Mûsa despatched a young and enterprising officer named Tarîf, to make a reconnaissance on the southern coast. The report was favourable, and in the auspicious month of Rajab,[1] Târick the son of Ziâd, one of Mûsa's ablest lieutenants, landed with a small force of 7000 picked men at a spot[2] which now bears his name. Having properly fortified the Rock to serve as a base of operations, he descended upon the adjacent province of Algeciras,[3] which was held by Theodomir on behalf of Roderick. The Goths who attempted to bar his progress were cut to pieces, and Târick commenced his memorable march upon Toledo.

Târick lands at Gibraltar. Thursday 8th Rajab 92 A.H. April 30, 711 A.C.

His army had, in the meanwhile, augmented to 12,000 by the timely arrival of some reinforcements despatched

[1] The month of Rajab is regarded by the Moslems as particularly auspicious, as it was in that month the Prophet saw the Vision of the Ascension.

[2] Gibraltar, Jabl(u)-Târick, "the Rock of Târick;" Ibn ul-Athîr, vol. iv. p. 444.

[3] This is an Arab name derived from al-Jazîra, a peninsula or island.

by the Viceroy. Roderick was engaged in quelling a disturbance in the north, but the moment he heard of the invasion he hurried to his capital, summoning all his feudal chiefs to join him at Cordova with their contingents. The royal army itself was immense; with the feudal auxiliaries the force at Roderick's disposal swelled to 100,000 men. The two armies thus unequally matched met on the banks of the Guadalete to the north of Medina Sidonia.[1]

86—96 A.H.

Battle of Medina Sidonia. Middle of Ramazân 92 A.H. Sept. 711 A.C.

The sons of Witiza, chafing under the wrongs inflicted on them by the king, broke away from Roderick after the first onslaught; but the force under his immediate command was numerous, well equipped and disciplined, and offered for a time a steady front to the Saracenic attacks; the fierceness of the last charge, led by Târick himself, however, was irresistible. The Gothic host was completely routed, and in his flight King Roderick was drowned in the waters of the Guadalete. The moral result of this magnificent victory was immense. It took the heart out of the Spaniards to meet the Saracens in the open.[2]

Defeat of the Goths; Death of Roderick.

Sidonia and Carmona opened their gates; Ecija, where Roderick's broken forces had taken refuge, offered some resistance, but ultimately capitulated on favourable terms.

1 "All agree," says Makkari, "that the battle was fought on the banks of the Wâdi-lakkèh (river of delight) in the district of Shidhûna." Dozy says the memorable battle took place on the banks of the Wadi-Becca, a small river which now bears the name of Salado, and which throws itself into the sea not far from Cape Trafalgar. The date of the battle he gives as July 19, 711 A.C.

2 Nothing—not even the defection of Witiza's sons—can minimise the greatness of this splendid victory. With barely 12,000 men the Moslem commander met and defeated a disciplined army at least five times as large.

705—715 A.C. Târick now divided his small force into four divisions, and directed one of his lieutenants to proceed towards Cordova; whilst the other marched upon Malaga, the third was to move upon Granada and Elvira. At the head of the main body he himself marched rapidly towards Toledo, the Gothic capital. Malaga, Granada, and Cordova fell one after another without much difficulty, and the whole of Algeciras held by Theodomir was quickly reduced to subjection. The Goths were dismayed by the rapidity of Târick's movements and the severity of his blows. "God," says the annalist, "filled the hearts of the idolaters with terror and alarm." The magnates either submitted or fled from place to place; the principal ecclesiastics betook themselves to Rome, whilst the people at large, the Jews, the serfs, the impoverished citizens, hailed the Moslems as their liberators. Târick found Toledo abandoned by the Spaniards; leaving a small detachment of Jews and Moslems in charge of the city, and confiding its government to Oppas, a brother of King Witiza, he pursued the retreating Goths as far as Astorga. In the meantime the octogenarian Viceroy, fired with jealousy or emulation, landed in Spain with 18,000 men to complete the conquest begun by his illustrious lieutenant. His army included many noble Arabs of the best families of Yemen, and several descendants of the Companions of the Prophet.
June 712 A.C. Taking an easterly course, Mûsa reduced successively Seville and Merida. At Toledo he was joined by Târick. The meeting of the two conquerors was attended by an unseemly dispute characteristic of the age, but they were soon reconciled, and uniting their forces they proceeded towards Aragon. Saragossa, Tarragona, Barcelona, and other principal cities of the north opened their gates in succession, and in less than two years

the whole of Spain, as far as the Pyrenees, was in the hands of the Saracens. Portugal was conquered a few years later, and was formed into a separate province under the name of al-Gharb,[1] "the West." In the mountains of Asturias alone the Christian Spaniards continued to make a stand against the Moslems. 86—96 A.H.

Mûsa's conquest.

Leaving to Târick the work of subjugation in Galicia, Mûsa crossed into France, and easily reduced that part of Languedoc which had belonged to the Gothic dominions. Standing on the Pyrenees, the dauntless Viceroy conceived the project of conquering the whole of Europe; and in all human probability had he been allowed to carry his plan into execution he would have succeeded. The West lay completely at his feet; there was no cohesion among the nations which divided Mûsa from the Caliphate; as yet no chief had sprung up to unite the forces of Christendom and oppose the progress of the Saracens. The cautious and hesitating policy of the Damascene Court lost the glorious opportunity, with the consequence that Europe remained enveloped in intellectual darkness for the next eight centuries. An order from Walîd stopped Mûsa whilst preparing to push farther into France with the object of crossing into Italy. He then turned his attention to the complete reduction of the mountainous parts of Spain, where the Christians were making a desperate stand. He entered Galicia, captured their fortresses, and drove the enemy into the rocky defiles of the Asturias. From Lugo, Mûsa directed the movements of his army, which now hemmed the insurgents on all sides. Cowed by the indomitable energy of the old warrior, the guerilla bands submitted one after another until there remained Pelayo alone with a few supporters. He too would have laid

[1] A province of modern Portugal is still called Algarve.

705—715 A.C. down his arms, but just at the moment when the conquest was near completion a messenger arrived from Damascus with peremptory orders for the return of the two conquerors. Whatever the motive which impelled

Recall of Mûsa and Târick. Walîd to recall Mûsa and Târick, there can be no doubt that it was most disastrous to Islâm. Mûsa's departure enabled Pelayo to fortify himself in the mountains, and there to form the nucleus of that power which in later times was to overwhelm with destruction the Moslem states towards the south. The Saracens, deprived of their two best captains, affected to look with contempt upon this handful of resolute defenders, and allowed them daily to increase in number and strength. "Would to God," says Makkarî, "that the Moslems had at once extinguished the sparks of a fire that was destined to consume the whole dominions of Islâm in those parts." Before leaving Spain, Mûsa made all necessary arrangements for the government of the country. He appointed his son, Abdul Azîz, the Viceroy of the new province, with Seville as the seat of government. Abdullâh, another son and a great warrior, was left in charge of Ifrîkia; whilst Abdul Malik, the youngest, ruled over Morocco (*Maghrib ul-Aksâ*), and Abdus Sâlèh held the command of the coast and of the fleet,

95 A.H. 714 A.C. with Tangiers for his head-quarters. After completing his arrangements for the proper government of his vice-royalty he commenced his journey towards Damascus attended by an immense number of followers.

The effect of the conquest. The conquest of Spain by the Saracens opened a new era for the Peninsula: it produced an important social revolution, the effect of which can be likened only to the best results of the great upheaval in France in the eighteenth century, without its evil or appalling consequences. It swept away the cruel rights and powers of the privileged classes, among whom the clergy and the 86—96 A.H. nobility occupied the most prominent position. It removed the heavy burdens that had crushed industry and ruined the middle strata of the population. Instead of grinding and capricious imposts, it introduced a just, equable, and intelligible system of taxation, viz. the usual poll or test-tax payable by non-Moslems, and the tax on culturable land to which all persons, Moslem and non-Moslem alike, were subject. The test-tax was extremely light in its incidence, for it varied according to the means of the payer, and was realised by twelve monthly instalments.[1] But people leading a monastic life, and women and children in general, were exempt from this tax; so were the lame, the blind, the sick, the mendicant, and the slave. As the land-tax was regulated by the productiveness of the soil it was never a burden upon agriculture. Many of the Spanish cities had obtained most favourable terms at the time of the conquest, and these conditions were religiously and faithfully observed. Excepting the estates of the nobles and the ecclesiastics, who had either fled from the country or had joined the ranks of the Galician rebels, there was no confiscation. Individual acts of violence or pillage committed by soldiers, inevitable with any invading army,[2] were severely repressed. The ruthless intolerance and fierce persecution which had characterised the former government made way for a large-hearted toleration. The persecuted and downtrodden Jews obtained the right to follow their religion without let or hindrance,

[1] It graduated from 12 to 48 dirhems. A dirhem was equal to a franc in value.

[2] We have only to read the record of a well-disciplined army like that of the Germans entering France during the invasion of 1870–71, or of 1914, to understand the evils that attend on a war.

705—715 A.C. and the Christians were secured in the unmolested enjoyment of their faith and laws, the administration of which was entrusted to their own judges. No one was troubled about his faith; every man, woman, or child was free to worship as he liked or what he liked. The Christians had governors of their own race to collect their taxes and to settle their disputes. Every branch of the public service, and all offices of rank and emolument were open equally to Moslems, Jews, and Christians. Many modern governments might well take a lesson from the Moslem administration of Spain. But the most beneficent effect exercised by the Moslem conquest was upon the condition of the servile classes. Hitherto they had been treated as worse than common beasts of burden; they now assumed their position as human beings. The slaves and serfs who worked upon the estates that passed into Moslem hands at once obtained enfranchisement, and were converted into tenant-farmers with a living interest of their own in the soil. The land became practically theirs, subject to the payment of a share of the produce to the Moslem landlords. The lot of those who still remained with Christian masters was considerably ameliorated, for a complaint of ill-treatment, or the confession of the Moslem Faith, led to their emancipation by operation of the law. The slaves and serfs adopted Islâm in order to obtain freedom and the blessings of existence that had been denied to them under the former *régime;* the magnates and nobles adopted it either from conviction or interest, but as earnestly and devoutly, as the sequel will show. The Christians themselves preferred the mild, generous, and beneficent rule of the Saracen to the grinding tyranny of the Goth or Frank, and flocked back into the cities and villages which they had at first abandoned through terror. Even the priests were not discontented with the change, "at least in the beginning," says Dozy. Another well-known writer expresses himself thus: "The Moors organised that wonderful kingdom of Cordova, which was the marvel of the Middle Ages, and which, when all Europe was plunged in barbaric ignorance and strife, alone held the torch of learning and civilisation bright and shining before the Western world." "It must not be supposed," he adds, "that the Moors, like the barbarian hordes who preceded them, brought desolation and tyranny in their wake. On the contrary, never was Andalusia so mildly, justly, and wisely governed as by her Arab conquerors. Where they got their talent for administration it is hard to say, for they came almost direct from their Arabian deserts, and the rapid tide of victories had left them little leisure to acquire the art of managing foreign nations." 86—96 A.H.

For administrative purposes they divided Spain into four large Provinces, each under a governor directly responsible to the Viceroy. The division of the Provinces.

The first Province comprised Andalusia—the country situated between the sea and the Guadalquiver—and the tract which stretched from this river to the Guadiana, with the cities of Cordova, Seville, Malaga, Ecija, Jaen, and Wosuna.

The second Province comprised the whole of Central Spain, with the Mediterranean to the east and the frontiers of Lusitania (modern Portugal) to the west, and extending to the Douro on the north. It included the cities of Toledo on the Tagus, Cuenca on the Xucar, Segovia on an affluent of the Douro, Guadalaxara, Valencia, Denia, Alicante, Carthagena, Murcia, Lorca, and Baeza.

705—715 A.C. The third Province comprised Galicia and Lusitania, with the cities of Merida, Evora, Beja, Lisbon, Coimbra, Lugo, Astorga, Zamora, Salamanca, etc.

The fourth extended from the borders of the Douro to the Pyrenees on both sides of the Ebro, with Galicia towards the west. It comprised the cities of Saragossa, Tortosa, Tarragona, Barcelona, Girona, Urgel, Tudela, Valladolid, Huesca, Jaud, Bobastro, etc.

Later on, when further conquests were made, a fifth Province was created beyond the Pyrenees, which included Narbonne, Nîmes, Carcassonne, Beziers, Agde, Maguelone, and Lodève.

The Arabs and the Berbers preferred to live in the cities. Here they grouped themselves in tribes, which, whilst affording a safeguard against isolated attacks by the Christians, led to the growth of a disastrous feeling of tribal jealousies.

The following table shows the tribes and people who settled in the different parts, and the character of their divisions—

Elvira (Cordova)	=	The Legion of Damascus
Seville Niebla	=	,, ,, of Hems
Jaen	=	,, ,, of Kinnisrin (ancient Chalcis)
Medina Sidonia Algeciras	=	,, ,, of Palestine
Rayah and Malaga	=	,, ,, of the Jordan
Xeres	=	,, ,, of Persia
Toledo	=	,, ,, of Yemen
Granada	=	,, ,, of Irâk
Merida Lisbon, etc.	=	,, ,, of Egypt.

And, lastly, ten thousand knights of Hijâz with their following settled themselves in the interior. Abdul Azîz, the son of Mûsa, who acted as Viceroy on the departure of his father for Syria, appointed a Diwân or Council for adapting the Islâmic laws and institutions to the requirements of the country and for promoting the fusion of the two people. By his wise statesmanship and mild and beneficent government he conciliated all classes. Like the first Mogul sovereigns of India, he encouraged intermarriages between the conquered and the conquerors, and himself set the example by marrying the widow of Roderick named Egilona, called by the Arabs Umm Aâsim. The Saracen settlers came chiefly from countries which were essentially agricultural, such as Egypt, Syria, and Persia. They were endowed like the Jews, who followed them in all their colonies, with the commercial instinct, and were led towards industry by the teachings of the Prophet, which made labour a religious duty. They accordingly took in hand with unequalled energy the material development of Spain, which had hitherto lain sterile under the Christian government. They introduced various agronomic works; they fertilised the uncultivated lands, repeopled the cities that were deserted, ornamented them with beautiful monuments, and united them by a number of industrial and commercial ties. They gave to the people a right which had never been permitted to them by the Gothic kings, the right of alienating their lands. Spain, emancipated from feudal servitude which had hung so long like a curse on the land, became the most populous and most industrious of European countries. The Arabs turned Spain into a garden; they organised a model administration, and gave impetus to the arts and sciences; but they could never put aside or repress, even in that distant land, the old tribal jealousies of the desert. They were offered the glorious opportunity of founding a lasting empire; they lost it from their own want of

86—96 A.H.

Development of Spain under the Arabs.

705—715 A.C. union and cohesion. In Spain, the discord was intensified by two additional elements bitterly opposed to the foreign domination. The intractable Berbers, who were to be found in large numbers in the Saracen army, hated the Arab officers. Mutiny and insurrections were frequent; and repression only tended to accentuate the bitterness of race-hatred. The Spanish Moslems, who were called *Bilâdiûn* (inhabitants of the country), hated both the Arabs and the Berbers—the former for their pride, the latter for their wildness. The democratic teachings of Islâm had levelled all distinctions of race and colour; but in distant lands, which he had entered with the help of his sword, the Arab could never rise superior to the intense pride of race which has always formed an essential characteristic of his nature. Like the Anglo-Saxon, he considers himself the noblest of God's creation. The relations of the Arabs and the Bilâdiûn remind us in a minor degree of the strong racial antipathy which divided the Austrians and Italians in Lombardy, or which still seem to divide the Celt from the Saxon in Ireland. Like the Irish, the Bilâdiûns insisted upon home rule in a modified shape; to be governed, in fact, by members of their own race. Many of their insurrections against the Arabs were fomented by the *Fakîhs* or Moslem legists, who fulfilled the roll of priests in Islâm. The Spaniards adopted Islâm with the same fierceness and unreasoning violence as they had, and have since, adopted Christianity. Under the instigation of the *Fakîhs* they often rose in revolt against the Arabs for their liberal interpretation of the laws and their general tolerance. All this discord tended to weaken the Empire; and, as Ibn Khaldûn pathetically deplores, led, before eighty years were over, to the loss of the northern portion of the conquest as far as Barcelona.

We must now turn our attention again towards the East; for Walîd did not live long enough to receive the generals whom he had recalled from the scenes of their triumphs. 86—96 A.H.

Like his father, he attempted before his death to alter, with the support of Hajjâj, Kotaiba, and most of the Modharite chiefs, the succession to the throne in favour of his son, but death came upon him before his object was achieved.

Walîd died at Dair-Marrân in the year 715, after a glorious reign of nine years and seven months. Both Masûdi and Ibn ul-Athîr regard him as a despot and a tyrant, but at this distance of time we may remember only his good actions. There can be no question that he was more humane than his father Abdul Malik, or his grandfather Merwân. Certainly more so than many of his successors. The Syrians naturally regard him as the most eminent of the Caliphs.[1] He built the cathedral mosque of Damascus, and enlarged and beautified those of Medîna and Jerusalem, and under his directions, mosques were built in every city which did not already possess a place of worship. He erected fortresses for the protection of the frontiers, and constructed roads and sank wells throughout the Empire. He established schools and hospitals, and stopped promiscuous charity by granting from the State fixed allowances to the infirm and the poor. He created asylums for the blind, the crippled, and the insane, where they were lodged and fed and looked after by attendants specially employed for that purpose. He established orphanages for the support and education of poor children bereft of their parents. He himself visited the markets and noted the rise and fall in prices, Jamâdi II., 96 A.H. February 715 A.C.

[1] Ibn ul-Athîr.

705—715 A.C. and was the first of the Ommeyades who encouraged literature, arts, and manufactures. In Walîd's reign died Ali II. (Zain ul-Aâbîdîn), the fourth Imâm of the House of Mohammed, regarded by the Shiahs as the rightful spiritual leader. He was succeeded in the apostolical chair by his son Mohammed, surnamed for his learning *al-Bâkir*, or the Profound.

Walîd's contemporaries on the throne of Constantinople were the cruel Justinian II., who was murdered in 711 A.C.; Philippicus, Justinian's successor, who was blinded and deposed in 713 A.C.; and Anastasius II., who was put to death by Theodosius III. in 716 A.C.

CHAPTER X

THE OMMEYADES (THE HAKAMITE BRANCH) (*continued*)

96—105 A.H., 715—724 A.C.

Accession of Sulaimân—Fall of Mûsa and Târick—Death of Abdul Azîz, son of Mûsa—Tribal dissensions—The Yemenites—The rise of Yezîd, son of Muhallib—Siege of Constantinople—Moslem Reverses—Death of Sulaimân—Accession of Omar II.—His wise and virtuous Reign—Retreat from Constantinople—Omar's Death—Accession of Yezîd II.—Insurrection of Yezîd, son of Muhallib—Destruction of the Yemenites—Tribal dissensions—Moslem Reverses—Death of Yezîd II.—The Abbassides.

In accordance with the covenant of his father Abdul Malik, Walîd was succeeded by his brother Sulaimân, who is described as generous and bluff, fond of pleasure and good cheer, "preferring justice," and amenable to the wise and humane counsels of his cousin, the good Omar bin Abdul Azîz, who afterwards succeeded him on the throne. Immediately upon his accession Sulaimân opened the prison-doors of Irâk, and gave their liberty to the thousands of beings whom Hajjâj had incarcerated. He removed the revenue-collectors of that tyrant, and abolished most of his oppressive ordinances. Had he rested content with removing the burdens that had been laid upon the people by Hajjâj there would have been nothing unworthy to record of him. But he allowed his vindictive feelings to master his judgment, and his hand fell heavily upon the Modharites who had sup-

715—724 A.C. ported Walîd in his design to alter the succession. The Yemenites were now in the ascendant, and they returned with interest the cruelties to which they had been subjected by Hajjâj. Yezîd, the son of Muhallib, the new Viceroy of Irâk, finding that his enemy had escaped him by death, wreaked his vengeance on the partisans and relatives of Hajjâj. In Khorâsân, the great general Kotaiba was killed in the civil war which now broke out afresh between the Modharite and Yemenite in every part of the Empire.

Mûsa and Târick.

Sulaimân's treatment of Mûsa and Târick, the conquerors of Spain, seems inexplicable, as both of them were Yemenites, and enjoyed the confidence of the favourite Yezîd. To the undying disgrace of the sovereign these two notable men were allowed to die in want. Sulaimân is even suspected of having connived at the murder in Seville of Abdul Azîz, the son of Mûsa, whose administration of Spain had been so successful and prosperous. Mohammed, the son of Kâsim, the conqueror of Sind and the Punjab, who had endeared himself to the Hindoos by his mild and equitable rule, was recalled from his government. Mohammed's only crime was that he was a nephew of Hajjâj, and for that he suffered terribly at the hands of Yezîd bin Muhallib. Habîb, a brother of Yezîd, was appointed to the command in India. Brave but tactless, he lost the hold which his predecessor had acquired over the Hindoos.

During this reign the Moslems in Spain were left much to their own devices. On the murder of Abdul Azîz the army elected Ayûb bin Habîb, a nephew of Mûsa, as their governor, but his appointment was not accepted by the Viceroy of Africa, of which Spain was regarded as a dependency. After an administration of a few months only, in the course of which he removed the seat of government from Seville to Cordova, Ayûb was replaced by al-Hurr, a Modharite. Al-Hurr is said to have brought in his train four hundred scions of the principal Arabian families of Africa, who became the stock of the Moslem nobility of Spain. From this time until the accession of the Abbassides the Peninsula was governed by a succession of governors, appointed sometimes by the Caliphs of Damascus and sometimes by the Viceroys of Africa, who held their court at Kairowân. The divided authority was a source of serious evil; it disorganised the administration, interfered with the continuity of policy, promoted disorders, and prevented efficient support of the outlying garrisons. Al-Hurr held the government for nearly three years, which were signalised by large conquests towards the north. 96—105 A.H.

Invasion of Byzantium.

In 98 A.H. Sulaimân happened to be at a place called Dâbik, near ancient Chalcis. Here he was visited by Leo, surnamed the Isaurian, a Byzantine general, who commanded the Roman forces in Asia Minor. This double-faced traitor painted in glowing terms to Sulaimân the ease with which Constantinople could be captured, and the advantages that would accrue to the Saracenic Empire from its conquest. To ensure success he offered himself to act as a guide to the invaders. Sulaimân, dazzled by the prospect of another Spain, and beguiled by the assurances of Leo, sent an army under Maslamah, which crossed the Hellespont without any opposition. Arrived under the walls of Constantinople they laid siege to the city. A detachment under a son of Sulaimân reduced Thrace and its capital, called Sakâlibat, "the City of the Slavs." The Romans thus hemmed in were panic-stricken; they offered Maslamah a large subsidy to raise the siege. This was refused, and the Romans were reduced to dire straits. At this juncture Theodo-

715—724 A.C. sius III., who ruled Constantinople, was either killed or deposed, and the terrified Romans invited Leo to assume the purple. Escaping from the Moslem ranks Leo entered Constantinople, and was proclaimed Emperor. Acquainted with the weak points of the besiegers, he was able to withstand all the Moslem attacks. He had already by a piece of treachery procured the destruction of a great portion of their provisions. The Moslem army and fleet now began to suffer severely from famine, pestilence, and frost; and yet bravely they held on to the siege. There was no talk of retreat until the Commander of the Faithful gave the order. Nothing shows so well Sulaimân's incapacity to fill the place of his brother Walîd as his inadequate support of Maslamah and his army under the walls of Byzantium. Had they been properly assisted there is no doubt Constantinople would have fallen then.[1]

These reverses were hardly counterbalanced by the success of Yezîd, the son of Muhallib, in Tabaristan and Kuhistan,[2]—countries lying to the south-west of the Caspian Sea, and hitherto held by native rulers who, from their impregnable strongholds, had frequently defied the Saracenic power. At last Sulaimân roused himself to conduct in person the reinforcements Maslamah demanded; but he had not proceeded beyond Dâbik, in the district of Kinnisrin, where he had met the traitor Leo, when he was stricken by a fatal illness. He died on the 20th Safar, 99 A.H., after a short and not very glorious reign of two years and five months.

Death of Sulaimân, September 717 A.C.

Like his brother, Sulaimân was anxious to leave the throne to one of his sons. Ayûb, the eldest, whom he had nominated as his successor, pre-deceased him, whilst the

[1] Of course the Greeks represent this episode differently.

[2] Ancient Media.

second, Dâûd, was engaged in that ill-fated expedition against the Romans, and it was uncertain whether he was alive or dead. Racked by this dreadful anxiety, and wishful to prevent the dissensions that were certain to arise in case he made no provision, he nominated on his death-bed his cousin, the good Omar, as his successor, and after Omar his brother Yezîd, another son of Abdul Malik. The two names were written on a piece of paper, which was sealed up and delivered to Rajâ, son of Ayûb, a trusted councillor, and the members of the household took the oath of fealty on that paper.

96—105 A.H.

The nomination of Omar bin Abdul Azîz.

Sulaimân's character was made up of contradictions. Generous towards his partisans, he was as cruel as his father towards his enemies. Fond of pleasure and ease, he could, like the famous Vendôme, rouse himself to great energy in moments of emergency. The act which won him most the affections of the people and the title of "the Key of Blessing" (*Miftâh ul-Khair*) was his opening the prison-doors of the tyrant Hajjâj all over the East. He not only gave to the prisoners their liberty, but conferred on them substantial donations.

Omar II., surnamed the pious Caliph (*al-Khalîfat-as-Sâlèh*), ascended the throne in the month of Safar 99 A.H. His father was Abdul Azîz, the brother of Abdul Malik, at one time Viceroy of Egypt, which he governed wisely and with justice. His mother was a grand-daughter of the second Caliph. Omar is regarded by the Sunnis as the fifth of the *Râshidîn* or lawful Caliphs.[1] Unaffected piety, a keen sense of justice, unswerving uprightness, moderation, and an almost primitive simplicity of life formed the chief features in his character. The responsibility of the office with which he was entrusted filled him

Omar II., September 717 A.C.

His character.

[1] Abû Bakr, Omar I., Osmân, and Ali I are regarded by the Sunnis as the lawful or *Râshidîn* Caliphs.

715—724 A.C. with anxiety, and caused many a heart-searching. Once he was found by his wife[1] weeping after his prayers; asked if anything had happened to cause him grief, he replied: "O, Fâtima, I have been made the ruler over the Moslems and the strangers, and I was thinking of the poor that are starving, and the sick that are destitute, and the naked that are in distress, and the oppressed that are stricken, and the stranger that is in prison, and the venerable elder, and him that hath a large family and small means, and the like of them in the countries of the earth and the distant provinces, and I felt that my Lord would ask an account of them at my hands on the day of resurrection, and I feared that no defence would avail me, and I wept."

Immediately upon his accession, he had the horses of the royal stables sold by public auction and the proceeds deposited in the State treasury. He also asked his wife to return to the treasury all the jewellery and valuable presents she had received from her father and brothers, and the request was cheerfully complied with. After Omar's death, when her brother Yezîd ascended the throne, he offered to return to her the jewellery. The noble answer was: "I did not care for the things in his lifetime, why should I care for them after his death?" He restored to the Christians and the Jews the churches and synagogues to which they were entitled under the ancient capitulations, and which had been wrongfully taken away from them. The garden of Fedak, which belonged to the Prophet, had been appropriated by Merwân. Omar gave it back to the family of Mohammed. Hitherto it had been customary under the Ommeyades to anathematise from the pulpits the

[1] Fâtima, a daughter of Abdul Malik, and a sister of the last two sovereigns.

memory of the Caliph Ali and his descendants. Omar ordered the discontinuance of the practice, and directed that, instead of the imprecation hitherto used, a prayer should be offered to turn the hearts of the people towards charity, forbearance and benevolence. Laxity of morals was reprehended; the smallest oppression met with condign punishment; and the burdens imposed by Hajjâj and his myrmidons on the converts of Irâk, Khorâsân, and Sind were removed. The reign of Omar II. forms the most attractive period of the Ommeyade domination. The historian dwells with satisfaction on the work and aspirations of a ruler who made the weal of his people the sole object of his ambition. 96—105 A.H.

During his reign the fanatical Khârijis withheld their hands both in Arabia and Africa. They even sent messengers to Omar to say they did not object to his rule, but protested against the succession of the reprobate Yezîd, who had been nominated by Sulaimân as Omar's successor. Omar's heart was set not upon the enlargement, but on the consolidation of the vast empire that had been committed to his care. The army of Maslamah, encamped under the walls of Constantinople, was recalled; all frontier expeditions were stopped; the people were encouraged in the pursuits of industry, and provincial governors were required to give a strict account of their stewardship. Omar had always looked upon Yezîd, the son of Muhallib, as a tyrant, whilst Yezîd called Omar a hypocrite. The hypocrite, however, was in thorough earnest in the discharge of his duty towards his subjects. He called upon Yezîd to account for the spoils of which he had sent such glowing descriptions to his deceased master. No satisfactory explanation being given, the presumable defaulter, instead of being tortured or otherwise ill-

715—724 A.C.

treated according to the practice of the times, was ordered to be imprisoned in the citadel of Aleppo, where he remained until Omar's death. In a rescript addressed to the prefect of Kûfa, Omar exhorted his governors to abolish all unjust ordinances and remove all causes of complaint, "for," said the good Caliph, "thou must know, that the maintenance of religion is due to the practice of justice and benevolence; do not think lightly of any sin; do not try to depopulate what is populous; do not try to exact from the subjects anything beyond their capacity; take from them what they can give; do everything to improve population and prosperity; govern mildly and without harshness; do not accept presents on festive occasions; do not take the price of sacred books (distributed among the people); impose no tax on travellers, or on marriages, or on the milk of camels; and do not insist on the poll-tax from any one who has become a convert to Islâm." His son, Abdul Malik, a promising youth of seventeen, who was in absolute sympathy with his father in his aspirations for the good of his people and the reform of the Moslems, one day asked Omar, half-reproachfully, why he did not make more serious endeavours to root out the evils that were beginning to eat into the heart of Moslem society. "My beloved son," was the father's answer, "what thou tellest me to do can be achieved only by the sword, but there is no good in the reform which requires the use of the sword."

Omar's ordinance.

Appointment of as-Samh as Viceroy of Spain.

In 719 A.C. Omar, apprised of the disorders that had broken out in Spain, and of the incapacity of al-Hurr to deal with them, removed him from office, and appointed in his place an Yemenite chief, as-Samh, son of Mâlik, of the tribe of Khoulân. As-Samh, equally celebrated as an administrator and a warrior, was charged with the duty of re-establishing order in the finances, and of thoroughly reorganising the government. Under instructions from the Caliph, as-Samh took a census of the divers nationalities, races, and creeds that inhabited the country. At the same time a general survey was made of the entire Peninsula—"the cities, mountains, rivers, and seas," the character of the soil, the nature of its products, the resources of the land were minutely and carefully described in the records. A great cathedral mosque was built at Saragossa, and numerous bridges were constructed or repaired.

96—105 A.H.

Repression of insurgents.

After restoring order in Spain, as-Samh took in hand the repression of the Christian insurgents and the settlement of Languedoc[1] and Provence, which had appertained to the Gothic dominions. The rebels were defeated and forced to take refuge in the mountainous defiles of the Asturias. Septimania was overrun, Narbonne opened its gates, and the other cities followed its example. As Narbonne was easy of access from the sea it was strongly fortified and garrisoned. As-Samh then marched upon Toulouse, the capital of Aquitaine, which was besieged, but owing to the garrisons that had been left behind, the force under his command was not large. Before he could deliver the final assault upon the city, Eudes, the duke of Aquitaine, arrived with an immense army to the relief of his capital. Outnumbered by ten to one, and placed between two enemies, the Saracens fought with their usual dauntless courage. The chiefs broke the scabbards of their swords and fought, determined to conquer or die. "It may be said of the Arab generals of those days as has been said of Napoleon's old guards

Advance into France.

[1] Called Septimania because of its seven cities—Narbonne, Agde, Beziers, Lodève, Carcassonne, Nîmes, and Maguelone.

715—724 A.C.

—they died, but never surrendered." The battle was terrible, and victory hung uncertain for a long time, when a chance arrow pierced as-Samh on the neck and felled him to the ground. Seeing their great leader fall the Moslems began to give way, but Abdur Rahmân, who immediately assumed the command, succeeded in withdrawing them from Provence with remarkable skill and courage which elicited the admiration even of the enemy. The battle of Toulouse, in which perished a great number of illustrious Saracens, took place in the month of May, 721 A.C., some time after the death of Omar.

Battle of Toulouse. Death of as-Samh.

The reign of strict and impartial justice initiated by Omar went against the grain of the Ommeyades. They saw power and influence fast slipping out of their hands. He had openly refused to have public offices polluted by their presence; and the expostulations of the fiery covenanters had made him think seriously of altering the succession. It was high time the descendants of Ommeya should employ their usual method to rid themselves of this virtuous member of their clan. A slave in the employ of the Caliph was bribed to administer the poison with fatal result. Omar was murdered at a place called Dair Simân (the convent of Simeon), near Hems, about the middle of 101 A.H.

Rajab, 101 A.H. January 702 A.C.

Accession of Yezîd II.

In accordance with the nomination of Sulaimân, Omar was succeeded by Yezîd, the third son of Abdul Malik. Yezîd was married to a niece of Hajjâj, and all his predilections and sympathies were on the side of the Modharites. Omar had carefully maintained the balance between the two rival tribes of Modhar and Himyar. Under Yezîd the latter were to feel the full weight of Modharite revenge. This was in part the result of the harsh, not to say cruel, policy which had been pursued under Sulaimân by Yezîd bin

Muhallib, against the family of Hajjâj to make them disgorge their ill-gotten gains. In extorting from them their wealth he had not spared even the niece of Hajjâj, the wife of Yezîd, and had put aside with contempt the pleadings of the husband, who swore that if he ever came to power he would have the son of Muhallib cut to pieces; whilst the other as bravely declared that he would meet him with a hundred thousand lances. Thus the moment Ibn Muhallib heard in his prison at Aleppo that Omar was fatally ill, he knew what he had to expect from his Ommeyade namesake. He bribed his guards, and escaped to Irâk, where, with his brother, he raised the standard of revolt. The great Imâm Hassan,[1] the founder of scholastic theology, who was then established at Basra, adjured his fellow-citizens not to side with either of the "reprobates"; but the volatile people, carried away by enthusiasm for Yezîd, the son of Muhallib, and his brother, whose bravery and munificence greatly influenced the Arab mind, flocked to his help, and even took an oath of fealty to him. Yezîd the Ommeyade sent a large force under Maslamah and Abbâs son of Walîd, the two warriors of the family, to crush the rising. The contending armies met on the field of Akra, on the right bank of the Euphrates. The rebel was out-generalled; deserted by most of his men, he and his brother Habîb fell fighting. The other brothers escaped to Kermân, where in a second fight some were slain; the rest took refuge with the Khâkân of the Turks. The revolt of Yezîd bin Muhallib, which at one time threatened the very existence of the Ommeyade throne, though crushed, had far-reaching consequences. The destruction in Kermân and Irâk of the Azdites, the

96—105 A.H.

Revolt of Yezîd bin Muhallib.

[1] Surnamed *Basri*, i. e. of Basra.

715—724 A.C.

The condition of the Empire.

branch of the Yemenite stock to which Yezîd belonged, convulsed the entire Saracenic world. Yemenite and Modharite became involved in a deadly struggle in Spain, in Africa, and in the East; and the enemies of Islâm triumphed on all sides, whilst the incapacity of the sovereign and his advisers, and the nomination of incompetent governors encouraged internal disorders. An expedition into the country of Azerbaijân was disastrously repulsed by the Khazars and Kipchacks who inhabited the Caucasian regions. In Transoxiana there were revolts and risings almost always brought about by the exactions of the new governors, which were suppressed with great difficulty and loss of life. In Asia Minor alone we read of successes against the Greeks. In Africa, the nomination of a former official of Hajjâj, who attempted to treat the Berbers with the harshness and cruelty his master had used towards the Irâkians, led to a rising which assumed within a short time formidable dimensions, and required for its suppression under Yezîd's successor all the resources of the empire. In Spain, where the balance had been held so equally under the rule of Omar, that neither faction had cause for complaint, the old story of tribal dissensions and jealousies had recommenced; and every city was distracted with its own intestine quarrels. The grinding imposts introduced into Yemen by the brother of Hajjâj in the reign of Walîd I., but which had been abolished by Omar II., were re-introduced with the result that the people of the province were thoroughly alienated. All the just ordinances issued by Omar were revoked. The Khârijis, who, during the last reign, had refrained from acts of aggression, now issued against the man whom they considered an unjust and ungodly tyrant. Whilst the empire was thus distracted on all sides, Yezîd spent his time with two ladies[1] of his harem to whom he was greatly attached. The death of Habâba so overwhelmed him with grief that he died a few days after, much to the relief of his family. The annalist records one meritorious act to the credit of this monarch which is worthy of note. His governor at Medîna, a man of the type of Hajjâj, had been importuning in marriage Fatîma, the daughter of Hussain, the martyr. The lady refused his proposal, pleading that she had devoted her life to the care of the orphan children of her family. The tyrant threatened them with ill-treatment; driven to extremities Fâtima appealed to Yezîd, who deposed the governor, and severely punished him.

96—105 A.H.

Death of Yezîd II. Rajab 105 A.H. January 724 A.C.

The Abbasside Propaganda.

It was in this reign that the Propaganda in favour of the descendants of Abbâs began to be actively prosecuted over the East. The Abbasside emissaries appeared in Khorâsân in the garb of innocent merchants; but their diligent canvass for Mohammed, who was now the head of the Abbasside branch, did not fail to reach the ears of the Ommeyade governor Saîd.[2] They were summoned before him and closely questioned; their ingenuous answers and the assurances of people whose friendship they had secured, induced Saîd to set them at liberty. His successors were either not so lenient or so easily duped; and the Abbasside emissaries worked, wherever they went, with their lives in their hands; if caught they were subjected to the barbarous punishments characteristic of the age. But in spite of all endeavours to crush this dangerous propaganda, the underground mining proceeded unceasingly, adherents were enrolled on all sides,

[1] Sallâma and Habâba. Both of them are said to have been great musicians.

[2] He was nicknamed Khozaina, as he used to dress himself like a Persian lady.

715—724 A.C. and within a short time Persia was honeycombed with secret organisations for the subversion of the hated family of the Banû Ommeya. Several causes combined at this moment to facilitate the development of the conspiracy and the eventual rising, which, like a sudden and colossal tidal wave, engulfed the Ommeyades a few years later in a terrible destruction. The cruelties of Hajjâj had hardly been effaced from the memories of men by the justice of Omar before Yezîd succeeded to the throne. His brutality towards the relatives of his rebellious namesake roused the animosity of the Yemenites. Besides this there was another potent cause which paved the way of the Abbassides to power. On every side there was an eager longing engendered by the vices and misrule of Yezîd II., that the House of Mohammed should be restored to its rights. The people looked wistfully to the Imâms to give the sign, but these saints had retired from the world; their domain was no more of this earth. It was in this state of suspense and unrest that the Banû-Abbâs appeared on the scene with their claims and pretensions.

The Banû-Abbâs. They were the descendants of Abbâs, an uncle of the Prophet, who died in 32 A.H., leaving four sons, Abdullâh, Fazl, Obaidullâh, and Kaisân. Abdullâh, better known in history and tradition as Ibn Abbâs, was born at Mecca in 619 A.C., three years before the Hegira. All four brothers were present at "the Battle of the Camel"; and at Siffîn, Ibn Abbâs, who was no less an accomplished soldier than a scholar, commanded the cavalry of Ali. He acted frequently as the envoy of the Caliph, and it was he whom Ali desired to nominate as the representative of the House of Mohammed when forced by his refractory troops to refer the dispute between himself and Muâwiyah to arbitration.

Ibn Abbâs died at Tâyef in 67 A.H., in the seventieth year of his age, of a broken heart, after the murder of Hussain. His son, who was named Ali after the great Caliph, walked in the footsteps of his father in his zealous attachment to the children of Fâtima. He died in 117 A.H., and was succeeded in the headship of his family by his son Mohammed. A man of great ability and unbounded ambition, Mohammed was the first to conceive the project of seizing the Caliphate for himself. He started a new doctrine to justify the claims of his house to the Imâmate: that on the murder of Hussain at Kerbela, the spiritual headship of Islâm was not transmitted to his surviving son Ali (Zain ul-Aâbidîn), but to Mohammed al-Hanafia;[1] that upon al-Hanafia's death his office descended upon his son Abû Hâshim, who had assigned it to Mohammed bin Ali bin Abdullâh. This story received credence in some quarters; but to the bulk of the people, who clung to the descendants of the Prophet, the emissaries[2] of the Abbassides affirmed that they were working for the apostolical family. The adherents of the Fatimides, little suspecting the treachery which lay behind this profession, without the knowledge of the Imâms and without their sanction, extended to Mohammed bin Ali and his party the favour and protection which was needed to impress upon his action the sanction of a recognised authority.

96—105 A.H.

The Abbasside Propaganda.

Before his death, which took place in 125 A.H., Mohammed named his sons Ibrâhim, Abdullâh Abu'l Abbâs (surnamed *as-Saffâh*), and Abdullâh Abû Jaafar (surnamed *al-Mansûr*), as his successors, one after the other. And the Propaganda started by him was conducted after his death with the same devotion, coolness, and courage as in his lifetime.

[1] See *ante*, p. 94.

[2] Called *Dâis* or *Nakîbs*.

CHAPTER XI

THE OMMEYADES (THE HAKAMITE BRANCH) (*continued*)

105—125 A.H., 724—744 A.C.

Accession of Hishâm—Troubled state of the Empire—Hishâm's character—Affairs in the East—In Armenia—In Africa—The Revolt of the Khârijis and Berbers—"The Battle of the Nobles"—Hanzala—Defeat of the Berbers—Spain—Intestine Dissensions—Frequent change of Governors—Appointment of Abdur Rahmân al-Ghâfeki—Invasion of Northern France—Battle of Tours—Monkish exaggeration—Fresh Invasion of France—Capture of Avignon—Okba's Victories—His Death—Internecine Quarrels—Ruin of the Arab Cause in France—Fall of Khâlid al-Kasri—Rising of Zaid in Irâk—His Death—The Abbasside Propaganda—Appearance of Abû Muslim—Death of Hishâm.

On the death of Yezîd II. his brother Hishâm[1] succeeded to an empire racked by tribal dissensions, and full of trouble at home and abroad. The wild hordes of Turkomans and Khazars pressing on the north, the Khâriji zealots seething within with discontent, and the emissaries of the house of Abbâs working underground, combined to sap the foundations of Ommeyade

[1] Shortly after his accession Yezîd had been persuaded, in consequence of the minority of his son Walîd, to nominate Hishâm as his immediate successor; upon Hishâm's death, the throne was to go to Walîd. As the latter attained his majority in his father's lifetime, Yezîd often cursed those who had persuaded him to postpone his son's succession. According to Masûdi, Hishâm reigned nineteen years nine months and nine days.

power in the East. The flower of the nation had perished either in the civil wars or under the suspicious policy of a jealous court. The blind confidence reposed by the last sovereign in his ministers had thrown the government into the hands of incompetent and self-seeking functionaries whose incapacity and misrule alienated the people. Here and there, a few men shone, like stars on a darkening horizon, for their devotion to duty, but generally amongst the official classes, the old patriotism and enthusiasm for the Faith had almost died out in the pursuit of individual ambition. At this crisis a master's hand was needed at the helm to save the ship of state from drifting to destruction. But Hishâm was little fitted by character or disposition to cope with the difficulties which now beset the empire. He was undoubtedly an improvement upon his immediate predecessor; the atmosphere of the court became purer, the laxity of the former reign gave way to decorum, the city was purged of the parasites that live on society, and greater regard was paid to the conventionalities and rules of life. But his austerity wore an aspect of sombreness, and his parsimony amounted to avarice. And these failings were aggravated by more serious defects of character. Bigoted in his views, narrow in his sympathies, and suspicious in nature, he trusted nobody, and relied chiefly on espionage and intrigue to prevent hostile combinations and conspiracies. Easily swayed by false reports, he often sacrificed the best servants of the state upon mere suspicion, and the frequent change of governors led to disastrous consequences. Of the few men who held office under him for any length of time, one was Khâlid son of Abdullâh al-Kasri, who was viceroy of Irâk from the accession of Hishâm until 120 A.H. A man of enlightened views,

105—125 A.H.

Khâlid al-Kasri, Viceroy of Irâk.

724—744 A.C. and himself a Yemenite, he held the balance between the two rival stocks with tact and judgment, and during the whole of his administration there was hardly a collision between Modhar and Himyar. His treatment of the Christians and Jews was considerate, just and liberal; he repaired their churches and synagogues, and threw open to them offices of emolument and trust. His wise and statesmanlike tolerance exposed him to the attacks of fanatics, a result not confined to any particular time or country, but the countenance of his master protected him from the malevolence of his enemies. His fall, however, was as sudden as his success for fifteen years was unprecedented.

Rising in Sogdiana.

Shortly after Hishâm's accession, a violent conflict between Modhar and Himyar broke out in Khorâsân, which was repressed with some difficulty. This was followed by a rising of the Sogdians, caused by the rapacity of the deputy-governor, who after promising the remission of the test-tax to such of the people as would embrace Islâm, tried to re-impose the burden when a great many had adopted the religion. The insurgents were joined by some of the colonists under an Arab chief named Hâris, who reprobated the breach of faith on the part of the governor. They also received support from the head of the Turkoman hordes who roamed towards the east of Transoxiana. Serious efforts were made to quell the insurrection, but without success, until

Asad al-Kasri, Governor of Khorâsân.

Khâlid, the viceroy of Irâk, deputed his brother Asad to restore order in the disturbed province. The insurgents were driven from Ferghâna and compelled to take refuge with the Turkomans. As these nomads kept the

Asad invades Khuttal, 119 A.H.

country in a continual state of ferment by their raids, in 119 A.H. Asad marched into Khuttal, which lay to the east of Ferghâna, and formed the special dominion of the Khâkân.[1] Beyond, however, repulsing an attack upon his vanguard and collecting a large booty, he made no impression on the enemy, for the approach of winter soon forced him to retire to Balkh. Here he took up his winter quarters, and the troops were dispersed to their homes. The Turkomans considered this a favourable opportunity to resume their depredations, and they again burst into Transoxiana killing and plundering on every side. Whilst thus engaged in rapine and slaughter they were set upon by the governor, who had collected his men by lighting beacons on the hill-tops, and literally annihilated. The Khâkân alone succeeded in making his escape, but was killed shortly after by one of his own chiefs. Hishâm at first would hardly believe the news, and special messengers were despatched to ascertain the true fact. When it became known that this redoubtable foe of Islâm was really dead, it caused great rejoicing at Damascus. Asad himself died in the year 120 A.H., shortly before the deposition of his brother Khâlid from the viceroyalty of Irâk. He was succeeded in the governorship of Khorâsân by Nasr, the son of Sayyâr, who in spite of all intrigues held the office until his death in 130 A.H. Nasr was a man of moderate views, and anxious to promote the well-being of the people entrusted to his charge. In the beginning, and before the dissensions which later broke out afresh between Modhar and Himyar, his administration was not only vigorous but just and generous. The insurgent Sogdians, who were still roaming within the Turkoman territories, were invited to return to their allegiance. They asked for two con-

105—125 A.H.

The Khâkân killed.

Nasr, the son of Sayyâr, appointed Governor of Khorâsân.

[1] This was the designation of the chief of the Turkoman hordes. It was also the title by which Chengîz and his successors were known to the Arabs.

724—744 A.C. ditions, *first*, that no one should be molested in his religion or punished unless in due course of law, and *second*, that apostasy from Islâm should not be treated as a crime. These conditions were accepted by the new governor, and the Sogdians returned to their homes.

Northern Persia and Armenia. Whilst these events were taking place in Central Asia, Northern Persia and Armenia were harassed by the incursions of the tribes inhabiting the Caucasian regions. The governorship of Armenia, which included Mesopotamia (designated the Jazîrah), Armenia, and the province of Azerbaijân, was at this time held by Hishâm's brother, 727 A.C. Maslamah. In 108 A.H. Persia was raided by a large body of Turks, who, issuing from the mountainous tract Incursion of the Khazars. beyond the Aras, laid waste Azerbaijân; they were eventually defeated and driven out of the province. The Jarrâh, governor of Armenia, killed. ease, however, with which they had entered Persia encouraged other tribes to follow their example, and four years later the formidable Turkish horde of the Khazars penetrated into Armenia. The Arab governor, Jarrâh, who had succeeded Maslamah, was overwhelmed and killed Saîd al-Harshi defeats the Khazars. near Ardebil, and the barbarians devastated the country as far as Mosul. Here they were met by an army chiefly composed of volunteers collected by Saîd al-Harshi, whom Hishâm had hurried off to the scene of disaster, and were defeated with terrible slaughter. The demoralised horde fled across the Aras, leaving behind their captives and the booty they had gathered, which was restored to the rightful owners.

Maslamah re-appointed. With the perversity of mind which characterised Hishâm, he now recalled Saîd and reappointed Maslamah. A year later Maslamah was again removed, and the post was given to Merwân,[1] who afterwards seized the throne.

[1] A grandson of the first Merwân, the founder of the family. His father's name was Mohammed.

Merwân signalised his entry into office by defeating the Khazars within their own territories. Georgia was conquered, and the Lesghis and other mountain tribes were subdued. But the incessant warfare Merwân had to maintain with the nomads of the north, who continued to press on him, formed a heavy drain on the resources of the empire.

105—125 A.H.

114 A.H. Maslamah removed again, and Merwân appointed.

In Southern Arabia also there were serious troubles; whilst in Irâk the Khârijis rose on several occasions, and necessitated the employment of large forces for their suppression.

Southern Arabia.

In Africa and Spain matters had gone smoothly for a time, and some additions were made to the empire. The Black Country was annexed in 115 A.H., and the following year Sardinia was conquered. In 122 A.H. Sicily was invaded, and Syracuse was reduced after a hard fight. Some conquests were made in France, and on the whole fortune seemed to smile on Hishâm in the West. But the year had hardly expired when the whole of Northern Africa was convulsed by a violent and sanguinary revolt of the Berbers and the Khârijis. A new sect of zealots had about this time appeared in Mauritania. They called themselves Soffarides, and in violence and bigotry equalled the Azârika of the East. Maddened like their Eastern brethren by persecution, they denounced their oppressors as worse than heathens, and proclaimed against them a war of extermination. All who submitted to the Ommeyade yoke were regarded as misbelievers. The oppression of the Viceroy's son, who was acting on behalf of his father at Tangiers, and his attempt to impose the test-tax on Moslems, roused them to fury, and, joined by the Berbers, they rose *en masse*, killed the governor and seized the city. From Tangiers they marched upon Kairowân. All further progress in

Africa and Spain.

Conquest of Sardinia and Syracuse in 122 A.H.

Revolt of the Khârijis and Berbers.

724—744 A.C. Sicily was now stopped, and the general[1] operating in that island was recalled to stem the Berber insurrection. On their way to the capital the insurgents were met by the son of the Sicilian commander with a force hardly adequate to check the advance of the barbarian host. Though terribly outnumbered, with the recklessness or audacity which characterised the Arabs, he engaged them at once. But heroic valour was of no avail against numbers; the Arab chiefs as usual broke their scabbards and fought on foot, and the men followed the example of their leaders. The Saracens were surrounded, overwhelmed, and killed almost to a man. This disastrous battle is known in Islâmic history as "the fight of the nobles,"[2] from the number of Arab cavaliers and knights who fell that day. The destruction of Ibn Habîb's army threw into disorder the whole of Northern Africa. Its effect was even felt in Spain, where the people rose in revolt against their governor, and elected in his place an officer who had been deposed by Hishâm.[3] The news of the reverse sustained by his army threw Hishâm into a violent rage; and he swore an oath that he would make the rebels feel the full weight of his wrath. The viceroy whose son's misgovernment had led to the revolt was recalled, and an able general of the name of Kulsûm (Kulthûm) was sent in haste to retrieve the disaster. An unseemly quarrel between two of his captains on the eve of battle was followed by the usual result: the Arabs were again defeated, and their principal leaders killed. A part of the Syrian army went off to Spain, whilst the remainder threw themselves into Kairowân, which was now beleaguered by the Berbers and the

"The Fight of the Nobles."

[1] Habîb the son of Obaidah.

[2] *Ghazwat ul-Ashrâf.*

[3] See *post*, p. 154.

zealots, led by a rebel chief named Okasha,[1] who had taken up arms at Cabes. Successive assaults delivered by the barbarians were repulsed with slaughter, and Okasha for a time retreated into the desert. Hishâm now appointed Hanzala, the son of Safwân, of the tribe of Kalb, to the governorship of Africa. Hanzala's first care on reaching Kairowân was to put the fortifications in order and rouse the courage of the defenders. It was not long before his generalship and resources were put to the test, for three hundred thousand Berbers swooped down on the African capital and prevented all egress and ingress. The Arabs were reduced to dire straits; but Hanzala was a hero of the old type. He combined the religious enthusiasm of the days of Omar with a gentleness of heart unusual in that cruel age. Standing in the great square in front of the Cathedral Mosque, he harangued the people that the struggle between the pent-up Moslems and the rebels outside was one of life and death, that a Berber victory would mean the promiscuous slaughter of the inhabitants, in which neither age nor sex would be spared. It was a crisis never to be forgotten in the history of Islâm. The beleaguering host raged round the city, whilst the wearied defenders stood and watched the struggle with beating hearts from the ramparts. To Hanzala's appeal for volunteers a ready response was made by the citizens. The women of the Arabs, accustomed to danger, and to the use of arms, have often proved valuable auxiliaries to their husbands and brothers on the field of battle. Hanzala formed a reserve of the women, who were to hold the city whilst the soldiers and volunteers attacked the enemy. All night long Hanzala and his officers were engaged in distributing arms and giving orders for the morrow's

105—125 A.H.

124 A.H.

Hanzala appointed Viceroy of Africa.

[1] A Khâriji of the Soffaride sect.

724—744 A.C. fight. After the morning prayers the defenders broke their scabbards and issued against the enemy. The battle was fierce and terrible, and lasted from daybreak till sundown, when the barbarians broke and fled. The pursuit was kept up until the rebels had lost all cohesion and power of resistance. One hundred and eighty thousand Berbers, with their principal leaders, are said to have been killed in this fight, whilst the Saracenic loss, though severe, was not great. The straits to which the Arabs had been reduced, and the importance of the victory gained by Hanzala, is shown by the fact that after the destruction of the rebels thanksgivings were offered up in all the mosques of Kairowân. Hanzala was now able to restore peace and order in the disaffected tracts, and so long as he held the reins of office the country was free from disturbance; under his mild and just government Northern Africa soon recovered its prosperity.

Andalusia or Spain. The vast dependency of Andalusia, which included the Iberian peninsula, with Gascony, Languedoc, and part of Savoy, formed at this period an integral part of the Ommeyade Caliphate. As usual in other countries and other times, with the Saracenic rule, the people inhabiting this region had, for the most part, assumed the manners and adopted the civilisation of their conquerors. But its distance from the heart of the empire weakened the central authority; and the system upon which the government was conducted was always productive of mischief. To use a designation borrowed from modern India, Spain was regarded as a subordinate presidency to *Ifrîkia*, and the Viceroy of Kairowân was vested with the power of appointing the governors of Andalusia without the sanction of the sovereign. Naturally, public interests were often sacrificed to tribal or family bias; and the frequent change of governors gave rise to civil wars. When as-Samh fell under the walls of Toulouse, Abdur Rahmân (*al-Ghâfeki*) was elected by the army in his place, but he held the office only for a few months until the arrival of Anbasah, who was nominated to the governorship by the Viceroy of Africa. Abdur Rahmân, who is described as "a man of great courage and considerable abilities, honest in his proceedings, and impartial in his judgment," kept under control the discordant elements within the Peninsula until the arrival of his successor, who took up the reins of government in the month of Safar 103 A.H. Shortly after Hishâm's accession Anbasah led an expedition into France, which resulted in the conquest of Carcassonne, Nîmes, and several other places of importance, and the formation of a defensive and offensive alliance with the Gothic communities of the neighbourhood. "The conquests of Anbasah," says Reinaud, following Isidore of Beja, "were due more to tact and management than to force; and his efforts to conciliate the good-will of the inhabitants strengthened the Saracenic position in Southern France." The hostages furnished by the French cities were sent to Barcelona, where they were treated with consideration, and helped in forming bonds of union between the people of the province and the Arabs. Unfortunately, Anbasah was killed in an ambush placed by the rebellious Biscayans in one of the Pyrenean defiles. His death again threw the Peninsula into disorder, all operations in France were stopped, and his lieutenant Uzrah (Udhrah) hastened back into Spain with the bulk of the army. During the five years that elapsed from the death of Anbasah to the reappointment of Abdur Rahmân in 113 A.H., five governors ruled over the province, some of whom held the office only for a few months. The administration of the country was completely paralysed

105—125 A.H.

Anbasah, Governor of Spain.

August 721 A.C.

Anbasah's death.

Shâbân 107 A.H. Jan. 726 A.C.

724—744 A.C. by these changes, and the rebels under Pelayo acquired strength. Under Haisem (Haithem), who came to Spain in 111 A.H., some endeavour was made to destroy their strongholds and to resume the work of conquest beyond the Pyrenees. Lyons, Macon, Chalons-on-the-Saone were captured; Beaune and Autun were seized and plundered, and other places were put under contribution. But in the end this invasion bore no fruit, for the Arabs, owing to their own differences, were unable to retain possession of these cities, and the excesses of the Berbers, who composed the bulk of the Saracenic army, converted the friendly-disposed Septimanians into bitter enemies. Upon the death of Haisem, Abdur Rahmân al-Ghâfeki was called by Hishâm to fill the office of Governor of Andalusia. His appointment was hailed by the Spaniards as a happy augury for the Peninsula; Abdur Rahmân was incomparably the ablest and most patriotic ruler that country ever had under the Ommeyade domination. He combined in an eminent degree a capacity for civil administration with military talents of the highest order. His influence over both Himyar and Modhar was unbounded; whilst adored by his soldiers, his gentleness of heart, generosity and justice endeared him to the people. He made a complete tour of the provincial cities and districts to settle the complaints that poured in from all sides; the *kâids* or local magistrates found guilty of breach of duty or trust were dismissed and replaced by men of position and probity; all classes were treated alike and with equal justice, without distinction of race or creed; the churches that had been wrongly taken from the Christians were restored to their rightful owners; the fiscal administration was carefully revised; and disorders against public peace were repressed with severity. But the task

Abdur Rahmân al-Ghâfeki appointed Governor of Spain.

His character and administration.

of reorganising the government did not distract his attention from the necessity of safeguarding the northern frontiers. Animated by a natural desire to avenge the check sustained by the Saracens before Toulouse, and anxious to emulate the glorious achievements of Târick and Mûsa, he persistently endeavoured to create an army which would prove irresistible in its advance towards the north. Religious zeal was still at its height, and service under a veteran and daring commander drew a large number of volunteers. The Moslem governor of Cerdagne, on the other side of the Pyrenees, called Munuza by the Christian writers of the time, but whose real name was Osmân bin Abû Nessa, or Abû Nêza, had married the beautiful Lampegie, daughter of Eudes, the Duke of Aquitaine, and entered into a defensive and offensive alliance with him. In concert with his father-in-law he raised the standard of revolt. Abdur Rahmân, however, was not the man to dally with insurrection. A body of troops was promptly despatched to al-Bâb,[1] where Munuza resided with his wife. The rebel chief fled to the mountains, but was overtaken and slain. His unhappy wife fell into the hands of Abdur Rahmân's lieutenant, and was sent with all respect to Damascus, where she afterwards married a son of Hishâm.

105—125 A.H.

Revolt of Munuza.

Munuza's death.

The defeat and death of Munuza threw into commotion the Christian principalities with whom he was in alliance, and Abdur Rahmân found himself compelled to take the field before his preparations for the projected invasion of the north were completed.

Taking the route through Aragon and Navarre, he

Invasion of Northern France.

[1] Al-Bâb signifies the gate, and indicates that this city was situated on one of the passages of the Pyrenees. It is said to have been situated to the west of Mount Louis, not far from Puycerda, with which it is often identified.

724—744 A.C.

entered France in the spring of 732 by the valleys of Bigoral and Bearn. Arles, described by the Arab writers as a city situated in a plain in a vast solitude, and built on a river three leagues from the sea, had agreed to the payment of a tribute. On the death of Munuza it refused to abide by the treaty. Abdur Rahmân marched first against Arles; a sanguinary battle on the banks of the Rhône was followed by the capitulation of the city. From Arles Abdur Rahmân retraced his steps towards Bordeaux, which was captured after a slight resistance. The Duke of Aquitaine, who tried to oppose the passage of the Dordogne, suffered a terrible defeat. God alone, says Isidore of Beja, could reckon the number of Christians who fell in the battle. With this victory all opposition was swept out of Aquitaine; Burgundy was overrun, and the proud standard of Islâm floated on the walls of Lyons, Besançon and Sens. Leaving strong garrisons in these cities, which, however, weakened the strength of his army, the victorious general marched towards the capital of the Frankish kingdom. After his defeat on the banks of the Dordogne, finding himself unable further to cope with the invaders, Eudes invoked the aid of Charles,[1] a natural son of Pepin of Heristal, who, as mayor of the palace in the Merovingian Court, exercised despotic sway over the Franks. Able and unscrupulous, Charles perceived in the appeal of Eudes a means of aggrandisement, and responded to it with alacrity. Collecting a vast horde of savage auxiliaries from the borders of the Danube, the Elbe and the wilds of Germany, he marched to the south. The Saracens in the meantime had advanced upon Tours, which was carried by assault. The Arabian writers ascribe the disaster which now overtook the Saracenic

Capitulation of Arles.

Bordeaux reduced.

Battle of the Dordogne; defeat of Eudes.

Charles, the son of Pepin of Heristal.

[1] Called Kârla, or Kâldus, by the Arab writers.

arms to divine wrath at the excesses committed in Tours by the half-disciplined Berbers, in spite of stringent orders. Misled by his spies as to the strength of the Franks, the Saracenic commander was endeavouring to cross the Loire, when the approach of Charles with his horde undeceived him. Finding the enemy vastly superior to him in number, he hurriedly drew in his outposts, and falling back from the banks of the river, took up a position between Tours and Poictiers. The condition of his own army was such as to cause Abdur Rahmân the gravest anxiety. The tribal legions, laden with spoil, and always jealous of each other, and unwilling to act for long in unison, were clamouring for retreat. The booty they had gathered in their march towards the north, and to which they clung, had introduced considerable laxity in their ranks, and slackened the bonds of discipline. Abdur Rahmân naturally feared, as Charles hoped, that at the moment of action the spoil acquired by the troops would prove a serious hindrance to the Saracens and a cause of embarrassment. He therefore thought of inducing the men to abandon a portion of the loot; at the same time he did not wish to create discontent by insisting upon obedience. The result of this weakness, if it can be so called, was, as the sequel shows, most fatal. The hordes of Charles, composed partly of horsemen, and partly of foot-soldiers clad in wolf-skins, with long matted hair hanging down over their shoulders, crossed the Loire a few miles above where the Arabs were encamped, and took up a position with the river at their back.[1] Several

105—125 A.H.

Battle of Tours.

[1] It is impossible to identify the exact spot where the fight took place, but there can be no doubt that the theatre of this memorable conflict between Frank and Saracen lay in the country between Poictiers and Tours. This tract, watered by a number of tributaries

724—744 A.C. days were spent in light skirmishes, in which the advantage lay with the Saracens; on the ninth day a general engagement began, which raged until the shades of night separated the two armies. Next morning the action recommenced; the Moslem warriors redoubled their efforts, and the Franks began to waver, when suddenly, whilst on the verge of a decisive victory, a cry arose that the Arab camp with all its treasure was in danger. At this news, the Saracens quitted their ranks and flew to the defence of their booty; in vain Abdur Rahmân endeavoured to restore order; all his efforts were useless, and he fell pierced by a lance. The fall of the general threw the whole army into disorder, and the enemy, taking advantage of the confusion, committed great havoc. But the Frank had felt the weight of the Arab's sword, and welcomed the darkness which again separated the foes; as the night closed in the two armies retired to their respective quarters.

Ramazân 116 A.H. October 732 A.C.

Abdur Rahmân killed.

Quarrels among his lieutenants.

No sooner had the Arabs reached their camps than furious dissensions broke out among Abdur Rahmân's lieutenants, and the legionaries turned their arms against each other. Victory over the Franks was now out of the question; a safe retreat was the only possible course open. Under cover of night, the Saracen generals quietly withdrew the army towards Septimania. At the dawn of day, the stillness of the hostile camp caused Charles and his ally Eudes to suspect some deep-laid design. Timorously and cautiously they approached the Saracenic encampment, and were overjoyed to find it empty and deserted, save for a number of wounded

Retreat of the Saracens.

of the Loire, forms a vast undulating plain interspersed with forest lands, meadows and pretty hamlets, which lend such charm to French landscape, but in those times it could only have furnished a vast field for the movement of mighty armies.

who could not accompany the retreating force. These were immediately butchered by the Franks. Charles, however, did not venture to pursue the retreating Saracens, and immediately retraced his steps northwards.[1] On the plains of Tours the Arabs lost the empire of the world when almost in their grasp. Insubordination and inter-tribal jealousies, which have ever been the curse of Moslem communities, led to that disastrous issue. The field of battle is called in Arabian history *Balât-ush-Shuhadâ*, or the *Pavement of Martyrs*, from the number of prominent men who lost their lives with Abdur Rahmân. And the pious still believe that the angels of Heaven may be heard there calling the Faithful to the Moslem vespers.

105—125 A.H.

Butchery of the wounded by the Franks.

The monkish writers represent the Arab loss to have amounted to 360,000 men, more than four times the number with which Abdur Rahmân actually entered France! The exaggeration is demonstrated by the fact, that before a few months were over the Saracens, in spite of intestine wars and disorders, again assumed the

[1] Most European writers, following in the footsteps of the early chroniclers, have extolled the prowess of the Frankish chief and his horde, and described the result of the battle as the salvation of Europe. The philosophic Gibbon gives a truer estimate of Charles's success. Speaking of the Arab loss alleged by the monkish writers, he says—"But this incredible tale is sufficiently disproved by the caution of the French general, who apprehended the snares and accidents of a pursuit, and dismissed his German allies to their native forests. The inactivity of a conqueror betrays the loss of strength and blood, and the most cruel execution is inflicted, not in the ranks of battle, but on the backs of a flying enemy." And yet there can be no question that the battle was decisive in one respect. Abdur Rahmân was the one man who could unite Modhar and Himyar; his loss was irreparable, for no one after him wielded the same influence, or exercised the same authority over the Saracenic forces.

724–744 A.C. offensive with a numerous army, although not so well equipped or organised as that under Abdur Rahmân.

Infuriated at the death of their great chief, the Saracens are said to have burnt the Abbey of Solignan at Limousin in their retreat towards the south.

The lieutenant of Abdur Rahmân sent in all haste to the Viceroy of Africa, and to Hishâm at Damascus, the news of the disaster. Hishâm at once despatched a new governor, Abdul Malik bin Kattan, with instructions to retrieve the prestige of the Saracenic flag. The people inhabiting the mountainous regions in the north of the Peninsula had attempted to profit by the death of Abdur Rahmân, and to throw off the Saracenic rule. The new governor directed his first efforts against Aragon and Navarre. The insurgents were defeated in several battles, and were compelled to sue for pardon. He then entered Languedoc, and strengthened the positions held by the Saracens in that province. In 734 A.C. the deputy governor of Narbonne, Yusuf, joining hands with Maurontius, Duke of Marseilles, who was in alliance with the Moslems, crossed the Rhône, captured Saint Remi (then called Fritta), and marched upon Avignon. In vain the Frankish hosts tried to oppose the passage of the Durance; they were beaten, and Avignon capitulated after a short siege.

Abdul Malik appointed Governor of Spain.

Avignon conquered.

After the capture of Avignon Abdul Malik returned to the south; but, owing either to a check received by his troops in the defiles of the Pyrenees, or, as the Arabian historian says, "owing to his cruel propensities and the excessive rigour of his judgment," he was deposed in the month of Ramazân, 116 A.H. (November, 734 A.C.). He was replaced by Okba, "a man of great justice and irreproachable conduct," says our author, "virtues which obtained for him the veneration of all

Okba appointed Governor of Spain.

Moslems." During the five years of his administration he entered France several times, and carried the Moslem arms far beyond the former limits. Under him the Saracens of Languedoc established fortified positions in all places susceptible of defence up to the river Rhône. These military stations were called *ribât*, and were intended for defensive purposes as well as observation. Okba converted Narbonne into a huge citadel, and stored it with provisions and arms. In 118 A.H. (736 A.C.) he entered Dauphiny, and captured in succession Saint Paul, Trois Chateaux, Donzère, Valence, and New Lyons. The Saracenic detachments spread into Burgundy and threatened the capital of France. Piedmont had been invaded a year earlier, and military colonies had been established in favourable situations. Charles, who had, since the battle of Tours, assumed the title of *Martel*, finding himself unable to cope unaided with the Saracens, invoked the assistance of Luitprand, king of the Lombards. Childebrand, his brother, brought a host of wild auxiliaries from the eastern territories of the Frankish kingdom, and the united horde descended upon the Saracenic possessions. At the same time Charles instigated the Basques and Gascons to create a diversion in the south by closing the Pyrenean passes. The Saracens were thus attacked from all sides. Avignon was taken by assault after a long siege, and all the Moslems were put to the sword. Narbonne was besieged, but although an army sent by sea for its relief was beaten by the allies, the defence was so vigorous that Charles lost heart and raised the siege. In order, however, to oppose an impassable barrier against any further Saracenic advance, he converted a vast tract of the country to the south of the Loire into a veritable desert. Bezier, Agde, and

105—125 A.H.

Saracenic garrisons established in France. Narbonne Arsenal created. Okbah invades Dauphiny.

Coalition formed by Charles Martel against the Saracens.

Charles Martel destroys a number of

724—744 A.C.

cities to create a barrier to the Saracenic advance.

other cities of importance, which had been beautified by the Saracens, were rased to the ground. Nîmes, with its magnificent amphitheatre and its glorious monuments of antiquity, was committed to the flames. Even the French historian is compelled to call this senseless vandalism a "deplorable thing." Maguelone, which had attained a pitch of prosperity it had never known under the Goths or Franks, was totally destroyed. Whilst these events were taking place in France, Africa was convulsed with the great Berber revolt which I have already described. The disorder in Africa incited troubles in Spain, and in 123 A.H. an insurrection, headed by old Abdul Malik bin Kattan, the deposed governor, broke out against Okba, who was taken prisoner and put to death by the rebels.[1] Abdul Malik then seized the reins of authority. But he had not been long in possession of his ill-gotten power, when the Syrians under Balj, who had escaped from the slaughter of Kulsûm's army in Africa, arrived in Spain, and added to the elements of strife within the Peninsula. In the struggle between Abdul Malik and Balj, the former was killed and his body ignominiously impaled on a cross. His enemy died shortly after from the effects of wounds received in a fight with Abdul Malik's son. The Syrians thereupon elected Saalaba (Thalaba), son of Sallâmah, one of their body, as governor of Andalusia, and the civil war proceeded merrily. The *Bilâdiûn*, or the Spanish Moslems, sided with the sons of Abdul Malik, the Syrians with the chief they had elected, whilst the Berbers fought for their own hand. The administration of Spain was completely paralysed, and the military stations and outposts in France were left to look after themselves. Narbonne was deserted by its commander,

December 740 A.C.

Insurrection in Spain; Okba killed. Abdul Malik seizes the government.

Abdul Malik killed.

Shawwâl 124 A.H.

[1] See *ante*, p. 142.

who had marched with his best troops to the succour of Abdul Malik and his sons, and the other cities possessed by the Saracens were equally bereft of their defenders. Had Pepin the Short, who had succeeded his father Charles in the mayoralty of the Merovingian Palace, attacked the Arab settlements then, the Saracens would have been powerless to offer any opposition. But the lessons learnt in former wars had not been forgotten, and the Franks waited to strike the blow until the Arabs were thoroughly weakened by their own dissensions. Whilst the Moslems in Spain were engaged in this fratricidal war, affairs at home, in spite of various successes in Asia Minor,[1] were going from bad to worse. 105—125 A.H.

The government of Irâk, as I have already mentioned, had been held ever since the accession of Hishâm by Khâlid, who had ruled the province with vigour and justice. His successful and tolerant administration had raised a host of enemies, and they poisoned the mind of Hishâm against him. The chief ground of suspicion against him was that he favoured the Hâshimides (the descendants of Hâshim). Probably Hishâm was also influenced by avarice, for he suspected that during the fifteen years Khâlid had held office, he had amassed a large fortune by peculation. In 120 A.H. Khâlid was removed from the viceroyalty of Irâk, and his place was taken by Yusuf (bin Omar), described as a hypocrite and a man of changeable temperament and cruel propensities. He was a Modharite and hated Khâlid. The deposed governor was put to the torture to discover his suspected wealth, but was released under the orders of the sovereign. Hishâm did not, however, interfere with Yusuf's persecution of the Hâshimides,

120 A.H.

Khâlid al-Kasri removed from office.

Yusuf al-Fazâri appointed in his place.

[1] Sundra and Matamer in Asia Minor were conquered in 121 A.H. by one of the sons of Hishâm.

724—744 A.C. who were subjected to cruel ill-treatment. Zaid, the grandson of Hussain, who went to Hishâm for redress, was driven from his presence with ignominy. Enraged at his ill-treatment, Zaid came to Kûfa, and against the advice of his relatives, who tried to dissuade him from the mad enterprise and from placing any reliance on the faithless Irâkians, he attempted a rising which failed. Zaid was killed, and his body was surreptitiously buried by his followers. But the vindictive Ommeyades discovered the grave; the body was exhumed and impaled on a cross; after a time it was taken down and burnt, and the ashes thrown into the Euphrates—an act of insensate barbarism which brought on the Ommeyades fearful and ruthless reprisals.[1] Zaid's son, Yahya, a high-minded youth of seventeen, escaped into Khorâsân. The death of Zaid strengthened the propaganda in favour of the Abbassides by removing from their path a possible rival, and was coeval with the appearance of Abû Muslim, who eventually wrought the downfall of the Ommeyade dynasty. Mohammed, the great-grandson of Abbâs, the real projector of the design to oust the Ommeyades from the sovereignty of Islâm, and to supplant the descendants of the Prophet, died in 124 A.H., leaving to his eldest son Ibrâhim the fulfilment of his ambitions. Abû Muslim, a native of Isphahân,[2] but descended from an Arab stock, had entered the service of Mohammed, who, struck by his intelligence and powers of organisation, had deputed

The rising of Zaid, grandson of Hussain the Martyr.

742 A.C.

Appearance of Abû Muslim.

[1] The first split among the Shiahs occurred about this time. Zaid and his followers (called Zaidias) accepted the first three Caliphs as the lawful vicegerents of the Prophet. Some of the bigoted Kûfans who denied their title to the vicegerency thereupon abandoned Zaid. These Kûfans received the name of *Abandoners*. The moderate Shiahs, the *Imâmias*, expressed no opinion, nor joined in the rising.

[2] According to Hamza Isphahâni.

him to Khorâsân to head the Abbasside propaganda. By his address and ability Abû Muslim drew over large numbers to the cause of the Hâshimides; and the death of Hishâm rendered his task easy. Hishâm died at Russâfa in the district of Kinnisrin (ancient Chalcis), on the 6th of Rabi II., 125 A.H., and was succeeded by his nephew Walîd II.[1]

105—125 A.H.

Death of Hishâm.

February 743 A.C.

The Imam Mohammed al-Bâkir died in this reign, in 113 A.H., and was succeeded in the apostolical chair by his son the celebrated Jaafar the True (*as-Sâdik*).

[1] A granddaughter of Witiza named the Princess Sarah visited the court of Hishâm to seek redress against her uncle, who had usurped her and her brothers' patrimony. Hishâm received her with kindness and consideration and lodged her in his queen's palace. He not only had her property restored to her by her uncle, but married her to an Arab noble, with whom she returned to Spain. She continued in her religion, but their children were brought up as Moslems. Her descendants occupied a distinguished position in the country. One of them, surnamed Ibn Gouthia (son of the Gothic Princess), was a scholar and well-known writer.

CHAPTER XII

THE OMMEYADES (THE HAKAMITE BRANCH) (*continued*)

125—126 A.H., 743—744 A.C.

The Extent of the Empire at Hishâm's Death—Character of his Successor—His cruelty towards his Relations—Khâlid al-Kasri put to Death—Yahya bin Zaid's Rising and Death—Its effect on the People of Khorâsân—Affairs in Spain—Husâm (Abu'l Khattâr) Governor of Spain—Submission of all Parties—His mild and just Government at the outset—His partiality for the Yemenites—Insurrection of the Modhar—Battle of Shekundah—Election of Thalaba—His Death—Election of Yusuf—The Knight of Andalusia—His Death—Arrival of Abdur Rahmân, grandson of Hishâm, in Spain—Invasion of Pepin the Short—Massacre of the Saracens—Siege of Narbonne—Captured by Treachery—Arab Power effaced in France—Affairs in Africa—Insurrection against Walîd II.—His Death—Yezîd III. proclaimed Caliph—His Death—Succession of Ibrâhim—Revolt of Merwân—Battle of Ain-ul-jâr—Flight of Ibrâhîm—Merwân proclaimed Caliph.

The extent of the Saracenic empire.

IN the year 743 A.C., when Hishâm died, the Saracenic empire had reached its extremest limit. In Europe, the south of France and the whole of the Iberian Peninsula, save and except some defiles in which robber-bands maintained a guerilla warfare, belonged to the Moslems. In the Mediterranean they possessed Majorca, Minorca, Ivica, Corsica, Sardinia, Crete, Rhodes, and Cyprus, with a part of Sicily, and many of the islands of the Grecian Archipelago also belonged to them. In Africa, their sway was recognised from the Straits of Gibraltar to the Isthmus of Suez; in Asia, from the deserts of Sinai to the Steppes of Mongolia. But whilst a vast and far-reaching conspiracy weakened the bonds of authority in the East, strife and discord in the West threatened the dissolution of the colossal fabric. It was at this moment of extreme gravity that the death of Hishâm removed a ruler who, with all his weakness, was at least virtuous and cautious.[1] His successor was totally different;[2] profligate to a degree, utterly oblivious of the ordinary rules of morality and addicted to drinking, he soon disgusted the people with his riotous and wicked life. Hishâm had tried to alter the succession, but the covenant of his brother[3] was binding and could not be departed from. He had also endeavoured, perhaps with some harshness, to repress the evil habits of his brother's son, which led only to unseemly quarrels and disputes. The sombre austerity of Hishâm's court went against the young man's grain, and he had removed to a place called Arrack in the district of Jordan (Ordûn), where he waited impatiently for the death of his uncle. Immediately on receiving the news he hurried to Damascus, and began his reign by driving out Hishâm's family from the palace. Even the funeral rites of the deceased monarch were not allowed to be performed without indecent interference. His cruelties to his cousins, the sons of Walîd I. and Hishâm, men of mature age who had distinguished themselves in the wars against the Romans, deepened the abhorrence felt by the people. In the beginning he tried to ingratiate himself with the legionaries by raising their stipends and distributing magnificent largesses among

125—126 A.H.

The character of his successor.

Walîd II.

His cruelty towards his relatives.

[1] Mansûr, the second Abbasside Caliph, is stated to have declared that Hishâm was the one grand man of the Ommeyade family (*Fatâ ul-Kawm*). This view, however, is somewhat exaggerated.

[2] Suyûti describes him as "a libertine, a wine-drinker, and a breaker of the divine commands."

[3] Yezîd II.

743—744 A.C.

the populace. To win public favour he increased the allowances of the poor, the lame, and decrepit. But these endeavours were neutralised and made abortive by a fickle temperament and debased nature, which often broke forth in cruel deeds. Khâlid, the governor of Irâk, had lived retired in Damascus since his release under the orders of Hishâm; he was now made over to his cruel enemy Yusuf, who put him to death. The youthful Yahya was hunted from place to place; goaded to desperation, he rose in arms, determined to fall with the sword in his hand rather than be killed like vermin. He met the death he courted; his head was severed from his body and sent to Walîd, and the body was impaled on a cross. The fate of Yahya created a great sensation in Khorâsân, and accelerated the downfall of the Ommeyades. The people went into universal mourning; every male child born on the day of Yahya's death was named after him, and when Abû Muslim stood forth as the "Avenger of the House," they flocked to his standard dressed in black, which thenceforth became the Abbasside colour. The names of the Ommeyades who had taken part in Yahya's death were ascertained from the Register, and they were pursued and killed without mercy.

Khâlid al-Kasri killed.

Yahya's rising and death.

Spain. Thalaba's election confirmed.

Modharite Insurrection.

I shall turn for a moment to the progress of events in Spain. Thalaba's election as governor was confirmed by Hishâm, but his partiality for the Yemenites caused an insurrection among the Modharites, who were joined by the Berbers and Bilâdiûn. He succeeded in defeating the allied insurgents under the walls of Merida. Ten thousand prisoners are said to have fallen into his hands; and it was Thalaba's intention to put them all to the sword the following day. The morning broke, and every one expected the bloody work to begin, when the sudden appearance in the distance of the Caliph's banner sent a thrill through the assemblage. In spite of the weakness that had crept into the Government, the Caliph's name still inspired awe and formed a spell to conjure with. The banner, the sight of which had stayed the hands of the merciless executioners, heralded the approach of a new governor, named Husâm (Abu'l Khattâr, of the tribe of Kalb), also a Yemenite, who had been sent by Hanzala the viceroy of Africa, under the orders of Hishâm, to re-establish public order, and to appease the troubles excited by the contending parties. Husâm (Abu'l Khattâr) entered Cordova in the month of Rajab, 125 A.H., five months after Hishâm's death; and "no sooner," says the historian, "did he land in Andalusia than all parties hastened to put down their arms." Thalaba himself swore allegiance and returned to Syria.

125—126 A.H.

Husâm (Abu'l Khattâr) appointed Governor of Spain.

May 743 A.C.

Abu'l Khattâr's government in the beginning was mild and just; but even he was not free from tribal bias. His partiality towards the Himyarites of Spain, and, an insult offered to a Modharite tribe in the person of its chief, provoked a revolt. The civil war broke out afresh and raged with more violence than ever. In a sanguinary battle in the suburbs of Cordova,[1] in which the Yemenites were worsted, Abu'l Khattâr lost his life. The Modhar then elected Sawâbah, a Yemenite, as their governor, with as-Sumail, one of their own chiefs, as second in command. Sawâbah held the nominal government for sixteen months, and upon his death a year later the army elected in his place Yusuf, a descendant of Okbah, the conqueror of Africa. His appointment was due to the suggestions of as-Sumail, and had the effect of reconciling for a while the rival tribes. Both parties laid down their arms, and enabled Yusuf to carry on the

Modharite Insurrection.

Abu'l Khattâr's death.

Election of Sawâbah. 127 A.H. 745 A.C.

Election of Yusuf. Rabi II. 129 A.H. December 746 A.C.

[1] Called Shekundah.

743—744 A.C. government for nearly ten years, without any confirmation from Damascus, or any interference from home. His rule, however, was not by any means peaceful. The Deputy-Governor of Narbonne, who bore the name of Abdur Rahmân,[1] and by his prowess and deeds of valour, joined to great physical strength, had won the surname of "the Knight of Andalusia" (*al-Fâris-ul-Andalûs*), rose in arms, but was treacherously killed by his own men. Another chief raised the standard of revolt at Beja, a third at Algesiras, and a fourth at Seville. Yusuf, however, successfully quelled these insurrections. Were it not for a grandson of Hishâm, who, fleeing from the Abbasside avengers, landed in June 755 A.C. on the shores of Spain, probably Yusuf would have founded a dynasty of his own. The arrival of this scion of the House of Ommeya completely altered the aspect of affairs. Gifted with energy, vigour, and administrative ability of the first order, and assisted by the prestige of his name, the Ommeyade prince conquered all difficulties, and finally made himself the founder of a new dynasty in Spain. Henceforth the history of the Saracenic rule in the Iberian Peninsula has to be treated separately from that of the central Caliphate.

The Knight of Andalusia.

Arrival of Abdur Rahmân, grandson of Hishâm, in Spain.

Invasion of Moslem France by Pepin the Short. 752 A.C.

Whilst Yusuf was engaged with his adversaries, Pepin the Short, who had been waiting to attack the Saracens in France until they were thoroughly weakened, swept down with an enormous horde of barbarians upon Languedoc, Septimania, and Western Savoy, which were still held by the Arabs. The beautiful cities were committed to the flames, the mosques, hospitals, and schools were destroyed by fire, the Arabs, regardless of sex and age, were put to the sword, and the whole

[1] His father's name was al-Kuman. He belonged to the tribe of Lakhm, and was hence called Abdur Rahmân al-Lakhmi.

country became one vast scene of carnage and destruction. The devastation wrought by the Franks resulted in a terrible famine, in which multitudes of people perished. In spite of their helplessness, the Saracens of Southern France maintained a stout defence for three years, contesting every inch of ground against tremendous odds. By 755 A.C., however, Narbonne alone was left in their hands, which Pepin besieged with all the resources at his command. The siege lasted four years, until the Christians within the city, taking advantage one day of the slackness of the guards, rose upon them, and after killing some, opened the gates to their brethren outside. The barbarians then poured into the city; the Moslems, men, women, and children, were put to the sword; all vestige of civilisation was rased to the ground, and Languedoc and Provence lapsed into the general darkness which then pervaded Christian Europe. Whilst Pepin was thus driving the Saracens out of their possessions in France, the difficulties in which they were involved in Spain led to the abandonment of the mountainous tract bordering on the Bay of Biscay, where the rebels were enabled to form the nucleus of a formidable kingdom.

125—126 A.H.

Narbonne captured by treachery. 759 A.C.

Spain.

In Africa, ever since the overthrow of the Berbers before Kairowân, Hanzala had ruled with unequalled success the vast province of which he held charge. Both the Berbers and the Khârijis recognised his honesty of purpose and the justice of his administration. The peace which reigned throughout his province gave an impetus to trade and commerce. The treachery and ambition of an exiled functionary named Abdur Rahmân bin Habîb again plunged the country into strife and dissension. In 127 A.H. he rose in rebellion in Tunis, and taking as his prisoners a number of notables whom

Africa.

Insurrection against Hanzala.

743—744 A.C. Hanzala had sent to dissuade him from his traitorous enterprise, he marched upon Kairowân. He threatened 744 A.C. to slay his prisoners if attacked. Hanzala, always averse to the shedding of blood, retired to Asia and into private life. Kairowân opened its gates to the rebel, who installed himself as the Viceroy of Ifrîkia. But the rule thus treacherously begun was disturbed by continuous risings and war. Abdur Rahmân bin Habîb, however, remained in power until he was killed in a fight with his own brother in 137 A.C.

Abdur Rahmân bin Habîb makes himself Viceroy of Africa.

In the foregoing pages I have, in order to maintain the continuity of the narrative, anticipated the course of events; for between the arrival of Husâm (Abu'l Khattâr) in the Iberian Peninsula and the loss of Narbonne, the Ommeyade dynasty had been swept out of Asia, and its place was taken by another family. I must, therefore, describe briefly the political convulsion which led to the fall of the House of Ommeya.

Hitherto Damascus had formed the stronghold of the Ommeyades, and whatever the character or disposition of the reigning sovereign, the members of the clan never wavered in their allegiance to him. Their loyalty, bred from kinship and fostered by self-interest, added to the prestige and safety of the dynasty. Under Walîd II., for the first time, a fatal change set in. His devotion to music and horse-racing, in the pursuit of which he neglected the affairs of state, though it made him unpopular among the bigots of the capital, was shared by the principal members of his family. But his profligacy and his open defiance of the ordinary rules of morality, says the chronicler, alienated his best supporters, and the bulk of the Ommeyades fell away from him. His connivance at the barbarous murder of Khâlid, the ex-governor of Irâk, by the cruel Yusuf, in the

Walîd II.

125—126 A.H.

Moharram of 126 A.H. (743 A.C.), infuriated the Himyarites of Syria. They rose in angry revolt against the sovereign who had permitted the cruel deed. Yezîd, a son of Walîd I., and grandson of Abdul Malik, placed himself at their head. They were joined by the populace of Damascus, and Walîd was besieged in a citadel in the suburbs of the capital. He tried to parley with the insurgents, but they hurled back the reply that it was his ungodliness and his dissolute life that had banded his subjects against him. The gate was burst open, and the luckless monarch was pursued and slain in his own palace; and his head severed from the body was paraded in the streets of Damascus. The circumstances connected with Walîd's death, and the ignominious treatment of his lifeless body, removed the halo which had hitherto surrounded the person of the "unanimously elected Caliph."

His death.

Jamâdi II. 126 A.H. April 744 A.C.

Yezîd III., surnamed "the Retrencher."

Upon the death of Walîd II., Yezîd, who led the revolt, was raised to the throne. He is described as a pious man, strictly observant of his religious duties, and faithful in his words and actions. In his public oration, after the people had taken the oath of fealty, he explained the reasons that had led him to rise against his cousin, and went on to promise that he would fortify the frontiers, place the cities in a proper state of defence, relieve the burdens that weighed on the masses, and remove the dishonest officers of government. Had he lived long enough it is probable that he would have proved a capable sovereign, but his reign was too short and too disturbed to admit of reform or improvement. The risings in Hems and Palestine were repressed. Merwân, the Governor of Armenia, refused at first to take the oath of fealty, and moved on Syria with the avowed object of placing one of the sons of the unfortunate

743—744 A.C. Walîd on the throne. His nominal submission was obtained with the bribe of the possessions held by his father; and the young sons of Walîd II. were thrown into prison. Yusuf, the murderer of Khâlid, was removed from office and incarcerated with the sons of Walîd; and Abdullâh, the son of Omar II., was appointed in his stead. Nasr, the deputy-governor of Khorâsân, however, refused to obey the orders of Abdullâh or to recognise the authority of Yezîd III. The paralysis which seized the central administration affected the remoter limbs of the Empire; and the rising of Abdur Rahmân in Africa against Hanzala passed unpunished. The only reform that Yezîd was able to introduce tended to make him unpopular with the legionaries. Walîd II. had increased their pay; Yezîd reduced it to the scale in Hishâm's time, which obtained for him the designation of *an-Nâkis*, or "the Retrencher." He died after a short reign of six months, at the end of 126 A.H.

The death of Yezîd III.

Zu'l Hijja 126 A.H. Sept. 744 A.C.

Ibrâhîm.

Yezîd III. was succeeded by his brother Ibrâhîm, whose authority was not recognised beyond the capital and its environs, and barely lasted two months and ten days. Ibrâhîm is not included in the category of Caliphs. Merwân again took up arms with the ostensible object of releasing the sons of Walîd, and marched upon Damascus. At Ain-ul-jâr, a small township between the Lebanon and the Anti-Lebanon, on the road from Baalbec to the capital, he was encountered by a large army sent by Ibrâhîm, composed chiefly of Yemenites. But Merwân's troops were seasoned soldiers, and trained to warfare in a long course of fighting with the Byzantines and the Turkish hordes. The Yemenite rabble were defeated with great slaughter, and the route to Damascus lay open to the victor. As Merwân approached the capital, Ibrâhîm and his myrmidons took

The revolt of Merwân

The battle of Ain-ul-jâr.

to flight, after killing the sons of Walîd in the vain hope of staying the rescuer's march. The murderer of Khâlid, who shared their prison, was also put to death by the son of his victim, thus meeting a doom which he well merited. The retainers of Walîd's family now rose in riot and slaughter against the followers of the fugitive Ibrâhîm and his dead brother, killed a number of them, sacked their dwellings, exhumed the body of Yezîd III. from his grave and impaled it on one of the city gates.[1] Damascus was now in a terrible state of anarchy and confusion, and the arrival of Merwân was welcomed by the respectable citizens. He was immediately proclaimed Caliph; and the people readily took the oath of fealty, in the expectation that a trained soldier would restore peace to the distracted country.

125—126 A.H.

Merwân II. Safar 127 A.H. Nov. 744 A.C.

[1] Such posthumous courtesies were not confined to Asia. To give one instance: In the fifteenth century Percy Hotspur's body was exhumed under the orders of Henry IV., quartered and gibbeted.

CHAPTER XIII

THE OMMEYADES (THE HAKAMITE BRANCH) (*continued*)

127—132 A.H., 744—750 A.C.

Merwân II.—His character—Insurrections—Rising in Khorâsân—Abû Muslim—The Persian Revolt—Defeat and death of Nasr, governor of Khorâsân—Death of Ibrâhîm, the Abbasside Imâm—Defeat of the Ommeyades at Nehâwand—Defeat of the Viceroy of Irâk—Proclamation of Saffâh as Caliph—Battle of the Zâb—Defeat of Merwân—His flight—Capture of Damascus—Abbasside vindictiveness—Death of Merwân—Last of the Ommeyades—The causes of the Ommeyade downfall.

MERWÂN II.[1] was a grandson of the founder of the Hakamite dynasty. He had governed his province of Armenia with vigour and ability, and had time after time rolled back the nomadic hordes in their attempts to overwhelm him from the north. His remarkable powers of endurance had obtained for him the surname of al-Himâr,[2] not in derision, but in acknowledgment of his physical strength and force of will. Unlike most of his predecessors, he was ascetic in his life and habits. In camp or on the march, he lived like his soldiers, and shared their simple fare as well as their privations; nor would he in his palace indulge in those luxuries which had become habitual among

[1] See Genealogical Table.

[2] "The Ass." The Arabian donkey is not the poor creature we see in Europe; it possesses great powers of endurance.

127—132 A.H.

Merwân's character.

the sovereigns of his house. He was devoted to the study of ancient history, on which he often discoursed to his secretary and companions. He was well advanced in years when he came to the throne,[1] but the celerity of his movements, and the promptitude with which he crushed the enemies that sprang up on all sides, showed that age had not dimmed his energies. However, something more than mere soldierly qualities in the sovereign was needed at this crisis to save the Ommeyade power from dissolution—the ability to rise above tribal bias; and this was the quality in which Merwân, like most of his family, was essentially wanting. Had he been gifted with the breadth of views and large outlook required of a statesman, and the spirit of conciliation which alone could bring the conflicting elements into harmony, the history of Asia would have been written otherwise. An ungovernable temper, combined with the obstinacy and hardness which characterised most of the Ommeyades, accentuated the defect. Instead of endeavouring to pacify the feuds which rent the Arab nation, he flung himself into the tribal dissensions with the blind zeal of a partisan; and the harshness, not to say cruelty, with which he treated the Yemenites gave rise to implacable hatred on their side. So the old rivalry, embittered by present wrongs, grew into rage under the attacks of poets. Komait, a Modharite, in a long poem[2] extolled the prowess and greatness of his tribe and the virtues and sufferings of the Hâshimides. He was answered in the same strain by an Yemenite poet named Dibli who attacked the Modharites, and sang of the glories of Himyar and of their kings. These poems were carried from the city to the tents, and by

[1] He is said to have been over sixty at the time.

[2] Called the *Hâshimiyyè*.

744–750 A.C. their raillery and sarcasm inflamed alike citizen and nomade.[1] Modhar and Himyar were now at each other's throats with unparalleled fury.

Insurrection. Western Asia was at this period in a state of chaos. The pious and the scholarly retired from the political strife which raged round them, leaving public affairs in the hands of the unscrupulous or the self-seeking. On all sides there was an expectant waiting for the convulsion that was in the air. Merwân had not been long on the throne before violent insurrections broke out against him at Hems and in Palestine. The Khâriji Zealots emerged at the same time from their desert fastnesses, denouncing the impious rule of the Ommeyades and inviting the people to Truth. Whatever may be said of the tenets of these fiery covenanters, it must be admitted that they were honest in their convictions and animated by a feeling of duty which took no note of obstacles. Though comparatively few in number, they overran and held for a while Yemen, Hijâz and the whole of Irâk. In dealing with these insurrections, Merwân displayed admirable generalship and soldierly promptitude. He swooped down in succession upon Hems and Palestine, scattered the rebels and impaled their leaders. He then marched back upon Irâk, and after some hard fights drove the Zealots across the Tigris. In Hijâz, Medîna

[1] Masûdi's thoughtful remarks on this subject are worth quoting—"Merwân's fanatical attachment to his family against the Yemenites detached the latter from his side, to the advantage of the Abbasside propaganda, and at last brought about those circumstances which passed the power from the sons of Ommeya to those of Hâshim. Later this rivalry provoked the invasion of Yemen by Maan, son of Zâidah, who, in his fanaticism for the Modharites, massacred the Yemenites and broke up the ancient alliance which united Himyar and Modhar. It led to sanguinary reprisals by Okba in Bahrain and Oman against the Modharite tribes settled in those provinces."

was captured by the Khârijis under Abû Hamza, after a fight in which the citizens were worsted, and was treated by them with a consideration which it did not receive from the Ommeyades. Yemen was in the hands of "the Summoner to Truth," *Dâi ul-Hakk.*[1] Merwân's lieutenant, a reckless and impious soldier of the type so common in Europe in the Middle Ages, who openly acknowledged himself not bound by the rules of the Korân, defeated the Zealots in several hotly-contested actions, and cleared Hijâz and Yemen. The bulk of the Khârijis, driven from Irâk, took refuge in Persia, where they added to the elements of disorder and discord already existing, whilst those defeated in Hijâz and Yemen betook themselves to Hadhramaut. On the restoration of peace, Merwân installed Yezîd bin Omar bin Hobaira, a devoted follower of his family, as the viceroy of the East, and then retired to his favourite residence in Harrân, leaving the practical work of administration to his sons Abdul Malik and Abdullâh. Here he abode until called to undertake the expedition which ended in disaster to himself and his dynasty.

127—132 A.H.

Defeat of the Zealots.

Whilst Merwân was beating down the insurrections in Syria and contending with the Zealots in Irâk and Arabia, the bitter feud between Modhar and Himyar was working out the destruction of the Ommeyade empire in Asia. Nasr, the governor of Khorâsân, was a Modharite, and against him was arrayed the entire Himyarite faction. The deadly conflict in which the two branches of the Arab nation who held guard over the subject races were involved, was deemed by the leaders of the Abbasside Propaganda to give the long-wished-for opportunity for applying the torch to the mine that had been so

129 A.H. 747 A.C.

Abû Muslim.

[1] This man was a native of Hadhramaut (Hazramaut), his name being Abdullâh bin Yahya Hadhrami (*i.e.* of Hadhramaut).

744—750 A.C. carefully laid. Abû Muslim, the leader of the revolt, was peculiarly fitted for the task entrusted to him by the Abbasside Imâm. An impassive exterior, which no adversity or success could affect, however slightly, concealed a pitiless and cruel heart. "The gravest events could hardly disturb the serenity of his countenance," says an old author. "He received the news of the most important victories without expressing the least symptom of joy; under the greatest reverses of fortune he never betrayed the slightest uneasiness; and when angered, he never lost his self-command." His unvarying urbanity and condescension conciliated enemies and secured adherents; whilst the capacity for organising the troops and administering public affairs extorted admiration. A Machiavellian dexterity in playing upon the vanity of Modhar and Himyar and the bitterness which animated both, enabled him to carry out his design with sufficient immunity from either side.

Revolt in Khorâsân.

I have already given a brief sketch of the Abbasside Propaganda, and described how gradually it grew into a power. The condemnation of force by the apostolical Imâms was regarded by many of their more violent adherents as quietism, and engendered a desire to look elsewhere for the leadership needed for the subversion of the hated family of Ommeya. But these causes alone are not sufficient to explain the intensity of the Revolt which carried the Abbassides to the throne on a wave of success, nor would they, by themselves, have sufficed to overthrow the Ommeyade power under a warlike and trained soldier like Merwân. The key to the phenomenal rise of the House of Abbâs is supplied in the character of the rule initiated by Hajjâj, which, in spite of the endeavours of Omar II., continued to be the traditional policy under the later sovereigns of the Ommeyade dynasty. The rulers were entirely out of touch with the subject races, nor was there any bond of sympathy between them and the people. In their racial pride the Arabs held themselves aloof from the natives and, in spite of the teachings of Islâm, looked down upon them as an inferior race, and were hated in consequence. The subordinate departments of the civil and fiscal administration were largely in the hands of the Persians; but they were excluded from military posts and the higher offices of state. When an appeal was made to that charter of emancipation—the Koran—as proclaiming the equality and brotherhood of man, it was either treated with contempt, or evaded by quibbles. With the exception of a few, whose names were borne on the register of the great Omar, or who had distinguished themselves by eminent services, the members of the subject race took no part in the social gatherings or the pleasures of their rulers, and brooded in sullen wrath and hatred over their lost greatness. But the Syrian Arabs, Modhar as well as Himyar, engaged in their own pastimes or tribal quarrels, recked little of the pent-up storm. Political disabilities and invidious social distinctions gave rise among the Persians to a strong and natural sense of injustice. A watch-word alone was needed to fire national enthusiasm; and that was found in "the rights of the *Ahl ul-bait*—People of the House," which became the rallying cry of the subject nationalities of the East. The Himyarite tribes, and the bulk of the Arabs of Hijâz and Irâk settled in Khorâsân, were equally discontented. The party in power, as is usually the case, strove to retain the monopoly of influence and emolument in its own hands, and to exclude any participation by the others, which bred bitter jealousy

127—132 A.H.

Its causes.

744—750 A.C. and disputes. In these elements of discontent and disaffection, Abû Muslim found his materials for the revolt. And Khorâsân became the centre for the adherents of the Banû Abbâs.[1]

Nasr, the governor of Khorâsân, was an able and vigorous administrator, and in happier circumstances would probably have left his impress on the province. But whilst his master was struggling with the Zealots in the west, he was endeavouring to make head against the Yemen faction led by a man called, after his birthplace, Kermâni. Finding the Arab garrisons thus off their guard, Abû Muslim issued the manifesto for the long-planned rising. The cause proclaimed was "the rights of the *Ahl ul-bait*" against the usurping Banû Ommeya; and the dubious words *âl-Hâshim*, "the children of Hâshim," whose champion he announced himself to be, secured the support of the adherents of the Fatimides.
Ramazân, 129 A.H. The gathering was to take place on the 25th of Ramazân, 129 A.H., and the people were summoned by large bonfires lighted on the hill-tops. Vast multitudes, all clothed in black, in sign of mourning for the chiefs that had fallen or been murdered, flocked to the trysting-places; and before a few weeks were over, the black standards of the Abbasside King-maker, called "the Cloud" and "the Shadow," flew from city to city on their onward march towards the west. The Ommeyade garrisons were expelled from Herat and other places in the far East. Kermâni's death in an ambush prepared by the Modhar, led to his sons joining Abû Muslim; and their combined forces drove Nasr out of Merv. The ominous sable standard of the *âl-Hâshim* brought the hitherto divided Syrians to their senses; they suddenly awakened to the gravity of the danger, and tried to patch up a semblance of union. But

[1] The *Shiiân* of the Banû Abbâs.

it was too late. The rising had now grown into a revolt, and was joined by many of the leading Arabs of Hijâz and Irâk. The unfortunate Viceroy, unable alone to contend with the force under Abû Muslim, which was all the while increasing in number and strength, invoked the assistance of his sovereign, but received no reply, as Merwân was just then pressed by the Zealots in Mesopotamia. Before leaving Merv, Nasr addressed a last pathetic appeal to Merwân for help. He pointed out that the fire of insurrection was yet in embryo and could still be stamped out, and wound up with the despairing cry which has become historical, "Oh that I knew whether the sons of Ommeya be awake or sunk in sleep! If they are sleeping in such times as these, say to them: 'Arise, the hour is come!'" In response to this urgent appeal, Merwân directed the viceroy of Irâk to despatch reinforcements for the assistance of Nasr; but before they could arrive on the scene of action, Ferghâna and Khorâsân had fallen entirely into the hands of Abû Muslim, and his resources had increased proportionately. Nothing shows the power of this remarkable man so well as his choice of men; the generals whom he employed were some of the ablest of the time. Kahtaba bin Shabîb, an Arab of Hijâz, settled in Fars, pursued Nasr to Sarrakhs, and inflicted on him a defeat which completely demoralised the Syrian forces. Nasr, then in his eighty-fifth year, fell back on Jurjân, where he suffered another defeat; he then fled towards Fars, but died on the way.

127—132 A.H.

130 A.H.

Flight and death of Nasr, the Governor of Khorâsân.

Whilst these events were passing in the east, Merwân endeavoured to discover the Hâshimide in whose interest the standard of revolt had been raised. At this time the descendants of Abbâs were living in a village called Humaima in Southern Palestine. Finding from his spies

744—750 A.C. that Ibrâhîm, styled by his adherents the Imâm (apostolical leader), was the originator of the risings, he immediately had him arrested and brought to Harrân. Here

Kahtaba's victories. Ibrâhîm was incarcerated, with several others, both Hâshimides and Ommeyades. Among the latter were Abdullâh, son of Omar II., and Abbâs, son of Walîd I., whom Merwân suspected of endeavouring to raise an insurrection. The arrest of Ibrâhîm had no effect, however, on the movement of Abû Muslim's forces. Kahtaba, after defeating Nasr in Jurjân, advanced rapidly westward. He was accompanied by Khâlid bin Barmek, a Persian, whose descendants became afterwards so famous in Arabian history and literature. All round, the country was in a state of utter disorganisation. Entering Rai (ancient Rhages), Kahtaba restored order in the province, whilst his son Hassan, and his lieutenant, Abû Ayûn, a Persian by birth, drove the Ommeyades and Khâriji Zealots before them. Nehâwand, where the famous battle which led to the conquest of Persia had been fought, was garrisoned by a strong Syrian force. Hassan bin Kahtaba laid siege to the city; whilst the father intercepted a large army sent by Merwân for its relief, and completely routed it. Two armies, one from Upper Mesopotamia under the command of Merwân's son Abdullâh, the other under Yezîd, the viceroy, were converging upon Nehâwand; Kahtaba pressed on the siege with vigour, and the city capitulated before the arrival of succour from either side. Kahtaba now detached a force under Abû Ayûn to oppose Abdullâh, whilst with his main army he slipped past Yezîd, who was encamped at Jalola, on the high-road from Kûfa, and made straight for the capital of Irâk. Yezîd, informed of this design, hastened to throw himself between Kûfa and the enemy. Kahtaba arrived at the Euphrates after Yezîd, and crossed the river several miles higher up, beyond reach of the opposing force. The two armies met on the same spot where Hussain had fallen; after a sanguinary struggle the Ommeyades were worsted, but Kahtaba was either drowned in the river or fell on the field. His son Hassan then took the command, and following up his father's success drove Yezîd from his camp and forced him to retire on Wâsit.[1] Kûfa, thus uncovered, fell without much opposition into the hands of Hassan. The news of the disaster made Merwân furious with rage, and impelled him to an act of barbarity which brought on the Ommeyades fearful reprisals. Finding that Ibrâhîm was in communication with Abû Muslim's forces, he ordered him to be killed by his head being thrust into a leather sack filled with quick-lime. The other prisoners were executed at the same time.[2] Before his death the unfortunate Ibrâhîm succeeded in passing a testament to his brother *Abu'l Abbâs* Abdullâh, which gave him the succession to the Abbasside Imamate. Abu'l Abbâs swore a terrible oath of revenge, and kept it so faithfully that he obtained the unenviable title of *as-Saffâh* or the *Sanguinary*, by which name he is known in history. On Ibrâhîm's death, his brothers fled to Kûfa, and there lay concealed until Hassan bin Kahtaba took possession of the city. Nothing as yet was divulged as to the ultimate purpose of the movement which had wrested Persia from the grasp of the Ommeyades. The *Ahl-bait* was the

127—132 A.H.

Defeat of the Viceroy of Irâk.

Death of Ibrâhîm, the Abbasside Imâm.

[1] A strongly fortified garrison town built by Hajjâj bin Yusuf, midway between Kûfa and Basra, and hence called *Wâsit*, the middle-placed.

[2] Ibn ul-Athîr gives a different account. According to him, Ibrâhîm died either through a house falling over him or from poison administered in a cup of milk; the other prisoners having died from the plague. Let us hope this is the correct version.

744—750 A.C. watchword which rallied round the black standard all classes of people, and enlisted the sympathy and support of the adherents (*Shiahs*) of the Banû Fâtima. On his entry into Kûfa, Hassan bin Kahtaba was joined by Abû Salma[1] al-Khallâl, "who," says the author of the *Rouzat us-Safâ*, "was designated the Vizier of the descendants of Mohammed." Apparently this man acted as the agent of the Fatimides, but without the formal sanction of the head of the family. He was received with the greatest consideration by the Abbasside general, "who kissed his hand, and seated him in the place of honour," and told him that it was Abû Muslim's orders that he should be obeyed in all things. Abû Salma's vanity was flattered. A proclamation was issued in the joint names of Abû Salma and Hassan bin Kahtaba, inviting the inhabitants of Kûfa to assemble on the following day, at the *Masjid ul-Jâmaa*,[2] to elect a Caliph. On that day Kûfa presented a strange aspect. Large crowds of people, clothed in the sable garments of the Banû-Abbâs, were hastening from every quarter to the *Masjid ul-Jâmaa*, to hear the long-deferred announcement. In due time Abû Salma appeared on the scene, and, strangely, dressed in the same sombre black. Few excepting the partisans of Abu'l Abbâs knew how he had come to sell himself to the Abbasside cause. He preferred his head to the interests of his masters. After leading the prayers, he explained to the assemblage the object of the meeting. Abû Muslim, he said, the defender of the Faith and the upholder of the rights of the House, had hurled the Ommeyades from the heights of their iniquity; it was

[1] This was his patronymic. His own name was Jaafar; his father's name was Sulaimân *al-Khallâl*, so called because he lived in the quarter of the vinegar-sellers.

[2] The Cathedral Mosque.

now necessary to elect an Imâm and Caliph; there was none so eminent for piety, ability, and all the virtues requisite for the office as Abu'l Abbâs Abdullâh, and him he offered for the election of the people. Up to this time Abû Salma and the Abbassides were dubious of the possible effect on the assembly. They were afraid that even the Kûfans might not view their treachery to the house of Ali with approbation. But the proverbial fickleness of the Irâkians was now proved. Again and again they had risen in arms in support of the Fatimide cause, and as often betrayed those whom they had pledged themselves to help or whose help they had invoked. Swayed by the passing whim of the moment, they had shown themselves equally to be traitors as the defenders of truth. No sooner had the words passed from the lips of Abû Salma, proposing Abu'l Abbâs as the Caliph, than they burst forth with loud acclamations of the *takbîr*,[1] signifying their approval. A messenger was sent in haste to fetch Abu'l Abbâs from his concealment, and when he arrived at the mosque there was a frantic rush on the part of the multitude to take his hand and swear fealty. The election was complete. He ascended the pulpit, recited the *Khutba*,[2] and was henceforth the Imâm (spiritual head) and Caliph of the Moslems. Thus rose the Abbassides to power on the popularity of the children of Fâtima, whom they repaid afterwards in such different coin.

127—132 A.H.

Proclamation of Saffâh as Caliph.

13th Rabi II. 132 A.H. 25th November 749 A.C.

Meanwhile, events were progressing rapidly in the

[1] *Allâho-akbar*, "God is great."

[2] The public sermon or oration delivered by the Imâm, or Caliph, or the leader of the congregation. The oration of Saffâh is preserved *in extenso* in the pages of Ibn ul-Athîr, and is a long laudation of the children of Abbâs, of their rights to the Pontificate, and of their enterprise in support of religion and law against the impious children of Ommeya.

744—750 A.C. north. Abû Ayûn came upon Merwân's son at Shahrzûr, east of the Little Zâb, and defeated him with great slaughter. The defeat of his son roused Merwân into his old activity. With an army 120,000 strong, he crossed the Tigris and advanced upon the Greater Zâb. Abû Ayûn had, in the meantime, been reinforced from Kûfa, and the cruel Abdullâh bin Ali, one of Saffâh's uncles, who brought the reinforcements, assumed the chief command of the Abbasside troops, with Abû Ayûn as lieutenant-general. The battle took place on the left bank of the Zâb[1] at a village called Kushâf. Merwân, against advice, threw a bridge across the river, and advanced with his usual boldness to the fight. The legions of Saffâh, clothed in black from head to foot, with standards, horses and camels all draped in black, marching up silently and in serried ranks like funeral mutes, must have struck the Syrians with awe. And an unusual occurrence, just as the opposing forces were waiting for orders, was taken by the Ommeyades as a portent of evil omen. A flight of ravens passed over the Syrian troops and settled themselves on the sable standards of the black-clad legions.[2] Merwân thought little of this incident, but plainly saw its effect upon his superstitious men. The first onset, led by Merwân himself, was successful, and the Abbassides gave way. But Abû Ayûn made his men dismount, and plant their lances on the ground; while Abdullâh bin Ali incited them, as the heroes of Khorâsân, to revenge the death of his nephew Ibrâhîm. He shouted, *Ya-Mohammed! Ya-Mansûr!* and the battle-cry was taken up by all the troops. Merwân, on his side, exhorted his people

[1] The river between Mosul and Arbela.

[2] Hence called the *Musawwidèh*, or the "black" or "black clad."

by their former achievements to maintain the prestige of his house. His appeal, however, was of no avail. The Syrians gave way before a fierce onslaught, and the sight of Merwân's riderless charger, which had broken loose from its groom, turned it into a rout. This memorable battle, which sealed the fate of the Ommeyade dynasty, took place on the 11th of Jamâdi II., 132 A.H. Merwân fled towards Mosul, but the city closed its gates upon him. He then hurried to Harrân, where he tarried a while, vainly endeavouring to raise another army. But the ruthless Abbassides were on his track; and he fled from Harrân to Hems and thence to Damascus. Finding no safety there, he hastened towards Palestine. But the pursuit was hot and unslacking, and Abdullâh bin Ali followed Merwân like a bloodhound. Mosul, Harrân, and Hems submitted to Saffâh without a blow. At Damascus, the Ommeyades offered some resistance; but the city was stormed, and the governor, Merwân's son-in-law, was slain, and the capital of Syria and practically of the whole empire, passed into the hands of the Abbassides. On the 5th of Ramazân, 132 A.H., five months from the entry into Kûfa, and three from the battle of the Zâb, the black standard floated in triumph over the palace of the Ommeya. With a barbarity which has few parallels in history, Abdullâh bin Ali did not rest content with wreaking his vengeance upon the living. Under his orders the dead were taken up from their last resting-places, the crumbling bones were burnt[1] and the ashes scattered to the winds. Abdullâh then pressed on after Merwân, who on leaving

127—132 A.H.

Battle of the Zâb. Defeat of Merwân.

11th Jamâdi II. 132 A.H. 25th January 750 A.C.

Capture of Damascus. 5th Ramazân, 132 A.H. March 750 A.C.

[1] The reason of this fierce vindictiveness is given by an eye-witness who is quoted by Ibn Khallikân. He says that the barbarous treatment meted out by the Ommeyades to Zaid and his son impelled Abdullâh bin Ali to this reprisal.

744—750 A.C. Palestine had thought of making his way into the Byzantine dominions and invoking the assistance of the successor of Constantine. He had read how a Persian king[1] had been restored to his patrimony by a Byzantine emperor, and doubted not that he would receive similar support. He was dissuaded from this step by the faithful few who still adhered to his fortunes. They advised his going to Egypt or Ifrîkia, where he might raise another army to reconquer the eastern empire, or found a new and more vigorous kingdom in the West. Merwân then hurried on to Fayûm, in Upper Egypt. Abdullâh bin Ali despatched his brother Sâlèh and Abû Ayûn to follow up the fugitive. At Fostât, Abû Ayûn came upon Merwân's traces, and the pursuit now turned into a hunt. The pursuers found the fallen monarch in a small Christian chapel at a place called Busîr, or Busiris, on the western bank of the Nile, where he had laid down to rest. Determined to sell his life dearly, the luckless sovereign rushed out, sword in hand, and fell transfixed with a lance. Thus perished one of the bravest and best of his house, and with him fell the House of Ommeya. Under the orders of Saffâh, who had assumed the title of "Avenger of the Hâshimides," the members of the fallen house were pursued with fearful cruelty. In the gratification of a ferocious vindictiveness, all feelings of humanity were stifled. The men were hunted and killed wherever found; search was made in the remotest spots, in the recesses of ruins, in solitary caves in the hillsides, and every fugitive discovered was put to death. We have to descend to later times, to the scenes of horror enacted in the Wars of the Roses, when whole families were destroyed, to understand the

Death of Merwân. 26th Zu'l Hijja, 132 A.H. 5th August 750 A.C.

[1] Khusrû Parvîz was restored to his kingdom by the Emperor Maurice.

bitter and savage hatred displayed by the Banû Abbâs. On the banks of the Abû Futrus, in Palestine, Abdullâh bin Ali inveigled into his tent eighty kinsmen and relatives of Merwân by a promise of amnesty, and then slaughtered them without mercy. Many, however, escaped the "Avenger's" sword,[1] and in later times received protection and patronage from the humanity of Saffâh's successors. Among those who evaded pursuit was Abdur Rahmân, a grandson of Hishâm, who escaped into Spain. The daughters of Merwân, who were with him at the time, were sent back to Harrân with other members of his family. Here they lived in poor circumstances until the accession of Mahdi, who settled a munificent pension on them, and treated them with the consideration due to their position and their misfortunes.

127—132 A.H.

With Merwân ended the rule of the mighty House of Ommeya in the East. Some of the sovereigns of this dynasty were undoubtedly great, whilst others were no worse than their contemporaries in the western world. Omar II., who has been deservedly styled the Marcus Aurelius of the Arabs, was a ruler far in advance of the times; and Walîd I. and Hishâm, though they cannot be placed on the same pedestal with him, were yet men of great capacity, honestly solicitous to promote the well-being of the people. Merwân himself, but for his unfortunate end, would have taken a front rank among the rulers of the world. He was brave and wise; but, says Ibn ul-Athîr, as destiny had put a term on his reign, both his valour and his wisdom came to naught.

The fate of the fallen dynasty is not without its lesson.

[1] In Medîna, a large number were saved by the descendants of Fâtima; in Irâk, Sulaimân bin Ali, an uncle of Saffâh, obtained an amnesty of protection, which put a stop to further massacres.

744—750 A.C. A member of Merwân's family, who had in his reign held a high office of state, thus described in later days, when the empire had passed into the hands of the Banû Abbâs, the causes which led to the downfall of the Ommeyade power—"We gave to pleasure," he said, "the time which it was our duty to devote to public affairs; the heavy burdens we imposed on the people alienated them from our rule; harassed by vexatious imposts and despairing of redress, they prayed for deliverance from us; our domains became uncultivated and our treasuries empty: we trusted our ministers, they sacrificed our interests to their selfish aims and ambitions, and conducted the administration without our participation and our knowledge. The army, whose pay was always in arrear, sided with the enemy in the hour of danger; and our allies failed us when we needed them most. But our ignorance of the public affairs and the events which were passing around us, was one of the principal causes of the fall of our empire."[1]

The total duration of the Ommeyade rule from the assassination of the Caliph Ali to the death of Merwân II. was little less than ninety-one years. But Masûdi deducts from this, the period during which Hassan held the Pontificate and Abdullâh bin Zubair was recognised as Caliph, and gives a thousand months, or eighty-three years and four months, as the term of their undisputed empire. Savage and selfish as was the struggle between Abbâs and Ommeya, it gave birth to factors which revolutionised the intellectual development of the Saracenic world, and brought to the fore more than one illustrious man.

[1] Masûdi.

DAMASCUS FROM THE RIVER.

CHAPTER XIV

RETROSPECT

The Government—Revenues—Administration—Military Service—Currency Reform of Abdul Malik—Damascus—Court life—Society—The position of women—Introduction of the system of seclusion—Dress—Habits—Literature—Religious and philosophical sects.

40—132 A.H. 661—750 A.C. The Government.

UNDER the Republic, the Caliph was elected by the suffrage of the entire population of Medîna, which election was accepted without demur by the outside Arabs. The ceremony was held at the public Mosque, where the Moslems assembled and took the oath of fealty. From Muâwiyah's time the reigning sovereign nominated his successor, and the grandees and military chiefs took the covenant in the royal presence; whilst in the provinces the oath was taken by the governor on behalf of the presumptive Caliph. This system combined the vices of democracy and despotism without the advantages of either. Once the oath was taken, the suffrage of the people, however obtained, whether by coercion, cajolery, or bribe, was supposed to give a sacramental character to the election.

Under Abû Bakr, Omar, and Ali, the Public Treasury[1] was in reality the property of the people, and every member of the Islâmic Commonwealth was entitled to an allowance out of the income of the state. With the establishment of an autocracy under Muâwiyah, the

[1] *Bait-ul-Mâl il Muslimîn.*

661—750 A.C. revenues of the empire became the private property of the sovereign, and subject to his absolute control. He was thus able to bestow the entire income derived from Egypt upon Amr, the son of Aâs, in return for his help against the Caliph Ali; Amr had in fact declined to take anything less, and refused in forcible terms "to hold the horns whilst somebody else milched the cow."

The Revenues. The revenues were derived from the same sources as under the Republic, viz. (1) the land-tax, (2) the test-tax on non-Moslem subjects, (3) the poor-rates, (4) customs and excise duties, (5) tributes paid under treaties, and (6) the fifth of the spoils of war. The taxes collected in each province were paid into the respective Provincial Treasuries. Decentralisation was the rule; all expenses connected with provincial administration were defrayed from the Provincial Treasury; the soldiers, the stipendiaries and public functionaries, stationed within or attached to any province, were paid out of its revenues. All works of utility, such as roads and canals, and public buildings, as mosques and schools, were likewise constructed at the cost of the particular province where they were required. Any balance that remained was remitted to the Imperial Treasury at Damascus. The collection of the revenue was entrusted to *Aâmils*, who appear to have also exercised executive functions and occupied a position similar to that of Collectors in British India. Sometimes the governors, when they happened to combine the office of *Sâhib ul-Kharâj* with their own proper functions, as was often the case after Omar II., broke the rule and gave the charge of collection to their secretaries or *Kâtibs*. This led to peculation, which was visited with severe punishment often accompanied by confiscation of the culprit's property.

Large domains were held by the sovereigns in their

private right, and by the princes of the royal blood. Until the second Walîd's accession, special care was devoted to their cultivation. During the civil wars that had preceded the rise of Abdul Malik to power, the great irrigation works of Omar in Chaldæa had been neglected and allowed to fall into ruin; vast tracts had thus turned into marshes. Maslamah, the brother of Hishâm, who held in fief the greater part of the *Sawâd* (the Lower Euphrates Valley), drained the country and reclaimed the lands. 40--132 A.H.

Taxes were not levied according to one standard, but varied in every province according to the conditions imposed, or privileges granted from time to time, by the early Caliphs. Attempts were sometimes made to go behind them, which gave rise to insurrections.

The Vice-royalties.

The empire was divided into five viceroyalties. Hijâz, Yemen, and Central Arabia were under one viceroy; Lower and Upper Egypt under another. The two Irâks, viz. Irâk-Arab (ancient Babylonia and Chaldæa) and Irâk Ajam (Persia proper), together with Oman, al-Bahrain, Kermân, Sistân, Cabul, Khorâsân, the whole of Transoxiana, Sind, and portions of the Punjab, formed one vast province under the viceroy of Irâk, whose seat of government was at Kûfa. Khorâsân and Transoxiana were ruled by a deputy-governor, who generally resided at Merv; al-Bahrain and Oman were under the deputy-governor of Basra; and Sind and the Punjab were governed by a separate officer.

Mesopotamia (the Jazîra of the Arabs), with Armenia, and Azerbaijân and parts of Asia Minor, formed another province. But the most important of all the vice-royalties was that of Ifrîkia, which included the whole of Northern Africa to the west of Egypt, Spain, and the south of France, together with Sicily, Sardinia, and the

661—750 A.C.

Balearic Isles. The seat of government was at Kairowân, and there were deputy-governors at Tangiers and the islands of the Mediterranean. Spain was ruled by a governor whose capital was Cordova.

Political and military administration.

The political and military administration of each province was in the hands of the viceroy, but the revenues were in the charge of another official, the *Sâhib ul-Kharâj*, wholly independent of the governor, who was appointed directly by the sovereign. The judges of the principal cities were vested with the power of appointing their own deputies. The administration of justice among the non-Moslem communities was wisely confided to their communal magistrates or priests. The presidency at the public prayers, a most important function, was entrusted either to the governor or to the chief Kâzi.

The head of the police (*Sâhib ush-Shurta*) was under the command of the governor. About the beginning of Hishâm's reign a new force was formed, which, under the name of *Ahdâs*, performed militia duties and stood half-way between the police and the regular soldiery. In order to facilitate correspondence between the sovereign and the provincial governors through the wide extent of the empire, and also to create a safeguard against the circulation of fraudulent edicts, Muâwiyah created a Chancery Department which bore the name of the Board of the Signet (*Diwân ul-Khâtim*). Every ordinance issued by the Caliph was copied in a Register, the original was then sealed and despatched to its destination. He also established a postal system, which afterwards was carried to such perfection by the Abbassides. It was not, however, from Muâwiyah that the policy of the Ommeyades, certainly in the Eastern provinces, derived its character, for Abdul Malik was its real

A Chancery Department established by Muâwiyah.

founder. With the object of excluding foreign influences from the affairs of state, he ordered that public offices should be held only by Arabs. This exclusive policy was carried to its furthest limit by his lieutenant in Irâk, the notorious Hajjâj, who endeavoured to exclude from the service of the state not only non-Moslems, but also Moslems who were not Arabs, and even re-imposed on the latter the test-tax paid by the *zimmis*. As a matter of fact, this exclusive policy did not succeed, for before long the Persians and Christians again held in large numbers the subordinate civil and fiscal employments. But it left a widespread feeling of discontent, which bore such bitter fruit in the time of Merwân II. Two other measures introduced by Abdul Malik were unquestionably beneficent in their tendency, and dictated by a wise and statesmanlike policy. Hitherto there was no regular and recognised currency in the Saracenic empire. The provincial governors had their own independent mints, which issued coin for local demands. The stamping and actual value were quite inexact, and counterfeiting was common. For ordinary purposes the Byzantine and the old Persian coinage were in general use. The extension of the empire and the development of commerce rendered it necessary to have a stable and uniform standard of currency. Abdul Malik established an imperial mint, withdrew all the variable coins in use in the country, and issued in lieu thereof his own coinage, both gold and silver.[1] His currency reform was based upon a mixture of Roman and Sassanide nominals. The Roman

40—132 A.H.

The Currency Reform of Abdul Malik.

77 A.H. 696 A.C.

[1] The precision with which the first Arabian gold coinage was issued is astounding. It weighed 4·25 grains. The relative weight of the gold to the silver coin (dirhem) was as 10 : 7; the actual weight of the latter was 2·97 grains.

661—750 A.C.

solidi formed the base of the gold coin, and the legal dirhems introduced by Omar the Great, of the silver. Counterfeiting was visited with severe punishment. The second reform introduced by Abdul Malik was equally remarkable and enduring. Before his time the state accounts were kept either in Persian, Greek, or Syriac, which encouraged malversation. Abdul Malik directed that henceforth the public registers should be kept in the Arabian language and character.

Introduction of the Arabian language in public offices.

Before the accession of Yezîd II., provincial appointments were made chiefly for political or administrative reasons, and viceroys and prefects were nominated either because they were fitted for their posts or had distinguished themselves by their services or devotion to the sovereigns or the dynasty. Under Yezîd II. the influence of the favourites became the guiding principle for public posts. The highest posts were conferred through their exertions, in utter disregard of the fitness of the nominees. Even Hishâm was not free from these outside influences. Another evil which at this time crept into the administration led to serious mischief later on. Hitherto the governors of distant provinces were required to reside within their governments. It became frequent now for members of the reigning family and even men of note at court who obtained these appointments to reside at the capital, leaving the administration to a deputy or proxy, whose sole object was to enrich his principal and himself with the income of the provinces.

The administrative machinery.

On the whole the administrative machinery under the Ommeyades was of a primitive character. There was no such elaboration as under the Abbassides, nor was there such a separation of duties as could promote efficiency. The practical work of administration was conducted by four principal departments—(1) the *Diwân ul-Kharâj* (the Board of Land-tax), which was in the nature of a Department of Finance; (2) the *Diwân ul-Khâtim*, or the Board of the Signet, where the ordinances of government were drawn up, confirmed and sealed; (3) the *Diwân ur-Rasâil*, the Board of Correspondence, which was vested with the control of provincial affairs and all communications from the governors; (4) the *Diwân ul-Mustaghillât*, or Board of Miscellaneous Revenue. 40—132 A.H.

Besides these there appear to have been two offices apparently subordinate to the Department of Finance which had charge of the pay of the police and the soldiers.

Military Service.

Military service was, in a manner, compulsory on all Arab-born subjects of the empire, who were bound at stated periods to attend the colours of their respective *Junds*, or legions, for the necessary training. On active duty the soldiers received a higher pay than when merely in the reserve; but every person liable to be called upon for service was entitled to a stipend from the state. I shall deal with the military organisation of the Saracens as a whole when I come to the Abbasside epoch, when the machinery of the state, both in war and peace, had attained such a high pitch of excellence. The fleet was under the command of an officer who was called the *Ameer ul-Bahr*, "Commander of the Sea."

Condition of the Towns.

The towns were all walled for defensive purposes. The various trades and guilds occupied separate quarters or streets, which were named after them. But this division of the town into blocks was not confined to crafts. The Arabs were always noted for their antipathy to centralisation. Hence, wherever they settled, they grouped themselves into separate clans. Each tribe had its particular quarter, its houses, its mosque, bazaar and burial-ground. This clannish tendency favoured *émeutes*

661—750 A.C. and risings against authority. In order to prevent combinations, each block or quarter, which formed a little town in itself, was separated from the rest by strong gates guarded by a warder or watchman (*Hâris*), whose duty it was to give egress and ingress, especially to belated wayfarers at night. But in times of trouble, all communication could be cut off between the different sections of the town by simply shutting the gates.

Damascus. At the period of the Moslem conquest, Damascus was a flourishing town and the seat of a Roman governor. Under the Ommeyades it became one of the most beautiful cities of the world, and the metropolis of the Islâmic empire. They adorned it with magnificent buildings, fountains, kiosks, and pleasure-houses. The embellishment began with the Green Palace (*Kasr ul-Khazrâ*) built by Muâwiyah, which received its name from its green colouring and ornamentation. Under his successors the city shone with the white domes and towers of innumerable palaces and mosques. Walîd I. in particular beautified Damascus and its environs with public structures, and erected for himself a lasting monument in the great mosque.

But the love of building was not confined to the rulers; the members of the reigning house and the grandees of the empire vied with each other in adorning Mosul. Damascus and other large cities. Hurr,[1] who held for 106 A.H. to 117 A.H. eleven years the governorship of Mosul under Hishâm, built a college, a caravanserai, and for his own residence a palace of exquisite beauty. The mansion[2]

[1] Hurr's father, Yusuf, was a grandson of Hakam, the father of Merwân I. He was thus a member of the reigning family.

[2] "This mansion was situated," says Ibn ul-Athîr, "near the bazaar of the harness-makers. It is now lying neglected and in ruins."

The Grand Mosque of Damascus.

was constructed of pure white alabaster; its walls were ornamented with inlaid stones of variegated colours; the ceilings rested on beams of highly-carved Indian wood (teak), and were beautifully painted and gilt. It was hence called the *Mankûsha*, or Painted Palace. Finding that the citizens of Mosul had great difficulty in obtaining good drinking-water, he constructed a canal, which in spite of the lapse of centuries still exists. The famous road by its side was planted with trees, and became the resort of the citizens and their families for evening recreation. 40—132 A.H.

The Water Supply of Damascus.

The water supply of Damascus, still unsurpassed in the East, is an imperishable memorial of the Ommeyade rulers. The Barâda, the Chrysorrhoas of the Greeks, certainly conducted a plentiful supply of drinking-water into the ancient town, but the merit of developing the system of water-courses to such an extent that up to this day even the poorest house has its particular fountain, is unquestionably due to the sovereigns of the house of Ommeya. There were seven principal canals running through the city besides innumerable aqueducts which connected each house with the main water-supply. The rulers of Damascus had certainly created for themselves a domicile of surpassing beauty in the town and its charming environs. The Caliph's palace was resplendent with gold and marble; costly mosaics ornamented the floors and walls; and running fountains and cascades diffused an agreeable coolness around the courts. The gardens were filled with rare and shady trees, and enlivened by innumerable singing birds. The ceilings of the apartments were painted in gold and white, or inlaid with jewels. Richly-attired slaves, in bright-coloured silk garments of the striped patterns still in vogue in Damascus, filled the rooms. Hishâm gave private

The Caliph's Palace.

661—750 A.C. audience "in a large hall paved with marble, each flag of which was separated from the other by a band of gold; seated on a red carpet woven with gold, dressed in red silk and perfumed with musk and amber."[1] Six imposing gates[2] gave access to the city, and their high towers were visible from a distance to the approaching traveller. When the Arabs conquered Syria, they had not yet had time to form an architectural style of their own, but they soon developed one which, in beauty of design and completeness of method, surpassed both the Persian and Byzantine. The architectural style of a nation derives its character from the original habitat of the people and their primitive conditions of life. In the graceful tracery of arches and pillars, minarets and domes of the Saracenic architecture, the strong resemblance to the arching and doming of the palm-groves, so dear to the Arab, forces itself upon our notice.

In the beginning, the Syrian houses were modelled after the neo-Roman style; and in the towns of Irâk they distinctly bore the stamp of Persian design and taste.

The lapse of time has made no change in the fashion of the buildings nor, generally, in the domestic arrangements. In the residences of the rich, then as now, a door-porter (*bawwâb*), whose usual seat was an estrade of stone, or a wooden bench in the doorway, gave admission to visitors. In the houses of the poor a big ring of iron or metal, fixed on the door, was used as a knocker. The doorway led into an oblong courtyard, which was often surrounded by pillared galleries. A

[1] Al-Harîri.

[2] Viz. the Gate of Paradise or gardens (*Bâb-ul-Farâdis*), the Jâbia Gate, the Eastern Gate (*Bâb ush-sharki*), the Tûma Gate, the Small Gate (*Bâb us-Saghîr*), and the Kaisân Gate.

variegated pavement of stone, marble, or pebbles tastefully designed ran round the courtyard, and a fountain, surrounded by a little garden filled with fragrant flowering shrubs, and shaded by orange, lemon, and citron trees, occupied the centre. On one side of the court was the raised *aiwân* (modern *liwan*) or hall, paved, like the courtyard, with marble or coloured stones, which in the hot season formed the reception-room. The mansions of the rich were sometimes two-storied, and had more than one hall, each differently decorated. To the right and left of the halls heavily curtained doors led to the reception and living rooms. In winter, the marble floors of the *aiwân* and of the apartments were richly carpeted; in summer, they were covered with matting. The *diwân*, or long couch round the wall, had not yet come into fashion, for we hear of it first under the Abbassides. If the master of the house was of high rank it was customary to place several rugs one upon another, so as to form a higher seat for him. Opposite the door was a niche ornamented with marble pillars, in which stood the ewer and basin used for the prescribed ablutions, and it is probable that, as now, an ornamental shelf ran along the wall in which were placed articles of use and luxury. The ceilings were adorned with arabesques, and richly gilt. In winter the rooms were warmed by means of a *manhal* or brazier placed in the centre of the room, while in summer the fountains and open windows kept the apartments cool.

Court life.

The sovereign was expected to preside at the Friday Cathedral service and the daily prayers. This duty was faithfully observed by Muâwiyah, Abdul Malik, and Omar II.; but the others often shirked attendance at the latter. The ruler's presence, however, was indispensable at the Friday service, when he delivered the

661—750 A.C. pontifical sermon. On these occasions he appeared in the *Jâmaa* Mosque clothed entirely in white, in a pointed white cap sometimes adorned with jewels. The signet-ring and staff of the Prophet formed the sole insignia of office. After prayers he ascended the pulpit and preached a sermon to the assembled congregation. Some of the gayer and more frivolous sovereigns of this dynasty found attendance even at Friday services too irksome. Yezîd II., for example, was often represented at public prayers by the chief of the body-guard (*Sâhib ush-Shurta*), and Walîd II. once indulged in a prank which greatly angered the religious people in the capital. He sent to the Mosque, enveloped in his cloak, a beautiful lady of the harem with whom he had been entertaining himself, and who entered fully into the spirit of the joke, to preside at the Friday service in his stead.

Besides these religious functions, the sovereign performed the duties of a high court of appeal, and received in audience the grandees of the state and the envoys of neighbouring princes. The receptions were either public (*aâm*) or private (*khâs*). At the public audiences the sovereign was seated on his throne in the large reception hall, with the princes of the royal blood ranged on his right; and the courtiers and dignitaries, and general retinue of the Court, on the left. Before him stood all the people entitled to enter and salute the sovereign—the notables of the town, the masters of crafts and guilds, poets, legists, etc. The private audiences were reserved for the members of the reigning house, dignitaries of state and special favourites, a custom not confined to the Ommeyades. At these receptions the sovereigns were dressed in gorgeous robes. The Ommeyade Sardanapalus, Walîd II., wore tunics of gold brocade and trousers of damask, whilst Sulaimân, his uncle, never wore anything but damask, and was buried in it. 40–132 A.H.

The first rulers of the Ommeyade dynasty spent most of their unoccupied time in listening to the stories of the wars, adventures, and deeds of heroism of the Arabs before the birth of Islâm. Poetical recitations also enlivened their entertainments. Under Yezîd I. the use of wine came into fashion. He himself drank immoderately, and his social gatherings, like those of Yezîd II. and Walîd II., were more like drinking bouts and orgies than convivial feasts. Before long recitations made room for singing and music. The best singers flocked to Damascus from Mecca and Medîna, in those days the home of the musical arts. The games of chess and polo had not yet come into vogue, but dice, and apparently cards, were not unknown. Cock-fights, though forbidden by Walîd I. and Omar II., were, as in England until recent times, fashionable pastimes. But the favourite form of outdoor amusement and diversion among all classes of the people was horse-racing. Horse-racing. Hishâm is said to have been the first to establish races with the object of improving the breed of horses. As many as four thousand horses from his own and other stables ran in the races organised by him, which, says Masûdi, is without precedent. Even princesses trained and ran horses.

Walîd II. was equally devoted to horse-racing, and there existed great rivalry between him and Hishâm on the subject of their horses. In this reign the love of music grew almost into a craze; and enormous sums Music. were spent on famous singers and musicians, who were summoned to court from the most distant parts. The large influx into the capital of the servile classes in pursuit of their vocation of dancing and singing naturally

661—750 A.C.

The Harem system.

demoralised society and gradually led to the segregation of the respectable section of the female community. A thoughtful historian[1] says, "the actual *harem* system commenced only under Walîd II., who, in imitation of the Byzantine custom, introduced eunuchs into his household. From that time forward these unfortunate creatures played a conspicuous part in the oriental courts as confidential servants and guards of female honour. The abominable custom of mutilation was practised by the Greeks, who afterwards traded with the objects of their avarice." So late as the third century of the Hegira, a learned Arab, the well-known rationalist (Mutazilite) al-Jahîz,[2] condemned the practice in the strongest terms. But though reprehended and denounced by Moslem doctors and divines, the system took root in the Ommeyade court.

Adoption of foreign customs.

As the Ommeyades borrowed from the Court of Byzantium the abominable custom of employing eunuchs, especially for the inner service of the palace, they also adopted various customs and rules of etiquette in vogue among the old Persian kings. Whilst the example of the sovereigns made the use of wine almost universal among the men, the ladies indulged in a beverage still sold in the bazaars of Damascus and Beyrut under the name of rose-sugar sherbet—a solution of rose-sugar and water, cooled in summer with snow. The ladies of the royal family seem to have been particularly addicted to this drink, and in later days a crystal and gold goblet of large proportions was exhibited in the treasury of Bagdad out of which

[1] Von Kremer.

[2] *Abû Osmân* Amr, of the tribe of Kinâna, generally known by the surname of al-Jahîz, "was a man," says Ibn-Khallikân, "celebrated for his learning and authorship of numerous works on every branch of science." He died in 255 A.H. (868-869 A.C.).

Umm Halîm, the wife of Hishâm, drank her sherbet. 40—132 A.H.
The second Caliph of the Ommeyade dynasty, Yezîd I., in imitation of some of the old Persian kings, intoxicated himself daily, and was hardly ever sober. Abdul Malik is said to have taken wine freely once a month, but the application of a remedy in use among the Roman emperors left him next morning fresh and lively, without any trace of the night's revels. Walîd I. drank every second day, whilst his brother Yezîd II., and his nephew Walîd II., were constantly drunk. Among the sovereigns of the Ommeyade dynasty only three did not indulge in wine —the pious Omar II., Hishâm, and Yezîd III. The wine-parties in the royal palace, as well as in the mansions of the great, were enlivened by music and song. On these occasions a thin curtain, hung in the middle of the hall, pretended to hide the august person of the sovereign and his immediate surroundings, from the view of the assembly of courtiers, singers, and musicians.

Women.

As I have already mentioned, the custom of female seclusion, which was in vogue among the Persians from very early times,[1] made its appearance among the Moslem communities in the reign of Walîd II. And the character and habits of the sovereign favoured the growth and development of a practice which pride and imitation had transplanted to the congenial soil of Syria. His utter disregard of social conventionalities, and the daring and coolness with which he entered the privacy of families, compelled the adoption of safeguards against outside intrusion, which once introduced became sanctified into a custom. To the uncultured mind walls and warders appear to afford more effective protection than nobility of sentiment and purity of heart.

Despite these unfavourable circumstances, women con-

[1] Comp. the story of Esther, vers. 9 and 12.

661—750 A.C. tinued down to the accession of Mutawakkil, the tenth Caliph of the House of Abbâs, to enjoy an extraordinary amount of freedom. The old chivalry was yet alive among men; Byzantine licence and Persian luxury had not destroyed the simplicity and freedom of the desert. Fathers were still proud to assume surnames after their accomplished and beautiful daughters;[1] and brothers and lovers still rushed to battle acclaiming the names of their sisters and lady-loves. The high-bred Arab maiden could still hold converse with men without embarrassment and in absolute unconsciousness of evil. To her the beautiful lines of Firdousi[2] were still applicable—

> "Lips full of smiles, countenance full of modesty,
> Conduct virtuous, conversation lively."[3]

She entertained her guests without shyness; and as she knew her own worth she was respected by all around her. A well-known author[4] relates that once returning from Mecca he halted at a watering-place not far from Medîna. The heat of the sun drove him to ask for shelter in a neighbouring house which appeared to be of some pretension. He entered the courtyard and asked the inmates if he might alight from his camel. A lady's voice gave him the sought-for permission.[5] He then asked for leave to enter the house, and receiving permission he entered the hall, where he found a "maiden fairer than

[1] Such as Abû Sufra, Abû Laila, etc.

[2] The Homer of Persia.

[3] "*Do lab pur ze khandah, do rukh pur ze sharm,*
Ba-raftâr nekô, ba guftâr garm."

[4] Abû Tayeb Mohammed al-Muffazal ad-Dibbi, who died in 308 A.H. (920 A.C.), quoted by al-Kharâiti in his *Itilâl ul-Kulûb.* This story illustrates equally the manners and customs under the early Abbassides. See also Ibn Khallikân under the title Zu'r-Rumma.

[5] In the original, "The lady of the house (*rabbat ul-bait*) called out 'Alight.'"

the sun" engaged in some household duty. She bade him to be seated, and they conversed, and the "words like pearls were scattered from her lips." Whilst they were conversing, her grandmother entered and sat down by their side, laughingly warning the stranger to beware of the witchery of the fair girl. 40—132 A.H.

Another incident related by the father of this author throws further light on the manners and customs of the age. He was proceeding to Mecca, and halted on the way at the house of a friend, who asked him if he would like an introduction to Kharka, the famous lady whose praises had been sung by one of the greatest poets of the Ommeyade times. On his expressing a desire to meet the beauty, he was taken to her residence, where he was received by a tall and extremely beautiful woman "in the force of age." He saluted her, and was asked to sit down. "We conversed for a time," continues the narrator, "when she asked me, laughingly, 'Did'st thou ever make the pilgrimage?' 'More than once,' said I.—'And what, then, has hindered thee from visiting *me?* Dost thou not know that I am one of the objects to be visited during the pilgrimage?'—'And how is that?'—'Hast thou never heard what thy uncle Zu'r-Rumma said: To complete a pilgrimage, the caravan should stop at Kharka's (*abode*) whilst she is laying aside her veil'?" Kharka.

Under the early Hakamites flourished *as-Syeda*[1] Sukaina,[2] or Sakîna, the daughter of Hussain, the Martyr Syeda Sukaina.

[1] *Syeda* (lady) is the feminine of *Syed* (lord), and is the title given to the descendants of Ali and Fâtima.

[2] Her real name is said to have been Omaima, Sukaina being a surname given to her by her mother. Sukaina died at Medîna in Rabî I. 117 A.H. (April 735), in the reign of Hishâm. Left a widow when quite young by the death of her first husband, Musaab bin Zubair, on the field of battle (see *ante*, p. 94), she married one

661—750 A.C. of Kerbela, who was regarded as "the first among the women of her time by birth, beauty, wit, and virtue." Her residence was the resort of poets, *fakîhs* (jurists), and learned and pious people of all classes. The assemblies in her house were brilliant and animated, and always enlivened by her repartees.

Umm-ul-Banîn, the wife of Walîd I., and sister of Omar II., was another remarkable woman of the time. Her influence over her husband was considerable, and was always exercised for the good of the people. The lecture she once administered to Hajjâj is famous in history. He had come to visit Walîd, and had the effrontery to advise him to shake off the influence of the Queen. When Umm-ul-Banîn heard this, she asked Walîd to send Hajjâj to pay his duties to her. Hajjâj came into the Queen's chamber. He was received with studied neglect, and was allowed to remain waiting for a long time. Umm ul-Banîn then entered the hall of audience, accompanied by her maids. His obeisance was acknowledged with reserve; and the Queen questioned him about his advice to the sovereign not to allow her interference in affairs of state. A prevaricating reply led to a memorable lecture. The royal lady recounted one by one all his misdeeds, and laid open before him how he had induced his masters to cruel deeds, in which the best followers of the Faith had been sacrificed, and how he had proved himself the evil genius of her family.

Abdullâh Hizâmi, by whom she had a son named Kurain. Abdullâh Hizâmi died shortly after. On his death a brother of Omar II. proposed to her, but was prohibited from marrying by Walîd I. She then married a grandson of the Caliph Osmân, who, however, was compelled to separate from her under the orders of the Ommeyade Sulaimân.

Then, after reproaching him for his cowardice, she ordered her attendants to thrust him out. 40—132 A.H.

The Arab ladies were extremely fond of poetry and recitations, and not a few have left compositions of great merit.

Saint Râbia.

The famous saint Râbia[1] lived about this epoch. She is described as one of the most eminent among the holy persons of the time.

Dress.

Men's dress had not undergone much change from early times, but evidently the tight-fitting *kaba* was now coming into use. The dress differed not only in quality and quantity according to the means of the wearer, but varied in style and shape according to his profession. The costume of a *fakîh* (lawyer or jurist) or a *kâtib* (clerk) differed widely from that of the soldier. For different pursuits there were also different dresses; for riding, short tight coats and tight trousers were worn instead of the loose flowing garments used indoors.

One can easily imagine the gay and lively scene Damascus presented when it was the seat of a wealthy and extravagant court, an important military station, and the commercial centre of a large empire. The grandees in rich attire, mounted on beautifully caparisoned horses, and surrounded by their retainers, hurrying to the palace; the Bedouin chiefs in their picturesque costume riding proudly through the streets; the sunburnt Arabs of the desert in their brown and white camel-hair cloaks with striped red and yellow *kufiyas*, gazing in astonishment at the bustle and excitement; the crowds of Syrian country folk in their purple cassocks, wide trousers, red-beaked shoes, and large white or blue turbans, driving their

[1] Surnamed *Umm ul-Khair*, "the mother of good," died in 135 A.H. (752-753 A.C.), and is buried on the Mount of Tir, to the east of Jerusalem. Her tomb is now a place of pilgrimage.

661–750 A.C. donkeys, mules, and camels laden with country produce; the jealously-watched Hâshimides with their finely-cut, aristocratic features, in long robes, walking with measured step; the ladies, surrounded by their maids, on shopping bent—all this must have formed an interesting and animated picture.

Mode of eating About this time we find mention made of napkins and spoons. The napkin was tied round the neck, or tucked in the *khaftân*, as is still the custom in many parts of the continent of Europe. The spoons were either of wood, with long handles to drink sherbet from the bowls, or were made of porcelain, and imported from China. Among the affluent the day generally began with a bowl of honied milk, or sugar and milk. Some time after sunrise breakfast was served in the inner apartments, at which all the members of the family were present; after breakfast the master of the house devoted himself to his duties. Noon was the usual hour for dinner, which was served in the reception-hall. At this meal guests were always present. Supper was laid after the *Aasr* prayers,[1] and was taken in company. They all sat on chairs; a table was placed on a stand and covered with a white cloth. First bowls of honied milk and other drinks were served, and then dishes of dressed meat. After supper, the host and his guests attended *Isha*[2] service, and then assembled in another apartment and spent the evening in conversation.

Association between the sexes became more and more restricted with the increase of Byzantine and Persian influence on Arab society.

[1] *Aasr* prayers may be offered at any time between four in the afternoon and sunset.

[2] *Isha* prayers may be offered any time between nightfall and midnight.

The term slavery is hardly applicable to the persons who hold that status in Islâm; for slavery among the Moslems bears no analogy to that practised among any other people. The Arabian Prophet forbade human chattelhood; he ordained that parents should not be separated from their children, nor one relative from another; he directed that "slaves" should be fed and clothed as their masters and mistresses, and should never be ill-treated. They should be allowed to ransom themselves, or to work out their emancipation. Enfranchisement of "slaves" was declared to be the highest act of virtue. The "slaves" were in reality members of the household. In spite, however, of their superior position compared to their status in other legal systems, their introduction in large numbers had an unwholesome effect on Arab society; it tended to lower the standard of ideals, and to relax the bonds of morality. Another mischievous result also began to show itself about this time. The Saracen settlers in foreign lands often intermarried with the daughters of the subject nations, with the result so often observable in history. If the people among whom they settled belonged to any of the higher races, like the Goths, the Franks, the Persians, or even the Greeks, their descendants improved; if they intermarried among the lower races, like the Ethiopians, their progeny deteriorated.

40—132 A.H.

Slavery.

Literature did not, like music, arts, or poetry, receive much encouragement from the Ommeyades. Under Omar II. jurists were esteemed and supported, and learned men in general were patronised. But the bent of the Ommeyade mind was not in this direction; in the whole course of their rule, they produced only one man of learning, Khâlid the son of Yezîd I., who was

Literature.

661—750 A.C. noted for his acquirements in the sciences and letters.[1] The members of the suspected families and the clients of Arab tribes took to commerce and literature. There was no established church such as grew up under the Abbassides; and the jurisconsults, who received allowances from the state, were not yet drawn into a vast hierarchy insisting in its own interests upon absolute conformity. As yet, the divisions were chiefly of a semi-political or dynastic character. The question of the Imâmate, or spiritual headship of Islâm, formed the principal point of difference between each group. The Ommeyade asserted, if he did not believe, that it belonged to his clan; the adherents of the descendants of Mohammed maintained that it was the right of the Prophet's family; the Abbassides claimed it for their branch; whilst the Khârijis held that the right of electing an Imâm appertained to the universality of the people, irrespective of race, clan, or family. Among the Ommeyades there was one cardinal doctrine, viz. the execration of Ali and his descendants; for the rest, each followed the rules of conduct supported by their traditions. Those who were inimical to the House of Ali were called *Nawâsib* (plural of *Nasabi*, a rebel), whilst their partisans were styled *ash-Shiat(u) li-ahl il-Bait*, "adherents of the people of the House." Among the Fatimides alone religious ideas took a philosophical turn. The general diffusion of learning had set free the spirit of inquiry. Philosophical discussions became common at every centre of population, and the lead was given by the school which flourished at Medîna, under a great-grandson of the Caliph Ali, named Imâm Jaafar, surnamed

Religious and philosophical sects.

[1] Khâlid, a great master of medicine and chemistry, has left writings on those subjects. He died in 85 A.H. (704 A.C.).

Sâdik. A man of inquiring mind and a keen thinker, well versed in most of the learning of the time, he was virtually the founder of the chief philosophical schools in Islâm. His lectures were attended not only by men who afterwards became the founders of schools of law,[1] but also by philosophers and students from distant lands. Imâm Hassan al-Basri, who founded a school of philosophy in his native city (Basra), was one of his disciples.[2] Wâsil bin Aata,[3] the founder of the great Mutazilite School, derived his inspiration from the same fountain-head. Wâsil, like the Fatimide Imâm, taught the liberty of human will.[4] 40—132 A.H.

Yezîd III. and Merwan II. were both Mutazilites; so also was Ibrahîm, the brother of Yezîd III. In Damascus, three men, Maabad al-Juhni, Jîlân Dimashki, and Eunas al-Aswâri, went further than Wâsil in asserting the absolute free agency of man, whilst Jahm bin Safwân upheld predestinarianism.

[1] Like Abû Hanîfa and Mâlik.

[2] Hassan died in Rajab 110 A.H. (October, 728 A.C.).

[3] Wâsil bin Aata was born in 80 A.H. (699-700 A.C.), and died in 131 A.H. (748-749 A.C.).

[4] I shall give a more detailed account of his doctrines when dealing with the reign of Mâmûn.

CHAPTER XV

THE ABBASSIDES

132—158 A.H., 749—775 A.C.

SAFFÂH AND MANSÛR

The reign of Saffâh—His death—Accession of Mansûr—His character—Revolt of Abdullâh bin Ali—Death of Abû Muslim—Bagdad founded—Manifestation of Mohammed and Ibrâhim al-Hassani—Their defeat and death—Invasion of Spain—Its failure—Irruption of the Khazars—Byzantine inroad—Death of Mansûr.

WITH the rise of the Abbassides, the aspect of Western Asia alters. The seat of government is removed from Syria to Irâk; the Syrians lose the monopoly of influence and power they had hitherto possessed; and the tide of progress is diverted from the west to the east. But the unity of the Caliphate was gone for ever. Spain from the first never acknowledged the authority of the Abbassides, and was easily reduced by the fugitive Abdur Rahmân, who founded a dynasty which rivalled in magnificence the House of Abbâs. Over Western Africa the early Abbassides exercised substantial dominion, but in time it dwindled into nominal suzerainty. The shrinking of the empire was not without its advantage, as it helped the founders of the Abbasside Caliphate to consolidate their power, to organise its resources, and to promote the material and intellectual development of their subjects. The first nine sovereigns of this house, with one exception, were men of extraordinary ability and politicians of a superior type, devoted to the advancement of the public weal. All of them combined warlike qualities with high intellectual attainments. And though the reigns of some were stained by deeds of cruelty, that was the characteristic of the age throughout the known world, and the outcome of dynastic policy. 132—158 A.H.

"The reign of the first Abbassides," says a distinguished French scholar and historian, "was the era of the greatest splendour of the Eastern Saracens. The age of conquest had passed; that of civilisation had commenced."

Abu'l Abbâs Abdullâh, *as-Saffâh*, 12 Rabi I., 132 to 136 A.H. 20th October, 749 A.C. to 754 A.C.

I have already mentioned how Abu'l Abbâs came to be proclaimed Caliph, and how by his reckless executions of enemies and suspects he acquired the title of Saffâh. In those days human life was accounted of little value either in the west or in the east;[1] and religion had little control in checking the natural ferocity of man. Yet, with all his cruelty, Saffâh was regarded as a generous sovereign, attentive to his duties, and not given to self-indulgence. Against the prevailing custom of the age and the people, he had only one wife, Umm Salma, to whom he was passionately attached, and who exercised unbounded influence over him. Even she, however, was at times unable to calm his mad frenzy against the Ommeyades.

Rising in Syria and Mesopotamia.

This ill-treatment brought its natural consequences. A revulsion of feeling took place in their favour in various parts of the country; and the partisans of the fallen House rose against Saffâh in Damascus, Hems, Kinnisrin, Palestine, and Mesopotamia. The usual mode adopted on these occasions was for the men to shave their face and disclaim fealty to the House of

[1] Sismondi says, "the shedding of human blood had in general nothing revolting to a prince of the Middle Ages."

749—775 A.C. Abbâs. These risings were quelled by more politic methods than had hitherto been in vogue, and the insurgents laid down their arms on favourable terms.

Capitulation of Yezîd bin Hobaira. Yezîd bin Hobaira, Merwân's viceroy over Irâk, was still holding Wasît, where he was hemmed in by Hassan bin Kahtaba and Abû Jaafar, Saffâh's brother and successor. The siege lasted eleven months; the besiegers sent burning boats down the river to set fire to the city, but the defenders seized or turned the boats aside by grappling-irons. Finding that the House of Ommeya had fallen beyond recovery, Yezîd addressed himself to a descendant of Ali[1] to take up the Caliphate, and thus supply a rallying centre to those who were opposed to the Banû Abbâs. Not receiving a reply in time, and despairing of making a longer stand, especially as the Yemenites within Wasît had been won over by Saffâh's emissaries, he made his submission to Abû Jaafar upon a solemn covenant of safety for himself, his family and followers, together with all their property. Abû Jaafar intended fully to abide by his covenant, but Saffâh was guided by Abû Muslim. This pitiless man saw in Yezîd a possible rival. Ibn Hobaira had still a large following; and his influence over his tribe (the Fezâra) was unbounded. Abû Muslim advised Saffâh to put Ibn Hobaira to death, and the latter wrote to his brother to do so. Abû Jaafar time after time refused to carry out the cruel order, but was at last compelled to give way.

His betrayal and death. A force was sent to Yezîd's house, where he was killed with his eldest son and a number of his followers.

Saffâh was now the undisputed master of Asia and Egypt; and West Africa acknowledged his authority. In the distribution of the governorships, he was careful to

[1] Abdullâh, son of Hassan II., son of Hassan I., son of the Caliph Ali.

entrust them either to members of his family or to men who had distinguished themselves by services in his cause. Abû Jaafar was the viceroy of Mesopotamia, Armenia and Azerbaijân; his uncle Dâûd bin Ali held Hijâz, Yemen and Yemâma; Abdullâh bin Ali, Syria; Sulaimân bin Ali, Basra and its dependencies;[1] Abû Muslim, Khorâsân; and Abû Ayûn, Egypt. Khalîd bin Barmek was chancellor of the exchequer, whilst Abû Salma, who was instrumental in proclaiming Saffâh as Caliph, was made vizier, and probably acted as confidential adviser. The influence exercised by Abû Salma roused the jealousy of Abû Muslim, and one night, while returning home from Saffâh's palace, he was set upon by Abû Muslim's myrmidons and assassinated. His death was ascribed to the Khârijis.

132—158 A.H.

Different Governorships.

Abû Salma's assassination.

In spite of the arrangements made by the new ruler, the empire was still unsettled, and the Byzantines seized the opportunity of ravaging the Moslem territories on the north. The peaceful inhabitants were either massacred or carried into captivity, and the country was laid waste.

Byzantine raid.

Saffâh died at Anbar, a place not far from Hîra, leaving a son named Mohammed and a daughter called Raita, who afterwards married her cousin Mohammed al-Mahdi.[2] Before his death he nominated Abû Jaafar,

Saffâh's death, Zu'l Hijja, 136 A.H. 9th June, 754 A.C.

[1] Al-Bahrain, al-Ahsa, Oman, Ahwâz, etc.

[2] The son of Abû Jaafar, who afterwards became Caliph. She died at the beginning of Hârûn ar-Rashîd's reign in 170 or 171 A.H., leaving a son named Ali. Of the son of Saffâh we hear repeatedly in Mansûr's reign as holding the post of governor in different provinces.

Nobody knew where Saffâh was buried. The Abbassides feared the same treatment for their dead as they had meted out to their fallen rivals; and therefore carefully concealed their graves. It was only for the eleventh sovereign of this dynasty (Muntassir) that a mausoleum was erected.

749—775 A.C.

his brother, as his successor to the throne, and his nephew Îsa as heir-presumptive.

Succession of *Abû Jaafar* Abdullâh, *al-Mansûr* (the Victorious), Zu'l Hijja, 136 A.H. June, 754 A.C.

Abû Jaafar was at this time absent on a pilgrimage to Mecca, and accordingly the oath of fealty to him was taken by the proxy of Îsa. Although Saffâh is the first sovereign of the Banû Abbâs, Abû Jaafar must be regarded as the real founder of the dynasty. The permanence of the family, the power they wielded, and the influence they exercised, even after they had lost their temporal sovereignty, were due to his foresight. He laid the foundations of the Church which maintained and enhanced the prestige of the pontifical throne, and in later years became the chief source of its strength and the mainstay of its influence. With a remarkable knowledge of human nature, he conceived and carried out, in the course of his long reign, the gradual formulation of those doctrines which, whilst they added to the hold of the sovereign on the imagination of the people, by enlisting other interests on the side of the throne, helped to create a powerful hierarchy bound and devoted to the new dynasty. The corner-stone of this far-reaching policy was the sacramental idea attached to "the consensus of the people."

Foundation of the Orthodox Church.

With Mansûr opens the series of those brilliant Caliphs whose names have become so popular in Asia. The first successors of Abu'l Abbâs have been compared to the Antonines and the Medicis. They applied their power to the amelioration and the well-being of the nation. "Respected by their neighbours, they endeavoured by an active and liberal administration, and by grand and useful enterprises, to merit the veneration and love of their subjects." They devoted themselves to the building of new cities, to the construction of roads, caravanserais, canals, fountains, the formation of charitable and educational institutions, the stimulation and protection of letters, and the promotion of commerce and all arts of peace. Schemes of conquest were abandoned. "In renouncing warlike enterprises," says Sédillot, "the Abbasside Caliphs acceded to the spirit of their times; the Eastern Saracens commenced to understand the benefits of civilisation; and the masters of Bagdad responded to the voice of the people in giving them regular administration, in establishing a strict system of justice, in spreading education, and connecting the different provinces of the Empire by intimate commercial relations." 132—158 A.H.

Abû Jaafar's character.

Abû Jaafar's character was a strange mixture of good and evil. As a politician, a statesman, and a sovereign, he is almost unsurpassed. Nor can he be said to be inferior to any in far-sighted wisdom or attention to the public weal. As a parent he was devoted to his children. As a man, however, he was both treacherous and unsparing of human life. Saffâh's cruelty was due to vindictive frenzy; his successor's bloodshed sprang from calculation. Cold-blooded, calculating, and unscrupulous, he spared none whom he thought in the least dangerous to himself or his dynasty. His treatment of the descendants of the Caliph Ali forms the darkest page in Abbasside history. Suyûti says that "Mansûr was the first who occasioned dissensions between the Abbassides and Alides, for before that they were united."

Revolt of Abdullâh bin Ali Safar, 137 A.H. Nov. 754 A.C.

Immediately on hearing of Saffâh's death, he hastened back to Kûfa and assumed the reins of government under the title of *al-Mansûr*, or the Victorious. Hardly had he been seated on the throne than Abdullâh bin Ali, his uncle, who was governor of Syria under Saffâh, rose in revolt. Mansûr, as we shall henceforth call him, directed Abû Muslim to crush the rebellion. In a well-

749–775 A.C. fought battle near Nasibîn, Abû Muslim inflicted a heavy defeat on Abdullâh bin Ali, who fled with his family to his brother Sulaimân bin Ali at Basra, and there remained in concealment until Sulaimân was removed from his government. Abdullâh and his two eldest sons then fell into the hands of Mansûr, and were imprisoned in a castle not far from Hâshimièh.[1] But the victor of Zâb was considered too dangerous a man to be allowed to live in such close proximity to the capital. A new house was built for him over foundations of salt, and Abdullâh was conducted into it with much ceremony. Death of Abdullâh bin Ali. The first heavy shower of rain, however, demolished the foundations, and the unhappy prisoner was killed under the crumbled house—a fate which he well deserved for his barbarity to the Ommeyades!

After the battle of Nasibîn, Abû Muslim desired to return to his government of Khorâsân, of which he had practically made himself the king. His power in the province was unbounded, and had indeed become a source of danger to the Abbassides. He had a large following, and there were sectaries who considered him a prophet. He could, by raising his finger, destroy the House of Abbâs as he had built it up. His attitude also now became overbearing. At Nasibîn, when the royal messenger arrived to make a list of the spoil, his language towards the careful sovereign was neither respectful nor conciliatory. The removal of such a dangerous subject now became the first consideration of Mansûr, and for this purpose it was necessary that he should not be permitted to return to Khorâsân, where he would be in the midst of his own devoted partisans. He was offered the government of Syria with

[1] Hâshimièh, or *Medînat ul-Hâshimièh*, the city of the Hâshimides, was built by Saffâh not far from Kûfa.

all its dependencies; but Abû Muslim was too wary to be caught thus. With the army which had crushed Abdullâh bin Ali, he commenced his return march towards Khorâsân. It was impossible for Mansûr to oppose him; so he had recourse to his favourite weapon. People who have employed treachery against others often fall easy victims themselves. Lavish promises made in Mansûr's name induced Abû Muslim to turn aside from his march and visit the court. He was received with consideration, and for a time the honours shown to him were almost regal. One unlucky day, however, whilst in the palace, his retainers were disarmed, and he himself murdered almost in the royal presence.

132—158 A.H.

Death of Abû Muslim, 137 A.H.

So long as Abû Muslim lived Mansûr did not think himself secure on the throne; he felt now that he was indeed the ruler, and began to cast about for the site of a capital. Damascus not only lacked attraction for the Abbasside, but was a place of peril, whilst the uncertain and fickle temperament of the people of Basra and Kûfa made those cities undesirable as the seat of government. After much questing, he fixed upon the locality where Bagdad now stands—six days' journey by river from Basra.

Bagdad is said to have been the summer retreat of Kesrâ Anushirvân, the famous monarch of Persia, and derived from his reputation as a just ruler the name it bears—the "Garden of Justice." With the disappearance of the Persian monarchy had disappeared the famous Garden, where the Lord of Asia dispensed justice to his multitudinous subjects; tradition however, preserved the name. The beautiful site, central and salubrious, attracted the eyes of Mansûr, and the glorious city of the Caliphs arose, like the sea-goddess issuing from

749—775 A.C. the waves, under the magic wands of the foremost architects of the day.

Bagdad. The Bagdad of Mansûr was founded on the western bank of the Tigris. Soon, however, another city—a new Bagdad—sprang up on the eastern bank under the auspices of the heir-apparent, the Prince Imperial of the Caliphate, and was named after him the Mahdièh. This new city vied in the splendour of its structures with the beauty and magnificence of the Mansûrièh. In the days of its glory, before the destroying hordes of Chengîz, sweeping over Western Asia, had engulfed in ruin every vestige of Saracenic civilisation, Bagdad presented a beautiful and imposing appearance—a fit capital for the Pontiffs of Islâm. The city was circular in shape, and surrounded by double walls. The palace stood in the centre, with the Cathedral Mosque close by. The mansions of the chief officers of state were beyond the space which was reserved for reviews and inspections. The streets were laid out regularly, and were forty cubits wide. The bazaars or market-places, being the haunts of vagabonds and suspicious characters, were placed outside the walls; but each street had a special set of provision-dealers at the corners, who were under police supervision. The barracks for the troops were on the eastern side of the river, and were divided into three blocks, one for the Modharite soldiery, another for the Yemenite, and the third for the Khorâsâni; each forming a check on the other. There were several gates to the city, each surmounted by a lofty tower, which was guarded night and day by relays of soldiers.

Bagdad was not completed until 150 A.H., and many events had happened in the meantime, all of which had turned out successfully for Mansûr. The murder of Abû Muslim caused an insurrection among his followers

in Khorâsân,[1] but they were defeated and dispersed. 132—158 A.H.
About the same time, the Râwendièh,[2] who professed to look upon the Abbasside Caliphs as incarnations of the Deity, raised a riot in Hâshimièh, which actually placed in jeopardy the life of Mansûr. The disturbance was quelled, and the ignorant and superstitious sectaries were expelled from the city. A Byzantine inroad was repulsed with great slaughter, and the Emperor of Constantinople was compelled to sue for peace, which resulted in a truce of seven years. After this, Mansûr applied himself to repair the ravages committed by the Christian raiders, to repopulate the ruined and deserted cities, and to put the frontier in a proper state of defence. With this object he himself made a tour of the provinces, and sent Hassan bin Kahtaba[3] into Cappadocia with a large army. Malatia (Melitene), Massîsa (Mopsuesta),

Rising in Khorâsân, 141 A.H.

Byzantine inroad.

[1] Masûdi says the followers of Abû Muslim formed a sect of their own called *Khurrami*. They acknowledged him as their Imâm and saviour, and were spread chiefly in Khorâsân and the mountainous regions of the East. After Abû Muslim's death they split up into two sections; one believed that he was still alive, and would soon re-appear to do justice on earth; the other believed that he was really dead, and that the Imâmate had passed to his daughter. The leader of the insurrection, Sanfâd, was one of the principal members of this sect. Ibn ul-Athîr and Mirkhond, however, say that he was a Magian.

[2] The Râwendièh looked upon Mansûr as the "Providence who supplied them with food and drink." They considered the commandant of his body-guard as the incarnation of the Angel Gabriel. Their unwelcome and blasphemous enthusiasm, which provoked the religious section of the people, caused Mansûr to imprison several of the Râwendièh, and hence the *émeute*. Mansûr's life was saved on this occasion by Maan bin Zâidah (celebrated for his generosity), an adherent of Merwân, on whose head a price had been put by the Abbassides. After this incident, he was not only received into favour, but made successively governor of Yemâma and Sijistân.

[3] See *ante*, p. 176.

749—775 and a number of other cities were thus rebuilt, repopulated, and strongly garrisoned. New fortresses were built at Claudia and other strategical points, to check Byzantine inroads.

Annexation of Tabaristân 142 A.H. In the mountains of Tabaristân, to the south-west of the Caspian, the inhabitants still followed the ancient cult, and were governed by their own chiefs under the nominal sovereignty of the Caliphs. Suddenly they rose upon the Saracens and massacred a number of them. An expedition followed of necessity. The native chiefs were either killed or expelled; and Tabaristân and Ghilân were definitively annexed to the Abbasside empire. Hardly had this conquest been achieved than the people of Deilem,[1] who also adhered to the old Magian religion, and were only nominally subject to the Moslem rule, raided into the Saracenic territories. They were driven back after some hard fighting, and military stations, carefully planted, prevented any further incursions on their part.
143 A.H. In 143 A.H. a new distribution was made of provincial governorships, and the system of employing newswriters, for the purpose of keeping the central government informed of all that occurred in the provinces, was inaugurated. An extensive ramification of detectives and spies, such as would take the palm from any modern government, whilst it helped the sovereign to watch the growth of combinations against his authority, certainly did not promote a sense of security among the people.

144 A.H., 761 A.C. The Banû Hassan—their ill-treatment. We now arrive at a page in the history of this remarkable monarch which reflects the least credit on the goodness of his heart, or the clemency of his nature.

[1] The mountainous tracts north of Ghilân, west of the Caspian. We shall hear a great deal about the Deilemites under the later Abbassides.

To understand the subsequent events, it is necessary to glance back for a moment at the position occupied at this period by the Alides.[1] The Banû Hassan, the descendants of the fifth Caliph,[2] had hitherto taken no part in politics; and, in spite of frequent ill-treatment, had never attempted a rising against the established government. The descendants of Ali II., the son of Hussain,[3] led a still more retired life, devoting themselves to literary and philosophical pursuits, standing wholly aloof from the agitations in which their kinsmen of the family of Abbâs were engaged. Zaid and his son had been driven by cruelty to take up arms against Hishâm and Walîd II., and had lost their lives. The Banû Hassan and the Banû Hussain lived in Medîna, where they maintained themselves with the income of the little property that was left to them, supplemented by the proceeds of commerce or the more uncertain profits of the lecture-room. But in spite of their comparative lack of means, they were held in the highest esteem by their fellow-citizens. Here dwelt also the descendants of the first three Caliphs, of Zubair, and other principal Companions of the Prophet, all of whom were connected in different ways with the Alides. The influence exercised by the latter, and the consideration they enjoyed, alarmed the dark and suspicious nature of Mansûr; and the ease with which the Merwanian dynasty had been overturned led him to fear a similar fate for his House. With the object of discovering if any conspiracy was afoot, he resorted to various methods of espionage; emissaries were sent with instructions to worm themselves

132—158 A.H.

[1] The Alawi, *i. e.* the descendants of Ali.

[2] Hassan I. He received from the adherents of his House the title of *Mujtaba* (the Well-Chosen).

[3] The Martyr of Kerbela.

749—775 A.C. into the confidence of the Alides, and to instigate them to speak incautiously, so as to furnish a ground for accusation afterwards. But this was not the only cause of the persecution of the Alides in this reign. When the Ommeyade Caliphate was falling to pieces, the family of the Prophet were naturally interested in the event. A meeting was held in Medîna, at which were present most of the members of the Banû-Hâshim, including Mansûr himself.[1] At this gathering, Mohammed,[2] a great-grandson of Hassan, regarded as the head of the Banû-Hassan, was chosen as Caliph, notwithstanding that his father was alive. His noble and pure character, his high aspirations and lofty standard of virtue, had obtained for him the name of *an-Nafs-uz-Zakiya*, or "the Pure Soul." There was a consensus of opinion regarding his worth and pre-eminence, and the entire assembly, including Abû Jaafar (Mansûr), took the oath of fealty to him. We have seen, however, how the Caliphate fell eventually into the hands of the Abbassides. When Mansûr was seated on the pontifical throne, the memory of that unforgotten oath darkened his life and deepened his suspicion. And his spies poisoned his mind with false accusations against the Banû-Hassan. He attempted to seize the person of Mohammed and his brother Ibrâhim, but they escaped. He then arrested all the leading members of the family, including the old father, Abdullâh, and the head of the Caliph Osman's descendants, named Mohammed al-Osmâni,[3] whose daughter was married to Ibrâhim. They were sent in

an-Nafs-uz-Zakiya "the Pure Soul."

[1] The apostolical Imâm Jaafar as-Sâdik was not present.

[2] Mohammed, son of Abdullâh, son of Hassan II. (*Mussana*), son of Hassan I., son of Ali.

[3] Mohammed, son of Abdullâh, son of Omar, son of Osmân the Caliph.

chains to Kûfa, and imprisoned in the castle of Hobaira. Mohammed al-Osmâni, owing to the veneration in which he was held by the Syrians, was regarded as a person likely to prove dangerous to the Abbasside throne. He was flogged, and afterwards put to death. The others were treated with great cruelty, so much so that the poor sufferers admitted that they had fared better even under the Ommeyades. Mohammed and Ibrâhim were now hunted on all sides. Bedouins were employed as detectives to haunt the watering-places; every hamlet likely to harbour the fugitives was searched, and any one suspected of giving them shelter was thrown into prison and flogged. Driven to desperation, Mohammed sent his brother Ibrâhim to raise Ahwâz and Basra, whilst he himself appeared in Medîna. The proclamation of Mansûr's deposition in Basra and Medîna was to be made simultaneously. Had this plan been successfully carried out, it is probable that the Abbasside rule would have come to an end. But Mohammed was forced to declare himself before his brother's preparations were completed; and Mansûr was thus able to attack them in succession. At first Mohammed carried everything before him. Mansûr's deputy in Medîna was seized and imprisoned, and in the course of a few days the whole of Hijâz and Yemen accepted Mohammed as the Caliph of Islâm. Imâm Abû Hanîfa and Imâm Mâlik, the founders of two of the great schools of law among the Sunnis, pronounced in favour of the validity of Mohammed's claim. Finding the movement more dangerous than he had expected, Mansûr had recourse to his usual method of duplicity. He addressed a letter to the *Nafs-uz-Zakiya* offering him absolute *Âmân* (quarter), permission to live anywhere he liked, a large pension, and free grace for his relatives.

132—158 A.H.

The appearance of Mohammed and Ibrâhim al-Hassani.

749—775 A.C. To this Mohammed replied, that it was for him to offer pardon and grace, as the Caliphate by right belonged to him, and concluded by asking if the *Âmân* that was offered by Mansûr was of the same character as had been given to Abû Muslim, to Abdullâh bin Ali, and to Yezîd bin Hobaira. Cut to the quick by this rejoinder, Mansûr answered *Nafs-uz-Zakiya* in a long recriminatory letter, in which he laid down the principles on which the Abbasside dynasty eventually came to be founded. He ignored the oath he had taken, but insisted that as the Prophet had died without leaving any male issue, his daughter's children were not entitled to his inheritance, which devolved on the descendants of his paternal uncle, Abbâs. Mansûr hurried Îsa, his nephew, with a large army to crush the *Nafs-uz-Zakiya*. Before the battle, Mohammed told his followers that they were free to leave, or abide with him; on this the bulk of his supporters, who were anxious about their families, departed for their homes, and he was left with 300 men to make head against the host of Mansûr. A heroic fight closed with death; his followers were killed to a man, and their bodies gibbeted as usual. A lady of the House obtained Îsa's permission to give them a burial, and they were interred in the Martyrs' Cemetery, near Medîna.

Mohammed killed.

15th Ramazân, 145 A.H. 762 A.C.

Ibrâhim's hands were forced by the premature rising of his brother; nevertheless he was able to collect a large force, with which he several times routed Mansûr's troops, until the Abbasside's position became so perilous that he resolved to fly from Kûfa. In his extremity he despatched Îsâ against Ibrâhim. In a battle on the bank of the Euphrates the Abbasside troops were driven back with great slaughter; but again the scrupulous humanity of the Alides led to the loss of their cause. Seeing the enemy flying, Ibrâhim stopped pursuit; as soon as the

Abbassides saw this, they turned, and many of their men who had thrown themselves down feigning to be wounded, jumped up. In the fight that followed, Ibrâhim was struck by an arrow and killed and his followers dispersed.[1]

132—158 A.H.

Ibrâhim killed, 24 Zul Kaada, 145 A.H.

Mansûr now vented his rage on Medîna and Basra. Many notables in Basra who had joined Ibrâhim were caught and executed. Their houses were rased to the ground; their date-groves cut down. In Medîna, the properties of the Banû Hassan and Banû Hussain were confiscated, all the privileges Medîna had enjoyed were withdrawn, and the supplies it received from Egypt were stopped. He even threatened with death the venerable Imâm Jaafar as-Sâdik for asking for a release of his properties. He threw into prison Imâm Abû Hanîfa, and had Imâm Mâlik cruelly flogged. Of the prisoners in the castle of Hobaira some were summarily put to death, others were allowed to die poisoned by the miasmatic exhalations of the prison-house. On receiving the head of Ibrâhim, Mansûr sent it to the victim's father, to add to the poignancy of his grief. Abdullâh's message in reply is memorable. "Tell thy master," he said to the messenger, "that the days of our adversity, like the days of his prosperity, are fast running their course, and we shall soon come before the Eternal Judge, who will judge between him and us." The narrator adds, he never saw a man so crushed as Mansûr after this message was delivered to him.

Mansûr's authority was now acknowledged over Western Asia and Africa, and although Spain was not subject to his temporal sway, the *Khutba* was read in his name even in that country, as he was the possessor and custodian of the Holy Cities.

[1] Ibn Khaldûn has given a concise but succinct account of these events (vol. iv. p. 4). Mine is an abridged paraphrase of his account.

749—775 A.C.

146 A. H.

In 146 A. H. he sent Jaafar, his son, as governor of Mosul, with Harb bin Abdullâh, a great warrior, as his deputy. Harb had a beautiful castle[1] in the neighbourhood of this city, where Jaafar took up his abode, and here his daughter Zubaida[2] was born.

Spain.

About this time an attempt was made by the governor of Ifrîkia to conquer Spain. The invading force was defeated by Abdur Rahmân the Ommeyade, and the head of the Abbasside commander was sent by a secret messenger and thrown in front of Mansûr as he was holding his court at Mecca. None knew who brought it. Mansûr was so struck with the audacity that he thanked the Lord who had placed a wide sea between him and the "falcon of the Koraish," as he called Abdur Rahmân.

Irruption of Khazars.

An irruption of the Khazars into Georgia was repelled, and measures were taken to prevent further incursions on the part of the nomades. As the Kurds were beginning to give trouble, Mansûr appointed Khâlid bin Barmek, his chancellor of the exchequer, governor of Mesopotamia. Khâlid, by a mixture of firmness and justice, soon brought the province into order, and effectually curbed the unruly Kurds.

Mohammed al-Mahdi nominated successor to the throne.

Mansûr now thought of forcing his nephew Îsa to resign the succession to the Caliphate. Coercive measures were employed with that object, and Îsa was

[1] The castle was in existence when Ibn ul-Athîr wrote his great work (*al-Kâmil*). In connection with Harb's castle, Ibn ul-Athîr makes an interesting statement. "In these days, close to it I have a village which is my exclusive property. I have dedicated it to a *ribât* (monastery) for Sûfis. I have a beautiful house in this village, where I have compiled the greater portion of this work."

[2] The famous wife of Hârûn ar-Rashîd. Her real name was Ammat-ul-Azîz. Zubaida, the diminutive of *zubda* (cream), was a pet name given to her by her grandfather Mansûr.

compelled to postpone his claim, whereupon Mansûr nominated his son Mohammed with the title of *al-Mahdi*, as his successor, and this nomination was accepted by the people, and the oath of fealty duly taken. 132—158 A.H.

In 148 A.H. the apostolical Imâm Jaafar as-Sâdik died at Medîna, but the school of learning he had founded did not fortunately close with his life. It continued to flourish under his son and successor, Mûsa, surnamed *al-Kâzim*. A further split now occurred among the Shiahs, or adherents of the House of Ali. The Imâm Jaafar had nominated as his successor his eldest son Ismâil, who predeceased him. He then appointed Mûsa. Some of his followers, however, refused their adhesion to Musâ, and accepted instead Habîb, the son of Ismâil, as their Imâm. This was the beginning of the Ismâilian sect, which afterwards founded the Fatimide dynasty in Egypt. 148 A.H. 765 A.C. Death of Imâm Jaafar as-Sâdik. Succeeded by his son Mûsa *al-Kâzim* (the Patient).

In the following year a violent insurrection broke out in Khorâsân, under one of the principal notables of the province named Ustâd Sis. The disturbance was quelled; Ustâd Sis and his family were brought as prisoners to Bagdad, where they were well treated. 151 A.H. Insurrection of Ustâd Sis.

Africa was a source of incessant trouble to Mansûr. Aghlab, a member of the tribe of Temîm, who was appointed in 148 A.H., ruled successfully for nearly two years, but he fell in an action with the Khâriji insurgents near Tunis. His successor Omar, son of Hafs, who proved himself a good and able governor, held the post for three years. The Khârijis rose again, and besieged Kairowân, which was reduced to dire straits. Africa.

Omar was killed during the siege, and the capital of Ifrîkia fell into the hands of the rebels. Mansûr's rage was unbounded, and he hurried off another army under a new

749—775 A.C. governor, named Yezîd Muhallibi,[1] a man of indomitable energy and great administrative power. He defeated the Khârijis, killed their leader, hunted their flying bands from place to place, and within a few months restored peace and order in the distracted country. He held the government of Ifrîkia for fifteen years, until his death in 170 A.H., when he was succeeded by his son Dâûd.

In 155 A.H., Mansûr built the city of Rafîka, and surrounded Kûfa and Basra with walls and trenches. He also ordered a census of the population.

The Roman Emperor, in violation of his convention, invaded the Moslem territories, and suffered a terrible defeat. A fresh treaty followed upon his undertaking to pay tribute. In 156 A.H., Mansûr made a new distribution of the provincial governorships, and actually appointed a member of the House of Hassan[2] as the governor of Medîna.

The energy with which he had worked to build up his empire had told upon his physical strength, and he now felt that he had not long to live. Sending for the Crown Prince, he gave him his last instructions for the government of the empire. Among the many counsels he gave his heir some are characteristic. "Never allow a thing which has to be done to-day, to remain over for to-morrow." "Keep the people and the army contented." "Never go beyond the bounds of moderation in inflicting punishment." "Never have your treasury empty." "Whatever you have to do, do it yourself." "Concentrate your energy on your work." "Associate with people from whom you can get good advice and counsel." "Do not

[1] Son of Haithem, son of Kabîsa, son of Abû Sufra. Kabîsa was a brother of the celebrated Muhallib (see *ante*, p. 96), hence the surname of Muhallibi.

[2] Zaîd.

neglect your friends and relatives." "Defend the frontiers religiously." "Nothing maketh a Caliph virtuous but piety, nor well disposeth a monarch but obedience, nor reformeth a people but justice; and the last of men to pardon is he who oppresseth him that is beneath him." "Do not proceed with any business until you have reflected upon it, for the meditation of a wise man is a mirror which showeth him his faults and his merits." "Seek the continuance of bounty by gratitude, and of power by pardon, and of obedience by conciliating affection, and of victory by humility and forgiveness of men." 132—158 A.H.

After a touching parting between father and son, the former left Bagdad for Mecca to end his days in the Holy Land, but died on the way at Bîr Maimûna, some hours' journey from Mecca. A hundred graves were dug for him, and he was surreptitiously buried in one, so that people might not know where he was interred. Mansûr's death, 6 Zu'l Hijja 158 A.H. October 775 A.C.

Mansûr reigned nearly twenty-two years. He was a thin, tall man, of fair complexion; exemplary in his conduct and life. Nothing unseemly or indecent was ever seen at his court. "He devoted the principal part of the forenoon to the issuing of orders, the appointment and removal of officers, to the consideration of measures for safeguarding the passes and frontiers, the protection of roads, the improvement of the condition of his subjects and their dwelling-places, in the examination of the receipts and disbursements, etc.;"[1] the afternoon he spent with his family and children, to whom he was devoted. After evening prayers, he listened to the dispatches of the day, and took counsel with his ministers, retiring to rest when one-third of the night was well spent. He slept little, and rose early for the morning prayers. He personally reviewed his troops and inspected the

[1] Ibn ul-Athîr, vol. vi. p. 17.

749—775 A.C. fortresses; the army was fitted throughout with improved weapons and armour. He was most careful in the scrutiny of the accounts of his intendants, "even to fractions of dirhems and grains, which obtained for him the designation of *Abu'd-Dawânîk*, or *ad-Dawânîki*."[1]

This despotic monarch, so tenacious of his rights, set an example to his subjects of strict obedience to the constituted courts of justice. Summoned by the Kâzi of Medîna, at the instance of some camel-owners, he attended in person accompanied only by his chamberlain, and stood as an ordinary litigant before the judge, who did not even rise from his seat to receive his sovereign. The suit was decided in favour of the plaintiffs; and Mansûr acknowledged the independence and integrity of the judge by presenting him on a fitting occasion with a large purse. He left a well-filled treasury, the contents of which, as he told his son, were sufficient for ten years expenditure.

[1] A dânik is the sixth part of a dirhem.

CHAPTER XVI

THE ABBASSIDES (*continued*)

158—170 A.H., 775—786 A.C.

MAHDI AND HÂDI

Accession of Mahdi—His magnificent reign—His humanity—The Zindîks—War with the Romans—Irene agrees to pay tribute—Mahdi's death—Accession of Hâdi—The separation of Mauritania—Hâdi's death.

Mohammed, *al-Mahdi* (the Well-Conducted), 158 to 169 A.H. 775 to 785 A.C.

MANSÛR was succeeded by his son Mohammed, surnamed *Mahdi*, who was descended on his mother's side from the old Himyarite kings of Yemen.[1] Mahdi's policy was totally different from that of his father. Naturally humane and generous, immediately on his accession to the throne he endeavoured to remedy the harshness and rigour of his father's rule. He inaugurated his reign by setting at liberty all persons, save the worst felons who were awaiting execution for murder, or were undergoing imprisonment for dangerous crimes. He released from prison Hassan the son of Ibrâhim, and conferred on him a substantial allowance. He restored to the Holy Cities their ancient privileges, that had been withdrawn by his father, and allowed them again to receive their supplies from Egypt. He also gave back to the descendants of the Prophet the properties confiscated by Mansûr. Heavy fines had, from time to time, been imposed by Mansûr upon dismissed servants of government on charges of extortion and defalcation. These were

[1] His mother's name was Umm Mûsa.

775—786 A.C. kept in a separate treasury, called the *Bait-ul-Mâl 'il Mazâlim*,[1] labelled with the names of those from whom the fines had been exacted. Mahdi restored these monies, even to the representatives of those that were dead.[2] In his campaign against the Romans, he passed by the mansion of the celebrated Maslamah. Remembering the dead warrior's kindness to his grandfather
160 A.H. Mohammed, he sent for the descendants and retainers of Maslamah, and bestowed on them a gratuity of 20,000 dinârs, besides valuable fiefs. In the course of his pilgrimage to Mecca in the year 160 A.H., which was conducted on an unprecedented scale of pomp and magnificence, he distributed nearly 30,000,000 dirhems in charity among the people of Hijâz, and gave away 150,000 garments in Mecca alone. The Mosque of the Prophet was rebuilt and beautified under his orders; the existing schools and mosques were enlarged in all the principal cities, and new ones built where none existed. With greater sagacity than his father, Mahdi selected 500 men from among the Ansâr of Medîna to form his bodyguard.[3]

He fixed pensions for lepers and poor people imprisoned for debt. In Saffâh's time rest-houses had been built on the road to Mecca only between Kâdessia and Zubala (a distance of about 300 miles). The road was now metalled and widened throughout under Mahdi's

[1] Treasury of the oppressed.

[2] It is said that Mansûr had counselled Mahdi in his last will to restore these monies, as such an act would add to his popularity.

[3] Had this force been maintained by his successors, the Turkish guard would never have acquired the mischievous preponderance they obtained in later times. But Mansûr's policy, which seems to have influenced the later sovereigns, was directed towards lowering the prestige of the Arabs, who still considered themselves the flower of Moslem chivalry.

orders; large and commodious houses, with wells and reservoirs, were built along the entire route to the Holy Cities, and guards were placed for the protection of pilgrims and travellers. 158–170 A.H.

A son of Merwân II. attempted a rising in Syria, but was defeated and taken prisoner. Mahdi kept him in durance for a while, then set him at liberty with a substantial pension. Merwân's widow, Mazûna, had apartments allotted to her by Khaizurân, Mahdi's queen, in the palace, where she was treated with consideration and kindness by all the members of the imperial family. Khaizurân is said to have had great influence over her husband. Her audience-hall, in consequence, was crowded with courtiers and grandees and seekers for office or patronage. The unlucky Îsa, Saffâh's nephew, was induced definitely to resign his right to the succession, and Mahdi nominated his two sons by Khaizurân, Mûsa and Hârûn, his successors to the pontifical throne one after the other; and the oath of fealty was duly taken to them as his heirs.

The impostor Hâshim bin Hâkim, who figures in Moore's *Lalla Rookh* as "the veiled Prophet of Khorâsân," appeared in the reign of Mahdi. Khorâsân has always been prolific in sects, and was in a peculiarly agitated condition at this period. Hâshim was a small, repulsive-looking man, and in order to hide his ugliness always wore a golden mask. He thus acquired the name of *Mokanna*, or the *veiled*. He taught his followers that the Deity had from time to time incarnated Himself in order to appear among mankind; that Adam, Noah, Abû Muslim, and himself were God incarnate; and that religion consisted in faith and not in work. His other doctrines were wildly revolutionary and immoral. He obtained a large following, Mokanna, 158-161 A.H.

775—786 A.C. and for a while successfully defied the imperial forces, but was finally overpowered and killed in Kish.

Mokanna's followers, like the Christian Taborites, dressed themselves in white, and were therefore called

Zindikism. *Mubaizzè*, "the white-clothed." Soon a new sect appeared in Jurjân, to the east of the Caspian, called the *Muhammirè*, "the red-clothed," with similar fantastical and immoral doctrines, and caused trouble. They were repressed without much difficulty. The old nihilistic communism of Mazdak, mixed with Manichæan doctrines, appears to have gained ground amongst a considerable number of people. Mazdak lived in the time of Kesra Anûshirwân (the great Chosroes), in the fourth century of the Christian era; he preached a wild and utterly lawless communism. His sect had been stamped out with fire and sword by the Persian king; but the snake had been scotched, not killed. Manes, or Mâni,[1] who flourished later, was a philosopher. In the reign of Mahdi, the nihilism of Mazdak, more or less mixed with the philosophy of Manes, began to spread in Khorâsân, and to find its way into parts of Western Persia and Irâk. It loosened the bonds of society, weakened the reins of authority, and afforded unlimited licence to the passions of man. The followers of this sect were called *Zindîk*, and one of the complaints against them was that they stole children from the public streets. Whether this was true or not, there is no doubt that the *Zindîk* undermined social conventions and religious beliefs by a pretence of obedience explained by glosses. Mahdi showed no mercy to these nihilists; they were hunted without pity, and placed under a ban as the enemies of morality, order, and authority.

[1] The term Manichæan is derived from Manes.

The Byzantines raided into the Moslem territories in 163 A.H., and ravaged the frontier province far and wide. They took Maraash (Germanicia), and reduced it to ashes, putting the people to the sword. On the approach of Hassan bin Kahtaba they retreated, and he avenged himself by destroying some of the Roman towns. A fresh inroad called Mahdi himself into the field. Leaving Mûsa his son as regent at Bagdad, he marched by Mosul towards the seat of war. Aleppo was made the head-quarters of the imperial army, and Hârûn was sent forward with generals like Îsa bin Mûsa, Abdul Malik bin Sâlèh, and Hassan bin Kahtaba against the Romans. Yahya bin Khâlid was the adjutant-general of the army. Samalion and other places either capitulated or were taken by storm. Mahdi then proceeded on a pilgrimage to Jerusalem. Harûn was appointed viceroy of the west, including Armenia and Azerbaijân. Sâbit bin Mûsa was made his financial secretary, while Yahya bin Khâlid held the portfolio. But Byzantine restlessness allowed no peace. A Roman army, under a general whose name is given as Megathakomes, again burst into Saracenic territory and spread havoc all around. Hârûn hurried to repel the invaders. The Romans were routed with slaughter, and the Saracenic army marched towards Constantinople. Irene, the widow of Leo IV., who held the government of Byzantium in the name of her son Constantine VI., and whose ambition had provoked this new war, now saw the camp-fires of the Saracens lighting up the shores of the Bosphorus. After another heavy defeat Irene sued for peace, which was granted upon her agreeing to pay an immense annual tribute, besides furnishing guides and provisions for the victorious army on its return march.

158—170 A.H.

Byzantine raid.

785 A.C.

In 168 A.H. an insurrection broke out among the nomades who wandered in the desert. They plundered

775—786 A.C. the caravans, "gave up prayers," and subjected the pilgrims to contemptuous treatment. The insurrection was quelled, but the culprits seem to have been treated with great leniency.

Death of Mahdi, 21st Moharram, 169 A.H.

The following year Mahdi undertook a journey towards the east, but died on the way, at a place called Mâsandân, where he had halted to enjoy some hunting, to which he was passionately devoted. He was after a stag which was pursued by the hounds; his horse rushing furiously along carried him against the gate of a ruined palace, and the concussion broke his spine. He died the same day.

Mahdi was forty-three years of age when he died, and had ruled ten years. He was a tall, fair, well-built man, with an amiable look.

In the beginning Abû Obaidullâh acted as Mahdi's vizier. Afterwards he appointed Yâkûb bin Dâûd as his prime minister. It was under Yâkûb's advice that most of the great and munificent works in this reign were undertaken and carried out. Towards the end the Caliph's mind was poisoned against the minister, and, suspecting him of conspiring with the Alides, he confined him in the political prison called the *Matbak*,[1] where Yâkûb remained for several years, until released by Hârûn.

Accession of Mûsâ *al-Hâdi* (the Guide).

Hârûn was present at his father's death, and in accordance with the deceased monarch's covenant he immediately proclaimed Mûsa *al-Hâdi* as the Caliph, and was the first to take the oath of fealty to him. He also despatched to Hâdi the imperial signet and the Prophet's staff and mantle.

Hâdi was twenty-four years of age when he ascended

[1] The Bastille of the Abbassides.

the throne, and ruled less than two years. He is described as headstrong, obstinate, and hard-hearted, but brave, energetic, and generous, and devoted to literature. 158—170 A.H.

Hâdi did not appreciate his brother's loyalty, and during his short reign strove hard to alter the succession in favour of his son Jaafar. With this object he threw into prison Yahya bin Khâlid Barmeki, Hârûn's principal adviser, and several other of his brother's servants whom he considered opposed to his design. There was also a breach between Hâdi and his mother, Khaizurân. This lady wanted to exercise the same influence over affairs of state in her son's reign as she did in her husband's time. Hâdi resented her interference, and threatened the courtiers and nobles who frequented her receptions with his displeasure. There were thus two parties at court—one ranged on the side of the young Caliph and his son, the other on that of Hârûn and the queen-mother. Hârûn tried by every possible means to conciliate his self-willed brother; and at last, acting under Yahya's advice, left the court for his own personal safety.

The governor of Medîna ill-treated some members of the Banû Hassan on a false charge of drunkenness. This led to a rising headed by Hussain,[1] a great-grandson of Hassan I., in which several members of this and other families were killed or put to death. A cousin of Hussain, Idrîs,[2] escaped to Mauritania, where he obtained the adhesion of the Berbers, and with their assistance founded the celebrated Idrîside dynasty. Maghrib al-Aksa was henceforth separated from the Abbasside Empire.

Whilst sojourning at Îsabad, a day's journey from Bagdad, Hâdi succumbed to an incurable disease. Find-

[1] Hussain, son of Ali, son of Hassan II., son of Hassan I., son of the Caliph Ali.

[2] Idrîs was a brother of the *Nafs-uz-Zakiya.*

775—786 A.C.

Death of Hâdi, Thursday, 15 Rabi I. 170 A.H. 786 A.C.

ing his end near, he sent for his mother. The meeting was sorrowful and touching. He told her that he had sometimes considered it his duty to take measures which were distasteful to her, but that he had never been an ungrateful son, and had always cherished her love and reverenced her. He then took her hand and placed it on his heart.[1] He also directed that Hârûn was to succeed him. He died on the 15th Rabi I.

He was tall, like his father, and ruddy. He left seven sons and two daughters. One of the latter, named Umm-Îsa, afterwards married Mâmûn, the son of Hârûn.

[1] Masûdi.

CHAPTER XVII

THE ABBASSIDES (*continued*)

170—198 A.H., 786—814 A.C.

RASHÎD AND AMÎN

Accession of Hârûn ar-Rashîd—His character—Glorious reign—The Barmekides—Grant of autonomy to Ifrîkia—Affairs in Asia—Arrangement for the succession to the Caliphate—Amîn and Mâmûn made successors—Division of the Empire—Fall of the Barmekides—An Arab Joan of Arc—The Roman war—Treachery of Nicephorus—His defeat—A fresh treaty—Byzantine breach of faith—Its result—Rashîd's death—Ascension of Amîn—His character—Declares war against Mâmûn—Tâhir defeats Amîn's troops—Siege of Bagdad—Mâmûn acknowledged as Caliph at Mecca and Medîna—Amîn's death.

Accession of Hârûn *ar-Rashîd* (Hârûn the Just).

UPON the death of his brother, Hârûn ascended the throne in accordance with the bequest of Mahdi; and Jaafar, the young son of Hâdi, resigned all claims to the succession.

The reign of Rashîd, as he is henceforth called in history, ushers in the most brilliant period of Saracenic rule in Asia. The stories of the *Arabian Nights* have lent a fascination to the name of the remarkable Caliph who was wont to roam the streets of Bagdad by night to remedy injustice, and to relieve the oppressed and destitute. The real man, however, stripped of all the glamour of romance, deserves well the admiration of posterity as indisputably one of the greatest rulers of the world. Faithful in the observance of his religious duties, abste-

786–814 A.C. mious in his life, unostentatiously pious and charitable, and yet fond of surrounding himself with the pomp and insignia of grandeur, he impressed his personality on popular imagination, and exercised a great influence by his character on society. A soldier by instinct and training, he repeatedly took the field himself; he frequently traversed his dominions in every direction to repress lawlessness and to acquaint himself with the condition of his subjects, personally inspected the frontiers and passes, and never spared himself trouble or labour in the work of government. The perfect immunity from danger with which traders, merchants, scholars, and pilgrims journeyed through the vast empire testify to the excellence and vigour of his administration. The mosques, colleges, and schools, the hospitals, dispensaries, caravanserais, roads, bridges, and canals with which he covered the countries under his sway, speak of his lively interest in the welfare of his people. As a patron of arts and literature, Rashîd was surpassed by his equally brilliant and gifted son; but in strength of character and grandeur of intellect he has no superior. And although his reign, unlike Mâmûn's, was not altogether free from the evils which often spring from the possession by one individual of unlimited and irresponsible power, the general prosperity of the people, and the unprecedented progress made in his reign in arts and civilisation, make amends for many of the sins of despotism.

The Barmekides. The glory and renown of Rashîd's administration are mostly due to the wisdom and ability of the men to whom he entrusted the government of the empire for the first seventeen years of his reign. I have already mentioned the distinguished position which Khâlid bin Barmek occupied under Saffâh and Mansûr. His son

Yahya, at one time governor of Armenia, was entrusted by Mahdi with the education of Rashîd. When his ward had attained majority and had been nominated successor to the Caliphate, he was made his counsellor and vizier. Rashîd called him "father" as a mark of affection, and always deferred to his counsel and advice, which were invariably for the good of the young prince and the subjects whom he was deputed to rule. Accordingly, the moment he came to the throne, Rashîd appointed Yahya as the Vizier of the empire, and vested him with absolute power. Yahya's administration was wise, firm, and benevolent; no detail was neglected, and the well-being of the people was made a primary duty. His sons, Fazl, Jaafar, Mûsa, and Mohammed, were also men of great ability, and possessed of administrative capacity of the highest order. Fazl had successively held the governorships of Khorâsân and Egypt, and had brought about the submission of Yahya bin Abdullâh,[1] who had succeeded in making himself the sovereign of Deilem (the northern part of ancient Media). Jaafar likewise had been governor of various important provinces, and when the old feud between Modhar and Himyar broke out afresh in Syria, was employed in bringing about peace between the rival tribes. Later on when, owing to old age, Yahya resigned the vizierate, Jaafar was entrusted with the office, the duties of which he discharged with signal success. For seventeen years this remarkable and gifted family governed the empire of Rashîd with fidelity. Their sudden fall furnishes an instructive lesson in the workings of intrigue under despotism.

170—198 A.H.

But at the period with which I am dealing the Barmekides were at the zenith of their glory.

[1] A great-grandson of the Caliph Hassan.

786—814 A.C. Africa. Mauritania had, as we have already seen, broken away from the Abbasside empire. Several attempts were made by the governors of Ifrîkia to reconquer Western Africa, but they all ended in failure. Ifrîkia was held by Yezîd bin Haithem Muhallibi until his death in 170 A.H. Troubles then broke out, which were suppressed by his brother Rûh, whom Rashîd appointed governor in 171 A.H. He died after having successfully governed the province several years. A mutiny among the troops against Rûh's son led Rashîd to send a noted general named Harsama[1] to quell the rebellion. Order was restored, and Harsama held the office for nearly three years. Upon his resignation Rashîd appointed an officer who proved himself wholly incapable of governing this unruly province. Up to this time Ifrîkia, instead of yielding any revenue, had been a constant drain on the resources of the empire, and a sum of 100,000 dinârs had to be remitted annually from the revenues of Egypt to defray the expenses of the Ifrîkian government. Ibrâhim, the son of Aghlab, offered to Rashîd, if the office was bestowed permanently on him and his family, not only to restore peace and order in the province, but, instead of asking for any contribution from the imperial treasury, to remit annually to Bagdad 40,000 dinârs. Harsama, who knew the character of the province and the difficulties of the government, advised Rashîd to accept Ibrâhim's offer. Ibrâhim was accordingly appointed governor of Ifrîkia, and the office was made hereditary in his family subject to investiture and confirmation by the sovereign upon each succession. Henceforth Ifrîkia became an autonomous principality.

In Asia, the government was conducted with vigour, and without difficulty, on settled lines. In 171 A.H. the

[1] Pronounced by the Arabs, Harthama.

whole of Kabul and Sânhar was annexed to the empire, and the frontier extended as far as the Hindoo Kush. At the same time Rashîd separated the Marches of Asia Minor from the ordinary governorship, and under the name of *Aawâsim*, placed them under the control of a special military governor. Tarsus in Cilicia was repopulated, and converted into a strong fortress.

170—198 A.H.

Affairs in Asia.

Khaizurân, the mother of Rashîd, died two years later, and in her Yahya bin Khâlid lost an ally who had materially helped to maintain his wise and noble influence over the young sovereign. Immediately on his accession, Rashîd had restored to his mother all the privileges which she had enjoyed under Mahdi, and of which she had been deprived by Hâdi; and her palace had again become the resort, as in her husband's reign, of courtiers and grandees. Shortly after the death of Khaizurân, Rashîd took the imperial signet from Yahya, and entrusted it to Fazl bin Rabii, the chamberlain who now begins to figure prominently in the history of the time.

173 A.H. 789 A.C.

In 175 A.H., under the pressure of the Empress Zubaida and her brother, Îsa bin Jaafar, backed by the entire Abbasside clan, Rashîd nominated his son Mohammed, who was then only five years of age, his successor to the Caliphate, under the title of *al-Amîn* (the Trusty). Seven years later, another son, Abdullâh, was made heir presumptive, and it was directed that the throne should go to him on the demise of Mohammed al-Amîn. Abdullâh received the title of *al-Mâmûn* (the Trusted). And subsequently a third son, Kâsim, under the title of *al-Motamin*,[1] was given the succession after Mâmûn. The three sons, during their lives, were to hold the empire in parts; the West was to be under the control of Amîn,

175 A.H. 791 A.C. Nomination of Mohammed, *al-Amîn*, as successor.

Nomination of Abdullâh, *al-Mâmûn*.

[1] "In whom trust is reposed."

786—814 A.C. the East under that of Mâmûn, whilst Mesopotamia and the Marches were to belong to Kâsim, as I shall continue to call him. Rashîd relied so entirely on the judgment and fidelity of Mâmûn that he vested him with the power of removing Kâsim from the succession if he thought proper. Mâmûn was confided to the tuition of Jaafar bin Yahya, whilst Kâsim was entrusted to the care of Abdul Malik bin Sâlèh, a cousin of the Caliph. In
802 A.C. 186 A.H. Rashîd made a pilgrimage to Mecca, accompanied by Amîn and Mâmûn, and deposited in the Kaaba two documents executed by the brothers respectively, binding themselves in solemn terms to abide by the arrangement made by their father. The one by Amîn, whose weak and uncertain character was already becoming apparent to the father, is given in full by Ibn ul-Athîr, and shows the anxiety of Rashîd to bind him by the most serious pledges not to violate his covenant with his brother.

Zubaida's visit to Mecca and Medîna. The Empress Zubaida's notable visit to Hijâz, memorials of which are still existing, was made in the same year. Finding that the inhabitants of Mecca suffered greatly from scarcity of water, she constructed at her own expense the famous aqueduct, which bears her name and which has proved an inestimable blessing to the city.[1]

183 A.H. 799 A.C. Khazar irruption. In 183 A.H. the wild hordes of the Khazars, instigated by the Greeks with whom they were on terms of amity,[2] again burst into Armenia from the north. Their atrocities and the devastations they caused are described as unheard-of and unparalleled. Rashîd despatched two of his best generals for the punishment of the barbarians;

[1] The cost of this aqueduct is said to have amounted to over a million and a half dinârs.

[2] The Emperors of Constantinople intermarried with the Khazar chiefs.

170—198 A.H.

and the chastisement inflicted appears to have been terrible and severe.

Death of Imâm Mûsa al-Kâzim.

In the same year the apostolical Imâm Mûsa al-Kâzim died. Ibn ul-Athîr says he received this title for his gentleness and patience, and "for always returning good for evil." He was greatly venerated in Medîna; and Rashîd, who had inherited some of his grandfather's suspicious nature, apprehensive that this saint would raise a revolt against him, had brought Mûsa with him from Hijâz to Bagdad. Here he was entrusted to the wardship of the sister of Sindi ibn Shâhik, the governor of the Bastille, "a virtuous woman," says the historian, who tended her prisoner with respect and devotion. Twice did Rashîd, conscience-stricken, bid the harmless saint go back to his home at Medîna, and as often allowed his suspicion to master the goodness of his heart. The health of the Imâm at last gave way, and he died in the house of the lady who had been his jailor for some years.[1] He was succeeded in the apostolical chair by his son Ali, surnamed *ar-Rizâ*[2] (the Agreeable), probably the most accomplished scholar and thinker of his day.

The fall of the Barmekides. 803 A.C.

The year 187 A.H. is noted for the event which has not only dimmed the lustre of Rashîd's reign, but must have darkened his future life with remorse, and the consciousness of ingratitude. For seventeen years the family of Barmek had served the monarch with unswerving fidelity and extraordinary ability. The people were prosperous and happy, the empire had grown rich and strong, national wealth had increased, and the arts of civilised life were cultivated everywhere. But their grandeur and magnificence, their benefactions and lavish

[1] Some say he was poisoned.

[2] See *post*, p. 265.

786–814 A.C. charity, which made them the idols of the masses, raised a host of enemies, who were determined by every means in their power to bring about their ruin. Many causes have been assigned for the fate which eventually overtook them. Ibn Khaldûn has examined the legends and stories that were circulated at the time, and which have been adopted by some historians to explain Rashîd's conduct towards this gifted family. He ridicules as baseless fiction the story of the marriage of Jaafar bin Yahya with Rashîd's sister Abbâsa. The true cause of the fall of the Barâmika, he says, is to be found "in the manner in which they seized upon all authority, and assumed the absolute disposition of the public revenue, so much so, that Rashîd was often forced to the necessity of asking for and not obtaining from the chancellor small sums of money. Their influence was unlimited, and their renown had spread in every direction. All the high offices of state, civil as well as military, were filled by functionaries chosen from their family, or from among their partisans. All faces were turned towards them; all heads inclined in their presence; on them alone rested the hopes of applicants and candidates; they showered their bounties on all sides, in every province of the empire, in the cities as well as in the villages; their praises were sung by all, and they were far more popular than their master." All this raised against them the hatred of the courtiers and the grand dignitaries of the empire; "and the scorpions of calumny came to wound them on the bed of repose on which they rested under the shadow of the imperial throne." Their most inveterate enemy, Fazl bin Rabii, the chamberlain, seized every opportunity, and from his position he had many, to poison Rashîd's mind against the Barmekides, and he had allies who in their burning

170—198 A.H.

jealousy forgot, as Ibn Khaldûn observes, even the ties of relationship. It was whispered to Rashîd that the Barâmika were plotting for the downfall of the Banû Abbâs. The faithful services of generations were forgotten in the blind fury of suspicion and despotic anger, influenced by persistent calumny. Suddenly one night the order issued for the execution of Jaafar the Vizier, and the imprisonment of old Yahya and his other sons, Fazl (the foster-brother of Rashîd), Mûsa and Mohammed. Jaafar was put to death by Masrûr, the attendant who accompanied Rashîd and his vizier in his nightly rounds through the city; the others were confined at Rakka (ancient Nicephorium), and their property was confiscated. At first they were not subjected to hardships, their servants were allowed to wait on them in prison, and their comforts were attended to. A year later Abdul Malik bin Sâlèh[1] was accused by his secretary, as well as his son, of plotting against the crown, and was thrown into prison. It was alleged that the Barmekides, if not accomplices, were cognisant of his plot. This led Rashîd to treat both his prisoners with harshness, and they were now deprived of the attentions hitherto shown to them. The old and faithful Yahya died in prison in 190 A.H. And his accomplished son Fazl followed him to the grave three years later. Mûsa and Mohammed appear to have been released after the death of their father; but Abdul Malik remained in prison until the accession of Amîn, who released him and made him governor of Syria. When Mâmûn came to the throne, he restored to the Barmekides their properties as well as their dignities.

Death of Yahya Barmeki, 806 A.C.

The Khârijis as usual rebelled several times in this

The Khârijis.

[1] A grandson of Ali bin Abdullâh bin Abbâs, and thus a cousin of Mahdi.

786—814 A.C. reign, but their risings were suppressed without difficulty. One of these insurrections is remarkable for the appearance of a young girl named Laila[1] as the leader of the zealots. The revolt was begun by her brother Walîd, son of Tarîf. When he fell she assumed the command, and repeatedly gave battle to Rashîd's troops, until a relative[2] who commanded the imperial forces induced her to lay down her arms, and return to a more maidenly life. This Arab Joan of Arc was noted for her beauty and accomplishment as a poet.

An Arab Joan of Arc.

The walls of Mosul pulled down.

The riotous conduct of the people of Mosul led Rashîd to demolish the walls of their city as a punishment. Damascus was harassed by Modharite and Himyarite strifes. For a time Rashîd, who knew the Syrians were not well-disposed towards his house, allowed the two factions to weaken themselves by internal dissensions. In the end he intervened, and with a firm hand put a stop to their disorders.

War with the Byzantines.

But Rashîd's wars with the Byzantines are the most interesting events of his reign. In 181 A.H. they broke the treaty concluded with Irene in Mahdi's time, and invaded the Moslem territories. Their army was repulsed with great slaughter, the cities of Matarah and Ancyra were captured, Cyprus, which had thrown off the Saracenic yoke in the civil wars, was reconquered, and Crete was overrun. A fresh convention followed, and the Greeks again bound themselves to pay regularly the tribute fixed by the former treaty. An exchange of prisoners took place, and there was every appearance that the peace now concluded would last for some time.
182 A.H. In 182 A.H. the unprincipled and merciless Irene blinded
792 A.C. her young son, Constantine VI., and seized the throne

[1] Ibn ul-Athîr. Ibn Khallikân gives her name as al-Fâria.

[2] Yezîd bin Mazaid.

under the title of Augusta (Arabicised into *Aatasa*). With the assistance of her favourite, the eunuch Ætius, she held the reins of government for five years, when the fickle Greeks rose against her. She was deposed and exiled; and her chancellor named Nicephorus[1] was invested with the purple. With characteristic want of fidelity, he determined "to break the peace that had been established between the Moslems and Irene," [2] and sent an insulting message to Rashîd. "From Nicephorus, the Roman Emperor, to Hârûn, Sovereign of the Arabs:—Verily the Empress who preceded me gave thee the rank of a rook and put herself in that of a pawn,[3] and conveyed to thee many loads of her wealth, and this through the weakness of women and their folly. Now when thou hast read this letter of mine, return what thou hast received of her substance, otherwise the sword shall decide between me and thee." "When Rashîd read this letter," says the historian, "he was so inflamed with rage, that no one durst look upon his face, much less speak to him, and his courtiers dispersed from fear, and his ministers speechless forbore from counsel."

170—198 A.H.

Then he wrote on the back of the Greek's letter: "From Hârûn, the Commander of the Faithful, to Nicephorus, the dog of a Roman:—Verily I have read thy letter; the answer thou shalt behold, not hear!" And he was as good as his word. He started the same day with his army, and did not tarry on the way until he reached Heraclea,[4] one of the Byzantine strongholds.

[1] Called by the Arabs, Nikfûr.

[2] Ibn Khaldûn.

[3] This had reference to the game of chess which Hârûn ar-Rashîd had recently introduced into Western Asia.

[4] Although the Arab historians mention Heraclea as the place where this battle was fought, it has been suggested by a modern writer that it was at Dorylæum on the Thymbris.

786–814 A.C. The boastful Greek met the Caliph at this place and sustained a heavy defeat.[1] "The warlike celerity of the Arabs could only be checked by arts of deceit and a show of repentance." Nicephorus implored for peace, and engaged to pay an increased tribute, which he promised solemnly to transmit every year. This was accepted, and the victorious Caliph returned to Rakka. Hardly had Rashîd taken up his quarters there than Nicephorus, deeming it impossible the Caliph would take the field again in that inclement season, violated his engagement. But he mistook his adversary. The moment Rashîd heard of the breach of faith, he retraced his steps. "Nicephorus was astonished by the bold and rapid march of the Commander of the Faithful, who repassed, in the depth of winter, the snows of Mount Taurus: his stratagems of policy and war were exhausted; and the perfidious Greek escaped with three wounds from a field of battle overspread with forty thousand of his subjects."[2]
188 A.H. Nicephorus again sued for peace, and his prayer was granted. Knowing the Byzantine nature, Rashîd, before leaving Phrygia, made such dispositions as would prevent any fresh infraction of the treaty. But "over and again when Hârûn was engaged elsewhere, Nicephorus broke his treaty, and as often was beaten."[3] In 189 A.H. Rashîd proceeded to Rai (ancient Rhages) to bring back to obedience a governor who had shown signs of refractoriness. This was too good an opportunity for the Greek to miss, and he accordingly attempted a fresh inroad, but was met by Kâsim, Rashîd's son, whom the Caliph had about this time invested with the command of the Marches, and "devoted him to holy warfare in the

[1] Suyûti calls it "a famous battle and a manifest victory."

[2] Gibbon.

[3] Muir.

way of God." Again was the violation of the treaty forgiven by the Caliph. 170—198 A.H.

Whilst at Rai, Rashîd received the Magian feudatories of Deilem and Tabaristân. A liberal and considerate treatment ensured their loyalty and won their attachment. Rashîd then returned to Bagdad on his way to Rakka, which had now become his permanent abode. From here he could keep an eye over the movements of the Greeks and the northern nomads, as well as the semi-loyal Syrian tribes, and here the overworked and harassed monarch came to enjoy a brief rest. But the faithless Greek would allow him no peace. An insurrection in Transoxiana gave Nicephorus the opportunity for which he waited. He burst into the dominions of the Caliph, and filled with devastation and havoc the frontier countries. Rashîd could brook this perfidy no longer. Leaving Mâmûn as regent at Rakka with absolute control over the government he started for the north. It was now, indeed, a *Jihâd*, a holy war for the preservation of peace and the maintenance of a solemn treaty sealed with the oath of the Greek. One hundred and thirty-five thousand soldiers receiving stipends [1] followed his standard, besides volunteers whose names were not on the military roll. They swept over the whole of Asia Minor as far as Bithynia on the north, and Mysia and Caria on the west. City after city opened its gates to Rashîd's generals; Kunîèh (Iconium) [2] and Ephesus in Lydia were captured by Yezîd bin Makhlad; Sakâllya, Thebasa (Dabsa), Malecopœa, Sideropolis, Andrasus and Nicæa [3] were reduced by Shurâbîl, son of Maan bin

The treachery of Nicephorus.

[1] *Murtazaka.* These were the regulars.

[2] This is the name given by Ibn Khaldûn; the other historians call it Malakunièh.

[3] The last four cities according to Theophanes; the Arab historians only mention a few names.

786—814 A.C. Zâida. The conquering army then invested Heraclea Pontica on the Black Sea. A force sent by Nicephorus suffered a disastrous defeat, and Heraclea was taken by storm. The Greek sued again for pardon, and the Caliph with shortsighted indulgence acceded to his prayer. Far better would it have been for the peace of the world and for civilisation, had a term been then put on the Byzantine rule, and Constantinople been taken by the Saracens. A fresh treaty was sworn to by Nicephorus and the princes of his family, and the grandees of his empire, by which he agreed to pay an increased tribute besides a personal impost on himself and on each member of his house. But in 192 A.H. the Greeks again broke their faith, and raided into the Moslem territories. "The end of it all," says Muir, "the bitter end of all such wars, was to inflame religious hate." The disorders which broke out just then in Khorâsân called Rashîd away to the east, and he was compelled to delay for a while the well-deserved punishment. Leaving Kâsim at Rakka with an experienced general, Khuzaima bin Khâzim, as his lieutenant, and Amîn at Bagdad, the wearied monarch started for the east. Mâmûn accompanied his father, but on entering Persia after traversing the mountainous range, he was sent in advance to Merv with a division of the troops, whilst the Caliph journeyed slowly with the main army. On arriving at a village named Sanabâd in the vicinity of Tûs,[1] the illness from which he had been suffering ever since he left Rakka, took a serious turn. Feeling that his end was approaching, Rashîd sent for all the members of his family (the Hâshimides) who were in the army, and addressed them thus: "All who are young will get old, all who have come into the world will die. I give you

Short-sighted magnanimity of Rashîd.

192 A.H. 808 A.C.

[1] The birthplace of the poet Firdousi.

three directions: observe faithfully your engagements, be faithful to your Imâms (the Caliphs), and united amongst yourselves; and take care of Mohammed and Abdullâh (Amîn and Mâmûn); if one revolts against the other, suppress his rebellion and brand his disloyalty with infamy." He then distributed considerable largesses among his attendants and troops. Two days later the end came; Rashîd died in the prime of life on a Saturday the 4th of Jamâdi II., after a glorious reign of twenty-three years and six months. 170–198 A.H. 193 A.H. 809 A.C.

Estimate of his character and rule.

Weigh him as carefully as you like in the scale of historical criticism, Hârûn ar-Rashîd will always take rank with the greatest sovereigns and rulers of the world. It is a mistake to compare the present with the past, the humanities and culture of the nineteenth century and its accumulated legacy of civilisation, the gift of ages of growth and development, with the harshness and rigour of a thousand years ago. The defects in Rashîd's character, his occasional outbursts of suspicion or temper were the natural outcome of despotism. That he should, with the unbounded power he possessed, be so self-restrained, so devoted to the advancement of public prosperity, so careful of the interests of his subjects, is a credit to his genius. He never allowed himself the smallest respite in the discharge of his duties: he repeatedly travelled over his empire from the east to the west to remedy evils, to redress wrongs, and to acquaint himself personally with the condition of his people. Nine times he himself led the caravan of pilgrims to the Holy Cities, and thus brought the nations under his sway to recognise and appreciate his personality, and to value the advantages of Islâmic solidarity. His court was the most brilliant of the time; to it came the learned and wise from every part of the world, who were

786—814 A.C. always entertained with munificent liberality. Unstinted patronage was extended to art and science, and every branch of mental study. He was the first to elevate music into a noble profession, establishing degrees and honours, as in science and literature.

Hanafi school of law.

It was in his reign that the Hanafi school of law began to acquire a systematic shape at the hands of the jurists, headed by Abû Yusuf, the Chief Kâzi[1] of the empire. Though called after Abû Hanifa, the Hanafi School is in reality the product of Rashîd's Chief Kâzi. Abû Yusuf combined with the pliability of Cranmer much of Bacon's greed. Owing either to the fact that it was in the vigour and freshness of its infancy, or to the absence of opposing forces, the religio-legal system of which Abû Yusuf was the founder, had not as yet acquired the rigidity of later times. The insistence of a church upon conformity varies in proportion to the forces with which it has to contend. At this stage, however, in spite of a growing tendency towards casuistry, the system possessed elasticity, and evinced undoubted signs of development. But the deference Rashîd paid to his legists, and the weight he attached to their enunciations, paved the way for the formation of a hierarchy whose preponderating influence under weaker monarchs stifled growth and barred all avenues of progress. Thus commenced the superstructure of the great Sunni School, the foundations of which were laid under Mansûr, although it was not completed until the later Abbassides, shorn of their temporal power, were compelled to devote themselves to the preservation of their religious influence. The upholders of the doctrine that the consensus of the people in the election of a chief possessed a sacramental efficacy, and constituted the person so elected the spiritual leader

[1] *Kâzi ul-Kuzzât.*

or Imâm of the Commonwealth, assumed now a distinctive designation. They called themselves *Ahl us-Sunnat wa'l Jamâat*, or "the followers of traditions and (the voice) of the universality of the people." 170—198 A.H.

Science and literature.

Rashîd enlarged the department founded by his grandfather Mansûr for the translation of scientific work into Arabic, and increased the staff, although it did not under him acquire the stupendous scale it attained under Mâmûn. Among the eminent men who flourished during the whole or part of his reign, may be mentioned Asmaï the grammarian, who was entrusted with the education of his sons, Shâfeï, Abdullâh bin Idrîs, Îsa bin Yunus, Sufiân bin Sûri, Ibrâhim Mosuli the musician; Gabriel, son of Bakhtiashú the physician. Rashîd, says Ibn Khaldûn, followed in the footsteps of his grandfather except in parsimony, for no Caliph exceeded him in liberality and munificence. Himself a poet,[1] he was specially liberal to poets. Communications were opened in his reign with the West as well as the Far East, and he was the first to receive at his Court embassies from the *Faghfûr* (emperor) of China and from Charlemagne. An account is still preserved of the magnificent presents sent to the latter, which gives some indication of the state of culture attained in the Caliphate. Among the presents sent was a clock, which is described as a marvellous work of art.[2]

[1] Some of Rashîd's verses addressed to Helen are beautiful. Whether Helen was a real or imaginary being, there is no doubt that he was deeply in love with the daughter of a Roman patrician whom he brought with him from Heraclea. He built for her a palace several miles from Rafîka on the borders of the Euphrates, and called it Heraclea in honour of her former home, and surrounded her with every luxury. The palace was in existence in the time of Masûdi.

[2] In this horologe the different hours were struck by means of

786—814 A.C. Of his surviving sons four are famous in history: Mohammed *al-Amîn*, Abdullâh *al-Mâmûn*, Kâsim *al-Motamin*, and Abû Ishâk Mohammed *al-Mutasim*.

Mohammed, *al-Amîn*, 193-198 A.H.; 809-813 A.C.

When Rashîd died Amîn was at the capital; Mâmûn was at Merv, which was the seat of the provincial government; Kâsim was at his post at Kinnisrîn, whilst Zubaida, the Empress, was at Rakka. The news of the Caliph's death was despatched to Bagdad by Hamawièh, the post-master-general (*Sâhib ul-Barîd*), and on the following day the imperial signet, sword and mantle were forwarded to Amîn by his brother Sâlèh, who was with Rashîd at the time of his decease. Amîn removed at once from the *Kasr ul-Khuld* (the Paradise Palace), where he was residing, to the *Kasr ul-Khilâfat* (the Imperial Palace). Next day he presided at the public prayers, and delivered the pontifical sermon and received the usual oath of fealty from the troops, the grandees, and the citizens. Mâmûn also sent to his imperial brother his loyal congratulations and presents. Immediately on receipt of the news of Rashîd's death, Zubaida left Rakka for Bagdad, and was received by her son at Anbar with great pomp and ceremony, and taken to the Imperial Palace, where she abided until Amîn's unhappy death.

Character of Amîn and Mâmûn.

It will be interesting at this stage to note the difference in the character of the two brothers, who soon became rivals and enemies. Both had been carefully brought up under the tuition of the most talented scholars of the day; Amîn in the charge of his mother and maternal uncle Îsa; Mâmûn, whose mother, a Persian lady, had died when he was an infant, under the

balls falling on a plate of brass; as the hour struck, a number of horsemen (varying with the number of the hour) issued from a door which opened suddenly, and as soon as the sound subsided they re-entered the door, which closed behind them, (see Marigny.)

guardianship of the unfortunate Vizier Jaafar. Both had received the same education; they were sedulously instructed in the course of studies in vogue at the time—rhetoric, *belles lettres*, jurisprudence, and traditions; but whilst Mâmûn's receptive mind imbibed and assimilated knowledge that was imparted to him, it had no effect on the volatile and pleasure-loving character of Amîn beyond giving him a superficial polish. In oratory, a necessary accomplishment for an Arab prince, both stood on an equal footing; but Mâmûn was a jurist and a philosopher as well. He knew the Koran by rote, and excelled in its interpretation. Rashîd knew the difference in the character of his two sons, and probably before his death foresaw the result of the arrangement he had so carefully made for them. He had willed that the army he had taken into Khorâsân with the treasure that he carried should belong to Mâmûn. It was a necessary measure for the defence of the Eastern Provinces. And Amîn was already in possession of the immense hoard left by his father at Bagdad. Amîn, who probably never intended to abide by the covenant he had made with his father, had, in anticipation of Rashîd's demise, sent emissaries to tamper with the army. Fazl bin Rabii, the chamberlain, who was with Rashîd at the time of his death, and was practically the prime minister since Jaafar Barmeki's fall, took the side of Amîn. He knew his weakness of character, and felt sure that with him he would be the virtual ruler. He persuaded the troops to abjure the oath Rashîd had made them take in favour of Mâmûn, and to hurry back with him to the capital. Taking with him the army and the treasure, Fazl bin Rabii came to Amîn, who invested him at once with the dignity of Vizier, and distributed two years' pay in advance among the troops.

170—198 A.H.

Treachery of Fazl bin Rabii.

786–814 A.C.

Deprived thus by the disloyalty of Fazl bin Rabii of both men and money, Mâmûn found himself in a difficult position, especially as the feudatories were beginning to show signs of agitation; but assisted by some able counsellors he applied himself vigorously to conciliate the chiefs and the people of his province. His principal adviser in this crisis was a Persian named Fazl bin Sahl, a man of great ability, but extremely jealous of his influence over the young prince. The famous Harsama, and a rising soldier of the name of Tâhir bin Hussain (al-Khuzâi), were also attached to his cause. Mâmûn treated the notables with consideration and generosity, and reduced the taxes. These and other measures won the affections of the provincials, and they rallied round him as "the son of their sister." His attitude all this while towards his brother, the Caliph, was dutiful, loyal, and circumspect.

Amîn's extravagance.

Whilst Mâmûn was thus engaged in organising the principality that had been left to him, Amîn was fast driving to ruin the country subjected to his rule. To secure the uncertain and mercenary loyalty of his rapacious soldiery, who, like the daughters of the horse-leech, cried for more as more was given, he wasted the public wealth in magnificent largesses. Jugglers and buffoons, astrologers and soothsayers were sent for from all parts of the country; and enormous sums were lavished in securing the services of the most beautiful *danseuses*, the most accomplished songstresses, or those unhappy specimens of humanity with which the Byzantine dominions abounded, and who were employed by the patricians of new Rome, not only in guarding their women, but also in conducting the affairs of state. We read of a real ballet in this reign arranged under Amîn's personal direction. A hundred beautiful girls, in splendid

A Saracenic ballet.

attire, decked with pearls and blazing with diamonds, danced in rhythmical unison to the soft harmony of music, advanced and retreated, waving palm-leaves; then breaking into groups often formed a labyrinthine maze, passing and repassing, turning and bending—a fairy circle of light and colour. For his *fêtes* on the Tigris (Dajla) he caused to be constructed five barges lavishly gilt and decorated in the shape of a lion, elephant, eagle, serpent, and horse. Spending his time in carousals and immersed in pleasure, surrounded by *danseuses*, singers, and the usual parasites borrowed from the effeminate Court of Byzantium, Amîn left the entire government in the hands of the ambitious but incompetent Fazl bin Rabii; and the enemies of Islâm waxed strong. Nicephorus was killed in a war with the Bulgarians, and was succeeded by his son Istibrâk (Stauracius). Upon his death after a short reign, the Byzantines raised to the throne Michael the son of George (Jurjis), who had married Istibrâk's sister. Michael, however, was forced to resign the throne in favour of Leo, one of his generals, and to assume the cowl. No sooner did Leo ascend the throne than he broke the terms of peace with the Moslems, and commenced to make depredations upon them. But Amîn had no ear for the wrongs of his subjects. Instead of employing his energy or resources for the defence of the empire, he involved himself in a war with his brother. Fazl bin Rabii, afraid that if Mâmûn ever came to the throne he would visit his treachery with condign punishment, instigated Amîn to set his brother aside from the succession. At first the young Caliph did not lend a willing ear to the suggestion, but the persistence with which Fazl applied himself to the task, enforced by the counsel of another equally unprincipled courtier named Ali bin Îsa bin Mâhân, induced Amîn

170—198 A.H.

A Saracenic ballet.

786–814 A.C. to take the fatal step. Mâmûn was summoned to Bagdad; he excused himself, saying that he could not safely leave the province. Amîn thereupon deposed him from his government, and directed that his name should henceforth cease to be mentioned in the prayers from the pulpits. Kâsim was also deprived of the provinces that had been given to him by Rashîd.

Breach between Amîn and Mâmûn.

195 A.H. 811 A.C. In supersession of Mâmûn, Amîn nominated his infant son Mûsa his successor to the throne under the high-sounding title of *Nâtik bi'l-Hakk*,[1] and shortly after his second son as heir-presumptive under the name of *Kâim-bi'l-Hakk.*[2] Mâmûn replied to this breach of faith by drawing a cordon on his western frontier. No person was allowed to enter the province without undergoing an examination in order that the emissaries from Bagdad might not tamper with his subjects. The breach between the brothers was now complete. Amîn sent for the two covenants solemnly suspended in the Kaaba, and tore them to pieces. An army, fifty thousand strong, was despatched under Ali bin Îsa bin Mâhân, towards Rai. Here they were met, and disastrously defeated, by Tâhir bin Hussain, who held guard for Mâmûn. Ali bin Îsa was killed, and his men either dispersed or joined Tâhir. The message of Tâhir, announcing his victory, was almost as laconic as the one sent by Julius Cæsar to the Roman senate. "The head of Ali bin Îsa," he wrote simply, "is before me; his ring on me (*i. e.* on his finger as a sign of victory); and his troops under me." The message was carried over a distance of 250 farsangs (750 miles) in three days.

Fazl bin Rabii now confiscated a sum of 100,000 dirhems presented to Mâmûn as a personal gift by his

1 "Proclaimer of the Truth."
2 "Firm in the Truth (of the Lord)."

father and all his private property which had been left in charge of Naufal, the guardian of his two infant sons. This high-handed act called forth a number of lampoons against the weak Caliph and the rapacious vizier. Amîn's parasites even suggested to him to hold Mâmûn's sons as hostages, and if he did not submit, to put them to death, but this advice he not only reprobated, but punished with imprisonment the persons who ventured to give him the shameful counsel. 170–198 A.H.

Several other armies despatched from Bagdad met with the same fate as the first; and Tâhir cleared the mountainous tract, seized Kazwîn and reached Holwan, which he made his head-quarters. From here he was sent to Ahwâz, leaving Harsama in the north. Mâmûn now assumed the title of *Ameer ul-Mominîn*, "Commander of the Faithful," and the whole of Persia accepted him as Caliph. Fazl bin Sahl was invested with supreme control throughout the principality, "from Tibet to Hamadân, from the Indian Ocean to the Caspian Sea." He combined the offices of minister of war (*Ameer ul-Harb*) with that of chancellor of the exchequer (*Ameer ul-Kharâj*). Ali bin Hishâm was placed in charge of the War Office; whilst the department of revenue was presided over by Nuaim bin Khâzim, assisted by Hassan bin Sahl as secretary. Mâmûn accepted as Caliph.

Whilst these events were happening in the east, Syria was disturbed by a rising headed by a descendant of Muâwiyah I.,[1] who invited the people to accept him as Caliph. A rival claimant appeared at the same time in the person of a grandson of the warrior Maslamah; but

[1] Ali bin Abdullâh bin Khâlid bin Yezîd bin Muâwiyah, known as Sufiâni. His mother's name was Nafîsa, a grand-daughter of Abbâs, son of Ali, who fell with Hussain at Kerbela.

786—814 A.C. their supporters soon melted away, and the two pretenders disappeared as they had risen.

In the meantime, Mâmûn's general had reduced Ahwâz, Yemâma, Bahrain, and Oman, and then making a detour towards the north, had captured Wâsit. The rapidity of his movement, and the submission of the East Arabian sea-board, had its effect upon other places. Abbâs, the son of Hâdi, who was Amîn's governor at Kûfa, acknowledged Mâmûn's authority. He was followed by Mansûr, the son of Mahdi, governor of Basra, and Dâûd, son of Îsa,[1] governor of the Holy Cities. They were all treated with marked consideration, and confirmed in their appointments. Tâhir then turned towards the north; after capturing Madâin, which was still a place of importance, he arrived in the suburbs of Bagdad, whilst Harsama moved down on the capital from the north. Another general, named Zuhair, the son of Musaib, arrived at the same time, and these three now laid siege to Bagdad. Tâhir was stationed in a garden at the Anbar Gate, whilst Harsama was posted at Noorbîn, one of the river exits. The siege lasted for several months; Amîn emptied the treasury for his soldiers and the commonalty who rallied round him; he ended by melting down gold and silver plate, and distributing it among his supporters. Great damage was done to Bagdad in the course of the siege; both sides pulled down palaces and mansions, that stood in the way of attack or defence; half the city was laid in ruin, and the sufferings of the people were heartrending. The notables and leaders began deserting Amîn, but the rabble continued the struggle with great pertinacity. At last, Amîn was driven to take refuge with his mother and family in

Siege of Bagdad.

197 A.H. 813 A.C.

[1] The Îsa whom Mansûr removed from the succession.

the citadel[1] built by Mansûr on the western bank of the river. Here also his position soon became untenable, and he was advised by the few counsellors that still remained by his side to make a dash for Syria. But his own inclinations chimed in with the suggestion of a surrender on condition of being taken to Mâmûn, for he knew and trusted his brother's fidelity. Negotiations were opened accordingly; but Tâhir insisted that Amîn should deliver himself into his hands, whilst the unlucky Caliph was equally obdurate in refusing to place himself in the power of the one-eyed man[2] whom he distrusted, and whom he believed to be personally inimical to him. He offered to surrender himself to Harsama, his father's old and faithful general. The matter at last was settled in this wise: Amîn was to give himself up to Harsama, whilst the signet, the mantle, and the sword were to be delivered to Tâhir. Both the generals were thus to share the glory of his submission. On the night of Sunday the 23rd of Moharram, 198 A.H., Amîn issued after a pathetic parting with his children to go on board Harsama's boat. He was received by the general with every mark of reverence and respect, and the boatmen were ordered to row rapidly towards Harsama's camp. Some of the Persian soldiers, cruel and heartless, who were on the watch, commenced to throw huge stones at the boat; one of them hit the frail Tigris gondola, which filled with water and capsized. Harsama narrowly escaped drowning, being saved by one of his boatmen; Amîn and the Town Magistrate, who was in their company, swam ashore. They were seized by the Persian soldiery, and taken to a neighbouring blockhouse, where

170—198 A.H.

Murder of Amîn, 23rd Moharram, 198 A.H. 814 A.C.

[1] Called the *Medînat ul-Mansûr*; see chap. xxii.

[2] Tâhir had only one eye, but this physical defect, the historians say, was made up by his being ambidexter.

786—814 A.C. they were confined. Amîn was shivering with cold, but the Magistrate covered him with his mantle, and they both lay down for a little rest. In the dead of night, some of the Persians burst open the door, and rushed upon the ill-fated Amîn. He tried to defend himself with a pillow, but the murderers cut him down. Next morning the assassins exhibited the head of the hapless victim on the walls of Bagdad.

When Mâmûn received the news of his brother's unhappy end, he was overwhelmed with grief. He had never dreamt that the consequences of their differences would have this disastrous result. He took immediate steps to punish the murderers, and in order to make up in some degree for the loss of their father, adopted the sons of Amîn as his own; they were confided to Zubaida's care, and when they grew up were married to his daughters. One of them died young. He also confirmed Amîn's family and servants in the enjoyment of the property they possessed.

Thus died Amîn in the twenty-eighth year of his age, after a troublous reign of four years and eight months.

CHAPTER XVIII

THE ABBASSIDES (*continued*)

198—232 A.H., 813—847 A.C.

MÂMÛN THE GREAT—MUTASIM—WÂSIK.

Mâmûn at Merv—Disorders in Bagdad—Death of Imâm Ali ar-Razâ—Mâmûn at Bagdad—War with the Greeks—Rationalism—Mâmûn's death—His character—Intellectual development of the Saracens under Mâmûn—Accession of Mutasim—Change of capital—Formation of the Turkish guard—Capture of Bâbek—Defeat of the Greeks —Death of Mutasim—Accession of Wâsik—His character—His death.

Mâmûn at Merv.

HAD Mâmûn moved at once upon Bagdad, the disorders of the next few years would have been avoided. But he relied on Fazl bin Sahl, his vizier, and was content to leave to him the absolute and uncontrolled direction of the government, spending his own time in philosophical discussions with the savants and scholars who formed his court. Fazl on his side was anxious to keep the sovereign at Merv, where he was entirely under the ambitious minister's influence. No information regarding the real state of affairs in the west was allowed to reach the Caliph, and he was thus kept in complete ignorance of the events that were taking place in Irâk and Syria.

Disorders in Irâk and Arabia.

Shortly after Amîn's death a partisan of the Ommeyades named Nasr[1] rose against Mâmûn in Mesopotamia, and defied the Imperial troops for over five years. In Irâk,

[1] Son of Shabas of the tribe of Okail.

813—847 A.C. the Bedouins, joined by all the bad characters of the neighbourhood, rose against Hassan bin Sahl, who had been appointed by his brother as governor of Irâk. The general confusion in the western provinces of the empire was not without its effects on the more ambitious scions of the House of Ali. They and some of the descendants of his brother Jaafar, surnamed Tayyâr, who had hitherto lived in comparative obscurity, perhaps felt that the time had arrived when they would be restored to their rights. Jamâdi II. 199 A.H. 814 A.C. An Alide commonly known as Ibn Tabâ-Tabâ appeared in Kûfa, and invited the people to take the oath of allegiance to the family of the Prophet. He was supported by Abû Sarâya, a quondam freebooter. Combining their forces they defeated Hassan bin Sahl, and made themselves masters of the whole of Southern Irâk. Ibn Tabâ-Tabâ was poisoned soon after by his supporter, who chose in his place a young lad belonging to the Alides.

Whilst these events were taking place on the banks of the Tigris, in Hijâz a son of the Imâm Jaafar as-Sâdik was elected Caliph. The whole country from the borders of Persia to Yemen was thus involved in internecine strife, and rapine and slaughter raged through the land. But none of this news was allowed to reach Mâmûn. At last the rising in Irâk assumed such formidable dimensions that Fazl was compelled, in spite of his jealousy, to send Harsama against Abû Sarâya. The rebel was defeated and killed, and the young lad whom he had elected as Caliph was sent to Merv, where he afterwards became a *protégé* of Mâmûn. After he had quelled the insurrection in Irâk, Harsama was ordered to go to Egypt, but the old warrior refused to obey the vizier's orders until he had opened the Caliph's eyes to the dangers that surrounded him. He hurried to Merv, and arrived suddenly in the royal presence. Hot words passed on both sides, and Harsama, with a soldierly bluntness, told Mâmûn how the empire was drifting to ruin. Hardly had he left the sovereign on his way to his residence, than he was set upon by the vizier's myrmidons, and so severely assaulted that he died of his injuries a few days after. To Mâmûn's inquiries he was represented as lying ill at home, and not until some time after did the Caliph know how the state had lost an invaluable servant. The news of Harsama's death caused a violent riot among the troops at Bagdad, with whom he was extremely popular, and fighting commenced anew all round. The people refused to obey Hassan bin Sahl, or his brother Fazl, calling him "a Magian son of a Magian," and elected in Hassan's place as governor, Mansûr bin Mahdi, who accepted the government provisionally on the express condition that he would hold it until such time as Mâmûn came himself or deputed somebody else.

198—232 A.H.

Harsama's death.

In the year 200 A.H. Mâmûn commenced to put into execution his long-formed project of making over the Caliphate to the House of Mohammed. With this object he sent for the Fatimide Imâm Ali III.,[1] son of Mûsa al-Kâzim, from Medîna. He openly avowed that he had searched for a successor in his own family,[2] as well as in that of the Alides, and had found none so qualified to fill the office of Pontiff as the son of Mûsa. Accordingly on the second of Ramazân in the year 201, the oath of fealty was taken to him as the heir apparent to the Caliphate, under the title of *ar-Rizâ min Âl-Mohammed*, "the acceptable among the children of Mohammed," —shortly *ar-Rizâ*, "the Acceptable." Henceforth he is

200 A.H. 815 A.C. Nomination of Imâm Ali *ar-Rizâ* as successor to the Caliphate.

2nd Ramazân, 201 A.H.

[1] See *ante*, p. 243.

[2] A census of the Abbassides taken at this time showed that they amounted to thirty-three thousand men, women, and children.

813—847 A.C. called in history ar-Rizâ.[1] Mâmûn directed at the same time that black, the colour of his house, should be abandoned and green, the colour of the Fatimides, adopted as the imperial livery. The news of the nomination of Ali ar-Rizâ as successor to the Caliphate, threw the Abbasside clan in Bagdad into frenzy. They raised Ibrâhim bin Mahdi to the throne, and expelled Hassan's officers from the capital. The disorders in Bagdad and the neighbouring cities became frightful; there was absolutely no government, and the robbers and bad characters indulged in rapine and violence in open daylight. Matters at last became so serious that the respectable classes were compelled to take measures for their own safety. They formed vigilance committees for the enforcement of law and the maintenance of order; and any ruffian caught in the commission of offence against society promptly met his deserts. These committees continued in working order until the arrival of Mâmûn at Bagdad. In Southern Irâk and Hijâz the condition of affairs was equally bad: neither Ibrâhim nor Hassan bin Sahl exercised any authority, and riots attended with murder and arson were rife in every city. It seemed as if under the selfish mismanagement of the Persian vizier, the empire of Mâmûn would fall to pieces. In this crisis the Imâm Ali ar-Rizâ betook himself to Mâmûn and acquainted him with the true state of affairs; he told him of the suppression of truth on the part of the vizier, of Ibrâhim's election, of the unpopularity amongst the Abbassides of his own nomination as Mâmûn's successor, and the whole history of events since the unfortunate death of Amîn. The Caliph was staggered, and naturally asked if any one else knew of the facts Rizâ had told him. The Imâm gave the names of some chiefs of

Disorders in Bagdad.

[1] His descendants are called Rizawî.

the army; they were sent for, and on receiving a guarantee of protection against the vizier's revenge, they corroborated every word the Imâm had said; they told him how the Caliphate had lost in Harsama a faithful and tried servant through Fazl's cruel vindictiveness, and that Ibrâhim bin Mahdi, far from being Mâmûn's deputy, as the vizier had represented him to be, was recognised by the Banû Abbâs as the *Sunni* Caliph in contradistinction to Mâmûn, whom they considered heretical. The scales fell from the Caliph's eyes; the order was issued for an immediate march towards the west; and the day following Mâmûn started with his whole Court for Bagdad. Fazl finding that his plot had miscarried, and unable to do any harm to the Imâm ar-Rizâ, who was protected by his position, wreaked his vengeance upon those who were in some way subordinate to him. He had some flogged; others were thrown into prison; whilst not a few had their beards plucked out. The Imâm ar-Rizâ again went to Mâmûn and told him of the vizier's cruelties. The Caliph replied that he could not at once deprive Fazl of his powers, but must do so by slow degrees. Mâmûn's resolve to dismiss Fazl was, however, anticipated by the host of irreconcilable enemies the Persian had raised against himself, and he was assassinated in his bath at Sarrakhs, a day's journey from Merv. The murderers were caught, and together with the instigators suffered the penalty of death.

198—232 A.H.

Mâmûn marches to Bagdad.

At Tûs, Mâmûn tarried a while by his father's tomb. Here he lost his faithful friend and adviser, the Imâm ar-Rizâ, who had practically saved his empire. The Imâm died suddenly,[1] and was succeeded by his son

Safar 203 A.H. August, 818 A.C. Death of Imâm Ali ar-Rizâ.

[1] The story that Mâmûn instigated the murder of Fazl, or had the Imâm ar-Rizâ poisoned, is a malicious fabrication, and does not stand the scrutiny of facts or the slightest historical criticism.

813—847 A.C. Mohammed, surnamed *Jâwwâd* (the generous) and *Takî* (the pious) in the apostolical chair. Mâmûn mourned for him with unaffected grief; and a mausoleum was built over the grave, which has since become the resort of Shiah pilgrims from all parts of the world, and is now known as Meshed (*Mash-had*, or *Mash-had Mukkaddas*, the holy sepulchre). After the obsequies of the Imâm were over, the Caliph continued his march towards the capital, stopping at every place of importance. The length of the stay varied with the importance of the city. At Nahrwân, where he stayed eight days, he was met by the military chiefs, the notables of Bagdad, and the members of his family (the Banû Abbâs). Up to this time everybody wore green; at the request of Tâhir, who had come from Rakka to wait on Mâmûn, and of other principal men, the Abbasside colour was resumed.

204 A.H. 819 A.C. Arrival of Mâmûn at Bagdad. Mâmûn's entry into Bagdad was of a triumphal character. The streets were decorated, the people wore gala dress, and on every side was rejoicing at the Caliph's return to the seat of government. With Mâmûn's arrival all disorders ceased, and the vigilance committees formed for the protection of the citizens were dissolved. Mâmûn applied himself vigorously to the work of reorganising the administration and repairing the ravages committed in the city during the siege. On one of his rounds of inspection, he was accompanied by his chamberlain Ahmed, son of Abû Khâlid,[1] who described to him the general distress of the times. Mâmûn observed in reply that there were three classes of people in Bagdad, one the oppressed (*Mazlûm*), the other the oppressors (*Zâlim*), whilst a third were neither the one nor the other, and that these latter were at the

[1] Nicknamed *Ahwal*, "the squint-eyed." He afterwards became Mâmûn's vizier.

root of all mischief. And the historian remarks this was the real fact.[1] 198—232 A.H.

The government of the Holy Cities was entrusted to an Alide; Kûfa and Basra were given to two brothers of the Caliph, whilst the captaincy of the guard was bestowed on Tâhir. The following year, Tâhir applied for and obtained the viceroyalty of the East, which he held until his death, two years later. Talha, his son, was then appointed in his place, and he governed the province for seven years.

Tâhir appointed Viceroy of the East. 205 A.H. 820 A.C. Death of Tâhir, Jamâdi I. 207 A.H. 822 A.C.

Another son of Tâhir, named Abdullâh, equally capable as a general, but a far more humane man, was entrusted with the government of Syria and Egypt, together with the task of reducing Nasr Okaili. After some hard fighting the rebel was forced to sue for quarter. His castle of Kaisân was rased to the ground and he himself was sent to Court, where, with his usual forbearance, Mâmûn pardoned him. After restoring order in Mesopotamia, Abdullâh bin Tâhir proceeded to Egypt, where also an insurrection was in progress. He crushed the rebels in a single battle. A large body of Spanish Moslems expelled from Andalusia by the Ommeyade sovereign of that country had arrived in Egypt accompanied by their families, and by their unruly conduct caused disturbances in Alexandria. Abdullâh called upon them either to deliver up their arms or to leave the province. They asked for permission to go to Crete (Ikritash), which was at once accorded. These unwelcome guests, on their departure, were furnished with supplies and such assistance as they needed for the

[1] In a well-regulated city every citizen is interested in the maintenance of order. The people who pharisaically stood aloof from public affairs, gave to the disorderly classes an opportunity to break the law with impunity.

813—847 A.C. conquest of the island. They and a number of volunteers who joined in the enterprise sailed for Crete, where

Conquest of Crete. 210 A.H. 825 A.C. they easily effected a landing; after a short struggle the bulk of the islanders submitted, and the invaders settled themselves in their conquest, where they and their descendants have dwelt ever since, and acquired as good a title to be there as the Saxon colonists in England.

Conquest of Sicily. 208 A.H. 823 A.C. Two years previously Ziâdatullâh Aghlab had brought the island of Sicily under the sway of the Caliph.

Rebellions in Yemen and Khorâsân were quelled without difficulty, and in both cases the insurgents were treated with exceptional leniency.

About this time Mâmûn was startled by the discovery of a dangerous conspiracy for his assassination, headed by several prominent Abbassides. The chief conspirators met with the just deserts of their crime, but the rank and file received a complete pardon.

Ramazân 210 A.H. 825-826 A.C. Marriage with Bûrân. In the Ramazân of this year Mâmûn married Khadîja, surnamed Bûrân, the beautiful daughter of his vizier Hassan bin Sahl, and to whom he was betrothed whilst at Merv. The splendour of the nuptials gives some idea of the magnificence of the Court of Bagdad at this epoch.

The marriage was celebrated with great festivals and rejoicings at a place called Fam us-Silh,[1] where Hassan resided at the time. Here the vizier entertained the whole company for seventeen days[2] on a lavish and gorgeous scale. Zubaida and her daughter with other ladies of the imperial household were present at this wedding; their surpassing beauty and the magnificence

[1] *The mouth of the Silh.* As-Silh was a large canal which joined the Tigris some miles above Wâsit. Fam us-Silh was situated on the junction of the canal and the river.

[2] The expenses of Hassan amounted to 50 million dirhems.

of their attire were sung by the poets invited on the occasion. But the most beauteous of them all was the bride herself. At the ceremony her grandmother showered upon the Caliph and his bride from a tray of gold a thousand pearls of unique size and splendour; they were collected under his orders, made into a necklace, and given to the young queen. The hymeneal apartment was lighted by a candle of ambergris, weighing eighty pounds, fixed in a candlestick of gold. When the imperial party was departing the vizier presented the chief officers of state with robes of honour, and showered balls of musk upon the princes and chiefs who accompanied the Caliph. Each of these balls contained a ticket on which was inscribed the name of an estate, or a slave or a team of horses, or some such gift; the recipient then took it to an agent who delivered to him the property which had fallen to his lot. Among the common people he scattered gold and silver coins, balls of musk, and eggs of amber. In order to recoup Hassan for his expenses, Mâmûn granted to him a year's revenue of Fars and Ahwâz (ancient Susiana). Bûrân is one of the most notable women in Islâm. By her wit and beauty, joined to her accomplishments and virtues, she succeeded in obtaining great influence over her husband, which was always exercised for the welfare of others. Her charity was profuse, and she was the founder of several hospitals and seminaries for women in Bagdad. She survived Mâmûn nearly fifty years, and thus witnessed the empire not only in the height of its glory, but also in the commencement of its decline.[1]

198—232 A.H.

Early in Mâmûn's reign, whilst the empire was convulsed by internecine struggle and warfare, a brigand of the name of Bâbek had made himself the master of a

201 A.H. 816 A.C.

Bâbek the Nihilist.

[1] She died in 883 A.C.

813—847 A.C. stronghold in one of the most inaccessible defiles of Mazendrân. He belonged to the Magian sect of Khurramièh, who believed in metempsychosis, and recognised none of the rules of morality enforced by Judaism, Christianity, or Islâm. From his mountain fortress he mercilessly harried the surrounding country, slaughtered the men and carried away the women, Christian and Moslem, into loathsome captivity. Army after army was despatched against him, but from his inaccessible position he continued for several years to defy all efforts to crush him. Hard pressed at one time by the imperial troops, he entered into relations with the Greeks, and instigated them to make a diversion in his favour by invading the Moslem territories. The throne of Byzantium was occupied by Theophilus, the son of Michael the Stammerer.[1] Joining hands with the nihilistic brigand, the Christian emperor raided into the Saracenic dominions and massacred a large number of Moslems. To repel this gratuitous and treacherous attack Mâmûn took the field in person, and in three successive campaigns so completely crushed the enemy that he was obliged to sue for peace. These incessant wars created a deadly hostility between the Greeks and the Arabs, and left a legacy of hatred and bitterness, the remains of which still linger in the West. After beating the Greeks the Caliph proceeded to Egypt; and a Turkish general of the name of Afshîn, who was now coming into prominence, reduced

War with the Byzantines.

[1] Ibn ul-Athîr calls this Michael also the son of Jurjis, and says he ruled for nine years. On his death, in 209 A.H., he was succeeded by his son Theophilus (Tôfîl). We know from Byzantine histories how Michael the Stammerer (the father of Theophilus) came to the throne. He was a general of Leo the Armenian; he was ordered by him to be burnt alive in the furnace of the private bath, but a short respite enabled the supporters of the condemned general to murder the emperor and place Michael on the throne.

al-Ferma, the farthest part of Upper Egypt, where the insurgents, driven from the lower tracts, had found refuge. To guard against the ever-recurring attacks of the Greeks, and the better to hold them in check, Mâmûn began the foundation of a strongly fortified military settlement at Tyana, seventy miles north of Tarsus. It was hardly finished when death overtook him. Encamped in the vicinity of a place called Bidândûn, not far from Tarsus, Mâmûn and his brother were sitting on a hot autumn day by the banks of a river which gave the town its name, laving their feet in its icy cold water. The same night they were attacked with violent fever. Mâmûn was brought in that condition to Tarsus, where he died shortly after, and was buried within the gardens of a faithful servant of his father. Mutasim recovered, and was able to receive his brother's dying injunctions. With his last breath Mâmûn enjoined his successor carefully to guard the interests of his subjects, to protect them from oppression, to do justice, and never to transgress the law in the punishment of offences. Mâmûn was born in the year 170 of the Hegira on the very day Hârûn, his father, ascended the throne, and reigned for twenty years and six months, besides the period "when prayers were offered for him in Mecca and Medîna and Amîn was besieged in Bagdad." He is described as a well-built, good-looking man of imposing appearance. "He was the most distinguished of the House of Abbâs," says one of the annalists, "for his prudence, his determination, his clemency and judgment, his sagacity and awe-inspiring aspect, his intrepidity, majesty, and liberality. He had many eminent qualities, and a long series of memorable actions are recorded of him. Of the House of Abbâs none wiser than he ever ruled the Caliphate."

198—232 A.H.

18th Rajjab, 218 A.H. 9th August, 833 A.C.

Death of Mâmûn.

His character

813—847 A.C.

Civilisation and culture.

Mâmûn's Caliphate constitutes the most glorious epoch in Saracenic history, and has been justly called the Augustan age of Islâm. The twenty years of his reign have left enduring monuments of the intellectual development of the Moslems in all directions of thought. Their achievements were not restricted to any particular branch of science or literature, but ranged over the whole course of the domain of intellect; speculative philosophy and *belles lettres* were cultivated with as much avidity as the exact sciences. Mathematics, astronomy, the science of medicine, etc., all made gigantic strides during this glorious period of Asiatic civilisation; its intellectual heritage passed both into Saracenic Spain and Christian Constantinople, whence it descended to modern Europe. Mâmûn considered that the true happiness of his people consisted in education and culture. He did not wish the progress of knowledge to depend on the accidental munificence of individual Caliphs or nobles of the state, and with a true regard for the dignity of letters, he made it independent of casual gifts by creating permanent endowments for its promotion and support. Schools and colleges were opened in all directions, and richly endowed. "We see for the first time," says Oelsner, "perhaps in the history of the world, a religious and despotic government allied to philosophy, preparing and partaking in its triumphs." In his sagacious tolerance, Mâmûn recognised no distinction of creed or race; all his subjects were declared eligible for public offices, and every religious distinction was effaced. After the fall of the republic and the establishment of an autocracy, the ministers were the only advisers of the sovereign.

State Council of Mâmûn.

Mâmûn established a regular Council of State, composed of representatives from all the communities under his sway. It thus included Moslems, Jews, Christians, Sabæans, and Zoroastrians. Liberty of conscience and freedom of worship had been always enjoyed by non-Moslems under the Islâmic *régime;* any occasional variation in this policy was due to the peculiar temperament of some local governor. Under Mâmûn, however, the liberality towards other religions was large-hearted and exemplary. In his reign we hear of eleven thousand Christian churches besides hundreds of synagogues and fire-temples. The patriarchs of Jerusalem and Antioch were the heads of the Christian Church. After the patriarch came the *Jasâlik* (*Catholicos*), then the *Metrân* (metropolitan), then the *Iskaf* (bishop), and lastly the *Kissîs* (the priest). They all retained the privileges and immunities they had enjoyed under sovereigns of their own creed. 198—232 A.H.

Rationalism under Mâmûn.

With the eye of genius Mâmûn foresaw the trend of the dogmas that were gradually coming into force in the Church of which he was the head; the rigidity they were acquiring with the efflux of time, and their ultimate consequences on society and state. In his judgment, adherence to those doctrines was worse than treason, for their tendency was to stifle all political and social development, and end in the destruction of the commonwealth. He foresaw the effect of swathing the mind of man with inflexible dogmas. He, therefore, applied himself vigorously, during the last four years of his reign, to the task of secularising the state, and of emancipating the human intellect from the shackles which doctors and jurists were beginning to place upon it. No one was better qualified than he for this great work of reform. In his knowledge of the traditions and jurisprudence he excelled most of the doctors of his time; his study of the Koran was profound and careful; he was a disciple of the

813–847 A.C.

apostolical Imâm ar-Rizâ, from whom he imbibed his love for philosophy and science and that liberalism which forms a distinguishing feature in the teachings of "the philosophers of the House of Mohammed." The first half of the second century had already witnessed the Dissent of Wâsil bin Aata.[1] Wâsil was originally a disciple of the Imâm Jaafar as-Sâdik, from whom he learnt the value of Human Reason. He afterwards attended the lectures of Hassan al-Basri,[2] from whom, however, he seceded on a question of religious dogma. His followers are, in consequence of his secession, called Mutazilas[3] or Dissenters, and the system that he founded was designated as the *Mazhab ul-Itizâl*, the Dissenting Church. The Established Church inculcated several doctrines which Wâsil considered as not only opposed to human reason, but as in direct conflict with the teachings of the Koran and of the Prophet. For example, it taught that every human act was pre-ordained—in other words, that man was not a free agent; that in the Day of Judgment there will be a corporeal resurrection, and that God will be seen with the corporeal eye; that the attributes of God were distinct from His Essence, and that the Koran was uncreated, existing from the beginning, co-eternal with Him. From the latter opinion it followed that every enunciation of a temporary character called for by the requirements of a primitive and changeable society must be converted into permanent immutable law.

Mazhab ul-Itizâl. The Dissenting Church.

The Mutazilas.

The Mutazilas, on the other hand, maintained in agreement with the apostolical Imâms that man was a

[1] See *ante*, p. 207.

[2] *Ibid.*

[3] Weil terms the Mutazilites, the Protestants and Rationalists of Islâm.

free agent in the choice of good and evil; that there would be no corporeal resurrection, nor could God be seen by corporeal sight, for that would imply that He Himself was a body; that the attributes of the Deity are not separate from His Essence, and that the Koran was created. They affirmed further that there is no eternal law as regards human actions; that the Divine ordinances which regulate the conduct of men are the results of growth and development,[1] and are subject to the same process of change to which the Creator has subjected the universe at large. Mâmûn adopted the Mutazilite doctrines and tried to introduce them in his dominions, as he considered the safety of Islâm, and all hope of progress, depended on their general adoption. In the year 217 A.H. he sent a mandate to the governor of Bagdad to summon the leading doctors, and to test them on the essential doctrines[2] and to report their answers. Most of the judges and doctors of Bagdad, either from conviction or from policy, expressed their agreement with the views of the Caliph. A few remained unyielding and rebellious. Among them all Ahmed bin Hanbal[3] proved the most reactionary. Had Mâmûn lived longer, his personality, his genius and erudition would have overborne the contumacious opposition of the few who viewed with rancour or alarm all signs of development. His two immediate successors followed in his footsteps, and tried to con-

198—232 A.H.

Islâmic Rationalism.

[1] For a full account of the Mutazilite doctrines, see the *Spirit of Islam*, new ed, pp. 416–422.

[2] The rescript issued by him is a remarkable document, and is worthy of serious study.

[3] Imâm Ahmed bin Hanbal became the founder of the fourth school of Sunni law. The fanaticism of Ibn Hanbal's followers was, under the later Caliphs, the cause of incessant disorders, riots, and bloodshed.

813—847 A.C.

tinue his work, but without his ability or the breadth of his comprehension. Under them Rationalism acquired a predominance such as it has perhaps not gained even in modern times in European countries. The Rationalists preached in the mosques and lectured in the colleges; they had the moulding of the character of the nation's youth in their hands; they were the chief counsellors of the Caliphs, and it cannot be gainsaid that they used their influence wisely. As professors, preachers, scientists, physicians, viziers, or provincial governors, they helped in the growth and development of the Saracenic nation.

Science and Literature.

Mâmûn's reign was unquestionably the most brilliant and glorious of all in the history of Islâm. The study and cultivation of humanitarian science is the best index to a nation's development. Mâmûn's court was crowded with men of science and letters; with poets, physicians, and philosophers from every part of the civilised world and of divers creeds and nationalities. To each comer was extended, without any racial difference, a lavish patronage which was shared equally by historians, philologers, grammarians, and collectors of traditions who had gathered in the capital. To use the expression of a great French historian, whose sympathy with the Arab genius is as marked as his appreciation of their civilisation and intellectual achievements is keen and true, Mâmûn gave his name to the century of which he assured the literary glory. To the son of Hârûn belongs the glory of completing the work commenced by his grandfather, Mansûr. Mâmûn, surrounded by the *élite* of savants and artists, collected afresh the writings of the school of Alexandria, and by his connection with the emperors of Constantinople secured from Athens the best philosophical works of ancient Greece. As soon as they were brought to Bagdad they were translated by competent scholars and issued to the public. The translation of works from Greek, Syriac, and Chaldaic was under the supervision of Costa the son of Luke; from ancient Persian, under Yahya bin Hârûn; from Sanscrit under Dûbân the Brahmin. Vast impetus was also given to original research and production by the establishment of special departments under qualified professors for the promotion and prosecution of special branches of study, and authorship was encouraged by munificent allowances. 198—232 A.H.

The astronomical observations made in Mâmûn's reign in connection with the equinoxes, the eclipses, the apparitions of the comets and other celestial phenomena were most important. The size of the earth was calculated from the measurement of a degree on the shores of the Red Sea—this at a time when Christian Europe was asserting the flatness of the earth. Abu'l Hassan invented the telescope, of which he speaks as "a tube to the extremities of which were attached diopters." These "tubes" were improved and used afterwards in the observatories of Marâgha and Cairo with great success. Innumerable works on arithmetic, geometry, philosophy, astronomy, meteorology, optics, mechanics, medicine, etc., were compiled and issued to the public. Special attention was devoted to the study of medicine, and the number of distinguished physicians who figure as the companions of the sovereign give some index to the character of Mâmûn. The first observatory in Islâm was established by Mâmûn at Shamâssia on the plains of Tadmor. Afterwards several others were created at Wâsit, Apamea, etc.

Cultivation of Persian Literature.

The Arab Conquest had naturally thrown into the background the language and literature of ancient Persia.

813—847 A.C. The people themselves in the pursuit of Arabic neglected their mother tongue. By an unstinted patronage, Mâmûn revived the old learning and gave an impetus to the cultivation of the Persian language, enriched as it was by thousands of Arabic words. The poet Abbâs (Marvazi),[1] the founder of modern Persian poetry, flourished in this reign.

Philosophical Reunions. Tuesdays were set apart for literary, philosophical, and scientific discussions. The scholars and savants attended at the palace in the forenoon, where they were entertained by the chamberlain at a royal breakfast. After the repast they were ushered into the chamber set apart for these reunions, at which the Caliph presided. The assemblage took leave of the sovereign after the evening prayers, when they were again entertained at supper. The other days of the week were scrupulously devoted to the business of the state; no detail was missed, no account passed unexamined, no petition overlooked. Exceptionally humane and forbearing, he never imposed punishment unless compelled by the exigencies of government. Mâmûn's tact. The tact with which he once silenced a zealot who, unbidden, had entered the royal presence, shows Mâmûn's genius for governing the people over whom he was placed. The Khâriji came fearlessly towards the Caliph, but stopped near the edge of the carpet and gave the usual salutation. Then he asked the Caliph, "Tell me regarding this seat which thou occupiest—dost thou sit there with the unanimous consent of the people or by violence and force?" Mâmûn at once replied, "Neither the one nor the other; but one who governed the affairs of the Moslems bequeathed it to me and to my brother, and

[1] Of Marv (Merv).

when the authority devolved upon me I felt that I needed the unanimous consent of the people, but I saw that if I abandoned the government, the security of Islâm would be disturbed, the highways would be infested with robbers, and public affairs would fall into confusion, and there would be strife and disorder by which the Moslems would be hindered from going on pilgrimage and doing their duty, wherefore I arose in defence of the people, until they should be of accord upon one man whom they should approve, and I would then resign the government to him: now when they agree upon a man, I will abdicate in his favour." The man replied, "Peace be to you and the mercy of God and His blessing," and he departed. Mâmûn sent one of his attendants to follow him. From the report of the messenger it appeared that he was the leader of a band of zealots who had gathered for the purpose of a rising, but were completely disarmed by Mâmûn's tact. 198—232 A.H.

Shortly before his death Mâmûn had issued a rescript nominating his brother *Abû Ishâk* Mohammed, surnamed *al-Mutasim b'Illâh*[1] (shortly Mutasim), his successor to the Caliphate. It is difficult to understand at this distance of time the reasons which led Mâmûn to supersede his son Abbâs, who was popular with the army, certainly with the Arabian section. Possibly he may have thought him impressionable and not likely to pursue the policy he had laid down for the guidance of the state. Perhaps he considered the stronger and maturer character of Mutasim as more certain of maintaining a continuity of action. *Abû Ishâk* Mohammed, *Mutasim b'Illâh.* 218—227 A.H. 833—842 A.C.

The soldiery were at first clamorous for the election of Abbâs, but he, mindful of his father's dying wishes, took the

[1] "He who is steadfast in the Lord." From this time the Caliphs began to use titles of this kind.

813—847 A.C.

oath of fealty to his uncle, whereupon the troops withdrew their demand and followed his example. Mutasim was accordingly proclaimed[1] Caliph at Tarsus. With a short-sightedness which is unintelligible, he stopped the building of Tyana and brought back to Tarsus the stores, provisions, and garrisons intended for that place. With this exception he endeavoured to follow scrupulously in the footsteps of his brother. His great mistake, however, was the formation of a standing military corps composed of Turks[2] and other foreigners, which ultimately proved the ruin of the Caliphate. This corps was recruited by Turkish *mamlukes*[3] and mercenaries from Central Asia and the highlands of Yemen and Egypt. Those who came from Transoxiana were called the *Ferâghina*,[4] whilst the Africans and Yemenis were named the *Maghâriba* or westerns. They were commanded by their own officers who were directly under the sovereign. They were thus completely separate from the Arab and Persian troops. And it is not surprising that before long they assumed the part of the Prætorian guards of the Roman Empire, deposing and setting up sovereigns at their own will and pleasure. Dressed in splendid uniform they galloped recklessly through the streets of Bagdad, knocking down everybody in their way. There was a howl of rage in the capital. The infatuated sovereign, apprehensive of a riot, removed with his favourite corps to a place called Sâmarra, several days' journey to the north-west of Bagdad. Sâmarra, or

19th Rajab, 218 A.H. 10th Aug. 833 A.C.

Formation of the Turkish Corps.

Change of capital.

[1] Masûdi mentions the 17th Rajab as the date of his accession.

[2] The Turks or Turkomans of those days must not be confounded with the modern Ottomans. There is as much affinity between them as between the Saxons of the eighth century and the Englishmen of the present day.

[3] Slaves.

[4] From Ferghâna.

Surra-man-Raa[1] as it now began to be called, became an Aldershot of Mutasim, who built for himself a palace there, with barracks for two hundred and fifty thousand soldiers and stables for a hundred and sixty thousand horses. Portions of the city were allotted to the Turkish chiefs, whose mansions vied in grandeur with the Caliph's residence. 198—232 A.H.

The Jâts in Irâk.

This reign is remarkable for the appearance on the banks of the Tigris, of the Indian tribe of Jâts, called by the Arab historians Zatt. How they came there we are not told, but it is said they numbered seventeen thousand souls. Their depredations caused Mutasim to send a small force against them, and they were brought in boats as prisoners to Bagdad for the Caliph to see the costume of their women. They were then settled on the frontiers of Cilicia. Here, without any cause whatsoever, they were attacked by the Greeks; the bulk were massacred, the survivors were taken away as captives and dispersed in Thrace.[2] In 835 A.C. the apostolical Imâm Mohammed at-Taki died at Bagdad, whilst on a visit to Mutasim with his wife Umm ul-Fazl, the daughter of Mâmûn. He was succeeded by his son Ali.

The ravages of Bâbek had latterly spread in every direction, and it became a matter of vital importance to reduce him. Mutasim sent Afshîn, one of his best Turkish generals, against the brigand. After a series of carefully conducted operations Afshîn captured Bâbek's stronghold. His son and other relatives submitted, and were sent to Bagdad, where they received the royal pardon, and were treated with kindness. He and his brother escaped to Armenia, where they were

[1] *Delighted was he who saw (it).*

[2] The Bohemians, the Zingaries, the gypsies, all seem to be the descendants of these poor captives, the remnants of the Zatt.

813—847 A.C.

Capture and death of Bâbek.

seized by an Armenian chief and delivered to Afshîn. They were brought to Bagdad; their crimes against humanity were too great and revolting for pardon. They were first paraded in the streets on an elephant, and then put to death.[1] Seven thousand women, Christian and Moslem, were released by Afshîn, and restored to their homes. The reception of the victorious general was royal, and he was covered with honours and presents, but his end was sorrowful.

War with the Byzantines.

Whilst Afshîn was engaged in Mazendrân, the Byzantine emperor, who was in alliance with Bâbek, attempted a diversion in his favour. He invaded Cappadocia, devastated the Moslem territories, sacked and burned their cities, put the men to the sword, and carried away the women and children into slavery. Zibatra (Zapetron), Mutasim's birthplace, was reduced to ashes; the men were either killed or blinded with red-hot irons; others were subjected to mutilation. The news of these barbarities threw Mutasim into a furious rage, and he swore dire vengeance. Rapidly collecting his army, he marched against the treacherous and brutal Greeks. His vanguard met Theophilus beyond Ancyra, and inflicted on him a terrible defeat. The Caliph then marched on Amorium, the birthplace of Theophilus. After a siege of fifty days it was carried by storm, and rased to the ground; thirty thousand men were put to the sword, the rest were carried away to Bagdad with Batis (Ætius), the Greek commander. Mutasim now directed his march towards the Propontis and Bosphorus with the object of striking a final blow at the Greek power. But the discovery of a dangerous plot within his own camp withheld

[1] As we descend into later times, the punishments approach gradually the character of those inflicted by the Byzantines, amputation of the limbs, blinding, etc.

him. Some of the Arab generals, jealous of the influence possessed by the Turks, and disgusted with the way in which they were treated by the Caliph, entered into a conspiracy with the young and misguided Abbâs to assassinate Mutasim. The plot was discovered by chance, and appeared to be so extensive, that it upset the Caliph's plans. Abbâs and his fellow-conspirators were executed, and Mutasim marched back to Sâmarra after concluding a convention with Theophilus, whom the capture of Amorium had thoroughly cowed. 198—232 A.H.

In the year 224 A.H. the Magian prince of Tabaristân, named Mâziâr, raised the standard of revolt. Under the impression that Abdullâh bin Tâhir would not be able to suppress Mâziâr's revolt, and that Mutasim would be compelled to appoint him as Viceroy of the East in place of Abdullâh, Afshîn secretly instigated the Magian chief to fight to the bitter end. But Mâziâr was captured by Abdullâh and sent to Bagdad. In the Caliph's presence, he exposed Afshîn's treachery, and showed the letters he had received. Mâziàr was executed, and Afshîn was imprisoned in his own house and starved to death. This Turkish chief was apparently a man of culture, for the story that he possessed books written in strange characters, and that his house was full of idols, seems to show that he was rather in advance of the times, and liked to surround himself with literature and curiosities gathered from different parts. Mutasim was seized with a fatal illness shortly after, and died on the 19th of Rabi I. 227 A.H. 839 A.C.

Mutasim's death, 19th Rabi I. 227 A.H. January 5, 842 A.C.

Mutasim is said to have promoted agriculture, and taken a great interest in the development of the natural resources of the empire. Though fiery in temper and somewhat hard of heart, the influence of the chief

813—847 A.C. judge, Ahmed, the son of Abû Duwâd, saved him from many cruel acts. The Kâzi's advice often neutralised the evil counsels of Mutasim's vizier. "Ahmed," says Masûdi, "was one of those privileged men on whom God bestows His gifts of nature, one of those whom He directs in the right path, and inspires with the love of truth and practice of virtue." Ahmed, son of Abû Duwâd, was a leader of the Mutazilites.[1]

Abû Jaafar Hârûn, *al-Wâsik b'Illâh.* 227—232 A.H. 842—849 A.C. Mutasim was succeeded on the throne by his son, *Abû Jaafar* Hârûn, *Wâsik b'Illâh.*[2] Wâsik's character has been grossly misrepresented by some of the orthodox writers. In reality, he was an excellent sovereign,—generous, "forbearing and patient under annoyance." His administration was firm and enlightened. Although fond of good cheer, his private life was above reproach. He patronised literature and science, and encouraged industry and commerce. With a literary turn of mind he joined great proficiency in music, and is said to have composed a hundred airs and melodies. His charity was unbounded, and under his government there was not a single mendicant within the empire. In this reign an interchange of prisoners on an extensive scale took place between the Greeks and the Saracens.

Wâsik continued the fatal mistake made by his father, of aggrandising the Turks at the expense of the Arabs and Persians. He appointed Ashnâs the Sultan or lieutenant of the empire, and decorated him with a jewelled girdle and sword. Wâsik tried hard to diffuse the Rationalistic doctrines among the people, but his endeavours were counteracted by the reactionary jurists, who secretly worked against him. His premature death

[1] Suyûti, in his orthodoxy, anathematises Ahmed's memory.

[2] "He who is trustful in (the help of) the Lord."

was an irreparable calamity, for with him ended the glory of the Abbassides. For the next two centuries their history presents a confused picture of sovereigns coming to the throne without power, and descending to the grave without regret. Wâsik died at *Surraman-ar-Raa* on the 24th Zu'l Hijja, 232 A.H.

198—232 A.H.

Death of Wâsik, 11th August, 847 A.C.

CHAPTER XIX

THE ABBASSIDES—(*continued*)

232—454 A.H., 847—1063 A.C.

MUTAWWAKIL TO KÂIM

Mutawakkil, the Nero of the Arabs—The Decline of the Empire—Muntassir—Mustaîn—Mutazz—The Negro Insurrection—The Suffârides—Muhtadi—Mutamid—The Negro Insurrection suppressed—Mutazid—The Rise of the Fatimides—The Carmathians—Their devastations—Muktafi—Restoration of Egypt to the Caliphate—The Sâmânides—Muktadir—Kâhir—Râzi—Muttaki—The Buyides—The Mayors of the Palace—Mustakfi—The Ghaznavides—Mutii—Tâii—Kâdir—Kâim—The Seljukides—Tughril Beg.

Abu'l Fazl Jaafar, *Mutawakkil aala Illâh.* 232—247 A.H. 847—861 A.C.

On the death of Wâsik, the chief Kâzi, the vizier and most of the other courtiers desired to raise his young son to the throne; but Wasîf the Turk objected, "as the crown, the robes, and the sceptre were much too big for the lad." Accordingly they elected Jaafar, a brother of Wâsik, with the title of *al-Mutawakkil aala Illâh.*[1] This "Nero of the Arabs" ruled for fifteen years, and under him commenced the decline of the empire. Sunk in debauchery and habitually drunk, he allowed the government to drift to ruin. Nevertheless he was keen for the restoration of orthodoxy. A rescript was issued

[1] "He that putteth his trust in the Lord."

placing Rationalism under the ban, and proclaiming the re-establishment of the old doctrines in their fullest rigour. The Rationalists were expelled from public offices, and lectures on science and philosophy were interdicted. Kâzi Abû Duwâd and his son, prominent Mutazilites, were thrown into prison, and their property was confiscated. But Mutawakkil's persecution was not confined to the Rationalists. Non-Moslems too suffered from his frantic zeal. They also were excluded from the employment of the state, and subjected to other galling disabilities.

232—454 A.H.

His persecution of the Rationalists.

In his unaccountable rancour against the Caliph Ali and his descendants, he rased to the ground the mausoleum of the martyr Hussain, and had a water-course turned over it. Pilgrimages to the consecrated spot were prohibited under the severest penalties, and the property of Fadak was re-confiscated. Ibn Zayyât,[1] the Vizier of Wâsik, was put to death for not having shown sufficient deference to the tyrant before he came to the throne. The Greeks took advantage of the general confusion to resume their raids. They burnt Damietta in Egypt, and devastated Cilicia, carrying away 20,000 prisoners, 12,000 of whom were put to death with the cruellest torture, by the Empress Theodora. Those alone who accepted Christianity were spared. The conduct of Mutawakkil became at last so outrageous that his Turkish guards conspired to put him to death.

[1] Ibn Zayyât was a cruel minister, but under Wâsik his cruelty was kept within bounds by Abû Duwâd. Ibn Zayyât had invented an instrument of torture for the punishment of criminals and enemies; and he was put into this by Mutawakkil. Ibn Zayyât's machine had the same object as the instrument invented in the fifteenth century by Sir W. Skevington, called after him "the Scavenger's Daughter"; the one burnt, the other crushed.

847—1063 A.C. It is said that his son Muntassir, who abhorred his cruelties, approved of the design. And accordingly one

His death. night, as the Arab Nero lay sunk in the stupor of drink, the conspirators entered his apartments and despatched him.

Abû Jaafar Ahmed, *Muntassir b'Illâh.* 247—248 A.H. 861—862 A.C.

Upon Mutawakkil's death *Muntassir b'Illâh*[1] was proclaimed Caliph. He is described as a pious and just sovereign, forbearing and generous in character, possessed of a keen intellect and honestly desirous for the welfare of his subjects. He rebuilt the desecrated mausolea of Ali and Hussain, restored to their descendants the property that had been confiscated by Mutawakkil, and withdrew

Rabi II. 248 A.H.

all the disabilities and restrictions that had been placed by his father upon non-Moslems. But unfortunately he died after a reign of barely six months.[2]

Abu'l Abbâs Ahmed, *Mustaîn b'Illâh.*

The Turkoman chiefs, who were at this time the virtual arbiters of the fate of the Caliphate, raised to the throne another grandson of Mutasim, under the title of *Mustaîn b'Illâh*,[3] but allowed him no power or authority. In the convulsions that followed the death of Muntassir, the provincial governors gradually converted themselves into feudatories, and the supremacy of the Caliphs dwindled into a more or less nominal suzerainty.[4]

The Tâhirides.

Abdullâh bin Tâhir, who had died in the reign of Mutasim, left his province in the hands of his son Tâhir, who received the investiture as of right. His administration, like that of his father, was enlightened, just, and liberal. The Tâhirides held their court at Nishâpur,

1 "Victorious by the help of the Lord."

2 Muntassir is the first Abbasside Caliph over whose grave a tomb was built.

3 "He who seeks the assistance of the Lord."

4 The history of the dynasties that appeared in the Arab empire between the death of Wâsik and the year 1055 A.C., resembles that of the powerful families who, in France, have occupied the duchies of Normandy, Burgundy, and Guienne.

232—454 A.H.

which was the capital of Khorâsân. Tâhir died in 862 A.C., and was succeeded by his son Mohammed, who governed the province until 873 A.C. The power exercised by the Tâhirides encouraged others, and the whole of the East soon escaped from the hands of the Banû Abbâs.

Mustaîn escapes to Bagdad.

Unable to stand the tyranny of his Turkish guards, Mustaîn escaped to Bagdad, where he expected the support of the Arab and Persian soldiery. The Turks failing to induce him to return, proclaimed the second son of Mutawakkil as Caliph, under the title of *al-Mutazz b'Illâh*,[1] and proceeded to besiege Bagdad. Mustaîn was persuaded to abdicate on the solemn engagement that he should be allowed to reside peaceably at Medîna, but at Wâsit, on the route to Hijâz, the deposed sovereign was treacherously murdered by an emissary of Mutazz.

Abû Abdullâh Mohammed, *al-Mutazz b'Illâh.*

Mustaîn's murder.

The Turkomans now commenced to quarrel amongst themselves. Two of the chief actors in the late scenes, Wâsif and Bughâ, were murdered by their rivals, and one Bâbikiâl seized the vizierate. He obtained from the worthless Caliph the viceroyalty of Egypt, and appointed the celebrated Ahmed bin Tûlûn as his deputy. On the murder of Bâbikiâl shortly after, Ahmed bin Tûlûn virtually became the independent ruler of Egypt. He proved himself an able, honest, and just administrator.[2] The Imâm Ali (*an-Naki*) died in the year 868 A.C., and was succeeded by his son Hassan, surnamed *al-Aaskari*.[3]

Jamâdi II. 264 A.H. June 868 A.C.

Mutazz occupied the throne for nearly three years. In

255 A.H. June 869 A.C.

[1] "He who is prepared with (the blessing of) the Lord."

[2] He left some splendid architectural monuments, the remains of which exist to the present day.

[3] This title was given him because he was born and died at the camp at Sâmarra, which was called *al-Aaskar* or the camp.

847—1063 A.C.

255 A.H. the troops became clamorous for their pay, and as Mutazz expressed himself unable to comply with their demands, they dragged him out of the palace, subjected him to various indignities, and forced him to abdicate. He was then thrown into prison, where he was assassinated. To this condition had the descendants of Mansûr and Rashîd now fallen!

Abdication of Mutazz.

His assassination.

Abû Abdullâh Mohammed, *al-Muhtadi b'Illâh.* 26th Rajjab, 255 A.H.

Upon the abdication of Mutazz, the Turkoman chiefs raised to the throne a son of Wâsik, under the title of *Muhtadi b'Illâh.*[1] He was a man of strong character, virtuous, just, and anxious to do his duty. In happier times he would have proved himself a capable ruler. He expelled from the palace the singers, musicians, dancing-women, and other parasites, and tried to rule the state according to law. This soon brought him into collision with the Turks. He met them bravely with a handful of men. Deserted by his supporters, he was seized by the insurgents, and after considerable ill-treatment was forced to abdicate. He was then thrown into confinement, where he died in a very short time.

256 A.H. 870 A.C. *Abu'l Abbâs* Ahmed, *Mutamid aala'llâh.*

The eldest surviving son of Mutawakkil, who was living at Sâmarra, was then proclaimed Caliph, under the name of *Mutamid aala'llâh.*[2] He was weak, unstable, and fond of pleasure. But his brother, Abû Ahmed, surnamed Muwaffik,[3] a man of ability and great military talent, in reality governed the empire, and proved the mainstay of the Caliphate until his death, shortly before that of Mutamid. Partly owing to Muwaffik's personality and partly to the fact that the Court was now again at Bagdad, where it was supported by national patriotism, during this and the two succeeding reigns, the Turkish guards

[1] "The directed by the Lord."

[2] "Confiding in the Lord."

[3] "He who prospers in the Lord."

were kept in check, and there were gleams of returning vigour and prosperity in the dismembered empire of Mâmûn. Tabaristân had broken away in 864 A.C. A descendant of Ali, named Hassan bin Zaid, converted the inhabitants to Islâm and made himself sovereign of that country. In 870 A.C. the famous Yâkûb, son of Lais the coppersmith,[1] the founder of the Suffâride dynasty, who had commenced life as a common soldier, conquered Sijistân from the Tâhirides, and gradually extended his power over the whole of modern Persia. In 873 he drove Mohammed, the grandson of Tâhir, out of Khorâsân, and shortly after annexed Tabaristân. His success so inflamed his pride that he invaded Irâk, but was met near Wâsit by Muwaffik, and defeated with heavy loss. Yâkûb then retired to his dominions. The following year, having repaired his losses, he again threatened the Caliph, when death surprised him at Jundisapur. His brother and successor, Amr bin Lais, made peace with Mutamid, and obtained by letters patent the free possession of all the country he occupied.

232—454 A.H.

Rise of the Suffârides. Yâkûb, the son of Lais.

879 A.C.

The Sâmân-ides.

Transoxiana, cut off from the seat of the empire by the Suffâride principality, became virtually independent under its governor, Ismâil the Sâmânide. Sâmân was an owner of camels and leader of caravans; his family owed their rise to Mâmûn, who in 819 A.C. appointed Sâmân's grandson Ahmed to the governorship of Ferghâna. Ahmed was succeeded in the office by Nasr, his son. Nasr died in 892 A.C., when Ismâil, his brother, became the ruler of the province. Ismâil was a man of great ability and strength of character. He neglected no measure for the consolidation of his power. He drove beyond the Jaxartes the Turkoman hordes who were pressing on

[1] Suffâr.

847—1063 A.C. Transoxiana, won the attachment of his subjects by a wise, liberal, and just administration, and placed his dynasty by these means on a solid foundation. As in the case of Amr bin Lais, the Caliph invested him with the government of the province, which was made hereditary in his family, subject to the payment of a nominal tribute.[1]

The Tûlûnides. Ahmed bin Tûlûn possessed Egypt and Syria. Ahmed died in 884 A.C., and was succeeded by his son Khumârwièh, who established his residence at Damascus.

The rise of these independent dynasties, though it weakened the empire, was not without benefit to the people of the countries over which they ruled, for they proved themselves liberal patrons of art and literature and promoted commerce and industry.

The Negro Revolt. The Negro Revolt in Chaldæa, which commenced in the reign of Mutazz, was most disastrous. It was headed by a Persian, who allowed the wildest licence to his followers, and thus acquired the name of *Khabîs* (Reprobate). Negro slaves from all parts of the country flocked to his standard, and he made himself master of Chaldæa and Ahwâz, and for several years defied all efforts to reduce him. In 882 A.C. he was attacked and annihilated by Muwaffik. His stronghold was destroyed, his followers were dispersed, and he himself was killed. In 882 A.C. the Caliph's dominion extended over Arabia, Mesopotamia, Babylonia and Chaldæa (Irâk Arab), Irâk Ajam, Azerbaijân, and Armenia, and the provinces bordering on the Indian Ocean. Still a vast empire worthy of being cherished and preserved.

The Byzantines took advantage of the troubles that beset the Caliphate and made several inroads into Moslem

[1] For the names of the Sâmânide princes, see Gen. Table.

territory. At first they carried everything before them, but when Syria fell into the hands of Ahmed bin Tûlûn they were opposed by the Tûlûnide governor of Tarsus, and defeated in a series of battles. 232—454 A.H.

The apostolical Imâm Hassan al-Aaskari died in the year 260 A.H., during the reign of Mutamid. Upon his death the Imâmate devolved upon his son Mohammed, surnamed *al-Mahdi* (the Conducted), the last Imâm of the Shiahs. The story of these Imâms of the House of Mohammed is intensely pathetic. The father of Hassan was deported from Medîna to Sâmarra by the tyrant Mutawakkil, and detained there until his death. Similarly, Hassan was kept a prisoner by the jealousy of Mutawakkil's successors. His infant son, barely five years of age, pining for his father, entered in search of him a cavern not far from their dwelling. From this cavern the child never returned. The pathos of this calamity culminated in the hope—the expectation—which fills the hearts of Hassan's followers, that the child may return to relieve a sorrowing and sinful world of its burden of sin and oppression. So late as the fourteenth century, when Ibn Khaldûn was writing his great work, the Shiahs were wont to assemble at eventide at the entrance of the cavern and supplicate the missing child to return to them. After waiting for a considerable time, they departed to their homes, disappointed and sorrowful. This, says Ibn Khaldûn, was a daily occurrence. When they were told it was hardly possible he could be alive, they answered that as the prophet Khizr was alive, why should not their Imâm be alive too? Upon this, Ibn Khaldûn remarks that the belief about Khizr being alive was an irrational superstition. This Imâm is therefore called the *Muntazzar*, the Expected One,—the *Hujja* or the Proof (of the Truth), and the *Kâim*, the living.

874 A.C. The last Imâm of the Shiahs.

265 A.H. 878 A.C.

847—1063 A.C. Muwaffik died in 278 A.H., and was shortly followed by the Caliph his brother. Mutamid was succeeded by
891 A.C. his nephew Ahmed, the son of Muwaffik, under the
Rajab 279 A.H. title of *Mutazid b'Illâh*.[1] During this and the succeeding
September reign there was no further dismemberment of the empire.
892 A.C. On the contrary, a combination of favourable circum-
Abu'l Abbâs Ahmed, *al-Mutazid b'Illâh*. stances contributed to strengthen the power of the Caliphs, who succeeded in reuniting to their dominions several of the detached provinces. Mutazid is called Saffâh the Second, as he is supposed to have restored the power of the House of Abbâs, which had become weak and effete. He is described as a bold and active man, a vigorous and wise administrator, and a capital soldier. Merciless like his ancestor, the first Saffâh, he seems to have kept in check the spirit of disorderliness among the people; and the awe and dread which he inspired lulled all dissensions.

The character of Mutazid.

He was successful in his wars with the Byzantines, and several cities were either recovered or taken from them. He drove the Kurds out of Mesopotamia, and repressed with firmness the insurrection of the Ameer Hamdân of Mosul, who had attempted to make himself independent. But his greatest achievement consisted in peacefully obtaining the practical restoration of Egypt to the Caliphate. Khumârwièh, the son and successor of Ahmed bin Tûlûn, of his own accord, solicited investiture as viceroy of Egypt upon payment of an annual tribute of a million pieces of gold. This willing submission was
282 A.C. further strengthened by the marriage of his daughter Katr-un-nadâ ("the Dewdrop") to Mutazid.

Restoration of Egypt.

Mutazid's rule was on the whole vigorous and firm, and some of his measures were undoubtedly beneficent.

[1] "One who recurs to the assistance of the Lord."

He expelled from the city vagabonds and bad characters, who in the day sat by the wayside plying the trade of story and fortune-telling, and at night indulged in robbery. But the reform which, more than anything, obtained for him the benedictions of the people was one connected with the law of intestate succession. Under the old Arabian custom, relatives connected to a deceased person through a female, such as daughter's or sister's children, were excluded from inheritance, and this archaic rule was at first embodied in the Sunni law. Accordingly, on failure of agnatic relatives, the property escheated to the state. Mutazid abolished the escheat office, and directed that relations in the female line should take after the agnates. Up to this time the beginning of the solar year was celebrated with the same festivities as among the ancient Persians. On the New Year's Day, called the *nairôz*[1] *khâssa*, the Caliph held an audience, received presents, and bestowed gifts. The people interchanged visits, sent round presents of coloured eggs,[2] delicate pastry and sweets, and amused themselves with letting off fireworks, and sprinkling on each other coloured or perfumed water.[3] As the sprinkling of water was sometimes carried to the verge of scandal, and promiscuous fireworks were dangerous, Mutazid prohibited both the customs. The prohibition regarding the sale of philosophical works by booksellers was, however, of problematical benefit. He also altered the New Year's Day from March to the Syrian month of

232—454 A.H.

Reform of the Law of Inheritance.

The New Year's Day.

[1] Persian *nourôz*.

[2] The egg is the emblem of the fecundity of the earth awakened by the rays of the sun. Does not the Western custom of Easter eggs and Easter offerings owe its origin to the same idea?

[3] Like the Hindoos on the occasion of the *Bassant* or Holi festival.

847—1063 A.C. Huzairân (June). It was thenceforth called Mutazid's New Year's Day.[1]

The rise of the Fatimides[2] in Africa, and the appearance of the communistic Carmathians (the *Karâmita*),[3] who soon filled with rapine and carnage the whole of Arabia, Syria, and Irâk, and ultimately brought ruin and disaster on the Moslem world, occurred in this reign.

The Carmathians. 278 A.H. 891—892 A.C. The Carmathians appeared first in the neighbourhood of Kûfa. Their doctrines were carried to al-Bahrain, the refuge of all the free-lances and revolutionaries of Islâm, and here, under the leadership of the notorious Abû Saîd

Abû Sâid al-Jannâbi. 900 A.C. al-Jannâbi (*i.e.* of Jannâba), they gained such strength that in 287 A.H. they were able to invade Chaldæa and inflict a disastrous defeat on the troops of Mutazid. Two years later they entered Syria, and devastated the

903—904 A.C. province. In 301 A.H., upon Abû Saîd's assassination, his son Abû Tâhir became their leader. Under him they seized Basra, and laid waste with fire and sword the countries within their reach. They continued in this course, defeating army after army, until in the year 317 of the Hegira (in the reign of Muktadir), they suddenly swooped down upon Mecca during the most important day of the Hajj, slaughtered the pilgrims, desecrated the Kaaba, and carried away the Black Stone. The cup of their iniquity was now full. The Moslems on all sides combined to destroy these enemies of humanity, and a cruel, sanguinary war, which lasted for nearly fifteen years, ended with the annihilation of this pestilential sect. However, the disastrous consequences of their rising were never effaced. Arabia and a great

[1] *An-Nairûz-ul-Mutazidi.* The reason of the alteration will be shown in the retrospect.

[2] See *post.*

[3] The followers of Karmath; see *The Spirit of Islam*, p. 495.

portion of Syria and Chaldæa were converted into a wilderness. The arm of the Caliphate, at the moment when it was recovering its strength, was paralysed. And the Byzantines, the natural enemies of the empire, were thus enabled to ravage Moslem territories with absolute impunity. 232—454 A.H.

Mutazid died in the year 299 A.H., and was succeeded by his son *Abû Mohammed* Ali, under the title of *Muktafi b'Illâh.*[1] Muktafi proved a wise, generous, and just ruler. He was at Rakka at the time of his father's death, and the oath of fealty was taken for him by the Vizier Kâsim, son of Obaidullâh, an honest and capable minister. Muktafi arrived at Bagdad in a ship which sailed down the Tigris amid the acclamations of the people. On his arrival he destroyed the underground prisons of his father, and converted them into places of worship. He restored to the rightful owners the lands and gardens that had been acquired by Mutazid for building his palace. He thus won the love of the people, who had been inspired with fear by his father. 22nd Rabi II. 299 A.H. 5th April, 902 A.C. Accession of *Abû Mohammed* Ali, *al-Muktafi b'Illâh.*

In spite of the Karmathian scourge, which kept the arms of the Caliphate incessantly occupied in Irâk, Hijâz, and Southern Syria, Muktafi had been able to bring Egypt under his direct control and to beat back the Byzantines and inflict some punishment on them. Antâlia (Adalia[2]), one of their most important cities, was taken by storm, and Thessalonica was sacked.

Muktafi unfortunately died after a short reign of five years, and was succeeded by his brother Jaafar, a lad of thirteen years, under the title of *Muktadir b'Illâh.*[3]

[1] "Restrained by the Lord."

[2] On the gulf of that name.

[3] "The Powerful in the Lord."

847—1063 A.C. He occupied the throne for nearly twenty-five years. The virtues and ability of the viziers,[1] who held the

12th Zu'l Kaada, 295 A.H. 13th August, 907 A.C. *Abu'l Fazl Jaafar, al-Muktadir b'Illâh.* real power, maintained the dignity of the empire in the beginning of this reign, but towards the end it declined rapidly, owing to the sovereign's recklessness. The Fatimide sovereign, Obaidullâh al-Mahdi, conquered the whole of Northern Africa, and drove out Ziâdatullâh bin Aghlab, the last Aghlabite prince of Ifrîkia, who fled to Egypt and thence to Irâk.

The Deilemites, who inhabited the northernmost part of ancient Media, were about this time converted to Islâm by a descendant of Ali named Hassan, also called al-Utrûsh (the deaf), who conquered Tabaristân

305 A.H. and Ghilân from the Sâmânides. In the year 305 A.H. we read of the arrival at Bagdad of an embassy from the Byzantine emperor, which was received with great pomp and ceremony, and of the opening in the following year of the great Muktadirièh hospital, for the maintenance of which an annual allowance of 7000 dinars was set apart.

Towards the end of Muktadir's reign, the actual government was in the hands of his mother, a woman of character and ability. She issued edicts and ordinances under her own hand, and on Fridays, surrounded by the Kâzis and nobles, held audiences to receive petitions and complaints. The reactionary Hanbalites acquired great influence in Muktadir's time. Their unruly fanaticism led to frequent riots in Bagdad.[2] Encouraged by the weakness of the government, they assumed the position of public

[1] Such as Ibn Furât and others.

[2] They carried their bigotry to the extent of not allowing the historian Tabari to be buried, because he had not praised Ahmed bin Hanbal in his great history. Tabari was consequently buried secretly by his friends.

censors. They invaded the privacy of houses, and, in these domiciliary visits, forcibly took and destroyed whatever offended their fanatical tastes. Their special hatred was directed against philosophical and scientific works, which they seized in the shops of booksellers and publicly burnt. 232—454 A.H.

In 320 A.H. Muktadir was killed in the course of a fight with one of his insurgent nobles. Another son of Mutazid, named *Abû Mansûr* Mohammed, was thereupon raised to the throne with the title of *al-Kâhir b'Illâh.*[1] He was cruel and depraved in disposition, and those who had proclaimed him Caliph themselves deposed and blinded him. In his reign Egypt again became independent under its famous governor, Ikshîd the Turk.[2] 31st October, 932 A.C. *Abû Mansûr* Mohammed, *al-Kâhir b'Illâh.* 6th Jamâdi I. 322 A.H. 25th April, 734 A.C.

The Turkish nobles then placed on the throne a son of Muktadir named *Abu'l Abbâs* Mohammed, and called him *ar-Râzi b'Illâh.*[3] With him vanished the last vestiges of power or dignity that had been left to the Caliphs. Soon after his accession, Mohammed bin Râik, governor of Wâsit and Basra, seized the supreme power, and was invested by the helpless Râzi with the title of *Ameer ul-Umrâ*,[4] a dignity specially created for him. With the exception of Bagdad and its environs, nothing now remained in the hands of the phantom Caliph; the governor of each province assumed an independent rôle. Hitherto the Ommeyades of Spain had scrupulously abstained from the assumption of the titles of *Abu'l Abbâs* Mohammed, *ar-Râzi b'Illâh.*

[1] "The Commander by the Lord."

[2] The founder of the Ikshidite dynasty.

[3] "Satisfied in the Lord."

[4] *Ameer of the Ameers.* The Ameer ul-Umrâ was, in fact, the mayor of the palace, and exercised absolute authority in the name of the Caliph.

847–1063 A.C. Caliph and Commander of the Faithful. But the degradation and practical effacement of the Abbasside sovereignty at this epoch led Abdur Rahmân III. to assume the dignity and insignia of the Caliphate.

Mohammed bin Râik was overthrown by his Turkish general Bajkam, who was then invested with the title and authority of *Ameer ul-Umrâ*.

940 A.C. Upon the death of Râzi in 329 A.H., *Abû Ishâk* Ibrâhîm, another son of Muktadir was proclaimed Caliph
329 A.H. 940 A.C. *Abû Ishâk* Ibrâhîm, *al-Muttaki b'Illâh.* under the title of *al-Muttaki b'Illâh.*[1] He was a mere puppet in the hands of Bajkam's secretary. Shortly after Bajkam was slain, and another Turk succeeded him in power, but he was routed by Ibn Râik, who again became the Ameer ul-Umrâ. Attacked by another Turkoman chief, Ibn Râik fled to Mosul, carrying the puppet Caliph with him. Here the grandsons of Ameer Hamdân, the Lords of Mosul and Tikrit, were holding at bay the Greeks, and making such head against Byzantine depredations as their limited resources could enable them to do. Ibn Râik was assassinated, and the two Hamdanite princes, Hassan and Ali, under the title of Nâsir ud-Dowla and Saif ud-Dowla respectively, became the guardians of the Caliph. Carrying Muttaki with them, they entered Bagdad in state, and again installed him on his throne. Another outbreak, headed by a Turkish general named Tûzûn, compelled them to leave Bagdad. Muttaki now fell into the hands of Tûzûn. Once he escaped to Rakka, but was induced by treacherous promises to return, when he was blinded and deposed. In this reign the Greeks raided as far as Edessa (Rohâ), slaughtering the Moslems on all sides. Edessa was saved only by the surrender of the reputed napkin

[1] "The Pious in the Lord."

of Jesus, which was preserved in the cathedral of the city. 232—454 A. H.

Tûzûn then installed Muttaki's brother, *Abu'l Kâsim* Abdullâh, as the Caliph, under the title of *al-Mustakfi b-Illâh*.[1] Tuzûn died shortly after Mustakfi's accession, and was succeeded in the office of Ameer ul-Omara by his secretary, Jaafar bin Shirzâd. The Deilemite princes, the sons of Buwaih, now began to press upon Irâk. In order to win their favour and support, Mustakfi conferred the title of Muiz ud-Dowla on Ahmed the eldest, that of Imâd ud-Dowla on his brother Ali, and of Rukn ud-Dowla on Hassan. Muiz ud-Dowla soon made himself master of Bagdad and of the Pontiff. He received the title of *Sultan*, and his name was inscribed on the coinage and recited in the Cathedral services along with the Caliph's. His position was like that of Charles Martel under the Merovingian kings of France, for he was the virtual sovereign, whilst the Caliph was merely his dependent, receiving a daily allowance of 5000 dinars from the public treasury. Muiz ud-Dowla, although a patron of arts and literature, was cruel by nature. He was a Shiah; and it was he who established the 10th day of the Moharram as a day of mourning in commemoration of the massacre of Kerbela. The Byzantines carried their arms everywhere, and the distracted empire of Islâm was powerless to oppose their progress or prevent their depredations.

Safar, 333 A.H. October, 944 A.C. *Abu'l Kâsim* Abdullâh, *al-Mustakfi b'Illâh.*

The Buyides. Mayors of the Palace.

341 A.H. 952 A.C.

Suspecting Mustakfi of conspiring against his power. Muiz ud-Dowla deposed and blinded him in January 946, *Abu'l Kâsim* al-Fazl, another son of Muktadir, was then installed as Caliph under the title of *al-Mutii b'Illâh*.[2]

324 A.H. 46 A.C. *Abu'l Kâsim* al-Fazl, *al-Mutii b'Illâh.*

1 "He who is contented with the Lord."

2 'Obedient to the Lord."

847—1063 The Buyides held the power for nearly a century almost without a rival to contest their title. The Turkish military element was annihilated, the Hamdanites were driven out of Mosul, and the whole of Mesopotamia, Irâk Arab, and Western Persia became subject to their rule. Some of them were undoubtedly cruel, but on the whole their mayoralty conduced to the prosperity of the people and the cultivation of literature and science.

Muiz ud-Dowla died in 356 A.H., and was succeeded in the office of Ameer ul-Umrâ by his son Bakhtyâr, who received the title of Izz ud-Dowla. Seven years later Mutii (the Caliph), struck with paralysis, abdicated on the requisition of the Buyide prince in favour of his son *Abû Bakr* Abdul Karîm, who was installed on the pontifical throne under the title of *at-Tâii b'Illâh.*[1] The munificence of the Hamdanite and Buyide princes, and their patronage of arts and letters, are shown by the number of eminent men who flourished at this time. Masûdi the historian, Abû Nasr Fârâbi the philosopher, Mutannabi the poet, Abu'l Farâj the author of the *Kitâb ul-Aghâni*, Abu'l Kâsim at-Tanûkhi, ad-Dinâwari the rhetorician, and a host of others—philosophers, scientists, poets, jurists—were contemporaries of Mutii b'Illâh.

13th Zu'l Kaada, 363 A.H. 5th August 974 A.C. *Abû Bakr* Abdul Karîm, *at-Tâii b'Illâh.*

The accession of Tâii b'Illâh was coeval with the conquest of Syria and Hijâz by the Fatimide Caliph, the great al-Muiz li-dîn Illâh, in whose name prayers were recited in the Holy Cities.

363 A.H. 974 A.C.

Shortly after, Izz ud-Dowla was deposed by his uncle Azud ud-Dowla, and the impotent Caliph was compelled not only to invest him with the insignia of office, but to allow him regal honours,[2] with the title of *Tâj ul-Millat*

[1] "Obedient to the Lord."

[2] Such as the beating of the drums at the gate of his palace in the morning, at sunset, and at nightfall.

("Crown of the Faith"). Azud ud-Dowla died in 372 A.H., 232—454
and was succeeded by his son Samsâm ud-Dowla,[1] who A.H.
received the title of *Shams ul-Millat* ("Sun of the Faith"). 372 A.H.
Samsâm ud-Dowla was deposed by his brother Sharf ud- 982 A.C.
Dowla, who held the office for nearly four years.[2] He died
in 379 A.H., and was succeeded by his son Abû Nasr, 376 A.H.
who received the title of *Bahâ ud-Dowla* and *Ziya ul-* 985 A.C.
Millat ("Glory of the State" and "Lustre of the Faith").

Both Azud ud-Dowla and Sharf ud-Dowla (949—989 379 A.H.
A.C.) re-animated the taste for letters and revived the 989 A.C.
School of Bagdad, which had suffered during the revolutions of the Caliphate. Among the scientists whom they patronised I may mention Ibn us-Salâm, Abdur Rahmân Sûfi, and the celebrated astronomer and geometrician Abu'l Wafâ. Besides supporting poets and *savants*, Azud ud-Dowla undertook works of public utility. Engineers of the highest merit were charged with the task of deepening the channels of the river Bendemir,[3] and making it navigable to ships as far as Shirâz. This when completed had the effect of stopping the periodical inundations hitherto so destructive to the surrounding districts. He also built a magnificent hospital and several colleges at Bagdad.

Tâii was deposed by Bahâ ud-Dowla, and forced to 19th Shâbân,
abdicate in favour of his brother, *Abu'l Abbâs* Ahmed, 381 A.H.
who was placed on the throne under the title of *al-Kâdir* 1st Nov.,
b'Illâh.[4] Tâii resided in the palace of his brother, and 991 A.C.
appears to have been treated with great consideration *Abu'l Abbâs*
and respect—an unusual circumstance for the times. He Ahmed, *al-Kâdir b'Illâh.*

[1] "The Sword of the Empire."

[2] Sharf ud-Dowla induced the Caliph to bestow on him the mighty title of *Shah in-Shah*, King of Kings.

[3] Near Shirâz.

[4] "Strong in the Lord."

847—1063 A.C. died in the year 373 A.H. (1002 A.C.). Kâdir b'Illâh is described as a virtuous man, distinguished for his piety and rectitude. He spent most of his nights in devotion, and gave a large portion of his income in charity. It cannot be denied, however, that he was narrow in his sympathies and bigoted in his views, and the circumstances of the times forced him to assume a strong reactionary attitude towards all development. The Fatimides were extending their power in every direction. Azîz, the successor of al-Muiz, had made himself the master of Emessa, Hamâh, and Aleppo, and his sovereignty was acknowledged in Mesopotamia. Mutazilaism also was making great progress. Kâdir, who himself was a jurist of some eminence, deprived of all temporal authority, now devoted himself to the consolidation of the spiritual authority and prestige of the Abbasside Caliphate. Synods of doctors were held, at which he presided as the Pontiff of the Church; anathemas were drawn up and fulminated against the Fatimides; Rationalism was condemned, and "conformity" was insisted upon as essential to orthodoxy. He himself wrote pamphlets against the Mutazilites, declaring Rationalism to be heresy. The consequence of all this was to inflame sectarian bitterness; and to impart a rigidity to the dogmas of the Church that has made the work of reform so difficult in later times.

The Ghaznavides. 999 A.C. The Sâmânides, who had ruled Transoxiana and Khorâsân with such brilliant success, disappeared at this epoch, and their place was taken by another dynasty. Their rule had lasted from 874 to 999 A.C. A Turkish soldier who had commenced life as a mameluke, had by his merits attained a high position in the service of his sovereign. Incurring the displeasure of the succeeding prince, Alptagîn escaped from Bokhâra and established himself in the mountainous regions of Afghanistan. 232–454 A.H. His seat of government was Ghazni, and here for sixteen years he defied all endeavours to subjugate him. On his death in 995 A.C., his power descended to his son-in-law, Subaktagîn, who by his wise and vigorous administration won the love of his subjects and the respect of his neighbours. His power and authority were recognised by the Caliph, which gave to his rule the coveted legitimacy. The title of Nâsir ud-Dowla, with the standard and customary robes of honour, was conferred on him from Bagdad, and Subaktagîn became the legitimate founder of the Ghaznavide dynasty. He carried his arms across the Hindoo Kush into the Punjab, and founded the cities of Bost and Kusdar. As the faithful ally of Nûh, the Sâmânide prince, he defended Transoxiana against the incursions of the Turkoman hordes. On his death there was a struggle for power between his sons Mahmûd and Ismâil. Mahmûd was willing to share the dominion with his brother, but the latter desired to rule alone. Mahmûd was successful in the fight, but treated Ismâil with great generosity and kindness. The Sâmânide power now broke to pieces, and in 1000 A.C. the Ghaznavide sovereign made himself the master of Khorâsân. The Caliph sent him the usual diploma of investiture, with the title of *Yemîn ud-Dowla* ("the Right Hand of the Empire"), and *Amîn ul-Millat* ("Custodian of the Faith"). Sultan Mahmûd's reign was one of the most brilliant in the history of Asia. He beautified Ghazni, and might have said, like the first emperor of Rome, that he found his capital a town of huts and left it a city of marble palaces. He was a patron of learning and arts; and although his generosity was sometimes marred by ill-timed parsimony and narrowness of views, his court was the resort of famous scholars and *savants*. Al-

Sultan Mahmûd.

847--1063 A.C. Beirûni, Firdousi, Dakîki, and many other philosophers and poets flourished in his reign.

Sultan Mahmûd entered India several times, but did not make any permanent conquest beyond the confines of the Punjab. Whilst Mahmûd was employed in the East, a large body of Turkomans from the Khirgiz steppes crossed the Jaxartes and settled themselves in Transoxiana. The Ghaznavide Sultan made the fatal mistake of leaving them in possession of this province, contenting himself with a nominal tribute and acknowledgment of fealty. With the object of weakening them as he thought, he deported into Khorâsân one of the tribes, under their leader Seljuk.[1] Here the Seljuks waxed in strength and number, until they were able successfully to measure swords with their former masters.

Sultan Masûd. Sultan Mahmûd died in 1030 A.C., leaving a glorious empire to his son and successor Masûd. He tried to remove from Khorâsân the redoubtable subjects whom a mistaken policy had implanted in the very heart of the kingdom. In a memorable battle near Herat, Masûd was vanquished, and the Seljukian power rose on the wreck of the Ghaznavide. Sultan Masûd's dominions were now confined to Afghanistan proper and the Punjab to the east; on his death the throne was occupied by several princes, in rapid succession, one after another. The affairs of the Ghaznavide dynasty remained in disorder until the accession of Sultan Ibrâhim, the friend and patron of the poet-philosopher, Hakîm Sanâï,[2] who concluded a peace with the Seljukian prince of Khorâsân,

The Seljukides.

[1] After whom the tribe was named.

[2] See the *Âtesh Kadèh*.

and directed his efforts solely to the consolidation of his power in the direction of India. 232—454 A.H.

Tughril Beg.

After the defeat of Sultan Masûd, the Seljuks had elected Tughril Beg, the grandson of the chieftain whose name they bore, to the over-lordship of the tribe. Tughril Beg is described by Ibn ul-Athîr as a wise sovereign, forbearing and generous, virtuous and simple in his life, and devoted to learning. Tughril rapidly reduced under his sway Jorjan, the Persian Irâk, Khwârism, and other important provinces to the west. He soon found himself in presence of the Buyide princes in Northern Persia, who were either driven from their principalities or compelled to acknowledge the suzerainty of the Seljukian chieftain. Whenever Tughril took a city, he established a mosque and a school in commemoration of his victory, and the fame of his piety enhanced and accelerated his success over his opponents.

11th Zu'l Hijja, 422 A.H. 29th November, 1031 A.C.

Whilst the power of Tughril was overshadowing that of the Buyides in Persia, the old orthodox Caliph, Kâdir b'Illâh, was breathing his last. He died in 422 A.H., at the age of 87, after having occupied the pontifical throne for over forty-one years. Many eminent scholars who have left a lasting impression on the history of Islâm flourished in his time, such as the Kâzi Abdul Jubbâr, the Mutazilite doctor, and his opponent, Abû Ishâk al-Isfaraini the Ashaarite; the Allâmah Shaikh Mufîd, the most learned of the Shiah legists; the poet Abû Omar bin Darrâj; the jurists Dâr Kutni and Ibn Shahîn, and others.

Abû Jaafar Abdullâh, *al-Kâim bi-amr-Illâh.*

On Kâdir b'Illâh's death, his son, *Abû Jaafar* Abdullâh, was installed on the throne, under the title of *al-Kâim bi-amr-Illâh.*[1] He is described as virtuous, pious, devout, and

1 "Who stands by the order of the Lord."

847—1063 A.C. learned, full of trust and faith in God, and charitable and patient. "He was assiduous in the cultivation of learning," says the annalist, "skilled in writing, and prompt to do justice and benevolence." He seems to have played quietly, for nearly twenty-four years, the part of a Pontiff without power, under the tutelage of the Buyides. In 466 A.H., a Turkish chief, Arslân al-Basâsîri, seized the supreme power, and practically displaced Malik Rahîm, the Buyide, from the office of Ameer ul-Umrâ, or Mayor of the Palace. At this juncture, Kâim invoked the assistance of the Seljukian sovereign. Tughril hurried to Bagdad, and on his approach, Basâsîri retired to Mosul. The moment, however, Tughril left Bagdad to suppress a revolt in Persia, Basâsîri returned to the capital, deposed the Abbasside Pontiff, and proclaimed in his place the Fatimide Caliph, al-Mustansir b'Illâh, the spiritual Head of Islâm. The mantle, sceptre, and pulpit were sent to Egypt, and prayers were recited for Mustansir in every mosque in Irâk. Tughril hurried back to Bagdad, Basâsîri was defeated and slain, and Kâim was replaced on the throne of his ancestors. The grateful Pontiff invested the Turkish sovereign with the supreme temporal power over the dominions of Islâm that still recognised the spiritual sway of the Abbassides. The ceremony of investiture took place in Bagdad. The Caliph himself placed two crowns on Tughril's head as the symbol of power over the Arabs and Persians, and invested him with seven robes emblematical of the seven countries of Islâm. The heralds then proclaimed Tughril Sultan of the East and the West.

Tughril Beg Sultan.

Gates on the Road to Shiraz.

CHAPTER XX

THE ABBASSIDES—(*continued*)

KÂIM TO MUSTAZHIR

455—503 A.H., 1063—1110 A.C.

THE COMMENCEMENT OF THE CRUSADES

Kâim bi-amr-Illâh, the Caliph—Tughril Beg—War with the Byzantines—Tughril's death—Accession of Alp Arslân—The Roman Invasion—Battle of Malâz Kard—Roman defeat—Diogenes Romanus made prisoner—Treaty of peace—Diogenes Romanus blinded and killed by his subjects—Death of Alp Arslân—Accession of Malik Shah—Death of Kâim—Accession of Muktadi bi-amr-Illâh as Caliph—Malik Shah's glorious reign—The Rise of the Assassins—Hassan Sabâh—Assassination of Nizâm ul-Mulk—Death of Malik Shah—Disputes among his sons—Death of Caliph Muktadi—Accession of Mustazhir b'Illâh—The beginning of the Crusades—Siege of Antioch—Its capture—Slaughter of the Moslems—Destruction of Maraa't un-Nomân—Butchery in Jerusalem—Sack of Tripoli.

455—503 A.H. 1063—1110 A.C.

The Seljuks.

UNDER Tughril the Seljuks became the dominant nation in Asia. This tribe formed a branch of the great Turkish or Scythian race, and derived their eponym from the chieftain under whom they had entered Transoxiana, and afterwards Khorâsân. Although the Turks and Mongols belonged to the same stock, there was this great difference between them, that whilst the latter lived and still live at the eastern extremity of Asia in a state of semi-barbarism verging on savagery, the western tribes had been much influenced by con-

1063—1110 A.C. tact with the civilisation of the Arabs. The Seljuks, who were the most advanced of them all, adopted Islâm with fervour and enthusiasm, and became its ardent champions. While the Arabs were cultivating the arts of peace, *they* devoted themselves to the extension of the power of Islâm. The latter half of the eleventh century forms the most glorious epoch of their history. During this period they recognised the over-lordship of one supreme monarch; the feudal vassals were united amongst themselves and faithful to the suzerain.

The Greeks had taken advantage of the growing weakness of the Caliphate to extend their power in Asia; the treacherous raids of former times had developed under some vigorous monarchs into attempts at conquest; and at the close of the tenth century of the Christian era, the Byzantine dominions extended as far as Antioch to the south and the boundaries of Armenia Proper to the east.

Death of Tughril Beg. Accession of Alp Arslân. 455 A.H. 1063 A.C.

In the year 1060 A.C., Tughril declared war against the Byzantines and swept them out of Cappadocia and Phrygia; but a permanent conquest of those regions was reserved for the reign of his brilliant nephew and successor, Alp Arslân[1] ("the valiant Lion"), who, upon the death of his uncle without male issue, succeeded to the over-lordship of the Seljuks, and was invested by the Caliph with the title and prerogatives of Sultan.[2] Alp Arslân is described by Ibn ul-Athîr as a noble, benevolent, just, and wise ruler: pure, pious, and devout in his life; humane of heart, charitable, and a friend of the poor; never indulging in anything reprehensible, and withal brave and chivalrous. After

[1] His father's name was *Jigri Beg* Dâûd.

[2] He received the title of Aazd ud-Dowla.

achieving the final conquest of Georgia and Armenia, he had retired to Khoi, in Azerbaijân, when he received news that Diogenes Romanus (called Armânûs by the Arabs), who had been raised from the scaffold to the throne by the favour of the Empress Eudocia, had burst into Asia Minor with an overwhelming force of over 200,000 men, with the avowed object of destroying Bagdad and reducing the whole of Western Asia under the Roman sway. A better equipped and more numerous army had never issued from Constantinople for conquest or plunder. As the Romans advanced, the Moslems fell back until they arrived at Malâz Kard,[1] an important fortress lying midway between the modern cities of Erzerum and Van. Here the Saracens were joined by the Sultan, and here the battle was fought which virtually destroyed the Byzantine power in Asia. The Moslems were out-numbered, but after a desperate and prolonged struggle they succeeded in inflicting a crushing defeat on the Roman army. The Emperor, with his patricians, was taken prisoner, and carried to the Sultan's camp, where he was treated with the kindness and courtesy due to his rank.

455—503 A.H.

Battle of Malâz Kard.

After protracted negotiations, a treaty of peace was concluded between the Sultan and Romanus, by which the latter agreed to marry his daughters to the sons of Alp Arslân, to pay a ransom of a million, and an annual tribute of three hundred and sixty thousand pieces of gold, and to surrender all prisoners of war. The Emperor and his nobles then took leave of their captor, and attended by a guard furnished by the Sultan, proceeded towards Constantinople, but on the way learnt that he had been deposed by his ungrateful subjects. The

[1] Ibn ul-Athîr : Mirkhond calls it Malâz Jard.

1063—1110 A.C. Sultan prepared to support him by arms, but before he could come to his assistance, Romanus was seized and blinded, and afterwards put to death, by the Greeks. After the battle of Malâz Kard, Asia Minor was bestowed as an appanage upon Sulaimân, the son of Kutlumish, a cousin, who held it as a feudatory of the Sultan. (465 A.H. 1072 A.C.) Sulaimân proved himself a wise ruler and a brave soldier. He extended his dominions to the Hellespont on the north, and to the Mediterranean on the west, and exacted tribute from the rulers of Byzantium. He established his capital at Nice in Bithynia, where it remained until the Crusades. On the capture of that place by the Crusaders, the seat of government was removed to Iconium. Asia Minor continued under his descendants until they were overthrown by the Tartars. They are commonly known as the sovereigns of Rûm,[1] and have left many monuments of their power and civilisation.

Death of Alp Arslân.

Alp Arslân died of a wound inflicted by a rebel whom he had sentenced to death. His rule was beneficent, wise, and just. During the whole of his reign he had as vizier the great Khwâja Hassan, surnamed Nizâm ul-Mulk, in whom was vested the absolute control of the civil administration. (466 A.H. 1073 A.C.) Alp Arslân was succeeded by his son, Malik Shah, who was invested with the Sultanate under the title of *Jalâl ud-Dowla* ("Glory of the Empire").

Accession of Malik Shah.

The Caliph Kâim died three years later, and was succeeded on the pontifical throne by his grandson, *Abu'l Kâsim* Abdullâh, under the title of *Muktadi bi-*

[1] For a list of the sovereigns of this dynasty see Genealogical Table. Aalâ ud-dîn, the fourteenth sovereign, was the friend, patron, and disciple of the celebrated mystic and poet Moulâna Jalâl ud-din Rûmi (of Rûm).

amr-Illâh.[1] Muktadi was only nineteen at the time of his accession, but had already given proof of his strength of character. He is described as pious, virtuous, and resolute, "magnanimous, and one of the noblest of the House of Abbâs." He administered his private domains with care; he expelled from the capital all the bad characters, and took other measures for promoting public decency and suppressing immorality. The fanatical Hanbalites were, however, a source of constant trouble, and riots between them and the Ashaarias (the Hanafîs) often led to heavy loss of life on both sides.

455—503 A.H.

The Caliph Kâim's death; 13th Shâbân, 467 A.H. 2nd April, 1075 A.C. *Abu'l Kâsim* Abdullâh, *al-Muktadi bi-amr-Illâh.*

But the interest of the Moslem world centred at this epoch not in the Caliph or his court, but in the great Sultan, the ruler of Asia.

Malik Shah's reign.

The beginning of Malik Shah's reign was disturbed by some insurrections, one headed by his own brother. The character of the Sultan is best indicated by an incident which occurred at Tûs. After his devotions at the mausoleum of the Imâm Ali ar-Razâ, Malik Shah informed his vizier that he had implored the Lord to give his brother the victory if he was more worthy than himself to rule over the Moslems. Wise, noble, and just, Malik Shah's renown as a ruler has been equalled by few sovereigns. He retained Khwâja Hassan, Nizâm ul-Mulk, in the office of vizierate, and invested him with absolute authority under the title of Atâbek[2] ("Prince Governor"). Nizâm ul-Mulk was probably, after Yahya Barmeki, the ablest minister and administrator Asia has ever produced. His work on administration and government[3] forms an enduring monument of his genius and capacity. Peace reigned throughout the vast dominions

Nizâm ul-Mulk, Vizier of Malik Shah.

[1] "Directing himself by the command of the Lord."

[2] Turkish, Atâbeg, arabicised into Atâbek.

[3] *Siâsat Nâmèh* (in Persian).

1063–1110 A.C. of the Sultan, which extended from the confines of China to the Mediterranean on the west, from Georgia on the north to Yemen in the south. Twelve times he traversed the wide extent of his dominions, and personally examined the condition and requirements of each province. Like Rashîd and Mâmûn, he established resting-places and guard-houses along all the trade and pilgrim routes for the protection of merchants and travellers. Hunting was the Sultan's passion, but in the pursuit of his pleasure he never forgot the poor or the peasant; and after a *battue* he distributed heavy largesses among the indigent inhabitants of the district where he hunted. Malik Shah's reign, in its grandeur and magnificence, and in the prosperity of the people, rivalled the best period of Roman or Arabian domination. Commerce and industry flourished; arts and literature were fostered by a lavish patronage; an unprecedented impetus was given to the cultivation of the Persian language; the cities of Asia were adorned with colleges, hospitals, mosques, and palaces, and the empire was covered with roads and canals to facilitate traffic and to fertilise the soil. The reformation of the Calendar, at the instance of the Sultan or his great vizier, was of importance to the world at large. A committee of scientists, under the presidency of the astronomer-royal, the celebrated poet Omar Khayyâm, was entrusted with the task. This assemblage of astronomers corrected all errors by a computation of time "which," says Gibbon, "surpasses the Julian and approaches the accuracy of the Gregorian." The new year's day was fixed at the first point of the sun's entry into Aries instead of, as heretofore, at the meridian of his passage through Pisces. The reformed era received, after the Sultan, the name *Jalâlian*.

Malik Shah's benign reign.

Reformation of the Calendar.

Sulaiman, the feudatory ruler of Rûm, had extended the Seljukian dominions up to the confines of Caria, and reduced many of the islands. Nicephorus Botaniates, who ascended the throne of Byzantium on the abdication of the son of Constantine Ducas, and Alexius Comnenus his successor, acknowledged Malik Shah as their suzerain, and paid him tribute. In the year 467 A.H., Sulaimân drove the Greeks from the principality of Antioch and reconquered the city in the name of the Sultan. This conquest was, however, counterbalanced by the loss, seven years later, of Sicily. In the year 1061 A.C. the island had been invaded by the Normans, whose progress was favoured by internecine disorders among the Saracens. And yet the struggle was protracted and sanguinary. After a long war, which extended over thirty years, the Norman Count Roger brought the island into his power.

455—503 A.H.

Conquest of Antioch, 467 A.H.

Loss of Sicily. 1091 A.C.

Towards the close of Malik Shah's reign, the Assassins,[1] the Nihilists of Islâm, made their appearance in the inaccessible defiles of Mazendrân, which had at one time harboured Bâbek and his confederates. This sanguinary fraternity, which was afterwards imitated with such remarkable success both in Europe and Asia, was founded by Hassan Sabâh, a school-fellow of Nizâm ul-Mulk, who, baulked in his ambition to play a part in the Seljukian empire, aimed at the destruction of legitimate authority by poison and the dagger. Becoming a follower of the Fatimide Caliphs of Egypt, he was appointed by them their nuncio in the East, with authority to make proselytes to the Ismâilia doctrines. Hitherto, the Ismâilites had only masters and fellows;

The Rise of the Assassins.

Hassan Sabâh.

The Ismâilias.

[1] The word *Assassin* is either a corruption of *Hassani* (a follower of Hassan) or *Hashîshîn*, *hashish*-taker.

1063—1110 A.C. namely, the *Dâïs* or emissaries, who, being initiated into all the grades of the secret doctrine, enlisted proselytes; and the *Rafîk*, who, gradually entrusted with its principles, formed the bulk of the secret society. Hassan saw at once that for the purpose of carrying out his project with security and energy, a third class was needed, composed of agents, who would be mere blind and fanatical tools in the hands of their superiors, who would yield implicit obedience to the master's orders without regard to consequences; these agents were called *Fedâïs* (*i. e.* the Devoted).

The grand-master of this murderous brotherhood was called "our lord," *Syedna* or *Sidna* (the *Sidney* of the Crusaders), and commonly *Shaikh ul-Jabal*, "the Old Man (or Lord) of the Mountain." And the *Fedâïs* formed his body-guard, and were the executioners of his deadly orders.[1]

"The Old Man of the Mountain."

The different degrees of the Order.

Immediately under the grand-master came the *Dâï ul-Kabîr*, the grand-prior, and each of the three provinces to which the power of the Order extended, namely Jabâl, Kuhistân, and Syria, was ruled by one of the grand-priors. Beneath them were the initiated masters, *Dâïs*, who acted as nuncios, and enlisted proselytes. The fellows or companions (*Rafîk*) were those who were advancing to the mastership, through the several grades of initiation into the secret doctrine. The devoted murderers (the *Fedâïs*) came last, and the *Lasîk* (aspirants) seem to have been the novices or lay brethren. From the uninitiated subjects of the Order, strict observance of the religious duties of Islâm was expected; from the devoted satellites was demanded

[1] The curious student of history will perceive the extraordinary analogy between this sanguinary Brotherhood of murderers, and the various Orders which sprang up afterwards in Europe.

only blind subjection. The initiated worked with their heads, and led the arms of the *Fedâïs* in execution of the orders of the Shaikh, who with his pen guided the daggers. These nihilists received the name of *Mulâhida* or the Impious. In 483 A.H., Hassan Sabâh obtained possession, partly by force and partly by treachery, of the inaccessible castle of Alamût ("the Eagle's Nest") on the mountains of Mazendrân, and from there commenced his attacks on constituted society. Two expeditions were directed by Malik Shah against the Assassins, but death overtook him before he could root out the hateful fraternity. In 1091 A.C., Nizam ul-Mulk was murdered by one of the emissaries of Hassan Sabâh. "He was universally beloved," says Ibn ul-Athîr,[1] "by the commonalty as well as the great, for his noble qualities and his spirit of justice." He left three sons, Muwayyid ul-Mulk, Fakhr ul-Mulk, and Izz ul-Mulk, who afterwards became the viziers of Malik Shah's successors. After the death of his great minister, the Sultan came to Bagdad. A marriage had been arranged between Malik Shah and a daughter of Alexius Comnenus,[2] but death prevented a union from which great results were expected, both for the East and the West. Malik Shah died at the age of thirty-nine, after a reign of about twenty-one years.

455—503 A.H.

Assassination of Nizâm ul-Mulk.

Death of Malik Shah 15th Shawwâl, 485 A.H., 18th November, 1092 A.C.

The greatness and unity of the Seljukian empire expired in the person of Malik Shah. At the instance of his wife Turkhân, surnamed *Khâtûn ul-Jalâlièh* (the glorious Lady), his infant son Mahmûd was invested by the Caliph with the dignity of the Sultanate, under the high-sounding title of *Nâsir ud-dunia w'ad-dîn*.[3] But the

[1] In his *History of the Atâbeks of Mosul.*

[2] Gibbon thinks that the lady must have been Anna Comnena herself.

[3] "Helper of the world and religion."

1063–1110 A.C. Accession of Barkyarûk. little child had to make way for his eldest brother Barkyarûk,[1] who seized the supreme power, and received the title of *Rukn ud-din.*[2] Shortly after, another competitor arose in the person of Mohammed, the second son of Malik Shâh. The civil war between the brothers Barkyarûk and Mohammed, concerning the territories of Irâk and Khorâsân, facilitated the execution of Hassan Sabâh's ambitious designs, and "in the bloody hotbed of intestine discord, the poisonous plant of murder and sedition flourished."

The Assassins by degrees made themselves master of some of the strongest fortresses in the mountainous tracts of Northern Persia, Irâk, and Syria, and pursued the best men of Islâm with their daggers.

15th Moharram, 487 A.H., February 1094 A.C. *Abu'l Abbâs* Ahmed, *al-Mustazhir b'Illâh.* The Caliph Muktadi died in 487 A.H., and was succeeded by his son *Abu'l Abbâs* Ahmed, under the title of *al-Mustazhir b'Illâh.*[3] He was only sixteen years of age at the time. Ibn ul-Athîr describes him as humane, virtuous, and liberal, of generous disposition and gentle manners, zealous in good works, and a patron of the learned. Had he lived in more favourable times, he would probably have made some figure in history. But the resources at his command were too inadequate to enable him to play an important part.

The Crusades. 491 A.H. 1097–8 A.C. It was at this period that the storm of savage fanaticism which in the annals of Christendom is called "the Holy Wars," burst in all its fury over Western Asia. In European histories the Crusades are surrounded with the halo of romance, and every knight or soldier engaged in it is regarded as the beau ideal of chivalry. It shall be my duty, in the interest of truth, to raise the veil

[1] Or Bek-Yâruk, "the brilliant Bey."

[2] "The pillar of religion."

[3] "Imploring help of the Lord."

455—503 A.H.

from this picture, and to reveal in the short space at my command the ghastliness of these wars, the cruel, savage, and treacherous character of those who were engaged in them, and the dire miseries they inflicted upon Western Asia. "The Crusades form," says a clever writer, "one of the maddest episodes in history. Christianity hurled itself at Mohammedanism in expedition after expedition for nearly three centuries, until failure brought lassitude, and superstition itself was undermined by its own labours. Europe was drained of men and money, and threatened with social bankruptcy, if not with annihilation. Millions perished in battle, hunger, or disease, and every atrocity the imagination can conceive disgraced the warriors of the Cross."

Condition of the Christians under the Islâmic *régime*.

Ever since the establishment of the Islâmic power, the Christians had enjoyed the utmost toleration; they were protected in the practice of their religion, and in the enjoyment of their civil rights and privileges. They were allowed to move freely about the empire, to hold communication with princes of their own creed in foreign countries, and to acquire lands and property under the same conditions as the Moslems. Public offices (excepting under some tyrannical governors) were open to them equally with the Moslems. Christian convents and churches existed everywhere, and Christian pilgrims from the most distant parts were permitted to enter Palestine without hindrance. In fact, pilgrimage to the Holy Land had been stimulated, rather than suppressed, by the conquest of the Arabs, and the Saracens contented themselves with maintaining order among the rival sects of Christianity, who would have torn each other to pieces in the very sepulchre they professed to worship. In Jerusalem, which was regarded as holy by the followers of both religions, a special quarter was set

1063— 1110 A.C. apart for the Patriarch and his clergy, which was inviolable on the part of the Moslems. When Palestine and Syria passed into the hands of the Fatimides in the year 969 A.C., the change of supremacy was to the advantage of the Christians, for the Egyptian sovereigns encouraged Christian trade and patronised the Christians. But no amount of toleration would conciliate the fanatics, who looked upon the presence of the Moslem in Jerusalem as an abomination. The pilgrims came under the protection of the Saracens, they enjoyed Saracen hospitality, and they carried away in their hearts a bitter hatred. Towards the end of the tenth century, the Millennium was believed to be at hand. Enormous crowds from the Latin world began to pour into the Holy Land; and in the eleventh century they increased to an appalling extent. About this time Palestine came into the possession of the Turkoman family of Ortok, who acknowledged a lax obedience to the Seljukian sovereign or his Syrian feudatory. The large influx of strangers and their furious zeal were equally unintelligible to the rude Turkomans, and the pilgrims were occasionally exposed to ill-treatment and robbery, just as Moslem pilgrims in the present day are often robbed and ill-treated by their Moslem brothers of the desert. The tales of ill-treatment, as usual grossly exaggerated, brought to a head the long-pent-up animosity of the Franks. Pope Urban II. summoned a council at Placentia in March 1095, and another at Clermont in November of the same year. Here the Pope commanded a crusade against the "infidels who were in possession of Christ's sepulchre, and promised a remission of sins to those who joined it, and paradise to those who fell in battle." Religious fanaticism was the chief motive of this Crusade, but it was mixed with others, such as a desire of carving

Councils of Placentia and Clermont, March and November, 1095.

out new kingdoms or acquiring riches; and "sensuality was allured by the fabulous flavour of Oriental wines and the magical beauty of Grecian women." "Avarice, ambition, and lust" thus co-operated with faith in exciting a religious outburst. 455—503 A.H.

"Every means," says Hallam, "was used to excite an epidemical frenzy." During the time that a Crusader bore the Cross, he was free from suits for debts and exempt from taxes, and his person was under the protection of the Church. To these material advantages were joined the remission of penances, the abolition of all sins, and the assurance of eternal felicity. "None doubted that such as perished in the war unfailingly received the reward of martyrdom."

1096 A.C. Peter the Hermit.

The first band, led by Walter (Gauthier) the Penniless, was massacred by the Christian Bulgarians. Peter the Hermit led the second host of forty thousand men, women, and children of all nations and languages. "Arriving at Malleville, they avenged their precursors by assaulting the town, slaying seven thousand of the inhabitants, and abandoning themselves to every species of grossness and libertinism." Hungary and Bulgaria became a desert before Peter's horde. Alexius shipped them across the Bosphorus without admitting them into the city. In Asia they recommenced their excesses. Michaud says that they "committed crimes which made nature shudder." They killed children at the breast, scattered their limbs in the air, and carried their ravages to the very walls of Nice. But the Sultan attacked them with fifteen thousand men. Their leader, Reginald, with some companions, embraced Islâm. The rest were exterminated.

The third wave, comprised of "the most stupid and

1063— 1110 A.C. savage refuse of the people,"[1] was commanded by Godeschal, a German monk. "They mingled with their devotion a brutal licence of rapine, prostitution, and drunkenness." According to Michaud, they gave themselves up to intemperance; they forgot Constantinople and Jerusalem "in tumultuous scenes of debauchery," and "pillage, violation, and murder was everywhere left on the traces of their passage." The Hungarians rose in arms against them; the plains of Belgrade were covered with the Crusaders' bones, and only a few of Godeschal's rabble escaped to tell the tale. The fourth wave issued from England, France, Flanders, and Lorraine. Mills calls them "another herd of wild and desperate savages." The Turks being far off, they took to murdering the Jews. Thousands of Jews were massacred and pillaged at Cologne, and in other towns on the banks of the Rhine and the Moselle. Seven hundred were slaughtered at Mayence alone.

"The infernal multitude hurried on to the south in their usual career of carnage and rapine;"[2] but at Memsburg they were destroyed by a Hungarian army.

1097 A.C. In the following year a more systematic onslaught was organised by the princes of feudal Europe. Their passage towards the East was attended by the same atrocities. Under the leadership of Godfrey of Bouillon, the Crusaders arrived at Constantinople. With considerable dexterity Alexius diverted their attack on Constantinople, and shipped the unwelcome visitors across the Bosphorus, and in May 1097 A.C. the Crusaders mustered on the plains of Nice, seven hundred thousand strong, an enormous host sufficient to sweep from the field any army the Seljuks could bring against them.

[1] Gibbon. [2] Mills.

Nice, the capital of the Sultan, was invested and threatened with destruction. But Alexius induced the Seljuk sovereign to deliver the place to him. The sight of his standard flying over the castle threw the fanatical horde into a frenzy. But the city was saved. From Nice the Crusaders marched to Antioch. Slaughter, rapine, and outrage marked their progress through Asia. The siege of Antioch lasted nine months. Provisions became scarce, and the soldiers of the Cross actually resorted to cannibalism. "Carrion was openly dressed," says Mills, "and human flesh was eaten in secret."[1]

455—503 A.H.

Siege of Antioch. Oct. 1097—June 1098.

Mutilation of the dead was indulged in as a sport. The heads of two thousand Turks, who fell in a sortie from Antioch, were cut off; some were exhibited as trophies, others were fixed on stakes round the camp, and others shot into the town. On another occasion they dragged the corpses of the Saracens from their sepulchres, and exposed fifteen hundred heads to the weeping citizens. "The son of the Seljuk Ameer commanding at Antioch," says Michaud, "fell into the hands of the Crusaders, and they tried to induce his family to deliver up the city as his ransom. On their demand being refused, they subjected their young captive to the most barbarous treatment. His cruel tortures were renewed each day for a month. At last they conducted him to the foot of the rampart, and there immolated him in the sight of his parents and fellow-citizens."[2]

Brutality often goes hand-in-hand with reckless indulgence, and the invaders gave the rein to their wildest passions. One author remarks that "seldom does the

[1] According to Von Sybel, Mills, and many other writers, cannibalism was openly practised among the lower ranks of the Crusaders, especially the camp followers.

[2] Vol. i. p. 462.

1063—1110 A.C. history of profane wars display such scenes of intemperance and debauchery."

And Michaud says, "if contemporary accounts are to be credited, all the vices of the infamous Babylon prevailed among the liberators of Sion."

Capture of Antioch by the Crusaders. An attempt at relief failed owing to the incapacity of the Seljukian general (Kerboghâ) and his ill-treatment of the princes and ameers who had joined him. Antioch at last fell by treachery. An Armenian traitor named

June 1098. Firûz, or as the Arabs call him Behrûz, lowered ropes in the night by means of which the Crusaders scaled the walls. Some towers were seized and the guards slain. A gate was then opened, and the whole army poured into the city shouting "*Dieu le veut*," and then commenced a frightful butchery. "The dignity of age, the helplessness of youth, and the beauty of the weaker sex, were disregarded by the Latin savages. Houses were no sanctuaries, and the sight of a mosque added new virulence to cruelty."[1]

Every habitation, from the marble palace to the meanest hovel, was converted into a shamble; the narrow streets and the spacious squares all alike ran with human blood. The lowest estimate puts the people massacred in Antioch at ten thousand souls.

After butchering the Saracens, the invaders abandoned themselves to the worst excesses. From Antioch they

Massacre at Marra't un-Nomân. proceeded to Marra't un-Nomân, one of the most populous and flourishing cities of Syria, which they captured. Here they slaughtered one hundred thousand people. "The streets ran with blood until ferocity was tired out." Bohemond then reviewed his prisoners. "They who were vigorous or beautiful," says Mills, "were reserved

[1] Mills, vol. i. p. 179.

for the slave-market at Antioch, but the aged and infirm were immolated at the altar of cruelty." At Marra also cannibalism was rampant, "and it is even said that human flesh was publicly exposed for sale in the Christian camp." From Marra the soldiers of the Cross marched upon Jerusalem,[1] which they took by storm.

455—503 A.H.

The capture of Jerusalem. Butchery by the Crusaders.

Michaud gives a graphic account of the massacre. "The Saracens were massacred in the streets and in the houses. Jerusalem had no refuge for the vanquished. Some fled from death by precipitating themselves from the ramparts; others crowded for shelter into the palaces, the towers, and above all into their mosques, where they could not conceal themselves from the pursuit of the Christians. The Crusaders, masters of the Mosque of Omar, where the Saracens defended themselves for some time, renewed there the deplorable scenes which disgraced the conquest of Titus. The infantry and cavalry rushed pell-mell among the fugitives. Amid the most horrid tumult, nothing was heard but the groans and cries of death; the victors trod over heaps of corpses in pursuing those who vainly attempted to escape. Raymond d'Agiles, who was an eye-witness, says, 'that under the portico of the mosque, the blood was knee-deep, and reached the horses' bridles.'"[2]

23 Shâbân, 492 A.H. 15th July, 1099 A.C.

There was a short lull in the work of slaughter whilst the Crusaders returned thanks to heaven for their success; but it recommenced immediately the prayers were over. "All the captives whom the lassitude of carnage had at first spared, all those who had been

[1] There is an extremely interesting description of Jerusalem as it existed at this epoch in the *Safarnâmèh* of Nâsiri Khusrû. It had been re-taken by the Fatimides shortly before its capture by the Franks.

[2] Vol. i. p. 236.

1063—1110 A.C. saved in the hope of a rich ransom, were butchered in cold blood. The Saracens were forced to throw themselves from the tops of towers and houses; they were burnt alive; they were dragged from their subterranean retreats, they were haled to the public places, and immolated on piles of the dead. Neither the tears of women, nor the cries of little children, nor the sight of the place where Jesus Christ forgave his executioners, could mollify the victors' passion."[1]

Another writer adds: "It was resolved that no pity should be shown to the Mussulmans. The subjugated people were therefore dragged into the public places, and slain as victims. Women with children at the breast, girls and boys, all were slaughtered. The squares, the streets, and even the uninhabited places of Jerusalem, again were strewed with the dead bodies of men and women, and the mangled limbs of children. No heart melted into compassion, or expanded into benevolence."[2] Over seventy thousand people perished in the city!

Treatment of the Jews. As special objects of malevolence, the Jews were reserved for a worse fate. Their synagogues, into which they were driven, were set on fire and they all perished in the flames. "Contemporary Christian historians," says Michaud, "describe these frightful scenes with perfect equanimity." Even amid recitals of the most disgusting details, they "never allow a single expression of horror or pity to escape them."

Godfrey de Bouillon. Godfrey of Bouillon was made King of Jerusalem. He was succeeded a year later by Baldwin, who laid siege to Cæsarea. After a brave resistance, the garrison

[1] Michaud, vol. i. p. 239.

[2] Mills, vol. i. p. 278. Michaud adds, "The carnage lasted for a week. The few who escaped were reduced to horrible servitude."

proposed to surrender on honourable terms, which were accepted. The gates were accordingly thrown open; but the Franks, once in the town, "paid no respect to the capitulation, and massacred without pity a disarmed and defenceless people." Tripoli, Tyre, and Sidon shared more or less the same fate. At this period the towns on the Phœnician sea-board were at the zenith of their prosperity. Nâsiri Khusrû describes the first-named city as a beautiful place; its suburbs and surrounding villages covered with fields of waving corn, smiling vineyards, luxuriant sugar-plantations, and gardens of orange, citron, dates, and other fruit-trees. The town itself was magnificent and populous, with houses "four, five, and even six stories" in height, with shops which looked like palaces, and markets stocked with every article of luxury and food. Fountains played in the public square and streets. Its cathedral mosque was a splendid structure of marble, "well adorned and decorated." It possessed besides a rich public library, a famous college, and a paper manufactory, which turned out paper "as good as that of Samarkand." In the year 1109 A.C., the Crusaders, under Tancred, assisted by a Pisan fleet, besieged this place. After a heroic defence, lasting several months, it was captured and sacked; the inhabitants were put to the sword, and the library, college, and manufactory were reduced to ashes.

455—503 A.H.

Sack of Tripoli.

Palestine and a part of Syria thus fell into the hands of the Franks, who introduced into their new possessions the feudal institutions of their native land. The Moslem population was reduced to serfdom or villenage; judicial investigation gave place to trial by battle or ordeal; and, as in Europe at that time, slaves chained in gangs were hawked about the streets. Ameer Osâma, who visited Jerusalem some years later, ransomed a number of these

1063—1110 A.C. poor wretches. The Templars appear, from his description, to have acquired a certain degree of polish, but the new-comers were uncouth barbarians; whilst his description of the laxity of morals among the Crusaders reveals a picture of unmitigated coarseness and depravity.

CHAPTER XXI

THE ABBASSIDES—(*continued*)

MUSTAZHIR—MUKTAFI—MUSTANJID

492—569 A.H., 1099—1174 A.C.

THE CRUSADES

Caliph Mustazhir—Sultan Barkyarûk—His wars with Tutûsh, his uncle, and his brother Mohammed—Death of Barkyarûk—Accession of Mohammed to the Sultanate—Discord among the vassals—The progress of the Crusaders—Death of Sultan Mohammed—Death of the Caliph Mustazhir—Accession of the Caliph Mustarshid—Sultan Sanjar, Sultan of the East—Sultan Mahmûd, of Irâk and Syria—Rise of Imâd ud-dîn Zangi (Sanguin)—Death of Mahmûd—Accession of Sultan Masûd—Assassination of Mustarshid—Election of Râshid as Caliph—Deposed by Masûd—Accession of Muktafi as Caliph—War of Zangi with the Crusaders—His victories—The death of Zangi—The accession of Nûr ud-dîn Mahmûd—His successes against the Crusaders—Death of Muktafi and accession of Caliph Mustanjid—The dispatch of Shirkûh to Egypt—Annexation of Egypt—Rise of Saladin—Death of Mustanjid—Accession of Caliph Mustazii—Death of Nûr ud-dîn Mahmûd.

492—569 A.H. 1099—1174 A.C.

WHETHER it was by design or by accident, Christendom could not have chosen a better opportunity to hurl itself on Asia. Feudalism sapped the foundations of the mighty empire of the Seljuk just as it had that of the Carlovingians. Alp Arslân had bestowed Asia Minor on his cousin Sulaimân; Malik Shah gave Syria to his

Feudalism in Asia.

1099—1174 A.C. brother Tutûsh.[1] Both these princes acknowledged the suzerainty of the Sultan. But besides these two kingdoms, Mesopotamia, Syria, and Palestine were parcelled among a number of vassal lords, whose sole duty to the suzerain was to render him military service. So long as the genius of Nizâm ul-Mulk and the grand personality of Malik Shah pervaded the empire, the chiefs and princes rendered a willing homage to the sovereign.

State of the Seljukide Empire.

The moment they ceased to breathe, dissensions sprang up on all sides; and peace and concord gave place to war and strife. First there was a struggle between Turkhân Khâtûn, on behalf of her son Mahmûd, and Barkyarûk. Mahmûd died shortly after, and Barkyarûk was thereupon acknowledged the over-lord of the Seljuks, and was invested by the Caliph Muktadi with the title of Sultan. Then followed a struggle between Barkyarûk and his uncle Tutûsh, who also aimed at supreme power. The defeat and death of Tutûsh did not bring peace to the distracted empire, for Barkyarûk became involved in a war with his brother Mohammed, which lasted several years.

The stream of fugitives fleeing from the Crusaders poured into Bagdad. It was the month of Ramazân, the season of fasting. The tale of horror told by the hapless few who had escaped slaughter or slavery plunged the city into sorrow. The fast was forgotten; the people assembled in the cathedral mosque and wept.[2] The Caliph Mustazhir b'Illâh hurried off three eminent men of his court to Barkyarûk and Mohammed, who were encamped at Holwan, to entreat them to settle their

[1] Surnamed *Tâj ud-Dowla*, "Crown of the Empire."

[2] One of the poets of the day, al-Muzzafar al-Abiwardi, expressed the universal grief in an elegy which has been preserved by Ibn ul-Athîr and Abu'l Fedâ.

quarrels and march against the common enemy. The appeal proved fruitless, for the brothers were soon again at each other's throat in consequence of the assassination of Barkyarûk's vizier. The historian pathetically adds, "the discord among the Sultans enabled the Franks to establish themselves in the countries of Islâm." 492—569 A.H.

On Barkyarûk's death in 498 A.H. (1104 A.C.), Mohammed[1] succeeded to the Sultanate,[2] which he held for fourteen years. He is described as valiant, virtuous, just, and generous, and his charity to the orphan and indigent have been praised by the poets of the time. Accession of Sultan Mohammed.

But the political condition of the empire was unfavourable to any united action against the common foe. The various chiefs who held the appanages of Syria and Mesopotamia were divided by mutual jealousies. The prince of Aleppo (Rizwân,[3] the son of Tutûsh) was a traitor; whilst the others, though willing enough to obey the Sultan, were more devoted to the advancement of their personal ambitions than to the furtherance of the national cause. The utter disorganisation of the Fatimide Caliphate, to which the Syrian sea-board and Palestine belonged at this period, rendered the assistance of the towns attacked by the enemy difficult or impossible. The Fatimide Caliphate.

[1] The celebrated philosopher and mystic Imâm Abû Hâmid al-Ghazzâli was a contemporary of Sultan Mohammed, by whom he was held in high esteem. One of the Sultan's daughters, named Fâtima, was married to the Caliph Muktadi. She is said to have been a woman of education and considerable political talent. She resided in the *Dargâh-i-Khâtûn*, "the Hall of the Princess."

[2] Under the title of *Ghyâs ud-duniâ w'ad-dîn* ("Redresser of Wrongs in the World and in Religion").

[3] Tutûsh left two sons, Rizwân and Dakkâk. Rizwân took possession of Aleppo and Dakkâk of Damascus. One of Dakkâk's sons was ousted by Toghtakîn, surnamed Zâhir ud-dîn, who was subsequently confirmed in his position by the Sultan.

1099—1174 A.C. The Fatimide Caliph (Mustaali) was wholly incompetent, whilst the Commander-in-Chief, who held the reins of government, instead of organising the military resources of the empire, and taking vigorous action, dallied in Cairo, or spent his time in intrigues against his rivals.

First Battle of Tiberias. Once or twice at the instance of the Sultan Mohammed the chiefs sunk their differences and joined hands to oppose the invaders. At the beginning of 1113 A.C., Baldwin,[1] the King of Jerusalem, raided into the seigniory of Damascus. 13th Moharram, 507 A.H. July 1113 A.C. Unable to oppose him single-handed, Toghtakîn, the Lord of Damascus, invoked the assistance of Moudûd of Mosul. In July 1113 the combined forces of the Lords of Mosul, Damascus, Sinjâr,[2] and Mâridîn marched into Palestine. In a battle near Tiberias, the Franks were routed with terrible loss, and a large number of them were drowned in the lake and in the Jordan. Battle of al-Balât. June 1119 A.C. In June 1119 they were again defeated at a place called al-Balât by Îlgâzi, the Lord of Mâridîn. Even the Egyptians won some successes on the sea-coast. But the Crusaders had the whole of Europe at their back; the reinforcements which poured in for them from all parts of Christendom, the assassination of Moudûd, who was stabbed by a Batinia after the battle of Tiberias, and the division of the chiefs, all helped them to recover their ground.

The Crusaders went on thus extending their power, capturing city after city, devastating the country, slaughtering the inhabitants or reducing them to slavery. 15th Zu'l Hijja, 511 A.H. 18th April, 1118 A.C. Sultan Mohammed died in 511 A.H., and was followed to the grave the year after by the Caliph Mustazhir. 16th Rabi II. 512 A.H. This Caliph had occupied the pontifical throne for

[1] Called by Ibn ul-Athîr, Baghdawîn; by others, Bardivîl.

[2] Tamîrik.

twenty-five years, and was succeeded by his son, *Abû Mansûr* al-Fazl, under the title of *al-Mustarshid b'Illâh.*[1] 492—569 A.H.

The death of Sultan Mohammed was not without effect on the fortunes of the Moslems and Christians. He was succeeded in the over-lordship by his brother Sanjar,[2] the last hero of a heroic race, and in the succession of his private dominions by his son Mahmûd. Under Sultan Mahmûd arose the first champion of Islâm, who not only withstood the shock of the Franks, but drove them inch by inch from their possessions. Imâd ud-dîn Zangi,[3] the Sanguin of the Christian writers, was the son of one of the principal chiefs of Sultan Malik Shah, named Ak-Sunkar[4] (*Kasîm ud-Dowla*), who played an important part in the history of the troublous times that followed the death of his great master Ak-Sunkar had died leaving his son Zangi, a lad of fourteen, to succeed him in the seigniory, but his vassals and retainers rallied round the youth and upheld him in his position, and he himself showed early the signs of an indomitable will, great energy of character, and administrative and military

6th Aug. 1118 A.C. *Abû Mansûr* al-Fazl, *al-Mustarshid b'Illâh.*

[1] "Taking the Lord for a guide."

[2] The friend and patron of the poet Anwarî.

[3] The Persian student must not confound this Zangi with the father of Atâbeg Saad, of Fars, the patron of the poet Shaikh Maslah ud-dîn Saadi, the author of the *Gulistân* ("the Rose-garden" of Persia).

[4] "The White Falcon." He was chamberlain or Hâjib to the Sultan. Ak-Sunkar was an able soldier and a wise administrator. Perfect justice reigned throughout his seigniory, the markets were moderate, the roads absolutely safe, and order prevailed in all parts. His policy of making a district pay for a misdeed occurring within its boundaries is not unknown in modern times. If a caravan happened to be plundered, the nearest villages had to make good the loss, and thus the whole population were interested in the protection of the travellers and the preservation of order.

1099— 1174 A.C. capacity of a high order. In 516 A.H., Zangi obtained from Sultan Mahmûd the city of Wâsit as an appanage, 1122-1123 A.C. and the post of Commissary (*Shahna*)[1] at Basra. Ramazân, 521 A.H. Sept.-Oct. 1127 A.C. Four years later the government of Mosul and Upper Mesopotamia was conferred on him, with the title of Atâbek ("Prince Tutor"[2]), and he was confirmed in this dignity by the letters patent of the Caliph. Imâd ud-dîn Zangi became the founder of the long line of the Atâbeks of Mosul. Ibn ul-Athîr describes most graphically the state of weakness among the Mussulmans at this epoch, and the strength of "the Polytheists." "Their army was numerous, their violence and depredations increased every day, and they committed every enormity without any fear of punishment. Their territories extended from Mâridîn in Upper Mesopotamia to the city of Aarîsh on the borders of Egypt; Harrân and Rakka were subjected to the greatest humiliations; their devastations were carried to the very gates of Nisibîn; they cut all the roads to Damascus save the desert route past Rahba; they levied tribute on towns without number, and blackmailed Aleppo to the half of its revenue, even to the profits of the mill that stands by the Garden Gate. They spared no one, neither those who believed in the unity of God nor those who denied it." Zangi set himself vigorously to the task of improving the government and organising his army; and before long he was able to take the field in sufficient force to drive the Franks out of Mesopotamia. The conquest of 522 A.H. 1128 A.C. Membij (ancient Bambace) and Bizaa or Buzaa made him the undisputed ruler of the vast principality of Mosul. In 1128 A.C., on the invitation of the people of Aleppo, who had suffered terribly from the depredations of the

Zangi appointed Atâbek of Mosul.

Occupation of Aleppo.

[1] See p. 408.

[2] Or "Prince-governor."

Crusaders,[1] he took possession of their city. Hamâh followed the example of Aleppo. The following year Zangi routed the Crusaders under the walls of al-Asârib, and captured the castle after a stout resistance. A short truce between Joscelin, the Count of Edessa, "the greatest demon of them all,"[2] enabled Zangi to take part in the inevitable civil war which broke out on the death of Sultan Mahmûd. Mahmûd was succeeded by his brother Masûd, but the succession was disputed by another brother named Seljuk Shah. After a short struggle, they made up their quarrel and marched against their uncle Sanjar, but were defeated at Damarj. Sanjar treated the rebels with kindness and confirmed them in their possessions. War then broke out between the Caliph Mustarshid and Masûd. Mustarshid was taken prisoner, and whilst in Masûd's camp was assassinated by the emissaries of the Batinias. Mustarshid was succeeded by his son, *Abû Jaafar* Mansûr, under the title of *Râshid b'Illâh*.[3] Râshid, however, did not occupy the pontifical throne beyond a few months. Differences between him and Sultan Masûd compelled him to leave Bagdad for Mosul. Masûd thereupon assembled the jurists and Kâzis, and after reciting Râshid's breach of faith, induced them to depose him. Upon Râshid's deposition, *Abû Abdullâh*, son of Mustazhir, was elected Caliph under the title of *al-Muktafi li'amr Illâh*.[4] As the power of the Seljuk sovereigns declined, Muktafi's influence proportionately increased in Irâk and Chaldæa, and in the end he succeeded in recovering his temporal authority in the home provinces.

492—569 A.H.

Sultan Mahmûd's death. 525 A.H. 1030-1031 A.C.

Battle of Damarj, Rajab 526 A.H. May 1132 A.C.

The Caliph Mustarshid assassinated, 16th Zu'l Kaada 529 A.H. 28th Aug., 1135 A.C.

Abû Jaafar Mansûr, *ar-Râshia b'Illâh.*

Abû Abdullâh Mohammed al-*Muktafi li'amr Illâh.*

[1] Ibn ul-Athîr calls them "the Demons of the Cross."

[2] *Âazim ush-Shiâtîn*, Ibn ul-Athîr.

[3] "Following the right path by the grace of the Lord."

[4] "Resting on the commands of the Lord."

1099—1174 A.C. Atâbek Zangi did not long concern himself with the troubles in the East. His great work lay in Syria. The Crusaders were again in a ferment; they had received large reinforcements from Europe, and had been joined by a Greek contingent under the personal command of the Emperor John Comnenus. They captured Buzaa, put to the sword all the male inhabitants, and carried into captivity the women and children. They then marched upon Shaizar (Cæsarea), a day's journey from Hamâh. The castle of Shaizar, the birthplace of Osâma,[1] was almost impregnable. Built on a rock, it could be approached only by a horse-path cut in the side of the mountains. This narrow road first spanned the dashing Orontes, then tunnelled through the rock, and finally ran across a deep ditch over a wooden bridge. The bridge once cut, nobody could approach the castle. Since the beginning of the fifth century of the Hegira, this place had belonged to the Banû Munkiz (Munkidh), of the Arab tribe of Kinâna, and they were the hereditary lords of the fortress and the surrounding district. Its strong situation, in close proximity to Hamâh as well as the crusading centres, made it important to both the Franks and the Saracens. No sooner, therefore, did Zangi receive the appeal of Abû Asâkir Sultan,[2] who was at that time the Lord of Shaizar, than he hastened to the relief of the place. On the approach of the Atâbek, the Franks and Greeks raised the siege and retreated, the Greeks returning to their country. Zangi lost no time in pursuing his advantage. The fortress of Arka, situated in the territories of the Count of Tripoli,

Shâbân 532 A.H. April-May 1138 A.C.

[1] Ameer *Muwayyid ud-Dowla* Osâma was one of the heroes of the early Crusades. His memoirs, called *Kitâb ul-Itibâr*, published in 1884, in Paris, are extremely interesting.

[2] Uncle of Osâma.

was carried by assault and rased to the ground. Baalbek 492—569 A.H.
was captured and placed under the command of *Najm ud-dîn* Ayûb, the father of Saladin. So long, however, as the principality of Damascus was held by an independent chief, it was impossible for the Atâbek to drive the Franks out of Syria.

In 534 A.H. he routed the Franks in the neighbourhood of Barîn (Mont-Ferrand), which fell into his hands. 1139 A.C.
It was one of the strongest fortresses held by the Crusaders, and formed the centre of their marauding excursions into the countries between Hamâh and Aleppo. His greatest conquest, however, was achieved in the year 539 A.H., when he captured Edessa (Rohâ), which belonged to Joscelin II, "their hero and demon." "It was in truth the conquest of conquests." "Rohâ was regarded by the Christians as one of the noblest of cities, for it formed one of their bishoprics, the most eminent of which was that of Jerusalem; after Jerusalem came in order Antioch, Rome, Constantinople, and Rohâ. It was in effect the eye of Mesopotamia. Its possession had enabled them to reduce the surrounding districts, and they possessed strong fortresses along the line of march."[1] On his approach he offered the inhabitants safety of life and property, but they rejected his terms with indignation. The city was carried by assault. He had thought of inflicting a terrible punishment in revenge for all that had taken place in Jerusalem and at Antioch, but his humanity overbore his anger. Save and except the fighting men and the monks and priests, who were found exciting the Frankish soldiery, none were killed. The men, women, and children who had fallen into the hands of the victors were set at liberty, and their goods and chattels were restored to them out of free grace.

Conquest of Edessa. Jamâdi II. 539 A.H. December 1144 A.C.

[1] Ibn ul-Athîr.

1099—1174 A.C.

Leaving a strong garrison, the Atâbek pursued his victorious course. He reduced in succession Serûj, al-Bira, and the other castles held by the Crusaders. Whilst engaged in the siege of Kalât-Jâbir, Imâd ud-dîn was murdered in his sleep by some of his own Mamlukes, who were instigated to the foul deed by his enemies. Thus perished one of the greatest heroes of the age.[1] Just, generous, and wise, the Atâbek Zangi was a father to his people. When he assumed the government of Mesopotamia, a considerable portion of that province, as well as of Syria, was lying uncultivated; the peasantry and citizens were ruined; and owing to the depredations of the Franks, commerce had ceased. Zangi devoted immense pains to revive agriculture and to restore the country to prosperity; the tillers of the soil flocked back to their lands; the ruined cities were rebuilt and re-embellished; disorders and brigandage were repressed with severity, and as the Frankish marauders and cut-throats were driven back towards the littoral, commerce resumed life. He was scrupulously guardful of women's safety, and any insult or outrage to them brought down the severest punishment. His charity was lavish. Every Friday he gave away "openly" a hundred dinârs in alms; on other days he distributed large sums in secret by the hands of a confidential servant. He was a faithful friend and considerate master; in camp, a strict disciplinarian. "His administration—in the abundance of its resources, in the prompt dispatch of business, in its numerous *personnel*—compared with that of the Sultan." He was a friend of the learned, and his vizier Jamâl ud-dîn, surnamed al-Jawwâd ("the Bountiful"), supported him as zealously in the patronage of learning as in the govern-

Imâd ud-dîn Zangi's assassination.

5th Rabi II. 541 A.H. 14th September 1146 A.C.

[1] Ibn ul-Athîr throughout calls him the *Shahîd*, "the Martyr."

ment of the kingdom. Jamâl ud-dîn[1] held the office of 492—569 A.H.
Inspector-General (*Mushrif*) of the principality and President of the Council of State. It was Zangi who said of himself that he loved the back of a saddle better than a silken bed, the din of battle better than the most enchanting music, the clash of arms more than the blandishments of a sweetheart. The great Atâbek left four sons, *Saif ud-dîn* Ghâzi the eldest, who succeeded to the principality of Mosul; *Nûr ud-dîn* Mahmûd (Noradinus of William of Tyre), on whom devolved the "heritage of championship," with the principality of Aleppo for his appanage; *Kutb ud-dîn* Moudûd and *Nusrat ud-dîn* Ameer Mirân. Both Saif ud-dîn and Nûr ud-dîn were trained in their father's camp. But the latter was not merely a soldier; he was a jurist[2] and a scholar as well, and a liberal patron of arts and learning. He founded colleges and hospitals in every part of his kingdom, and was the munificent patron of scholars and *savants*, who flocked to his court. He was the first to establish a regular High Court of Justice, called the *Dâr ul-aadl*. "The true praise of kings," says Gibbon, with his usual acu-

Nûr ud-dîn Mahmûd.

[1] Abû Jaafar Mohammed surnamed Jamâl ud-dîn ("the beauty of religion"). Amongst the numerous monuments which he left of his beneficence, Ibn Khallikân mentions the aqueduct by which water was brought from a great distance to Arafât during the days of the Hajj, the stairs leading from the foot to the summit of that mountain, and the wall around Medîna. Every twelvemonth he sent to Mecca and Medîna money and clothing sufficient for the wants of the poor and destitute during the year. He had a special register for the persons to whom he granted pensions or who applied for pecuniary assistance. During a famine which afflicted Mosul, he spent all he possessed in alleviating the misery of the people.

[2] His collection of the traditions of the Prophet relating to justice, alms, and piety, called the *Fakhr un-Nûrî*, formed the ground-work of his policy, morals, and discipline, during a long and glorious reign of twenty-eight years.

1099—1174 A.C. men, "is after their death and from the mouth of their enemies." William, Bishop of Tyre, whilst calling him the greatest persecutor of the Christian name and faith, is forced to admit that he was "a just ruler, energetic, prudent, and religious, according to the traditions of his people." The prosperity of his people was the sole object and aim of his life, and his subjects adored him for his justice, his clemency, and his moderation. Soon after Nûr ud-dîn's accession to the throne of Aleppo, the Christians of Edessa, assisted by a large body of Franks under Joscelin, treacherously rose against the garrison, and massacred the soldiers and Moslem inhabitants in the city. Nûr ud-dîn swooped down upon the devoted town, which this time felt the full weight of a justly indignant sovereign. The soldiers of Joscelin, and the traitors who had assisted him, were put to the sword. The Armenians, who were the chief promoters of treasonable communications with the Crusaders, were expelled, and the walls were pulled down.

His character.

The Second Crusade. 542 A.H. 1147 A.C.

The double fall of Edessa created a great commotion in Europe, and St. Bernard of Clairvaux preached a fresh crusade against Islâm. In 1147 A.C. Conrad III., Emperor of Germany, and Louis VII. undertook this "Holy War" to support "the failing fortunes of the Latins." Contemporaneous history records that they led over 900,000 men under their united banners for the help of their brethren in Syria and Palestine. Louis VII. was accompanied by his wife, Eleanor of Guienne, who afterwards married Henry II. of England, and her example attracted a number of women to join the ill-fated expedition. A considerable troop of women, armed with spears and shields, rode among the Germans. Nor were the French behind in this mixture of sexes, which naturally led to much depravity of morals. The fate of the two armies is well known. Both sovereigns suffered disastrous defeats on their march towards Syria; a large portion of Conrad's army was annihilated in the neighbourhood of Laodicea, whilst the forces of Louis, whose route lay along the sea-coast, were overwhelmed and destroyed by the Seljuks on the heights of the Cadmus, now called Bâba-Dâgh. When Louis arrived in the principality of Antioch, which was held by Raymond of Poictiers, an uncle of Eleanor, he had lost three-fourths of his army. The voluptuous city contained at this time within its walls the Countess of Toulouse, the Countess of Blois, Sybille of Flanders, Maurille, countess of Roussy, Talcquery, duchess of Bouillon, and many other ladies celebrated for their birth or their beauty. But the queen of them all was Eleanor of Guienne. In Antioch the warriors of the Cross abandoned themselves to unbridled licence, whilst the *fêtes* of Raymond degenerated into orgies, and Queen Eleanor scandalised everybody by her freedom of manners. After the Crusaders had sufficiently refreshed themselves in Antioch, their united forces marched upon Damascus, which they held in leaguer for several months; but the approach of Saif ud-dîn Ghâzi[1] and Nûr ud-dîn Mahmûd to the relief of the city, compelled them to raise the siege and hurriedly to retreat towards Palestine. Conrad and Louis then left for Europe, and thus the Second Crusade ended.

492—569 A.H.

6th Rabi I. 543 A.H. 25th July, 1148 A.C.

End of the Second Crusade.

Nûr ud-dîn Mahmûd now commenced his career of conquest against the Franks. He captured the castle of al-Aareima, one of their strongest fortresses on the borders of Syria, and a few months later inflicted on

[1] Saif ud-dîn Ghâzi died in Jamâdi II. 544 A.H. (November 1149 A.C.), and leaving no male issue was succeeded in the Atâbekship of Mosul by his brother, Kutb ud-dîn Moudûd.

1099–1174 A.C. them a heavy defeat at Zaghrâ, in the neighbourhood of Antioch. In a battle under the walls of Anneb (ancient
1148–1149 A.C. Nepa), the proud Raymond of Poictiers, prince of Antioch, was killed, and his troops routed with great slaughter. He left a young son named Bohemond (called by the Arabs, Beemend), under the guardianship of his wife. This lady did not, however, remain long a widow, but the fate of her second husband was almost as disastrous as that of Raymond, for he fell into Nûr ud-dîn's hands in a skirmish, in which the Franks were again discomfited.

Capture of Apameas. 544 A.H. 1149-50 A.C.

In 544 A.H. he reduced the important fortress of Apameas (Afâmièh), about a day's journey from Hamâh. Two years later Nûr ud-dîn suffered a defeat at the hands of Joscelin II. This reverse was soon compensated by the capture of Joscelin, which was regarded by the Saracens as a splendid success; "for," says Ibn ul-Athîr, "Joscelin was one of the most bigoted demons among the Franks, and surpassed all others in his hatred against the Moslems. Whenever the Franks undertook any expedition they confided the command to him, as they appreciated his bravery, his prudence, his animosity against Islâm, and the hardness of his heart against its professors." The capture of this redoubtable foe facilitated the task of Nûr ud-dîn, and he rapidly reduced a number of cities and fortresses belonging to the Crusaders, such as Tell-Bâsher, Ain-Tâb, Nahr ul-jazz, Burj ur-Rassas, etc.

Nûr ud-dîn Mahmûd's defeat. 546 A.H. 1151-52 A.C. Capture of Joscelin.

Battle of Dulûk.

Another battle at Dulûk, which was equally disastrous to the Franks, led to the subjugation of the greater part of the principality of Antioch.

Sultan Masûd died in 547 A.H. (1152-53 A.C.), and was succeeded on the throne by Malik Shah, a son of his brother, Sultan Mahmûd. He was the last of his family who was recognised as a Sultan.

492—569 A.H.

But so long as Damascus was held by an independent prince, whose fidelity was by no means certain, Nûr ud-dîn, like his father, experienced great difficulties in his operations against the Crusaders. These, on their side, emboldened by the successful capture of Ascalon on the sea-coast, resumed their design of conquering the capital of Syria.[1] In this crisis, the inhabitants of Damascus appealed to Nûr ud-dîn, who immediately responded to their call. The prince[2] of that city received for his appanage the city of Emessa, and the son of the great Zangi was installed as the sovereign of Damascus, amidst the acclamation of the citizens.

Loss of Ascalon. Nûr ud-dîn Mahmûd takes possession of Damascus. 10th Safar, 549 A.H. 26th April, 1154 A.C.

This peaceful but important conquest obtained for him from the Caliph the title of *al-Malik al-Aâdil* ("the Just King"), which he fully deserved. There was a short peace between Nûr ud-dîn and the Crusaders, which enabled him to repair the havoc caused by the earthquake that about this time afflicted Syria and ruined so many monuments of antiquity.

The Caliph Muktafi's death. 2nd Rabi I. 555 A.H. 12th March 1160 A.C. *Abu'l Muzzaffar* Yusuf, *al-Mustanjid b'Illâh.*

The Caliph Muktafi died in the year 1160, and was succeeded in the pontificate by his son *Abu'l Muzzaffar* Yusuf, under the title of *al-Mustanjid b'Illâh.*[3]

Six years later Nûr ud-dîn sent the memorable expedi-

[1] In the time of Toghtakin the Crusaders had entered into a coalition with the Assassins and attacked Damascus, but were disastrously repulsed.

[2] Mujîr ud-dîn Abak. He entered afterwards into treasonable communications with the Franks, and was removed from Hems to Balès, which he held up to his death. Toghtakin was succeeded by his son, Tâj ul-Mulûk Bûri, as the Lord of Damascus. Bûri was succeeded by his son Shams ul-Mulûk Ismâil. Upon his assassination the seigniory fell into the hands of his brother, Shihâb ud-dîn Mahmûd. Mujîr ud-dîn was Shihâb ud-dîn's son. The government was practically in the hands of Muîn ud-dîn Anâr, the friend of Osâma, with whom he visited Jerusalem.

[3] "Seeking victory from the Lord."

1099—1174 A.C. tion to Egypt, which bore such important results for both Franks and Saracens. The Fatimide dynasty was tottering to its fall. The last Caliph of this race, al-Aâzid li'dîn Illâh, was a confirmed valetudinarian, and all the power of the state rested in the hands of his minister, Shâwer as-Saadi. Ousted from office by a cabal, Shâwer betook himself to the Prince of Damascus, Jamâdi I. 559 A.H. April 1164 A.C. and sought his assistance, promising in return the support of the Egyptian troops against the Crusaders, cession of certain territories, and a large subsidy. After some hesitation, Nûr ud-dîn acceded to his prayer, and sent him back to Egypt with an escort under the command of *Asad ud-dîn* Shirkûh ("the Lion of the Mountain"), the uncle of the famous Saladin. No sooner did the traitor recover his power, than, joining hands with the Franks, he called upon Shirkûh to evacuate Egypt. Zu'l Hijja 559 A.H. October—November, 1164. The small force under Shirkûh's command offered a stout resistance to the allies at Bilbais or Bilbîs (ancient Pelusium); but in the end was forced to evacuate the place with all the honours of war.

559 A.H. August 1164 A.C. In the Ramazân of 559 A.H., Nûr ud-dîn was attacked by the united armies of the Franks and Greeks. The battle, which took place under the walls of Hârim, was one of the severest of the Crusades; the Franks suffered a terrible defeat, and most of their chieftains, such as Bohemond, Prince of Antioch, Raymond of Tripoli, Joscelin III., and the Greek general, Duke of Calamar, were taken prisoners. As the fruit of this splendid victory, Nûr ud-dîn captured Hârim, Paneas, al-Monetara (al-Munaitira), etc.

Rabi II. 562 A.H. January—February 1167 A.C. In 562 A.H. Shirkûh again entered Egypt, and again Shâwer called in the Franks to his assistance. Amaury, who now occupied the throne of Jerusalem, hoping to obtain possession of the country on his own account, hurried off an army to the help of Shâwer. The marches and counter-marches of Shirkûh, and his final victory at Bâbain, over the allies, "show," says Michaud, "military capacity of the highest order." "Never has history," remarks Ibn ul-Athîr enthusiastically, "recorded a more extraordinary event than the rout of the Egyptain forces and the Franks of the littoral, by only a thousand cavaliers." After this brilliant success, Shirkûh captured Alexandria and installed himself there. Subsequently a peace was concluded between the Egyptians and the Franks on one side, and the lieutenant of Nûr ud-dîn on the other, by which Amaury agreed to withdraw his troops from Egypt, and to refrain from all interference in its affairs; Shirkûh, to evacuate Alexandria on payment of 50,000 pieces of gold, and to return to Syria. But the Franks, by a secret convention with Shâwer, obtained the right of keeping a resident at Cairo, of occupying some of the cities by their troops, and receiving an annual subsidy of 100,000 pieces of gold. This was in direct breach of the terms of peace with Shirkûh. At last, the conduct of the Crusaders who occupied Cairo and other places became so overbearing, and their tyranny so great, that al-Aâzid himself appealed for help to Nûr ud-dîn. In response, Nûr ud-dîn again sent Shirkûh to Egypt with a sufficiently large force to make head against the Franks. On Shirkûh's approach the Crusaders hurriedly left the country with all their spoil. On the 8th of January, 1169 A.C., Shirkûh re-entered Cairo, and was welcomed by the people and the Fatimide Caliph as the saviour of Egypt. Shâwer was put to death by his enraged sovereign, and Shirkûh was appointed in his place as prime minister and commander-in-chief.[1] Shirkûh, dying two months after, was succeeded in the

492—569 A.H.

Battle of Bâbain.

7th Rabi II. 564 A.H. 8th January, 1169 A.C.

[1] *Ameer ul-juyûsh.*

1099—1174 A.C.

22nd Jamâdi II. 564 A.H. 23rd March, 1169 A.C.

office by his famous nephew, *Salâh ud-dîn* Yusuf (the great Saladin), with the title of *al-Malik un-Nâsir*.[1] Whilst purporting to hold the vizierate of al-Aâzid, Saladin regarded himself in reality the lieutenant of Nûr ud-dîn, who always addressed him as *al-Ameer al-Isfah Salâr*[2] (Ameer, General-in-Chief).

Saladin won all hearts by his liberality and justice. Al-Aâzid was dying, and during his mortal illness, Saladin, who was a strict Hanafî, quietly restored in Egypt the spiritual authority of the Abbasside Caliph.

In the year 1170 A.C., the Caliph al-Mustanjid died, and was succeeded by his son, *Abû Mohammed* Hassan, under the title of *al-Mustazii bi'-amr Illâh*.[3]

9th Rabi II. 506 A.H. 21st December 1170 A.C. Death of al-Mustanjid. Accession of *Abû Mohammed* Hassan, *al-Mustazii bi'-amr Illâh.*

Mustanjid is described by Ibn ul-Athîr as the best of the Caliphs in his conduct towards his subjects. He ruled them with justice and treated them with generosity; he abolished all oppressive and illegal imposts within his territories, and maintained order and peace with firmness.

In 565 A.H. (1170 A.C.) died Kutb ud-din Moudûd, the third son of Zangi, and was succeeded in the Atâbekship by his son, Saif ud-dîn Ghâzi II.

Under Saif ud-dîn Ghâzi II. the affairs of Mosul fell into disorder. Nûr ud-dîn hastened to his nephew's dominions, re-organised the state, and replaced Saif ud-dîn on the throne of Mosul, keeping the control of the army in his own hands.

In the Moharram 567 A.H. died the last of the Fatimides,[4] and Egypt was restored to the spiritual control of the Caliphs of Bagdad. From this time

[1] "The victorious king."

[2] Arabicised form of the Persian Sipah Sâlâr.

[3] "Seeking illumination from the Lord."

[4] Their rule extended over 266 years.

492—569 A.H.

Saladin became the virtual master of Egypt, ruling until the death of Nûr ud-dîn Mahmûd as his viceroy and lieutenant, and afterwards as an independent sovereign. He was then about thirty-five years of age.[1] His father, Najm ud-dîn Ayûb, son of Shâdi, was, like his brother Shirkûh, a trusted officer of Zangi, as well as of Nûr ud-dîn Mahmûd. Saladin himself held various offices under this monarch before he proceeded to Egypt with his uncle. He is described by his biographer[2] as a chivalrous, just, generous, and high-minded sovereign; most tender-hearted, pious in his life, never indulging in anything reprehensible or unseemly, and devoted to the promotion of his people's welfare.

569 A.H. 1173-74 A.C.

11th Shawwâl, 569 A.H. 15th May, 1174 A.C.

In 569 A.H. he sent, with the sanction of his suzerain, his brother Turân Shâh to reduce Yemen, which was successfully accomplished. And the death of Nûr ud-dîn soon after enabled Saladin to consolidate his independent authority over the whole of Egypt, part of Nubia, and Hijâz and Yemen. Nûr ud-dîn left an only son, named Ismâîl (al-Mâlik us-Sâleh),[3] barely eleven years of age at the time.

[1] Saladin was born in 1137-38 A.C. (532 A.H.).

[2] Kâzi Bahâ ud-dîn Abu'l Mahâsin Yusuf, generally known as Ibn Shaddâd, Saladin's *Kâzi ul-aasker* and privy councillor.

[3] "The good king."

CHAPTER XXII

THE ABBASSIDES (*continued*)

576—589 A.H., 1181—1193 A.C.

THE CRUSADES

The Caliph Nâsir—Malik Sâlèh Ismâil, Prince of Damascus—Saladin invited to Damascus—War between Saladin and Malik Sâlèh—Saladin ruler of Syria—Invested with the title of Sultan—Malik Sâlèh's death—Saladin's power—The kingdom of Jerusalem—The Crusaders break the truce—Battle of Tiberias—Rout of the Crusaders—Conquest of Acre, Naplus, Jericho, etc.—Siege of Jerusalem—Its capitulation—Humanity of Saladin—The Third Crusade—Siege of Acre — Heroic defence—The Crusaders' defeats—Death of Frederick Barbarossa—Arrival of the Kings of France and England—Acre taken—Cruelty of Richard Cœur de Lion—Ascalon rased to the ground by Saladin—Peace with Richard—Death of Saladin—His character.

Malik Sâlèh, son of Nûr ud-dîn Mahmûd.

IMMEDIATELY on learning of the death of his patron and master, Saladin sent his condolences to Malik Sâlèh with the customary presents, offering his services and expressing his devotion. He continued the prayers and the coinage, the chief tokens of suzerainty, in the name of Nûr ud-dîn's successor. But the minority of Malik Sâlèh encouraged the ambitions of his father's vassals and courtiers, and each tried to aggrandise himself at the expense of the young king. Their intrigues compelled Saladin to write in stern language, warning them against treachery, and threatening that if matters did not mend, he himself would come to Damascus to look after his sovereign. On this one of the Ameers (Gumushtagîn) hurried off Malik Sâlèh to Aleppo, leaving Damascus exposed to a Frankish attack. The Crusaders would not forgo the opportunity, and laid siege to the city, which was only raised on the payment of a large ransom. Enraged at this and invited by some of the chief men, Saladin hurried to Damascus with seven hundred horse and took possession of the city. He did not enter the palace of Nûr ud-dîn, but abode in his own house where his father, Najm ud-dîn Ayûb, lived whilst at Damascus. From here he wrote to the young Atâbek a respectful letter, containing his homage, and the assurance that he had come to Syria only for his suzerain's protection. The answer which was drawn up by his enemies contained, instead of thanks, accusations of ingratitude and disobedience. Provoked at this he marched towards Aleppo, with the object of having a personal interview with Malik Sâlèh. The young lad, instigated by Gumushtagîn, did not look upon him with friendly eyes. When Saladin approached the northern city, the son of Nûr ud-dîn, although only twelve years of age, came riding into the market-place and reminded the people of the gratitude they owed to his father, and called upon them to help him against "the ungrateful man outside." The Aleppins issued in arms against Saladin. "God is my witness," exclaimed he, "that I wish it not to come to arms, but since ye will have it so, they shall decide." The troops of Aleppo were defeated and fled in disorder into the city. Finding himself helpless, Gumushtagîn unsheathed against Saladin the daggers of the Assassins. Their attack failed, and the unworthy guardian of young Malik Sâlèh appealed for help to the Crusaders and to

576—589 A.H.

1181— 1193 A.C. Saif ud-dîn Ghâzi II., Atabek of Mosul.[1] The former laid siege to Emessa, but fell back on the approach of Saladin, who once more attempted to come to an amicable arrangement with the son of Nûr ud-dîn. He offered him, in a respectful letter, the restoration of Hamâ, Emessa, and Baalbek, on condition of holding Damascus and Egypt as Malik Sâlèh's lieutenant. His offers were haughtily refused. In a battle under the walls of the city, Malik Sâlèh's troops were again defeated and Aleppo was besieged in earnest. Gumushtagîn and Saif ud-dîn Ghâzi were compelled to sue for peace; they sent the young daughter of Nûr ud-dîn, a mere child, to the camp of Saladin to excite his pity and to obtain favourable terms. Saladin received the maiden with the greatest kindness, covered her with presents, and at her request gave back all the cities he had taken in the principality of Aleppo. By the treaty, Damascus was definitely made over to him. From this time Malik Sâlèh's name was removed from the *Khutba* in Syria, Hijâz, and Egypt; and the Caliph, the fountain of all legitimate authority, ratified Saladin's assumption of independent power by the usual investiture and the title of Sultan.

Saladin invested with the title of Sultan.

Malik Sâlèh's death. 1181-82 A.C.

In 579 A.H. Malik Sâlèh died at the age of nineteen, leaving his principality to his cousin Izz ud-dîn, who had succeeded Saif ud-dîn in the Atâbekship of Mosul. Izz ud-dîn exchanged with his brother Imâd ud-dîn the principality of Aleppo for the seigniory of Sinjâr. After a while Imâd ud-dîn accepted Saladin as his suzerain, and, in return for some valuable fiefs, made over Aleppo to the great monarch of Egypt. Mosul followed suit, and the Atâbek was guaranteed in his riverain territories lying between the Tigris and the Euphrates. By the end of 1182 A.C. the authority of Saladin was acknowledged

[1] Cousin of Malik Sâlèh.

by all the sovereigns of Western Asia, including the Sultan of Iconium and the Prince of Greater Armenia,[1] and he was entitled to call upon them in any emergency to take the field with him. 576—589 A.H. The power of Saladin.

But the Frankish kingdom of Jerusalem drew its supplies of men and materials from all parts of Europe; knights in quest of glory, adventurers in search of riches, fanatics anxious to war against the "infidels," criminals escaping from justice, all flocked to the Syrian coasts. Amaury had died about this time, leaving the throne to his son Baldwin IV., but this poor youth was afflicted with a fell disease[2] which soon made him a pitiable object and prevented his taking any part in the government of his kingdom. His sister Sybilla was married to the Marquis of Montferrat, by whom she had a child, also named Baldwin. On Montferrat's death she married Guy de Lusignan, and him Baldwin appointed as Regent. Shortly after, he deposed Guy de Lusignan from the Regency and entrusted it to Raymond, Count of Tripoli. At the same time he resigned the throne in favour of his nephew, Baldwin V., who was then only five years of age. The infant king is supposed to have been murdered by, or with the connivance of, his own unnatural mother. Whether that be true or not, on his death Sybilla was accepted as the Queen of Jerusalem, and she herself placed the crown on her husband's head. Thus in the year 1187 A.C. the throne of Palestine came to be occupied by Sybilla and Guy de Lusignan. The kingdom of Jerusalem. Sybilla and Guy de Lusignan, Queen and King of Jerusalem, 1187 A.C.

In the time of Baldwin the Leper, a truce had been concluded between the Sultan and the Franks. "It is worthy of remark," says Michaud, "that the Mussulmans

[1] Whose capital was Khilât. It was ruled by a Mussulman sovereign.

[2] He was a leper.

1181—1193 A.C. respected their pledged faith, whilst the Christians gave the signal for a new war." Renaud, or Reginald, of Chatillon,[1] who married Constance the widow of Raymond of Poictiers, was for a long time a prisoner in the hands of Nûr ud-dîn Mahmûd. Malik Sâlèh gave him his freedom. He then married the widow of Humphrey of Thorun, from whom he obtained the seigniories of Karak[2] and Montreal. In the year 1186, in violation of the truce existing between the Christians and Moslems, he attacked a rich caravan passing by his castle, massacred a number of the people, and pillaged their goods. The enraged Sultan demanded redress from the King of Jerusalem; on its refusal, Saladin himself took in hand the work of punishment. Karak was besieged, whilst a small force under Ali, surnamed al-Malik ul-Afzal (Saladin's eldest son), was sent towards Galilee to keep an eye on the Franks. No sooner, however, did they learn of the siege of Karak, and of the advance of al-Malik ul-Afzal, than uniting their forces they marched against him. The Sultan on his side hastened to the support of his son. The two armies were equally matched; the Franks had gathered on the plains of Safûria or Sepphoris,[3] but by a skilful manœuvre, Saladin drew them into an enclosed valley among the mountains in the neighbourhood of Tiberias near the hill of Hittîn.[4] The Franks came

Breach of the treaty by the Franks, 1186 A.C.

[1] Called Arnât by the Arabs.

[2] Karak lies to the east of the south-eastern extremity of the Dead Sea.

[3] Ancient Diocæsarea was one of the principal villages of Galilee in the Roman times.

[4] The southern slope of the chain of hills, of which Hittîn is the highest, formed the battle-field of Tiberias. It is a vast plateau covered with grass, at an hour's distance from the Lake of Tiberias, between three valleys, that of Bâtûf to the west, of Hittîn to the north, of Hâma to the south-east. The exact spot where the battle took place has for its boundaries the angle formed by the hill of

down the hills "like mountains in movement," with their face towards the Lake of Tiberias, whilst the Sultan's force was posted in front of the lake, thus cutting off the Crusaders from the water. It was the evening of Thursday, the 2nd of July, as the two armies stood face to face. The Sultan was up the whole night making his dispositions for the fateful fight of the next day. The battle of Friday and the following morning, the 25th Rabi II., 583 A.H., gave the death-blow to Guy de Lusignan's kingdom. A hotly-contested fight ended in a terrible rout; ten thousand Crusaders fell on the field, and their principal leaders were either killed or taken prisoner. Among the latter were Guy de Lusignan, his brother Geoffrey, Renaud of Chatillon (the main cause of the war), the son of Humphrey of Thorun, Count Hugh of Jubail, the son of the Lord of Tiberiade, and the grand-masters of the two orders. The only persons who escaped were Raymond of Tripoli, the Lord of Tiberiade, Renaud of Sidon, the son of the Prince of Antioch, and Balian of Ibelin. These evaded pursuit and managed to reach the coast. Guy de Lusignan was well treated, but Renaud of Chatillon and several others, who like him had violated the treaty and massacred the Moslems during the truce, were put to death. The Sultan did not allow the enemy time to recover from his defeat, and rapidly followed up the victory of Hittîn. The castle of Tiberiade was captured, and the wife of Raymond of Tripoli fell into the hands of the Sultan; she was sent to her husband with every courtesy and respect; no woman was insulted or child hurt. Soon Ptolemais[1] saw him under its ram-

576—589 A.H.

23rd and 24th Rabi II., 583 A.H., 2nd and 3rd July, 1187 A.C.

Battle of Tiberias, or Hittîn, 4th July, 1187 A.C.

Hittîn to the north, the hill of "the Multiplication of Pains" to the north-east, the steep horn of the lake towards the east, and the village of Lubia to the south.—(Michaud.)

[1] St. Jean d'Acre, or shortly Acre; called Akka by the Arabs.

1181—1193 A.C. parts. This city, which had resisted the most formidable armies of Christendom for two years, fell into Saladin's hands in two days. Naplus, Jericho, Ramlah, Cæsarea, Arsûf, Jaffa, Beyrut, and a number of other cities opened their gates without any opposition. On the sea-coast, Tyre, Tripoli, and Ascalon alone remained in the hands of the Crusaders. Ascalon submitted after a short siege, and received generous terms.

Jerusalem. The Sultan then turned his attention towards Jerusalem, which contained within its walls over sixty thousand soldiers, besides an immense civil population. On approaching the city he sent for the principal inhabitants and spoke to them in the following terms—"I know, as you do, that Jerusalem is a holy place.[1] I do not wish to profane it by the effusion of blood; abandon your ramparts, and I shall give you a part of my treasures and as much land as you can cultivate." With characteristic fanaticism the Crusaders refused this generous and humane offer. Irritated by their refusal, Saladin vowed he would avenge on the city the butchery committed by the comrades and soldiers of Godfrey de Bouillon. After the siege had lasted a while, the Crusaders lost heart, and appealed for mercy "in the name of the common Father of mankind." The Sultan's kindness of heart conquered his desire for punishment. The Greeks and Syrian Christians within Jerusalem received permission to abide in the Sultan's dominions in the full enjoyment of their civil rights, and the Franks and Latins who wished to settle in Palestine as subjects of the Sultan were permitted to do so. All the combatants within the city were to leave with their women and children within forty days, under the safe-conduct of the Sultan's soldiers and betake

Capitulation of Jerusalem; the humanity of Saladin.

[1] Lit. "The house of God."

themselves either to Tyre or Tripoli. Their ransom was fixed at ten Syrian dinârs for each man, five for each woman, and one for each child. On failure to pay the stipulated ransom, they were to remain in bondage. But this was a mere nominal provision. The Sultan himself paid the ransom for ten thousand people, whilst his brother Saif ud-dîn[1] (the Saphadin of the Christians) released seven thousand more. Several thousand were dismissed by Saladin's clemency without any ransom. The clergy and the people carried away all their treasures and valuables without the smallest molestation. Several Christians were seen carrying on their shoulders their feeble and aged parents or friends. Touched by the spectacle, the Sultan distributed a goodly sum to them in charity, and even provided them with mules to carry their burdens. When Sybilla, the Queen of Jerusalem, accompanied by the principal matrons and knights, took leave of him, he respected her unhappiness, and spoke to her with the utmost tenderness. She was followed by a number of weeping women, carrying their children in their arms. Several of them approached the Sultan and addressed him as follows—"You see us on foot, the wives, mothers, and daughters of warriors who are your prisoners; we are quitting for ever this country; they aided us in our lives, in losing them we lose our last hope; if you will give them to us, they can alleviate our miseries and we shall not be without support on earth." Saladin, touched by their prayers, at once restored to the mothers their sons, to the wives their husbands, and promised to treat whoever remained in his power with kindness. He distributed liberal alms among the orphans and widows, and allowed the Knights Hospitallers, although they had been in arms against

576—589 A.H.

The humanity of Saladin.

[1] *Saif ud-dîn* Abû Bakr, surnamed al-Malik al-Aâdil.

1181— him, to continue their work of tending the sick and
1193 A.C. wounded and looking after the Christian pilgrims.

Saladin's humanity was in striking contrast with the brutality of the nearest Christian prince. "Many of the Christians who left Jerusalem," says Mills, "went to Antioch, but Bohemond not only denied them hospitality, but even stripped them. They marched into the Saracenian country, and were well received." Michaud gives some striking details of Christian inhumanity to the exiles from Jerusalem. Repulsed by their brethren of the East, they wandered miserably about Syria, many dying of grief and hunger. Tripoli shut its gates against them, and "one woman, urged by despair, cast her infant into the sea, cursing the Christians who refused them succour." Out of respect for the feelings of the vanquished, the Sultan had abstained from entering the city until all the Crusaders had left. On Friday, the 27th of Rajab,[1] 583 A.H., attended by the princes and lords and the dignitaries of the empire who had arrived in camp to congratulate him on his victory, he entered Jerusalem. The ravages of war were repaired on all sides, the mosques and colleges that had been demolished by the Franks were either restored or rebuilt, and a liberal and wise administration was introduced in the government of the country, quite different from the rude tyranny of the Crusaders.

From Jerusalem Saladin marched upon Tyre, where somewhat unwisely the Crusaders whom his humanity had liberated had been allowed to betake themselves. The garrison of Tyre, thus enforced from every direction, prepared for an obstinate defence. It was commanded by Conrad, Marquis of Montferrat,[2] a man of ability

[1] The anniversary of the Vision of the Ascension of the Prophet.

[2] Called by the Arabs simply Markîs or Mârkîs.

and great cunning. He refused to obey the summons of the Sultan to surrender the city, alleging that he was under the commands of a sovereign over the seas. Without wasting time upon the siege of Tyre, Saladin turned aside for a while, and marching along the northern sea-board, reduced successively Laodicea, Jabala, Saihûn, Becas, Bozair, Derbersâk, and other strong places still held by the Franks. He set at liberty Guy de Lusignan on his solemn word of honour that he would immediately leave for Europe. No sooner, however, did this Christian knight recover his freedom than he broke his pledged word, and collecting a large army from the *débris* of the crusading forces and new arrivals from the west, laid siege to Ptolemais. And it was now round this place that the interest of three continents became centred for the next two years. 576—589 A.H.

The Third Crusade.

The fall of Jerusalem threw Christendom into violent commotion, and every effort was made by the ecclesiastics to rouse the frenzy of the people and induce the sovereigns and princes of Europe to embark on another crusade. Their efforts were crowned with complete success. Reinforcements poured into Tyre as well as the camp before Acre, and the three principal sovereigns of Christendom, Frederick Barbarossa, the Emperor of Germany, Philip Augustus, King of France, and Richard Cœur de Lion, King of England, engaged in the enterprise. Had Saladin at this juncture, with his usual perspicacity and foresight, united the fleets of Egypt and Syria, and established a strict blockade of the Phœnician sea-board, he would have crippled the Crusaders in Palestine, and prevented the landing of the strong contingents that soon arrived from Europe. He forgot that the safety of Phœnicia lay in immunity from naval incursions, and that no victory on land could ensure

1181— 1193 A.C. against an influx from beyond the sea. As it was, the Pisans, the Genoese, and the Venetians brought daily, with provisions and munitions of war, enormous accessions to the Crusaders. The following passages relating to the memorable siege, in the course of which the two personalities of Saladin and Richard of England stand forth in such bold relief, are drawn from the narratives of Ibn ul-Athîr and of Ibn Shaddâd, and are to some extent in their own words.—"Whenever Salâh ud-dîn took a city or fortress, he spared the lives of the inhabitants, and the Franks hastened to Tyre with all their riches, their women and children. Thus a large body of the enemy collected at this place, and they continually received reinforcements from beyond the sea."[1] Every means, he goes on to add, were taken to rouse the fanaticism of the people of Europe. The Patriarch of Jerusalem, whom Saladin had treated with such kindness, perambulated the Frankish cities with the figure of the Messiah wounded by an Arab, and thus excited the indignation of the Christians to the wildest pitch; in this manner he collected large armies for the help of the Franks in Palestine. Even women enrolled themselves for the war. A young Christian prisoner, the sole child of a widowed mother, whose only possession was a small house, told the historian how she sold the house, equipped him for the war, and sent him forth to fight with the Saracens. "The Franks came from all directions by land and by sea with all their forces," and when they were all united at Tyre, they thought first of attacking Sidon, but eventually determined on reconquering Acre. They accordingly marched upon this place, an enormous host, their route along the sea-coast, and their ships keeping alongside of them. The sea in fact was

Commencement of the siege of Acre by the Crusaders, 15th Rajab, 585 A.H. 29th August, 1189 A.C.

[1] Ibn ul-Athîr.

their great auxiliary, for it brought them materials, provisions, and help from their native countries. They arrived before Acre on the 15th Rajab, 585 A.H., and at once laid siege to the city. 576—589 A.H.

As soon as Salâh ud-dîn heard of the movement of the Franks, he held a council of war. His own opinion was to attack them *en route;* but he was dissuaded by his ameers, who advised an attack on the open ground before Acre. When Salâh ud-dîn reached the place, he found the Crusaders encamped round Acre with their wings resting on the sea, thus closely encircling the city and cutting off all communications landward. Had, says the historian, Salâh ud-dîn acted according to his own opinion and attacked the Franks before they had taken up position before Acre, he would have saved the city, "but when God wills a thing He provides means therefor." The Sultan encamped in front of the Crusaders, and established his tent on the hill of Kaisân (Tell-Kaisân). His right wing stretched to the Tell-Ayâzia, and the left wing rested on the river Belus.[1] He was now joined by some reinforcements which arrived from Mosul, Diâr-Bakr, Sinjâr, and Harrân. Whilst the Moslems were thus reinforced on the land side, succour poured in for the Franks from over the seas. At the beginning of Shâbân 585 A.H., Saladin attacked the Crusaders. Takî ud-dîn, his nephew, delivered a terrific charge, drove them from their positions, and restored communication with Acre. "Had the Mussulmans," says Ibn ul-Athîr, "continued the fight up to the night, they would have completely attained their object, but after gaining half the positions of the Franks, they rested to resume the battle next day." Saladin now changed the

The siege of Acre.

1st Shâbân, 585 A.H. 14th Sept., 1189 A.C.

[1] The *Nahr ul-Jâri* (the flowing river) of Ibn ul-Athîr, the *Nahr ul-Halw* (the river of sweet waters) of Ibn Shaddâd.

1181– 1193 A.C. garrison and re-provisioned Acre. Among the ameers whom he sent into the city was Husâm ud-dîn (Abu'l Haija, nicknamed *as-Samîn*, or the Stout). On the 6th of Shâbân the battle was begun by the Franks, who issued from behind their entrenchments and vigorously attacked the Saracens. They were repulsed with frightful slaughter and compelled to retreat behind their trenches.

19th Sept., 1189 A.C.

At this time, Saladin's forces were dispersed all over the country; one army watched Bohemond, Prince of Antioch; another was stationed at Emessa, in front of Tripoli, for the defence of that frontier; a third watched Tyre, and a fourth held Damietta, Alexandria, etc., to guard against Frankish incursions from the sea. In spite, therefore, of the reinforcements he had received, the Sultan's force was numerically weaker than that of the Crusaders, and they, wanting to crush him before he received any further accession, delivered another attack, which, partially successful in the beginning, ended in a fearful rout. The number of Crusaders killed in this battle amounted to 10,000 men. In spite of Saladin's endeavours to keep the place clean and to throw the dead bodies into the sea, the exhalations from the numerous unburied corpses poisoned the atmosphere, and a deadly pestilence broke out. The Sultan himself was affected, and under the advice of the doctors and generals the camp was broken up, and Saladin and the troops moved to the neighbourhood of al-Kharrûba.[1] When the Saracens had departed, the Franks "recovered their tranquillity," and resumed the siege of Acre. And in order to protect themselves against Saladin's attacks,

4th Ramazân, 585 A.H. 16th Oct., 1189 A.C.

[1] Al-Kharrûba is a fortress on the Mediterranean, three miles to the south of Haïta on Mount Carmel.

they made a deep ditch round their camp, and raised a high wall behind which they could shelter themselves when defeated. 576—589 A.H.

Saladin spent the winter at al-Kharrûba. In the spring of 1190 he descended again into the plains of Acre, and took up his former position. The Franks had constructed huge towers of wood filled with men in armour for attacking the ramparts of the city; the besieged, under the direction of a Damascene engineer, threw grenades filled with naphtha and Greek fire, which set fire to the movable towers, and they were burnt to the ground. About this time the Sultan was joined by some troops from the side of Mesopotamia. The Egyptian flotilla also arrived with provisions and munitions of war for the garrison of Acre. In a naval engagement, the Franks were worsted, and the Egyptian ships entered the harbour. The Saracen camp was, however, greatly disquieted by the news which came just then that Frederick Barbarossa, the Emperor of Germany (*Malik ul-Almân*), was marching upon Palestine with an enormous horde. He was harassed on the way by the Ouj Turkomans, who hung on his flanks, but he succeeded in crossing into Upper Cilicia (*Bilâd ul-Arman*), held by Lafûn (Leo), the son of Istefân (Stephen). The Sultan hurried off messengers to his allies for assistance; he even sent an embassy to Yâkûb al-Mansûr, the Sultan of Morocco, but they all showed themselves lukewarm in his support. Saladin was thus thrown upon his own resources to make head against the combined forces of Europe. The emperor, however, was never fated to reach his goal; he was drowned in the river Salaf (ancient Calycadnus) near Seleucia. Discord then broke out among his men; a large number returned home, whilst a small body under his son (the Duke of Swabia)

Safar 586 A.H. 10th March, 1190 A.C.

Frederick Barbarossa

His death 10th June, 1190 A.C.

1181— came to Antioch, and thence to Palestine. They finally
1193 A.C. took ship for home, but were wrecked on the way, and many were drowned.

20th Jamâdi II., 586 A.H. 25th July, 1190 A.C. On the 20th of Jamâdi II. 586, the Franks issued from their entrenchments and gave battle. They suffered a heavy and murderous defeat, and the field was covered with their slain and wounded. The Crusaders now lost heart. Two days later a formidable contingent arrived for them from beyond the seas under the command of

Arrival of Count Henry. al-Kond Heri (Count Henry of Champagne). This young man was the son of a half-sister of the King of England, and was also connected with the King of France. He landed his troops without difficulty in the neighbourhood of Acre, and formed a junction with the Crusaders already encamped there. He strongly fortified the camp, and concentrating his forces, announced his

27th Jamâdi II., 586 A.H. 1st Aug., 1190 A.C. intention of attacking the Sultan. Saladin thereupon moved his troops back to al-Kharrûba so as to have more space for the deployment of his army, and to avoid the terrible stench before Acre. The withdrawal of the Sultan's troops enabled the Crusaders to press the siege with vigour, but the Saracens confined within the city supported the horrors of this fierce attack with a heroic constancy. The ameers Karakûsh and Husâm ud-dîn ceaselessly animated the courage of the soldiers. Vigilant, present everywhere, employing every force and every artifice, they allowed no occasion to escape either to surprise the Franks or to defeat their assaults.[1] They burnt the machines of the besiegers, and in several "sorties drove the enemy back into their camp." Count Henry thereupon turned the siege into a blockade. But the Sultan relieved the garrison by sending provisions by sea from Beyrut.

[1] Michaud.

The Franks then addressed a letter to the Pope (Arabic, Bâbâ), "the sovereign of Rome the great,"[1] "who is their (religious) head, and whose words among them have the same authority as the directions of the Prophet among us." And at his instance help arrived for them from every quarter. When these reinforcements had joined Count Henry, he issued from his entrenchments to give battle to the Sultan, who met them "with an army ranged in good order." His sons Ali, Khizr, and Ghâzi commanded in the centre, whilst his brother Saif ud-dîn with the Egyptian troops was on the right; the princes of Hamâh, of Sinjâr, and other feudatories commanded on the left. Unfortunately Saladin himself was ill that day with a disorder to which he was subject, and could only watch the battle from a small tent pitched on a hill from which he could overlook the field. The battle continued for a long time; eventually the Franks were driven back to their defences with great loss. "Had Salâh ud-dîn not been indisposed that day, the fight would have been decisive." "The Franks now began to suffer from famine, and the approach of winter compelled them to send off their ships for shelter to the neighbouring isles of Greece." Saif ud-dîn Ali, son of Ahmed al-Mashtûb, was placed in command of the city, but unfortunately the weakened garrison was not changed, nor, in spite of the Sultan's order, was the opportunity taken by the ameers to re-provision the place.

576—589 A.H.

Siege of Acre.

With the spring the Frankish vessels of war returned in enormous numbers and again interrupted communication with the garrison of Acre. Only a diver with letters could reach the Sultan's camp. On the 12th of Rabi I., 587 A.H., fresh help arrived for the Franks encamped before Acre. "The King of the French,

9th April, 1191 A.C.

[1] Rûm ul-Kubrâ.

1181 — 1193 A.C. Filîb (Philip Augustus), one of the noblest of their monarchs, although his dominions are not extensive," landed with an immense army. Salâh ud-dîn, who was then encamped at Shafra-aam,[1] sent for reinforcements to his feudatories, but before these could reach him the Crusaders received great accessions to their strength by the arrival of Malik Ankiltâr[2] (the King of England) with twenty ship-loads of fighting men and munitions of war. The Crusaders were now in overwhelming force, and in consequence the evil they caused to the Moslems redoubled; "for Malik Ankiltâr was noted in his time for bravery, deceit, activity, and endurance." When Salâh ud-dîn received news of his coming, he ordered that a ship filled with provisions should be sent to Acre from Beyrut. This vessel was attacked by the Crusaders before it could run into harbour; its commandant, Yâkûb al-Halebi (*i.e.* of Aleppo), one of the captains of the *corps d'élite*,[3] finding that his ship would fall into the hands of the enemy, went into the hold and scuttled the vessel. It was engulfed with all on board.

Arrival of the King of England.

13th Jamâdi I., 587 A.H. 8th June, 1191 A.C.

The siege of Acre was now conducted with the greatest violence. For a time the garrison maintained a stout defence and drove back all assaults. The assistance promised by the feudatories had not arrived yet, and, in spite of repeated battles, the Sultan found himself unable to force the Crusaders to raise the siege. Enfeebled by war, pestilence, and famine, the defenders began to feel the pinch of a struggle which had lasted two years. In their extremity, Mashtûb, the commandant of

[1] A village three miles from Acre; *Mujam ul-Buldân*.

[2] Roi d'Angleterre.

[3] The *Jândâr*. Soon after their arrival, the Kings of England and France fell ill of fever. Saladin, on hearing of their illness, sent them the snow of Lebanon, and cooling drinks, and fresh fruit during the whole time they were ill.

the city, betook himself to Philip Augustus and said to him, "We have been masters of this city for four years. When we took Ptolemais, we allowed all the inhabitants perfect freedom to go where they listed with all their goods and families; to-day we offer the city to you, and ask for the same conditions that we accorded to the Christians." The King of France refused to spare a single one of the inhabitants or garrison of Acre unless the Saracens restored Jerusalem and all the cities taken from the Crusaders since the battle of Tiberias. The Saracen ameer returned to the city bent on fighting to the last and burying himself under the ruins of the city. For a time the hopeless struggle continued, but famine was fast decimating the defenders, whilst the Sultan's army lay crippled for want of reinforcements. At last the Saracens within the city capitulated on the solemn condition that no life should be sacrificed by the Franks; that the Moslems on their side should restore the wood of the true Cross with 1600 prisoners, and give 200,000 pieces of gold to the chiefs of the Crusaders. Some delay occurred in the payment of the ransom; the *lion-hearted* King of England took out from the city the garrison, and butchered them in cold blood within sight of their brethren.

576—589 A.H.

Butchery of the Saracens.

The capture of Ptolemais cost the Crusaders 60,000 lives.

"The victorious Crusaders," says Michaud, "enjoyed at last in Ptolemais a repose which they had not known since their arrival in Syria. The pleasures of peace, the abundance of food, the wine of Cyprus, the women who arrived from the neighbouring isles, made them forget for the moment the object of their enterprise." After refreshing themselves in the usual way, they marched under Richard's command upon Ascalon. Saladin

1181—1193 A.C. marched alongside, and the 150 miles were signalised by eleven Homeric battles. At the battle of Arsûf, Saladin lost 8000 of his bravest men. Finding his troops too weak to prevent the strongest place in Palestine from falling into the hands of the Crusaders, he hurried on to Ascalon, removed the inhabitants, and rased it to the ground. When Richard arrived, he saw the uninhabitable ruins of a great fortress and city. And he saw more. He saw opposed to him a man of indomitable will and unceasing energy. Impressed with the personality of Saladin, Richard became anxious for peace. He himself was tired of the fruitless, harassing, and decimating struggle, and was anxious to return to his disturbed dominions. He accordingly sent messengers to demand a conference with the Sultan's brother, Saif ud-dîn (al-Malik al-Aâdil). The two princes met, the son of Hunferi[1] (Humphrey of Thorun) acting as an interpreter. Richard dilated on his desire for peace, and mentioned the conditions he proposed, which were, however, found to be impossible, and nothing came of the interview. The Marquis of Montferrat, disgusted with the conduct of Richard, sent an envoy to the Sultan to make peace on his own account, on condition of obtaining Sidon and Beyrut. The Sultan agreed to his terms, provided he first carried out his part of the compact. Fresh messengers arrived from the King of England with proposals of peace and letters to "his brother and friend," al-Malik al-Aâdil, and to the Sultan. This time the sole conditions asked were that the Crusaders should be allowed to retain the cities they possessed on the littoral, and that Jerusalem, with the wood of the true Cross, should be restored to them.

Richard's desire for peace.

[1] "I saw him," says Bahâ ud-dîn ibn Shaddâd, "on the day the peace was concluded; he was really good-looking, but had his beard shaved according to their custom."

The Sultan emphatically rejected the demand for the retrocession of Jerusalem, but expressed his willingness to give back the wood of the Cross, provided peace was made according to his wishes. The King of England renewed his overtures to al-Malik al-Aâdil, and came to an agreement subject to the sanction of the Sultan and his council. The terms were that the sister of Richard, the widow of the King of Sicily, should be married to al-Malik al-Aâdil, that Richard should give for her dowry the cities held by him on the sea-coast; that the Sultan should give to his brother the cities he had conquered; that Jerusalem should be possessed by husband and wife as a neutral city free to the followers of both religions; a general exchange of prisoners, restoration of the Cross to the Christians, and the Hospitallers and Templars to maintain their privileges. The Sultan saw in these proposals the means of restoring peace between the two creeds so long arrayed against each other in sanguinary combat, and at once acceded to them. Had Richard's priests allowed the treaty to be concluded, probably it might have been the means of bridging the gulf that still divides Christendom from Islâm. They raised an outcry against the idea of a Christian princess marrying a brave and chivalrous knight like Saif ud-dîn; they threatened Richard with excommunication; they played on the religious fears and superstition of the ex-Queen of Sicily. Richard, alarmed at their threats, sent envoys to "his brother and friend" requesting him to change his faith. This suggestion was, of course, declined. In the meantime fresh messengers arrived from the Marquis. The King of England thereupon entered into relations with the chief of the Assassins at Massiat to rid him of his inconvenient ally, and Conrad was set upon by

576—589 A.H.

Negotiations.

Assassination of Conrad.

1st May, 1192 A.C.

1181— 1193 A.C. two *fedâis* and assassinated on the 16th of Rabi II., 588 A.H.[1]

An expedition against Jerusalem, commanded by Richard in person, ended in absolute failure, and this strengthened his desire to leave Palestine. He sent envoys to the Sultan with fresh proposals, in which all the previous demands were withdrawn. "I desire your affection and friendship," was the message of the King of England to the Sultan; "I have no wish to dominate over this land. I know you must be as unwilling to lose more of your people as I am of losing mine. I have given to Count Henry,[2] the son of my sister, the country I hold, and now I commend him to you, and he will obey you and accompany you in your expeditions to the East. And I ask of you the Church (in Jerusalem)." The Sultan, with the advice of his council, who saw the necessity of giving peace to the land and rest to the army, returned a favourable answer. The same envoy, accompanied by the son of Count Humphrey, again arrived in the Sultan's camp with presents from the King of England, definitively abandoning all pretensions to Jerusalem, but asking for the three cities of Ascalon, Dârûm, and Gazza in good condition and a general peace. The Sultan replied that with the Prince of Antioch he would make peace separately, and that instead of Ascalon he was willing to give Richard Lydda, but not the other cities. Learning that the Crusaders were marching on Beyrut, Saladin broke up his camp and took the field again. Jaffa was taken by assault, but the citadel was

[1] Von Hammer, in his *History of the Assassins*, proves conclusively that the assassination of Conrad, Marquis of Montferrat, was due to the instigation of Richard of England.

[2] Of Champagne. On the death of Guy de Lusignan, Sybilla married this Count, and he thus acquired the kingdom of Jerusalem.

relieved by Richard. The King of England again asked for a conference with delegates from al-Malik al-Aâdil. On their arrival in his camp, he spoke enthusiastically of the Sultan. He then asked the chief ameer to implore the Sultan, "in the name of God to make peace." In response to this appeal, the Sultan offered to Richard the sea-coast from Tyre to Cæsarea. Richard asked for Jaffa and Ascalon. Saladin expressed his willingness to give Jaffa, but refused Ascalon on any condition. At last the King of England renounced the demand for Ascalon, and the terms of peace were concluded on both sides. "A proclamation was then issued, announcing that peace was at last established between the Moslems and Christians, and declaring that the territories of both should equally enjoy repose and security; that persons of either nation might go into the territory of the other and return again, without molestation or fear. That day crowds assembled to hear the news, and the joy felt on both sides was extreme. The troops which were arriving from distant countries for the purpose of reinforcing the army, received permission to return home, and departed." Richard left soon after for his home. The sequel is known to every student of English history.

576—589 A.H.

Peace concluded. 22nd Shâbân, 588 A.H. 2nd September 1192 A.C.

Thus ended the Third Crusade, in which an enormous number of human beings perished, thousands of homes both in the East and the West were rendered desolate; Germany ingloriously lost one of its greatest emperors, and France and England the flower of their chivalry. Their only gain was the capture of Acre!

End of the Third Crusade.

On the departure of Richard, Saladin rested a while at Jerusalem and then proceeded with an escort of cavalry to the sea-coast to examine the state of the maritime fortresses and to put them in repair. At Jerusalem he built a hospital and college under the direction

1181—1193 A.C. of his secretary and biographer. He then returned to Damascus and remained with his family until his death on Wednesday, the 27th of Safar, 589 A.H. "The day of his death," says a Moslem writer, "was, for Islâm and the Mussulmans, a misfortune such as they never suffered since they were deprived of the first four Caliphs. The palace, the empire, and the world were overwhelmed with grief, the whole city was plunged in sorrow, and followed his bier weeping and crying."

Death of Saladin, 4th March, 1193 A.C.

His character.

Thus died one of the greatest and most chivalrous monarchs the world has produced. Before his death he distributed large sums in charity among the poor, irrespective of any distinction of creed. The messenger who took the news of Saladin's death to Bagdad arrived there with the Sultan's coat of mail, his charger and one dînar and thirty-six dirhems, which was all the property he left. His character can be judged by the accounts of his contemporaries, who describe him as tender-hearted, kind, condescending and affable, full of patience and indulgence. "He befriended the learned and the virtuous, admitted them into his society, and treated them with beneficence." No man with any talent ever left his court without some mark of recognition. He covered his empire with colleges and hospitals. The Sultan's vizier, al-Kâzi al-Fâzil,[1] who held office under three sovereigns of the Ayûbide dynasty, vied with his master in the patronage of learning and arts. Saladin's council was composed not only of warriors like Karâkush, Husâm ud-dîn, Mashtûb, but men of letters like the Kâzi, the Kâtib Imâd ud-dîn, surnamed *Alûh* (the

[1] Abû Ali Abdu'r Rahîm, surnamed *Majîr ud-dîn*, "protector of religion," and *al-Kâzi al-Fâzil*, "the learned Kâzi." He was a pure Arab of the tribe of Lakhm, and was born at Ascalon, a member of a family of judges.

Eagle), who was the Sultan's Secretary of State, the jurist al-Hakkari, who often exchanged the flowing robes of his profession for a soldier's uniform, and many others.[1] 576—589 A.H.

[1] The famous traveller, Abdul Latîf, who saw Saladin after the peace with Richard, speaks of him in the most enthusiastic terms as a great sovereign, whose countenance "inspired love and respect in every heart." "The first evening I spent in his company," he continues, "I found him surrounded with learned men who discoursed on every branch of learning. He listened to them with pleasure, and frequently joined in the discussion himself. He was engaged just then in building the walls and a moat round Jerusalem. He superintended the work personally, and often carried the stones on his own shoulders. He went to the place before sunrise, and returned for breakfast at noon, after which he rested. At *Aasr* he rode again to the spot and returned only by torch-light. He spent the great part of the night in transacting the business of the next day." The same writer describes the solicitude of Saladin for his soldiers, and says that at the camp before Acre the market occupied a vast space of ground, and contained over seven thousand shops besides booths and tents for farriers, and one thousand baths kept by the maghribins.

CHAPTER XXIII

THE ABBASSIDES (*continued*)

589—661 A.H., 1193—1268 A.C.

THE ERUPTION OF THE TARTARS

Saladin's sons—Rise of al-Malik al-Aâdil—The Fourth Crusade—The sons of al-Malik al-Aâdil—General review of the Islâmic world in the East—The Caliphate—Caliph Az-Zâhir—The Caliph Mustansir—The Caliph Mustaasim—Eruption of the Tartars—Fall of Bagdad—Destruction of Islâmic civilisation.

The sons of Saladin. The division of the Empire. UNFORTUNATELY, Saladin made no provision before his death to regulate the succession, and this want of foresight proved the ruin of his empire, which now split up into three independent monarchies under his three elder sons. Ali, *al-Malik al-Afzal* (*Abu'l Hassan, Nûr ud-dîn*), obtained Syria and Palestine; and the possession of Damascus, the capital of the empire, gave him pre-eminence over his brothers. Osman, *al-Malik* Afzal. Azîz. Zâhir. *al-Azîz* (*Abu'l Fath, Imâd ud-dîn*), who held in his father's lifetime the command in Egypt, was proclaimed sovereign of that country; whilst Ghazi, *al-Malik az-Zâhir* (*Ghyâs ud-dîn*), obtained the principality of Aleppo. Al-Malik al-Aâdil (*Saif ud-dîn, Abû Bakr*), Lord of Karak and Shaubek and brother of Saladin, who was most popular with the army, held part of Mesopotamia and several cities in the neighbourhood of the Euphrates. The children of Shirkûh were established at Emessa, and other important fiefs were held by other cadets of the family. Yemen was ruled by another brother of Saladin. Had the sons of the great Sultan remained united, probably in spite of the division of the empire they would have been able to hand down the power to their descendants. Their dissensions and incapacity helped al-Aâdil to acquire the dominions of his brother. The quarrels which broke out between Afzal and Azîz led to the former being driven from Damascus, which was then given to Aâdil, Afzal resting content with the city of Sarkhad. On the death of Azîz, leaving a minor son,[1] Afzal was called to undertake his tutorship. Dissensions then broke out between Afzal and Aâdil, who thereupon expelled both Afzal and his nephew Mansûr from Egypt. They received some fiefs in Mesopotamia, where they and their descendants abode. Aâdil established himself in Cairo on the 16th of the Rabi II. 596 A.H. Soon after he obtained possession of Syria, Eastern Mesopotamia, Khilât, and Greater Armenia, and in 612 A.H. became master of Yemen, to which country he despatched (as governor) his grandson Yusuf.[2] Saif ud-dîn (al-Malik al-Aâdil) is described as a sovereign possessing great knowledge and foresight, and gifted with consummate prudence, always animated with the best intentions, virtuous in his conduct, and resolute in his undertakings. Like his brother he was a patron of learning. Al-Aâdil now became supreme sovereign of Syria, Upper Mesopotamia, Egypt, and Arabia, with an empire almost as extensive as that of his great brother. The

589—661 A.H.

Accession of Aâdil. 2nd February, 1200 A.C.

1207-8 A.C.

1215-16 A.C.

[1] *Al-Malik ul-Mansûr* Mohammed.

[2] Surnamed *al-Malik al-Masûd* ("the fortunate prince"), Salâh ud-dîn Abu'l Muzzaffar.

1193— 1268 A.H. *Khutba* was recited in his name from all the pulpits, and the coins bore his seal.[1]

The Fourth Crusade.

Two years after the death of Saladin, Pope Celestine III. inflamed another Crusade. But with the conflict between Saladin and Richard, the wars of the giants had ended. Henceforth the struggles between Islâm and Christendom were comparatively weak and spasmodic. In spite of the division that prevailed in the Moslem camp, this onslaught of the Franks proved as abortive as its predecessors. "All the powers of the West," says Michaud, "miscarried in an attempt upon a little fortress in Syria." In flagrant breach of the treaty concluded with Saladin, which had been solemnly sworn to by all the Christian princes then in Syria, a large force of Crusaders landed on the Phœnician coast and seized Beyrut. At this time, the sons of Saladin still held their kingdoms, but al-Malik al-Aâdil, as the most experienced champion of Islâm, hastened from his principality to resist the Franks. He carried Jaffa by storm, whilst the Crusaders were besieging Tibnîn. The siege ended in disastrous failure, and they were compelled to sue for peace. A truce of three years was accordingly concluded. This Crusade too was marked by the wildest excesses on the part of the soldiers of the Cross.

Siege of Tibnîn.

594 A.H. 1197–98 A.C.

1200 A.C.

Three years later Innocent III., "who simply wanted to raise money," says an European writer, "for the gratification of his luxury and avarice," proclaimed another Crusade, and invited the princes of Christendom to engage in it. Richard of England refused to pay any heed to the exhortations of the Pope. "You advise me," he said in wrath to the emissaries of the Roman Pontiff, "to dismiss my three daughters, pride, avarice,

The Fifth Crusade.

[1] Abu'l Fedâ.

and incontinence. I bequeath them to the most deserv- 589—661 A.H.
ing—my pride to the Knights Templars, my avarice to the monks of Cisteaux, and my incontinence to the prelates." But the other princes of Europe were not so wise, and an immense force sprang up for a fresh invasion of the East. Luckily for Islâm, instead of marching against Syria, they turned their arms against Constantinople. Ibn ul-Athîr's account of this Crusade agrees wonderfully with that given by European historians. He tells briefly how the usurper blinded his brother,[1] and threw him into prison; how the young son[2] of the latter escaped to the horde that had been collected for the invasion of Palestine; how they turned aside on his appeal to the assistance of the blind and deposed sovereign of Byzantium; he describes in a few graphic sentences the surrender of the city, its conflagration, and the subsequent atrocities committed by the warriors of the Cross on a Christian city. The conflagration, "which reduced to ashes one fourth of Constantinople,"[3] began with the bigotry of some Flemish pilgrims, who "were scandalised by the aspect of a mosque or a synagogue in which one God was worshipped, without a partner or a son. Their effectual mode of controversy was to attack the infidels with the sword, and their habitation with fire, but the infidels and some Christian neighbours presumed to defend their lives and properties, and the flames which bigotry had kindled consumed the most orthodox and innocent structures. During eight days and nights the conflagration spread above a league in front, from the harbour to the Propontis, over the thickest and most populous regions of the city."[4]

[1] Isaac Angelus.
[2] Alexius.
[3] Ibn ul-Athîr.
[4] Gibbon.

1193—1268 A.C. When the Crusaders took the city by force, they put to the sword every Greek they met. "It was a horrible spectacle," says old Villehardouin, "to see women and young children running distractedly here and there, trembling and half dead with fright, lamenting piteously and begging for mercy." According to Mills and Gibbon, the atrocities perpetrated by the pilgrims were bitterly lamented by Pope Innocent III., atrocities too horrible to describe. The Crusaders were insensible to pity. For several days they enacted the worst scenes of outrage and spoliation, within and without the walls of Constantinople. "Villages, churches, and country houses," says Michaud, "were all devastated and given over to pillage. A distracted crowd covered the roads and wandered about at hazard, pursued by fear, bending under fatigue, and uttering cries of despair." Nicetas, the Byzantine historian, whose daughter was with difficulty preserved from harm, reproaches the Crusaders with having surpassed "the Turks" in barbarity. He reminds them of the example of Saladin's soldiers, who, when masters of Jerusalem, neither violated the modesty of matrons and virgins, nor subjected the Christians to fire, sword, hunger, and nakedness.[1]

"After stripping the gems and pearls, they converted the chalices into drinking cups; their tables, on which they gamed and feasted, were covered with pictures of Christ and the saints, and they trampled underfoot the most venerable objects of the Christian worship. In the Cathedral of St. Sophia, the ample veil of the sanctuary was rent asunder for the sake of the golden fringe, and the altar, a monument of art and riches, was broken in pieces and shared among the captors. Their mules and horses were laden with the wrought silver and

[1] Michaud, vol. ii. p. 295.

gilt carvings which they tore down from doors and pulpits; and if the beasts stumbled under the burden, they were stabbed by their impatient drivers, and the holy pavement streamed with their impure blood. 'A follower of the demon and a priestess of the furies' was seated on the throne of the patriarch, and the daughter of Belial, as she is styled, sang and danced in the church to ridicule the hymns and processions of the Orientals." 589—661 A.H.

In 1216–17 A.C., Innocent III. preached the Sixth Crusade. "Women, children, the old, the blind, the lame, the leprous, all were enrolled in the sacred militia. The King of Hungary, the Dukes of Austria and Bavaria, and all the potentates of Lower Germany, united their forces for the projected invasion of the East." Two hundred and fifty thousand men, chiefly Germans, landed first in Syria, and after devastating portions of the sea-coast, turned their attention towards Egypt. Arrived at the eastern mouth of the Nile, they laid siege to Damietta. Al-Malik al-Aâdil was hurrying from Northern Syria to Egypt, but died in the neighbourhood of Damascus. His reign of nearly twenty years was by no means inglorious. He had repeatedly defeated the Franks, and foiled their attacks by land and sea. His empire was divided by his sons. Mohammed, surnamed *al-Malik al-Kâmil* (*Abu'l Maâli*, *Nâsir ud-dîn*),[1] obtained Egypt. The second son Îsa, surnamed *al-Malik al-Muazzam* (*Sharf ud-dîn*[2]), received the kingdom of Syria, extending from Emessa to al-Aarish on the Egyptian frontier, and including Palestine, Jerusalem, al-Karak, etc.; whilst Mûsa, *al-Malik al-Ashraf* (*Muzzaffar ud-dîn*[3]), held the principality of Aleppo.

The Sixth Crusade, 1216–17 A.C.

Death of al-Malik al-Aâdil, 7th Jamâdi, 615 A.H. 21st Aug., 1218 A.C.

The sons of Aâdil.

[1] "The perfect king, helper of the Faith."

[2] "The mighty prince, nobleness of religion."

[3] "Noble prince, the victor of the Faith."

1193—1268 A.C. After a siege of eighteen months, Damietta fell into the hands of the Crusaders, and they entered the city with the same ruthless feelings as had maddened the early Crusaders, when they first leaped on the battlements of Jerusalem. But revenge sought its victims in vain. Damietta was one vast charnel-house; of a population which at the beginning of the siege consisted of more than seventy thousand souls, three thousand only remained to tell the story of their sufferings. Even this awful sight did not dismay or excite the pity of the Crusaders, and they massacred the famished survivors without mercy. They then marched upon Cairo; Kâmil, although reinforced by his brothers, felt himself unequal to contend successfully with the overwhelming forces of the Crusaders. He accordingly offered to restore to them all the conquests of Saladin, provided they gave up Damietta. Feeling certain of the conquest of Egypt they refused Kâmil's offer. The Nile was just beginning to rise, and the Saracens opened the dykes and suddenly inundated the country. The Crusaders found themselves now entirely cut off from their base; a convoy bringing up provisions was surprised, and famine began to stalk in their camp. At the same time the Moslem troops kept up an incessant attack. The Franks were forced to sue for peace, hostages were exchanged, and finally a treaty was concluded by which the Crusaders agreed to evacuate Damietta on condition of a safe retreat to the sea-coast, some concessions to the pilgrims, and the restoration of "the doubtful relic" of the true Cross.

Siege of Damietta, 10th Ramazân, 616 A.H. 19th November, 1219 A.C.

The defeat of the Franks.

19th Rajab, 619 A.H. 8th Sept., 1221 A.C.

No sooner had the Christians left than quarrels broke out between the brothers; al-Malik al-Muazzam entered into an alliance with the ambitious Jalâl ud-dîn, son of Aala ud-dîn Khwârism Shah,[1] with the object of ousting

[1] See post.

Kâmil, who on his side opened negotiations with Frederick II., Emperor of Germany, just then preparing a Crusade on his own account, against the wishes of the Pope. 589–661 A.H.

Al-Malik al-Muazzam died in 1227, leaving the principality of Damascus to his son *al-Malik un-Nâsir* Dâûd; Kâmil and Ashraf then combined to seize Damascus, and to give to Nâsir in return Harrân, Rôha (Edessa), and Rakka. Damascus was accordingly taken from him, and he had to content himself with the three cities his uncles agreed to give him. In the year 1229 A.C. (629 A.H.), Frederick (called by the Arabs the *Anberûr* or *Anbertûr*[1]) arrived in Syria. There were many communications between him and Kâmil; finally a treaty was concluded between the two for ten years six months and ten days, by which Frederick obtained the peaceful retrocession of Jerusalem, Bethlehem, Nazareth, and all the cities situated between the route from Jaffa to Acre. The only privilege reserved for the Moslems was the free exercise of their religion in the ceded towns. In Jerusalem, they were allowed to retain the Mosque of Omar. This treaty was approved neither by Moslems nor by Christians; it was grievous to the former, because they lost by it almost all that had been won by Saladin; to the Christians, because the Moslems were permitted the free exercise of their religion! Frederick returned soon after to Europe to defend his dominions against papal aggressions.

Death of al Malik al-Muazzam. Zu'l Kada, 624 A.H. Oct.-Nov., 1227 A.C.

4th Feb., 1229 A.C.

Kâmil died on the 8th of March 1238. The ameers

Death of al-Malik al-Kâmil, 21st Rajab, 635 A.H.

[1] Abu'l Fedâ gives the name as "Ferderîk," and says that he learnt from Kâzi Jamâl ud-dîn, who had been sent on a mission to Europe by Sultan Baibers, that "the Anberûr was distinguished among all the kings of the Franks by his learning, and his taste for philosophy, logic, and medicine; he was fond of the company of Mussulmans, as he had been educated in Sicily, *where most of the inhabitants were Moslems.*"

1193—1268 A.C.

Zu'l Kada, 637 A.H. 1240 A.C.

thereupon raised to the throne his son Abû Bakr, *al-Malik al-Aâdil*, a young man of weak character and given to pleasure. He was deposed by his brother Ayûb, *al-Malik as-Salèh*, who was better fitted to deal with the unruly military mamlukes who now formed the aristocracy of Egypt. In 637 A.H. (1239–40), *Abû Nasr* Dâûd, the Lord of Harrân, re-took Jerusalem from the Christians and demolished its walls.

Jerusalem re-taken.

State of Asia.

At this time Western Asia was in a state of chaos; the territories held by the Caliph alone seemed to enjoy peace and repose. In order to understand the events that now rapidly follow one another, and the causes of the fast approaching catastrophe which engulfed Saracenic civilisation, it is necessary to retrace our steps for a while.

Under Muktafi, Mustanjid, and Mustazii, the Caliphs had succeeded in regaining their temporal power over Irâk, Lower Mesopotamia, Fars, Ahwâz, and the Deltaic province. Their spiritual authority was more powerful than at any time since the death of Wâsik.

Death of Mustazii, 1179-80 A.C.

Ahmed *Abu'l Abbâs, an-Nâsir li dîn-Illâh.*

622 A.H. 1225 A.C.

Abû Nasr Mohammed, *az-Zâhir bi-amr-Illâh.*

Mustazii died in 575 A.H., and was succeeded by his son Ahmed *Abu'l Abbâs*, under the title of *an-Nâsir li dîn-Illâh.*[1] He is described as an able and successful ruler. According to az-Zahabi, his long reign of forty-seven years was glorious and blessed with splendour. He created a powerful army, and seems to have been respected and feared by all the neighbouring princes; his dominions enjoyed perfect repose, and peace and prosperity reigned everywhere. Upon his death his son *Abû Nasr* Mohammed ascended the throne under the title of *az-Zâhir bi-amr-Illâh.*[2] Ibn ul-Athîr says he was a just, mild, and benevolent sovereign, recalling the

[1] "The helper of the religion of the Lord."

[2] "Pre-eminent by the decree of the Lord."

days of Omar bin Abdul Azîz. He died after a reign of barely a year. 589—661 A.H.

His son *Abû Jaafar* Mansûr, who ascended the throne under the title of *al-Mustansir b'Illâh*,[1] maintained the power and grandeur of the Caliphate. The historians speak of him as a brave and chivalrous man, and a just, wise, and pious ruler. He established on the eastern bank of the Tigris, a college which was richly endowed and furnished with every requisite for the comfort and instruction of the students; and organised a large army for the defence of his dominions against the Tartars. 13th Rajab, 623 A.H. 10th July, 1226 A.C. *Abû Jaafar* Mansûr, *al-Mustansir b'Illâh.*

The vast steppes of Mongolia, or the tract commonly known as Chinese Tartary, stretching from the eastern borders of Ferghâna far away to the Amur, were then, as now, inhabited, if one may use the expression, by savage hordes of nomades bearing different names, but springing from one stock. Abdul Latîf, who was almost an eye-witness of the harrowing scenes enacted by these savages in the various seats of civilisation, describes them thus: "Their women fight as well as their men; their principal weapons are arrows, and their food any flesh they can get, and there is no exception or quarter in their massacre, for they slay even women and children. They are accustomed to cross deep rivers with bladders or else holding on to the manes and tails of their shaggy horses as they swim, knowing no fatigue, reckless of death, and pitiless to others." Towards the close of the twelfth century of the Christian era, these wild and teeming hordes of Tartars were united, as they probably may be again, under one banner by Chengîz or Jingis, the Devastator, the veritable "Scourge of God." Chengîz, whose real name was Temujin, was born in 1155 A.C., and was proclaimed Khâkân, or the over-lord The eruption of the Tartars. Rise of Chengîz, "the Scourge of God."

[1] "Seeking the help of the Lord."

1193—1268 A.C. of the hordes, in 1189 A.C., and from this time commenced his march towards the south and the west. By the year 1219 he had conquered China and the whole of Tartary. At this period the Moslem world was ruled by several new dynasties. The Seljukian empire of Persia had passed away. After a glorious reign of nearly half a century the great Sultan Sanjar was defeated and taken prisoner with his queen, Turkhân Khâtûn, by a rebellious tribe of Turkomans called Oghuz. These marauders, after their unexpected victory over their sovereign, sacked Merv and Nishâpur, but the work of destruction was left to be completed by the Tartars. For four years Sanjar remained a prisoner in the hands of the Oghuz. After the death of his wife, whom he did not like to leave in captivity, Sanjar escaped from his captors and arrived at Nishâpur only to find his capital a wreck and his empire ruined. He died shortly after of a broken heart. Upon his death a nephew, who bore the name of Tughril, was raised to the throne, but he was assassinated, and his kingdom seized by one of the nobles of the court.

Sultan Sanjar's unhappy end.

552 A.H. 1157 A.C. End of the Seljukide dynasty.

545 A.H. 1150 A.C. About the year 1150 A.C. a new dynasty had risen in Eastern Afghanistan, which displaced and eventually destroyed the Ghaznavides. Aalâ ud-dîn Hussain *Jehânsûz* ("the burner of the world"), the founder of the Ghori dynasty, sacked Ghazni in 550 A.H., and forced the scions of the house of Subaktagin to retire to Lahore, where they soon became domesticated Indian sovereigns. Aalâ ud-dîn Hussain's ambitions westward were restrained by Sanjar, then in the plenitude of his power; and he was compelled to find a vent for his energy in the direction of India. In 1156 A.C. Aalâ ud-dîn was succeeded by his son Saif ud-dîn, who died shortly after. The throne then went to his cousin Ghyâs ud-dîn. In 569 A.H. Ghazni was finally annexed to the Ghorian king-

Aalâ ud-dîn Hussain (Ghori).

The Ghoride dynasty.

1163 A.C.

dom. In 571 A.H. Ghyâs ud-dîn's brother Shihâb 589—661
ud-dîn,[1] who acted as his generalissimo in the East, A.H.
conquered Multan, and in 582 A.H. Khusrû Malik, the 1175 A.C.
last of the Ghaznavides, was seized by stratagem and put 1187 A.C.
to death. In 589 A.H. he defeated the combined armies 1193 A.C.
of India on the memorable field of Narâin, on the banks of the Saraswati. By this single victory the Moslems became the virtual masters of Hindustan. In 599 A.H. Shihâb ud-dîn succeeded his brother Ghyâs ud-dîn.
Upon his assassination in 602 A.H., without leaving any 1206 A.C.
issue, his mamluke Kutb ud-dîn (Aïbek)[2] obtained Hin- Hindustan.
dustan; whilst Ilduz, another slave or retainer, received 1206-1210
the principality of Ghazni. Aïbek was succeeded by his A.C.
son Abu'l Muzaffar Ârâm, but after a short reign of barely a year he was ousted by his brother-in-law Altamsh (*Shams ud-dîn*), who ruled Hindustan for twenty-five
years. He was the first of the Indo-Mahommedan 1210-35
sovereigns who received the coveted diploma of investi- A.C.
ture from the Pontifical Court of Bagdad. The kingdom was held by his children up to the year 1265 A.C. The celebrated Queen Regnant of Moslem India, Razia, the daughter of Altamsh, was raised to the throne in accord-
ance with her father's wishes in 634 A.H., and Eastern 1236-39
eyes beheld for the first time the spectacle of an unveiled A.C.
and diademed empress. The commencement of Razia's reign was attended with considerable danger and difficulty, caused chiefly by the refractory governors, who hesitated in conceding their allegiance. Eventually, however, quiet was established throughout the empire, and Razia's sway was acknowledged "from Daibal to Lakhnauti."[3] Her end was unfortunate. In attempting to quell a rebellion

[1] Known in history as Muiz ud-dîn Mohammed bin Sâm.

[2] The brilliant "bek," or chief; *Aï-Khâtûn*, brilliant lady.

[3] *Minhâj us-Sirâj.*

1193— 1268 A.C. she was taken prisoner and afterwards assassinated by the Hindoos.

Khwârism. The principality of Khwârism (modern Khiva) had been bestowed as a fief by Sultan Malik Shah upon his cupbearer,[1] or chamberlain, Nushtagîn. He was succeeded by his son Kutb ud-din Mohammed, who obtained from Sanjar the title of Khwârism Shah. Atsiz, his son and successor, rebelled against his sovereign, and towards the end of Sultan Sanjar's reign became virtually independent. The grandson of Atsiz added Irâk Ajam to his dominions, and on the murder of the last Seljuk ruler, Tughril, the nephew of Sanjar, he was invested by the Caliph with the sovereignty of Persia, Khwârism, and Khorâsân. Takish was succeeded by his son Aalâ ud-dîn Mohammed. By the conquest of Balkh and Herat he completed the subjugation of Khorâsân, and added to his dominions Mazendrân, Kermân, Ghazni, and finally Transoxiana, which was held by a lieutenant of the Khan of the Kara Khitai horde. In 1214 A.C. he marched against the Caliph, but was stopped by a snowstorm which overtook his troops on the mountains of Asadabâd, near Hamadân.[2] He then retraced his steps towards his capital. Four years later he was overwhelmed by the Mongolian avalanche, owing chiefly to his own cruel and savage folly.

Mosul. At the time of the Mongolian eruption the great Zangi's dynasty had passed away from the rulership of Mosul. The last Atâbek[3] had left an infant son named Masûd under the guardianship of his faithful mamluke Badr ud-dîn Lûlû. Masûd died in 1218 A.C.,

[1] *Tashtdâr.*

[2] The road by Hamadân and Kermanshah is to this day in winter the terror of travellers.

[3] Nur ud-dîn Arslân Shah.

and was within a short space of time followed to the grave by his son. Badr ud-dîn Lûlû then became the Atâbek of Mosul. He had held the principality for thirty-seven years when the Mongols invaded the country. 589—661 A.H.

The throne of Iconium in the year 1235-37, when the Mongols made their first raid into Asia Minor, was occupied by (Aalâ ud-dîn) Kai Kobâd, the seventh in descent from Sultan Sulaimân. In 641 A.H. they defeated Kai Kobâd's son and successor Ghyâs ud-dîn Kaikhusrû, and compelled him to pay tribute and receive a resident at his court, who was called a *Perwânah*. Rûm, 1243-44 A.C.

I have already mentioned how Malik as-Sâlèh Ayûb made himself master of Egypt in 638 A.H. He gradually extended his power over Syria, and compelled the princes of the Ayûbide dynasty, who held sway in that country, to acknowledge his suzerainty. Whilst he was endeavouring to introduce peace and order in his dominions, the troops of Mohammed Khwârism Shah, flying before the Mongols, entered Syria and plunged it into disorder. They took service first under one chief and then another. They finally threw off allegiance to the princes of Syria, and gave themselves up to slaughter and rapine. After a series of battles they were finally destroyed in 644 A.H. Egypt, 1240-41 A.C. 1246-47 A.C.

Whilst al-Malik as-Sâlèh was engaged in Syria, the Franks launched the eighth Crusade. This was headed by Louis IX. of France, called by the Arab historians *Rîdafrans* (Roi de France). Louis landed at Damietta, which was evacuated by the Moslems, turned the mosques into churches, and fixed his residence there. Once in possession of Damietta the Crusaders fell into their usual habits of life. The barons emulated each other in the splendour of their banquets, and the commonalty abandoned themselves to the lowest vices. "So general The Eighth Crusade, 647 A.H. 1249-50 A.C.

1193— 1268 A.C. was the immorality, that the king could not stop the foul and noxious torrent."

"The passion," says Michaud, "for gaming had got entire possession of the leaders and soldiers: after losing their fortune they risked even their horses and arms. Beneath the shadow of the standard of Christ the Crusaders gave themselves up to all the excesses of debauchery; the contagion of the most odious vices pervaded all ranks." "To satisfy the boundless taste for luxury and pleasure, recourse was had to all sorts of violent means. The leaders of the army pillaged the traders that provisioned the camp and the city; they imposed enormous tributes upon them, and this assisted greatly in bringing on scarcity. The most ardent made distant excursions, surprised caravans, devastated towns and plains, and drove away Mussulman women, whom they brought in triumph to Damietta." Joinville says that "the common soldiers indulged in the wildest

15th Shâbân, 647 A.H. 23rd Nov., 1249 A.C. violence towards matrons and maidens." Al-Malik as-Sâlèh Ayûb died whilst the Franks were still at Damietta, after a reign of nearly ten years.[1] He is described as taciturn, just, and upright in his conduct, faithful in his words, and martial and imposing in his character. He never took any action without consulting his generals and councillors. He organised the military corps of Bahrite Mamelukes.[2]

Ayûb left him surviving one son named Tûrân Shah (*al-Malik al-Muazzam*—"the grand prince"), who was absent on the borders of Syria. Shajr ud-Durr, the wife of Ayûb, a woman of great capacity and courage, concealed the Sultan's death until the principal officers had

[1] He was surnamed *Najm ud-dîn*, "the star of religion."

[2] So called from their barracks being over the river Nile—Bahr-un-Nîl.

taken the oath of allegiance to Tûrân Shah. On the death of Ayûb the Franks issued from Damietta for the conquest of Egypt, but they were defeated with great slaughter, and Louis and his principal noblemen fell into the hands of the Moslems. Tûrân Shah's favouritism towards the rival military corps (the Burjites) led to his assassination by the Bahrite Mamelukes. They then raised to the throne Shajr ud-Durr. The *Khutba* was recited in her name, and the coins were inscribed with her title, *al-Mustaasimièh* (the servant of the Caliph al-Mustaasim, who then ruled at Bagdad), *as-Sâlèha* (the wife of as-Sâlèh Ayûb), *al-Malikat ul-Muslimîn* (Queen of the Moslems), *mother of al-Malik al-Mansûr Khalîl.*[1] With her was associated as commander-in-chief,[2] the *Chashnigîr,*[3] Muiz ud-dîn Aïbek. Before long the commander-in-chief deposed the princess, and constituted himself the virtual sovereign. But the ameers were not satisfied, and wishing to raise to the throne a descendant of the royal blood, their choice fell on a young lad named Mûsa, a great-grandson of al-Malik al-Kâmil. He was associated with Aïbek under the title of al-Malik al-Ashraf. At this time an-Nâsir Yusuf was the sovereign of Damascus and Aleppo, and virtually of the whole of Syria. By the mediation of the Caliph a peace was concluded between an-Nâsir Yusuf and Aïbek, by which the country up to the Jordan was left in the hands of the Egyptians. In the following year Aïbek seized the sovereignty, and sent al-Malik al-Ashraf back to his relatives in Yemen. This lad was the last of the Ayûbides in whose name the *Khutba* was read in Egypt. The Bahrite Mamelukes, persecuted by Aïbek, fled to Syria, and war broke out afresh between an-Nâsir and Aïbek.

589—661 A.H.

1250 A.C.

5th August 1250 A.C.

651 A.H. 1253-54 A.C.

The last of the Ayûbides.

[1] She had a son named Khalîl, whom she lost in infancy.

[2] *Atâbek ul-Aasakir.*

[3] The taster (to the prince).

1193—1268 A.C. Again the Caliph interfered, and peace was patched up by which an-Nâsir extended his territories to al-Aarish on the frontiers of Egypt. Two years later Aïbek was assassinated, and his son Nur ud-dîn Ali was placed on the throne, with the title of al-Malik al-Mansûr. After the death of Aïbek, the Caliph sent al-Malik an-Nâsir Yusuf the diploma and pelisse of Sultanate for which he had long prayed. Syria. Although he was master of Syria from the Euphrates to the borders of Egypt, there were several petty princes within its borders who, before his aggrandisement, were doubtless his peers, and who belonged to the Ayûbide family. Emessa was held at the time of the Mongolian eruption by al-Malik al-Ashraf Mûsa, a grandson of Shirkûh. He was deprived of his principality by Nâsir about 1248, and received in exchange the district of Tell-Bâshir. Ashraf was reinstated by the Mongols, and became their deputy in Syria. Hamâh was held by the descendants of Tâkî ud-dîn Omar, the nephew of the great Saladin, by whom he was appointed Lord of Hamâh. His son Mohammed, *al-Malik al-Mansûr I.*, had gained considerable renown in the war with the Crusaders, and by his patronage of the learned. His grandson Mansûr II. held Hamâh when the Mongols invaded Syria.[1] Karak and Shaubek were held by the descendants of Aâdil (Saif ud-dîn Abû Bakr), the brother of Saladin. His great-grandson *al-Malik al-Mughîs* Taki ud-dîn Omar ruled over the principality at the invasion of the Mongols. Besides their possessions in Syria, the Ayûbides still retained a small portion of Saladin's dominions in Mesopotamia. This consisted of the principality of Mayâfârikîn. It

[1] The historian Abu'l Fedâ, Prince of Hamâh (*al-Malik al-Muwayyid, Imâd ud-din Ismâil*), was a descendant of Takî ud-din Omar (*al-Malik al-Muzzafar*), being fifth in descent.

was governed by a dynasty descended from another son of al-Aâdil. At the time of Hulâku's invasion it was subject to Malik Kâmil, who was its fifth ruler. He was killed by the Mongols. 589—661 A.H.

Such was the position of the Moslem sovereigns and princes at the time of the Mongol invasion. In 1218 A.C., the dominions of Chengîz were conterminous with those of Mohammed, the Shah of Khwârism. An interchange of courtesies between the barbarian lord of several millions of armed nomades, and the reckless and haughty Turkoman sovereign of Transoxiana, was followed by an act of cruelty on the part of the latter which unloosed upon Islâm the whirlwind of savagery that converted Western Asia in the course of a few years into a vast charnel-house. A body of traders who had arrived from Mongolia were put to death and their goods seized by the Khwarismian governor of a frontier town, on the pretence that they were spies. The Mongol asked for the surrender of the guilty governor; the Khwarismian king replied to the demand by killing the envoy. Upon receipt of the news of this outrage upon humanity and international courtesy, the Mongol issued from the steppes with a savage following of a million, and moved upon Ferghâna. It was in the year 615 A.H. that the storm burst. At the time of the Mongol eruption, in spite of the frequent wars of which the plains of Transoxiana, Khorâsân, and Persia had been the theatre, these countries were most flourishing; the people were prosperous; literature, arts, and crafts of every kind were cultivated, encouraged, and patronised; the cities were populous, and embellished with fine public and private structures, the outcome of centuries of prosperity and civilisation. Herat and Balkh each

Barbarous folly of Khwârism Shah.

The Tartaric invasion.

1218 A.C.

1193—1268 A.C. had a population of a million; in Bokhâra[1] and Samarkand it far exceeded that number. The forces of Khwârism Shah were simply swept away as by a torrent. Leaving out the minor cities and towns, it is enough to describe what happened in the principal centres of civilisation and trade. Khojand was rased to the ground, and its inhabitants passed under the sword. Bokhâra was reduced to ashes. Ibn ul-Athîr's account of the sack of this seat of learning depicts in vivid terms the terrible cruelties inflicted by the savages upon the helpless inhabitants; space, however, does not permit my quoting his description. Advancing along the beautiful valley of the Soghd, "The Scourge of God" arrived at Samarkand, which was not only the capital of Transoxiana, but also one of the greatest *entrepôts* of commerce in the world. It was three miles in circumference, and surrounded by a wall pierced by twelve iron gates, with castles at intervals. Its garrison consisted of 110,000 men, of whom 60,000 were Turkomans and Kankalis and 50,000 Tâjiks or Persians. The three armies that had overrun Northern Transoxiana now converged upon the doomed town, and an immense body of men invested it. The Turkish mercenaries, who thought they would be treated as compatriots by the Mongols, deserted in a body with their families and goods, and were immediately put to death. Upon this the Imâms and the notables issued and offered to surrender. In spite of their submission the city was sacked, and an immense number of people were killed; 30,000 artisans were assigned by Chengîz as slaves to his several sons; an equal number were set aside

Bokhâra reduced to ashes.

June 1219 A.C.

Samarkand destroyed.

[1] Bokhâra, which was studded with palaces, parks, and gardens, stretched for miles on both sides of the river Soghd, which traversed its suburbs.

for military works, transport service, etc. Of its million inhabitants, 50,000 alone remained to tell the fate of the ruined city. Warned by the fate of Bokhâra and Samarkand, the citizens of Balkh sent him presents and offered their submission, but he was afraid to leave it behind him. On pretence of counting its inhabitants, he enticed them out of the city, and then slaughtered them; the town itself was reduced to ashes. In May 1220 A.C. the savage horde captured Urganj (old Khiva), after a desperate fight, which was followed by a general massacre. They then destroyed the city by opening the dykes of the Oxus. At Nessa they made a hecatomb of over 70,000 people; men, women, and children were told to lie down side by side, they were then tied by cords and destroyed by arrows. Nishâpur, the capital of the Tahirides, and the Persian Seljukides, was destroyed in April 1221 A.C. It was rased to the ground, and its site was sown with barley; only 400 artisans escaped, and they were transported to the north. According to Mirkhond 1,747,000 men lost their lives in the massacre at Nishâpur and the surrounding districts. In Herat, and its environs, they killed, burnt, and destroyed for a week, and it is said that 1,600,000 people were killed; the place was entirely depopulated,[1] and the neighbourhood turned into a desert. Rai, Dinâwar, and Hamadan were sacked, and a large portion of the population put to the sword. The Mongols then marched upon Irâk, which belonged to the Caliph, but were beaten back by Mustansir's troops.

589—661 A.H.

Massacre in Herat.

Rai and Hamadan sacked.

Whilst his empire was being thus devastated, and his people destroyed, Mohammed, the primary author of

[1] It is said that after the retreat of the Mongols, forty persons assembled in the charred remains of the Cathedral Mosque—the miserable remnants of Herat's once teeming population.

1193—1268 A.C.

Death of Khwârism Shah.

22nd Zu'l Hijja, 617 A.H. 1220 A.C.

these calamities, was hunted from place to place; no heroism could make headway against the numbers that fell upon him. He was pursued, his family were captured by the Mongols, and all the males were put to death; only three sons escaped, one of whom alone was able to offer any resistance to the savage invaders. Mohammed took refuge in an island on the Caspian Sea, where he died of pleurisy, alone and abandoned—a poor atonement for the disasters he had brought on Islâm. His heroic son Jalâl ud-dîn was pursued by the Tartars with ruthless bloodhound pertinacity. He retreated by Khwârism, Herat, and Ghazni, collected fresh forces, and succeeded in two successful actions in inflicting considerable losses on the Mongols. Chengîz himself pursued Jalâl ud-dîn with tremendous impetuosity across the Bamiân and Kabul, past Ghazni. Hurrying on, by forced marches, he overtook the fugitive prince on the western banks of the Indus, and attacked him furiously. Jalâl ud-dîn fought with his accustomed bravery. He rushed upon the Mongols again and again, until he was driven into a corner. Two horses had already been killed under him; he sprang on to a third, with which he plunged from the bank, some thirty feet high, into the waters of the Indus, and succeeded in reaching the opposite shore in safety. The appearance of the troops of Sultan Bulban, who then ruled India, prevented Chengîz from crossing the Indus, and he withdrew his men towards the west.

In Transoxiana and Khorâsân the civilisation of centuries was completely destroyed, and the people were plunged into a depth of barbarism in which the remembrance of their former greatness and their whole future were alike engulfed. The great high-roads of Central Asia, by which the products of China and India were conveyed to Western Asia, and to Europe, were deserted; the tracts well known for their fertility lay barren and neglected, or finally destroyed; the arts and manufactures, so celebrated throughout Islâm, decayed for ever. The towns were in ruins, the peasants either murdered or compulsorily enrolled in the Mongolian army, and the artisans sent off by thousands to the farthest east to adorn and beautify the home of the barbarian conqueror. 589—661 A.H.

The Mongolian eruption put an end to the intellectual life of Central Asia, for although Persia and the west gradually recovered from their misfortunes, Bokhâra and Samarkand never regained their former mental activity, and their intellectual labours were henceforth entirely devoted to casuistry and mysticism. After converting Central Asia and Persia into a desert Chengîz retreated to the steppes, where he subsequently died. Jalâl ud-dîn was thus able to reconquer some portion of his patrimony. But the Mongols were soon upon his track again before he had time to organise an army. He was obliged to take refuge in the mountains of Kurdistan, where he was treacherously murdered by one of the inhabitants.

Death of Jalâl ud-dîn.

The Caliph Mustansir died in 1242 A.C., at the most critical period in the destiny of his house and of Saracenic civilisation. He was succeeded by his son *Abû Ahmed* Abdullâh, who received the title of *al-Mustaasim b'Illâh.*[1] Weak, vacillating, and fond of pleasure, his reign was one continuous record of disturbance and disorder at home and disaster abroad, culminating in his destruction and that of his family. The quarrels of the Hanafîs with the Hanbalites, who were the source of constant trouble in Bagdad; of the Sunnis with the Shiahs who inhabited

Death of Caliph Mustansir. 10th Jamâdi II., 640 A.H. 5th Dec., 1242 A.C. Accession of *Abû Ahmed* Abdullâh, *al-Mustaasim b'Illâh.*

[1] "Strong in the Lord."

1193–1268 A.C. the western suburb of Karkh, and most of all the quarrels of the rabble and the *budmashes* with the monied classes and the aristocracy, made Mustaasim's life a burden. And he accentuated these disorders by disbanding his father's army, and directing them to take to trade and husbandry. A riot between the Shiahs and the Sunnis led him to give an order to his son, Abû Bakr, and his secretary to demolish the suburb of Karkh, and reduce the Shiahs to slavery. *Muwayyid ud-dîn* Mohammed bin al-Kami, the vizier, who was a Shiah, was grieved at this, and is said to have invited the Tartars to come to Bagdad. The Arab historians, Ibn Khaldûn, Abu'l Fedâ, Makrîsi, and Suyûti, all describe the Vizier as a traitor; in this they are supported by Mirkhond and Wassâf, who wrote under one of the Mongols. Rashîd ud-dîn[1] alone describes him as a faithful servant anxious to save the dynasty from the impending ruin, but helpless under the imbecility and vacillation of the nerveless pontiff. However it be, Halâku, who was acting in Persia as the lieutenant-general of his brother Mangu Khan, after exterminating the Assassins and destroying their castles, marched towards Tabrîz, whence he sent some envoys to Mustaasim with the following message: "When we went out against Rudbâr, we sent ambassadors to thee, desiring aid; thou didst promise it, but sentest not a man. Now, we request that thou wouldst change thy conduct, and refrain from thy contumacy, which will only bring about the loss of thy empire and thy treasures." The misguided Caliph, without an army, with half-hearted councillors and a city torn by intestine dissensions, instead of bowing to the storm, returned a haughty reply, and the rabble insulted the departing Mongols. This threw the heathen savage into

Halâku marches upon Bagdad. Rabi I., 555 A.H.

[1] *Jâmaa ut-Tawârîkh*

a rage. Halâku advanced on the capital of the Abbassides with a force which could beleaguer the city all round. The Caliph's troops attempted to make some stand against the invaders before they arrived in the neighbourhood of Bagdad. But divided counsels led on one occasion to a disastrous repulse, and on another to a fruitless loss of life. The Mongols now resolved on blockading Bagdad. On all the heights without the city, and on all the towers and palaces which commanded it, were placed projectiles and engines, throwing masses of rock and flaming naphtha, which breached the walls, and set the buildings on fire. After the siege had lasted forty days, the vacillating Caliph commenced a parley with the savage. His messages of submission were, however, fruitless. Halâku then inveigled into his camp the principal officers of Mustaasim, who were massacred on a slight pretext along with their retainers and followers. Mustaasim's position was now hopeless. At last he was persuaded to save his life and the lives of his people by a surrender. He repaired to the Mongol camp, attended by his brother and his two sons, together with a suite of nearly three thousand persons—kâzis, shaikhs, imâms, and other notables; only the Caliph and the three princes, his brother and two sons, together with three of the suite, were admitted to an audience. The savage chief concealed the perfidy of his designs under the mask of smooth words and a most friendly reception. He requested the Caliph to send word into the city that the armed inhabitants should throw away their weapons, and assemble before the gates, in order that a general census might be taken. At the order of the Caliph the city poured out its unarmed defenders, who were immediately secured. The next day, at sunrise, Halâku issued commands for the sack of the devoted city and the massacre

589—661 A.H.

Mustaasim surrenders himself. 4th Safar, 656 A.H.

Sack of Bagdad.

1193—1268 A.C.

Universal massacre.

of its inhabitants. The destruction of Bagdad requires the pen of a master like Gibbon. The women and children who came out of their houses with the Koran in their hands, imploring quarter, were trampled to death. Delicately nurtured ladies who had never braved the sight of crowds were dragged into the open streets and subjected to the grossest brutalities; the artistic and literary treasures, collected with such labour and industry by sovereign after sovereign, with the remains of the old Persian civilisation, were destroyed in the course of a few hours. For three days the streets ran with blood, and the water of the Tigris was dyed red for miles along its course. The horrors of rapine, slaughter, and outraged humanity lasted for six weeks. The palaces, mosques, and mausolea were destroyed by fire or levelled to the earth for their golden domes. The patients in the hospitals, and the students and professors in the colleges, were put to the sword. In the mausolea the mortal remains of the shaikhs and pious imâms, and in the academies the immortal works of great and learned men, were consumed to ashes; books were thrown into the fire, or, where the Tigris was near, buried in its waters. The accumulated treasures of five centuries were thus for ever lost to humanity, and the flower of the nation was completely destroyed. After the carnage had lasted four days, Mustaasim was beaten to death, together with his sons and the principal members of his family. A few obscure scions of the house of Abbâs alone escaped the destruction. Bagdad, the abode of learning, the seat of culture, the eye and centre of the Saracenic world, was ruined for ever. The population before the sack was over two millions; according to Ibn Khaldûn, one million six hundred thousand people perished in the slaughter of six weeks. With the destruction of Bagdad

Death of Mustaasim. 20th Moharram, 651 A.H. 27th Jan., 1258 A.C.

Tomb of Tamarlane, Samarkand.

the gloom of night settled on Western Asia! The Arab and Persian authors speak in harrowing strains of the havoc and ruin caused by the myriads of savages and heathens who swept over the Islâmic world in the middle of the thirteenth century, and none but a fanatic can help shedding a tear over the fearful loss of human life and the destruction of intellectual treasure, or the carnage and atrocities committed by the Mongols. "The invasion of the Tartars," says Ibn ul-Athîr, "was one of the greatest of calamities and the most terrible of visitations which fell upon the world in general and the Moslems in particular, the like of which succeeding ages have failed to bring forth, for if one were to say that the world, since God created it to the present time, was never so afflicted, one would speak truly, for history has nothing which approaches it." Abdul Latîf calls the Mongol eruption "a misfortune that reduces to insignificance all other misfortunes." Juwaini, the author of the *Jahân Kushâ*, who was in the service of Chengîz about this time, says, "the revolution which has overwhelmed the world, has destroyed learning and the learned, especially in Khorâsân, which was the focus of light and the rendezvous of the learned. The men of learning have become the victims of the sword. This is a period of famine for science and virtue." 589—661 A.H.

After destroying Bagdad, the savage horde crossed the Euphrates and passed into Mesopotamia, carrying havoc and slaughter wherever they went. The inhabitants of Edessa, Harrân, and Nasibin were put to the sword. In Aleppo, fifty thousand people were massacred, and ten thousand women and children were sold as slaves. Harrân surrendered on a promise that the city would be spared; but the savages destroyed the inhabitants—even to the children at the breast. The Mongols marched thus west- 9th Safar, 658 A.H. 25th Jan., 1260 A.C.

1193—1268 A.C. ward, carrying destruction everywhere, assisted in their progress by the divisions prevailing among the Mussulmans
15th Ramazân, 658 A.H. 1260 A.C. themselves, until they were met at Ain Jalût, a town below Nazareth in Palestine, by the celebrated Sultan Baibers, who afterwards became the sovereign of Egypt, and were defeated with terrible slaughter. Baibers pursued the
25th Ramazân, 658 A.H. 3rd Sep., 1260 A.C. Mongols beyond Aleppo, and cleared Syria and Mesopotamia of their loathsome presence. At this time the son of Aïbek had been deposed by one of his generals named Saif ud-dîn Kotûz, who had assumed the sovereignty. Kotûz was assassinated shortly after the battle of Ain
October 1260 A.C. Jalût, when Baibers was raised to the throne under the title of *al-Malik az-Zâhir.*

For two years the Sunni world felt keenly and in sorrow the want of a spiritual head—a want which has been pathetically voiced by Suyûti.[1] Baibers appreciated
Revival of the Caliphate. the necessity of reviving the Caliphate, and he invited to Cairo Ahmed (*Abu'l Kâsim*), a scion of the house of Abbâs who had escaped the massacre of his family.

On the arrival of the young prince in the environs of Cairo, the Sultan went forth to meet him with the Kâzis and officers of state. After his descent had been formally proved before the Chief Kâzi, he was acknowledged as Caliph under the title of *al-Mustansir b'Illâh.*

The first to take the oath of allegiance was the Sultan; next came the Chief Kâzi Tâj ud-dîn, the principal shaikhs, and lastly the nobles, according to their
13th Rajab, 659 A.H. May 1261 A.C. rank. This occurred on the 13th of Rajab (12th of May, 1261), and the new Caliph's name was impressed on the coinage and recited in the *Khutba.* The following Friday (17th Rajab) he rode to the mosque in procession, wearing the black mantle, and delivered the pontifical

[1] "Thus began the year 657, and the world without a Caliph. The year 658 began, and the age still without a Caliph."

sermon. Having been formally installed the Caliph of the Faithful, he proceeded to invest the Sultan with the robe and diploma so essential in the eyes of the orthodox for legitimate authority. 589—661 A.H.

Thus was revived at Cairo the Abbasside Caliphate under the auspices of the warrior Sultan. Henceforth it is a purely spiritual office. In the sixteenth century Sultan Selîm, the great Osmanli conqueror, obtained a renunciation of the office in his favour from the last Caliph. Since then the Osmanli sovereigns have assumed the title of Caliph, and have been recognised by the bulk of the Sunni world as their legitimate Pontiffs.

CHAPTER XXIV

RETROSPECT

The Caliphate—Nominally elective—The Oath of Allegiance—Its sacramental character—Government—The political machinery—Policy — Administration — The Governorships — Provincial divisions—The Vizier—The Departments of State—Courts of Justice—Agriculture—Manufacture—Revenues of the Empire—The Army—Military tactics—The Navy.

WE have already seen how since the time of Hajjâj, with a slight intermission during the reign of Omar II., the Syrian Arabs had monopolised the high offices of state, and how sedulously they had excluded outsiders from all avenues to posts of emolument and honour. This selfish policy, based on material force, was successful so long as the subject nationalities had not learnt their strength. The revolution which wrested the supreme power from the Ommeyades and transferred it to their rivals broke their monopoly. Henceforth the non-Arabs, as common subjects of a great and civilised empire, assumed their proper place as citizens of Islâm, were admitted to the highest employment of state, and enjoyed equal consideration with the Arabs. A greater revolution than this has scarcely been witnessed either in ancient or modern times ; it gave practical effect to the democratic enunciation of the equality and brotherhood of man. To this mainly is due the extraordinary vitality of the Abbasside

Caliphate and the permanence of its spiritual supremacy, even after it had lost its temporal authority. The acceptance of this fundamental principle of racial equality among all their subjects helped the early sovereigns of the house of Abbâs to build up a fabric which endured without a rival for over five centuries, and fell only before a barbarian attack from without.

The Abbasside Caliphate.

The Caliph was not merely a secular sovereign; he was the spiritual head of a church and a commonwealth, the actual representative of divine government. The honours that were paid to some of the Pontiffs, even when they were puppets in the hands of their mayors, and the halo that surrounded their personality, show the genius of Mansûr in devising the system which constituted the Caliph the divinely-appointed Imâm or leader of the great Sunni congregation.

Mode of nominating a successor.

As under the Ommeyades, the ruling Pontiff almost invariably nominated his successor in his lifetime. When the nomination had been made, the chief dignitaries of the empire, including the Kâzis, the generals of the army, the subordinate civil and military officers, were called upon to take the oath of allegiance to the heir designate. This was called the *biat;* the person taking the oath placed his hands in those of the Prince and swore that he would be loyal and faithful. The high functionaries and the grandees of the empire took the oath to the heir designate in person; with the rank and file, he was generally represented by a proxy. To impart greater validity to the Imperial title, the *biat* was renewed upon the decease of the reigning sovereign. The Spanish historian [1] gives a graphic account of the ceremonial observed on these occasions in Cordova, which in most particulars copied the etiquette of the Caliph's court at

[1] Makkarî.

Bagdad. The Caliph sat enthroned under the gilded pavilion called the Tâj, whilst the neighbouring apartments were filled with public functionaries and courtiers who had a right to be present at such ceremonies. The ceremony commenced by the princes of the royal blood approaching the throne, and reading the formula of inauguration, after which they took the oath of allegiance, "with all its sanctions and restrictions." They were followed by the viziers and their sons, the body-guard, and the servants of the palace. This done, the brothers of the Caliph, the viziers, and the nobles, ranged themselves in a circle on each side of the throne, and the Chamberlain, who stood in one corner of the hall, swore in the people as they entered.

The Caliphate.

The oath of allegiance to the elected Caliph possessed a sacramental virtue, and imparted a sacredness to his personality of which we, in these times and living under such different conditions, can have but little conception. And this sacredness was enhanced and accentuated by prayers offered for the accepted Pontiff in the mosques of Medîna and Mecca. It was a fresh enunciation of the saying, *vox populi vox Dei.* The sacramental virtue attached to the *biat* was based upon the following idea. All the rules and ordinances which regulate the conduct of the general body of Moslems are the utterances of the voice of God. This is in substance the *Ijmâa ul-Ummat,* "the consensus of the people," and when they unanimously, or almost unanimously, choose a spiritual leader and head of the congregation of Islâm, a divine sanction is imparted to his spiritual authority; he becomes the source and channel of legitimate government, and he alone has the right of "ordaining" deputies entitled to rule, decide, or to lead at prayers. It was due to this conception of the sacramental character of the Caliph's election that long after he had lost every vestige of temporal power, conquerors and chieftains like Mahmûd of Ghazni solicited from him the consecration of *their* power. The Caliph's confirmation legitimised their authority, vested in them the lawful government of their states, and made every popular rising against them illegal and impious. This ordination was effected by the grant of a formal diploma which was invariably accompanied by a pelisse of honour (*tashrîf*), often by a turban studded with jewels, swords and banners.

The political machinery. The political machinery which existed under the Abbasside Caliphate, and was afterwards adopted either wholly, or with some modifications by the states that came into existence on the break-up of the Arab empire, was founded by Mansûr, and derived its character from his genius. During the Ommeyade rule the government of the Caliphs was a pure autocracy tempered by the freedom of speech possessed by the desert Arabs and the learned or holy which enabled them, often by a phrase or verse from the Koran or from the poets, to change the mood of the sovereign. Under the first five Caliphs of the Abbasside dynasty also the government continued to be more or less autocratic, although the departmental ministers and prominent members of the family formed a body of unauthorised councillors. The Caliph was the fountain of all power, and all orders relating to the administration of the state emanated from him. The vizier was practically the lieutenant of the Caliph, and wielded in his name the full authority of the empire. He could appoint and displace the functionaries; he supervised the taxation and the receipt and disbursement of revenues; all the state correspondence was in his hands, and he acted as the mandatary of the sovereign and united in his person the civil and military administration, besides the ordinary duties of counselling and helping the Caliph. Such were the viziers who held the office under the early Abbassides; they derived their authority from the Caliphs and purported to carry out his mandates. In time it was found that the duties were too heavy for one man to discharge, and it became necessary to appoint some minor functionaries for the work of the various departments in subordination to the vizier. Under the great Mâmûn government by the will of one man gave way to constitutionalism. A regular council of state, representing every community owning allegiance to the Caliph, was for the first time established in his reign. The representatives of the people enjoyed perfect freedom in the expression of their opinions, and do not seem ever to have been hampered in their discussions. The Caliph's council in later times, when they had lost their temporal authority, and their influence rested on their spiritual prestige, turned into a synod of divines and doctors of law. But the Buyides, the Sâmânides, the Seljukides, and the Ayûbides, all had their councils in which the people were more or less represented. Saladin's council met regularly, either under his presidency or that of the vizier (al-Kâzi al-Fâzil), for the transaction of business, and seems to have followed the Sultan in his campaigns.

Constitutionalism under Mâmûn.

With the exception of the ill-fated Amîn, the first eight sovereigns of the Abbasside dynasty were men of exceptional ability, who, like the Tudors, maintained a tight hold on their governors. It was a settled policy never to keep a governor too long in any province; confidential messengers were stationed at each provincial capital to keep the Court at Bagdad fully acquainted with the events transpiring from day to day in their respective provinces. Sometimes the head of the post offices[1]

[1] Also called the *Sâhib ul-Khabar*.

(*Sâhib ul-Barîd*) acted as the official newsagent, so to speak, of the Caliph. Besides these recognised agents and commissaries, there existed a large body of secret police or detectives in all parts of the empire, who kept a strict watch over all conditions of people. They even extended their operations to foreign countries, for under Mahdi, Rashîd, Mâmûn, and Mutasim, secret agents were maintained at Byzantium, and other important places, to keep the Caliph informed of every movement of the Byzantine emperors. These detectives were of both sexes, and seem to have done their duty with remarkable fidelity and success. It is probable that during the ascendency of the Turkish guards, and the mayoralty of the Buyides, when the Caliphs were either prisoners or in tutelage, the system fell into abeyance or desuetude. But with the partial recovery of their temporal power, they re-employed the old machinery for obtaining information. It is stated that an-Nâsir li-dîn-Illâh[1] kept himself so well posted in everything which transpired, either within his own dominions, or in neighbouring countries, that people believed "he was ministered to by the Jinns."[2] As in modern times, unofficial agency was frequently resorted to for these purposes, and spies were chosen from all classes, especially merchants, pedlars, and such like, who kept the Caliph informed of every occurrence, however trivial. When the provincial governors became feudatories of the empire, and the sovereignty of the Caliph dwindled into a more or less effective suzerainty, the confidential messengers were turned into legates of the Pontiff, and acted as his resident agents in the Courts of Nishâpur, Merv, Mosul, Damascus, etc. Like the Papal legates in the later mediæval

[1] *Ante*, p. 382.
[2] Az-Zahabi.

times in Europe, they accompanied the sovereigns to whom they were accredited in their military marches. We find them not only in the camps of Alp Arslân and Malik Shah, but also in those of Nûr ud-dîn Mahmûd and Saladin, ever active, and sometimes meddlesome; occasionally, as under the later Ayûbides, reconciling contending princes, and settling fratricidal strifes.[1]

Each sovereign on his side maintained a commissary called *Shahna*, at the Pontifical Court, charged with the duty of keenly watching the moves of the game on the part of his rivals, for the struggle for predominating influence over the source of all legitimate authority was as great at Bagdad as in papal Rome. *Shahnas*[2] were usually stationed, besides the capital, in places like Wâsit, Basra, Tikrit, etc.

Policy.

One great object of the early Abbassides was the consolidation of the empire; and in order to attain this end, aggressive enterprises and foreign conquests were abandoned. The advance into Upper Egypt, and the countries of Deilem and Cabul, were due to the turbulence of the wild and savage tribes inhabiting these regions, whilst the frequent wars with the Byzantines were always the result of inroads and violations of treaty-pledges on their part.

The administration.

The administration was conducted on definite lines analogous to modern civilised systems; in some directions it may be said to have been in advance of our own times. All offices of state, as under the Ottoman Empire in the present day, were equally open to Moslems, Jews, Christians, and Hindoos. Nothing marks so distinctly the difference between the Ommeyade and Abbasside

[1] The Caliph's envoy, says Abu'l Fedâ, settled the dispute between the sons of al-Malik al-Muazzam.

[2] This word has now come to mean a watchman.

rule, as the complicated machinery for the conduct of government which came into existence under the Caliphs of the house of Abbâs, and which were afterwards copied by all the succeeding Moslem states.

The Governors.

The provincial administration was, as under the last dynasty, conducted by governors appointed by the Caliph, but their powers and jurisdiction were considerably circumscribed. Mansûr never kept a governor in one province for any length of time. On being relieved of office he was required to give a full account of his administration, and the smallest suspicion of breach of trust led to confiscation of his properties. Under Mansûr the office of a provincial governor was by no means a sinecure. Their position was more satisfactory under his successors, although their powers of initiation were equally limited. They were merely the administrative and military heads of the provinces entrusted to their charge, liable to dismissal at pleasure of the sovereign. The judicial authority was entrusted to the provincial Kâzi, who was assisted by a number of deputies, stationed in the different towns. The governors of certain provinces, however, gained for themselves special privileges by services rendered to the state by liberal aid from the territories under their charge, or by special loyalty.

The several Governorships.

Western Africa beyond the Libyan Desert, together with Sicily, formed one government, and was held in Saffâh's time by Abdur Rahmân bin Habîb, whilst Egypt was entrusted to the faithful Abû Ayûn. The Jazîra (Mesopotamia), Azerbaijân, and Armenia; Medîna, Mecca, and Yemâma (Western and Central Arabia); Yemen or Southern Arabia; Kûfa and its neighbourhood (the *Sawâd*, the great Euphrates valley); Basra with the Delta, Bahrain, and Oman; the Persian Irâk, Khorâsân, and Transoxiana; Sind and the Punjab; Ahwâz (Susiana) and Southern Persia; the principality of Mosul; and lastly Syria with the Phœnician littoral, formed the remaining governments. Saffâh afterwards separated Palestine from Syria and placed it under a separate governor. Rashîd in some measure recast the previous divisions; he separated the marches of Syria and Cilicia from the governorship of Mesopotamia and Kinnisrin, and formed them into a separate governorship under the name of Awâsim.[1] When the office was entrusted to a prince of the royal blood, a military officer of high rank was always associated with him as his adviser and lieutenant. The governor of the Awâsim was in fact the warden of the marches,[2] and was charged with the duty of guarding the frontiers and the mountain passes. Tarsus, in Cilicia, which was built and fortified by Rashîd, was made the capital of this important governorship. Like his grandfather, Rashîd was a great builder of cities; Mansûr had rebuilt Massisia (ancient Mopsuesta); Rashîd built Tarsus, Adana, Maraash (Germanicia), and a number of other places which were strongly fortified and garrisoned by the regular soldiers of the Caliphate.

The Vizier.

Although the office of vizier[3] existed among the Persians, and was known to the Arabs, it was not until the Abbassides came into power that any functionary actually held office under that name. With the loss of the Caliph's actual authority, the vizier lost his predominant position, and his place was taken by the *Ameer ul-Umrâ*,[4] or general-in-chief. The Buyides after-

[1] It means the marches.

[2] The Persian word *marzbân* has the same signification.

[3] The word "vizier" means "the bearer of a burden." Abû Salmah was the first who bore this title.

[4] See *ante*, p. 301.

wards transferred the title to their own ministers, leaving to the Pontiff only a secretary who bore the name of *Raîs ur-Ruasâ*.[1] When the Caliphs under the Seljuk Sultans resumed their temporal power, they again nominated their viziers, and the office of cabinet-secretary and the vizierate were combined in one person.[2]

The *Ustâd ud-dâr* or intendant of the palace was another important personage. Under the weaker sovereigns, the Ameer ul-Umrâ was also the *Ustâd ud-dâr*, and the Buyide princes did not hesitate to distinguish themselves by this title. When they lost their power, the office of *Ustâd ud-dâr* became reduced to what its name really implies, viz. *maître d'hôtel*. Under the Caliph al-Mustanjid,[3] Abdullâh (Aazd ud-dîn) ibn ul-Muzzaffar, and after him his son Abdul Fârigh Mohammed (Imâd ud-dîn), a grandson of the *Raîs ur-Ruasâ*, acted as *maîtres d'hôtel*.

The *Ustâd ud-dâr*.

The title of *Sultan*[4] was for the first time bestowed by Wâsik upon Ashnâs, the commandant of the Turkish guards, who was decorated with a jewelled crown and double girdle. It seems virtually to have remained in abeyance until the Buyides rose to power, when it was conferred on those princes. The investiture was attended with great pomp and ceremony. The recipient of the title was first dressed in royal robes, a jewelled crown was placed on his head, a collar round his neck, a bracelet on his arm, and a sword was buckled round his waist. Finally, to mark the combination of both civil and military powers, two banners were handed to

The Sultan.

[1] *i. e.* Chief of the chiefs.

[2] In the reign of al-Kâim (p. 309) the vizier Ali bin Ahmed bin Maslamah bore the title of *Raîs ur-Ruasâ*.

[3] See *ante*, p. 345.

[4] An Arabic word meaning a ruler.

him by the Caliph personally, "one ornamented with silver, fashioned as is customary among the nobles, and the other with gold in the manner of those given to the successors designate to the Caliph." The diploma was then read out in the presence of the assembled multitude, after which the Sultan kissed the Caliph's hand.

The title of Sultan was not, however, confined to the Buyide princes. It was conferred on mighty conquerors like Mahmûd of Ghazni, Tughril, Alp Arslân, Malik Shah, Saladin, etc. Practically once assumed or conferred it became hereditary in the family, although on each succession, a formal investiture was applied for, and almost as a matter of course granted with the usual robes of honour.

The Malik.

Later, another title was created, that of Malik,[1] or king, which, sometimes jointly with the designation of Sultan and sometimes separately, but always with a qualifying phrase, was bestowed on ruling princes. The first to obtain this honour was the great Nûr ud-dîn Mahmûd, the son of Zangi, who received from the Caliph the title of *al-Malik al-Aâdil*, the just king.

The Vizierate.

Regarding the position of viziers under the Abbassides, the Moslem legists and writers on political economy recognise two grades of *vizierate:* (1) the unlimited (*vizârat ut-tafwîz*), (2) the limited (*vizârat ut-tanfîz*). To viziers of the first class the sovereign "delegated" all his powers; they were vested with absolute and unfettered discretion in all matters concerning the state. They could make any disposition and report it afterwards to their master. Under Saffâh, Mansûr or Mahdi, there were no such viziers; under Rashîd, Jaafar Barmeki, and under Mâmûn, Fazl bin Sahl alone held the delegated authority.

The viziers of the second class did not possess such

[1] An Arabic word analogous to the Latin Rex.

wide powers. They could not act of their own initiative, but were authorised to carry out the orders of the sovereign. The viziers were required to have a thorough knowledge of administration and taxation, of the local circumstances of the provinces, and their several needs and requirements. Non-Moslems were eligible for the office, although their appointment might not have been viewed with approval by the orthodox.[1]

The manner of the vizier's appointment is not without interest. The person on whom the imperial choice fell was summoned to the palace by a *Mutâlia* (a notification or official letter), which was delivered to him by two of the prominent grandees (*Ameers*) of the empire. On his arrival at the door of the *Hujra* (the Caliph's cabinet) he was introduced into the presence by the Chamberlain. After he had made his obeisance, the Pontiff held a short conversation with him ; he was then led to another room, to be robed in the usual dress of honour (*tashrîf*). Returning to the Caliph's presence he kissed the hand and withdrew. On arrival at the gate a richly-caparisoned horse was brought to him. He then rode to his office at the *Diwân*, preceded by the great functionaries, the officers of the empire, the Ameers attached to the Court, the Caliph's servants, and the chamberlains of the *Diwân*. At the office he dismounted with great ceremony, and after he had taken his seat the proclamation of appointment was read.[2]

[1] This feeling was not peculiar to the Saracens. The Buyide Azud ud-Dowla's Christian vizier (Nasr bin Hârûn) wielded great influence. The Fatimides of Egypt had frequently Hebrew and Christian viziers.

[2] Among the most noted viziers may be mentioned Abû Ayûb al-Muriyâni and Rabî bin Yunus of Mansûr, Jaafar of Rashîd, Fazl and Hassan of Mâmûn, Fakhr ud-Dowla bin Tahir of Muktadi and

The Diwân ul-Azîz.

The Departments of State.

The government of the Caliph was called *ad-Diwân al-Azîz* or the *August Board*, as the government of Turkey is called now *al-Bâb ul-Aâli*, the *Sublime Porte*. The grand vizier presided over the Board and received the designation of *al-Vizier ud-Diwân il-Azîz*.[1] The administrative machinery under the Abbassides, in its effective distribution of work and its control of detail, ranks with the best modern systems. The following were the principal departments of state:—the *Diwân ul-Kharâj* (Central Office of Taxes) or Department of Finance; the *Diwân ud-Diâ* (Office of the Crown Property); the *Diwân uz-Zimâm* (Audit or Accounts Office); the *Diwân ul-Jund* (War Office); the *Diwân ul-Mawâli wa'l Ghilmân* (Office for the Protection of Clients and Slaves), in which a register was kept of the freedmen and slaves of the Caliph, and whence their support was assigned to them; the *Diwân ul-Barîd* (the Post Office); the *Diwân uz-Zimâm an-Nafakât* (Household Expense Office); the *Diwân ur-Rasâil* (Board of Correspondence or Chancery Office); the *Diwân ut-Toukia* (Board of Requests); the *Diwân aan-nazr fi'l Mazâlim* (Board for the Inspection of Grievances); *Diwân ul-Ahdâs w'ash-Shurta* (Militia and Police Office); and the *Diwân ul-Aatâ* (Donation Office), analogous to the paymaster-general's department, charged with the payment of the regular troops.[2] The protection

Kâim, Rudâwari of al-Muhtadi, Ibn Hobaira of Mustanjid, al-Âmid al-Kunduri of Tughril Beg, Nizâm ul-Mulk of Alp Arslân and Malik Shah, and al-Kâzi al-Fâzil of Saladin.

[1] The chiefs of the various departments were sometimes designated viziers or ministers, but they were always in subordination to the principal vizier, who was practically at the head of the administration. The principal or Prime Minister received the title of grand vizier, *al-Vizier al-aâzam* or *as-Sadr al-aâzam*.

[2] In the reign of Mansûr the president of this department was one Habîb bin Abdullâh bin Raghabân.

of the interests of non-Moslems was entrusted to a special office, the head of which was called the *Kâtib ul-Jihbâzèh.*[1]

Besides these principal departments of state there were a few minor ones, administrative, political, and judicial. Among these, the Board of Government Grants, *Diwân ul-Mukâtiât*, and the one charged with the supervision of canals, aqueducts, and irrigation works (*Diwân ul-Akriha*) deserve special notice. With all these offices there was far less bureaucratism and officialdom, if I may use the expression, under the Caliphs than in the Byzantine Empire, and the government carried its policy of non-interference with the concerns of separate communities sometimes to the extremest verge, to the detriment of its own interests. Each village, each town administered its own affairs, and the government only interfered when disturbances arose, or the taxes were not paid. It, however, maintained a close and strict supervision upon all matters which concerned agriculture. It superintended the construction and repairs of the canals and all irrigation works, upon which depended the crops and the revenues of the state. Abû Yusuf, the Chief Kâzi of the empire under Rashîd, in a letter addressed to the Caliph, emphasises the duty of government to build new canals at its own cost for the promotion of agriculture, and to cleanse and keep in repair the existing ones, the expense of maintenance and of distributing the waters being shared by the state and the recipients. He dwells on the necessity of an efficient river police, and of removing all hindrances to navigation upon the large rivers, particularly on the Tigris and Euphrates.

Diwân uz-Zimâm.

One of the most effective arrangements for improved administration was the introduction by the Caliph

[1] In Spain this officer was called the *Kâtib uz-Zimâm.*

Mahdi of the Audit or Accounts Office (*Diwân uz-Zimâm*) in the large centres. As under the Ommeyades the Central Taxation Office (*Diwân ul-Kharâj*) formed the most important Department of State. Its duty was to collect the taxes of the whole of Irâk, the richest province of the empire, and to keep an account of the taxes in other provinces. The collection of the payments in kind (*Maawin*) was also included in its duties.

The *Diwân ur-Rasâil*, or Chancery Office, was another important institution. The duties of the president of this bureau, who may be regarded as one of the principal Secretaries of State, was to draw up the imperial mandates, diplomas, letters patent, and political correspondence generally, and after these had been approved by the sovereign, or the vizier, to seal them in red wax with the pontifical seal bearing the Caliph's device. He also revised and corrected official letters, and sealed them himself. He attended the public audiences, where the Caliph heard the complaints or petitions of the people, and took down the royal decision on the paper presented by the suitor; often in such cases a copy was given to the complainant whilst the original was kept in the state archives. From the nature of the work transacted in this office, and the style of the writing which was and has always been elaborately elegant, the secretaries and clerks were necessarily selected from among men of talent and education belonging to the higher classes of society. The next office in importance was the *Diwân ut-Toukia*, or Board of Requests. In this office, called under the Ommeyades the office of the Seal of State, the answers to memorials presented to the sovereign were drawn up; they were registered, marked with the royal letters, and sealed; and the motto of the Caliph, or a verse from the Koran generally written on them before despatch.

In each provincial capital a postmaster (*as-Sâhib ul-Barîd*) was charged with the control of the postal establishment. He not only superintended the regular despatch of the imperial mails, but also kept the Caliph informed of all important occurrences. He was in fact a direct confidential agent of the central government, and periodically submitted confidential reports on the condition of the province, the working of the administration, the state of the peasantry and agriculture, the attitude of the local authorities, the condition of the mint and the amount of gold and silver coined. He also had to be present at the mustering and paying of the troops. Private letters were carried with the government despatches and safely delivered to the addressees, but it is difficult to say what private individuals had to pay for this boon. In Persia relays of horses and mules, in Arabia and Syria camels, were used for the conveyance of the mails. There were 930 stages in the whole empire, and the relays of animals at each stage must have been very numerous, as they were available upon proper payment for public use. A governor with all his retinue would travel to his appointed province by stages, and even troops were conveyed in that manner. The imperial mail horses bore distinctive marks, and could not be mistaken for private ones. The cost of feeding the animals, the purchase of new ones, the salary of the postmen and postal officials for Irâk alone amounted to 154,000 dinârs, about £100,000. Under the Ommeyade Caliph Hishâm the postal expenditure in the province of Irâk had amounted to four million dirhems. The *Sâhib ul-Barîd*, head of the postal department, had to lay the reports of the postmasters and other

Postal Department.

officers before the Caliph, and sometimes to make extracts from them. Besides this, he had in his hands the appointment of the postal officials in all the provincial towns, their general superintendence, and the payment of their salaries. Accurate postal directories containing the name of every station and their distance from one another were kept in the government offices. It is stated that the employment of pigeons for carrying news was known to the Greeks and the Romans;[1] but the earliest authentic record is found in the reign of Mutasim, when the news of the capture of Bâbek was carried to Bagdad by a carrier pigeon.[2] After this pigeons were employed for regular postal work. In the reign of the Caliph Nâsir li dîn-Illâh they seem to have been in great requisition, and Nûr ud-dîn Mahmûd had regular establishments of carrier pigeons for military purposes in every important station.

Military Inspection Office.

Another department, but apparently connected with or subordinate to the war office, was the *Diwân ul-Aarz*, or military inspection office. The arsenals were under a special officer who was called the *Mushrif us-Sanâat bi'l Makhzan.*[3] Each government office was presided over by a director who was designated the *Raîs*, or *Sadr*, and the practical work of control and supervision was carried on by inspectors, called *Mushrifs*, or *Nâzirs*. The inspector of agriculture and irrigation bore the designation of *Mushrif ul-Akriha*; of taxes paid in kind, *Mushrif ul-ikâmat il-Makhzania*;

[1] It is said that Taurosthenes announced to his father his victory at the Olympic games by sending to him at Ægina a pigeon stained with purple, and that Hirtius and Brutus corresponded by means of pigeons at the siege of Modena.

[2] Masûdi.

[3] Inspector of the manufactory at the magazine.

of the government stores, *Mushrif bi'l Makhzan ;* of the board of government grants, *Nâzir ud-Diwân il-Mukâtiât.* The sub-director of the account and audit office was called the *Nâib aan-Diwân iz-Zimâm.*[1]

Besides these and other officers, there was a general controller, whose duty it was periodically to inspect the government offices and report in detail to the sovereign. He was called the *Mushrif ul-Mumlikat.* The order of precedence among the different dignitaries seems to have been as follows; first came the Vizier, then the *Hâjib*, or Lord High Chamberlain, the presidents of the various boards, the Chief Kâzi, the chief of the guards, the several secretaries, etc. The Hâjib[2] introduced foreign ambassadors, princes, and nobles into the imperial presence, and naturally exercised great influence.

Each city had its own special police, called the *Shurta*, under a chief who was designated the *Sâhib ush-Shurta.* As under the Ommeyades, the *Shurta*, or city guards, were distinct from the municipal police, and were divided into groups according to the urban districts. To them was entrusted the protection of the person and property of the citizens, and they patrolled the city at night under the divisional commandants. The *Shurta* held military rank, and being always well paid were honest and zealous in their work. The office of commissary of police at Bagdad ranked almost as a governorship. Under Mâmûn the general Tâhir held the post for some time until he sought for, and obtained the governorship of Khorâsân. In later times the *Sâhib ush-Shurta* occasionally assumed the position of vizier.

The police.

[1] Abû Ghâlib al-Asbâghi, surnamed *Tâj ur-Ruasâ* ("crown of the *raises*"), held this office in the reign of the Caliph al-Muktadi. The *Kâtibs* of Irâk "drew up the public accounts after the system introduced by him."

[2] In Spain, the Hâjib was practically the vizier.

The Muhtasib.

The municipal police was under a special officer called the *Muhtasib.* This useful and important office was created by the Caliph Mahdi, and has existed ever since in Islâmic countries. The *Muhtasib* was both superintendent of the markets and a public censor. He went through the city daily, accompanied by a detachment of subordinates, and assured himself of the due execution of the police orders, inspected the provisions, tested the weights and measures used by tradespeople, and suppressed nuisances. Any attempt to cheat led to immediate punishment. Abu'l Hassan al-Mâwardi, "the Hugo Grotius of Islâmic public law," after describing[1] the extent and limits of judicial and executive authority, says that the police (*hisbat*) stand half-way between judicial utterances and the application of executive force. "The duties of the police," says he, "are circumscribed within the limits imposed by law, to enforce what is incumbent and to prevent from committing what is forbidden when it comes into prominence."

Corporation of merchants.

A responsible syndicate was constituted from among the merchants themselves to supervise commercial transactions and repress frauds. The syndicate was either a corporation of merchants, or was composed of representatives from among their body. It was always presided over by one of their most influential and respected members, who was called *ar-Raîs ut-Tujjâr.*[2] The syndics of the corporation were called *Amîns.* Not only did each centre of commerce possess its corporation of merchants, but most cities of importance had their town councils (*Diwân ush-Shûra*) composed of the notables of the place, and sometimes of nominees of the governor or sovereign, and presided over by an elected *Sadr.*

[1] In his *Ahkâm us-Sultâniyeh.*

[2] "The chief of the merchants."

Self-government was specially fostered, and municipal institutions were protected and encouraged. The historian of *Culture under the Caliphs* justly observes that "fortunately the Moslem world had no absolute bureaucracy. The administration was as simple as possible and left entirely to the community; the only thing that the supreme power exacted was the correct payment of the taxes." To this I may add the preservation of irrigation works. As an example of this non-interference I would refer to the system pursued in Persia. Each town with its dependencies administered its own affairs, levied its own taxes, and paid the fixed revenue to the state. The governors were consulted when there arose any question of new taxation or dispute between a neighbouring town. These cities thus formed so many semi-independent principalities. Their position was almost similar to that of the free cities of Europe. Balkh, with its dependency, extended over ten leagues, and was defended by earth works thrown up all round it. Soghd, Samarkand, Herat, Bokhâra, Khwârism,[1] Rai, Hamadân, and other townships were as extensive. These municipalities had thus a great influence upon the culture of the nation. The central government merely nominated the deputy governor, generally chosen from the local patrician family, and the judges and other dignitaries. The office of deputy governor in these free towns was of such importance that sometimes it was given to princes of the royal blood.

I have already mentioned how the Caliphs built caravanserais and rest-houses, and made cisterns along the whole route from Bagdad to Mecca and from Bagdad to other important centres, so that the pilgrims and caravans should find shelter in bad weather and get relief

[1] Medînat ul-Fîl (city of the elephant).

from the sufferings of thirst. In order to protect pilgrims from the depredations and attacks of the Bedouins, they also established the important office of a superintendent of the Hâjis (*Ameer ul-Hâjj*), whose duty it was to accompany the pilgrims with a body of troops.

Ameer ul-Hâjj.

The management and control of the nomadic tribes was entrusted to some prominent chief, who was called the *Ameer ul-Arab*,[1] and was responsible for their good conduct.

The administration of justice.

The administration of justice was a subject of extreme importance. All questions relating to civil rights among non-Moslems were left to the decision of their own religious heads or magistrates; among Moslems, to the Kâzis. Each city had its own Kâzi; and in large towns there were several *nâib* (deputy) Kâzis. The Chief Kâzi of Bagdad was called the Kâzi ul-Kuzzât,[2] and was in fact the chief judiciary of the empire. In order to assist the Kâzis in the administration of justice, another class of officers was established analogous to the notaries public of modern times, who were called *aadls*.

Criminal justice was apparently in the hands of magistrates called *Sâhib ul-Mazâlim*. But the highest tribunal was the "Board for the inspection of grievances," *ad-Diwân aan-Nazr fi'l Mazâlim*, which was presided over by the sovereign himself, or in his absence by one of his chief officers. The other members of this Board were the Chief Kâzi, the Hâjib, the principal secretaries of state, and some of the Muftis or jurisconsults especially invited to attend. The establishment of this Court was rendered necessary by the difficulty of executing the decrees of the Kâzi when the defendant was of high

[1] He was the phylarch of the Roman and Byzantine times.

[2] The first person to hold this office was Abû Yusuf, appointed by Rashîd.

rank or employed in the service of government. None dared disobey a citation before this Court, and none were powerful enough to escape its severity.

A regular High Court of Justice, however, was not established until the time of Nûr ud-dîn Mahmûd.[1] He instituted for the first time the *Dâr ul-Aadl*, locating in one place the different Courts, and organised and improved the judiciary, which had seriously deteriorated in the decline of the Caliphate.

In Courts of Justice nobody could give evidence or witness any document unless he bore a good character. This wise provision, like all others framed by human ingenuity, often miscarried.

Agriculture.

The province between the Euphrates and Tigris was the richest and most important in the whole empire, and being under the direct administration of the supreme government, particular attention was devoted to its agricultural development and prosperity. A network of canals lent fertility to the soil, and a complicated system of drainage works drained the marshy tracts. Mahdi built a canal in the Wâsit district, which brought into cultivation a vast area of land. The Îsa canal, built by an uncle of Mansûr, extended from the Euphrates at Anbâr to Bagdad, and ran into the Tigris in the western part of the town; it was navigable to big ships all the way. The Dujail[2] canal, which branched from the main stream at Tikrit and had many off-shoots, was used for the purpose of irrigating the districts to the north of Bagdad. The districts east of the Tigris enjoyed the same agricultural facilities. These were not confined to any particular province; all over the empire the work of promoting agriculture and horticulture was regarded as a

[1] See *ante*, p. 341.

[2] *Dujail* is the diminutive of *Dajla*, the Tigris.

religious duty. In those days Irâk and Southern Persia presented, say the annalists, the appearance of a veritable garden, and the whole country, especially between Bagdad and Kûfa, was covered with prosperous towns, flourishing villages, and fine villas. The mineral resources of the empire too were carefully examined and utilised. The iron mines of Khorâsân, and the lead and silver mines in Kermân, were worked under competent overseers. Porcelain and marble were obtained from Tabriz; rock-salt and sulphur from Northern Persia; bitumen and naphtha from Georgia. Manufacture of every kind was fostered and encouraged. The glass and soap manufactories of Basra were famous all over the civilised world; under Mutasim these manufactures acquired fresh impetus, for he opened new workshops at Bagdad, Sâmarra, and other important cities. He also established paper manufactories at different places, for which workmen and foremen were brought from Egypt, where the art of paper-making had flourished from ancient times. Royal factories for gold embroidery existed in all the principal towns of Persia, and the manufacture of silk, satin, brocade, carpets, etc., was maintained at a high standard by distinctive marks. In fact, the industrial progress of the Saracens is attested by the exquisite fabrics that were turned out from the innumerable looms of Persia, Irâk, and Syria. Kûfa was famous for its silk and half-silk kerchiefs for the head, which are still used in Western Asia and known as *Kuffiyèh*. Khuzistân (ancient Susiana) was also noted for its textile fabrics. The beautiful brocades of Tostar, the rich carpets of Korkub, and the silks and satins of Sus were in request all over the world. The other provinces were equally famous for their splendid manufactures. Susangird contained a royal factory for the gold embroidery of damask, camel-hair fabrics, and carpets. It

Manufactures.

also produced embroidered curtains made of spun silk (*kazz*) for the Sultan, and raw silk and camel and goat hair materials. Here were manufactured splendid cloaks of spun silk, considered superior to the striped woollen cloaks of Shirâz. The wealthy cities of Khorâsân were active in the production of brocades, carpets, rugs, hangings, coverings for cushions, and woollen fabrics of all kinds. In short, every city in the empire had its own particular manufacture in metal, glass, wool, silk, or linen.[1] Syria was famous for its manufacture of glass, and as early as the second century of the Hegira parti-coloured and enamelled glass was produced. The art of ornamenting it with gold and other colours was carried to perfection, and many famous pieces of ornamental crystal are mentioned by the old writers. One particular goblet from the treasury of the Fatimides was sold for 360 dinârs.[2] Sconces of glass with enamelled inscriptions in white and blue were hung up in the mosques and palaces, and vessels of every shape and description were in demand as articles of use or luxury.

The country was equally rich in raw produce; barley, wheat, rice, dates, and fruit of all kinds, also cotton, were grown in large quantities all over the empire.[3] Fruit culture was pursued as a science with remarkably productive results. Ahwâz and Fârs were noted for their sugar plantations and manufacture. The numerous

[1] Kazerûn was noted for its linen fabrics.

[2] Makrîsi.

[3] Nâsiri Khusrû's vivid account of the flourishing state of cultivation in the various countries through which he passed, gives some idea of their agricultural condition in the palmy days of the Caliphate. In the neighbourhoods of Mayâfârikîn, Khilât, Aleppo, Tyre, Sidon, Beyrut, etc., he saw miles of waving corn, vast fields of sugar plantations, groves upon groves of fruit trees, citron, olive, date, orange, etc.

refineries and factories which existed in these provinces supplied not only a great part of Asia but also Europe. Jundisapûr was in those days the seat of the world-famed college of natural sciences, and the home of the most eminent physicists of the time. It is probable that this college gave an impetus to industry and commerce. The knowledge of sugar-refining certainly originated in that city, and was first applied and started in a commercial manner in Khuzistân itself, and from there, like many other arts, carried to Spain. The ordinary articles of export were barley, wheat, rice, fruit, the famous flowers of Mazendrân, sugar, glass and hardware, silk, woollen and linen stuffs, oil and perfumes of all kinds, such as rose-water, saffron and lily-water, a perfume made of date blossoms, aromatic pomades, grape syrup, oil of violets, etc. The imports consisted of spices and drugs from India and the Archipelago, sandalwood, precious stones and jewellery, bamboo, ebony, and ivory.

Farsistân was rich in minerals; it had salt, silver, iron, lead, sulphur, and naphtha mines. Silver was also found in the neighbourhood of Yezd.

The Revenues.

The revenues of the empire were derived from (1) the land tax; (2) tithes or income tax (*ushr*, *zakât*, *sadakât*); (3) the fifth of the produce of mines and pasturage; (4) the tax on non-Moslems (in lieu of military service); (5) customs dues; (6) salt and fishery tax; (7) tax paid by shopkeepers for the use of public places, in other words, for erecting shops or putting up stalls in the streets and squares; (8) tax upon mills and factories; (9) tax upon conveyances and luxuries; and (10) tax upon imports. Wâsik, however, abolished the tax upon imports with a view to reviving maritime trade.

"All this proves," says von Kremer, "that the financiers

General View of Ispahan.

of those days were no fools, as one might think." The peasantry were an object of great solicitude to the Abbasside sovereigns, and every effort was made to lighten their burdens. Mansûr abolished the payment of the wheat and oat tax in money, and introduced the *Mukâsimèh* system, viz. of paying the taxes in kind according to a certain percentage of the crop. Upon the less important cultivations and for date palms and fruit trees, the old system of levying the tax in money was continued. As this led to extortion on the part of the revenue collectors, Mahdi extended the application of the rule introduced by his father, and directed that in every case the tax should be levied in proportion to the actual out-turn. If the lands were peculiarly fertile and required no labour, the cultivator gave to the government half the crops; if the watering of the ground was difficult and expensive, one-third; where it was still harder only one-fourth, and sometimes even one-fifth. In taxing vineyards, date-groves, orchards, and such like, the crops were valued in money, and the rates calculated at half or one-third the sum. This system of taxation was called the productive rate system (*Mukâsimèh*),[1] in contradistinction to the older system which was based upon measurement (*Muhâsibèh*).

In the year 204 A.H. (819-20 A.C.) Mâmûn introduced a further reduction in the land tax, by which even in case of the most fertile lands the produce-rates were fixed at two-fifths of the whole instead of half. But in Babylonia, Chaldæa, Irâk, Mesopotamia, and Persia there were numerous landowners and peasant freeholders whose rents were permanently fixed upon the basis of agreements entered into at the time of the Conquest. No variation could be made in the tax leviable from them, and they were thus protected from all harassment. The same

[1] The term is still in use in India.

boon was enjoyed by the village communities of Northern Persia and Khorâsân. There were thus three methods of taxing the land:—1st, by measurement (*Muhâsibèh*) with fixed amounts in money or kind or both; 2nd, according to the produce, payment being made in kind (*Mukâsimèh*); 3rd, according to a fixed settlement based upon leases or agreements between the government and private people (called *Mukâtièh*). The last class contained most of the crown-lands. Remissions of taxes were frequent even under the hardest reigns. For example, Mutazid remitted a quarter's tax by postponing the financial year[1] from the middle of March to June 17 (11th of Rabi I.). Later, a further remission appears to have been granted by a fresh postponement to July 21. When we bear in mind the flourishing state of the empire, the prosperous condition of the peasantry, the briskness of trade and commerce, we do not feel surprised at the account that the annual revenue of Rashîd was 272 million dirhems and four and a half millions of dinârs, or that Mâmûn's daily expense was 6000 dinârs.

Military organisation.

Simultaneously with the annexation of Syria, the Saracens had to take steps to guard the northern frontiers of the acquired territories against the destructive inroads of the Byzantines. The work was begun in the Caliph Omar's time and was continued throughout the Ommeyade rule; but it was only systematically undertaken when Mansûr ascended the throne. The most important strategical points, such as Tarsus, Adana, Massisia

[1] As there was no fixity in the lunar year and it bore no relation to the seasons, the financial year of the Saracens proceeded on the basis of the (Persian) solar year, which before the reform of Malik Shah began at the meridian of the sun's passage through Pisces. As we have already seen, in his reign the commencement of the solar year was put at the first point of the sun's entry into Aries, which coincides with March 21.

(Mopsuesta), Maraash (Germanicia), Malatia (Melitene), which were situated at the junction of high-roads or at the end of mountain passes through which alone large forces could debouch, were occupied and held by strong garrisons. In 133 A.H. (750-51 A.C.) Malatia was rased to the ground by the Byzantines. In 139 A.H. Mansûr rebuilt the place and garrisoned it with 4000 men who occupied commodious barracks and received special pay, every soldier receiving besides rations 10 dinârs over and above his usual allowance of 100 dinârs a year. Mansûr built castles at Hadat in Cilicia, at Zibatra (the Zapetron of the Byzantines), at Laodicia, and several other places in Phrygia and Cappadocia. Rashîd fortified Maraash and raised Tarsus, the ancient town on the Cydnus, from its ruins, and placed strong garrisons there. In the neighbourhood of Maraash he erected the castle of Harûnièh; whilst the Empress Zubaida rebuilt Iskanderûn (Alexandretta). One of the measures adopted by Rashîd for the security of the frontiers has been already described.[1] He constituted the marches that had formerly belonged to the military district of Kinnisrin into a separate province which comprised Antioch, Membij (Bambace or Hierapolis), Dulûk (Doleche), Kuris (Cyrrhoes), etc., and organised it on a military basis; troops were placed at all the important points, and numerous new fortifications and block-houses were erected. The troops stationed in these parts, besides their fixed pay, received rations and gratuities. They were required to keep their arms, accoutrements, and horses in good order. Often plots of land were allotted to them and their families for cultivation. This system was continued by Mâmûn and Mutasim. In order to revivify the tracts laid waste and depopulated by the continuous raids of the Greeks, and to strengthen

[1] See *ante*, p. 410.

the Moslem population, whole tribes were transplanted from the distant provinces to this border-land.

The history of the border towns clearly represents the changeable phases in the development of these two powers, which were for centuries engaged in a deadly strife. There is perhaps no place in the world, not even excepting the borders of the Rhine, or the plains of Lombardy, where every spot has been so saturated with blood, every foot of which has been so bitterly quarrelled over as these marches between Syria and Asia Minor. Under the more vigorous and capable sovereigns of the Ommeyade dynasty the Arabs had spread their sway and carried their arms into the interior of Cilicia and Cappadocia. Under Yezîd II. and his feeble successors the Byzantines had recovered their lost ground. Upon the accession of the Abbassides the empire gained fresh strength and they soon won back the border towns. Byzantine raids and violations of treaty compelled the Caliphs every summer to set in motion a large army. Sometimes these annual movements (*as-Sâifèh*) developed into campaigns; at other times they simply remained as annual manœuvres. But the system of fortified watch-posts (*ribât*) was not confined to Cilicia or the Syrian borders. In Transoxiana, Georgia, and Armenia the same system was pursued, and blockhouses were maintained in every defensible position.

The army. On active service the army consisted of two classes of soldiers, the regulars,[1] who were in the pay of government, and volunteers,[2] who joined from a sense of duty and who only received rations whilst in the field. During their absence from home, their women and children received gratuities either in kind or in money. The

[1] The *Murtazikèh.*

[2] The *Mutatawwièh.*

regulars included different classes of arms. The infantry (*Harbièh*) were armed with lance, spears, swords and shields; the archers (*Râmièh*) had swords and shields, as well as bows and arrows. The foot-soldiers wore helmets and breast-plates, and their arms and legs were protected by iron sheaths. To each corps was attached a body of naphtha-firemen (*Naffatîn*), who shot at the enemy with naphtha or Greek-fire, or with fire-balls specially prepared; and a company of sappers who carried spades in addition to their swords and shields. The firemen were protected, it is said, with fire-proof suits in which they could penetrate with impunity into the burning ruins of the enemy's strongholds. A corps was generally composed of 10,000 men, and was commanded by an *Ameer* or general. The *Kâid* was at the head of a battalion of 1000 men; whilst the captain of a company of 100 soldiers was called a *Nakîb* (centurion); over ten men was the *Aârif* (decurion). The troops were uniformed according to their corps and arms. Under Mutawwakil all the regulars were given light brown cloaks, and were required to wear their sword according to Persian fashion buckled round the waist.[1]

A special corps, composed principally of foreign soldiers, formed the imperial guard.[2] They received higher pay and wore splendid uniforms. Mutasim arrayed his body-guard in damask with gold girdles.

Besides the imperial guard there was another body of men occupying apparently a somewhat inferior position, who were called the household troops.[3] In later times the *corps d'élite* received the name of *Jândâr*.

[1] The Arabs wore their sword slung from the shoulder.

[2] They bore the name of *ar-Rajâl ul-Musâfiat*. After the death of Muntassir they in fact played the part of the Prætorian guards.

[3] *Al-Manâat*. Under Mutasim a Turkoman of the name of

The *aides-de-camp* were called, under the Abbassides, *al-ghilmân ul-hujaria* ("boys of the chamber").[1] They were the Caliph's pages, but those who were grown up also acted as *aides-de-camp*. These youths received their education at Court, and after a careful training in military exercises, they were taken into service. They had separate barracks, where they lived under a discipline, partly conventual and partly military.

Engineers. A selected staff of engineers[2] accompanied the army in all its movements; and a number of these officers were stationed at every fortress and city. The chief of the engineers was called the *Ameer ul-Manjanîkîn*. They generally commenced their career in the regular army (*Jund*), and afterwards were posted to their own special corps, or stationed at places to which they were appointed. One of the ablest of these engineers was Yâkûb bin Sâbir al-Manjanîkî (the engineer). He, like the others, commenced his career by serving in the regular army, and became chief of the engineers stationed at Bagdad. He was noted both for his studies and his military exercises, and won renown by his pen as well as his sword. He composed a work on engineering which is called *Umdat ul-Masâlik*.[3] Of this work, Ibn Khallikân speaks thus: "It treats of everything relating to war—the order of battle, the taking of fortresses, the building of castles, horsemanship, engin-

Itâkh was in command of these troops. When Mutawwakil came to the throne, Itâkh was raised to the highest positions, and at one time held the post of general of the Maghribîn and Turkish guards, grand treasurer, postmaster-general, and grand chamberlain. It will thus be seen that plurality was not unknown to the Arabs !

1 Under the Fatimides they were called *Sibyân ul-Hujâr*, "Youths of the Chamber."

2 Called *Manjanîkîn*.

3 Its full title is *Umdat ul-Masâlik fi siâsat ul-Mamâlik*.

eering, the blockading of strongholds, of sieges, equestrian exercises, war-horses, the management of all sorts of arms, the construction of military engines, close fighting, the different sorts of cavalry, and the qualities of horses."

Field hospitals and ambulances.

During operations in the field the army was accompanied by a staff of physicians and a well-supplied hospital, to which were attached ambulances for the wounded in the shape of litters carried by camels. The field-hospital of Rashîd and Mâmûn required a large number of camels and mules for the carriage of tents, stores, and medicines. Even in later times, under less important sovereigns, such as Sultan Mahmûd the Seljuk, the army hospital requisites amounted to forty camel-loads.

Depôts of arms and arsenals[1] for their manufacture were established in every important station. These were frequently inspected by officers[2] of experience and position. The cavalry had the same equipment as under the Ommeyades, viz. swords, battle-axes, and lances, and were almost always clad in mail with iron helmets. To each corps was attached a body of mounted archers, either Khorâsâni, or North Persian, who were noted in ancient times for shooting from horseback.[3] Iron stirrups were introduced as early as the time of Abdul Malik by the famous al-Muhallib.[4]

As I have already mentioned every able-bodied Arab was liable to military duty. In the majority of cases the reservists joined their colours, not only willingly, but

[1] *Dâr us-sanâ.* The word *arsenal* is, in fact, derived from the Arabic.

[2] Called *Nâzirs.*

[3] The Parthians were famous for this accomplishment.

[4] See *ante*, p. 96.

with alacrity, but when that failed, conscription was resorted to, and Hajjâj once made wholesome use of this at Basra.

Decline of the Saracenic military power.

The decline of the military power of the Saracens really commenced in the reign of Muktadir, and was brought about principally by a change in the system of payment to the soldiers. Henceforth the troops did not receive their pay directly from the Imperial treasury, but from the governors, or divisional commanders, to whom certain provinces were assigned for the purpose. This change was, in fact, due to the depleted state of the exchequer. Some of the provinces yielded no revenue; others only a fraction of what they had previously contributed. With an extravagant and luxurious Court, it was impossible to meet the state expenditure with the normal receipts. Muktadir accordingly conferred provinces on his nobles on condition that they should collect the whole income on their own account, discharge therewith the expenses of administration, pay the troops, and remit a certain sum annually to the Court at Bagdad. These grants were called *Iktiât*. This insane policy had its natural result in the rapid dissolution of the empire. The Buyides instead of pay gave the soldiers land. These military grants were free from every tax, and the produce belonged to the grantees, *i. e.* the officers and soldiers. "The consequence of this was, that civilisation receded, and the richest and the most productive provinces were soon impoverished and depopulated. The Arabian nation was gradually ejected from the possession of the land by foreigners." Just before the commencement of the Crusades, the political and social condition of Western Asia was identical in many respects with that of Europe. It was divided into a number of small states and feudal principalities which acknowledged the Caliph as their religious head, as the Pope was accepted in the West. Without any solidarity of interest, frequently opposed to each other, they weakened the empire by their selfish rivalries and ambitions.

Under the Seljuks the military feudal system developed still further. Every member of the ruling family, every Ameer, received a grant of a town or district over which he ruled with absolute power, and exercised all the functions of a feudal lord (*Sâhib ul-Maakâl*). The seignior paid the Sultan a yearly tribute, and in time of war marched into the field under the Sultan's banner with a fixed number of soldiers, which he equipped and supported at his own expense. In Irâk alone there were forty such seigniories. Few were held by Arab families.[1] This military feudal system was introduced wherever the Turks and Tartars, who now figured as the conquering and ruling nation throughout Western Asia, unfurled their victorious flag—into Egypt and Western Africa, into Persia and India, and finally even across the Bosphorus into Eastern Europe. In Turkey it fell into disuse after the reforms of Sultan Mahmûd and the establishment of a regular army.

Military feudal system.

Under the Ommeyades the average pay of an infantry soldier was 1000 dirhems (about £40) a year. Saffâh seems to have reduced this to eighty dirhems a month. The cavalry soldier received double this amount, with periodical gratuities like his brother-in-arms. But the pay of the troops seems to have varied according to the provinces where they were stationed. For example, Mâmûn gave to his foot-soldiers in Irâk [2] twenty dirhems

Pay of the soldiery.

[1] The family of Dubais held Hillah, and the Munkiz ruled over Shaizar. Besides these there were a few others.

[2] The army of occupation in Irâk in Mâmûn's time (201 A.H. or 816–17 A.C.) amounted to 125,000 men.

a month, besides rations; to the mounted soldiers, forty dirhems and the usual allowances; whilst in the military division of Damascus they received forty and one hundred dirhems respectively. The causes which led to a reduction in the pay of the soldiery in the later times were of a twofold character; first, the appreciation of gold,[1] and second, the vast recruiting grounds which the wide extension of the empire placed at the disposal of the Caliph. The great democratic principle that every alien who embraced Islâm was placed on the same level as the pure-bred Arab in the enjoyment of political and civil rights, helped in the diffusion of the faith. Another method of attaching members of the conquered races to the ruling nation was equally effective. It was the system of *walâ*, or clientage. A Persian, Greek, Berber, or Sclavonian was immediately, upon the adoption of Islâm, received into the confederacy of some one of the great Arabian tribes, or became a client of some prominent man, or even perhaps of the reigning family, and according to the principle of *walâ*, came to stand in direct relation to the patron. Hence the later Caliphs were not restricted for their fighting materials to the military clans of the Peninsula. Varangians, Franks, Persians, Greeks, Africans, Berbers, attracted by the love of pay, flocked to their standard. But this, whilst it opened a large field for recruiting, destroyed the old *esprit de corps*.

Clientage.

These mercenaries were unreliable, and the dissolving influence of their presence in the army made itself felt under the weaker sovereigns. Under Mansûr the army consisted of three large divisions: (1) the Modharites,

[1] In the Caliph Omar's time a dinâr was worth 10 dirhems. In Mâmûn's time it was worth 15. A dinâr was about 13*s*. 6*d*. in value.

(2) the Himyarites, and (3) the Persians. To these Mutasim added a fourth corps, composed of Turkomans and Africans. From the earliest times the army in the field, as on the march, was composed of five divisions; (1) the centre (*Kalb*), where the general in command was usually posted; (2) the right wing (*Maisarèh*); (3) the left wing (*Maimanèh*); (4) the vanguard (*Talîèh*), and (5) the rear-guard (*Sâkèh*). In marching, the vanguard, consisting of light cavalry in gleaming coats of mail and shining helmets of steel, with their long lances surmounted by bunches of black ostrich feathers, was always several miles ahead of the main body. Scouting was well known. Kotaiba[1] employed his scouts not only for reconnoitring, but also for making maps of the countries on the line of advance; and this became the practice from his time. Every general either prepared his own maps by means of the scouts, or obtained them from head-quarters.

Military formation.

The sight of an Arab army, winding its way across the enemy's territory in endless columns, must have been overwhelmingly grand. In front marched the heavy cavalry, flanked by large bodies of archers, who ran almost as fast as the others rode. Behind them came the infantry moving in dense masses and with splendid regularity. In their midst went the long rows of camels, carrying provisions, tents, and ammunition, while the ambulances or stretchers for the sick and wounded, and the war machinery, such as mangonels, catapults, etc., packed on camels, mules, and horses, followed in the rear. If the Caliph, or one of the princes, happened to be with the army the scene was still more imposing. The bright uniforms of the body-guard, the standards with the imperial device embroidered in gold, the generals

[1] *Ante*, p. 103.

and chiefs in their magnificent attire, made a brilliant picture. The vanguard, immediately on arrival at the appointed place of encampment, threw up entrenchments, for an Arab army never encamped at any place without taking every precaution against sudden attacks. When the main army arrived tents were put up in regular order with streets, markets, and squares as in an ordinary town. There was no confusion and no disorder; rations were distributed, camp-fires were soon alight, kettles boiled, and after the simple evening meal, and the *Ishâ* prayers, led by the Caliph, or, in his absence, the *Kâzi ul-Aaskar*,[1] the people formed rings, and listened to stories of war and adventure, or to the recitations of their ancient poems, accompanied by flute or violin. Not till the stars were beginning to set did stillness and rest spread over the camp and its inhabitants.

Formation of the troops.

The oldest formation of the Arabian troops was in lines, the troops being closely ranged in simple or double lines, both for purposes of attack and defence. By the time of Merwân II. a great development had taken place in the system of fighting, and attacks were delivered and received in solid, compact bodies. This was the mode adopted on both sides at the battle of the Zâb. The next great battle, of which a description is given by Ibn ul-Athîr, took place on the field of Nasibîn, in which

Tactics.

Abû Muslim crushed Abdullâh bin Ali.[2] The tactical skill of the Khorâsâni general on this occasion, and the manner in which he employed his troops show the military advance of the Saracenic nation. Posted on an eminence, he watched the fight, giving orders, remedying defects, making dispositions by means of messengers

[1] The army judge.

[2] *Ante*, p. 214.

or *aides-de-camp*, who were constantly going to and fro between him and the divisional officers.[1] When receiving an attack, squares were formed by the infantry; they planted their long lances in front inclined towards the enemy, and knelt on one knee, with the shield before them resting on the ground, and waited thus behind the improvised *chevaux de frise*, ready to receive the enemy with the thrusting spears. The position of the archers was just behind the heavy infantry, whilst at the back and on the flanks were posted the cavalry. On the approach of the enemy, the archers delivered tremendous volleys of arrows, whilst the infantry, immovable in their places, used their spears. At the same time, the cavalry burst forth through the intermediate space, and charged the advancing foe. The victories of the Saracens were often won in this way. The moment the enemy was perceived to be falling back, the thrust was carried home by a forward movement of the main force or reserves. The pursuit was always conducted by the cavalry and mounted archers. In an attack similar formation and tactics were observed.

The great superiority of the Saracens over the neighbouring nations consisted not only in their military organisation, but also in the celerity of their movements. Whilst the Greeks dragged their baggage and commissariat in wagons drawn by mules, donkeys, and horses, the Arabs mostly employed camels. Hence marches were made, and troops, provisions, baggage, ammunition, etc. were transported with surprising rapidity. In fact, remarks a modern historian, the Arabs conquered Syria by the camel. When long distances were to be traversed, the infantry were also provided with horses or camels;

[1] At Kâdessia, Saad bin Wakkâs directed the movements by written orders.

often on short, forced marches each horseman took a foot-soldier up behind him. We have an interesting account of the military tactics of the Saracens from an enemy. Leo VI.,[1] surnamed the Wise, a contemporary of Mutamid, Mutazid, Muktafi, and Muktadir, when the Arab empire had already lost its greatness and strength, speaks with some degree of admiration of "the barbarians," whom he professes to despise. Their battle-order, he says, was invariably a long square, and consequently difficult to attack, and affording the greatest advantages for defence. This order was strictly preserved, both on the march as well as in battle. The Saracens held their position firmly and unshakably, so that they should not be tempted to attack hastily, nor to end quickly a fight once commenced. They generally preferred to wait for attack, but as soon as they saw the first attack was repulsed, they advanced with all forces. They employed these means both by land and sea. First they shot at the enemy with spears and arrows, then closed their shields tightly one against the other, and in serried ranks commenced the attack. In warfare the Saracens distinguished themselves above all nations for their circumspection and excellent arrangement. They went to war of their own free will, not forced by conscription. The rich joined to fight for their country and to die for it; the poor for booty's sake Their countrymen gave them arms, and men as well as women eagerly contributed towards providing the poor and indigent with weapons. The historian of *Culture under the Caliphs*[2] remarks upon this that "the emperor evidently did not think the Saracens, whom he calls barbarians and unbelievers,

[1] Died in 912 A.C.

[2] Von Kremer, to whom I am largely indebted on this subject.

were far above the decayed Byzantines in culture, that, at that time, they represented progress and civilisation." And he goes on to add, "many things prove how much more the Byzantines deserved the name of barbarians, which they gave to others. We learn from Leo, that they shot at the Saracens, especially at the cavalry, with poisoned arrows, and as the latter loved their horses more than their own lives, they frequently preferred retreat to allowing their horses to be killed with poisoned shafts. Pillaging and burning the enemy's villages was a Byzantine regulation, whilst the Arabs permitted it with great restriction." "With regard to booty the Byzantines possessed no regulations, but the religious laws of the Moslems had prescribed rigid principles, which were generally strictly observed so long as the old rules were not shaken. The moral superiority of the Arabs over the Greeks is evidenced by the foregoing passage respecting the voluntary military service of the Saracens." The use of *zarebas* was by no means infrequent, when the general had only light cavalry under his command. The troops formed a *zareba* of baggage, and if the first charge failed, generally retreated behind this defence to reform and make a fresh attack on the enemy.

In mountain warfare the Saracens were great adepts. The operations of Afshîn, in the campaign against Bâbek, appear to have been planned with care and conducted with skill. The rebels knew the use of breastworks and stone *sangars*, and they hurled huge rocks on their assailants from the mountain-tops. Afshîn cleared the heights by his archers and stones thrown from the mangonels; and afterwards occupied them with his troops, and thus gradually advanced into the heart of the enemy's country. The siege machinery of the Saracens consisted of the ballista and catapults (*manjanîk*), and the tortoise (testudo, *dabbâbah*), with which the walls were battered. They made the thrusting-machine so strong that the blocks of rock thrown flew in a straight line against the walls and penetrated them.

About the middle of the thirteenth century the Arabs introduced the use of gunpowder, and Sultan Baibars, who overthrew the Tartars at Ain-Jâlût, had a body of arquebusiers in his army.

The Navy. With the conquest of Syria and Egypt a long stretch of sea-board had come into the Saracenic power; and the creation and maintenance of a navy for the protection of the maritime ports as well as for meeting the enemy became a matter of vital importance. Great attention was therefore paid to the manning and equipment of the fleet (*asâtîl*). The sailors were at first drawn from the Phœnician towns, whose inhabitants were famous for their daring voyages. Afterwards they were recruited from Syria, Egypt, and the coasts of Asia Minor. In 28 A.H. Cyprus was occupied by troops landed by a fleet; and in 34 A.H. the governor of Egypt, with a fleet of 200 ships, defeated the Byzantines, who had borne down on him as he lay on the Lycian coast with an array of 600 vessels. The Saracens accepted the fight unflinchingly, but seeing that they would succumb if they fought ship by ship, they hastened to bring about a hand-to-hand fight between the men. They caught the enemy's vessels with grappling-irons, drew them up alongside, and rushed upon the Greeks with spear and sword. A sanguinary struggle was followed by a brilliant victory. The Byzantine fleet was shattered, and the prince, who was in command, barely escaped with his life. From this time the naval tactics of the Saracens were to avoid all manœuvring and close with the enemy as soon as possible. Ship-building was carried on in the dockyards of almost all the Syrian and Egyptian sea-ports, as also at Obolla and Bushire on the Persian Gulf. The Arabian ships were of a larger size than the Byzantine, but probably not so fast in sailing capacity.

The mercantile navy was equally efficient, and maritime trade was fostered and encouraged. Almost every sea-port possessed a lighthouse, called *Khashâb.* It appears that the fleet consisted not only of ships that the government had built for war purposes, but every province or sea-port was bound to produce a certain number of crafts when the state issued the order. This was especially the case under the Fatimides in Egypt, and the same practice was followed by Saladin. The fleet of the Spanish Caliphs was similarly collected from all the ports of the empire. Each warship was commanded by a captain (*kâid* or *mukaddam*), who was in command of the marines on board, and looked after their exercise and equipment; while a second officer, called a *raîs*, exclusively devoted himself to the navigation. The general in command of the fleet was called the *Ameer ul-Mâ*, or *Ameer ul-Bahr*, from which the word "admiral" is derived.

CHAPTER XXV

RETROSPECT (*continued*)

Bagdad—Its structures—Architecture—The Caliph's Court—Social life—Dress—Women—Their position—Music—Literature—Philosophy—Science and Arts—Rationalism—The *Ikhwân us-Safâ* (the Brothers of Purity).

BAGDAD was the centre of the great civil and military organisation described in the preceding pages. It was "the capital of Islâm, the eye of Irâk, the seat of empire, the centre of beauty, culture, and arts."[1]

The city of Mansûr.

Yâkût in his geographical encyclopædia[2] says that Mansûr planned the city of a circular shape, surrounded by a strong wall and a deep moat, pierced by four gates with massive iron doors. Each gate was surmounted by a gilt cupola, and was of sufficient height to allow the passage of a horseman holding aloft his lance. Inside, and at some distance from the *ceinture* of the city, came the inner walls, within which arose majestically the imperial palace of *Khuld* with its golden gate (*Bâb uz-zahab*). Not far from the residence of the Caliph, and within the enclosure, stood the Cathedral Mosque, the mansions of the princes and nobles, the arsenal, the treasury, and other government offices. This enclosure, which formed a city in itself, was called the *Medînat ul-*

[1] Yâkût (*Shihâb ud-din* Abû Abdullâh).

[2] *Mujam ul-Buldân.*

Mansûr. As a matter of fact, after the completion of the Mahdièh, the city formed two vast semi-circles on the right and left banks of the Tigris, twelve miles in diameter. The numerous suburbs, covered with parks, gardens, villas, and beautiful promenades, and plentifully supplied with rich bazaars and finely-built mosques and baths, stretched to a considerable distance on both sides of the river. In the days of its prosperity the population of Bagdad and its suburbs amounted to over two millions! The Mahdièh was, if possible, more magnificent than the city on the western bank. The palace of the Caliph (*Kasr ul-Khilâfat*) stood in the midst of a vast park "several hours in circumference," which, besides a menagerie and aviary, comprised an enclosure for wild animals reserved for the chase. The palace grounds were laid out in gardens, and adorned in exquisite taste with plants, flowers, and trees, reservoirs and fountains, surrounded by sculptured figures. On this side stood the palaces of the Tâhirides and other great nobles. Immense streets, none less than forty cubits wide, traversed the city on both sides of the river, from one end to the other, dividing it into blocks or quarters, each under the control of an overseer, or supervisor, who looked after the cleanliness, sanitation, and the comfort of its inhabitants. At the corner of each street were posted sentries (*ashâb ul-arbuu*) to maintain order. One of the principal streets or quarters was called the Mâmûnièh. "It was of great breadth, and extended from the canal (*al-Muallâ*) to the gate of *al-Azaj*."[1]

The city gates.

Among the numerous gates which gave access to the western city, the most important were: (1) the *Bâb ush-Shamâssia*; (2) the *Bâb ul-Kazz* (the Gate

[1] The *Marâsid ul-Itilaâ*.

of Silk); (3) the Basra Gate; (4) the *Bâb ud-Dair* (the Convent Gate); (5) the *Bâb ush-Shâm* (the Gate of Syria); (6) the *Bâb ul-Bustân* (the Garden Gate); (7) the *Bâb ut-Tâk* (the Gate of the Pavilion); (8) the Shirâz Gate; (9) the Khaizurân Gate; (10) the *Bâb us-Sibyân* (the Gate of Boys); (11) the *Bâb ut-tîn* (the Gate of Figs); (12) the *Bâb ul-Azaj*. On the Mahdièh side there were five, the names of which have been preserved: (1) the *Bâb ul-Gharâbeh* (the Gate of the Willow); (2) the *Bâb sûk ut-tamar* (Gate of the Date Market); (3) the *Bâb un-Nûbi* (Gate of the Nubians), where the threshold was which the ambassadors were expected to kiss; (4) the *Bâb ul-Aâmmah* (the People's Gate); and (5) the *Bâb ul-Marâtib* (the Gate of Steps).

The water exits, both on the north and the south, were, like the city gates, guarded night and day by relays of soldiers stationed in the watch-towers on both sides of the river. Every household was plentifully supplied with water "at all seasons" by the numerous aqueducts which intersected the town; the streets, gardens, and parks were regularly swept and watered, and no refuse was allowed to remain within the walls. The hall (*aiwân*) of the *Kasr ul-Khuld* was surmounted by a green dome eighty cubits high, which was "the crown of Bagdad, the emblem of the city and a memorial of the house of Abbâs." Over the cupola was the statue of a horseman with a spear in its hand.[1]

The Square.

An immense square in front of the imperial palace,

[1] There was a legend that the statue gave warning to the Caliph of any rebellion by pointing the spear in the direction in which it broke out. Yâkût characterises it as a gross superstition and "distinct falsehood." The summit of this dome together with the statue succumbed in a night of rain and thunder in the reign of Muttaki (329 A.H.—940 A.C.), after having stood about 190 years.—*Mujam ul-Buldân*, vol. i. p. 684.

called the *Murabbaa*, was used for reviews, military inspections, tournaments, and races; at night the square and the streets were lighted by lamps. Mansûr reviewed his troops in full military attire, either standing on a daïs or seated on a throne, whilst Rashîd, Mâmûn, and Mutasim always rode, and frequently took part in military tournaments. Horse-racing has always been a passion with the Arabs,[1] and was so in Bagdad, as in Damascus. The Persian game of polo (*choukân*),[2] of which Rashîd set the fashion, was also played on the *Murabbaa*.

On the Mahdièh side also there was a vast open space (*Maidân*), where the troops whose barracks lay on the left bank of the river were paraded daily.[3] The long, wide estrades at the different gates of the city were used by the citizens for gossip and recreation, or for watching the flow of travellers and country folk into the capital. The different nationalities in the capital had each a head officer to represent their interests with the government, and to whom the stranger could appeal for counsel or help. These officers were also responsible for the good conduct of their compatriots.

The Palaces of Bagdad.

Bagdad was a veritable City of Palaces, not made of stucco and mortar, but of marble. The buildings,

[1] Betting on horses is the only form of gambling *permissible* (*mustahal*) under the Moslem ecclesiastic law.

[2] In Persian, *chougân*. An officer called the *choukândâr* was in charge of the polo establishment of the Caliph and the other sovereigns. The Greek name Τζυχάνιον shows the source from which the Byzantines borrowed this game. The French received it from Cordova, and called it the game of *chicane*. The modern English words "*chicane*" and "*chicanery*" are derived from *choukân*, the turning and twisting of the game furnishing the idea of fraud.

[3] Every city had its *maidân* (hippodrome) for practising archery, horse-racing, and the games of polo, *jerîd*, etc., and here the citizens with their families took their evening recreation.

although not different in structure or style from those in Damascus, were usually of several stories, and the influence of Persian taste was distinctly visible in the decorations. The palaces and mansions were lavishly gilt and decorated, and hung with beautiful tapestry and hangings of brocade or silk. The rooms were lightly and tastefully furnished with luxurious *diwâns*, costly tables, unique Chinese vases, and gold and silver ornaments. The imperial *Kasrs* were resplendent with inlaid jewels; and the interminable halls bore distinctive names according to their ornamentation. The special feature of one was a tree made entirely of gold, with birds perched on its branches made also of gold and studded with gems. Another, the Hall of Paradise (*Aiwân ul-Firdous*), with its magnificent chandeliers, its inlaid jewels on the walls and ceiling, its colouring and adornments, was a perfect fairy sight. Both sides of the river were for miles fronted by the palaces, kiosks, gardens, and parks of the grandees and nobles;[1] marble steps led down to the water's edge, and the scene on the river was animated by thousands of gondolas called *zourak*, decked with little flags dancing like sunbeams on the water, and carrying the pleasure-seeking Bagdadi from one part of the city to the other. All along the quays, which stretched for miles along the river-banks, lay whole fleets at anchor, sea and river craft of all sizes and kinds, from the Chinese junk to the old Assyrian raft resting on inflated skins. Among these towered the war-ships of the Caliph, interspersed with police boats (*Shazawât*). The cathedral mosques were magnificent structures, and in the beauty of their design, the im-

The Mosques.

[1] The river-banks down to Obolla, says Nâsiri Khusrû (see *post*), were covered with mansions, kiosks, gardens, and parks, and this in the eleventh century!

mensity of their conception, and the excellence of their finish rivalled, if they did not surpass, the grand mosque of Walîd at Damascus. Besides the *Masjid al-Jâmaa*, each quarter of the city had its own special place of worship, and every town throughout the empire had a finely-constructed cathedral mosque of its own.[1]

Colleges and Hospitals.

In the capital as well as in the provincial towns were numerous richly-endowed colleges, hospitals, and infirmaries[2] for both sexes. Each college had a separate principal; and the state hospitals were under the control of a prominent physician, called the Director (*Dabîr*) of Hospitals. In the reign of Muktafi, the celebrated Abû Bakr ar-Râzi[3] (the Rhazes of European science) held this high and responsible office. A Kâzi seems to have been attached to each infirmary,[4] but it is difficult to say what his duties were.

The Nizâmieh college, built by Nizâm ul-Mulk in 1067 A.C., and the Mustansirièh, built by Mustansir b'Illâh in 623 A.H. (1226 A.C.), have become famous in the annals of Islâm; but the older institutions were equally efficient, and students from all parts of the world flocked to them as well as to the newer colleges. The other cities of the empire vied with the capital in the magnificence of their colleges, established by the munificence of royal personages or private individuals.[5]

[1] Nâsiri Khusrû.

[2] *Dâr ush-shafâ* or *Mâristân* (see *post*). Hospitals existed in every city; the one built by Nûr ud-dîn Mahmûd in Damascus, and called after him the *Mâristân un-Nûri*, was a magnificent institution. Hospitals for lunatics also existed everywhere.

[3] Died in 923 A.C.

[4] This officer was called the *Kâzi ul-Mâristân*.

[5] Herat and Nishâpur each had a Nizâmièh college established by that great Mæcenas of the Arabs, Nizâm ul-Mulk. Saladin opened

The pomp and pageantry which surrounded the Abbasside sovereigns were on a much grander scale than what had been witnessed in Damascus. A body-guard in splendid uniform attended the Caliph whenever he issued from the Palace gates. Hâdi introduced the practice for the guard to march with swords drawn, bows bent, and lance at rest; although Rashîd and Mâmûn often rode or walked in the city with only one or two attendants. The Caliph's *cortège*, especially on Fridays[1] and festive occasions when they presided at the cathedral service in the great mosque, was unusually impressive. Troops marched in front with banners flying, drums beating, and trumpets sounding;[2] then followed the princes of the royal blood on splendidly caparisoned horses, and behind them came the Caliph on a milk-white horse, followed by his principal dignitaries. The rest of the body-guard brought up the rear. On these occasions he was dressed in a black or violet-coloured *kabâ* reaching below the knees, with a shawl-girdle or jewelled belt round the waist, a rich black mantle over the shoulder, and wearing a high-peaked

a college at Jerusalem, which was called after him the Nâsirièh. At Damascus there were several of these; the Rawâhièh and the *Madrassat us-Sitt ish-Shâm* ("the college of the Lady of Syria"), founded by a sister of Saladin, were the two most famous. In Mosul there were the Nûrièh, the Izzièh, the Zainièh, the Wafîsa, and Alièh.

[1] The Abbassides were undoubtedly more cultured than the sons of Ommeya, and with rare exceptions they attended and presided at the Friday service, and often delivered the usual sermon themselves.

[2] The imperial band was called the *Tabal Khânâh*, and was composed, among other instruments, of trumpets (*nafîr*), drums (*daff*), tambours (*tabal*), hautboys (*zamûr*), and fifes (*shabâba*), and was presided over by a master or chief, who was called the *Mihtâr* or *Raîs*.

hat called *kalânsuèh.*[1] The *kalânsuèh* was usually ornamented with a single diamond of great value. The signet and staff of the Prophet were indispensable accompaniments. Generally a gold chain studded with gems hung round the neck, and the shoes had jewelled buckles. The *kabâ*, which closely fitted the body, came below the knees and was worn slightly open at the neck, showing the embroidered *khaftân* underneath. The sleeves were worn buttoned till Mustaîn set the fashion of wearing them loose; and his *kabâs*, we are told, had sleeves three cubits wide.

The receptions of the Caliphs, which served as models to the grandees, and were afterwards copied by Moslem rulers in every age and country, were held on a magnificent scale. As under the Ommeyades there were two receptions—one public (*aâm*) and the other select (*khâs*). Three big halls, one opening into the other, were thronged by courtiers and magnates of all ranks The doors were hung with heavy embroidered curtains, which, on the entrance of a courtier, were raised by a page of the Hâjib (Lord Chamberlain) stationed at the entrance. The Caliph was seated on a throne; a hundred men in splendid uniforms and with drawn swords stood round him, whilst the dignitaries of the empire and the princes were ranged on the right and left of the royal seat. As the last curtain was raised the Chamberlain

Receptions.

[1] The shape and character of this head-dress have greatly exercised the minds of orientalists like Dozy, Lane, and De Slane. It was, however, only a very high-peaked hat just as was once worn in England under the Plantagenets, made either of felt or lamb's-wool, and was always black. The *kalânsuèh* was evidently borrowed from the ancient Persian hat, and was introduced by Mansûr. They were worn inordinately high until Mustaîn reduced the size. Zamakhshri explains the word *kalânsuèh* as meaning a *kulâh*. The modern Persian *kulâh* or hat is a truncated form of the *kalânsuèh.*

called the name of the person who presented himself. He then made his obeisance,[1] and took his stand by the side of those already in the room.

The private receptions reserved for princes of the blood, the dignitaries of the empire and men of learning, talent, and note, were more or less informal, and were held without guards or armed men. On these occasions the heir-apparent occupied a seat next to the Caliph, whilst the courtiers sat in two rows along each side of the throne "according to the nobleness of their descent and the eminence of the offices they held."[2] At these gatherings the Pontiff conversed unceremoniously with those present; physicians and astronomers dilated on the newest discoveries of science, poets recited their poems, and travellers told their tales of wonder. In the month of Ramazân it was customary for the Caliph to give an entertainment (*simât*) to the great officers of the empire, sometimes in his own palace, oftener in the official residence of the Vizier. This repast was called the *tabak*, at which seats were allotted according to the office held by the guests.[3]

[1] The usual mode among the Arabs of making an obeisance was to place the right hand on the breast, bow the head bending the body slightly, and then lift the hand to the forehead. The Persian custom of bowing almost to the ground, or prostration, which gave rise to the phrase, "kissing the ground," was never practised by the Arab, and was wholly opposed to his independent and manly character. In private receptions the sovereign extended his right hand to be kissed. When an obeisance was made to a lady the skirt was touched with the lips. Muktadir's mother presented in this way the hem of her garment.

[2] "*Aala kadr ansâbihim wa marâtibihim*," Ibn Khallikân.

[3] The poet Hais Bais (d. 1179 A.C.) was once so offended at seeing a number of persons, "who had no other merit than of being paid functionaries," passing before him to a higher place, that he wrote to the Vizier to be excused in future from attendance at the State Repast!

At the feast of the *Îd ul-Fitr*, which is held on the conclusion of the Moslem Lent, the Caliph entertained the city notables. At the upper end of the saloon was placed the royal sofa, mostly occupied by some dignitary representing the sovereign. If he himself was present the Vizier and some princes of the blood attended him.

The dress. The dress of the magnates and nobles was of course modelled after that of the sovereign; but professors of theology or law wore a turban, over which was thrown a scarf called the *tailasân*, in imitation of the one worn by the Prophet. Sometimes the *tailasân* was worn over the shoulders.[1] The laity, if I may so call them, wore the *kalânsuèh* by itself. Another light hat, made of white silk, was worn inside the thick black one, and was kept on indoors when the black one was put aside at informal gatherings. In the privacy of the house, this also was discarded for a violet skull-cap. In later times the *kalânsuèh* gave place to the modern *tarbûsh*, or fez. Loose trousers, pantaloons, shirt (*kamîs*),[2] under-vest, jacket, *khaftân*, *kabâ*, with the outer mantle (*abâ* or *jubba*), and the *kalânsuèh* as head-gear, formed the ordinary costume of a gentleman in the Abbasside times. Occasionally a dust cloak was worn over the *kabâ* instead of the *abâ*. Socks or stockings were not unknown, and seem to have been worn by the rich. They were made either of silk or wool, or leather, and were called *môzaj*.[3] There were

[1] As Lane very rightly suggests, from these doctoral scarfs have sprung the modern (European) academical scarfs and hoods.

[2] The word chemise is derived from the Arabic *kamîs*. The illustration gives an idea of the change in men's dress from the days of the Abbassides.

[3] The Persian *môza*. From the Arabs it passed to the Byzantines. The Greek *μουιζάκιον*, says Dozy, is derived from the Arabic *môzaj*.

marked differences, however, in the costumes of the different professions. As under the Ommeyades, for travelling or riding or military exercises men wore costumes different from those used indoors. Night garments were called *kumâsh un-nawm*. Among the commonalty the usual dress consisted of the *izâr* (pantaloons), shirt, a vest, and a long jacket—tied round the waist by a belt or *kamarbund* (*mizâr*), with a *rida* over the shoulders. Boots as well as shoes were in use among men; the former particularly among soldiers. Sometimes two pairs were worn simultaneously, one drawn over the other. The outer pair called the *jurmûk* was pulled off on entering a mosque or palace, whilst the inner was kept on.

Women's dress.

The dress of the ladies had altered considerably since the Ommeyade times.[1] Ladies of high rank or great wealth wore for head-dress a dome-shaped cap studded with jewels. At the bottom of this cap was a circlet of gold inlaid with jewels. This head-dress was introduced by Olaiyèh, a half-sister of Rashîd. Some sort of charm, with ancient characters inscribed on it, was often worn as a chatelaine hanging from the girdle.[2] Among the middle classes the women generally adorned their heads with flat ornaments of gold, a kind of fillet, often interspersed with pearls and emeralds. These were extremely tasteful in design and are worn even now. Anklets (*khalâkhal*) and bracelets were also in common use. Adventitious aids to beauty were not unknown.

[1] Like her husband, the Empress Zubaida exercised a great influence on the fashion of her age. She invented the sedan chair, and introduced among her sex the use of jewelled girdles and jewelled shoes.

[2] Although men's dress altered considerably during the succeeding centuries, the fashion of women's dress did not undergo much change.

The art of tinting the cheeks and lips[1] was evidently borrowed from the Persians, among whom it seems to have been in vogue from the earliest times, although artificial beauty-spots had always been in fashion among the Arabs. The Arab maiden, in order to be considered beautiful, had to be tall, of slender figure, well-proportioned, fair, with large, long, black eyes.[2]

The position of women.

Under the early Abbassides the position of women was in no way different from that under the Ommeyades. In fact, the system of absolute seclusion and segregation of the sexes does not seem to have become general until the time of Kâdir b'Illâh, who did more to stop the progress of the Moslem world than any other sovereign. In the time of Mansûr we hear of two royal princesses (his cousins) going to the Byzantine war clad in mail, in performance of a vow taken during the struggle with Merwân. In Rashîd's time, too, we have seen how Arab maidens went to fight on horseback and commanded troops. The mother of Muktadir herself presided at the High Court of Appeal, listened to applications, gave audiences to dignitaries and foreign envoys. Reunions and conversaziones at the residence of cultured women of rank and position did not cease until the time of Mutawwakil. Under Rashîd and Mâmûn we read of ladies holding their own against men in culture and wit, taking part in poetical recitations, and enlivening society by their grace and accomplishments. The empress Zubaida was a gifted woman and an accomplished poetess. She frequently sent poetical epistles to Rashîd, and the letter she addressed to Mâmûn, after the death of her son Amîn, displays high talent and feeling. Of Bûrân I

[1] *Chehrà bar afrôkhtan*, "lighting up the cheeks."

[2] But the fame of Zarka, the blue-eyed maid of Yemâma, shows the admiration of the Arab for deep blue eyes.

have already spoken. Obaidah, the tambourinist (*at-tambûria*), who lived in the reign of Mâmûn and Mutasim, is described by the author of the *Kitâb ul-Aghâni* as a woman of great beauty, virtue, and talent.[1] She played exquisitely on the instrument from which she derived her title, and also composed.

Fazl the poetess flourished under Mutawwakil, in whose palace she appears to have lived for a while. After her enfranchisement by Mutawwakil she married and lived in Bagdad. Her poetry is considered equal in merit to that of the foremost poets of the time.

The Shaikha Shuhda, who flourished in the sixth century of the Hegira, lectured in Bagdad on history and *belles lettres*, and was renowned for the excellence of her handwriting. One of the most famous lady-jurists was Zainab Umm ul-Muwayyid, who lived about the beginning of the twelfth century of the Christian era, and the middle of the sixth of the Hegira.[2] She had received from some of the prominent doctors of the age diplomas of competency, and was licensed to teach law.

In the time of Saladin flourished Takièh, daughter of Abu'l Faraj, who lectured on the traditions; she also was a poetess of eminence.

The pages of Ameer Osâma give a very vivid picture of the high position occupied by women among the Arabs. In the midst of the great turmoil of the eleventh century, when the social and political fabric of Western

[1] "She was one of the most virtuous women of former times, and her worth and accomplishments have been testified to by Ishâk" (the famous musician), "and Abû Khashîsha used to honour her, and acknowledged her superiority and genius. She was beautiful, and possessed a voice of great melody."—*Kitâb ul-Aghâni*, part ix. p. 134.

[2] She was born in 524 A.H. (1130 A.C.) and died in 615 A.H. (1218–19).

Asia was almost in a state of dissolution, woman was still, especially at Shaizar, the object of chivalrous adoration, and of delicate care and attention. Marriage was regarded as a solemn act, the domestic hearth a sanctuary, and the birth of children, especially of sons, a blessing from heaven. To the mother belonged the training of her sons and daughters; the sons were brought up by her until they passed into the hands of tutors; the daughters were trained to be virtuous, pure-souled women—the future "mothers of men."[1]

Music had not yet been placed under the ban by the legists of Islâm, and people of the highest rank, both men and women, cultivated it. The Princess Olaiyèh, a devout and pious woman, was one of the most accomplished musicians of her time. She had an exquisite taste for music, and her compositions are mentioned with high eulogium by the author of the Book of Music (*Kitâb ul-Aghâni*).[2] Her brother Ibrâhîm was equally talented, and the Caliph Wâsik distinguished himself both as a composer and performer. Princesses and ladies of high rank often gave musical soirées (*noubat ul-Khâtûn*), the orchestra being composed of as many as a hundred musicians, led by a conductor beating time with a stick. Music.

Chairs (*kursi*) and raised seats had already come into fashion under the Ommeyades, but the *diwân*, or the sofa, placed along three sides of the apartment, was to be seen in almost every household under the later dynasty. People dined at tables placed by the side of the *diwâns*. The tables were of wood inlaid with mother-of-pearl, Household furniture.

[1] "*Ummahât ur-rijâl*," *Kitâb ul-Itibâr*, p. 100.

[2] Abu'l Faraj al-Isphahâni, part ix. p. 83. His great work is a musical anthology. He is also the author of a biography of female musicians (*Kitâb ul-Kyân*).

Mode of eating.

ebony, or tortoise-shell. Wâsik had a table made entirely of gold. A large round tray of silver, tinned copper, or brass, covered with a white cloth, was placed on each of these tables with the dishes, which were either of silver or china (among the commonalty, of tinned copper). China or ebony spoons were placed by each plate, and flat cakes of bread on each tray. Two-pronged forks, called *ianjâl* (Persian, *changâl*), were common in the houses of the grandees. For each person there was a napkin, and after the repast a servant poured water over his hands from an ewer into a bowl.

The usual beverage in the houses of the wealthy was sherbet served in covered glass cups, composed of water sweetened with sugar, and flavoured with a hard conserve of violets, roses, mulberries, or cherries.

The *Nebîz*, prepared from dates or raisins, and *bâl*, or hydromel, were also very common; but the use of wine was not unknown, and we hear of convivial gatherings in the houses of viziers in which Kâzis and jurists indulged in the intoxicating drink.[1] The profession of *nadîm*, or boon companion, is first heard of in the reign of Rashîd. There was no opprobrium attached to the word. His duty was to amuse his patron by his wit, recite to him if he was a man of parts, and act generally as a *convive*.

Games.

Among indoor games chess was the universal favourite. Introduced by Rashîd into Western Asia it spread rapidly among the Saracenic people, and practically displaced cards and dice. Archery, and in later times shooting

[1] See Ibn Khallikân, Tit. Vizier al-Muhallabi. Coffee is said to have been discovered only in the year 656 of the Hegira by a holy personage of the name of Shaikh Omar, in the neighbourhood of Mocha, but its use did not become general until the following century.—De Sacy, *Chrest. Arabe*, vol. ii. p. 481.

with the arquebus, polo (*choukân*), hockey (*sulajân*),[1] throwing of spears (*jerîd*), horse-racing, wrestling, and fencing on foot and on horseback, were the principal outdoor games. Tourneys and jousts were held periodically in the capital and other large towns, at which challenges (*rihân*) were given and received. Cricket was not unknown; and rackets and tennis (*lub ul-kurah*) were played by both sexes, and women also practised archery. At first dancing was not confined to the servile classes, and young ladies often engaged in it for their own amusement. But the large influx of professionals led to rapid national deterioration.

Hunting was the common pastime of sovereigns and chiefs. With very rare exceptions, the Abbassides were keenly devoted to this exhilarating exercise; and so late as the time of Mustanjid we read of regular hunting-parties. Saladin's passion for the chase, in which he was generally accompanied by his sons, once brought him to the verge of capture by the Crusaders. Lions, panthers, leopards, and deer of all kinds, besides the feathered tribe which each winter brought into Western Asia, were the usual objects of pursuit. Falconry was another favourite pastime.

Social reunions.

Social reunions and conversaziones were frequent in the houses of the magnates, where people of divers talents and accomplishments met and held discussions. Literary clubs, however, had sprung up since the time of Mâmûn, where scholars flocked and discussed philosophical sub

[1] *Choukân* and *sulajân* are often considered convertible terms. Among the Saracen sovereigns and chiefs who were passionately fond of polo, besides Rashîd and Mamûn, I may mention Malik Shah, Nur ud-dîn Mahmûd, Najm ud-dîn Ayûb, and Saladin. Nur ud-dîn Mahmûd, according to the author of the *Rouzatain*, hardly allowed the ball to drop on the ground.

jects; and although several attempts were made for their suppression, notably in the time of Mutawwakil and Mutazid, they continued to flourish until the destruction of Bagdad. The booksellers occupied an important position in society in those days; and their shops were the resort of students and the learned generally. Here, as it were on neutral ground, Mutazali and Ashaari debated together on predestination, on the corporeal vision of God, on corporeal resurrection, and so forth. The bookseller was not merely the disseminator of knowledge but often the producer of books. The art of writing had been carried to such perfection that they were able to place in the hands of the public some of the best books at the average price of one dinâr, about 13*s.* 6*d.*

Intellectual development of the Saracens.

It is impossible, within the space of a few pages, to give an adequate idea of the intellectual progress made by a nation in the course of five centuries. And yet this retrospect will hardly be complete without a brief sketch of the work done by the Arabs in promoting the development of the world. I have already referred in passing to the patronage of arts, letters, and science under Rashîd and Mâmûn. Here I shall confine myself to the principal features of the intellectual side of Saracenic history.

The mariners' compass.

The Arabs invented the mariners' compass, and voyaged to all parts of the world in quest of knowledge or in the pursuit of commerce. They established colonies in Africa, far to the south in the Indian Archipelago, on the coasts of India, and on the Malayan Peninsula. Even China opened her barred gates to Moslem colonists and mercenaries, and Basra was an active port of commercial interchange with India and Cathay.

The commercial activity of the Arabs was not confined to the sea. One great caravan route extended along the countries of Northern Africa, another stretched southwards across the desert into the very heart of the Dark Continent. From the numerous ports in the Mediterranean this northern trade was carried into Spain, Sicily, Italy, and France. Trebizonde was the junction of a brisk trade with Byzantium. Other routes led into Central Asia and Northern India along the shores of the Persian Gulf; whilst a third, starting from Bagdad to the Caspian Sea, was connected by ships with the countries of the far north. This accounts for the Abbasside coins still found in Russia and Sweden, and seems to prove a lively intercourse with the Saracens in those early times. The Arabs discovered the Azores, and it is surmised that they even penetrated as far as America. Within the confines of the ancient continents they gave an unprecedented and almost unparalleled impulse in every direction to human industry. The Arabian Prophet had inculcated labour as a duty; he had given the impress of piety to industrial pursuits; he had recommended commerce and agriculture as meritorious in the sight of the Lord. These precepts had their natural result; the merchants, the traders, the industrial classes in general, were treated with respect; and governors, generals, and savants disdained not to call themselves by the title of their professions.

Commercial activity of the Arabs.

Arab discoveries.

The host of *littérateurs* and savants who flourished during this long period directed their minds to every branch of human study. They wrote on grammar, *belles lettres*, rhetoric, philology, geography, the "traditions," and travels; they compiled lexicons and biographies, and enriched the world with thoughtful histories and beautiful poetry; they added to the sum total of human knowledge by their discoveries in science, and gave an impetus to the movement of thought by their philosophical discussions. When we consider the immense range over which the Arabs exercised their intellect from the eighth to the thirteenth century of the Christian era, the estimate of the thoughtful historian[1] to whom I have often referred can scarcely be said to be exaggerated. "The vast literature which existed during this period, the multifarious productions of genius, the precious inventions, all of which attest a marvellous activity of intellect, justify the opinion that the Arabs were our masters in everything. They furnished us on the one hand with inestimable materials for the history of the Middle Ages, with travels, with the happy idea of biographical dictionaries; on the other, an industry without equal, architecture magnificent in execution and thought, and important discoveries in art."

During the period under review the physical sciences were diligently cultivated, and chemistry, botany, geology, natural history, etc., occupied the attention and exercised the energies of the ablest men. Abû Mûsa Jaafar of Kûfa (the Geber of Christian writers) is the father of modern chemistry. He was followed by others, whose originality and industry, profoundness of knowledge, and keenness of observation evoke the astonishment of modern students. The science of medicine and the art of surgery were developed to the highest degree. The Arabs invented chemical pharmacy, and were the founders of those institutions which are now called *dispensaries*. They established in every city public hospitals, called *Dâr ush-Shafâ*, "the house of cure," or *Mâristân* (an abbreviation of *bimâristân*, "the patient's house"), maintained at the expense of the state.

Regular gardens for the study of botany and herbalogy existed both in Bagdad and other places, for the

[1] Sédillot.

education of pupils, where discourses were delivered by the most learned in the sciences. The same intellectual movement, which led at the beginning of the ninth century to the rapid development of science and art, gave birth to works on geography and travel. Muslim bin Humair,[1] Jaafar bin Ahmed al-Marvazi (of Merv), Ibn Fuzlân, Ibn Khurdâbèh,[2] Jaihâni, Masûdi, al-Istakhri,[3] Ibn Haukal,[4] al-Beirûni,[5] Yâkût,[6] al-Bakrî, al-Mukaddasi, and Idrîsi are the most famous of Arab geographers.

Al-Beirûni[7] travelled into India, lived among the Hindoos, studied their language, their sciences, their philosophy and literature, their customs and manners, their law, their religion and their peculiar superstitions, the geographical and physical conditions of the country, and embodied his observations in a work diversified by quotations from Homer and Plato and other Greek writers and philosophers. Besides his great work on India, he wrote on astronomy, mathematics, and mathematical geography, chronology, physics, and chemistry. Shortly after Beirûni came that brilliant *littérateur* and traveller, Nâsiri Khusrû. He was born in a village called Kubâdiân, on the Jaxartes, and lived at Merv. He left this city in the year 1046 A.C., and travelling by Nishâpur, Kum, Tabriz, Akhlât or Khilât, Mayâfârikîn, Aleppo, he

[1] In 845 A.C.

[2] Lived under Mutazid, died about 912 A.C.

[3] Lived about 951 A.C.

[4] Died about 976 A.C.

[5] Died at Ghazni A.C. 1038.

[6] The author of the *Mujam ul-Buldân*, born in 1175 A.C., died in 1229 A.C. Al-Bakrî (Abû Obaid Abdullâh) was a Spaniard, died in 1094 A.C. Idrîsi is too well known to require a detailed account. He died 1164 A. C.

[7] Abû Raihân Mohammed bin Ahmed was a native of Khwârism and flourished in the age of Mahmûd of Ghazni and Masûd.

came to Syria, visited Tyre, Sidon, Beyrut, Jerusalem, then went to Egypt; from Egypt to the Holy Cities, and then by al-Ahsâ to Basra and back to Balkh. His *Safarnâmèh*[1] is one of the most entertaining works of travel in any language.

History. Archæology and ethnology were included in history, and great minds applied themselves to the pursuit of this captivating branch of study. Balâzari, who died in 279 A.H. (A.C. 892), was born at Bagdad, where he lived and worked. His history of the Conquest (*Futûh ul-Buldân*) is written in admirable style, and marks a distinct advance of the historical spirit.

Hamdâni, who flourished towards the end of the third and the beginning of the fourth century of the Hegira, gave to the world a comprehensive history of Southern Arabia, with an account of its tribes, its numerous ruins of interest, with explanations of their inscriptions, as well as the ethnography and geography of Yemen. It is, however, in the monumental works of Masûdi, of Tabari, and of Ibn-ul-Athîr that we see the full activity of the Saracenic mind during this period. Like their successors,[2] these men were encyclopædists, philosophers, mathematicians, geographers, as well as historians. Masûdi was a native of Bagdad, but by descent a northern Arab, who in his early youth travelled and saw the greater part of the Islâmic world. He first went to India, visited Multan and Mansûra, then travelled over Persia and Kerman, again went to India, remained for some time at Cambay (Kambâja) and in the Deccan, went to Ceylon, sailed from there to Kambâlû (Madagascar), and went from there to Oman, and perhaps even

[1] This book, with a French translation by M. Schefer, has been published in Paris.

[2] Such as Makrîsi, Ibn Khaldûn, Abu'l Fedâ, etc.

reached the Indo-Chinese peninsula and China. He had travelled far in Central Asia, and reached the Caspian Sea. At the close of his travels he lived for some time in Tiberias and Antioch, and afterwards in Basra, where he first published his great work, called the *Murûj uz-Zahab*. Subsequently he went to reside at Fostat (old Cairo), where he published the *Kitâb ut-Tanbîh*, and later the *Mirat uz-Zamân* or *The Mirror of the Time*, a voluminous work, which is only partially preserved. In the *Murûj uz-Zahab* (the "Golden Meadows") he tells the rich experiences of his life in the amiable and cheerful manner of a man who had seen various lands, experienced life in all its phases, and who takes pleasure in amusing as well as instructing his reader. Without burdening us with the names of the authorities, without losing himself in long explanations, he delights in giving prominence to that which strikes him as wonderful, rare, and interesting, and to portray people and manners with conciseness and anecdotic skill. Masûdi.

Tabari (Abû Jaafar Mohammed ibn Jarîr), surnamed the Livy of the Arabs, who died in Bagdad in 922 A.C., brought his work down to the year 302 of the Hegira (914 A.C.). It was continued to the end of the twelfth century by al-Makîn or Elmacin. Tabari.

Ibn ul-Athîr, surnamed *Iz ud-dîn*, "Glory of the Religion," was a native of Jazîra bani-Omar, in Irâk, but resided chiefly in the neighbourhood of Mosul, where his "beautiful house"[1] was the resort of the most distinguished scholars and savants of the time. His universal history, known as the *al-Kâmil*, which ends with the year 1231 A.C., may be compared with the best works of modern Europe. He also wrote a history of the Atâbeks of Mosul. Ibn ul-Athîr.

[1] See *ante*, p. 224.

The exact sciences among the Arabs.

The great work performed by the Arabs in the different branches of the exact sciences needs only a short mention. Mâsha Allâh and Ahmed bin Mohammed al-Nehâvendi, the most ancient of the Arab astronomers, lived in the reign of Mansûr. Under Mamûn flourished famous astronomers like Send bin Ali, Yehya bin Abi Mansûr, and Khâlid bin Abdul Malik. Their observations concerning the equinoxes, the eclipses, the apparitions of the comets, and other celestial phenomena, added greatly to human knowledge.

Astronomy

Mohammed bin Mûsa al-Khwârismi, under the orders of Mâmûn, translated the *Siddhanta*, or the Indian Tables, with notes and observations. Al-Kindi wrote two hundred works on various subjects—arithmetic, geometry, philosophy, meteorology, optics, and medicine. Abû Maashar (corrupted by the Europe of the Middle Ages into Albumazar) made the celestial phenomena his special study; and the Table of Abû Maashar has always remained one of the chief sources of astronomical knowledge. Mûsa bin Shâkir was a great engineer in the time of Rashîd. But his sons, who flourished under Mâmûn, Mutasim, and Wâsik, made astronomy their special study, and made wonderful discoveries as to the movement of the sun and other astral bodies. They ascertained the size of the earth, the obliquity of the ecliptic, the variations in the lunar latitudes, the precession of the equinoxes, etc. Abu'l Hassan invented the telescope, of which he speaks as "a tube to the extremities of which were attached diopters." An-Naizèri and Mohammed bin Isa Abû Abdullâh continued the great work of Mûsa bin Shâkir's sons. Albatâni[1] (the Albategnius of mediæval Europe) was another distinguished astronomer. His Astronomical Tables,

[1] Died in 929 A.C.

translated into Latin, furnished the ground-work of astronomy in Europe for many centuries.

Among the numerous astronomers who lived and worked in Bagdad at the close of the tenth century, the names of two men, Ali ibn Amajûr and Abu'l Hassan Ali ibn Amajûr, generally known as Banû Amajûr, stand prominently forward. They are noted for their calculation of the lunar movements.

Under the Buyides flourished a host of astronomers, physicists, and mathematicians, of whom only two need be mentioned here, Alkôhi and Abu'l Wafâ. Alkôhi studied the movements of the planets. His discoveries concerning the summer solstice and the autumnal equinox were extremely important. Abu'l Wafâ was born in 939 A.C., at Buzjân in Khorâsân. He established himself in Irâk in 959, where he applied himself chiefly to mathematics and astronomy. He introduced the use of the secant and the tangent in trigonometry and astronomical observations.

Ibn Yunus, another great astronomer and mathematician, died in 1009; his discoveries were continued by Ibn un-Nabdi, who died in Cairo in 1040, and Hassan bin Haisem (Haithem), commonly called in Europe Alhazen, and famous for his discovery of atmospheric refraction. He flourished about the end of the eleventh century, and was a distinguished astronomer and optician. He was born in Spain, but resided chiefly in Egypt. He is best known in Europe by his works on optics, one of which has been translated. Ibn Shâthir, who lived in the reign of Ibn Tulûn, and Omar Khayyâm, better known as a poet, were also distinguished mathematicians and astronomers.

Philosophy.

Metaphysics and philosophy were cultivated with as much zeal as the exact sciences. Al-Kindi, al-Fârâbi, and Abû Ali ibn Sina (Avicenna), are the most noted of Arabian philosophers.[1]

Al-Kindi, Yâkûb bin Ishâk,[2] usually called "the philosopher of the Arabs," and known in Europe as Alchendius, was a universalist. Abu Nasr Fârâbi[3] (Alfarabius), called by the Arabs a second Aristotle, was the master and precursor of Avicenna. Ibn Sîna[4] (Avicenna) was undoubtedly one of the greatest thinkers and physicians the world has produced.

Avicenna.

Poetry.

Among the innumerable poets of this period who wrote both in Arabic and Persian, it is difficult to make a selection. The names of those who composed in Arabic will be found in the glowing pages of Isphahâni and Ibn Khallikân. Those given here are chosen at random only to show the fecundity of the Saracenic mind. Abû Nawâs[5] flourished under Amîn, and is regarded as the equal of the famous Imr ul-Kais, the pre-Islâmic poet. Otbi[6] and Abû Tammâm Habîb[7] came immediately after him. Of the latter, Ibn Khallikân speaks as follows: "he surpassed all his contemporaries in the purity of his style, the merit of his poetry, and his excellent manner of treating a subject." Al-Buhtari flourished in the ninth century and, like Abû Tammâm, is the author of a Hamâsa. But the fame of Mutannabi[8] has overshadowed that of most of his predecessors. He enjoyed the patronage of Saif ud-Dowlah, a prince of the

[1] For the Spanish names see the *Spirit of Islâm*, p. 630.

[2] Died A.D. 861.

[3] Died in 950 A.C.

[4] Died in 1037 A.C.

[5] Born in 763 A.C.

[6] Otbi died in 842 A.C.

[7] Abû Tammâm died in 845 A.C.

[8] He was killed in a fight with brigands in 965 A.C.

Hamdanite dynasty of Mosul. An-Nâmi was another talented poet. He died in 1008 A.C., at Aleppo.

Among the Persian poets, the most distinguished are Dakîki and Firdousi under Sultan Mahmûd, Unsurî under Sultan Masûd, Anwarî under Sultan Sanjar, Farîd ud-dîn the druggist, who was murdered by the Tartars, Jalâl ud-dîn under Sultan Aalâ ud-dîn of Iconium, and Sanâï under Sultan Ibrâhim the Ghaznevide. Abu'l Faraj Mohammed bin Ishâk,[1] surnamed an-Nadîm, a native of Bagdad, first conceived the idea of a bibliographical dictionary. His *Kitâb ul-Fihrist* deals with every branch of learning. It gives the names of many authors and their works which have ceased to exist, and proves the literary productiveness of the Arabs. Ibn Khallikân's [2] great work is a biographical encyclopædia replete with the most varied information.

Saif ud-Dowlah was also the magnificent patron of Abu'l Faraj Ali bin Hussain al-Isphahâni,[3] the author of the famous *Kitâb ul-Aghâni*. This work is not a mere book of songs, as its name would imply. It contains biographical notices of all those whose songs are reproduced, discusses their grammatical constructions, and occasionally treats of history and science.

Penmanship.

The art of Arabic writing is stated to have been introduced among the Koraish shortly before the promulgation of Islâm. It was invented first by one Murâmir bin Marâsa, a native of Anbâr, near Hîra.[4] From Anbâr it went to Hîra; Harb, the father of Abû Sufiân,[5] acquired it on a visit to the capital of the Munzirs,[6] and

[1] In 987 A.C.

[2] Born in 1211 A.C., died in 1282 A.C.

[3] Died in 967 A.C.

[4] See *ante*, p. 24.

[5] The father of Muâwiyah.

[6] His teacher is stated to have been one Aslam bin Sidra.

introduced it among his fellow-citizens at Mecca. After that it spread rapidly among the Koraish.

The Himyarites of Yemen appear to have had a separate system of writing, probably phonetic. Ibn Khallikân says, "the Himyar had a sort of writing called *al-Musnad*, the letters of which were separate, not joined together; they prevented the common people from learning it, and none dared employ it without their permission. Then came the religion of Islâm, and there was not, in all Yemen, a person who could read and write."

At the close of the Ommeyade dynasty the archaic Kufic character had developed into several forms, the commonest being the *Naskh*, or *Naskhi*. Towards the end of the tenth and the beginning of the eleventh century of the Christian era (the fourth and fifth centuries of the Hegira) the *Naskh* was still further improved by two great masters of Arabian penmanship, Abû Hassan, commonly known as Ibn Bawwâb, and Abû Talib al-Mubârak.

In the reign of Saladin we hear of a big, round writing called *suls*,[1] which seems to have been a development of the *Naskhi* approaching the *nastâlîk* of Persia.

Sects. Sects, as was to be expected, had multiplied during this period; but the state religion was Hanafïsm, or, as it was in those days often called, *Ashaarïsm*.[2] The Hanafi

[1] Abd ul-Latîf.

[2] After its founder, Abu'l Hassan al-Ashaari, whose denunciations of Rationalism exercised a strong reactionary tendency. "But for al-Ashaari and al-Gazzâli," says the learned editor of al-Beirûni's *al-Âsâr*, "the Arabs might have been a nation of Galileos, Keplers, and Newtons." Al-Ashaari died in Bagdad 331 or 340 A.H. (941 or 952 A.C.). See *The Spirit of Islâm* about *Ashaarïsm*.

synods, however, were dominated over by the Hanbalites, who, as the most noisy and turbulent sectarians, possessed considerable authority among the rabble of Bagdad. Shâfeïsm was also spreading among the learned. In the Syrian cities and the towns on the sea-coast of Phœnicia, Shiahism found a large number of adherents, who doubtless exercised a certain dissolving influence on the rigid dogmatism of the Hanbalis. The most notable feature in the religio-philosophical history of the fourth century of the Hegira (which corresponded with the tenth century of the Christian era) is the extraordinary resuscitation of the Rationalistic movement. This was most probably due to the writings of thinkers like Masûdi and Zamakhshri, and of philosophers like al-Kindi and al-Fârâbi. The Mutazilites endeavoured to reconcile faith with reason, religion with philosophy, and naturally attracted all minds not content to be driven in a common groove. Thus many Hanafis who adhered on ordinary doctrinal points to the tenets of their school, adopted the Mutazilite views on philosophical questions. In spite of all this, however, the general tendency was retrogressive, and towards the close of the century the prospects of development were decidedly reactionary. It was at this critical juncture that the first society for the diffusion of knowledge came into existence. The illiberal formalism of the theologians, the self-indulgent epicureanism of the rich, the ignorant fanaticism of the poor, led a small body of thinkers who were deeply interested in the renovation of Islâm, to form themselves into a brotherhood to introduce a more healthy tone among the people, and to arrest the downward course of the Islâmists towards ignorance and rigidity. They called themselves the "Brothers of Purity," *Ikhwân us-Safâ*. The society of the "Pure

Mutazila-ism.

The "Brothers of Purity."

Brethren" was established in Basra. To this "Brotherhood" none but men of unsullied character and the purest morals were admitted. The members met together quietly and unobtrusively at the residence of the head of the society, Zaid, the son of Rifaâ, and discussed philosophical and ethical subjects with a catholicity of spirit and breadth of views which would be creditable even in modern times. They formed branches in every city of the Caliphate, wherever, in fact, they could find a body of thoughtful men, willing and qualified to work according to their scientific method. Their system was eclectic in the highest and truest sense of the word, and their views on social and political problems were highly practical and intensely humane. As the result of their labours they gave to the world a general *résumé* of the knowledge of the time in separate treatises, which were collectively known as the *Tracts of the Brothers of Purity*. These tracts or *risâlas* range over every subject of human study—mathematics, including astronomy, physical geography, music, and mechanics; physics, including chemistry, meteorology, and geology; biology, physiology, zoology, botany, logic, grammar, metaphysics, ethics, the doctrines of a future life, etc. They constituted, in fact, a popular encyclopædia of all the sciences and philosophy then extant.

The Final Collapse.

Thus when the star of Avicenna rose on the horizon, the ground was prepared for the reception of his advanced conceptions in the domains of sociology and the cognate sciences. And at the beginning of the eleventh century the outlook of a renaissance in the Saracenic world was decidedly hopeful. But the death-struggle in which the Moslems soon became involved with the Crusading forces of the West diverted all energy to one subject, that of self-preservation. And hardly had the successes of Zangi, Nûr ud-dîn, and Saladin rescued them from the dangers of the Frankish onslaught, when came the Tartaric wave which swept away all the civilisation and culture of the East.

CHAPTER XXVI

THE SARACENS OF SPAIN—THE OMMEYADES

138—300 A.H., 756—912 A.C.

ABDUR RAHMÂN I. (*ad-Dâkhil*)—HISHÂM—HAKAM—ABDUR RAHMÂN II. (*al-Ausat*)—MOHAMMED—MUNZIR—ABDULLÂH

Abdur Rahmân lands in Spain—The battle of Masârah—Revolt of the nobles—Frankish intrigues—Invasion of Charlemagne—Battle of Roncesvalles—Abdur Rahmân's death—His character—Accession of Hishâm I.—His character—His just and mild rule—War with the Franks and Christian tribes—Mâliki doctrines introduced—Hishâm's death—Accession of Hakam I.—His character—His unpopularity among the *Fakîhs*—The revolt in Cordova—Suppressed—Rioters expelled—Toledo—Death of Hakam—Accession of Abdur Rahmân II.—His prosperous reign—The raids of the Christian tribesmen—Their submission—The appearance of the Normans—Christian agitation in Cordova—Abdur Rahmân's death—Accession of Mohammed—His character—Christian mutiny stamped out—Fresh inroad of the Normans—Their defeat—Rebellions—Death of Mohammed—Accession of Munzir—His death—Succeeded by Abdullâh—His disturbed reign—His death—The Saracens enter Savoy, Piedmont, Liguria, and Switzerland.

Abdur Rahmân I. (surnamed *ad-Dâkhil*, or the Enterer).

SIX years had not elapsed from the battle of the Zâb[1] when a new Ommeyade kingdom sprang up in the west. Among the members of the proscribed family who eluded the vengeance of Saffâh was a grandson of Hishâm, named

[1] See *ante*, p. 180.

Colonnade of the Mihrâb, Cordova.

Abdur Rahmân ("the servant of the merciful").[1] His flight from Syria to Mauritania, his hairbreadth escapes, his sojourn among the hospitable Berbers, make a romantic story full at times of a thrilling pathos. Whilst living with the Berbers he could not resist casting longing eyes on the beautiful country across the straits which once belonged to his ancestors. Determined to make a bid for its sovereignty he sent a faithful emissary to his clansmen and clients to enlist their support in his struggle for power. His message was received with enthusiasm, and he was invited to appear in person. In the month of September 755 A.C. this youthful scion of an unhappy race landed on the shores of Spain at a place called Almuñecar (al-Munakkab). The Yemenites, smarting under recent wrongs inflicted on them by the dominant Modhar, flocked to his standard, and he was soon able to meet in open field the governor Yusuf, who had hitherto ruled the Peninsula virtually as an independent sovereign, although owning a nominal allegiance to the Abbasside Caliph. The battle which gave Abdur Rahmân the throne was fought[2] at Masârah, and proved a second Marj Râhât.[3] Yusuf was defeated with heavy loss, and was forced to submit. In 141 A.H. he attempted an unsuccessful rising in which he lost his life.

138—300 A.H.

Lands in Spain, Rabi II. 138 A.H. Sept. 755 A.C.

The battle of Masârah, May 13, 756 A.C.

The proscribed fugitive, the homeless wanderer, had now attained the summit of his ambition. He was the master of a kingdom; but he was not allowed to enjoy peaceably what he had gained by his ability and valour. The Arab nobility, as usual impatient of control, hated

[1] He was the son of Muâwiyah son of the Caliph Hishâm. He was therefore called Ibn Muâwiyah, which the old Christian chroniclers corrupted into Benemaugius.

[2] On the day of the sacrificial festival (*Yeum ul-Azhâ*); Ibn ul-Athîr, vol. v. p. 378.

[3] See *ante*, p. 91.

756—912 A.C. a personal rule. Their dislike was shared by the Berbers. Both these races, with their republican proclivities, wished to dissolve Saracenic Spain into a conglomeration of petty semi-oligarchical states, at liberty to war with each other when they listed, and to unite, when the danger appeared pressing, against the Christian raiders of the north. Owing to this feeling Abdur Rahmân's endeavour to introduce order, cohesion, and homogeneity was opposed by the nobles, who constantly rose against him. The Arab rebels, like the Christians of Leon, Catalonia, and Navarre, received support from Pepin, and, after him, from his son Charlemagne. It was the policy of both these rulers to favour by all the means in their power the attempts of the Saracen governors to make themselves independent of the sovereign of Cordova. Often their revolts were directly instigated by the Frankish kings; but Abdur Rahmân met these risings with unequalled energy. Forced to fight unceasingly for his kingdom and in the interests of peace and order, he adopted a policy which may not commend itself to us for its humanity or straightforwardness, but it was suited to the circumstances under which he was placed. It was the struggle of feudalism with monarchy. Happily for Abdur Rahmân there was no union among the Arab chiefs; they felt in a confused way that to vanquish the Ameer a confederation of the whole body of the nobility was necessary, but they did not know how to act together. In the course of a few years the Ommeyade cleared his path of all enemies; the rebellions were stamped out, the Arab noblesse were crushed, and the authority of the Ameer was supreme in the land.[1] But his power

Frankish intrigues.

[1] Ibn ul-Athîr says that it was owing to the rising at Seville and the malevolence of the Arabs (*Ghish'shul-Arab*) that Abdur Rahmân began to enlist mercenaries (*lit.* slaves, *Ubaid*). Vol. vi. p. 5.

rested upon his mercenaries; he was no more the popular sovereign, the young hero of his first arrival; he could no more wander about the streets of Cordova without a guard. He had now to surround himself with numerous retainers as a protection from the vengeance of those whom he had defeated or conquered. Whilst Abdur Rahmân was engaged with his insurgent nobles, the Moslems of Spain were terribly harried by their Christian neighbours. Their cities were burnt, their homes and fields devastated, and they themselves were either massacred or carried away into hopeless captivity and servitude. During this period of anarchy and turmoil the Saracens lost a large portion of their northern possessions. Fruella,[1] the son of Alfonso (Adfunsh), captured Lugo, Oporto, Salamanca, Castile[2] (Kastiâla), Zamora, and Segovia.[3] In the year 777 A.C. one of the numerous rebels[4] who rose in arms against Abdur Rahmân fled across the Pyrenees to Charlemagne,[5] to implore his help.

138—300 A.H.

[1] Called Tadvîlia by Ibn ul-Athîr.

[2] The Arab writers call old Castile and Alva as the country of Alaba and the Castles (*Alaba wa'l Kallâa*, rendered into old Latin as *Alava et Castella Vetula*). Navarre they called the *country of the Bascones*. Sometimes this denomination included a portion of Gascony bordering on the Pyrenees, which was named *al-Jabâl ul-Burt*, "mountains of the ports or passes." There were five passes for entering France from Spain, one or other of which was used by the Saracens in their frequent invasions of that country—(1) the route by Barcelona to Narbonne by Perpignan; (2) that by Puycerda across to Cerdagne; (3) that from Pampeluna to Saint Jean-Pied-de-Port across the defile of Roncesvalles, which passed along the country of Cize, and is called by Idrîsi *Bâb ush-Shazrî*; (4) the route from Tolosa to Bayonne, and (5) the route which led to Jaca in the Bearn.

[3] Ibn ul-Athîr, vol. v. p. 382; Makkarî, vol. i. p. 213.

[4] Sulaimân bin Yukzân al-Kalbi.

[5] Called Kârla by Ibn ul-Athîr.

756—912 A.C.

Invasion of Spain by Charlemagne.

The Emperor of the Franks, who wanted nothing better than to extend his authority, believed the occasion favourable for rendering himself master of Spain. Collecting a vast army he crossed the mountains, sweeping everything before him until he arrived under the walls of Saragossa, which was defended by Hussain bin Yahya al-Ansâri.[1] Here he sustained a disastrous repulse. Suspecting treachery he seized the person of the rebel chief, and retreated towards his country. Whilst crossing the

Roncesvalles.

Pyrenees he was attacked in the defiles of Roncesvalles by Matrûh and Aishûn, the sons of Sulaimân; his rearguard was cut to pieces, and some of his best paladins were killed.[2] After this a peace was concluded between Charlemagne and Abdur Rahmân.

The authority of the Ommeyade was now firmly established in the land of his adoption; and although his reign continued to be disturbed by risings and conspiracies, even in his own family, it was uniformly successful.

788 A.C. He died in the year 173 A.H.,[3] after a reign of thirty-three years. Although in resisting the attempts against his authority he often employed harsh and cruel measures, he was naturally of a mild disposition,[4] and fond of arts and letters. Ibn ul-Athîr describes him as a tall, thin man with sharp aquiline features, learned, accomplished, and a poet, endowed with indefatigable energy, keenness of intellect and foresight, devoted to work, generous and liberal. In industry and administrative ability he was compared to Mansûr.[5] He embellished Cordova with magnificent buildings and parks, and commenced

1 A descendant of Saad bin Ubâda.

2 Ibn ul-Athîr, vol. vi. p. 8.

3 Ibn ul-Athîr puts it in 171 A.H.

4 Reinaud, p. 98.

5 Ibn ul-Athîr, vol. vi. p. 76.

a cathedral mosque, which he did not live to finish. 138—300 A.H.
Although in the year 156 A.H. he had discontinued the *Khutba* in the name of the Abbasside Mansûr, he 776 A.C.
never assumed the title of Commander of the Faithful (*Ameer ul-Mominîn*), "out of respect for the seat of the Caliphate, which was still the abode of Islâm and the meeting-place of the Arabian tribes,"[1] and was content with the simple title of Ameer (ruler or sovereign).[2]

Accession of Hishâm.

Abdur Rahmân was succeeded by his son Hishâm. He was a just, mild, and generous ruler, "truly religious, and a model of virtue."[3] "In fact he is likened in character to Omar bin Abdul Azîz."[4] Dressed in simple garb he was wont to perambulate the streets of Cordova, mix with the people, and acquaint himself with their complaints and grievances; he frequently watched by the bedside of the sick and lowly, visited the poor in their own houses, and listened with tender solicitude to the tales of their cares and burdens. Often he would sally forth at night in rain and snow on errands of mercy, carrying food with his own hand to some poor invalid. His charity was unbounded; and he would distribute sums among the indigent pious who, undeterred by the inclemency of the weather, came to offer their orisons in the mosques. In him the persecuted and poverty-stricken never failed to find a protector. At the same time his administration was firm and vigorous; disorders were repressed with a strong hand, and no misdeed was allowed to pass unpunished. The people prospered

His character.

[1] Makkarî. Masûdi says so long as the Holy Cities were in the possession of the Abbassides, the Ommeyades of Spain did not assume the title of "*Ameer ul-Mominîn.*"

[2] Ibn ul-Athîr always calls him *Sâhib ul-Andalus*, the Lord of Andalusia.

[3] Dozy.

[4] Ibn ul-Athîr, vol. vi. p. 102.

756—912 A.C. under the rule of this virtuous monarch. He restored the great bridge of as-Samh, completed the cathedral mosque begun by his father, and embellished the cities of his kingdom with fine public buildings.

But neither the firmness of his rule nor the mildness of his character withheld the ameers from revolting. Soon after his accession he had to deal with a rebellion on the part of his own brothers. After reducing them to submission he marched towards the Ebro to quell the insurrection of Matrûh, the son of Sulaimân, who had invited Charlemagne into Spain. The rebel was killed, and Saragossa and Barcelona again acknowledged the authority of the Ommeyade sovereign.

The restoration of peace within his own dominions enabled Hishâm to turn his attention towards the north. The repression of the Christian frontier tribes had become a matter of vital necessity, for their raids were incessant and disastrous. They burnt, they massacred, they devastated wherever they went. It was then, as now, a conflict between civilisation and barbarism. Unfortunately the former was hampered by frequent intestine troubles, and the latter was helped by continuous aid from outside. Hishâm considered it necessary to teach a lesson to the Franks, whose rulers had hitherto pursued a most treacherous policy towards Saracenic Spain, and had for some time past fomented all the disorders within the Peninsula. With this object he sent forward two armies—one, marching through Catalonia, entered France, overran Cerdagne, recaptured Narbonne (Arbûna) and several other places, and inflicted, on the banks of the river Orbiena, at a place called Villedaigne, a terrible defeat on the Count of Toulouse, who held guard in Septimania for the son of Charlemagne. The other corps was equally successful;

War with the Franks, 792 A.C.

the Galician tribesmen, under their chief Bermudah (Bermundah), were routed with great slaughter, and compelled to sue for peace.

Mâliki doctrines introduced in Spain.

Hishâm entertained a profound respect for Imâm Mâlik,[1] the Medinite doctor, and the founder of one of the four principal Sunni schools of law, and did his utmost to introduce the Mâliki system into the Peninsula. From this time it became practically the state religion of Andalusia. The *fakîhs*, who combined the functions of theologians and jurists, and whom the pious king held in great consideration, acquired in this reign great influence and authority among the people and in the state.

Death of Hishâm, 796 A.C. Accession of Hakam (*al-Muntassir*).

Hishâm died in 180 A.H., and was succeeded by his son Hakam, surnamed *al-Muntassir* (the conqueror). Ibn ul-Athîr describes him as wise, courageous, and accomplished, and the first among Andalusian sovereigns who surrounded himself with pomp and pageantry. His reign, nevertheless, was continually disturbed by internal troubles. He was by temperament unfitted for the life of an anchorite as the divines wished. His nature was gay and expansive, and richly organised for the enjoyment of existence. He was fond of hunting, and not satisfied with the society of lawyers and theologians, loved to surround himself with poets, musicians, and scholars. All this tended to make him unpopular among the *fakîhs*. But there were other and stronger reasons for their discontent. Owing to the generous, though perhaps mistaken, policy of Hishâm, the *fakîhs* had become a power in the land. Hakam, on the other hand, although he never failed to treat them with deference, or to give

His character.

His unpopularity among the *Fakîhs*

[1] See *ante*, p. 221. The learned Imâm on his side extolled the piety and virtues of the Spanish sovereign as the ideal of a Moslem prince alone worthy of occupying the chair of the Caliphs.

756—912 A.C. effect to the decisions of the constituted courts of justice, excluded them from all interference in affairs of state. Frustrated thus in their hopes of power, and "full of clerical pride,"[1] they became demagogues. They denounced him from the pulpits as impious and irreligious,[2] and prayed for the salvation of his soul. They tried in this way to inflame the bigotry of the Moslem Spaniards, among whom their influence was unbounded. The bulk of the population throughout the Peninsula consisted of converts to Islâm. In the principal cities, like Cordova, Seville, Toledo, and Madrid, the converts belonged to the highest families. Marriages between Arabs and Berbers on one side and the Spaniards, both Moslem and Christian, especially in the northern provinces, were common. The issue of such unions were called *Muwallad*,[3] or *born* (*in the Arab race*). The pure-bred Arab professed to look down on the *Bilâdiûn* and the *Muwallad*, treated them with hauteur, and, as in Persia under the Ommeyades, attempted to exclude them from the high offices of state. The consequence was that he was hated in return by both. The Moslem Spaniards rose time after time in angry revolt against the Arab dominancy. The *fakîhs*, instead of pacifying these bitter racial differences, made themselves the partisans of the natives, and encouraged them in their rebellious attitude towards the sovereign.

Racial antipathies.

Whilst these evils were breeding mischief within Andalusia, the two uncles of Hakam, Sulaimân and

[1] Dozy.

[2] These denunciations are echoed in the pages of Ibn ul-Athîr, vol. vi. p. 128.

[3] The Spanish *mulatto* and the French *mulâtre* are corruptions of the Arabic *muwallad*. In Persia the children of Arab fathers and Persian mothers were called *abnâ*, "the children."

Abdullâh, whose rebellion had been pardoned by Hishâm, again took to arms. Abdullâh proceeded to Charlemagne at Aix-la-Chapelle to solicit the assistance of that ambitious and intriguing monarch. With the help of the Franks, Abdullâh seized Toledo, and Sulaimân obtained possession of Valencia. At the same time the sons of Charlemagne, Louis and Charles, burst into the northern provinces with fire and sword; and Alfonso, the Galician chief, raided into Aragon. In these critical circumstances Hakam displayed the greatest energy. Leaving a small portion of his army to watch Toledo, he marched towards the Galicians, defeated them in a pitched battle, and ravaged their country; then turning towards the Franks, he drove them headlong across the Ebro[1] and beyond the Pyrenees. After these successes, he returned to Toledo. Sulaimân was killed in a battle; Abdullâh submitted and was pardoned. Whilst Hakam was thus occupied, the Franks seized Barcelona. The loss of this valuable and important town was primarily due to the treachery of its governor, who, in the hope of being allowed by Charlemagne to hold it as an independent king, had invited the Franks to his assistance. Charlemagne thus obtained a strong foothold in Spain. His Spanish possessions were divided into two Marches—the March of Septimania, which embraced Catalonia, with Barcelona for its capital; and the March of Gascony, comprising the Frankish cities of Navarre and Aragon. In 809 A.C., however, the March of Gascony fell again into the power of Hakam. In 805 A.C., riots broke out in Cordova, which were leniently dealt with. In the following year, whilst

138—300 A.H.

Frankish inroads.

Their defeat.

Barcelona lost, 185 A.H. 801 A.C.

Revolt in Cordova.

[1] These victories obtained for him from his soldiers the title of *al-Muzaffar* (the victorious), corrupted by the Christian chroniclers into *Abulafer*.

756—912 A.C. the king was engaged in quelling the rebellion of the people of Merida, the Cordovans rose again. Hakam hastened back to the capital, and this time repressed the *émeute* with severity, which added to his unpopularity. In 807 A.C. Tortosa was besieged by Ludwig, son of Charlemagne, but was relieved by Hakam's son Abdur Rahmân; and in 811 he himself undertook an expedition against the Franks, in which he was eminently successful.

Toledo. The Toledans had never forgotten that their city was once the capital of Spain, and the memory of their past grandeur rankled in their hearts and increased their animosity against the Arabs. Proud of their wealth, their numbers, and their riches, they refused to obey the orders of the sovereign or to receive as their governor any one who was not acceptable to them. The first rebellion (in 181 A.H.) was easily suppressed. Amrûs bin Yusuf, one of Hakam's generals (*Kâid*), who held command at Talavera, himself a *Muwallad*, was deputed to restore order. He won over some of the principal inhabitants,[1] and with their help induced the people to acknowledge the authority of the king. Ten years later they revolted again. Thoroughly sick of their unruliness, and failing to bring them to reason by conciliatory means, he reappointed Amrûs, who now held command in the upper marches, as governor of the city. His appointment was accepted by the Toledans, as they believed him to be inimical to the king. They went so far as to allow him to build a fortified residence within
191 A.H. the city. Having succeeded so far, he one day inveigled
813 A.C. the principal citizens into the castle and put them to
The incident of the Hufra. death.[2] Deprived thus by violence and treachery of its

[1] The Banû Makhshî.

[2] Ibn ul-Athîr, vol. vi. p. 135.

chief notables, the turbulent city maintained a submissive attitude for the next seven years. 138—300 A.H.

In the year 198 A.H. the turbulence of the Cordovans reached its limit. One day in the mosque, a common man had the insolence to insult and menace the sovereign to his face. The well-deserved punishment led to a furious rising in the suburb of Cordova, called Shekundah. The mob actually besieged the king in his palace. The peril was extreme, but Hakam met the anger of the populace with his usual energy and presence of mind. The rioters were beaten back, their principal leaders were either killed or executed, and the rest of them expelled. Some crossed the straits and settled near Fez; the bulk went to Alexandria, and thence to Crete,[1] which they conquered and held until it was re-taken by the Greeks. In 816 A.C. a peace was concluded between the son and successor of Charlemagne and Hakam, which, however, did not last long. *Émeute* in Cordova, 814 A.C.

Hakam died in 206 A.H., after a reign of twenty-six years, and was succeeded by his son, Abdur Rahmân, surnamed *al-Ausat*.[2] "His reign," says the Arab historian, "was one of peace and splendour; the people were prosperous and the revenues ample." He was devoted to arts and letters, and loved the society of men of talent and learning. At his instance the famous musician Ziryâb came from Bagdad to Cordova, and became at once the favourite of the palace and the city. The love of music, which became afterwards a national characteristic of the Spanish Arabs, began at this time to develop itself among all classes of the people. In the brilliancy Death of Hakam, Zu'l Hijja 206 A.H. May 822 A.C. Accession of Abdur Rahmân II. (*al-Ausat*). His character.

[1] See *ante*, p. 270. The city they founded derived its name (Candia, Candax, *Khandak*) from the fosse or ditch they constructed for its defence.

[2] The *Middle*.

756—912 A.C. and superb magnificence of his court, Abdur Rahmân surpassed all his predecessors. The splendid culture, the polished chivalry, the delicacy, grace, and elegance of Arab manners, which European chivalry afterwards attempted to imitate, date from this epoch.[1]

His love of music.

The raids of the Christian tribesmen.

Soon after Abdur Rahmân's accession to the throne the chief of Leon (Alfonso II.)[2] made an incursion into the district of Medîna-Sâlim (Medinaceli), in Aragon,[3] and his example was followed by the other tribesmen, who raided into the Saracenic territories. A strong force was despatched for their punishment; they were thoroughly beaten, their towers and fortresses were rased to the ground, and Leon itself was destroyed. On their submission they were required to pay a heavy fine over and above the fixed tribute, to release their Moslem prisoners, and to give hostages for future good behaviour. The Franks had also attempted to profit by the occasion; they had entered with fire and sword those parts of Catalonia which were under Arab sway. They suffered a disastrous defeat, and were driven across the frontier.

Their submission.

The first appearance of the Normans.

It was in this reign that the Northmen or Normans (called Majûs by the Arabs) appeared on the coasts of Spain. They plundered several places within reach of the sea, but fled on the approach of a fleet and army sent by the King of Cordova. The Christians of Merida, instigated by Louis le Débonnaire of France, several times rose in arms, but were easily reduced to subjection. A fresh revolt in Toledo, in which the Jews and Christians took part, was finally crushed in 837 A.C.

The agitation of the Christians in Cordova.

Towards the close of Abdur Rahmân's reign, the fanatical section of the Cordovan Christians assumed

[1] Sédillot.

[2] Called by the Arabs Ludherik.

[3] The Saghr of the Arabs.

a dangerous and menacing attitude, which virtually amounted to a revolt. The bulk of the Christian community, and that the most enlightened in the capital and throughout the country, had no cause of complaint under the Arab *régime*. On the contrary, they had every reason to be satisfied with their lot; they were not persecuted or troubled for their faith, they were permitted the free and unrestricted exercise of their religion and the full enjoyment of their laws. Many of them served in the army; the highest and most lucrative civil and military posts were open to them equally with the ruling classes; they were employed largely in missions to foreign states; whilst the rich Arab magnates utilised the talents of Christian stewards in the management of their estates Fascinated by the brilliancy of the Saracenic literature,[1] the cultivated classes, and especially men of taste, spoke and wrote in the language of the conquerors. And with the language of the Saracens they adopted Arab manners and customs. These Arabicised Christians were hated by their fanatical brethren, who denounced them as irreligious, and the priests fanned the flame of discontent and increased the bitterness of the bigoted sections. "They had," says a Christian writer of our times,[2] "an instinctive hatred for the Mussulmans, and entertained thoroughly false ideas about Mohammed and the doctrines he preached. Living in the midst of the Arabs, nothing was more easy than to instruct themselves on this subject; but they refused obstinately to go to the sources which could be found at their doors, and were satisfied with believing and repeating all the absurd fables which they retailed about the Prophet of Mecca." But it was not the religion of the Arabs only that they hated; they had a strong aversion to the frank gaiety and refinement of

138—300 A.H.

Tolerance of the Arabs.

The Arabicised Christians.

Denounced by the bigoted.

[1] Dozy. [2] *Ibid.*

756–912 A.C.

manners of the ruling race. The hatred bred by these causes was deepened by some little affronts by the *gamins* and roughs of Cordova, such as those of modern cities are apt to show to strangers or outsiders. Under Abdur Rahmân their religious zeal grew into agitation. "In the sierras and mountains they became bandits or partisans. In the capital they could only become martyrs." They publicly cursed the Arabian Prophet and his religion; they entered the mosques at prayer time and repeated their maledictions; they tampered with the religion of the youth of both sexes, and frequently abducted them from their homes. Blasphemy of the Arabian Prophet is a capital offence under the Islâmic state law, as calculated to lead to riot and bloodshed. The offenders were brought before the Kâzi; in his court they repeated their maledictions. They were condemned to death. When taken to the Council of state for confirmation of the sentence, they were implored by the councillors, in the name of common-sense and humanity, to withdraw their words. Instead of complying with the request, here again they repeated the offence. The law was then allowed to take its course. Struck by the gravity of the situation, Abdur Rahmân convoked a synod of the ecclesiastics within his kingdom, and as he could not be present in person at their meeting, he deputed an eminent Christian,[1] a councillor of state, to represent him at the assembly. The bishops passed a decree prohibiting all public imprecations against Mohammed, and adopted severe measures against the agitators. But nothing could quell the ardour of these fanatics; the turbulent and impetuous arrogantly defied

The outrageous conduct of the agitators.

[1] His name was Gomez, son of Antony, son of Julian. He was cursed by the fanatical Christians for taking part in the convocation of the bishops.

the authority of their bishops. Some had the audacity to enter the Grand Mosque and to call out—"The kingdom of heaven has come for the faithful, and for you, infidels, the taste of hell-fire." The people were thrown into fury and would have killed the offenders, but the Kâzi interposed his authority and saved them from the vengeance of the congregation. The metropolitan was firm and the government energetic; several of the fanatics were imprisoned. But their agitation continued up to Abdur Rahmân's death, which took place in 852 A.C.

138—300 A.H.

Abdur Rahmân's death, Sept. 852 A.C.

Accession of Mohammed.

He was succeeded by his son Mohammed. "In justice," says Ibn ul-Athîr, "he followed in the footsteps of his father. He was the first to organise the government of Andalusia (on a regular basis) and to frame rules and regulations for the administration of the state. He improved the condition of the commonalty by his generosity. In the organisation of the kingdom he is likened to Walîd, son of Abdul Malik (Walîd I.)." Immediately on the death of Abdur Rahmân the Toledans, assisted by an army sent by the chief of Leon, had again revolted. Mohammed hastened in person against the united forces of the Toledans and Leonese, and met them near Guadacelete (Wâdi Salîtèh). The rebels, relying on their numbers, attacked him with great fury, but falling into an ambuscade were literally annihilated. After this, the Toledans made their submission on terms which left them a large share of self-government. The traitors and agitators of Cordova began now to feel the full weight of a justly angered sovereign. Repressive measures were adopted to stamp out the mutiny in the capital, and the fanatical enthusiasts who instigated the people to rebellion, or who carried on treasonable correspondence with the enemy beyond the frontier,

His character.

854 A.C.

R 2

756—912 A.C. suffered the penalty of death. Deprived of its chief promoters, "the singular enthusiasm," to use the mild language of the Christian historian, which had for several years reigned at Cordova, "gradually submitted to the common law, and after a while there remained nothing but its memory."[1]

Christian mutiny in Cordova stamped out.

The Franks as usual took advantage of the internal troubles to make incursions into the northern provinces; and Mohammed had to keep an army always employed
859 A.C. in those quarters. In the year 245 A.H. the Normans, after devastating Provence, re-appeared on the coasts of Spain and committed great depredations. They were pursued by the Spanish fleet, and after a hotly-contested fight, were driven off with the loss of several ships. Punitive expeditions were despatched at regular intervals against the Christian princes of Galicia,
251 A.H. Leon, and Navarre. In 861 A.C. "the country of the
861 A.C. Baskones" (Navarre) was overrun and its capital (Pampeluna) captured. Four years later the Prince of Leon sued for peace, which was granted on an unconditional submission. But more serious disturbances broke out in different parts of the kingdom towards the end of Mohammed's reign. In Aragon a Moslem Spaniard[2] descended from the Visigoths of Spain, made himself master of Saragossa, Tudela, and Huesca, and assumed the kingly title. In the west, a native of Merida named Ibn Merwân,[3] assisted by the chief of Leon (Alfonso
884 A.C. III.), raised the standard of revolt. A more formidable rebel appeared soon in Bobastro. The mountainous range between Ronda and Malaga, specially adapted for guerilla warfare, has always been the home of bandits

The Normans.

Navarre and Galicia overrun.

Rebellions.

Ibn Merwân.

[1] Dozy.

[2] Mûsa, belonging to the Banû Kasî family.

[3] Called by Ibn ul-Athîr the *Jalîki*, "or the Galician."

and brigands. Here the generals of Napoleon in later times met with the greatest resistance; and here Omar bin Hafsûn, a deserter from the Sultan's army, gathered a numerous band of brigands and established an independent state. The example of these rebels was contagious, and insurrections, fomented partly by the frontier Christian princes and partly by the King of the Franks, broke out in every part of the country. It is surprising that the Arab kingdom did not break to pieces under the weight of these troubles. The success with which it passed through the ordeal at this period shows considerable vitality in the dominant race, and no little ability on the part of the rulers. Too old himself to take the field, the king employed his son Munzir, the heir-apparent, to repress these dangerous risings. Munzir proceeded first towards the north. Saragossa, Rûta, Carthagena, and Lerida were reduced. Abdul Wâhid Rûti, "the bravest man of the age"[1] was captured; and Ismâil, the son of Mûsa, who held a part of Aragon, tendered his submission. In 271 A.H. Munzir marched against Ibn Merwân; he was defeated and his stronghold was rased to the ground. Saragossa had again fallen into the hands of the Aragonese rebels, who were led by Mohammed,[2] a grandson of Mûsa, who had entered into an alliance with the brigand of Bobastro.[3] It was only after a regular siege that the place was recaptured. Mohammed and his ally Omar bin Hafsûn fled into the mountains. No sooner had the royal army retired than they emerged again. In 886 A.C. Munzir again took the field against Omar bin Hafsûn. Alhama, where the rebel had taken refuge, was besieged and

138—300 A.H.

Omar bin Hafsûn.

[1] Ibn ul-Athîr, vol. vii. p. 258.

[2] The son of Lup (Lopez), son of Mûsa.

[3] Called by Ibn ul-Athîr, Babastar, by Makkarî, Yabastar.

756—912 A.C. reduced to dire straits. At this moment news reached the prince's camp that the old king was dead.

Death of Mohammed, August 4, 886 A.C. Safar 273 A.H. Accession of Munzir. Munzir hurriedly raised the siege and hastened to Cordova to assure his succession to the throne. Omar profited by the occasion, and by treachery or force made himself master of a great many castles. Mohammed was a patron of learning and "a lover of science"; "he was discreet and wise, and well versed in the rules of administration."[1] Munzir, who succeeded him, was gifted with energy, prudence, and bravery. Had a longer life been vouchsafed him, there can be no doubt he would have succeeded in restoring complete order in his kingdom. He applied himself vigorously to the work which lay before him, and marched in person against the rebels. Archidona was captured, and Bobastro, the stronghold of Omar, was besieged. Reduced to extremities, the rebel submitted, but immediately after broke the pledge under which he had obtained the royal pardon. Munzir took the field again, but was killed in a fight near Bobastro.[2] Although his reign barely lasted two years, the country had prospered, and wealth and comfort had increased among the people.

His character.

Death of Munzir. Safar 275 A.H. July 888 A.C. Accession of Abdullâh.

Munzir was succeeded by his brother Abdullâh. "In his time," says Ibn ul-Athîr, "Andalusia became filled with disturbance, and rebels arose on every side, and thus it remained throughout his reign."[3] Abdullâh ascended the throne under the most fatal conditions. The state, undermined for a long time by racial antipathies, seemed rapidly marching towards ruin and

[1] Ibn ul-Athîr, vol. vii. p. 297.

[2] Dozy says he was poisoned by his physician. He gives the date of his death as June 29, 888 A.C. Ibn ul-Athîr puts it in Safar 274 A.H., whilst Makkarî has 275 A.H.

[3] Vol. vii. p. 303.

decomposition. The Ameer of Cordova found himself opposed not only to the Spanish mountaineers but also to the Arab aristocracy, who, in the general disorder, perceived an opportunity for independence. Insurrections and revolts broke out in every quarter. There were sanguinary riots between the Arabs and the Bilâdiûn in the districts of Seville and Elvira. Various Berber chiefs established themselves in some of the strongest castles and defied the royal authority. Mentesa, Medîna Banî-Salîm (in the district of Sidona), Lorca, and Saragossa were held by Arab lords; whilst Ibrâhim ibn Hajjâj, a descendant of the Gothic princess Sarah,[1] through whom his family, the Banû Hajjâj, had received considerable property in the district of Seville, possessed himself of this principality. Here he ruled in great state; his government was firm and vigorous, more so than that of the king. All acts of brigandage and breach of public peace were repressed with great severity. Trade, commerce, and arts were encouraged, and every endeavour was made to repair the ravages caused by the riots. Algarve, Beja, San Esteven, Jaen, Murcia, and various other places were held by Moslem Spanish chiefs. Badajoz was in the possession of Ibn Merwân; whilst in Aragon, Mohammed, the son of Lopez, held court as an independent sovereign. Omar bin Hafsûn took advantage of these troubles to extend his authority in every direction. He even aspired to the possession of Cordova. The Sultan, who had hitherto indulged in a temporising policy, determined at last to fight for the throne of his fathers, which was in deadly peril of being altogether lost. His general Obaidullâh was successful in beating Ibn Hafsûn near Polei. This was the turning-

138—300 A.H.

His distinguished reign.

Seville.

Omar bin Hafsûn marches on Cordova.

His defeat, April 15, 891 A.C.

[1] See *ante*, p. 157.

756–912 A.C. point in the fortunes of the king, and the victory of Obaidullâh saved the monarchy. Polei, Ecija, Archidona, Elvira, and Jaen submitted at once to his authority. Later, an act of humanity, done at the instance of the faithful vizier Badr, brought the willing submission of Ibn Hajjâj. His favourite son had been sent as a hostage to Cordova. Abdullâh restored the youth to the father with many marks of consideration, and won the heart and loyalty of Ibn Hajjâj. The reconciliation of the Sultan with this powerful chief was the commencement of a new era. The royal authority began gradually to be re-established in the disaffected tracts. The districts from Algesiras to Niebla submitted without any fight, and their example was followed by several other places of importance. Even the Banû Kâsi of Aragon showed signs of returning to subjection. At this stage the old king died at the age of sixty-eight, after a troubled and inglorious reign of nearly twenty-six years.[1]

Rabî I. 300 A.H. Oct 15, 912 A.C.

The observant traveller cannot fail to notice on the Ligurian coast, as also on the Alps, in Piedmont as in Dauphiny, the recurrence of the Arab type, and he will probably ask himself, was that due to accident or any other cause? At the period I am describing (889 A.C.), the Saracens had again entered Southern France, this time by the Gulf of Saint Tropès, and spread themselves over Provence and Dauphiny. It was an independent movement, conducted by several adventurous spirits gathered from the seaports of Spain and Africa. Their principal castle was called *Fraxinetum*. In 906 A.C. they traversed the gorges of Dauphiny, and crossing the Mont Cenis, they occupied Piedmont, Liguria, and part

The Saracens enter Savoy.

Piedmont.

[1] Twenty-five years and eleven months (Ibn ul-Athîr). Dozy says he ruled twenty-four years.

of Switzerland. They penetrated into this country as far as the Lake of Constance, where they established a colony. In France they occupied Frejus, Marseilles, and Grenoble, and Nice was held by them for a considerable time, and it is due to their sway that a part of the town is still called *the Canton de Sarrazins.* 138—300 A.H. Switzerland.

CHAPTER XXVII

THE SARACENS OF SPAIN

THE OMMEYADES (*continued*)

300—366 A.H., 912—976 A.C.

ABDUR RAHMÂN III. (AN-NÂSIR)—HAKAM II. (AL-MUSTANSIR)

Accession of Abdur Rahmân III.—Reduces the insurgents—His wars with the Christian tribes of the north—Their punishment—Assumes the title of *Ameer ul-Mominîn*—Fresh raids by the Galicians—Introduction of the Slavs into state service—Battle of *al-Khandak*—The tribes sue for peace—Boundaries withdrawn to the Ebro—War in Africa—Fresh war with the Galicians—Sancho expelled by his subjects—Tota—Sancho implores Abdur Rahmân's help—Leon, Castile, and Navarre dependencies of the Caliphate—Abdur Rahmân's death—His character—Accession of Hakam II.—His benignant reign—Successes over the Galicians and Navarrese—Expedition into Africa—Hakam's love of learning—Cordova—Its splendour—Its extent—Az-Zahra—Chivalry.

Abdur Rahmân III. (*an-Nâsir li dîn Illâh*).

ABDULLAH was succeeded by his grandson, Abdur Rahmân.[1] He was barely twenty-two years of age when the oath of allegiance was sworn to him, but his accession was hailed by his uncles and kinsmen, who were older and more experienced than himself, as a happy

[1] His father Mohammed had, says Ibn ul-Athîr, suffered the penalty of death for some capital offence under the orders of Abdullâh. Abdur Rahmân was then only three weeks old, but was brought up most tenderly by the old king, who wanted to make amends to the child for his severity to the father.

augury for the kingdom. They had all perceived in him, says the historian, the signs of greatness, and accepted him as the saviour of the distracted empire of the Ommeyades. Abandoning the tortuous and temporising policy of his grandfather, he adopted towards the rebels a course of conduct which was alike bold and straightforward. Disdaining any middle course, he announced to the insurgents, Spanish, Berber, and Arab, that he did not wish for their tribute, but for their castles and their cities; if they submitted he promised them a complete pardon; otherwise they were to receive exemplary punishment. Most of the principal cities submitted spontaneously. In April 913 A.C. Abdur Rahmân appeared in person among his troops. The frank and chivalrous manners of the handsome young king, and his evident desire to share with them, not only their glory but also their fatigues and perils, evoked an extraordinary enthusiasm among his soldiers, and exercised a wonderful influence on their morale. In a campaign of less than three months he reduced to subjection the province of Elvira and Jaen. The strongest castles were captured, and the entire tract purged of brigands and pacified. In the inaccessible height of the Sierra Nevada he was as successful as in the plains, and the bandit chiefs who had harassed the country either submitted or were put to death. Mohammed, the son of Ibrâhim ibn Hajjâj, who had succeeded his father in the principality of Seville, came to Abdur Rahmân and offered his services. The Sevillans were at first refractory, but after a short siege they opened their gates. The Sultan then marched against the insurgents of the Serrania of Regio (called by the Arabs Rayyia), and one by one their leaders tendered their submission. Even the Christian Spaniards, who were the most inveterate enemies of the

300—366 A.H.

His straightforward policy.

The submission of the rebels, Dec. 913 A.C.

912—976 A.C. king, convinced of his generosity as well as firmness, began to lay down their arms. The Christian historian adds here, "the government, be it said to its honour, conducted itself with the greatest justice towards the Christians who had capitulated."[1] Omar bin Hafsûn died in 917 A.C., but the war in the Serrania did not end with his death. For ten long years the king had to keep a large body of troops employed in that mountainous range. In 928 A.C. Bobastro was captured, and the other castles reduced and rased to the ground, and the Serrania finally pacified. Similarly the rebels in the west were brought to subjection. Having nothing to fear now in the south, the king turned all his forces against the rebels in the north and the east. Badajoz fell after a siege lasting over a year. Toledo, instigated by the Christian chief of Leon, had again risen in revolt. The king sent to this stiff-necked and rebellious city a deputation of learned men inviting their obedience. The rebels, relying on the help of the Leonese, returned a haughty answer. Seeing that nothing but force would bring the Toledans to reason, he took his measures with promptitude and characteristic vigour. After a siege lasting two years the Toledans capitulated unconditionally. At last the embers of discord were stamped out, every vestige of rebellion was crushed, and the king was the undisputed sovereign of the patrimony of his ancestors.

Capture of Bobastro, Jan. 2, 928.

Badajoz reduced, 930 A.C.

Capitulation of Toledo, 932 A.C.

But whilst thus engaged in pacifying his kingdom, Abdur Rahmân had to wage war with two enemies whose designs on fair Andalusia were unmistakable; one being the Christian nationalities or tribes of the north, the other, the Fatimides of Africa. A terrible famine which in the middle of the eighth century raged for five years

[1] Dozy.

300—366 A.H.

in Spain had led to a vast emigration into Africa of the Arabs who had, after the conquest, settled in the north of the Peninsula. Profiting by this exodus the Galicians rose in insurrection, massacred a large number of the Saracens who were still left, and elected Alfonso as their chief or king. Some years later, the Berbers who principally occupied that tract, owing to the paucity of their numbers, evacuated several important cities, such as Astorga, Leon, Zamora, Salamanca, Simancas, Segovia, and Miranda. Alfonso, however, did not establish himself in the abandoned country, but contented himself with massacring the few Moslems who had remained behind, and then retiring to his mountains. His successors took advantage of the civil wars which decimated the Arab kingdom to make Leon their capital; and in the middle of the ninth century, when Andalusia was convulsed with insurrections against the Sultan, they advanced their borders up to the Douro, where they built four strong fortresses.[1] From here they raided into the territories of Islâm and harried the defenceless Moslems with fire and sword. Barbarous and poor to such a degree that they could only buy and sell by barter, they cast longing eyes on the wealth of Andalusia, regarding the distracted kingdom as an easy prey. Fanatical, cruel, and pitiless they rarely gave quarter; when they took a city they indulged in promiscuous slaughter, sparing neither age nor sex.[2] As for toleration such as the Saracens had accorded to the Christians, they were wholly unaware of the phrase. What the fate of the Moslems would be if such people carried out their designs of conquest can be easily imagined. They hated the brilliant civilisation which developed day by day among the Arabs. The task before Abdur Rahmân was thus not only of saving

The Christian tribes of the north.

The incessant raids.

[1] Zamora, Simancas, San Estevan, and Osma. [2] Dozy.

912—976 A.C. his kingdom but also civilisation. The young sovereign understood his mission and applied himself to the work with the same energy with which he endeavoured to pacify his insurgent subjects.

Abdur Rahmân had no intention of turning his arms against the barbarians of the north; he would gladly have remained at peace with them, but they forced him
914 A.C. into a war. In 914 A.C. the Leonese, under their chief Ordono II.,[1] burst into the province of Merida, and ravaged the country with fire and sword. They captured Alange,[2] and massacred the male inhabitants and carried away the women and children into slavery. Laden with booty and driving an enormous number of prisoners, they re-crossed the Douro. Abdur Rahmân, who was at this time engaged with the Fatimides in Africa, contented himself with sending a punitive expedition under his vizier Ahmed, son of Abû Abda. Ahmed inflicted severe punishment on the enemy; but a check before San Estevan, where the Saracens were repulsed with heavy loss, emboldened Ordono and his ally Sancho,[3] chief of Navarre, to ravage the environs of Tudela and Valtierra. Abdur Rahmân now resolved at all hazards to teach the Christian tribesmen a lesson they would not be likely
305 A.H. July 918 A.C. soon to forget. In July 918 A.C. an army was despatched under the Hâjib Badr, who found the raiders entrenched in their mountains; they were attacked and defeated. Believing that the Leonese were not yet sufficiently
308 A.H. 920 A.C. Defeat of Ordono. humiliated, in June 920 A.C. Abdur Rahmân took the field in person. Ordono was beaten, and Osma, San

[1] Makkarî calls him Urdûn, son of Adifunsh, whilst Ibn Khaldûn gives the name of his father as Razmîr or Radmîr.

[2] Arabic, al-Hans (al-Hanth).

[3] Sanja of the Arabs; he is called by Ibn Khaldûn the chief of the Baskones or Basques.

Estevan, Clunia, and several other places of importance were captured. Leaving a small force to watch the Leonese, the king turned his attention towards Navarre. Sancho, the Navarrese chief, suffered a disastrous defeat at the hands of Mohammed bin Lope, Governor of Tudela, who was in command of the advanced guard. Wholly unable to resist the royal troops by himself, Sancho sought the assistance of his brother chief of Leon, and their joint forces posted themselves on the heights to overwhelm the Saracenic army as it wended its way through the narrow Pyrenean defiles. They hurled stones and missiles, and rolled down huge rocks on the Saracens. The king saw the danger, and as soon as his men arrived at a place called Junquera, where the pass widened into a fairly broad valley, he ordered them to halt and put up their tents. "The Christians now committed a serious mistake," says Dozy; "instead of remaining on the mountains, they descended into the plains, and audaciously accepted the battle the Mussulmans offered. They paid for their temerity by a terrible defeat. The Mussulmans pursued them until they were concealed from sight by the darkness of night; and many of their chiefs fell into the hands of the victors, among them two bishops, who were fighting clad in mail." After this brilliant victory the king traversed Navarre from end to end without the least opposition from the Navarrese. After rasing to the ground their towers and fortified places, he re-entered his capital on September 24. In 921 A.C. Ordono and Sancho were again on the war-path; they suddenly came down on Najera and Viguera, and massacred the Saracen families abiding there, among them some of the most illustrious of the Arabs. Even if the king had wished to avoid a war, public opinion would have compelled him to avenge this wanton out-

300—366 A.H.

Defeat of Sancho.

Fresh tribal rising.

912—976 A.C. rage. But he himself was exasperated and furious at the ceaseless massacres and ravages committed in his territories by the northern barbarians. Without waiting for the spring, he at once took the field. On the 10th of July he entered Navarre, but the terror his name inspired was so great that the enemy abandoned their fortresses on his approach. Sancho tried several times to oppose the king, but was as often beaten. The royal troops reached Pampeluna,[1] Sancho's capital, without any trouble and barely any loss. As a punishment, Sancho's citadel, palace, and other buildings were rased to the ground. The chief of the Basques was now completely subdued and rendered incapable of doing further mischief for some time. On the side of Leon, the king was equally successful, and his task was materially helped by a civil war which broke out in 925 A.C. between the sons [2] of Ordono. Leaving the Leonese to cut each other's throats as they pleased, he applied himself now vigorously to stamp out the insurrections within his own dominions, and by 929 A.C., as I have already described, he had succeeded in reducing the whole kingdom into order. Hitherto, the Ommeyade sovereigns had been content with the designation of Ameer or Sultan; they recognised that the titles of Caliph and *Ameer ul-Mominîn* appertained to the custodian of the Holy Cities,[3] and had accordingly abstained from assuming these honours so long as the house of Abbâs was in virtual possession of Mecca and Medîna, and prayers were recited for them in those places.

312 A.H. April 924 A.C.

Exemplary punishment.

317 A.H. Jan. 16, 929 A.C. Assumes the title of *Ameer ul-Mominîn.*

At this period the Abbasside Caliphate had reached its lowest stage of decrepitude and weakness; Râzi was a

[1] Al-Banbalûna.
[2] Sancho and Alphonso.
[3] Masûdi.

pensioner, if not a prisoner of the Buyide mayors of the palace; and the Holy Cities were held by al-Muiz, the Fatimide. The sovereign of Cordova naturally considered that the deference the Ommeyades of Spain had hitherto shown to the Caliphs of Bagdad was now misplaced, and felt himself justified in assuming the titles of Caliph and *Ameer ul-Mominîn.*[1] 300—366 A.H.

In the midst of a vast conclave of his subjects, representing all classes, he was accordingly invested with the Caliphate under the title of *an-Nâsir li dîn-Illâh.*[2]

In the year 933 A.C. Ramire II. had seized the chieftaincy of Leon after putting out the eyes of his brother Alphonso IV. and several others of his kinsmen. He entertained a ferocious and implacable hatred against the Saracens, and as soon as he got the power he commenced raiding into the Moslem territories.

Abdur Rahmân at once marched against him, and endeavoured to draw him into a battle. But Ramire judged it prudent to remain behind the walls of Osma (Washma). Leaving a detachment in front of this place, the Caliph continued his march towards the north. The Galicians and Leonese were joined at this time by the Navarrese. Sancho was dead, and Navarre was now held by Garcia, his son, under the regency of his mother, Tota (Theuda), who hated the Saracens with as fierce a hatred as Ramire himself. The Caliph swept through Castile and Alva, rasing to the ground the fortresses and towers of the Galicians. Ramire was powerless to prevent even the destruction of Burgos, which was the capital of Castile. At this juncture the Christian tribesmen obtained an invaluable ally in the rebel Governor

Ramire's raid.

His punishment.

[1] Corrupted by the Christians into Miramolin.

[2] "The Helper of the Religion of the Lord."

912—976 A.C. of Saragossa (Mohammed bin Hishâm[1]), who for some fancied wrong rose in arms against his sovereign. The whole of the north was thus arrayed against Abdur Rahmân; the danger was one of extreme magnitude,
937 A.C. but he met it with his usual energy. Saragossa was besieged with such vigour and promptitude that the rebel capitulated. He was pardoned and re-appointed to his post. But the tribesmen were not treated with the same leniency; the country of the Basques was again overrun, and the villages and towns laid under contribution. Tota, after sustaining reverse after reverse, sued for pardon, and definitely acknowledged the Caliph as the suzerain of Navarre. Ramire was beaten in several actions until he dared not meet the Caliph in the open, and skulked behind his hills.[2] With the exception of the principality of Leon and a part of Catalonia, which was a dependency of France, the whole of Spain was now at the feet of the great monarch of Cordova.

The introduction of "Slavs" into State service.

In his dislike towards the Arab aristocracy and their factious and turbulent spirit, Abdur Rahmân had been throwing of late a great deal of power into the hands of foreigners. They were chiefly mamelukes of various nationalities—Germans, Franks, Italians, Scandinavians, Varangians, Russians, etc.—brought from their native countries into Spain, when quite young, by the Venetians, Genoese, and Pisan traders, and sold to the Saracens.[3] With the religion of Islâm they adopted the Arab

[1] Ibn Khaldûn gives the name as Hishâm, whilst Dozy has Hâshim.

[2] Ibn Khaldûn, vol. vi. p. 4.

[3] Some of them were mutilated before being sold In Verdun and several other places in the south of France, the French had established large manufactories for the mutilation of human beings (Reinaud's *Invasions des Sarrazins*). These places supplied the demand from Byzantium, the Vatican, Spain, and other countries.

language, culture, and manners. In the Arab households they were treated as members of the family, and often entrusted with the discharge of confidential business. An-Nâsir surrounded himself with a large number of these foreigners, whose generic designation was *Iskalâbi* or Slavs; invested them with important military and civil functions, and compelled "men of the highest families, who counted in their ancestry the heroes of the desert, to pay homage to these upstarts." And the Slav corps formed his most trusted soldiers. This favouritism alienated still further the Arab nobles. In 939 A.C. the Galicians and Basques were again in arms, which necessitated a fresh punitive expedition. On this occasion the Caliph made a fatal mistake; he gave the chief command to a Slav general named Najd. The Arab officers were furious, and in their anger vowed that they would leave the Slavs in the lurch at the most critical moment. The disaster to the Saracen army, resulting from the Caliph's favouritism or the jealousy of the Arabs, is differently described by different authors. Masûdi and Makkarî state that the Saracens marched unopposed until they arrived at Zamora, which was besieged. This city was surrounded by several walls, one within the other, with a large ditch filled with water within the inner circle. The Arab soldiers succeeded in forcing their way through a breach across the outer walls, when they suddenly found themselves in front of the ditch; here they were met by showers of arrows and spears. At this juncture the Arab corps took it into its head to retire. Thus deserted and cooped within the walls, the Caliph's force lost an enormous number of men. Condé's account is fuller. The Saracens, in spite of the check before the ditch and the retreat of some of their comrades, continued the attack; they poured in

300—366 A.H.

Battle of al-Khandak.

912—976 A.C. through the breach, and crossing the ditch over the dead bodies of their comrades, fell upon the Christians, who, unable to sustain the shock, fled into the city pursued by the Saracens, and the entire place "became one field of carnage; the children and women alone being spared."[1] This battle, which took place within the walls of Zamora, is called the fight of *al-Khandak* or the Ditch. The account given by Dozy taken from Spanish Christian chroniclers is totally different. He says that the Saracen army was attacked by the enemy near the village of al-Khandak (Alhandaga), not far from Salamanca, when the Arabs left the field in a body; the flanks thus left open, the Leonese and Navarrese penetrated into the heart of the Caliph's army; the Slavs fought with great determination, but were almost annihilated.

The loss sustained within the walls of Zamora did not damp the courage or energy of the Caliph. He immediately set in motion another force which exacted
740 A.C. terrible retribution from the Galicians and Basques. In November 940 A.C. his Governor of Badajoz[2] inflicted a murderous defeat on Ramire, and laid waste his country with fire and sword. These expeditions were
Ordono III. sues for peace. continued for some years until the spirit of the tribes was completely broken. In 955 A.C., Ordono III., the son and successor of the fanatical Ramire,[3] sued for peace, which was concluded on terms honourable to both sides. The Galician chief bound himself to recognise the suzerainty of the Caliph, to abstain from all intrigues with the Christians of Andalusia or any foreign power, to demolish within a fixed time his principal fortresses on the borders of the Cordovan dominions, and not to

[1] *Domination des Arabes en Espagne*, vol. i. p. 430.

[2] Ahmed bin Îla.

[3] Ramire II. died in 950 A.C.

commit any raids on the Moslem territories. The Caliph on his side agreed to respect the independence of Navarre and Leon, and to be content with the customary homage and a stipulated tribute.[1] 300—366 A.H.

Boundaries withdrawn to the Ebro.

In accordance with this treaty the Moslem frontiers were withdrawn to the Ebro. Henceforth they stretched from Tortosa on the Mediterranean along the great river, which formed an excellent defensive boundary, past the strong fortress of Afraga (Fraga) to Lerida on the Atlantic sea-board.

War in Africa.

Whilst engaged in these wars against the frontier tribes, Abdur Rahmân was equally involved in hostilities in Africa. In order to guard against the Fatimide menace and to prevent the extension of the Mahdi's power in Mauritania, he had, since 917 A.C., been helping the minor principalities of Western Africa. He had no doubt that the Mahdi, who had already been in communication with the rebel Omar bin Hafsûn, entertained aggressive designs against Spain. In order to forestall them, the Caliph tried to take possession of Western Africa. He was at first successful, but on the accession of the great al-Muiz on the Fatimide throne, the troops of the Spanish sovereign, just then busily engaged with the Christian tribesmen, were driven out of Africa. Ceuta, the key of Mauritania, alone remained in his hands. After the peace with Ordono III., the indefatigable Caliph felt himself able to give his undivided attention to Africa. The death of Ordono, however, compelled him to abandon his projected invasion of the Fatimide dominions. Sancho, who succeeded to the chieftaincy of Galicia and Leon, refused to abide by the treaty concluded with his brother. The Caliph was constrained to employ the

Fresh war with the Galicians.

[1] One of the envoys of the Caliph on this occasion was the Hebrew savant Hasdaï (son of Shabrût), the Director-General of Customs.

912—976 A.C. army he had prepared for Africa against the refractory tribesmen. His brave general, Ahmed bin Îlâ, who held the governorship of Toledo, was entrusted with the conduct of the campaign, and in the month of July 957 A.C. July he won a grand victory over the Galicians and Leonese.

Sancho expelled by his subjects. Before long, Sancho was expelled from his dominions by a combination of his subjects and Ferdinand Gonzalez,[1] Count of Castile. Sancho fled to his grandmother Tota at Pampeluna, whilst the Leonese elected his cousin Ordono as their chief or king. Tota, unable Implores the help of the Caliph. herself to render any assistance to her grandson, implored the help of the Caliph. They repaired to Cordova, where they were received in great state. Their prayers were granted, and a Saracenic army accompanied Sancho to his principality. The usurper was defeated and fled April 959 A.C. to the mountains, and by the month of April 959 A.C., Sancho's authority was re-established. Leon, Castile, Galicia, and Navarre were now practically the dependencies of the Caliphate of Cordova.

Death of Abdur Rahmân an-Nâsir. Ramazân 350 A.H. Oct. 16, 961 A.C. The great Caliph enjoyed this triumph only for two years, for he died on October 16, 961 A.C., at the age of seventy-three, after a reign of a full half-century.

Abdur Rahmân an-Nâsir was unquestionably the ablest and most gifted of all the Ommeyade sovereigns who have ruled in Spain. He had found the kingdom in a chaos, torn by factions, and parcelled among a number of feudal chieftains belonging to different races; a prey to anarchy and civil war, and exposed to continual raids on the part of the Christian tribes of the north. In spite of innumerable obstacles he had saved Andalusia, and made it greater and stronger than it ever was before.

[1] Called *Kums* or *Komes* by the Arabs.

Order and prosperity reigned throughout the empire. 300—366 A.H.
The police organisation was so perfect that the stranger or trader could travel in the most inaccessible tracts without the least fear of molestation or danger. And the cheapness of the markets, the excellence of the clothes worn by the peasantry, and the universal habit of riding, even by the poorest, testified to the general prosperity of the people. The smiling fields, the well-stocked gardens, the immense wealth of fruit, spoke of the wonderful impetus given to agriculture under his liberal and benignant government. The splendid hydraulic works and the scientific system of irrigation which made the most sterile lands fruitful, evoked the admiration of the traveller. But it was not agriculture alone that was fostered by an-Nâsir. Commerce and industry, the arts and sciences were encouraged and developed. Cordova, Almeria, Seville, and other cities had numerous special industries which enriched the population and added to the wealth of Spain. The commerce of the country had increased to such an extent that the customs dues alone supplied the most considerable part of the state revenue, which in an-Nâsir's time amounted to over twelve million dinârs.[1] The military resources of an-Nâsir were formidable. A splendid navy permitted him to dispute with the Fatimides for the supremacy of the Mediterranean, and a numerous and well-disciplined army, "perhaps the best in the world," says Dozy, gave him the preponderance over the Christians of the north. The great sovereigns of Europe courted his alliance, and the Emperor of Constantinople, and the kings of Germany,

[1] Of this vast income, one-third was appropriated for military purposes, one-third was devoted to public works and the development of trade and commerce, and the encouragement of letters and arts, whilst the remaining one-third was put by.

912—976 A.C.

France, and Italy, all sent him ambassadors.[1] "But what excites the admiration and wonderment of the student of this glorious reign is less the work than the workman." The grasp of his intellect, which allowed nothing to escape, showed itself as admirably in the minutest detail as in the sublimest conception. "This sagacious man," continues the historian, "who centralised, who founded the unity of the nation and that of the monarchical power, who by his alliances established a kind of political equilibrium, who, in his large tolerance, called to his counsel men of every religion, is especially a king of modern times rather than a ruler of the Middle Ages." After this enthusiastic estimate, the description of Abdur Rahmân given by the Arab historians sounds weak and colourless.[2]

Accession of Hakam II. (*al-Mustansir b'Illâh*).

Abdur Rahmân was succeeded by his son Hakam, under the title of *al-Mustansir b'Illâh*.[3] Hakam had, for

[1] The year 947 A.C. (336 A.H.) was remarkable for an influx of embassies to Cordova. Besides the envoys from Constantinople who solicited an alliance with Abdur Rahmân, there were ambassadors from the king or duke of the Slavonians (called by the Arabs, Zuka or Duka), the Emperor of Germany (Otho), "the King of France called Kaldah or Karla (Charles the Simple), and another prince of the Franks beyond the *Jabâl ul-Burt* (the Pyrenees) named Ukoh" (Hugo).

[2] This was the monarch who said that in reviewing his long life he could only remember fourteen days of unalloyed happiness. A son had attempted a revolt. He was condemned to suffer the penalty of death. His brother, the heir-apparent, threw himself with tears at the father's feet to rescind the sentence passed by the Council. "As a father I shall shed tears of blood all my life," said the old Caliph, "but I am a king as well as a father; if I interfere in this case the empire will fall to pieces." The sentence of death was allowed to take effect. From that day, Abdur Rahmân was never seen to smile.

[3] "Imploring the succour of the Lord."

some years before his father's death, taken an active part in the administration of the state, and the fame of his justice and wisdom had already spread into distant lands.[1] The chiefs of Leon and Navarre, instead of regarding the death of the great Caliph, who had rendered them such services, as a loss, looked upon it as a means of evading compliance with the treaties, and of throwing off the Saracenic suzerainty. Under the impression that Hakam, who was known to be of a pacific and scholarly disposition, would not insist on the execution of the terms of their compacts, and, if it came to war, would not be so successful as his father, both Sancho and Garcia adopted an evasive attitude, which boded treachery, and delayed the demolition of the frontier fortresses by every device. At the same time Ferdinand Gonzalez, Count of Castile, recommenced his raids. The ungrateful chiefs were soon undeceived as to the real character of the new sovereign; for a short campaign showed that the scholar could be a soldier, that he could strike as well as study. The first expedition against Gonzalez was led by Hakam in person; the rebel suffered a disastrous defeat, and had to fly across the frontiers. On his return from the expedition against the Count of Castile, Hakam was visited by Ordono (the Wicked), who had been ousted by Sancho with the help of the late Caliph. He was received with great honour,[2] and a treaty was signed by which Ordono bound himself always to live at peace with the Moslems, to give his son Garcia as a hostage, and never to join with the rebel Gonzalez. An army under the command of the general Ghâlib was then placed at his disposal,

300—366 A.H.

Treachery of the Leonese chief.

February 962 A.C.

[1] Masûdi, who wrote his *Murûj uz-Zahab* in the lifetime of Abdur Rahmân, speaks of Hakam "as the most distinguished man of his time for his justice and excellent qualities."

[2] Ibn Khaldûn.

912—976 A.C. with orders to drive Sancho out of Leon and Galicia, and instal Ordono in the chiefship. Sancho, whose position was still precarious, was frightened at the preparations, and hurried off to Cordova an embassy consisting of the principal ecclesiastics and nobles of his principality to implore the Caliph's pardon, and to promise solemnly the immediate fulfilment of his treaty engagements. As Ordono died a few months after,[1] he again became refractory, and, relying on the help of the Navarrese chief and the Castilian and Catalonian counts, he flatly refused to abide by the treaty. Hakam was thus compelled to declare war against the Christian tribes. He turned his arms first against Castile, took by storm San Estevan de Gormaz (Shant Eshtibân), and forced Gonzalez to sue for peace, "but it was broken as soon as concluded." Ghâlib was despatched against Leon. Marching by Medinaceli (Medîna Sâlim) he arrived at a place called Atienza (Asta) in the territories of Sancho, where he was met by a large body of Galicians. They suffered a disastrous defeat, and Galicia was overrun. Joining hands with Yahya, son of Mohammed Tajîbi, Governor of Saragossa, he then invaded the country of the Basques, whose chief had also broken the treaty.[2] The Navarrese chief was beaten, and his principal cities were taken by storm. "The capture of Calahorra (Kalharra) at the hands of Ghâlib in the country of the Baskones was the most important among these conquests."[3] Hakam rebuilt its fortifications, and occupied it with his troops. Several other places in Navarre, Galicia, and Alava and Castile were similarly garrisoned. In a word, although Hakam did not love war, and had to engage in it against his own wishes, he

Submission of Navarre.

[1] Towards the end of 962 A.C.

[2] Ibn Khaldûn. [3] *Ibid.*

soon forced the enemies of his realm to sue for peace. Sancho of Leon made his submission in 966 A.C. The Counts of Catalonia, Borrel, and Miron,[1] who also had suffered some disastrous reverses, followed his example, and solicited a renewal of the treaty of peace, engaging to dismantle all the fortresses and towers in the vicinity of the Moslem frontiers, from which marauding parties usually started; to lend no assistance to the people of their faith in their wars with the Saracens, and lastly to deter other Christian tribes and nations from joining their forces against the Moslems. "Garcia, the chief of the Baskones, sent ambassadors accompanied by a body of his counts and bishops to ask for peace." They were kept waiting for a time until Ghâlib had thoroughly beaten the Navarrese, when Hakam acceded to their prayers on the same terms. About the same time, "the mother of a powerful count, named Luzrik, son of Balakash (Rodrigo Velasquez), whose territories bordered on Galicia," visited the court of Hakam to pray for peace on behalf of her son. The Caliph received her in great state, covered her with presents, and granted her request. The death in 970 A.C. of the rebel Count of Castile at last brought tranquillity to that province.

300—366 A.H.

Submission of Sancho. Peace concluded with them.

Two years later Hakam sent an expedition into Mauritania (*Maghrib ul-Aksa* and *Ausat*) to stem the tide of Fatimide conquest. His general Ghâlib seems to have been successful in restoring the Ommeyade supremacy in Western Africa. The Berber tribes of Zenata, Maghrâwa, and Miknâsa abandoned their allegiance to the Caliph of Cairo, and prayers were recited in Hakam's name from their pulpits. Many of the Alide princes, long settled in Fez, came over to Spain, where they were received with kindness. The Idrîsides were brought to

362 A.H. October 972 A.C. Expedition into Africa.

[1] Barîl and Munîra of Ibn Khaldûn.

912–976 A.C.

the country of the Riffs,[1] and thence to Cordova. But later some of them were exiled to Alexandria.

Hakam's love of learning.

"Hakam," says Ibn Khaldûn, "loved literature and the sciences, and showered his munificence on men of learning." He was a great collector of books, and although all his predecessors were men of culture, and fond of enriching their libraries with rare and precious books, none had engaged in the work with the same zeal as Hakam. A special officer was entrusted with the charge of the imperial library, the catalogue of which alone consisted of forty-four volumes.[2] Hakam converted Spain into a great market, where the literary production of every country was immediately brought for sale; he sent out agents to every part of the world in search of interesting and valuable works, and spent large sums in their purchase. The publication of original works was encouraged by munificent donations, and every endeavour made to obtain the first copies. Abu'l Faraj (Isphahâni) sent him a copy of "his great work[3] even before it had appeared in Irâk," and received from the grateful monarch of Cordova a thousand dinârs as reward. Several rooms in the palace were set apart for the work of copying, illuminating, and binding books, over which were employed the most skilful men of the time. Hakam was not merely a book-hunter, but a studious scholar. He not only read the books in his library, but what is more, he made copious notes on the fly-leaf relative to the author and the work. His liberality towards Spanish as well as foreign scholars, scientists, and philosophers was unbounded. He encouraged and protected "even the philosophers, who could now pursue

[1] Ibn Khaldûn.

[2] The library is said to have contained 400,000 volumes.

[3] See *ante*, p. 469.

their studies without fear of persecution by the bigots." All branches of learning and science flourished under this enlightened sovereign. The elementary schools, founded by his predecessors, were numerous and well endowed. "In Spain almost everybody knew how to read and write, whilst in Christian Europe, save and except the clergy, even persons belonging to the highest ranks were wholly ignorant."[1] Hakam believed that knowledge could never be too widely diffused, and in his benevolent solicitude for the poorer classes, he established in the capital twenty-seven schools, where the children of parents without means received gratuitous education, even the books being supplied from the state, whilst the University of Cordova was one of the most renowned in the world, and equalled the Azharièh of Cairo and the Nizâmièh of Bagdad.

300—366 A.H.

Death of Hakam al-Mustansir, Safar 2, 366 A.H. Oct. 1, 976 A.C.

This good and virtuous Caliph died on October 1, 976 A.C., and with him ended the glory of the Ommeyades of Spain.

Cordova.

Cordova, called by the Arabs Kurtuba,[2] is situated in an extensive and fertile plain at the foot of the ridge of mountains called the Sierra Morena, forming a kind of semicircular amphitheatre on the right bank of the Guadalquiver.[3] This city had been adorned by the Arab governors with numerous beautiful structures, but its systematic embellishment on a scale of grandeur of which we can have but little conception in these days began under Abdur Rahmân ad-Dâkhil. One of his first acts, after his accession to power, was to build an aqueduct for the supply of pure water to the capital

[1] Dozy.

[2] Cordoba of the Romans. It was also called by these people Colonia Patricia.

[3] Corrupted from the Arabic *Wâdi ul-Kabîr* (the great river).

912—976 A.C. from the hills in the vicinity. His successors continually added to the number until the water supply of Cordova surpassed in excellence that of every other city. The water was brought in leaden pipes and then distributed over the town and suburbs. The reservoirs and cisterns were either of Grecian marble wonderfully carved or of plated brass. In some of the palaces they were even of gold and silver. The Saracens loved water in every shape; no mansion of any pretension was without its garden, its running rills of water, its fountains. In the year 940 A.C. Abdur Rahmân III. constructed another great aqueduct which threw into shade the works of his predecessors. It was built over arches scientifically designed, and conveyed the water from the neighbouring mountains to the waterworks of the city. There the water was discharged into a vast reservoir, in the middle of which was the figure of a lion covered with plates of gold, spouting water from its mouth. By the side of the lion stood the gigantic statue of a man pouring water over the lion. After supplying the city the surplus water ran into the river. The famous garden of Rusâfa, which became the model for the civilised countries of Europe, was made by Abdur Rahmân I. It was stocked with choice and rare plants from all parts of the world. An exquisite palace enhanced the charm of the garden; but he was not content with building for his own pleasure or indulgence, for he "erected mosques, baths, bridges, and castles in every province of his dominions." The great cathedral mosque which became one of the ornaments of Spain was begun by him although completed by his son. The magnificence of Cordova in the days of its glory can be judged from the statement of an old author to the effect that one could travel for ten miles "by the light of lamps along an uninterrupted extent of buildings."

Another writer says—"The city extended twenty-four miles one way and six on the other, and the whole space was occupied by houses, palaces, mosques, and gardens along the banks of the Guadalquiver." Beyond the city walls stretched the suburbs, divided into twenty-seven quarters, inhabited by a thriving population. In each division there were mosques, markets, and baths adequate for the wants of its inhabitants, "so that there was no need for people of one quarter to go to the other." The capital derived its supplies from three thousand townships and villages appertaining to it. The magistrates of the places in the immediate vicinity of Cordova made their reports every Friday to the Caliph after the public prayers. The grand mosque begun by ad-Dâkhil and completed by Hishâm I. was further beautified by an-Nâsir. It was a magnificent structure, resplendent with gold and silver, and decorated in the most exquisite taste. Cordova contained innumerable libraries, and rich people, however illiterate, spared no labour or expense in amassing books, merely for the sake of having it reported that they had libraries, or were possessed of unique works. The beautiful palace of az-Zahra,[1] built by an-Nâsir, at a distance of four miles from the capital, was one of the wonders of the world. It was made of pure marble—white, onyx, rose-coloured, and green—brought from different parts of the globe. The eastern hall was adorned with fountains, in which were placed figures of animals, made of gold, set with precious stones, through the mouths of which water flowed continuously. The audience-chamber was an exquisite piece of workmanship in marble and gold, studded with jewels. According to the old writers it was impossible to give in words a proper description of "the boldness of the

300—366 A.H.

The palace of az-Zahra.

[1] "The Beautiful."

912—976 A.C. design, the beauty of the proportions, the elegance of the ornaments and decorations, whether of carved marble or of molten gold, of the columns that seemed from their symmetry as if cast in moulds, of the paintings that equalled the choicest bowers themselves, the vast but firmly constructed lake, and the fountains with the exquisite images."

Attached to the gardens were large enclosures for wild beasts, as well as aviaries containing birds of all kinds and from all climes. Over the central gate was placed the statue of the queen after whom the palace and the city were named. Besides the actual palace with its gardens, there were enormous buildings appropriated to the use of the Caliph's retinue and court. Contiguous to them was the town of az-Zahra.[1]

Under its great Ommeyade sovereigns, Cordova, with its three thousand eight hundred mosques, its sixty thousand palaces and mansions, its two hundred thousand houses inhabited by the common people, its seven hundred baths, its eighty thousand shops, besides hostels and serais, vied in splendour and extent with Bagdad. Its fame had spread even into the heart of Germany, and the Saxon nun Hroswitha "called it the ornament of the world."[2] In the days of its glory the population of Cordova numbered one million inhabitants; under the present rule it does not exceed thirty-five thousand![3]

[1] A donation of four hundred dirhems to each person who came to reside in the vicinity of the palace brought a large influx of inhabitants from all parts of the country. For twenty years ten thousand men were employed over the palace.

[2] Dozy says this writer was celebrated in the last half of the tenth century for her poems and Latin dramas.

[3] Murphy. The prosperity of Cordova was typical of the other cities; such as Seville, Almeria, Jaen, Malaga, Ecija, Madrid, and Saragossa.

But Cordova was not merely the abode of culture, of learning and arts, of industry and commerce; it was the home where chivalry received its first nourishment. Chivalry is innate in the Arab character, but its rules and principles, the punctilious code of honour, the knightly polish, the courtliness, all of which were so assiduously cultivated afterwards in the kingdom of Granada, came into prominence under an-Nâsir and his son. "It was at this period that the chivalrous ideas commenced to develop themselves, joined to an exalted sense of honour and respect for the feeble sex."[1] Another competent writer states that chivalry with all its institutions, such as came later into existence among the Christian nations of the West, flourished among the Saracens in the time of an-Nâsir, Hakam, and al-Mansûr.[2] Here came foreign knights under guarantee of peace and protection to break lance with Saracen cavaliers. The old custom of warriors rushing to battle shouting the names of their sisters and sweethearts had gone out of fashion; the knight now entered the lists wearing some token of his lady-love on his shoulder or helmet. The Saracen lady was an undisguised spectator at the frequent jousts and tournaments which enlivened the capital, and her presence at the public festivals lent a charm and fascination to the scenes. The dignified association of the sexes gave rise to a delicacy of sentiment and refinement of manners, of which the domiciled Moslem of India in the present day can have but a faint conception; the polished courtesy and exalted sentiment of honour, which distinguished the Arab cavaliers to the very end of their empire in Spain, "might have graced

300—366 A.H.

Chivalry.

[1] Reinaud.

[2] Viardot, *Scènes de mœurs Arabes en Espagne au dixième Siècle.*

912–976 A.C. a Bayard or a Sidney."[1] The ten qualities essential to a true knight were "piety, valour, courtesy, prowess, the gifts of poetry and eloquence, and dexterity in the management of the horse, the sword, lance, and bow."

1 "When the empress queen of Alfonso VII. was besieged in the castle of Azeca, in 1139, she reproached the Moslem cavaliers for their want of courtesy and courage in attacking a fortress defended by a female. They acknowledged the justice of the rebuke, and only requested that she would condescend to show herself to them from her palace; when the Moorish chivalry, after paying their obeisance to her in the most respectful manner, instantly raised the siege, and departed."

CHAPTER XXVIII

THE SARACENS OF SPAIN

THE OMMEYADES (*continued*)

366—428 A.H.; 976—1037 A.C.

HISHÂM II.—MAHDÎ—SULAIMÂN—ABDUR RAHMÂN IV.—MOHAMMED II.—HISHÂM III.

Accession of Hishâm II.—Hâjib al-Mansûr—His intrigues—Seizes all the powers of the State—His victories over the Christian tribes—His death—Is succeeded by his son, al-Muzzaffar—His successful government—Al-Muzzaffar's death—Hajib Abdur Rahmân—Mahdi seizes the throne—Abdication of Hishâm II.—Sulaimân kills Mahdi—Convulsion in Cordova.

HAKAM left him surviving a son named Hishâm, barely eleven years of age. He had tried in his lifetime by every means in his power to assure the young lad's peaceable succession to the throne. A few months before his death he held a convocation of the magnates and nobles; and all took the oath of fealty to Hishâm, and subscribed the document by which Hakam devised the Caliphate to the son of his old age whom he so tenderly loved. On his death-bed he confided the care of the child to the Hâjib Mashafi and to the secretary of state, Mohammed bin Abi Aâmir. He trusted that under the guardianship of his mother, the Empress Subh,[1] a woman of great ability, and with the help of these favoured servants, his

366—428 A.H. 976—1037 A.C.

Accession of Hishâm II. (*al-Muwayyid b'Illâh*).

[1] It means the Dawn. Dozy has rendered it happily as "Aurora."

976—1037 A.C. son would rule peaceably and successfully. Hishâm was accordingly proclaimed Caliph under the title of *al-Muwaiyyid b'Illâh.*[1] But the deceased Caliph had miscalculated the fidelity or ambition of Mohammed bin Abi Aâmir. Before long he overthrew Hâjib Mashafi and the other nobles who were opposed to his ascendency. He put to death many leading *walîs* and magnates, "and when the kingdom was denuded of its leading men,"[2] he seized all power and authority, and kept the young Caliph almost confined in his palace. The state officials were not allowed to come near him except on festive occasions, when they made their obeisance and departed. After seizing on the vizierate Ibn Abî Aâmir assumed the title of the Hâjib al-Mansûr,[3] and built a magnificent palace for himself which was named the Zâhira. "His name was borne on the coins, and all orders and edicts were issued under his seal, and prayers were offered for him along with the Caliph from the pulpits." After ridding himself of the rivals who inspired alarm or jealousy, he turned his attention to the army, which he re-organised by removing the Arab element and introducing in its place large bodies of Berbers, on whose devotion he could rely. "In fact, he relegated the Arabs to a secondary position."[4]

According to Ibn Khaldûn he undertook fifty-two[5] campaigns, in which he was invariably successful. "Never was a detachment of his army cut up, or his standard lowered." The Galicians and Basques had, immediately on the death of Hakam, risen against the Saracens and

[1] "The Aider of the religion of the Lord."
[2] Ibn Khaldûn.
[3] "The victorious Lord Chamberlain."
[4] Ibn Khaldûn.
[5] According to another writer, fifty-six.

resumed their raids. By a series of brilliant operations, Mansûr, as I shall now call him, reduced Leon and Navarre to the condition of tributary provinces, and garrisoned the capitals of those principalities with his troops. He then turned his arms against Catalonia; sacked Barcelona, and drove out the French counts. The boundaries of the empire were thus again extended beyond the Pyrenees. In Mauritania, his arms were equally successful, and a large part of Western Africa was reduced to subjection by his generals. In the year 991 A.C. he conceived the design of making the office of Hâjib hereditary in his family He would have, if he could, removed the son of his patron from the throne, and made himself sovereign *de jure* as he was *de facto*, but he was afraid of the nation, among whom the idea of legitimacy was ingrained. The nobles, perhaps, would have considered a change of dynasty useful; but the people, chiefly of Spanish origin, thought otherwise. "Like the religious sentiment, the love of dynasty was a part of their being; and although Mansûr had given the country unprecedented glory and prosperity, they hated him for keeping their sovereign in a condition of pupilage." Aware of this feeling, but hopeful that it might change in time, he contented himself with declaring his son Abdul Malik his successor to the vizierate, under the nominal orders of the Caliph. In 996 A.C., he assumed the titles of *Syed* (lord) and *Malik Karîm* (generous king).

366—428 A.H.

This remarkable man died in 1002 A.C., and was buried at Medîna Sâlim (Medinaceli). None of the rulers of Andalusia was so dreaded by the Christians of the north as the Hâjib al-Mansûr. His military ability and wonderful talent for organisation had made him the idol of the soldiery. His solicitude for their well-being

Hâjib al-Mansûr's death, 1002 A.C.

976—1037 A.C.

and discipline was constant and unceasing; and with the splendid army he had created and trained, he had given to Spain a power "which it had not enjoyed," says Dozy, "even in the times of Abdur Rahmân III." But this is not his sole claim to the gratitude of his people. Although he was forced by political considerations to show himself intolerant to free-thinkers and philosophers, he did not hesitate to protect them when he could do so without wounding the susceptibilities of the legists.[1] During the whole period of his rule, with the glory of arms was combined a taste for letters and arts and the love of industry and agriculture. "Never was Mussulman Spain," says Reinaud, "more prosperous than under his domination." He fostered learning, and patronised learned men with generous munificence. Although the means he had employed to attain to power must be strongly condemned, it cannot be denied that once he got it he exercised it nobly. In character he was generous, just, and loyal to his word. His sagacity and love of justice passed in fact into a proverb.

Hâjib Abdul Malik, *al-Muzzaffar*.

Mansûr was succeeded in the Hâjibate by his son Abdul Malik, surnamed *al-Muzzaffar* (*the Victorious*). He followed in the footsteps of his father in the management of the state. He won several victories over the Christian tribes, and under his successful rule the country advanced still further in prosperity. "They were days of festivity," says an old writer.

The unpopularity of the Banû-Aâmir.

And yet the Banû-Aâmir were not loved. Had they remained content with ruling in the name of the sovereign, their mayoralty in all probability would have lasted some time, but their vaulting ambition over-stepped all bounds. They aimed not only at the reality of power under the shadow of the throne, but at the throne itself.

[1] Dozy.

They thus made the princes of the blood and the whole Ommeyade clan their bitter enemies, and completely alienated the *fakîhs* and the people. At the same time, the change which had taken place in the peninsula since the accession of Nâsir favoured a revolution. The old Arab society, "with its virtues and its faults," had disappeared. The unification of the nations which had been the aim of an-Nâsir and of the great Hâjib, had been attained at the expense of the ancient aristocracy, which, ruined and impoverished, were fast disappearing, and gradually the old historic names faded away from the memories of men. The court-nobility, allied to the Ommeyade by ties of clientage, had no doubt withstood the shock, and hitherto maintained intact their wealth and influence. But the most powerful men at this epoch were the Berber and Slav generals who had made their fortunes under the Hâjib al-Mansûr. Material development had brought into prominence another social factor, viz. an opulent middle-class; and the merchants, traders, and the industrial classes generally began now to play an important part in the economy of the country. But this very fact gave birth to new difficulties, for with the increase of wealth and the rise of a new order commenced the struggle of classes. One can see mirrored in the history of those times all the troubles which beset the statesman of the present day—the mutual aversion of the military and the civilian, the hatred of the proletariat against employers, the envy of the commonalty towards the upper ranks of society. In the capital the social conditions were such that the smallest disturbance was sure to result in a fearful conflict between the rich and the poor. "Cordova had become a vast manufactory filled with thousands of workmen, ready at the slightest notice to take part in any riot or revolt which promised

976—1037 A.C. a harvest of loot. But the opulent classes forgot the danger in their detestation of the Banû-Aâmir."[1]

October, 1008 A.C. Death of the Hâjib al-Muzaffar. The death of Muzaffar in the flower of his age brought about the catastrophe which was feared by some and hoped for by all. The Banû-Aâmir fell, but, like blind Samson, they brought down with them the whole fabric of the empire.

Hajib Abdur Rahmân Sanchol. He was succeeded by his brother Abdur Rahmân, called Sanchol.[2] He was hated by the people for his flagrant immorality, and yet he was ambitious of making himself the Caliph. He forced Hishâm II. to declare him heir-presumptive to the pontifical throne. His audacity brought the discontent of the Cordovans to a head. Sanchol had hardly left the capital on an expedition to the north than a revolt, headed by a member of the royal family named Mohammed, broke out in Cordova. The palace of the Banû-Aâmir (az-Zâhira) was plundered and reduced to ashes. Hishâm signed his own abdication in favour of Mohammed, who assumed the title of *Mahdi*. Immediately upon his accession he proclaimed the attainder of Sanchol. The enthusiasm of the capital communicated itself to the provinces, and in a short time a large army gathered round the Mahdi's standard, officered, as in the French Revolution, by members of the middle-class, or "men of the people," doctors, butchers, saddlers, etc. Mahdi had, however, raised in the popular excitement a Frankenstein which he could not lay, and which practically caused the destruction of the Ommeyades in Spain. Sanchol, deserted by his followers, was taken prisoner and put to death.

Mohammed *al-Mahdi*.

Death of Sanchol.

[1] Dozy.

[2] The Sanjûl of the Arabs. Dozy says he was nicknamed Sanchol, that is, little Sancho, because his mother was a daughter of Sancho, King of Navarre.

But the new Caliph did not reign long; he soon alienated all parties by his conduct. The ferocious Berbers fell off, and put forward another candidate to the throne. He, too, was an Ommeyade, and bore the name of Sulaimân. Cordova now became the theatre of frightful riots, in which the worst excesses were practised on both sides. Baited by the wild troops, Mahdi brought out Hishâm II. and again placed him in the pontifical chair. Sulaimân thereupon invoked the assistance of the Christians of Castile and Leon, whilst Mahdi applied for help to the Catalonians. Thus, in the course of a few months, from the death of Muzzaffar, the Saracens, instead of dictating the law to the Galicians and other tribesmen, were supplicating their aid, which was granted only on the retrocession of all the conquests made by an-Nâsir and the great Hâjib. Two hundred fortresses and cities were thus abandoned to the Christians. Cordova was alternately captured and recaptured by the allies of Sulaimân and Mahdi, and treated as a city taken by storm. The beautiful az-Zahra of Abdur Rahmân III. was sacked and partially destroyed. Mahdi was at last killed; Sulaimân then seized the person of the helpless Hishâm, who was either put to death or allowed to escape to Mecca. The usurper, who assumed the title of Mustaîn b'Illâh, did not, however, long enjoy the fruits of his ill-gotten victory. Another revolt led to his fall and death. A member of the Idrîside family[1] then seated himself on the throne. Upon his assassination, shortly after, his brother Kâsim was raised to the supreme power. Kâsim's administration was mild and just. But he was before long deserted by the Berbers. A struggle with his nephew ended in his expulsion from Cordova. The Cordovans then raised an

366—428 A.H.

July 1010 A.C.

Sulaimân.

Ali bin Hamûd.

1017 A.C. 408 A.H.

[1] Ali bin Hamûd.

976—1037 A.C. Ommeyade[1] to the throne, which, however, he did not occupy long. Two other Ommeyades[2] followed in rapid succession. With the last of these unfortunate sovereigns, sovereigns[3] merely in name, the Ommeyade dynasty came to an end in Spain. The Cordovans submitted for a while to Yahya, the son of Ali bin Hamûd.[4] Upon his assassination in 1035 A.C. they established a republic in their city, which continued in existence until its reduction forty years later by the King of Seville.

[1] Abdur Rahmân, surnamed *al-Mustazhir b'Illâh* ("He who implores the assistance of the Lord").

[2] Mohammed, *al-Mustakfi b'Illâh* ("He who is contented with the Lord"). This Al-Mustakfi was the father of the celebrated poetess Wallâdèh. She was the most eloquent woman of her age, and in learning and taste rivalled the best poets of her father's court. The histories of the time are filled with anecdotes respecting this princess. She was equally celebrated for the nobility and purity of her character as for her beauty. She lived to a great age, and died unmarried in the year 480 A.H. (May 8, A.C. 1087).

[3] Hishâm III., *al-Mutazz b'Illâh* ("He who is prepared in the Lord"). "Hishâm," says Makkarî, "was a mild and enlightened ruler, and possessed many brilliant qualities; but, notwithstanding all that, some time after his entrance into the capital, the volatile and degenerate citizens of Cordova grew discontented with his rule, and he was deposed by the army in 422 A.H. (A.C. 1031)."

[4] Surnamed *al-Mutaali.*

CHAPTER XXIX

THE SARACENS IN SPAIN (*continued*)

428—871 A.H.; 1037—1466 A.C.

The *Mulûk ut-Tawâif* or Petty Kings—Their mutual divisions—Gradual extension of the Christian power—The Almoravides—Yusuf bin Tâshfîn—The Battle of Zallâka—Death of Yusuf bin Tâshfîn—Is succeeded by his son Ali—His death—Collapse of the Almoravide Empire—The Almohades—Abdul Momîn—*Abû Yâkûb* Yusuf—*Abû Yusuf* Yâkûb (al-Mansûr)—Battle of Alarcos—Death of Yâkûb—Accession of Mohammed an-Nâsir—Disaster of al-Aakâb—Collapse of the Almohade Empire—Rise of the Banû-Ahmar—The kingdom of Granada.

428—871 A.H. 1037—1466 A.C.

The *Mulûk ut-Tawâif*, "the petty kings."

THE political convulsions in the capital gave to the provincial governors and magnates the opportunity for proclaiming their independence. Malaga, Algeciras, and the neighbouring districts were seized by the Banû Hamûd,[1] who assumed the title of *Ameer ul-Mominîn.* They continued to rule in these parts until dispossessed by the king of Granada in 1057 A.C. Granada fell into the hands of the Berber chief Zâwi. His family held this kingdom until 1090 A.C. Seville with the western districts (including Algarve) was possessed by the Banû

The Banû Hamûd.

The Banû Abbâd.

[1] Descended from the Idrîsides of Mauritania, they were the descendants of Hamûd, son of Maimûn, son of Ahmed, son of Ali, son of Obaidullâh, son of Omar, son of Idrîs. Hamûd had fled from Africa and taken refuge in Cordova during the administration of the Hâjib al-Mansûr, who received him with kindness, and gave him a command in the armies of the Caliph Hishâm.

1037—1466 A.C. Abbâd. The founder of this family was the Chief Kâzi of Seville, *Abu'l Kâsim* Mohammed, surnamed Ibn Abbâd.[1] The last of the Banû Abbâd was Mutamid, who was deported to Africa by Yusuf bin Tâshfîn.[2]

The Banû Zu'n-nûn. Toledo was held by the Banû Zu'n-nûn, who made themselves famous by their lavish splendour. The last of the Zu'n-nûn, Kâdir, surrendered the city to Alfonso

478 A.H. 1085 A.C. The Banû Hûd. VI. in 1085 A.C. The Banû Hûd, descended from one of the generals of Abdur Rahmân III.,[3] held Saragossa until 1118 A.C., when it was captured by the Christians under Ramire. Badajoz, Valencia, Murcia, and Almeria were similarly ruled by independent chiefs. Denia and the islands of the Mediterranean were in the hands of

Mujâhid al-Aâmiri. Mujâhid bin Abdullâh al-Aâmiri,[4] surnamed *Abu'l juyûsh* ("the father of the army"). "He was an undaunted warrior and an experienced sailor. He kept a considerable fleet always ready for sea, with which he made descents on the coasts of France and Italy. As long as he lived no Christian vessel dared to furrow the waters of the Bahr ush-Shâm (Sea of Shâm)."[5] These petty sovereigns, collectively designated *Mulûk ut-Tawâif*,[6] were one and all munificent patrons of learning and arts. In fact, each endeavoured to outvie the other in his encouragement of letters. Many of them were themselves accomplished *littérateurs* and poets.[7] And the Arab historian justly

[1] Abbâd was one of his ancestors. He was succeeded by his son, Abû Amr Abbâd, surnamed Mutazid b'Illâh.

[2] See *post*, p. 533.

[3] Mohammed bin Hâshim at-Tajîbi, Governor of Saragossa.

[4] He was a Moula of the Hâjib al-Mansûr.

[5] The Mediterranean Sea. Dozy calls Mujâhid the greatest pirate of his time.

[6] *Tawâif*, plural of *Tâifeh*, tribe, a band of people.

[7] Mutamid, the last King of Seville, was distinguished for the excellence of his style and the elegance of his poetry. Muzaffar

remarks that "when, after the breaking of the necklace and the scattering of its pearls, the petty kings divided among themselves the patrimony of the Banû-Ommeya, the cause of science and literature, instead of losing, gained considerably by the division." 428—871 A.H.

Their divisions.

Had they been united among themselves, or possessed any solidarity of interest, they might have opposed a steady front to the attacks of the Christian Spaniards, which at this time naturally increased in violence. Their mutual dissensions and jealousies paved the way for their destruction. Some even entered into alliance with the Christians against their Moslem rivals. In the year 1055 A.C., Ferdinand I., King of Castile and Leon, fell on the disunited Saracens with all his forces, and drove them from many important places.[1] Mutazid, the King of Seville, saved himself by argreeing to pay tribute to the Leonese. He died in 1069 A.C., leaving the kingdom to his son Mutamid. In 1075 A.C. Mutamid captured Cordova, and shortly after reduced the entire Toledan country, stretching from the Guadalquiver to the Guadiana. On the death of Ferdinand I., in 1065 A.C., his son Alfonso VI. had ascended the throne of Castile. Ambitious and unscrupulous, he expelled his brothers from their kingdoms, and made himself the supreme ruler of Leon, Castile, Galicia and Navarre, and assumed the title of emperor. Not satisfied with the tribute paid by his Arab vassals, he determined to reduce the whole peninsula under his direct sway. Possessed of a splendid army composed of hardy warriors drawn from all parts

Ferdinand I.

Mutamid, King of Seville.

Alfonso VI.

ibn Aftas, the King of Badajoz, left a magnificent history consisting of fifty volumes called the *Kitâb ul-Muzaffari*.

[1] As usual the Christian Spaniards indulged in fiendish atrocities on the capture of every town or city. The excesses committed at Bobastro are indescribable.

1037—1466 A.C.

Surrender of Toledo, 1085 A.C.

of Europe, he declared himself ready to fight with "genii, demons, or the angels of heaven." In 1085 A.C. Kâdir, the last of the Zu'n-nûn kings, surrendered to him the important city of Toledo. His pride now knew no bounds. Granada, Badajoz, Seville, and the few other cities that still remained in Moslem hands, saw clearly the fate in store for them, and looked on all sides for help against the threatened danger. Within the peninsula, however, internecine disputes made a general combination against the common foe hopeless. They therefore cast their eyes abroad.

The rise of the Almoravides.

Whilst the Islâmic empire in Spain was falling to pieces, a new Power had sprung up in Western Africa. The Berbers of the Sahara, called the *Mulassamîn*,[1] had recently been converted to Islâm. Under their spiritual leaders, who bore the title of *marbût*,[2] or saints, they had made vast conquests, and, at the time we are speaking of, their empire extended from Senegambia to Algeria. Their kings were called the *al-Marâbita*,[3] corrupted into Almoravides. The famous

Yusuf bin Tâshfîn, *Ameer-ul Muslimîn*,

Yusuf bin Tâshfîn, who had shortly before been invested by the Caliph of Bagdad with the proud title of *Ameer ul-Muslimîn*, "Commander of the Moslems," was their ruler. And to him, persuaded by the ministers of

[1] The People of the Veil, from *lisam* (*litham*), the veil. This name was given to them because their men always wore a veil as a protection against the burning sands of the desert. The women of the *Mulassamîn* appear to have enjoyed great freedom, and moved about unrestrained and unveiled. As they did not engage in forays, they do not seem to have required the protection of a veil against the flying sands.

[2] *Marâbit*, *marbût*, *râbit*, *rabît*, all derived from the same root, mean a pious or holy man.

[3] The plural of *marbût*. The word *marbût* is common in modern Algeria.

religion, the Saracen kings of Spain addressed their appeal for help. In response to their prayers, Yusuf bin Tâshfîn crossed to Spain in October 1086 A.C. Near Seville he was joined by the forces of Mutamid and the other Andalusian chiefs, and the united army marched towards Badajoz (Bâzios or Batlios). Alfonso met them at a place called Zallâka,[1] about four leagues to the south of Badajoz. The Saracens numbered twenty thousand all told, whilst the force under Alfonso amounted to over sixty thousand seasoned soldiers. A frightful and sanguinary battle took place on Friday, October 23, 1086 A.C. Alfonso fled, says Ibn ul-Athîr,[2] from the scene of action with only three hundred cavaliers, whilst the rest lay dead or dying on the field. The victory of Zallâka paralysed for a time the Christian kingdom of Leon. Yusuf bin Tâshfîn did not on this occasion tarry long in Spain; on his return in the following year he expelled the Spanish kings from their dominions, which he incorporated with the Almoravide empire.[3] The whole of Andalusia as far as the Tagus was now virtually under the sceptre of the Emperor of Morocco. The *fakîhs* who had so actively co-operated in bringing over the Almoravides acquired great influence under these sovereigns. "One must go back," says Dozy, "to the times of the Visigoths to discover another example of a clergy so powerful as the Moslem clergy were under the Almoravide rule." They carried their narrow prejudice so far as to place under the ban Imâm al-Ghazzâli's celebrated work on "the Revival of Learning and Religion."[4]

428—871 A.H.

crosses into Spain, October 1086 A.C.

12 Rajab 479 A.H. 23 October 1086 A.C. The victory of Zallâka.

[1] The Sacralias of the Christians.

[2] Vol. x. p. 100.

[3] Mutamid, the King of Seville, was deported to Morocco, where he died in 1095. The account of his fall forms a pathetic story.

[4] *Ihyâ-ul-ulûm w'ad-dîn*, a thoroughly orthodox work.

1037—1466 A.C. Whilst Yusuf lived the Christians were in continual terror of his arms. He died in the year 1106 A.C., and was succeeded by his son Ali, surnamed Abu'l Hassan.[1] He followed in the footsteps of his able father, "although," says the historian, "he fell short of him in some things." He defeated the Christian tribes several times and took from them Talavera, Madrid (Majrît),[2] Guadalaxara (Wâdi ul-Hijâra),[3] and many other fortresses and towns, whilst his general, Sîr Ibn Abî Bakr, re-took the cities of Santarem (Shanterim), Badajoz, Oporto (Bortokal), Evora (Teborah), and Lisbon (Alishbûna). These gains, however, were counterbalanced by the loss of Saragossa (Sarâkustèh), Calatayud (Kalât Ayûb), and other important places beyond the Tagus, which were captured by a combined army of Aragonese, Catalonians, and Franks from beyond the Pyrenees. Whilst the Almoravides were thus engaged in Andalusia, a new development, fraught with the most disastrous consequences to their rule, was taking place in Africa.

Death of Yusuf bin Tâshfîn Moharram 500 A.H. September 1106 A.C. Accession of *Abu'l Hassan* Ali.

1119 A.C.

In the year 514 of the Hegira, a man of the name of Mohammed, surnamed Ibn Tumârt,[4] a native of Sûs in Western Africa, appeared among the Berbers inhabiting the vast chain of mountains which intersects Mauritania. He was an Arab by descent, but belonged by adoption to one of the Berber tribes. In his youth he had travelled in the East and studied philosophy and jurisprudence under various masters, such as al-Ghazzâli, Abû Bakr at-Tartûshi (of Tortosa), and others. On his

The Almohades (*al-Muwahhiddûn*), 1120 A.C.

Mohammed ibn Tumârt, al-Mahdi.

[1] He is described by Ibn Khallikân as a powerful prince, mild, devout, just, and of great humanity.

[2] Ancient Majoritum.

[3] "The river of stones." The city got its name from the river.

[4] *Abû Abdullâh* Mohammed, son of Abdullâh, son of Tumârt, an Alide, descended from Hassan I.

return to his native land, disgusted with the laxity of morals prevailing among all classes of society, and the excessive veneration paid by the commonalty to saints, he commenced to preach a reform among the wild inhabitants of the Atlas, and announced himself as the Mahdi whose advent had been foretold by the Prophet. An enormous following soon gathered round him. Ibn Tumârt chose for his lieutenant a young man of the name of Abdul Momin, the son of a rich merchant. His followers and disciples styled themselves *al-Muwwahhidîn*,[1] or Unitarians. Gradually the power of the Unitarians increased, and before long they formed an extensive kingdom, chiefly at the expense of the *Murabite* empire. So long as Ali bin Tâshfîn lived they were kept in check. He died in 1143 A.C., and was succeeded by his son Tâshfîn, who was wholly incapable of coping with the Unitarians. He was killed in the year 1145 A.C., and the empire of Morocco passed into the hands of Abdul Momin.[2] The struggle between Almoravide and Almohade furnished a glorious opportunity to the Christian Spaniards for ravaging the Moslem territories in Spain, and committing the most appalling atrocities on the Saracens. Alphonso VII., who, like his grandfather Alphonso VI., had assumed the title of Emperor, carried fire and sword to the very walls of Cordova, Seville and Carmona; pillaged and burnt Xeres, and penetrated as far as Gaudix (Wâdi-Ash). Five years later he devastated the fertile districts of Jaen, Baeza, Ubeda and Andujar. Again the Andalusian Moslems appealed for help to their brethren across the straits. In the year 541 A.H., Abdul Momin sent an army and

428—871 A.H.

Abdul Momin.

Death of Ali bin Tâshfîn, 1143 A.C.

Succeeded by his son Tâshfîn.

His death, 1145 A.C.

Alphonso VII.

1147 A.C.

[1] Corrupted by the Christians into Almohade.

[2] Mohammed ibn Tumârt died in 524 A.H. (1130 A.C.), leaving the headship of his disciples to Abdul Momin.

1037—1466 A.C. fleet to their assistance.[1] His generals beat back the Christians, reduced the Almoravide governors who had assumed independent authority in several districts, and practically brought Andalusia under his sway. Four years later he divided his vast empire into provinces, and appointed his sons as governors over them.[2] In the
1160 A.C. year 554 A.H. he took Mahdièh[3] from the Franks, and
The Almohade Empire. assumed the title of *Ameer ul-Mominîn.* With the conquest of this important city he became the master of the whole of Northern Africa, from the deserts of Barca westward to the Atlantic.

Death of Abdul Momin, 1163 A.C. Abdul Momin died in the year 1163 A.C., after a successful reign of over thirty-three years. He was a fair man with blue eyes, austere, brave, wise and energetic, and favoured learned men. Learning and arts flourished in all parts of his empire, especially in Spain. He had established in Morocco numerous public colleges and schools. Upon his death his son Mohammed was first raised to the throne, but owing to his incapacity and idleness, the grandees of the empire deposed him, and
Accession of *Abû Yâkûb* Yusuf. elected in his place his brother *Abû Yâkûb* Yusuf. He was a humane and generous prince, and his elevation promised to the people a happy and prosperous reign. He came to Spain several times and re-conquered many
His death, Rabi I. 580 A.H. July 1184 A.C. cities, among others Tarragona and Santarem. Yusuf died in the year 1184 A.C., and was succeeded by his famous son Yâkûb, under whom the empire of the Almohades attained the highest pitch of glory. He is described as a wise and accomplished sovereign. A successful war

[1] Ibn ul-Athîr, vol. xi. p. 75.

[2] For example, Abû Mohammed Abdullâh, who succeeded him, held Bugia and its dependencies; Abu'l Hassan Ali, Fez, and Abû Saîd, Ceuta (*Sibta*), Algeciras (*al-Jazîrat ul-Khazrâ*, the Green Isle), Malaga, etc.

[3] See *post*, p. 594.

with Alfonso IX. of Castile had ended in a truce for five years. Hardly had it expired when the Castilian army, swelled by large bodies of volunteers from across the Pyrenees, invaded Andalusia, "plundering and slaying all before them, and committing horrible depredations and ravages." On receipt of this news Yâkûb crossed over from Africa. The Franks on their side collected troops "from the remotest parts of Christendom," and with a large army attacked the Almohade sovereign at a place called Alarcos (*al-Aark*) in the neighbourhood of Badajos.[1] They suffered a fearful defeat, in which it is said they lost one hundred and forty-six thousand men, besides thirty thousand prisoners. The remnant of the Christian army fled to Calatrava, where they fortified themselves, but the place was stormed. Alfonso fled to Toledo, where he gathered another large army to oppose the Almohade sovereign; he was again disastrously beaten. Calatrava, Guadalaxara, Madrid, Escelona, Salamanca, and other cities and fortresses, both in Spain and Portugal which had fallen into his hands were reconquered. In November 1196 A.C. Yâkûb laid siege to Toledo, which was reduced to the last extremity. "The mother of Alfonso, accompanied by his wives and daughters, then came out of the city, and, with tears in her eyes implored the conqueror to spare the city. Being moved to compassion, Yâkûb not only granted the request, but after paying them due honour, dismissed them with splendid presents in jewels and other valuable articles." After relieving Madrid, which was blockaded by the Aragonese, who incontinently took to flight on his approach, he returned to Seville. Here he abode

428—871 A.H.

Abû Yusuf Yâkûb, *al-Mansûr b'Illâh.*

Rajab 591 A.H. 1195 A.C.

Battle of Alarcos, 9 Shâbân, 591 A.H. 19 July 1195 A.C.

593 A.H. November 1196 A.C.

[1] Some say this battle took place at Marj ul-Hadîd (the *Iron Meadow*), a plain in the neighbourhood of Kalât Rabâh (Calatrava) to the north of Cordova.

1037—1466 A.C. for a year, discussing terms with the envoys of the Christian princes "who had come to sue for peace, which he granted."[1] He also made various dispositions regarding

Returns to Spain, 594 A.H. November 1197 A.C. His death, 22 Rabi II. 595 A.H., February 1199 A.C.

the government of Andalusia. Towards the end of 1197 he returned to his African dominions, where he remained until his death in 1199 A.C. Yâkûb was a contemporary of Saladin, and it was to him that the great sovereign of Asia had sent as ambassador the nephew of Ameer Osâma, soliciting his aid against the Crusaders. Yâkûb was a munificent patron of arts and letters. "He protected the learned," says an old writer, "because he was a scholar himself; he respected religion and manners because he was virtuous and pious." His army was well-disciplined, and kept under strict control. His government was firm and just. He established hospitals and infirmaries in every city within his dominions, where the sick and ailing received treatment, and the indigent and infirm were maintained and taken care of. The famous physicians Avenzoar (Ibn Zuhr) and Avenpace (Ibn Bâja) flourished in his reign. So did the philosopher and scientist Averroes[2] (Ibn Rushd), who held the post of Kâzi of Cordova. Like the Abbasside Rashîd and Mâmûn, and the Ommeyade sovereigns of Spain, he paid great attention to the irrigation of the country, and the comfort and safety of merchants and travellers, and embellished the cities of his empire with fine buildings. The famous observatory at Seville, now called the Giralda, was built by him after the battle of Alarcos.[3]

[1] Ibn Khaldûn.

[2] In 1196, it appears the bigots had complained to the Almohade Sultan about the heretical notions of Averroes, which led to his being sent to prison. But he was soon after released and restored to favour.

[3] The Christian Spaniards converted it into a belfry!

Yâkûb al-Mansûr was succeeded by his son Mohammed, who assumed the same title as Abdur Rahmân III., *an-Nâsir li-dîn-Illâh.*[1] An-Nâsir was very different from his father both in character and ability. Fond of pleasure and devoid of capacity, he became the primary cause of the ruin of the Almohade empire, and with it of the Saracenic cause in Spain. 428—871 A.H. Mohammed, *an-Nâsir li-dîn-Illâh*

The death of Yakûb al-Mansûr was the signal for the Christians to resume their attacks on Andalusia. Alphonso IX. of Castile (Ibn Adfunsh) again inundated the country round Seville and Cordova with his troops, and laid it waste with fire and sword. To avenge the atrocities committed on his subjects, an-Nâsir with a large army crossed over from Ceuta (Sibta). Shortly after his arrival in Seville he put to death Yusuf ibn Kâdis, the governor of Calatrava (Kalât Rabâh), for surrendering it to Alfonso. The execution of this officer, who was highly respected by the Andalusian Moslems, not only caused great discontent among them, but led to their defection on the field of battle. The news of an-Nâsir's preparations had caused a ferment among the Christian nations. Driven from Asia by the victorious arms of Saladin, the hordes of adventurers who, under the name of Crusaders, had harried Palestine and Syria, betook themselves to Spain. Innocent III. proclaimed a crusade, and Roderiquez, the Archbishop of Toledo, who had gone to Rome to solicit the aid of the Pope, preached everywhere a holy war against the Saracens. The kings of Castile, Aragon, Portugal, Leon, and Navarre, joined by a host of Crusaders from France, Italy, and Germany, marched against the Almohades. The two armies met at a place called al-Ukâb by the Arabs, and Las Navas de Tolosa by the Spaniards. At Battle of al-Aakâb, 29 Safar, 609 A.H. July 1212 A.C.

[1] "The helper of the religion of the Lord."

the first shock of battle the Andalusian contingent either left the field or deserted to the enemy. The Africans fought heroically, but were overwhelmed and destroyed to a man. An-Nâsir was with difficulty induced to leave the scene of disaster. From Seville he went to Morocco, where he died, it is said of grief and shame, in the year 1214 A.C.

Death of an-Nâsir, 611 A.H. May 1214 A.C.

Nâsir was succeeded on the throne of the *Muwwahaddîn* Caliphate by his son Yusuf, who assumed the title of *al-Mustansir b'Illâh.*[1] He was only sixteen years of age at the time, and naturally all the power fell into the hands of "the Shaikhs of the *Muwwahhidîn.*" He died in 1223 A.C., when Sîd[2] Abû Mohammed Abdul Wâhid was placed on the throne. Under him the Almohade princes and governors in Spain became practically independent. Upon Abdul Wâhid's assassination in the following year, the Almohades elected as their sovereign a son of al-Mansûr named Abû Mohammed, under the title of *al-Aâdil.* In the year 1227 A.C. a revolt broke out against al-Aâdil, who was killed by the rebels. Thereupon his brother Idrîs, who held the governorship of Seville, proclaimed himself Caliph, under the title of *al-Mâmûn.* Murcia and the greater part of Eastern Andalusia, however, under the leadership of Ibn Hûd,[3] fell away from him. In 1228 A.C., Mâmûn proceeded to Africa with a number of Christian auxiliaries furnished by the King of Castile.[4] His departure was

Yusuf *al-Mustansir b'Illâh.*

His death, 620 A.H. 1223 A.C.

Accession of Abdul Wâhid.

His assassination, 621 A.H. 1224 A.C.

Accession of Abû Mohammed *al-Aâdil,* 624 A.H. 1227 A.C.

Idrîs *al-Mâmûn.*

[1] "He who seeks help from the Lord."

[2] All the Almohade chiefs bore the title of *Sîd* (Syed), hence the Spanish Cid. The *Cid,* over whose name romance has thrown so much glamour, was a turncoat and a common brigand.

[3] Mohammed bin Yusuf bin Hûd.

626 A.C. 1228 A.H.

[4] On the conquest of Morocco, al-Mâmûn abolished all the institutions peculiar to the Muwwahhidîn. He died in 1242 A.C. (640 A.H.), and was succeeded by his brother as-Saîd, who was

the signal for a revolt in Seville, which, throwing off the yoke of the Almohades, acknowledged the authority of Ibn Hûd, who thus became the master of the greater part of Andalusia. The Almohades were either expelled or killed "by the infuriated mob." But Ibn Hûd[1] was not the only Spanish Arab who rose to power on the *débris* of the *Muwwahhidîn* empire. Zayyân (Abû Jamîl)[2] assumed the kingly title in Valencia; whilst Mohammed bin Yusuf, commonly known as *Ibn ul-Ahmar*, established himself in the city and fortress of Arjona.[3] Of all the aspirants to royal dignity Ibn ul-Ahmar proved the most successful, for he founded a kingdom in which centred for the next two centuries and a half the splendid civilisation of the Arabs. Ibn Khaldûn, who resided at Granada in the court of one of Ibn ul-Ahmar's successors, describes the rapid rise of this remarkable adventurer.[4] His ancestors had long been settled in Spain under the name of the Banû-Nasr, and under the Ommeyade Caliphs had held important offices in the *jund* or army. Mohammed, who was generally styled *the Shaikh*, was at this period the head of the Banû-Nasr, and by his character and ability exercised great

428—871 A.H.

Rise of Mohammed Ibn ul-Ahmar.

killed two years later, when Omar, another descendant of Abdul Momin, was raised to the throne under the title of *Murtaza b'Illâh* ("the accepted of the Lord"). Murtaza was put to death by Wâsik (Abû Dabûs) in 1266 A.C. Wâsik himself fell in 1269 A.C. (668 A.H.), in a battle with the Banû Marîn, a Berber tribe, who subjected the whole of Mauritania to their rule.

[1] He assumed the title of al-Mutawakkil.

[2] A descendant of Mardânîsh (Martinus), who had been removed from the chieftaincy of Badajoz by Yusuf bin Tâshfîn.

[3] Within the jurisdiction of Cordova.

[4] He was descended from Saad bin Obâda, chief (Syed) of the Khasraj in the time of the Prophet. The Banû-Nasr bore accordingly the title of al-Ansâri and al-Khasraji (*i.e.* belonging to the Ansâr and the tribe of Khasraj).

1037—1466 A.C. influence among his kinsmen. "When the fortunes of the *Muwwahhidîn* began to decline, and their affairs became weak, and the chiefs began to give up their castles to the enemy, Ibn ul-Ahmar also assumed the title of Sultan."[1]

629 A.H. 1231 A.C. "The whole of Andalusia," adds Ibn Khaldûn, "now became a prey to civil war," and the Castilians did not fail to take advantage of "the divisions and perversity" of the Saracen chiefs. They set one against the other, and destroyed each in turn. In the beginning of his reign, Ibn ul-Ahmar had entered into an alliance with the King of Castile,[2] in order to obtain his assistance against Ibn Hûd. The latter on his side gave the Christian thirty castles for similar aid against Ibn ul-Ahmar. And thus the conflict proceeded. In 1236 A.C. the Castilians captured Cordova; Valencia[3] fell into their hands two years later. In 1239 A.C. they took Acira, and in 1246 A.C. Murcia, finally driving Zayyân to Tunis. In 1248 A.C., after a protracted siege of fifteen months, Seville[4] capitulated to them.

The Castilians capture Cordova and Valencia.

Whilst the Castilians were thus destroying his rivals, Ibn ul-Ahmar contrived to gain possession of Xeres, Jaen, Granada, Malaga, and Almeria, and, by a combination of tact and ability of the highest order, consolidated his power in this small and shrunken kingdom, which was to make head for the next two hundred years against the combined forces of Christian Spain and

[1] Ibn Khaldûn, vol. iv. p. 170. The feudal lords were called *ashâb ul-maakâl*, "lords of castles."

[2] Ferdinand III.

[3] The city surrendered to Jayme (Jakmek), King of Aragon.

[4] For the last two years Seville (Ashbîlia) was practically a republic, the administration of affairs being vested in a council of five, presided over by Abu Fâris ibn Abu Hafs. Ibn ul-Ahmar co-operated with Ferdinand in the siege of Seville, as well as in the reduction of Carmona and other places.

Pavilion in the Court of Lions, Alhambra, Granada

Portugal, assisted by frequent relays of Crusaders from beyond the Pyrenees. But from the outset it was an unequal contest, and the final collapse of Ibn ul-Ahmar's kingdom was only a question of time. Still the struggle was heroically sustained to the very end. 428—871 A.H.

After the conquest of Granada Ibn ul-Ahmar made it the seat of his government, and assumed the title of *al-Ghâlib b'Illâh*.[1] He built for himself here the famous castle and palace of Alhambra (*al-Hamra*),[2] which was enlarged and still further embellished by his successors. Assumes the title of *al-Ghâlib b'Illâh.* The Alhambra.

The keystone of Ibn ul-Ahmar's policy was to keep in close amity with the Marînide sovereigns of Mauritania. And for this reason their names were joined with his in the prayers offered at the mosques within his kingdom. In 660 A.H. (1261 A.C.) a war broke out between him and his quondam ally, the Christian King of Castile, who invaded the kingdom of Granada, but was beaten back. Ibn ul-Ahmar died in 1272 A.C., and was succeeded by his son, *Abû Abdullâh* Mohammed. Himself a scholar and jurist,[3] he was a great patron of learning. In 1274 A.C. Granada was again invaded by the Castilians under a general called by the Arabs Don Nunoh (Nuño Gonzalez de Lara), but with the assistance of the Marînide sovereign[4] Mohammed defeated them in an action in which the Castilian chief lost his life. Eleven years later a fresh war broke out between the Castilians and Saracens, which lasted to the close of the century, and in which Mohammed was equally successful. He died in 1302 A.C., after a prosperous reign of over thirty years, Death of Ibn ul-Ahmar. 29 Jamadi II. 671 A.H. 24 Sept. 1272 A.C. Accession of *Abû Abdullâh* Mohammed (II.) *al-Fakîh.* 1295 A.C. His death, Shâbân 701 A.H. April 1302 A.C.

[1] "The conqueror by (the grace of) the Lord."

[2] The Red Palace. See *post*, p. 567.

[3] He bore the title of *al-Fakîh*, or Jurist.

[4] Yâkûb bin Abdul Hakk, and his son Yusuf, were two of the most powerful sovereigns of this dynasty.

1037—1466 A.C.

Accession of Abû Abdullâh Mohammed III. His abdication. Accession of Nasr. His abdication, 713 A.H. 1314 A.C. Accession of Abu'l Walîd Ismail. 716 A.H. 20 Rabi, 719 A.C. 12 May, 1319 A.C. Battle of Elvira; destruction of the Castilian army.

and was succeeded by his son, who bore the same name. He reigned with wisdom and ability until 1307 A.C., when a revolt on the part of his brother Nasr led to his abdication. Nasr proved an unlucky king. Immediately after his elevation he was attacked by the kings of Castile and Aragon, and was only able to buy them off by consenting to pay an annual tribute. In 1314 A.C. he was forced to vacate the throne in favour of Ismâil,[1] a grandson of Ismâîl, the brother of Ibn ul-Ahmar, the founder of the dynasty. In 1316 A.C. the Castilians captured from him a number of cities, although three years later he succeeded in inflicting on them a memorable defeat at Elvira.[2] In the year 1319 A.C., a large army was despatched by the Castilian king under the command of his son Pedro (Don Betroh) for the final subjugation of Granada. The Infante was accompanied by twenty-five princes, among them a prince of England who had joined the Castilians with an English contingent. All of them, including Don Pedro, fell in the action.

Assassination of Ismâil, 27 Rajab, 725 A.H. 18 July, 1325 A.C. *Abû Abdullâh* Mohammed IV. *Abu'l Hajjâj* Yusuf, 733 A.H. August 1333 A.C.

On the assassination of Ismâil in the year 1325 A.C., his son, *Abû Abdullâh* Mohammed, was raised to the throne. He proved a vigorous and successful ruler. In 1333 A.C. Gibraltar, which had been seized by the Christians, was wrested from their hands. Whilst returning from an inspection of the fortifications, Sultan Mohammed was attacked and killed by a band of assassins who lay concealed behind a rock. He was succeeded by his brother, *Abu'l Hajjâj* Yusuf, one of the most enlightened sovereigns of the Banû-Nasr dynasty. Under his just and liberal administration the kingdom

[1] His full name is given as Abu'l Walîd Ismâil bin Faraj bin Ismâil.

[2] Al-bîra of the Arabs, Illibiris of the Romans.

prospered, and the people were happy and contented. Like his ancestors he was a zealous patron of literature and science. Unluckily for the Moslems of Andalusia his reign did not last long, for in the year 1354 A.C. he was stabbed by a madman whilst performing his devotions in the mosque of his palace. He was succeeded by his son, also named Mohammed, who assumed the title of *al-Ghanî b'Illâh.*[1] Al-Ghanî was a cultured and scholarly sovereign, and encouraged and fostered learning and arts within his dominions. He had for his vizier the famous Ibn ul-Khatîb, surnamed *Lisân ud-dîn*, or "the Tongue of Religion," the historian of the Banû-Nasr dynasty.[2] During a temporary absence from the capital, al-Ghanî found himself displaced by his half-brother Ismâil. Al-Ghanî then proceeded to Africa, and took up his abode in Fez. Ismâil did not hold his ill-gotten power for long, for he was killed in a revolt headed by Abû Saîd, also called Abû Abdullâh Mohammed. Two years later Abû Saîd was forced to take refuge with the King of Castile, who murdered him for his riches. On the death of Abû Saîd, al-Ghanî returned to Granada, and was received by the fickle people with wild acclamations of joy. The remainder of his reign passed undisturbed, and the peace which, by his tact and skill, he maintained with the Castilians, enabled the kingdom to advance in wealth and prosperity. Arts and industry recovered their old activity in Granada; commerce brought to its door all the treasures of the Levant and the far East, and the country was fertilised by numerous new irrigation works. Al-Ghanî died in 1391 A.C., amidst universal mourning,

428—871 A.H.

His murder, 755 A.H. 1354 A.C.

Accession of Mohammed, *al-Ghanî b'Illâh.*

Displaced by Ismâil, 1359 A.C.

Revolt of Abû Saîd, 1360 A.C.

Murder of Abû Saîd, 1362 A.C.

Restoration of Al-Ghanî, 765 A.H. 1364 A.C.

Death of Al-Ghanî. 793 A.H. 1391 A.C.

Yusuf II.

[1] "Rich with the grace of the Lord."

[2] His history is called the *Târîkh Dowlat un-Nasrîeh*. He was a contemporary and friend of Ibn Khaldûn, "the Montesquieu of the Arabs." See *Appendix*.

1037— and was succeeded by his son, *Abû Abdullâh* Yusuf.
1466 A.C. The reign of this sovereign was not fortunate. Wishful himself to follow in the footsteps of his father, he desired to maintain amicable relations with the Castilians; but, as has often happened in modern times, popular excitement caused him to engage in a war which was not uniformly successful. The enthusiasm of the Granadans did not, however, last long, and Yusuf was able to conclude a peace on favourable terms with the young king Henry III.

Death of Yusuf II., 799 A.H. 1396 A.C. Mohammed VI.

Yusuf II. had designated his eldest son, also named Yusuf, a prince endowed with talent and virtue, as his successor; but on his death in 1396 A.C., the throne was seized by the younger Mohammed, who confined his brother in the castle of Salobrena. In 1405 A.C. the Castilian frontier guard raided into the territories of Granada. Instead of asking for redress from their king, Mohammed took in his own hand their punishment.

Death of Mohammed VI., 811 A.H. 1408 A.C. Accession of *Abû Abdullâh* Yusuf III.

In the war which followed the losses on the two sides were fairly balanced. On the death of Mohammed VI., in 1408 A.C., Sîd Yusuf was brought out from his prison and proclaimed king. The first care of Yusuf was to obtain a prolongation of the armistice with the Castilians. Two years later war broke out afresh between the two nations, which was equally inconclusive; and a short truce was followed by a treaty of peace, which lasted during the whole of Yusuf's lifetime. At this period the throne of Castile was occupied by the infant son of Henry III. under the regency of his mother. The Castilian Queen held the Saracen sovereign in the highest estimation, and the relations between the two were extremely cordial. Every year they forwarded rich presents to each other, and carried on a warm and active correspondence. Castilian and Aragonese cavaliers, aggrieved by their own government, frequently took shelter in Yusuf's court. Many came to Granada to settle questions of honour, which they invariably referred to his arbitration; and if it came to combat he often interfered to stop the battle and to bring about reconciliation between the contending parties. His kindness of heart, his justice, benevolence, and virtues endeared him to foreigners equally with his own people. The harmony which prevailed during his reign between the Castilians and the Saracens helped the latter in part to repair their losses, and to enjoy the blessings of peace, which had not been known for a long time. 428—871 A.H.

This good king died after a reign of fifteen years, to the sincere grief of all his subjects. With him ended the happy days of Granada. He was succeeded by his son Mohammed, surnamed *al-Aisar*, or the *left-handed*. Proud and morose, he soon made himself extremely unpopular among the Granadans. He stopped the tournaments and public fêtes so dear to Granada, and introduced various other regulations highly distasteful to its pleasure-loving people. Suddenly they rose in revolt and drove him from the capital. Recalled, he was again expelled, and the throne was seized by a noble named Yusuf, belonging to the royal family, who was assisted by John II.,[1] the King of Castile. Yusuf, however, died in a few months, and Mohammed VII. again recovered his kingdom. In 1433 A.C. the Castilians invaded Granada, and although they suffered a murderous defeat under the walls of Archidona, they laid waste a considerable part of the districts of Guadix (Wâdi-Âsh) and Granada proper. In 1444 A.C. Mohammed was finally deposed by his nephew, Ibn ul-

Death of Yusuf III. 827 A.H. 1423 A.C. Accession of Mohammed VII. (*al-Aisar*).

Yusuf al-Ahmari, 836 A.H. 1432 A.C.

848 A.H. 1444 A.C.

[1] The usurper expressly acknowledged himself the vassal of the Castilian king.

1037—1466 A.C. Ahnaf, also named Mohammed; and the people, won over by his largesses, acknowledged him as their king. A large body of nobles, however, betook themselves to Castile, and gave their adhesion to Saad, surnamed Ibn Ismâîl,[1] a cousin of Ibn ul-Ahnâf, who had taken refuge with John II. With a large body of Castilians, and accompanied by the malcontent nobles, Ibn Ismâîl invaded Granada, and for five years the Saracens were plunged in a cruel and sanguinary civil war. Ibn ul-Ahnaf was finally defeated in 1454 A.C., and Ibn Ismâîl seated himself on the throne of the Banû Ahmar. His first care was to send ambassadors and presents to Henry IV., the King of Castile, to obtain a renewal of the peace. The Castilian, however, refused the request and invaded Granada. The devastating war lasted several years, and the Saracens suffered grievously from the ravages of the Christian Spaniards. Their homesteads were reduced to ashes, their fields and plantations were ruthlessly destroyed, their beautiful palaces and mansions and the works of irrigation which fertilised the soil were irrevocably ruined. In such a conflict, the advantages were all on the side of the Christians, for even the victories of the Saracens brought no fruit; the Castilian centres of population were far away, and the kingdom of Granada was now cooped between the sea, the mountains of Elvira, and the chain of the Alpuxarras (*al-Bushârât*).[2] The Castilians surprised and captured Archidona and Gibraltar. These disasters broke the spirit of Ibn Ismâîl. He saw that if the war continued

Accession of Ibn Ismâîl, 859 A.H. 1454 A.C.

[1] A grandson of Sultan Yusuf II., by his son, the *Ameer* Ali.

[2] The valleys of the al-Bushârât were extremely fertile, and the flocks and herds of the hardy and warlike population who inhabited them, their vines, oranges, pomegranates, citron and mulberry-trees, added to the wealth of the kingdom.

longer the kingdom would be ruined altogether; he accordingly made every sacrifice for obtaining peace. He acknowledged Henry IV. as his suzerain, and bound himself to pay an annual tribute of twelve thousand pieces of gold, and this treaty was ratified in a personal interview between the two kings in the neighbourhood of Granada. The peace thus concluded lasted until the death of Ibn Ismâil in 1466 A.C.

428—871 A.H.

868 A.H. 1463 A.C.

Death of Ibn Ismâîl, 871 A.H. 1466 A.C.

CHAPTER XXX

THE SARACENS IN SPAIN (*continued*).

871—1016 A.H.; 1466—1610 A.C.

The last struggle—The siege of Granada—The capitulation—Treachery of Ferdinand and Isabella—The persecution of the Spanish Moslems—Final expulsion—The loss to Spain.

Accession of *Abu'l Hassan* Ali.

IBN ISMÂÎL was succeeded by his eldest son Ali, surnamed *Abu'l Hassan.*[1] Brave, chivalrous, and gifted, had he been supported by an united people he would probably have rivalled the glory of his ancestors, and kept his kingdom intact; but with a nation divided and torn by factions, the task before him was hopeless. The ruin was hastened by his own fiery recklessness and the rebellion of his son.

Ferdinand and Isabella, 1469 A.C.

In the year 1469 A.C. the marriage of Ferdinand and Isabella united the forces of Castile, Aragon, and Leon under one common standard. Both equally fanatical, both alike regarding it a pious duty to burn or slaughter infidels and heretics, both alike determined to put an end to the last remnant of civilisation in Spain, they waited impatiently for the termination of the truce which, at their instance, and in consequence of the troubles within their own dominions, had been concluded with Abu'l Hassan. But the haughty refusal of the King of Granada to pay the tribute agreed upon by his father[2]

[1] Corrupted by the Spaniards into Alboacen.

[2] His message in answer to the demand for tribute was proud and haughty. "Tell your master the kings who paid tribute are dead; our mints no longer coin gold but only spear-heads."

rankled within them. The longed-for opportunity was supplied by Abu'l Hassan himself. No sooner did the truce expire, than he recklessly commenced the war by attacking and carrying by assault, in a storm of wind and rain, the township of Zahara. The capture of this township unloosed upon him and his kingdom the avalanche of savagery and fanaticism, which only the internal convulsions in Northern Spain had hitherto prevented from rolling down on Granada. Thinking men among the Saracens considered the rashness of the King as the harbinger of evil to their own principality. In the reception-hall of the King an old *fakîh* gave expression to this foreboding. "Woe is me!" said he. "The ruins of Zahara will fall on our own heads; the days of the Moslem Empire in Spain are now numbered!" Perceiving the difficulty of recapturing Zahara, which had been strongly garrisoned by Abu'l Hassan, the Castilians on their side made a sudden night attack on the fortified township of al-Hamah (Alhama), which, situated at the foot of the mountains fifteen leagues from the capital, guarded the entrance into the Granadan territories. In spite of a heroic defence the place was taken by assault and turned into a human shamble. Even the women and children, who had taken refuge in the cathedral mosque, were mercilessly slaughtered by the Castilians. Thus fell Alhama—one day a flourishing city, the next a vast tomb; its beautiful streets one day promenaded by a happy people, the next heaped with slaughtered corpses. The fall of Alhama foreshadowed the doom of Granada; and a general wail went up from the Moslem population at the cruel fate of its citizens and garrison. They cursed the folly which had led to the disaster. Abu'l Hassan made two attempts to retake the city: the first failed; in the second he was

Capture of Zahara, 871—1016 A.H.

The fall of Alhama, 887 A.H. February 1482 A.C.

1466–1610 A.C. nearly successful, when the news of an insurrection in the capital, headed by his son Abû Abdullâh Mohammed,[1] paralysed his arms. The evils of polygamy showed themselves at this grave crisis in the fortunes of the Spanish Moslems. Abu'l Hassan had two wives, one the daughter of his uncle, named Âyesha, the other a Spanish (Christian) lady of high birth.[2] To the latter and her children he was devotedly attached. Âyesha, jealous of the influence exercised by her Spanish rival, instigated her son, the notorious Boabdil, to rise against his father. Bribed by the mother, a portion of the garrison and the people accepted the young man as their king. Abu'l Hassan hastened back to Granada, which became a field of carnage on both sides. A short truce between father and son enabled the old King to relieve Loja or Loxa
27 Jamâdi I., 887 A.H. July 1482 A.C. (Losha), which was besieged by the Castilians, and to capture Canète. But these successes were of no avail, for he learnt that his rebel son had succeeded in seizing the Castle of Alhambra, and had virtually made himself master of the whole of Granada. Abu'l Hassan then fell back on Malaga, of which his brother Abû Abdullâh Mohammed, surnamed az-Zaghal,[3] was the governor. The cities of Guadix and Baeza (Basta) alone remained under his authority.

Safar, 888 A.H. March 1483 A.C. Ferdinand and Isabella, burning to avenge the check sustained by their troops before Loxa, dispatched a strong force into the province of Malaga, which at first

[1] Corrupted by the Spaniards into Boabdil. The Granadans called him the Little King, *as-Sultan as-Saghîr*; and accordingly in the Spanish chronicles he is called *El-Rey-Chico*. In the following pages I shall call him Boabdil.

[2] She was the daughter of the Castilian Alcayde of Bedmar. Her name was Isabel de Solis, but among the Saracens she was called Zuhrâ (Venus).

[3] "The valiant or comely (youth)."

met with great success, "if we can call by that name the 871—1016 A.H.
burning of harvests, the cutting down of olive trees and vines, the destruction of flourishing villages, the lifting of cattle, and the butchery of defenceless human beings."[1] The Castilians, who were thus pleasantly engaged, were attacked by az-Zaghal and his lieutenant Rizwân in the mountains of Axarquia (*ash-Sharkia*) and routed with terrible slaughter.[2] The Saracen cause was not entirely hopeless, but a new incident, of which the traitor Boabdil was the author, altered the whole course of events. Desirous of emulating the achievements of his uncle, az-Zaghal, whose name was now on the lips of the volatile Granadans, the unlucky Boabdil attacked the Castilian town of Lucena, was disastrously beaten and taken prisoner. At this juncture Abu'l Hassan abdicated the throne in favour of the brave az-Zaghal, and retired with his family and effects to Illora,[3] and thence to Almuñecar, where he died soon after. The capture of Boabdil was regarded by Ferdinand and Isabella as a providential help rendered to their cause, for they saw in him the fittest instrument for perpetuating the discord in Granada, dividing its military resources, and ultimately destroying the ill-fated kingdom. Weak, vacillating, and pusillanimous, he was "mere wax" in the hands of the astute and masterful Ferdinand. He was soon persuaded to become their faithful vassal. "As soon as they felt they had completely mastered their tool," they sent him back towards Granada well supplied with men, money, and other requisites. With the assistance of the Castilians who formed his escort, and a number of Granadans

[1] Condé.

[2] This Castilian disaster is graphically described by Washington Irving.

[3] Ancient Illiris.

1466–1610 A.C. who had been bribed by Âyesha, he seized the suburb of Albaezin,[1] and Granada was again plunged in a destructive civil war. Az-Zaghal proposed to Boabdil that they should reign together, and jointly oppose the common enemy; but the incapable young man refused all overtures.[2] The Castilians took advantage of this suicidal struggle between az-Zaghal and Boabdil to capture in succession Alora, Kasr-Bonela, Ronda, and other important cities. Loxa, before which they had failed several times, was reduced in 1486 A.C., and Malaga fell a year later. Once did az-Zaghal issue to relieve this city, but was actually prevented by Boabdil, who was base enough to congratulate Ferdinand on the conquest of this Moslem city. Although these places had surrendered or capitulated on a solemn pledge of security and protection to the inhabitants, once in possession the saintly Ferdinand did not hesitate to break his pledged word; the people were either reduced to slavery or expelled from their homes and country. Baeza, Almeria, Vera, Huescar, and a few other places alone remained in the hands of az-Zaghal. The perfidious Ferdinand entered into a secret compact with Boabdil to give to him all the territories he would conquer from az-Zaghal; and the miserable traitor fully relied on this promise in the fear that if he did not help the Castilians, az-Zaghal, who had beaten Ferdinand in several engagements, would turn him out of Granada. Ferdinand was thus able to fall with all his forces upon Baeza. Az-Zaghal, driven

[1] So called because it was inhabited by people from Baeza, "people at all times noted," says an old writer, "for their proneness to rebellion."

[2] It was at this time that the patriotic family of the Banû Sirâj (the Abencerrages) were inveigled by the Zegris (the partisans of the traitor Boabdil) and destroyed to a man.

to desperation, appealed to the Moslem sovereigns of Africa, just then fighting amongst themselves. The appeal proved fruitless; nevertheless the Saracens maintained a sturdy defence, and az-Zaghal repeatedly drove back the Castilians from the walls of his capital; but the tactics of Ferdinand finally starved the city into capitulation. As usual, the terms on which the submission was obtained were broken immediately afterwards, and the citizens were ruthlessly expelled from their homes, and their goods and chattels seized by the pious King and Queen. The governors of the castles and towns in the Alpuxarras (al-Bushârât) were gradually bribed into submission. Az-Zaghal, who had, until now, fought heroically for the freedom of his people, was at last induced to make his submission to Ferdinand and Isabella. He was allotted the district of Andarax, with the title of king, but was not allowed long to remain in the enjoyment of his small territory, for a year later he was exiled to Africa. Nothing now remained in the hands of the Saracens except Granada and its immediate dependencies. Boabdil, to whom the fall of az-Zaghal had come as a relief, was speedily undeceived as to the intentions of his Christian patrons regarding himself. No sooner was az-Zaghal disposed of than they called upon Boabdil to surrender Granada. His refusal supplied to Ferdinand the pretext for laying waste with fire and sword the fertile territories of Granada. After converting the Vega into a "vast expanse of desolation" he retired to Cordova. It was now war to the knife; the Saracens, under the leadership of Musa bin Abi'l Ghâzân, one of their most valorous knights, whose words had put some life even into the heart of the pusillanimous Boabdil, resolved once more to carry the war into the enemy's country, and they actually succeeded

871—1016 A.H.

Fall of Baeza, 10 Moharram, 895 A.H. 4 Dec. 1489 A.C.

1466–1610 A.C.

Jamâdi II. 896 A.H. March 1491 A.C.

in capturing some of the frontier posts. But with the return of spring Ferdinand again entered the plains of Granada with an army consisting of forty thousand foot and ten thousand horse, and commenced anew the work of devastation. The crops and fruit trees were destroyed, the homesteads reduced to ashes, and the defenceless inhabitants either butchered, outraged, or mutilated. The cordon was drawn tighter and tighter round the last stronghold of civilisation in Spain, and the harried people of the Vega took refuge within the walls of the capital.

Granada besieged.

"For ten years they had disputed every inch of ground with their invaders; wherever their feet could hold they had stood firm against the enemy. But now there was left to them nothing beyond their capital, and within its walls they shut themselves up in sullen despair." The dispositions for the defence were excellently conceived, and for a time were ably carried out. As yet the communications between the capital and the Alpuxarras (al-Bushârât) were not interrupted, and convoys with provisions came constantly for the besieged from the districts of Sierra Nevada (the Jabâl-Shulair), whilst vigorous sorties led by Mûsa himself kept the enemy at bay. In the single combats, which were of daily occurrence in front of the Castilian camp, the Saracen cavaliers almost invariably killed their antagonists. The loss of his best knights in these encounters determined Ferdinand to convert the siege into a blockade, and to starve the Saracens into surrender. "Every patch of ground beyond the city walls was seized by the enemy, and all

Moharram, 897 A.H. November 1491 A.C.

access from outside was barred, so that it became impossible for the besieged to gather any crops or to receive supplies from the neighbouring districts. Provisions grew every day more scarce, and by the month

Famine in the city.

of Safar the privations of the people became almost

intolerable."[1] A desperate attempt to break the cordon failed owing to the weakness of the famished infantry of Granada. Reduced to terrible straits, the besieged at last determined upon a surrender. "Famine did the work that no mere valour could effect." Delegates were sent to the Castilian camp to arrange the conditions of capitulation, and after a long conference the following terms were settled: That, in case the Saracens were not relieved within the space of two months, either by land or sea, the city of Granada should be delivered over to the Christians; that the King, his generals, viziers and shaikhs, with all the people, should take the oath of obedience to the Castilian sovereigns, and that Boabdil should receive some property in the Alpuxarras; that the Moslems "great and small," should be perfectly secure in person, and that they should preserve, with their liberty, the full and unrestricted enjoyment and possession of their property, their arms, and their horses; that they should be allowed the free and unmolested exercise of their religion; that their mosques and religious foundations should remain intact; that the *muezzin* should not be interrupted in his call to prayers; that they should retain their manners, usages, customs, language, and dress; that their laws should be administered to them by their own magistrates; that transactions between them and the Christians should be dealt with by mixed tribunals; that they should not be subjected to any taxes beyond what they paid to their sovereigns; that no Christian should enter forcibly the house of a Moslem, or insult him in any way; that all the Moslem captives should be liberated; that all Saracens who might wish to cross over to Africa should be allowed to take their departure within a fixed time, and be conveyed thither

871—1016 A.H.

Safar, 897 A.H. December 1491 A.C.

Terms of capitulation.

[1] Makkarî.

1466–1610 A.C. in the Castilian ships, without any payment except the mere charge for passage; and that after the expiration of that time no Moslem should be hindered from departing, provided he paid, in addition to the price of his passage, a tenth of whatever property he might carry along with him; that no one should be prosecuted and punished for the crime of another man; that any Christian who had embraced Islâm should not be compelled to relinquish it, and adopt his or her former creed; that any Moslem wishing to become Christian should be allowed some days to consider the step he was about to take, after which he was to be questioned both by a Moslem and a Christian judge concerning his intended change, and if, after this examination, he still refuse to return to Islâm, he should be permitted to follow his own inclination; that no Moslem should be subject to have Christian soldiers billeted upon him, or to be transported from his home against his will; that any Moslem choosing to travel or reside among the Christians should be perfectly secure in his person and property; and that no badge or distinctive mark should be put on them, as was done with the Jews.

Mûsa alone raised his voice against the capitulation. He warned them not to rely on the delusive and treacherous promises of the Castilians, and implored them to make one supreme effort to break the leaguer. "Death is sweeter," he said, "than the pain and shame of servitude. Do you believe that the Castilians would observe faithfully their promises? You are deceived. The enemy is thirsting for our blood. But death is nothing to what he has in store for us—injury, outrage, humiliation, degradation; the plunder of our homes, the dishonour of our wives and daughters, the profanation of our mosques—in a word, oppression, injustice, and intolerance. Already the fagots have been alighted to reduce us into cinders."[1] His words had no effect. The brave knight, with a glance of contempt and indignation at his compatriots assembled in council, mounted his charger and rode forth from the city by the gate of Elvira never to return. "It is said that as he rode he encountered a party of Christian knights, half a score strong, and, answering their challenge, slew many of them before he was unhorsed, and then, disdaining their offers of mercy, fought stubbornly upon his knees till he was too weak to continue the struggle: with a last effort he cast himself into the river Xenil, and, heavy with armour, sank to the bottom."

871–1016 A.H.

Death of Mûsa.

Messengers had been despatched to implore the help of the Sultans of Egypt and Rûm, but the period of grace expired without any sign of relief; and on January 3, 1492 A.C., the Castilians took possession of Granada. It was indeed "an ill-omened hour when the Cross supplanted the Crescent on the towers of Granada;" for with the conquest of that city by the Christian Spaniards died for ever the intellectual life and industrial activity of the Peninsula.

Surrender of Granada, 2 Rabi I. 897 A.H. January, 1492 A.C.

Boabdil and his family took the road to the Alpuxarras, where he was to abide. When he reached the mountains of Padul he cast a last long look at Granada and wept. His mother, hitherto his evil genius, turned upon him with the words, "Yes, you may well weep like a woman at the loss of what you could not defend like a man."[2] At Andarax Boabdil lived for a while, but

[1] The Inquisition was started in Seville in 1480 A.C., and it commenced its murderous work by burning seven Jews in one *auto da fe*.

[2] The spot whence Boabdil took his sad farewell look of Granada bears to this day the name of *El ultimo sospiro del Moro*—"The last sigh of the Moor."

1466-1610 A.C. his presence in Spain was regarded by Ferdinand as dangerous to the Castilian sovereignty, and he was soon banished to Africa. He then went to Fez, where he abode until his death in 1538 A.C.[1]

Death of Boabdil, 940 A.H. 1538 A.C.

Neither the pious Ferdinand nor the saintly Isabella meant to abide by the capitulation concluded with the Moslems, who were soon reminded of the ominous warning of their last hero by the fate of the Jews. These people had prospered under the tolerant rule of the Saracens; their wealth attracted the cupidity of the Castilian sovereigns. In 1492 A.C., Ferdinand, who always concealed his perfidious policy in the cloak of religion, and lavished promises where he meant to deceive, promulgated a decree that they should either abandon their religion or leave the country. They were burnt, tortured, or exiled. Simultaneously with the decree against the Jews, the terms settled with the Moslems began to be infringed; they were subjected to every humiliation and injury; their religion and laws were proscribed, and many of them were forcibly baptised. The treachery of the Castilians caused great resentment among the Moslem population, and the Albaezin rose in arms, which only led to further ill-treatment. In 1498 A.C. the ferocious Ximenes started a universal persecution. They were enjoined within a certain time to embrace "the religion of the idolators" or to submit to death. Some yielded, but a majority clung to their faith, and betook themselves to the mountains of Alpuxarras. Here they were attacked by their persecutors. Not content with massacring the men, the Castilians blew up

The beginning of the persecution.

904 A.H. 1498 A.C. Persecution by Ximenes.

Castilian cruelty.

[1] He left two sons, Yusuf and Ahmed, whose descendants were visited by an Arabian writer of the seventeenth century; they were reduced to the necessity of living on the charity dispensed from mosques.

by gunpowder a mosque where the women and children of a wide dictrict had taken refuge. In spite of the odds against them the Moslems defended themselves bravely, and in 1501 A.C. gained a victory at Jabâl Balânsa, which obtained for the survivors and their families an exit to Morocco, Turkey, and Egypt. Their goods and chattels, however, were seized by their Christian majesties. Those that remained, and they were still numerous, were compelled at the point of the sword to make a profession of Christianity. Although nominally Christians, "they were not so in their hearts, for they worshipped God in secret, and performed their prayers and ablutions at the proper hours."[1] "They took care to wash off the holy water with which their children were baptised as soon as they were out of the priest's sight; they came home from their Christian weddings to be married again after the Mohammedan rite. A wise and honest government, respecting its pledges given at the surrender of Granada, would have been spared the danger of this hidden disaffection, but the rulers of Spain were neither wise nor honest in their dealings with the Moriscoes, and as time went on they became more and more cruel and false."[2] These nominal Christians were watched with the greatest vigilance, and any sign of backsliding brought upon the hapless offender the punishment of the Inquisition. The fires of the *auto da fé* were lighted at Granada, at Cordova, and at Seville, and from day to day the flames devoured numbers of men, women, and children. In order to prevent a rising the use of every sharp instrument, even to the smallest knife, was interdicted, and so the unlucky descendants of the race that had conquered Spain bore patiently the tortures and outrages to which they were subjected. In

871–1016 A.H.

[1] Makkarî. [2] Lane-Poole.

1466–1610 A.C. 1568 A.C. their condition became intolerable. Not satisfied with despoiling their victims of property and privileges, reducing them to a hideous servitude in the land where they had once reigned, "the Christians sought their extermination—the destruction of the very memory of their glorious existence." The mad fanatic Philip II. occupied the throne of Spain at this time. And the Archbishop of Granada, equally ferocious and fanatical, obtained from him a decree requiring the Arabs to abandon their language, their customs, their manners, and all their institutions in a day. "'The infidels' were ordered to abandon their picturesque costume, and to assume the hats and breeches of the Christians; to give up bathing, and adopt the dirt of their conquerors; to renounce their language, their customs and ceremonies, even their very names, and to speak Spanish, behave Spanishly, and re-name themselves Spaniards." "The wholesale denationalisation of the people was more than any folk, much less the descendants of the Almanzors and the Abencerrages, could stomach."[1] Driven to desperation they rose in arms. It was a hopeless struggle. After three years of incessant fighting the insurrection was crushed by the notorious Don Juan of Austria,[2] by wholesale butchery and devastation. Men and women and children were butchered under his own eyes, and the villages and valleys of the Alpuxarras were turned into November 1570 A.C. human shambles. The poor people who took refuge in caves were smoked to death. There still remained a large number of Moriscoes, as they were called, in Valencia and Murcia. In 1610 A.C. Philip III. completed the work begun by his father; over half a million of inoffensive people were forcibly deported

[1] Lane-Poole.

[2] A natural son of Charles V. by his mistress, Barbara Bromberg.

to Africa and thrown upon its shores without means or money. Those who lived in the interior, and whose number is said to have amounted to no less than two hundred thousand, unhappy remnant of a once powerful and prosperous nation, were mercilessly driven across the frontier into France, whence such as survived the cruelties of the Spaniards or the hardships of the road, took ship to the countries of Islâm. From the fall of Granada to the reign of Philip III. three millions of people were driven out of the Peninsula!

871–1016 A.H.

Final expulsion of the Spanish Arabs.

Thus disappeared from the soil of Spain a brave, ingenious and enlightened nation, whose active industry had brought back to life the Peninsula that had lain dead and barren under the indolent pride of the Goths; who had turned Andalusia into a garden, and had held aloft the torch of knowledge when all around lay in darkness; who had spread culture, given impetus to civilisation, and established chivalry—who had, in fact, created modern Europe. And what has Spain gained by the expulsion of the Moors? Fair Andalusia, for centuries the home of culture, learning, and arts, has relapsed into sterility and become a synonym for intellectual and moral desolation. "An eternal gloom," to use the eloquent words of Condé,[1] "envelopes the countries which their presence had brightened and enriched. Nature has not changed; she is as smiling as ever; but the people and their religion have changed. Some mutilated monuments still dominate over the ruins which cover a desolate land; but from the midst of these monuments, of these cold ruins comes the cry of Truth, 'Honour and glory to the vanquished Arab, decay and misery for the conquering Spaniard.'" Another European writer describes still more graphically the loss inflicted by fanaticism in Spain.

[1] Himself a Spaniard.

1466–1610 A.C. "The misguided Spaniards knew not what they were doing. The exile of the Moors delighted them; nothing more picturesque and romantic had occurred for some time. Lope de Vega sang about the *sentencia justa* by which Philip III., *despreciando sus barbaros tesoros*, banished to Africa *las ultimas reliquias de los Moros.* Velazquez painted it in a memorial picture; even the mild and tolerant Cervantes forced himself to justify it. They did not understand that they had killed their golden goose. For centuries Spain had been the centre of civilisation, the seat of arts and sciences, of learning, and every form of refined enlightenment. No other country in Europe had so far approached the cultivated dominion of the Moors. The brief brilliancy of Ferdinand and Isabella, and of the empire of Charles V., could found no such enduring pre-eminence. The Moors were banished; for a while Christian Spain shone, like the moon, with a borrowed light; then came the eclipse, and in that darkness Spain has grovelled ever since. The true memorial of the Moors is seen in desolate tracts of utter barrenness, where once the Moslem grew luxuriant vines and olives and yellow ears of corn; in a stupid, ignorant population where once wit and learning flourished; in the general stagnation and degradation of a people which has hopelessly fallen in the scale of the nations, and has deserved its humiliation." [1]

[1] Lane-Poole.

CHAPTER XXXI

RETROSPECT

The Kingdom of Granada—The city—The Alhambra—Al-Generaliffe—Arts and learning in Granada—Dress—General Review of Spain under the Arabs—Government—The Functionaries—Economic condition - Manufactures—Agriculture—The fine arts—Learning—Position of women—The women scholars—Pastimes.

THE kingdom of Granada comprised those parts of Spain which lie in the south-eastern corner of the peninsula; and, in its most flourishing period, never exceeded seventy leagues in length from east to west, and twenty-five in breadth from north to south. Within this narrow circuit it contained all the physical resources of a great empire. Its broad valleys were intersected by mountains rich in mineral wealth, whose hardy population supplied the state with husbandmen and soldiers. Its pastures were fed by abundant streams, and its coasts were studded with commodious ports, the principal marts of the Mediterranean. It possessed thirty cities, eighty fortified towns, and several thousand walled townships and villages.[1] The plain or Meadow (*Ghoṭat*) of Granada, now called the Vega de Granada, the arena of the death-struggle, covered a space of thirty leagues.

The Kingdom of Granada.

[1] Under the Arab domination, on the banks of the Guadalquiver alone there were twelve thousand villages or small towns.

Watered by the Shenîl[1] (Xenil), Daroh (Darro),[2] and three other rivers issuing from the neighbouring mountains of the Jabâl Shulair (Sierra Nevada), and studded in every direction with orchards, gardens, groves, palaces, mansions, villas, and vineyards, the Meadow presented a rare spectacle of luxuriance and beauty. Around the gardens lay fields clothed with perpetual verdure. The Arabs exhausted on the Vega all their elaborate powers of cultivation. They distributed the waters of the Xenil and Darro into numberless channels, and obtained by their skill and labour a succession of fruit and cereals throughout the year. They successfully cultivated products of the most opposite latitudes. Large quantities of silk and flax were exported from the ports of Almeria and Malaga to the Italian cities then rising into opulence. Their manufactures were varied and numerous, and each city was noted for a special industry. The ports of the Ahmarite kingdom swarmed with the shipping of Europe, Levant, and Africa, and its capital, as the chief centre of a remarkable commercial activity, had "become the common city of all nations."[3] The citizens of Granada were universally reputed and honoured for their probity and trustworthiness, and their mere word was considered surer than the Christian Spaniard's document. Besides textile fabrics and precious metals they exported large quantities of raw produce, especially flax and silk. Florence derived her principal supply of this article from the ports of Almeria and Malaga.

Granada, called by the Arabs Gharnâta, stood "like a watch-tower" in the Meadow. It rested, as it does now,

[1] Also called Shinjîl, the Singilis of the Romans.

[2] The Hadârah of Ibn ul-Khatîb, and the Salon of the Romans.

[3] The Genoese and Florentines had mercantile establishments in Granada.

partly in the Vega and partly on the slope of the hills, on which her elevated and populous suburbs were entirely built. The rippling Darro flowed through the city, and after supplying its numerous mansions, markets, mills, and baths, winded its course into the plain below. In the days of the Banû-Nasr, Granada was encompassed by a strong wall, pierced with twenty gates, and was flanked by a thousand and thirty towers. The castle (Kassâba) stood in the centre. Every house in the city had its own garden planted with orange, lemon, citron, laurel, myrtle, and other odoriferous trees and plants, and its separate supply of running water. Beautiful fountains for the comfort and convenience of the public were to be found in large numbers in every street. The houses were extremely elegant, and beautifully ornamented with damasquina work. The population of the city towards the middle of the fifteenth century amounted to four hundred thousand souls.

The city of Granada.

On the summit of one of the hills opposite, Ibn ul-Ahmar built the fortress or city of *al-Hamra*,[1] which was capable of holding within its circuit forty thousand men.

It is impossible within the space at my command to do justice to "this fabric of the genii." The towers, citadels, and palaces, with their light and elegant architecture, the graceful porticos and colonnades, the domes and ceilings still glowing with tints which have lost none of their original brilliancy; the airy halls, constructed to admit the perfume of the surrounding gardens; the numberless fountains over which the owners had such perfect control, that the water could be made high or

[1] *Medînât ul-Hamrâ* (corrupted into Alhambra), "the Red City or Palace," called either from his name of Ibn ul-Ahmar ("the son of the Red Man"), or from the colour of the materials used in its construction.

low, visible or invisible at pleasure, sometimes allowed to spout in the air, at other times to spread out in large, oblong sheets, in which were reflected buildings, fountains, and serene azure sky; the lovely arabesques, paintings and mosaics finished with such care and accuracy as to make even the smallest apartments fascinating, and illuminated in varied shades of gold, pink, light blue, and dusky purple; the lovely dados of porcelain mosaic of various figures and colours; the beautiful Hall of Lions with its cloister of a hundred and twenty-eight slender and graceful columns, its blue-and-white pavement, its harmony of scarlet, azure and gold; the arabesques glowing with colour like the pattern on a cashmere shawl, its lovely marble filagree filling in the arches, its beautiful cupolas, its famous alabaster cup in the centre; the enchanting Hall of Music, where the Court sat and listened to the music of the performers in the tribunes above; the beautiful seraglio with its delicate and graceful brass lattice work and exquisite ceilings; the lovely colouring of the stalactites in the larger halls and of the conical linings in the smaller chambers—all these require a master's pen to describe.

Al-Generaliffe.

Opposite to the al-Hamrâ, on the side of a steep mountain, stands the celebrated royal villa of Al-Generaliffe,[1] and like the Red Palace, is within the enclosure of the walls of the city. "It also," to use the words of a clever writer, "was a marvel of beauty with fountains, groves, and flowers, though little is left of their old glory but a few gigantic cypresses[2] and myrtles." The gardens were terraced in the form of an amphitheatre, and were

[1] Corrupted from the Arabic *al-Jâmaa-ul-Aârif*, "the mosque of the Knower (or Supervisor)," from an exquisite mosque attached to the villa.

[2] Still called the Queen's Cypresses.

irrigated by streams issuing from the summit of the mountains, which, after forming numerous cascades, lost themselves among the trees and flowering shrubs.

The sovereigns of Granada[1] rivalled the Caliphs of Cordova in their patronage of learning and arts, and in the construction of sumptuous public works; and under their liberal and enlightened government, Granada became the home and birth-place of eminent scholars, distinguished poets, accomplished soldiers, "men fit in every respect to serve as models." Her daughters were no less famous in literature, and the names of Nazhûn,[2] Zainab, Hamda,[3] Hafsah, al-Kalayyèh,[4] Safia,[5] Maria[6] shed an ineffaceable lustre on the land of their birth. It was not polite literature alone that was fostered and encouraged by the Arab kings of Granada. History, geography, philosophy, astronomy, the naturai and exact

Learning and Arts.

Women scholars.

[1] They also appear to have assumed the title of Caliphs.

[2] Nazhûn, the daughter of Abû Bakr al-Ghassâni, an eloquent poetess, well versed in history and literature, flourished towards the end of the sixth century of the Hegira.

[3] Zainab and Hamda were the daughters of Ziâd, the bookseller, and lived at a place called Wâdi ul-Hama (pronounced as Waudi), in the neighbourhood of Granada. Ibn ul-Abbâr in his *Tuhfat ul-Kadîm* says, "They were both excellent poetesses, thoroughly versed in all branches of learning and science; they were beautiful, rich, amiable, and modest. Their love of learning brought them into the company of scholars, with whom they mixed on perfect terms of equality with great composure and dignity, and nobody could accuse them of forgetting the rules of their sex."

[4] Hafsah and Kalayyèh were both natives of Granada.

[5] Safia was a native of Seville. In addition to distinguished oratorical and poetical talents, she excelled all others in the calligraphic art; "so that her penmanship was at once the subject of admiration and an example to be copied by the most skilful scribes."

[6] Maria, the daughter of Abû Yâkûb al-Faisali, has been called the Arabian Corinna; she also was eminent for her learning and scholarship.

sciences in general, medicine and music were cultivated with equal earnestness.

Universities. The government of each academy was entrusted to a rector, who was chosen from among the most distinguished scholars. In the middle of the thirteenth century of the Christian era this high office in the university of Granada was held by Sirâj ud-din Abû Jaafar Omar al-Hakami. No religious distinction was made in these appointments, and learned Jews and Christians were often appointed to the post of rector. Real learning, in the estimation of the Arabs, "was of greater value than the religious opinion of the literate."

It was customary in the Spanish Arabian universities to hold annual commemorations and periodical meetings, to which the public were invited. On these occasions poems were recited and orations delivered by the most eminent persons in the universities. Every college had the following lines inscribed over its gates—"The world is supported by four things only: the learning of the wise, and the justice of the great, the prayers of the good, and the valour of the brave."

Chivalry. After the fall of Cordova chivalry found a congenial home at Granada, where it attained its highest development. As in the capital of the Caliphs, women occupied a pre-eminent position, mingled freely in the society of men, and by their presence enlivened the fêtes, tourneys, and the perpetual succession of spectacles which delighted the Granadans. Much of the chivalrous spirit and gallantry for which the Saracens of Granada were conspicuous was undoubtedly due to the ennobling influence of women. The Arab cavalier entered the lists, or went to war with some device emblazoned on his arms, either a heart pierced with darts, a star directing a vessel, or the initial letter of the name of his lady-love. The knights contended openly in her presence for the prize of valour, and often joined her in the graceful dance of the zambra. It is said that the women were handsome, mostly of a middle stature, witty, and brilliant in conversation. Their dress consisted of costly robes of the finest linen, silk, or cotton with a girdle and kerchief. The historian, Ibn ul-Khatîb, characterises their "luxury of dress" as a madness. Perfumes were used to a lavish extent, and women, especially ladies of rank, were passionately fond of decorating themselves with hyacinths, chrysolites, emeralds, and other gems, together with ornaments of gold and precious stones; and such was the variegated splendour of their appearance when in the mosques, that they have been compared to "the flowers of spring in a beautiful meadow."

Men's head-dress.

The turban as an article of head-dress was long ago discarded among men who followed the profession of arms. In Valencia, Murcia, and the Eastern provinces generally even the Kâzis and *Fakihs* had abandoned its use, and taken to caps.[1] A contemporary writer[2] speaks of a distinguished *Allâmah* (*Ulema*) entering bare-headed the presence of the Sultan of Murcia. "And," he goes on to say, "Ibn Hûd[3] never wore a turban, nor did Ibn ul-Ahmar."

In the western districts, like Cordova and Seville, Kâzis and *Fakîhs* generally wore turbans, but they were of much smaller dimensions than those in vogue in Asia. And we are told that the Spanish Moslems

[1] These caps were probably the *kalansuèh* (see *ante*, p. 451) reduced to a reasonable size, something in the shape of the Persian *kulâh*, but most likely not so high. Dozy, in his *Dictionnaire des Noms des Vêtements Arabes*, quoting Nuwairi, says the *kalansuèh* was in use in Spain (p. 371).

[2] Ibn us-Saîd, a contemporary of Ibn ul-Ahmar.

[3] See *ante*, p. 541.

were moved to mirth by the sight of the huge head-dress of their Eastern brethren. The sovereigns and princes, the aristocracy and military, with a large proportion of the civil population, followed in dress the fashion of their Frankish neighbours, and dressed like them. The Arab cavaliers, instead of the light armour of their ancestors, their bows and scimitars, were clad in heavy mail, and used the same weapons as the Franks—the crossbow, the spear, and shield.[1] Over the mail they generally threw a short scarlet tunic embroidered with devices.

The Spanish Moslems were said to be the cleanest people on earth in their person and dress, and in the interior of their houses; "indeed they carry cleanliness to such an extreme that it is not an uncommon thing for a man of the lower classes to spend his last dirhem in soap instead of buying food for his daily consumption, and thus go without his dinner rather than appear in public with dirty clothes."

General Review. I have so far dealt separately with Granada and Cordova. It now remains to give a general review of the system of administration and mode of government among the Spanish Arabs, of the economic condition of the country, and the state of culture under them.

Government. Whilst the Sultan was the supreme head of government the practical work of administration was conducted by ministers who, as in the East, bore the title of *vizier*. Each department of State was in the charge of a separate minister. There seem to have been four principal offices, viz., finance, foreign affairs, the administration of justice

[1] Apparently under the influence of the Marînides, a change was made in the equipment of the troops, which may perhaps account for some of the later defeats. For an account of the frontier guard, see Appendix.

or "redress of grievances," and the management, pay, and supervision of the army. The title of vizier[1] was also conferred on the Privy Councillors; but in order to distinguish the ministers who held portfolios from the ordinary members of the Caliph's council, the former were styled *vizier zu'l vizâratain.* The President of the Council, called in Asia *Grand Vizier*, was the *Hâjib*, or Chamberlain. He held direct communication with the sovereign, received the royal mandates, and acted generally as the chief of the ministers. They all sat in one hall, but the seat of the President was more elevated than those of the others. The Privy Councillors, like ministers, had the privilege of sitting with the Caliph in the Council chamber.

Secretaries of State.

There were several Secretaries of State, or *Kâtib ud-Dawal*, among whom the chief of the correspondence office (*Kitâbat ur-Rasâil*) occupied the most prominent position. Another officer, named *Kâtib uz-Zimâm*, was entrusted with the security and protection of non-Moslems. The supervision of the public accounts was in the charge of an officer called *Sâhib ul-ashgâl.*[2] He was practically the Finance Minister, for his department received the revenues, imposed taxes, made disbursements, and "checked extortions." In the kingdom of Granada the functionary entrusted with the keeping of accounts, the private expenses of the Sultan and other pecuniary concerns, was called the *Vakîl.* There being no Secretary of State in Granada, the Board of Correspondence was in the charge of the Vizier, whilst the sovereign himself sealed the diplomas and despatches. Under the

[1] The Arabic *al-vizier* was, as usual, corrupted by the Spaniards into Alguazil.

[2] "The master of occupations."

Banû Ahmar and the Banû Marîn of Africa the *sâhib ul-ashgal* became a mere collector of revenue.

In Spain the position of Kâzi was one of great dignity, and the Chief Kâzi was often designated *Kâzi ul-Jamâat* (Kâzi of the People) instead of *Kâzi ul-Kuzzât*.

The Kâzis.

The police.

The head of the police was, as in the East, called *Sâhib ush-Shurta*, and under the Caliphs of Cordova was vested with very large powers. Under the later dynasties he became a mere Commissary of Police. The town magistrates were called *Sâhib ul-Medîna*,[1] and sometimes *Sâhib ul-Lail*,[2] and were subject to the Kâzis' control and supervision. The *Muhtasib* exercised the same functions as in the cities of Asia and Africa. He examined the weights and measures used by traders, inspected the markets, prevented nuisances, and took summary cognisance of attempts at cheating by shop-keepers. The night-watchmen were called *ad-dârabûn*, or *gate-keepers*, to whom was entrusted the duty of closing the interior gates of the cities after the last evening prayers. They were always well-armed, and carried lanterns, besides being accompanied by a huge watch-dog.

In early times the naval commander was called *Ameer ul-Mâ*,[3] which was corrupted by the Franks and Spaniards into *Almirant*. This was again re-imported to the Arabs in the form of *al-miland*. Under Abdur Rahmân an-Nâsir and his successors this high officer was styled *Kâid ul-Asâtil*, or Commander of the Fleet. The Ommeyades and the Almohades maintained the navy in a high state of efficiency, and their maritime force was superior to that of all the Christian nations combined. It was the

[1] City magistrate.

[2] Night magistrate. They were sometimes called also *al-Kâids*, which the Christian Spaniards corrupted into alcalde.

[3] Commander of the Sea.

loss of this superiority, as Ibn Khaldûn points out, which materially contributed to the decay of Moslem power.[1]

No country in the world ever enjoyed a higher degree of agricultural prosperity than Spain under the Arabs.[2] They raised agriculture into a science, and by an extraordinary application of industry, skill, and knowledge developed the resources of the country in a wonderful manner. Thoroughly acquainted with the adaptability of certain crops to the nature of certain kinds of soil, and the application of various kinds of manure to particular species of trees, plants, etc., they made the most sterile tracts bloom into luxuriance. The Spaniards are indebted to the Arabs for the introduction of rice, sugar-cane, the cotton-tree, saffron, spinach, and that infinite variety of fine fruits which have now become almost indigenous to the peninsula, whence the use and culture of many of them have gradually been introduced into various parts of Europe.

Agriculture.

Every kind of soil was appropriated to that species of culture which was best adapted for it. At Elchar in the province of Valencia they have left vast groves of palm trees. Rice was cultivated in enormous quantities near Albufera. Sugar-cane and cotton were grown at Oliva and Gandia. Xeres, Granada, and Malaga were covered with vines; while the country around Seville and the greater part of Andalusia were planted with olives.[3]

Economic condition of Spain.

[1] Ibn Khaldûn's view of the rise and decay of the Moslem power in the Mediterranean (*Bahr ur-Rûm*, also called *Bahr ush-Shâm*) is extremely interesting. Evidently in his time (he was a contemporary of Tamerlane) attempts were being made to resuscitate the Moslem navy.

[2] Compare the eloquent words of Murphy on this point.

[3] The agricultural development of Spain under the Saracens is sufficiently evidenced by the fact, that in 1255 A.C., when Ferdinand I. took possession of Seville, that province contained several millions of olive trees and nearly 100,000 mills for turning out olive oil.

They levelled the earth by means of an instrument called the *marhifal*, and the science of irrigation was carried to high perfection. The whole country was covered with aqueducts and canals for the fertilisation of the soil.[1] They manufactured iron and steel in large quantities, and their steel was so excellent, that the swords of Granada were preferred to all others in Spain. The manufacture of silk and cotton was introduced by the Arabs into Spain; and woollen cloths were made of very fine quality. They excelled specially in dyeing, and the art of dyeing black with indigo is said to be their invention. The superb vases still preserved in the palace of the Alhambra, and the glazed tiles which form a distinguished ornament of that magnificent edifice, show their progress in the manufacture of porcelain. Their exports consisted of gold, silver, copper, raw and wrought silk, sugar, cochineal, quicksilver, pig and cast iron, olives, woollen manufactures, ambergris, yellow amber, loadstone, antimony, talc, marcasites, rock crystal, oil, sugar, sulphur, saffron, ginger, myrrh, and various other drugs; corals fished on the coast of Andalusia, pearls obtained from that of Catalonia, rubies from the mines of Malaga and Beja, and amethysts procured from near Carthagena. They were specially renowned in the art of tanning, currying, and dyeing and embossing leather, which has almost completely died out in Spain since the expulsion of the Moors. Carried from Spain to Fez, it was brought from there to England, where it is now known under the name of *Morocco* and *Cordovan*. They also introduced into Spain the manufacture of gunpowder, sugar, and paper. The fine arts were not neglected, and the Spanish Arabs excelled their Chris-

The Fine Arts.

[1] The aqueducts of Carmona carried water over a distance of several leagues.

tian neighbours both in sculpture and painting. We know how the palaces of the Caliphs in Cordova, especially az-Zahra, were decorated with statuary and paintings, whilst the sculptured lions and historical paintings [1] still preserved in the Alhambra show the development of both the arts in Granada. No town, however small, was without colleges and schools; whilst each principal city possessed a separate university. Those of Cordova, Seville (Ishbîlia),[2] Malaga, Saragossa, Lisbon (Alishbûna), Jaen, Salamanca, among others, occupied the most distinguished position.

Among the host of historians produced by Moslem Spain the following are the most prominent:—Ibn Hayyân,[3] Ibn ul-Abbâr,[4] Abû Obaidullah al-Bakri, Ibn Bushkûwâl (Abu'l Kâsim Khalf[5] bin Abdul Malik bin Masûd bin Mûsa), Ibn us-Saîd (Abu'l Hassan Ali),[6] Ash-Shakandi (Abu'l Walîd Ismâil, a native of Shakunda),[7] Ibn ul-Khatîb (Lisân ud-din).[8] I have mentioned in a preceding page the names of a few of the literary women of Granada. It will be interesting to add here the distinguished poetesses and cultured ladies who flourished in earlier times in Cordova and other places. Hassâna

[1] The paintings are a species of encaustic, and represent a council-meeting, a battle-field, a cavalcade, and various hunting scenes.

[2] Hispalis of the Romans.

[3] He wrote two histories of Spain—one in ten volumes, the other in sixty!

[4] Died in 1076 A.C.

[5] Born in Cordova in 1101 A.C.; died in 1183 A.C.

[6] Was born at Granada in 1214 A.C.; died in 1286-7 A.C. He was educated at Seville.

[7] Died in 1231-32 A.C.

[8] Born in 1313 A.C. He was Vizier to Yusuf Abu'l Hajâj, seventh king of Granada, and his successor al-Ghani. Suspected of treason, he was executed in 1374 A.C. As Ibn Khaldûn was born at Tunis, I have given a short account of his life in the Appendix.

at-Tamîmiyèh, daughter of Abu'l Hussain the poet, and Umm ul-Ulâ, both natives of Guadalaxara, flourished in the sixth century of the Hegira. Ammat ul-Azîz, a descendant of the Prophet, and therefore styled ash-Sharîfa, and al-Ghusânièh, a native of Bejenah in the province of Almeria, flourished in the fifth century. These ladies held high rank among the scholars of the time.

Al-Aarûzzièh, who lived at Valencia, was a distinguished grammarian and rhetorician. She died at Denia in 450 A.H. Hafsah ar-Rakûnièh, "renowned for her beauty, her talents, her nobility and her wealth," flourished under the Almohades. Hafsa, the daughter of Hamdûn, also a native of Guadalaxara, was one of the most illustrious poetesses and scholars of the fourth century of the Hegira. Zainab al-Murabiyyèh, a native of Wadi Âsh (Guadix), lived in the time of Hâjib al-Muzaffar, with whose family she was on terms of intimacy. Mariam, daughter of Abû Yâkûb al-Ansâri, was a native of Seville; she was a learned and accomplished woman, and taught rhetoric, poetry, and literature, "which, joined to her piety, her good morals, her virtues, and amiable disposition, gained her the affection of her sex, and gave her many pupils." She died towards the end of the fourth century of the Hegira. Asma al-Aâmariyèh, also a native of Seville, was a distinguished scholar. Umm ul-Hinâ, daughter of the Kâzi Abû Mohammed Abdul Hakk ibn Aatiyyèh, was both a poetess and a jurisconsult. Bahja, a native of Cordova, a friend of Wallâdèh,[1] the daughter of al-Mustakfi, was equally renowned for her beauty and her verses.

Itimâd ar-Ramîkkiyèh and Busîna, the wife and daughter of Mutamid, the last king of Seville, also held high rank among the scholars of the day.

[1] See *ante*, p. 528.

A sketch of the Spanish Moslems can hardly be complete without some further account of the distinguished physicians and philosophers who have shed such lustre on the country of their birth.

Abû Bakr Mohammed bin Yahya, surnamed Ibn us-Sâigh ("son of the goldsmith"), commonly known as Ibn Bâja (Aven-Pace or Avenpace), was a native of Saragossa, and a Tajîbite by descent. He was eminent as a physician, philosopher, mathematician and astronomer. To his learning and scientific attainments he joined the highest proficiency in music. He died at Fez in 533 A.H. (1138 A.C.).

Ibn Tufail (*Abû Bakr* Mohammed bin Abdul Malik ibn Tufail) was one of the most remarkable philosophers of the Arabs in Spain. He was born at Wâdi Âsh (Guadix), and was celebrated as a physician, mathematician, philosopher, and poet. He was held in the highest estimation by *Abû Yâkûb* Yusuf, the second sovereign of the Almohade dynasty. Ibn Tufail died in Morocco in 581 A.H. (1185 A.C.), and Yâkûb al-Mansur, the son and successor of Yusuf, personally assisted at his funeral. Probably Ibn Tufail's famous work, *Hai ibn Yukzân*,[1] is one of the first works on natural religion.

Ibn Zuhr[2] (Abû Bakr al-Iyâzi) was a native of Seville,

[1] This book has been translated into Latin by Pococke, and in an abridged form also into English by Ashwell (1686 A.C.).

[2] Avenzoar, *ante*, p. 538. His father's name was *Abû Merwân* Abdul Malik, Chief Physician to Abdul Momîn, founder of the Almohade dynasty. His grandfather was "the vizier of that epoch and its grandee, the philosopher of that age and its physician." He died at Cordova, A.H. 525 (A.C. 1130-31). His great-grandfather, Abdul Malik, travelled to the East, where he long practised as a physician, and became head of the faculty in Bagdad; he then removed to Egypt, and afterwards to Kairowân. At a later period, he took up his residence at Denia, whence his reputation spread over

and belonged to a remarkably gifted family, of which all the members were scholars, physicians, or viziers. "Many of them attained to the highest offices in the State, enjoyed the favour of sovereigns, and exercised great authority." Ibn Zuhr was chief physician to *Abû Yusuf* Yâkûb al-Mansûr. He died in 595 A.H. (1199 A.C.).

Ibn Rushd, the great Averroes (Abu'l Walîd Mohammed bin Ahmed ibn Rushd), was born in 520 A.H. (1126 A.C.). His grandfather and father were Chief Kâzis of Andalusia under the Almoravides. Ibn Rushd enjoyed the friendship of Abû Merwân ibn Zuhr, and of Ibn Tufail, who introduced him to *Abû Yâkûb* Yusuf. In 1109 A.C. Ibn Rushd was Kâzi of Seville. In 1182 he was appointed to the same office at Cordova. He died on the 9th of Safar 595 A.H. (December 1198 A.C.).

all the regions of Spain and Maghrib. "His pre-eminence in the art of medicine was so conspicuously displayed that he outshone all his contemporaries." He died at Denia.

Tombs of the Caliphs, Cairo.

CHAPTER XXXII

THE SARACENS IN AFRICA

169—567 A.H.; 785—1171 A.C.

The Idrîsides—The Aghlabides—Invasion of Sicily—Its Conquest—The fall of the Aghlabides—The rise of the Fatimides—Conquest of Egypt—Foundation of Cairo—Conquest of Syria, Hijâz, and Yemen—Decline of the Fatimides—The end of the dynasty—Cairo—The Grand Lodge of the Ismâilias.

169—567 A.H. 785—1171 A.C.

UP to the time of Mahdi, the third Caliph of the House of Abbâs, the whole of the African possessions acknowledged the Abbasside sovereignty. In the reign of Hâdi, Idrîs, a descendant of Hassan I., escaped into Western Mauritania,[1] and there, with the assistance of the Berber tribes, who accepted him as their chief and Imâm, established a powerful kingdom, which for a long time flourished in Northern Africa. He built the city of Fez, and made it his capital; under his enlightened administration it soon became a famous seat of culture and learning. He is said to have been poisoned by an emissary of the Abbassides, and was succeeded on the throne by his infant son, also called Idrîs, under the regency of the mother and the Vizier Ghâlib. Idrîs II. proved himself a great warrior, and made large conquests towards the south. Ibn Khaldûn says, "The rule

The Idrîsides (the *Addrisa*) Idrîs I.

Idrîs II. *al-Asghar*

[1] See *ante*, p. 235.

785—1171 A.C. (*daawat*) of the Abbassides was at this time effaced in the west (Mauritania) from Sûs ul-Aksâ to Shilf (Silves)." On his death in 213 A.H. his son Mohammed became Caliph. His policy of entrusting the provincial governorships to members of his family appears to have succeeded admirably, for, with one exception, his brothers whom he appointed as governors remained loyal to the end.

Death of Idrîs II., 213 A.H. 825 A.C. Accession of Mohammed.

Mohammed died in 221 A.H., and was succeeded by his son Ali, who was only nine years of age at the time. Ali's accession was loyally accepted by all his subjects, and the government was conducted with such success by the faithful servants of his father that the historian observes, "his reign was extremely prosperous." On his death without issue in the twenty-second year of his age, his brother Yahya bin Mohammed was raised to the throne. During his long reign, he extended his power in all directions, and the kingdom advanced in wealth and prosperity. He enlarged and embellished Fez,[1] to which peopled flocked from all directions.

Death of Mohammed, 221 A.H. 833 A.C. Accession of Ali.

Death of Ali, 234 A.H. 856 A.C. Accession of Yahya.

Yahya died in 264 A.H., and was succeeded by his son, also named Yahya. His oppression led to a revolt, in which he was expelled from the kingdom. He fled to Spain, where he died.

Death of Yahya, 264 A.H. 878 A.C. Accession of Yahya II.

Upon the dethronement of Yahya II., his cousin, Ali bin Omar,[2] made himself master of the capital. He did not, however, remain long in possession of Fez, as a Khâriji rising compelled him to take shelter in Spain. On the flight of Ali the people of Fez proclaimed a grandson of Idrîs II. named Yahya[3] their Imâm and Caliph. He was a scholar and jurist, and well-versed in traditions. He succeeded for a time in reducing under his

His dethronement.

Yahya III.

[1] Arabic, Fâs.

[2] Omar was a brother of Yahya I.

[3] His father's name was Kâsim.

power the whole of the old Idrîside possessions. His rule, however, came to an abrupt end in 309 A.H., for in that year he was driven out of his kingdom by the Fatimide governor of Miknâsa. He then retired into private life, and lived at Mahdièh until his death in 331 A.H. With the fall of Yahya III. ended the Idrîside Caliphate. The various princes of this dynasty possessed themselves of the outlying provinces, and assumed the kingly title. In 319 A.H. Abdur Rahmân III. (an-Nâsir) sent an expedition into Africa; a large part of Mauritania was annexed, and many of the Idrîside princes were deported to Cordova. Western Morocco then fell into the hands of the Spanish Caliphs, whilst the east acknowledged the sway of the Fatimides.

169—567 A.H.

His expulsion and death.

I have already mentioned how in the year 184 A.H. Ifrîkia[1] became an autonomous principality.

The Aghlabides (the *Aghâliba*). Moharram. 184 A.H. 801 A.C.

The first prince of this dynasty was Ibrâhim bin Aghlab, a man of great administrative talent and energy of character. He founded in the vicinity of Kairowân, a new city, which he named Abbâsièh, and made it the seat of his government. He reigned for over twelve years, and was succeeded by his son Abdullâh. In his time there was no war or disturbance of any kind; the principality enjoyed perfect peace, and the people prospered and grew rich.[2] He died in 201 A.H., and was succeeded by his brother, Ziâdatullâh. He is described as a prince of great talent and ambition, and a distinguished patron of arts and learning, but with a haughty and reckless temper, which gave rise to a violent insurrection. After a protracted struggle the rebels were finally defeated, and peace was restored in the country in 208 A.H., or 209 A.H.

Death of Ibrâhim Aghlab, 196 A.H. 812 A.C. Accession of *Abu'l Abbâs* Abdullâh.

His death 6 Zu'l Hijja, 201 A.H. 817 A.C. Accession of Ziâdatullâh.

[1] See *ante*, p. 240.

[2] Ibn ul-Althîr, vol. vi. p. 108.

785—1171 A.C. The Arabs had long possessed a settlement in the south of Sicily.[1] The systematic subjugation of the island was undertaken under this Aghlabide sovereign.

Conquest of Sicily. In 212 A.H. he despatched into Sicily a large force under Asad bin Furât,[2] the Kâzi of Kairowân. The primary cause of this invasion is somewhat differently given by the Arab and Christian historians.[3] The latter say that a Byzantine youth, Euphemius, who had stolen a too willing nun from her cloister, was sentenced by the emperor to the amputation of his tongue. He fled to the Saracens of Ifrîkia, and induced them to send into the island the expedition which eventually brought the whole of Sicily into Arab power. The Arab historians mention nothing about the nun. "The emperor of the

826–27 A.C. Romans, who lived at Constantinople, Kustuntunièh," says Ibn ul-Athîr, "sent in the year 211 A.H. a patrician, Constantine, as governor of Sicily. Constantine appointed a Roman of the name of Fîmi (Euphemius), a brave and wise soldier, to the command of the fleet, and he invaded Ifrîkia, and did great damage to the Moslems. In the meantime Constantine received orders from the emperor to throw Fîmi into prison and subject him to torture. Fîmi, on hearing this, rose in arms, drove Constantine into Catania (Katânia), and proclaimed himself King of Sicily. War then broke out between Fîmi and his lieutenant, Balâta,[4] who was assisted by Michael (Mikhâil), governor of Palermo.[5] Fîmi suffered a heavy

[1] Called *Sikilièh* (with a *sâd*) by the Arabs.

[2] The author of the *Asadièh*, a work on the Mâliki doctrines and jurisprudence.

[3] Professor Amari, in his *Storia dei Musulmani di Sicilia*, gives both versions.

[4] Spelt Palata by Amari.

[5] Balaram of the Arabs.

defeat at the hands of Balâta, who made himself master of Syracuse (Sarakûsa).[1] Fîmi thereupon invoked the assistance of Ziâdatullâh Aghlab, offering him the sovereignty of Sicily. This brilliant offer induced Ziâdat-ullâh to send an army into Sicily. The Saracens landed in the Rabi I. of 212 A.H., at a place called Mazura (Mazar of the Arabs). Balâta, Fîmi's enemy and rival, met them here, and suffered a sanguinary defeat. He fled to Calabria (*Kallûria*),[2] where he died shortly after. "The Moslems rapidly reduced into their power a great many fortresses in the island." Syracuse was besieged, but a pestilence, which broke out in the Saracen camp, carried away Asad and a large number of his troops, and Mohammed bin Abi'l Jawâri, Asad's successor, was forced by the Byzantine army sent for the relief of Syracuse to raise the siege. The Moslems succeeded, however, in capturing Mineo (*Minâo*) and Girgenteo (*Jurjunt*), where they placed strong garrisons. At Kasr-Iânna (modern Castrogiovanni)[3] they lost their ally Fîmi, who was treacherously murdered by the inhabitants of the place. Mohammed bin Abi'l Jawâri dying shortly after, the command was assumed by Zuhair bin Ghous. The Byzantines, who had, in the meantime, been largely reinforced from Constantinople, now made a supreme effort to drive the invaders from the island. The Saracens were besieged in Mineo, which was reduced to dire straits. Luckily reinforcements arrived for them from Spain as well as Africa. The Byzantines fell back upon Syracuse, and the Saracens again assumed the offensive. In the Rajab of 216 A.H.[4] Palermo, the capital, capitu-

169—567 A.H.

Conquest of Sicily.

Death of Fîmi.

[1] Italian Siracusa.

[2] May also be read as *Kalavria*.

[3] *Castrum Ennæ* of the Romans.

[4] August 13 to Sept. 11, 831 A.C.

785—1171 lated on favourable terms. "The occupation of Palermo
A.C. was, in truth, the beginning of that of the Island."[1]
Conquest Although a great part of the country had submitted to the
of Palermo, Rajab Arab rule, systematic administration was not introduced
216 A.H. until the arrival of *Abu'l Aghlab* Ibrahîm bin Abdullâh, a
831 A.C. kinsman of Ziâdutullâh, as the civil and military governor
15 Ramazan, of Sicily. Under him the districts in the neighbourhood
220 A.H. of Mount Etna ("the Mountain of Fire")[2] were brought
Sept. 11, 835 A.C. into subjection.

Ziâdatullâh died in the year 223 of the Hegira, and
was succeeded by his brother *Abû Ikâl* Aghlab. His
14 Rajab, 223 A.H. rule was prosperous and successful. Reinforcements
June 10, were sent to Sicily, and the work of conquest in that
883 A.C. direction proceeded apace. The Saracens about this
time made a descent into Southern Italy, and captured
Accession of *Abû Ikâl* Aghlab. several strong places on the Calabrian coast.

Aghlab died in 226 A.H., after a short reign of two
years and seven months, and was succeeded by his son
Death of Aghlab, *Abu'l Abbâs* Mohammed. He was a great builder, and
Rabi II. wise administrator.

226 A.H. In the year 228 A.H. Fazl bin Jaafar Hamdâni, the
Accession of *Abu'l* lieutenant of the viceroy of Sicily, landed an expedition
Abbâs Mohammed. by sea near Messina (Messîn). Assisted from Naples,
October 9, (Nâbîl[3]) Messina resisted the Saracenic attack for two
842, years; but in the end capitulated and received generous
Sept 28, 843 A.C. terms. In the year 232 A.H. Fazl captured the city of
Lentini, and carried his victorious arms far into the
mainland (*Arz ul-Kubrâ*). Calabria and Campania were
overrun, and a hundred and fifty towns either reduced or
laid under contribution. An Arab fleet sailed up the Tiber,
846 A.C. plundered Fundi, and the suburbs of Rome, and laid siege

[1] Amari.

[2] *Jabl un-Nâr.*

[3] Also called *Nâblûs.*

to Gaëta, but the capital was saved by the internal divisions of the Arabs. In 233 A.H. the Saracens took up their "abode" in the city of Târant (Taranto). In 234 A.H. they obtained the submission of Ragusa (Raghûs). In 235 A.H. they renewed their attack on Rome. A sudden and fearful tempest "which confounded the skill and courage of the stoutest mariners" came to the rescue of the Pope (Leo IV.). The Saracen fleet was dashed to pieces among the rocks and islands of a hostile shore. The viceroy Ibn Abdullâh died in Rajab 236 A.H. at Palermo. The Arab colonists thereupon elected Abbâs the son of Fazl as their commander, and their election was confirmed by the sovereign of Ifrîkia. Abbâs continued vigorously the work of conquest in Sicily as well as on the mainland. In 239 and 240 A.H. Catania, Caltavuturo (Kalât Abi-Sûr), and several other places were reduced in rapid succession.

169—567 A.H.

849 A.C.

853-5 A.C.

Abbâs, the governor of Sicily, died in 247 A.H., and the colonists thereupon elected in his place his son Abdullâh, and their choice was confirmed by the Aghlabide prince Abû Ibrâhim. Some time after he was replaced by Khafâja bin Sufiân. In 250 A.H. the Moslems took possession of the ancient and important city of Noto (Notos), and in the course of the next few years reduced Syracuse, which had hitherto resisted their arms, Abba, Satas, and Castelnuovo (*Kasr ul-jadîd*). In 254 A.H. Khufâja's son Mohammed again besieged Gaëta and laid the suburbs of Rome under contribution. Khufâja died in 255 A.H., and was succeeded in the governorship by his son Mohammed. During his tenure of office Malta was captured by a fleet under Ahmed bin Omar. Mohammed the son of Khufâja was assassinated in his palace on the 3rd of Rajab 257 A.H.

Conquest of Notos.

869 A.C.

Malta.

To maintain the continuity of the narrative relating to

870 A.C.

May 27, 871 A.C. Accession of *Abû Ibrâhim* Ahmed.

His death 20 Zu'l Kaada, 249 A.H. 862 A.C. Accession of Ziâdatullâh (*al-Asghar*) "The Little."

His death, 19 Zu'l Kaada, 250 A.H. 863 A.C. Accession of *Abû Abdullâh* Mohammed.

Sicily I have had to anticipate the history of the Ifrîkian principality, for Abu'l Abbâs Mohammed died in 242 A.H. He was succeeded by his son *Abû Ibrâhim* Ahmed. Under his rule peace reigned throughout the principality; and there were no disturbances. He treated his subjects well, and they were happy and prosperous. He built ten thousand forts and outposts made of "stone, brick, and mortar," to protect the country against the inroads of the enemy. Abû Ibrâhim Ahmed died in 249 A.H., when his brother,[1] *Abû Mohammed* Ziâdatullâh ascended the throne and "walked in the footsteps of his ancestors," but reigned barely eighteen months before he died. His brother *Abû Abdullâh*[2] Mohammed was then raised to the throne. Ibn ul-Athîr says he was learned, wise, and endowed with good qualities. In his reign the Byzantines recovered some of their lost possessions in Sicily. Mohammed thereupon built a number of fortresses and outposts to keep them in check. He is said to also have made some conquests on the mainland. *Abû Abdullâh* Mohammed died in 261 A.H., and was succeeded by his brother Ibrâhîm.

Death of Abû Abdullâh Mohammed. Jamâdi II. 261 A.H. 874 A.C. Accession of Ibrâhim.

In the beginning of his reign he distinguished himself by justice and benevolence towards his subjects, but towards the end developed a ferocious homicidal mania which led him to slaughter even his own children. The account of his atrocities roused the anger of the Caliph Mutazid, who sent a peremptory order deposing Ibrâhîm from his government. His son *Abu'l Abbâs* Abdullâh, who was in Sicily, was appointed by the Caliph to the

[1] Ibn Khaldûn says he was Ahmed's son and not brother: vol. iv. p. 201.

[2] Ibn Khaldûn gives his surname as *Abu'l Gharânîk*, and says "he was addicted to pleasure and wine, and wars and disturbances broke out in his time."

government of Ifrîkia. Ibrâhîm put on the garment of a hermit, set free the crowds of captives whom he had thrown into prison, and crossed over to Sicily to fight the Byzantines. Here he died shortly after.

169—567 A.H.

Abu'l Abbâs Abdullâh was a kind-hearted and just sovereign, and skilled both in war and in the administration of affairs. But he was assassinated in his sleep by some of his slaves, at the instigation of his own son, *Abû Mozar* (Modhar) Ziâdatullâh. The parricide was the last of his family who reigned over Ifrîkia. After executing the slaves whom he had employed to murder his father, he abandoned himself to debauchery and "the company of buffoons and clowns," and the principality was allowed to drift to ruin. In the meantime a revolution was taking place in Northern Africa, which altered the entire aspect of affairs.

Appointment of *Abu'l Abbâs* Abdullâh as Viceroy of Ifrîkia. 289 A.H. 902 A.C.

Accession of *Abû Mozar* Ziâdatullâh, the last of the Aghlabides.

The schism that occurred among the Shiahs on the decease of the apostolical Imâm Jaafar[1] has already been described. The majority accepted the Imâmate of Mûsa (*al-Kâzim*), whom the Imâm had, upon the death of his eldest son Ismâil, named as his successor, whilst the rest gave their adhesion to Ismâil's son Mohammed, surnamed *al-Maktûm* (the *concealed*, or *unrevealed*).[2] The Ismâilias, as they were henceforth called, in the course of time amalgamated with their doctrines many esoteric motions borrowed from the philosophy of Mâni (Manes)[3].

The rise of the Fatimides.

The Ismâilias Mohammed *al-Maktûm*.

[1] See *ante*, p. 225.

[2] The Ismâilias designate their next five spiritual leaders, *concealed* or *unrevealed* Imâms, as they did not "reveal" themselves (openly avow their title), owing "to the oppression of their enemies."

[3] A Persian philosopher of great genius and versatile talents, who flourished in the third century of the Christian era. The influence of his teachings is markedly visible in Christianity as well as Islâm, and all the later esoteric sects are traceable to him.

785—1171 A.C.

Some of them were decidedly Manichæan[1] in their views, and considered the hidden meaning in words as of more importance than the positive law, and, differing from the general body of Moslems, believed in "justification by faith" and not by work.[2] This extreme section of the Ismâilias received the name of Esoterician (Bâtinia).[3] Their secret teachings and pretensions naturally aroused the suspicions of the Abbassides, and they were strictly watched, and sometimes ill-treated.

Jaafar *al-Mussadak.*

Mohammed *al-Maktûm* was succeeded in the Ismâilia Imâmate by his son Jaafar, surnamed *al-Mussadak* (the Veracious). Upon his death his son Mohammed, who bore the title of *al-Habîb* (the Friend), became their Imâm. He was a man of great ability and ambition, and closely resembled in character the other Mohammed, the father of Saffâh and Mansûr. He lived at a place called Salâmièh, near Hems (Emessa), and from here he sent out missionaries (*dâis*) in all directions to enlist adherents and diffuse the Ismâilia cult. The doctrines of his sect thus spread rapidly in Yemen, Yemâma, Bahrain, Sind, India, Egypt, and Northern Africa. One of his most zealous and indefatigable missionaries was *Abû Abdullâh* Hussain,[4] at one time *Muhtasib* of Basra, who afterwards became famous under the designa-

Mohammed, *al-Habîb.*

Abû Abdullâh *The Shiah.*

[1] Derived from Mâni.

[2] In other words, so long as they believed implicitly in their Imâms, it was not necessary for their future welfare to act in accordance with the dictates of religion. Hence their blind subjection to their spiritual leaders. The doctrine of "justification by faith" is not confined to these ultra-Ismâilias.

[3] The *Karâmita* (the Carmathians) and the Assassins were two offshoots of this sect. In Arabian histories, the latter are invariably called *Bâtinias.*

[4] Son of Mohammed, son of Zakaria.

tion of *the Shiah.*[1] In the year 288 A.H. Abû Abdullâh proceeded to Africa, and by his wonderful preaching and force of character, which, joined to his piety and asceticism, gave him great influence among the impressionable Berbers, he soon secured the adhesion of the powerful tribe of Kitâma to the Imâmate of the *Ahl ul-Bait.* At this time Ibrâhim bin Mohammed was the ruler of Ifrîkia; and he tried to suppress the Ismailite movement. Abû Abdullâh, however, surmounted every difficulty, and the accession of the incompetent Ziâdatullâh paved his way to success. Whilst the Aghlabide was "lying immersed in pleasure in Rakkâda, Abû Abdullâh's power waxed in the country, and his missionaries announced to the inhabitants the immediate advent of the Mahdi."[2] Two armies sent by Ziâdatullâh to oppose the Shiah suffered ignominious defeats. Ziâdatullâh then fled to Tripoli, and from there to Asia.[3] 169—567 A.H.

Abû Abdullâh made his triumphal entry into the capital of the Aghlabides on Saturday the 1st of Rajab, 296 A.H. Governors were at once despatched throughout the province to assume charge of the cities and preserve order. The wise and merciful policy inaugurated by Abû Abdullâh had the effect of conciliating public opinion, and preparing the people to give a hearty and loyal welcome to the master in whose name the conquest was made. March 26, 909 A.C.

[1] *Ash-Shiï*, the Shiah *par excellence*; he was also often called the *Sûfi* for his mysticism, and the *Muallim* (the Preceptor), as he taught the people the Shiah doctrines.

[2] Ibn Khaldûn, vol. iv. p. 34. Rakkâda lay three miles from Kairowân. The place was renowned for the extreme salubrity of the air and its delicious climate. It was an immense cluster of fortified palaces, enclosing beautiful gardens, baths, fountains, and large reservoirs.

[3] He died at Rakka (according to Ibn Asâkir) in 296 A.H. (908-9 A.C.).

785—1171 A.C. Obaidullâh *al-Mahdi*, 1st Caliph of the Fatimides.

Mohammed al-Habîb died towards the close of the third century of the Hegira, leaving the Imâmate to his son Obaidullâh.[1] "You are the Mahdi," said the dying father; "after my death you will have to fly to a far country, where you will meet with severe trials." Obaidullâh, however, abode quietly at Salâmièh, until the Shiah, having brought the tribe of Kitâma absolutely under his influence, sent messengers to the Mahdi, imploring him to come to Africa and place himself at the head of the movement. Obaidullâh started at once with his son Abu'l Kasim, Abu'l Abbâs (a brother of the Shiah), and a few devoted followers, all disguised as merchants. In spite of the strict secrecy observed by Abû Abdullâh in his communications with the Mahdi, the Abbassides got wind of Obaidullâh's flight from Salâmièh. The Caliph Muktafi distributed throughout the provinces of the empire a description of the fugitive, with orders to seize and imprison any one answering to it. At Tripoli Abu'l Abbâs left the Mahdi's party and proceeded to Kairowân. Here he was discovered and thrown into a dungeon. Obaidullâh and his son succeeded in evading pursuit or discovery, and in 296 A.H. reached Sijilmâssèh,[2] a beau-

[1] The genealogy given in the text is according to Makrîsi and Ibn Khaldûn. Ibn ul-Athîr mentions two different names for Jaafar al-Mussadak and Mohammed al-Habîb. In the reign of Kâdir the Abbasside the leading Sunni jurisconsults and divines under the presidency of the Caliph of Bagdad fulminated an anathema against the rival Caliphs of Egypt, impugning their legitimacy as the real descendants of Fâtima and Ali. That it was a calumny and the outcome of dynastic jealousy no Mussulman historian of any note has ever doubted. Makrîsi, Ibn ul-Athîr, Abu'l Fedâ and Ibn Khaldûn all accept Obaidullâh as a real descendant of Ali. Ibn Khaldûn's exposure of the falsity of the Abbasside aspersions is a master-piece of historical criticism, vol. iv. p. 31.

[2] Sijilmâssèh was founded, says al-Bakri, in 140 A.H. (757 A.C.). It is not far from modern Morocco.

tiful city on the southern slope of the Grand Atlas, then the capital of the Banû Midrâr. Here their luck deserted them. At this time Sijilmâssèh was ruled by a Berber prince named Elisaa bin Midrâr, who at first received them kindly; but on receipt of a letter from Ziâdatullâh, threw them into prison. The Shiah, however, was soon afoot with a great army. After releasing his brother Abu'l Abbâs from Ziâdatullâh's dungeon at Kairowân, he marched against Elisaa, who was defeated and slain. Abû Abdullâh then hurried to the prison where the Mahdi and his son lay confined. Placing father and son on horseback, and himself proceeding on foot in front of them, accompanied by all the chiefs of the Kitâma, he conducted them to the camp, "shedding tears of joy as he went, and calling out to the people who thronged the streets, 'Behold your master.'"[1] They remained forty days at Sijilmâssèh, and then came to Rakkâda, where the people of Kairowân took the oath of allegiance to the Mahdi as the Caliph. His rule was now established throughout Ifrîkia, and the people with few exceptions acknowledged his authority. *Wâlis* were appointed to the government of the different provinces, including Sicily, and efforts were made to repair the ravages of war. The vigour with which Obaidullah applied himself to the task of government aroused the animosity of Abu'l Abbâs, the brother of Abû Abdullâh, who had hoped to find in the Mahdi only a *roi fainéant*. Chafing under the loss of power, he entered into a conspiracy with some of the chiefs of the Kitâma for overthrowing the Fatimide Caliph. Abu'l Abbâs even drew the hitherto faithful Abû Abdullâh into his mischievous toils. The Mahdi made every effort to conciliate the two brothers. His endeavours were met by a stubborn refusal. The dis-

169—567 A.H.

August 909 A.C.

The Mahdi.

June 910 A.C.

[1] Ibn ul-Athîr.

785—1171 A.C. covery of a plot for his assassination determined the Mahdi to put them to death, and they were accordingly executed in their palace. The death of the king-maker did not stop the work of conquest, and Obaidullâh succeeded in bringing under his sway the greater part of the tract that stretched from the Libyan Desert to Western Mauritania. In spite of all his efforts to maintain discipline and prevent excesses the ferocious Berbers, who formed the bulk of his army, committed great atrocities in the course of his wars, which gave rise to a fierce revolt in the succeeding reign. The Mahdi saw that he must have a strongly fortified capital in case of any sudden outburst against his dynasty. Setting out from Tunis he inspected the entire sea-coast to choose an impregnable site, and at last fixed upon a slip of land jutting out into the sea. Here the city of Mahdièh[1] was begun in 303 A.H., and completed in five years. A strong wall, with gates of iron, enclosed it; and within were built splendid marble palaces, and vast tanks and underground storehouses, which were filled with provisions. "I am now at ease," said Obaidullâh, when he saw the finished city, "regarding the [fate of the] Fawâtim (the Fatimides)." Obaidullâh's rule was firm and vigorous. Even the orthodox Suyûti admits that "Obaidullâh extended justice and beneficence to the people, and they inclined towards him." In 309 A.H. he reduced the Idrîsides to subjection, but failed to conquer Egypt. Not satisfied with the possession of Mauritania, he cast longing eyes on Spain, when death put an end to his dreams.[2]

Death of *The Shiah*. Jamâdi I. 298 A.H. February 911 A.C.

916 A.C.

922 A.C.

[1] Mahdièh was captured by the Normans in 543 A.H. (1148 A.C.). It was wrested from them by Abdul Momin in 1160 A.C.

[2] The rise of the Fatimide power, although no doubt it promoted the civilisation of Northern Africa, was in many respects disastrous to Islâm, for the rivalry and wars of the later sovereigns of this

169—567 A.H.

Death of Obaid-ullâh al-Mahdi, 15th Rabi I. 322 A.H. March 934 A.C.

Accession of *Abu'l Kâsim* Mohammed Nizâr, *al-Kâim bi-amr Illâh.*

After a successful reign of twenty-four years, Obaid-ullâh al-Mahdi died in 322 A.H., and was succeeded by his son *Abu'l Kâsim* Mohammed Nizâr, who assumed the title of *al-Kâim bi-amr Illâh.*[1] Kâim was a great warrior, and personally conducted most of his military operations. He was the first of the Fatimide Caliphs who, in order to obtain the command of the Mediterranean, applied himself to the creation of a powerful fleet. After re-establishing his authority in Mauritania, save and except the district of Fez, which had been recovered by the Idrîsides, he turned his attention towards the continent of Europe. His ports had been harassed by Italian pirates from the Ligurian coast, from Pisa and other places. In reprisal, Kâim overran Southern Italy as far as Gaëta; and his ships of war captured Genoa, which was held by the Saracens for a considerable time. A part of Lombardy (*al-Ankaburda*) was also brought into subjection. But for a domestic convulsion which taxed all his resources and military skill, there is little doubt that Kâim would have reduced Italy under his power. Unfortunately the pent-up wrath of the people at the excesses of the savage Berbers burst into a furious flame just at the moment when the prospects were most favourable. The revolt was headed by a Khâriji named *Abû Yezîd* Makhlad, son of Kîrâd, a school-master by profession, who had by his preachings collected a large following among the Berbers of Mount Auress (*Aurâs* of the Arabs). With political foresight unusual among fanatics, he invited the Spanish

dynasty with the Seljukide Sultans of Asia, prevented the latter from subjugating the Byzantine empire, and extending their sway in Eastern Europe. But for this rivalry, probably the Crusaders too would have been beaten back.

[1] "Firm in the ordinances of the Lord."

785—1171 A.C. Caliph an-Nâsir, to despoil the heretic and take his kingdom. In the year 333 of the Hegira, Abû Yezîd, who received from his followers the title of *Shaikh ul-Muslimîn*,[1] swept down from the mountains with an enormous horde of savages. The Fatimide troops were defeated again and again, city after city was taken by storm, and frightful atrocities were committed by the fanatics. Before long what the Mahdi had foreseen came to pass. The greater part of the country fell into the hands of the Khâriji school-master, whilst the rule of Kâim was confined to the walls of Mahdièh and a few other fortified towns on the sea-coast. Abû Yezîd tried to carry the capital by assault. Four times he delivered desperate attacks, and each time was repulsed with frightful slaughter. Turning the siege into a blockade, Abû Yezîd proceeded towards Susa (Sûs of the Arabs), which he tried to take by storm.

Revolt of Abû Yezîd Makhlad 333 A.H. 942-3 A.C.

Whilst Abû Yezîd was laying siege to Susa, Kâim died. He was succeeded on the throne by his son *Abu't Tâhir* Ismâil, surnamed *al-Mansûr bi-amr Illâh*[2]—a young man of rare energy and determination. Step by step he beat back the fanatical horde. They had shown no pity in the hour of their success, and none was shown to them in the day of defeat. Those only who submitted received immediate pardon and absolute safety. Abû Yezîd fled to Jabl Sâlât[3]—a precipitous and inaccessible rock rising from a parched desert, which needed eleven days to traverse. Mansûr pursued him with relentless fury, and at last cooped up the fanatic and his dwindled following in a castle among the mountains of the Kitâma.[4]

Kâim's death, 13th Shawwâl, 335 A.H. 18th May, 946 A.C. Accession of *Abu't Tâhir* Ismâil, *al-Mansûr bi-amr-Illâh.*

336 A.H. 947 A.C.

1 "The old man (or chief) of the Moslems."

2 "Victorious by the command of the Lord."

3 Spelt with a *sîn*.

4 Amari reads this as Kiâna.

The struggle round this place was long and terrible. Abû Yezîd endeavoured to cut his way through the besiegers, but was captured and executed. Although the son of Abû Yezîd and some of his adherents continued for a while to give trouble, practically the whole of Ifrîkia again submitted to the Fatimide rule. Sicily and Calabria, where their authority had been hitherto only partially acknowledged by the Arab colonists, were brought under control. In 339 A.C. Mansûr appointed Abu'l Kâsim Hassan bin Ali bin Abi'l Hussain al-Kalbi as the viceroy of Sicily and its dependencies. The office remained in Hassan's family for a long time.[1] The Franks, who had made an inroad into Calabria, were defeated in a naval action off the coast of Italy. Mauritania, however, was lost to Mansûr, for Abû Yezîd's revolt had enabled an-Nâsir, the Ommeyade Caliph of Spain, to seize the whole of the Idrîside possessions.

169—567 A.H.

Abû Yezîd's death.

950 A.C.

Mansûr[2] died in 341 A.H., when his son *Abû Tamîm* Maad ascended the throne under the title of *al-Muiz li-dîn-Illâh.*[3] Al-Muiz is described, even by historians inimical to his family, as a wise, energetic, and chivalrous sovereign, an accomplished scholar, well versed in science and philosophy, and a munificent patron of arts and learning. He was unquestionably the Mâmûn of the West, and under him North Africa attained the highest pitch of civilisation and prosperity. The people were contented and happy; internal dissensions and disturb-

Death of Mansûr, Ramazân 341 A.H. March 943 A.C. Accession of *Abû Tamîm* Maad, *al-Muiz li-dîn-Illâh.*

[1] It remained in Hassan's family for a hundred and eight years. The anarchy which prevailed in the island during the reign of the Ameer Hassan, son of the Ameer Abu'l Fath Yusuf, enabled the Normans under Count Roger (the Rujâr of the Arabs) to establish their domination in the year 1152 A.C.

[2] Mansûr built a splendid city in the neighbourhood of Susa, which was named, after him, al-Mansûrièh.

[3] "The Exalter of the religion of the Lord."

785—1171 A.C. ances were repressed with vigour; the administration was placed on a systematic basis; rules were framed for the conduct of business; the provinces were divided into districts, which were entrusted to qualified officers who had under them a number of militia and regulars to maintain order. The army and fleet were re-organised, and a great impetus was given to commerce and industry. Humane in disposition, and gifted with wonderful tact and ability, he won the friendship, if not the attachment, of the chiefs who were most bitterly opposed to his father and grandfather. He received them with marked courtesy and kindness, and from enemies converted them into supporters.[1] His General-in-Chief Jouhar[2] recovered Mauritania from the hands of an-Nâsir, who was just then engaged with the Christian insurgents in the North of Spain, whilst Zîri bin Manâd, chief of the Sanhâja, crushed the malcontents in the districts of Oran and Bugia. "And the power of Muiz became firmly established in Ifrîkia and Maghrib, and his dominion became extensive." In 344 A.H. the Andalusian ships captured a vessel of al-Muiz carrying dispatches to Maghrib. In his rage at the insult, the Fatimide Caliph ordered the Viceroy of Sicily, Hassan bin Ali, to proceed to Spain and lay waste the coast of Almeria. An-Nâsir's captains
344 A.H. retaliated by devastating the neighbourhood of Susa and
955 A.C. Marsikhizr. Henceforth the two Moslem sovereigns, instead of joining their forces for the conquest of Europe,
Loss of Crete. wasted their strength in warring upon each other. Crete

[1] Ibn Khaldûn.

[2] The *Kâid ul-Kuwwâd* Abu'l Hassan Jouhar, son of Abdullâh, who bore the surname of *Kâtib ur-Rûmi*, was a native of Sicily. He died at Misr on the 20th of Zu'l Kaada, 381 A.H. (January 29, 992 A.C.). He was generous and liberal; "his beneficence," says Ibn Khallikân, "ceased only with his death."

had been conquered in the time of Mâmûn by the Saracens exiled from Cordova. They had held it since then; had introduced civilisation, arts, and industry, and made it prosperous and flourishing. In 350 A.H. the Byzantines made a supreme effort for its reconquest. A fleet consisting of seven hundred ships of war landed an overwhelming force; the Saracens were overpowered and destroyed. The atrocities committed by the Greeks beggar all description; men were tarred and then burnt alive; no mercy was shown even to the infant in arms, and the women were subjected to terrible outrages. 169—567 A.H.

The loss of Crete was in some measure compensated by the extermination of the Byzantine power in Sicily. They still held in the island several strong places whence they were accustomed to harass the Saracens. Ahmed bin Hassan, the viceroy, applied himself vigorously to the conquest of these cities. The army sent from Byzantine for the relief of the Greeks sustained a heavy defeat on land, and were forced to betake themselves to their ships. These slipped anchor and tried to escape, but were pursued, disastrously beaten, and sunk. By the end of 351 A.H. the whole island was brought into subjection. Sicily has never been so prosperous as under the Kalbite Ameers: mosques, colleges, and schools sprang up on all sides; learning and arts were patronised, and the people prospered. The university of medicine at Palermo rivalled those of Bagdad and Cordova.

Final Conquest of Sicily.

966 A.C.

In 356 A.H. serious troubles broke out in Egypt,[1] and the notables of the province invited Muiz to take possession of the country, and to give them peace and order. In response to their solicitations Muiz despatched a well-appointed army under his lieutenant Jouhar. The Fatimide general entered the capital (Fostât) with-

Egypt, 968 A.C.

[1] On the death of Kâfûr al-Ikhshîdi.

785—1171 A.C. out opposition, and on the 15th of Shâbân 358 A.H. read the *Khutba* in the public mosque in the name of

July 5, 969 A.C. Muiz. In 359 A.H. he introduced in the call to prayers (*Azân*) the additional sentence: "Hasten to good work."[1] Jouhar inaugurated the Fatimide rule by founding the

Foundation of Cairo. city of *al-Kâhira*[2] (modern Cairo), which became later the capital of Muiz and his successors. He also obtained the submission of Hijâz and Syria; and prayers were recited in the name of al-Muiz in the Holy Cities. The Karmathians, who were still levying blackmail from the Moslem princes within their reach, were crushed in a single battle near Fostât. Hitherto Muiz had remained in Ifrîkia, but on the urgent solicitations of Jouhar he determined to proceed to Egypt. Before doing so he made a careful inspection of his ancestral kingdom.

Zu'l Hijja, 361 A.C. October 972 A.C. He appointed Bulukkîn,[3] the son of the faithful Zîri, to the viceroyalty of Ifrîkia with the title of *Saif ud-Dowla* ("Sword of the Empire"); confirmed Ahmed in the government of Sicily, and made other arrangements for

Muiz leaves for Egypt, November 972 A.C. the safety and wise administration of Northern Africa. He then left for the East in the Safar of 362 A.H. He entered Cairo during the Moslem Lent, and on the 15th of Ramazân, seated on a throne of gold, received the

His entry into Cairo, June 19, 973 A.C. oath of allegiance from the assembled delegates of Egypt, Syria, and Hijâz.

In spite of their defeat at the hands of Jouhar, the

[1] "*Hai aala khair ul-aaml.*" This additional phrase in the *Azân* forms a point of distinction in these days between the Shiahs and Sunnis.

[2] *Al Kâhira* ("the Victorious City").

[3] Instead of the uneuphonious Berber name, Muiz called him Yusuf Abu'l Futûh ("the father of victories"). Bulukkîn became the founder of the famous Zîride (often also called the Banû-Bâdîs) family which ruled Ifrîkia with such magnificence until the rise of the Almoravides.

audacity of the Carmathians was still unbounded. They had hitherto levied blackmail from Damascus; the refusal of the Fatimide governor to continue the payment brought them in great force against him. He was defeated and slain, and the city fell into their hands. They then proceeded to invade Egypt, but were met by Muiz at Ain ush-Shams (Heliopolis) and routed with frightful slaughter. This defeat finally broke their power.[1] Whilst the Fatimides were engaged with the Carmathians, a Turkish retainer of the Buyide Muiz ud-Dowla,[2] named Iftikîn, made himself master of Damascus and the surrounding country. 169—567 A.H.

Muiz died on Friday the 15th of Rabi II. 365 A.H., and was succeeded by his son *Abu'l Mansûr* Nizâr, who assumed the title of *al-Azîz b' Illâh.*[3] He is described as generous, brave, wise, and humane, "prone to forgiveness even with the power of punishing." He confirmed Bulukkîn bîn Zîri and the other officers of his father in their respective governments. Iftikîn, who had attempted to extend his power in the direction of Palestine and the Phœnician littoral, was defeated and taken prisoner. Azîz received him with such kindness that he became the faithful adherent of the Fatimide Caliph until his death. Death of Muiz, 15 Rabi II 365 A.H. Dec. 20, 975 A.C. Accession of *Abu'l Mansûr* Nizâr, *al-Azîz b' Illâh.*

Under Azîz the Fatimides succeeded in conquering the whole of Syria and part of Mesopotamia, and the *Khutba* was read in his name not only in Hijâz and Yemen, but also in Mosul, Aleppo, Hamâh, Shaizar, and other places. At this time the Fatimide Empire extended from the borders of the Euphrates to the Atlantic, and included the greater portion of Arabia. Hitherto the

[1] There is an interesting account of their capital (al-Ahsâ) in Nâsiri Khusrû's *Safarnâmèh.*

[2] See *ante* p. 303.

[3] "August by the grace of the Lord."

785—1171 A.C. Kitamians, who had helped in the establishment of the dynasty, had supplied the most trusted soldiers of the Fatimides, and their power naturally was great. Azîz formed a corps of Turks and Persians (Deilemites) apparently as a counterpoise against the Berbers.

Death of al-Azîz, 28 Ramazan, 386 A.H. Oct. 14, 996 A.C. Accession of *Abû Ali* al-Mansûr *al-Hâkim bi-amr-Illah.*

Azîz died in the year 386 of the Hegira at Bilbais, or Bilbîs, on his way to Syria, and with him ended the glory of the Fatimides. He had on his deathbed confided his young son and heir Mansûr to the chief Kâzi Mohammed bin an-Nomân[1] and Abû Mohammed Hassan bin Ammâr,[2] surnamed *Amîn ud-Dowla* ("warden of the empire"), in the hope that under their guidance the lad would prove himself a wise and successful ruler. Mansûr was proclaimed Imâm and Caliph, with the title of *al-Hâkim bi-amr-Illâh*,[3] but he soon fell under the influence of an unscrupulous intriguer named Barjâwân. The latter was opposed by Ibn Ammâr, and their quarrels and rivalry occasioned serious disturbances both in Syria and Egypt. Before long Hâkim himself began to show signs of madness. He often issued strange and contradictory orders; the smallest neglect exposed the offender to the punishment of death. In time this mental aberration developed into homicidal mania, and he put to death without any reason a number of prominent men. Yet in his lucid moments he was a liberal and generous patron of learning and science,[4] and built numerous

[1] Mohammed bin an-Nomân was the Chief Kâzi of the whole of Egypt, Hijâz, and of the military colonies in Syria. Many members of his family occupied high judicial functions under the later Caliphs. He died in 999 A.C.

[2] He was the *Shaikh* and commander of the Kitâmian troops, and himself was a member of that tribe.

[3] "He who governs by the orders of the Lord."

[4] He was the patron of the celebrated astronomer Ibn Yunus.

mosques, colleges, and observatories both in Syria and Egypt. For five-and-twenty years Hâkim occupied the throne of his forefathers in this insane manner, but fate at last overtook him. He was fond of solitude, and accustomed to wander about at night. Often he went to a lonesome house on the hill of Mokattam,[1] "either to watch the stars," says Ibn Khaldûn, "or to offer his devotions." One night, the night of the 27th of Shawwâl, 411 A.H., he had as usual gone there with two attendants, whom, however, he dismissed at the foot of the hill. From this visit to Mokattam he never returned. His prolonged absence caused alarm, and a search party was sent out to scour the country. On the top of the hill they found the pony he had ridden with its forelegs hacked by a sword, and in a cistern not far off his clothes pierced by daggers, still buttoned up, but the body was never discovered. No doubt whatever remained that he had been assassinated.[2]

169–567 A.H.

Death of Hâkim, 27th Shawwâl 411 A.H. Feb. 13, 1021 A.C.

Hâkim was actually the founder of a new cult, in which he occupied the central figure, and was regarded as the emanation of the Deity. His followers and disciples believed him to have only disappeared from the earth to appear again in the fulness of time, or to use their own expression, "when it shall please him."

1 In the neighbourhood of Cairo.

2 Several authors have given currency to the story that Hâkim was assassinated at the instigation of his sister, the Sitt ul-Mulk ("the Lady of the Empire"), whom he had threatened with death for her gallantries. Makrîsi, however, who lived nearer the time, characterises the story as absolutely false, and states that four years later (415 A.H.) a man, who was arrested for having raised a rebellion in Upper Egypt, confessed to having murdered Hâkim with three accomplices, "for the glory of God and religion." The details given by this man are so circumstantial as to leave no doubt that the confession was genuine.

785—1171 A.C.

This cult is still extant among the Druses[1] of the Lebanon.[2]

Accession of *Abû Hâshim* Ali, *Az-Zâhir li-Izâz din-Illah.*

Hâkim's son, *Abû Hâshim* Ali, was then raised to the throne under the title of *Az-Zâhir li Izâz dîn-Illâh.*[3] For the first four years his aunt, the Sitt ul-Mulk, held the regency. After her death the government was carried on by Mizâd and Nâfir, who had been officials under Hâkim. In this reign the greater portion of Syria escaped from the hands of the Fatimides; and an Arab chief of the name of Sâlèh bin Mirdâs made himself master of Aleppo and the surrounding districts.

Zâhir's death, 15th Shâbân, 427 A.H. June 1036 A.C. Accession of *Abû Tamîm* Maad, *al-Mustansir b'Illâh.*

Zâhir died in the thirty-first year of his age and the sixteenth of his reign, and was succeeded by his son *Abû Tamîm* Maad, under the title of *al-Mustansir b' Illâh.*[4] He was only seven years of age, and the government fell into the hands of a number of intriguers, under whose mismanagement the empire rapidly declined in strength and prosperity. In 1047 A.C. the Holy Cities disclaimed their allegiance to the Fatimide Caliph; and five years later the Zîride prince of Ifrîkia, al-Muiz bin Bâdîs,[5] who bore the title of *Sharf ud-Dowla*, threw off the Fatimide yoke, discontinued the *Khutba* in the name of Mustansir,[6] and acknowledged the Abbasside sovereign al-Kâim as

452 A.H. 1060 A.C.

the Pontiff of Islâm. The rebellion of Bassâsiri[7] and the flight of Kâim from Bagdad created a diversion in favour

[1] Ad-Durziyyèh, Durzi or Durûz of the Arabs; see the *Radd-ul-Muhtâr*.

[2] In their religious books he is described "our Lord al-Hâkim, may his name be glorified."

[3] "The assister in exalting the religion of the Lord."

[4] "Imploring the help of the Lord."

[5] Abû Tamîm Muiz, son of Bâdîs, son of Mansûr, son of Bulukkîn. (See *ante*, p. 600).

[6] This happened when Nâsiri Khusrû was sojourning in Cairo.

[7] See *ante*, p. 310.

of Mustansir; and for a whole year the *Khutba* was read in his name in Irâk and its dependencies. But Tughril soon restored the spiritual supremacy of the Abbasside Caliph in Western Asia; and under Alp Arslân, Tughril's successor, the Seljuks drove the Fatimides beyond al-Aarîsh. To add to the misfortunes of the people, a terrible famine desolated Egypt, and continued, says our author, for seven years. The administration became completely paralysed, and a great part of the country was deserted or ruined. During the height of the distress Mustansir called to his help the famous Badr ul-Jamâli,[1] governor of Acre, and invested him with absolute control. Badr ul-Jamâli proved a second Joseph to the Fatimide Pharaoh. He restored order in the kingdom, relieved the people, and re-established the authority of the sovereign throughout Egypt. He failed in his attempts to recover Damascus, but succeeded in recapturing the cities of the Phœnician coast. Badr ul-Jamâli died in the year 1094 A.C.,[2] and was followed a month later by the master who had experienced so much adversity in his life, "that at one time there was nothing left to him but the prayer-mat on which he was seated."[3]

169—567 A.H.

466 A.H. 1074 A.C.

Death of Mustansir, 18th Zu'l Hijja 487 A.H. January 6, 1095 A.C.

Mustansir had nominated his eldest son Nizâr[4] as his successor to the throne. But al-Afzal, the son of Badr ul-Jamâli, who had succeeded to the office held by his

Accession of *Abu'l Kâsim* Ahmed, *al-Mustaali b'Illâh.*

[1] His titles show the power with which he was vested: "the Glorious Lord, Commander-in-chief, the Custodian of the Affairs of the Moslems, the Chief Missionary of the Faithful, *Dâi ud-Daawât il-Mominîn.*"

[2] According to Ibn Khaldûn he died in Rabi I. of 487 A.H., whilst Ibn Khallikân puts it in 488 A.H.

[3] Ibn ul-Athîr, vol. x. p. 161.

[4] The Eastern Ismâilias, the Assassins of Alamût (the followers of Hassan Sabâh), acknowledged the Imâmate of Nizâr, and not of his brother. Their Imâms or spiritual leaders claimed descent from him.

785—1171 father, raised to the throne a younger brother of Nizâr
A.C. named *Abu'l Kâsim* Ahmed, under the title of *al-Mustaali*
b'Illâh.[1] Nizâr fled to the governor of Alexandria, who
proclaimed him Caliph.[2] Both were defeated and taken
Shâbân prisoner by Afzal. The governor was publicly put to
489 A.H. death, whilst nobody knew the fate of Nizâr.[3] Jerusalem,
1096 A.C. which had been held by the Banû-Ortok under the
The Crusades, Seljukide sovereign of Damascus, was recaptured by al-
Zu'l Kaada Afzal in 1096 A.C. But he did not hold it long, for
490 A.H. November the crusading storm soon burst upon Syria and Pales-
1097 A.C. tine, and swept away both Seljukide and Fatimide.

Death of Mustaali died in the Safar of 495 A.H., when al-Afzal,
Mustaali, 16th Safar the real master of the Fatimide kingdom, raised to the
495 A.H. throne the deceased Caliph's infant son *Abû Ali* al-
December Mansûr under the title of *al-Aâmir bi-ahkâm Illâh.*[4]
1101 A.C. Afzal governed the empire with absolute power until
Accession Aâmir attained majority, and his rule seems to have been
of *Abû Ali* al-Mansûr, on the whole successful and prosperous. In spite of
al-Aâmir some successes gained by the Egyptians under Afzal's son,
bi-Ahkâm Illâh. Sharf ul-Maâli, over the Crusaders, the cities on the
Phœnician littoral, which only a short time before had
11th Zu'l been reconquered by Badr ul-Jamâli, fell gradually into
Hijja 502 A.H. the power of the Crusaders. The sack of Tripoli[2] has
July 12, already been described. "The Egyptian troops sent to
1109 A.C. the relief of the place arrived when all was lost!"

When Aâmir attained majority he proved himself a

[1] "Grand (by the grace) of the Lord."

[2] Under the title of *al-Mustafâ li-dîn Illâh* ("the Chosen of the Religion of the Lord").

[3] Some say he was secretly murdered, whilst the Eastern Ismâilias believe he escaped into Asia, and became the progenitor of the Ismâilia Imâms of Alamût; see the *Spirit of Islâm*, p. 462.

[4] "The Commander who executes the decrees of the Lord."

[5] See *ante*, p. 329.

vicious and evil-minded young man, addicted to low pleasures, tyrannical, haughty, and inconsiderate; chafing under the tutelage of his all-powerful vizier, he contrived to have him murdered. Nine years later the same fate overtook him; on his way to a garden "on the island" he was attacked and stabbed to death by a number of *Fedâis*[1] (assassins), who had plotted his murder. 169—567 A.H. 515 A.H. 1121 A.C.

As Aâmir's queen was expecting a child, his cousin *Abu'l Maimûn* Abd ul-Majîd[2] undertook the regency under the title of *al-Hâfiz li-dîn Illâh*[3] until the birth of the heir to the throne. The child, however, happened to be a girl; Hâfiz was then proclaimed in his own right Caliph and Imâm of the Fatimides. Shortly after the people had sworn allegiance to him he was deposed and placed in confinement by the vizier Abû Ali Ahmed, the son of al-Afzal, a man of great ability and towering ambition. He was a follower of the Apostolical Imâms;[4] and partly in furtherance of his own designs to become the absolute ruler of Egypt, and partly under the influence of his sectarian predilections, he substituted the name of the last Imâm,[5] the unfortunate child who disappeared in the cave of Sâmarra, on the coinage and in the prayers.[6] This continued for a time, but Hâfiz plotted from his prison the vizier's death; and on the 15th of Moharram 526 A.H., he was attacked and killed in the Great Garden

Abu'l Maimûn Abd ul-Majîd, *al-Hâfiz li dîn-Illâh.*

Moharram 526 A.H. Dec. 1131 A.C.

[1] Ibn ul-Athîr calls them by the name of Bâtinias.

[2] His father Mohammed was a son of Mustansir.

[3] "Guardian of the Religion of the Lord."

[4] The followers of the twelve Apostolical Imâms are called Isnâ-aasharias or Duodecimians; see the *Spirit of Islâm*, p. 314.

[5] See *ante*, p. 295.

[6] He also had the words "hasten to good work" omitted from the call to prayer. The titles assumed by this ambitious vizier are given in full by Ibn ul-Athîr (vol. x. p. 473), and convey some idea of the extraordinary pretensions of the age as well as of the man.

785—1171 A.C. (*al-Bustân ul-Kabîr*) outside the capital. Upon Abu'l Ali Ahmed's death Hâfiz was re-instated on the throne; but his restoration was of no advantage to the state, for, without any strength of character, he proved a mere tool in the hands of his vizier, the Ameer ul-Juyûsh Yânis al-Hâfizi, "a fearful man, and great in wickedness,"[1] although
1132 A.C. far-sighted. Yânis was assassinated at the instance, it is said, of Hâfiz in the month of Zu'l Hijja of 526 A.H. Hâfiz then appointed an Armenian of the name of Bihrâm as his vizier. The rivalry between Bihrâm and Rizwân, one of the principal secretaries of state, plunged the country into internecine strife and warfare. Bihrâm was seized and imprisoned by Hâfiz, when Rizwân became vizier.[2] He also rose in arms against his sovereign, but
1148 A.C. lost his life in the struggle. The conduct of these officers determined Hâfiz to keep all the power in his own hands and not to have any vizier in future. And this resolve he maintained up to his death.

Death of Hâfiz, 5th Jamâdi II. 544 A.H. Oct. 10, 1149 A.C.

Hâfiz died in 1149 A.C. His last days were darkened by the gloom of intestine dissensions within the capital. During the whole of his reign, says Ibn ul-Athîr, he was subject to the influence of those who surrounded him, especially his viziers.

Accession of *Abû Mansûr* Ismâil, *az-Zâfir bi-amr Illâh.*

Hâfiz was succeeded by his son *Abû Mansûr* Ismâil, under the title of *az-Zâfir bi-amr-Illâh.*[3] Addicted to pleasure of all kinds, and passing his time with unworthy favourites, he was a mere cypher in the state; and all the power and influence fell into the hands of the vizier Abu'l Hasan Ali ibn us-Salâr, surnamed *al-Malik ul-*

[1] *Kasîr ush-Sharr.*

[2] It was in the vizierate of Rizwân that Ameer Osâma went to Egypt (539 A.H., 1144 A.C.).

[3] "Conquering by the commands of the Lord."

Mosque in Cairo.

Aâdil.[1] Ibn us-Salâr was assassinated in 1153 A.C. by 169—567
his stepson Abbâs, who then became the vizier of Zâfir. A.H.
The position occupied by the Egyptian Caliphs at this Moharram
time is graphically described by Ibn ul-Athîr. "In Egypt 548 A.H.
the vizierate belonged to him who had force under his April 3
command; the Caliphs were powerless; the viziers were 1153 A.C.
like kings; no one obtained the vizierate (in Egypt) after al-Afzal except by war and murder and such like (crimes)." The authority of the Caliph hardly extended beyond the limits of his own palace. In the pages of Osâma we see pictured the same symptoms of decadence that he saw in the kingdom of Jerusalem. The revolts, the rivalries, the plots and counterplots, the anarchy that had transformed Cairo into a field of battle given up to the violence of factions, foretold an early dissolution. Up to this time the Egyptians had managed to hold Ascalon,
but the dissensions which broke out in Egypt on the 548 A.H.
murder of Ibn us-Salâr gave to the Crusaders the oppor- 1153 A.C.
tunity of reducing that important city.[2]

In the month of Moharram 549 A.H., Zâfir was assas- Assassination of Az-Zâfir, Moharram 549 A.H. April 1154 A.C.
sinated by Nasr the son of Abbâs.[3] In order to divert

[1] Osâma was employed by this vizier as ambassador to Nur ud-dîn Mahmûd.

[2] "Ascalon (Aaskalân)," says Mukaddasi, "is a beautiful city on the sea-coast. The cereals and fruits are abundant. The mosque is in the Market Place, where they sell clothes; it is of marble, an edifice of great beauty, and solidly built. Life here is easy; the bazaars are good and the country charming." The head of Hussain the Martyr was kept in a *meshed* at Ascalon up to 549 A.H. (1154 A.C.), when it was taken to Cairo.

[3] Zâfir created several endowments, one notably for the maintenance of the mosque named az-Zâfiri, built by him at the Zawîla gate at Cairo. He also established the *Khazânat ul-bunûd* (the "magazine of standards") where three thousand skilled workmen were employed in the manufacture of arms, military machines, etc.; Makrîsi, *al-Khittat.*

785—1171 A.C.

Accession of *Abu'l Kâsim* Isâ, *al-Fâiz ba-nasr Illâh.*

suspicion from himself and his son, the treacherous and cruel vizier put to death az-Zâfir's brothers, Jibraîl and Yusuf, on the false charge of having murdered the Caliph. He then placed on the throne *Abu'l Kâsim* Îsa, the infant son of Zâfir, under the title of *al-Fâiz ba-nasr*[1] *Illâh*, and attempted to rule the kingdom as its absolute master. But the punishment of his crime was not long in coming. The sisters of Zâfir soon discovered the truth. They cut off their hair and sent it in a letter in deep black to Talâii bin Ruzzik,[2] governor of Upper Egypt, invoking his help to avenge the murder of Zâfir. Talâii marched upon Cairo with a large body of soldiers and a troop of nomadic Arabs all in mourning. Abbâs and Nasr, deserted by the army, fled with all their treasure towards Syria. They were accompanied by Ameer Osâma and a large following. The sisters of az-Zâfir had, in the meantime, written to the Crusaders at Ascalon, offering them a large sum of money to intercept Abbâs and his son. Incited by the promised reward, the Franks sallied from the castle to meet the fugitives; in the fight which ensued Abbâs was killed with a number of his followers, and Nasr was taken prisoner.[3] The Franks then put Nasr into an iron cage and sent him to Cairo, where, after being cruelly tortured, he was impaled on

March 6, 1156 A.C.

a cross. Talâii then assumed the vizierate with the title of *al-Malik as-Sâlèh*, and took charge of the infant Caliph.

Death of al-Fâiz, 17th Rajab 555 A.H. July 1160 A.C.

Al-Fâiz died before attaining his majority. The vizier, instead of proclaiming any of the adult members of the royal family, who were numerous and able, selected the

1 "Successful with the help of the Lord." *Fâiz* is spelt with a *zay*.

2 Or Ruzzaik. He was of Armenian parentage.

3 Osâma and his companions escaped.

infant son of Yusuf, the brother of Zâfir, for the dignity of Caliph. The child's name was *Abû Mohammed* Abdullâh Ali, and he was placed on the throne with the title of *al-Aâzid li-dîn-Illâh.*[1] As-Sâlèh continued to exercise absolute authority, and his conduct grew gradually most violent.[2] As-Sâlèh was assassinated by a palace conspiracy according to Ibn Khaldûn, or by a Bâtinia according to Makrîsi, in 1161 A.C. His son Ruzzik then became the vizier with the title of *al-Malik al-Aâdil,* but he was soon displaced by Shâwer as-Saadi,[3] who was driven out by Zirghâm,[4] an Arab, descended from the Munzirs of ancient Hîra, who held the office of Sâhib ul-Bâb,[5] a position similar to that of the Hâjib in the Abbasside court. Shâwer fled to Nûr ud-dîn Mahmûd at Damascus, and returned with assistance from the son of Zangi. Zirghâm was killed in a battle between his troops and the Syrians, and Shâwer again assumed the vizierate. The rest of the story of the Fatimides has already been told.[6]

169—567 A.H.

Accession of *Abû Mohammed* Abdullâh Ali, *al-Aâzid li-dîn Illâh.*

Ramazân 556 A.H. September 1161 A.C.

Ramazân 558 A.H. August 1163 A.C.

Al-Aâzid died in 1171 A.C., and with him ended the dynasty founded by Obaidullâh al-Mahdi.

12th Moharram 567 A.H. September 1171 A.C.

The circuit of Cairo was traced by Jouhar on the 24th Jamâdi II. 359 A.H. (May 14, 969 A.C.), and the walls were completed before the arrival of al-Muiz. Magnificent structures rapidly sprang up on all sides, giving to "the victorious city" a most imposing appearance. It

Cairo.

1 "Herdsman to the Faith of the Lord." *Aâzid* is spelt with a *zâd.*

2 Ibn Khaldûn, vol. iii. p. 73.

3 Of the tribe of Saad.

4 *Abu'l Ashbâl* Zirghâm, "father of the whelps, Lion," surnamed *al-Fâris ul-Muslimîn,* "the cavalier of the Moslems." Zirghâm is spelt with a *zâd.*

5 "Lord of the Gate," or Prefect of the Palace.

6 See *ante*, p. 348.

785—1171 A.C. was traversed by numerous roads and streets; the former leading into the suburbs were called *Harât*, whilst the latter apparently ended within the walls, and were designated *Akhtât*.[1] The Caliph's principal palace, composed of twelve pavilions, was situated in the eastern part of Cairo, and was called the *al-Kasr ul-Kabîr ush-Sharki* (the grand eastern palace), or *Kasr ul-Muizi* (the Palace of Muiz). Ten gates gave access to the Palace, which was guarded by a select body of troops, composed of five hundred foot-soldiers and an equal number of mounted men. Twelve thousand servants ministered to the wants of the inmates. A subterranean passage led to another magnificent palace, which was situated on the Nile in the western part of the city, and was called *Kasr ul-Gharbi* (the Western Palace), or *Kasr ul-Bahr* (Maritime Palace). There were other palaces and villas belonging to the Caliph both in the suburbs and the city, lavishly decorated by the best artists of the time. The mansions of the Ameers vied in splendour, although not in size or extent, with those of the sovereigns. Beautiful gardens surrounded the houses of the rich and opulent citizens. The number of these gardens and the magnificence of the houses seem to have struck with surprise travellers from Europe who visited Cairo so late as the fifteenth and sixteenth centuries of the Christian era.[2] Mosques, colleges, hospitals, and caravanserais of immense size adorned the city. The four cathedral mosques [3] were

[1] Plural of *Khatt*.

[2] Jehan Thenaud, "Master of Arts and Doctor in Theology," who accompanied Andre le Roy, sent by Louis XII. to the Mamluke Sultan Ghôri, has left an interesting account of Cairo, its gardens and palaces.

[3] (1) *Al-Jâmaa ul-Azhar* (the Brilliant Mosque); (2) *al-Jâmaa un-Nûr* (the Mosque of Light); (3) *Jâmaa ul-Hâkim* (the mosque of Hâkim bi-amr Illâh); (4) *Jâmaa ul-Muiz* (the mosque of Muiz).

specially grand and beautiful. One special feature of Cairo under the Fatimides was the *Hussainièh*, a building[1] where, on the anniversary of the murder of the martyr Hussain on the field of Kerbela, they held meetings of mourning. Finely-built public baths were to be found in large numbers in every part of the town both for men and women. Those set apart for the latter were easily distinguishable from the others by their ornamentation. The markets, which contained twenty thousand shops, were superb, and stocked with the products of the world. The city was surrounded by a strong wall pierced by several gates.[2]

169—567 A.H.

Cairo.

Among out-door amusements, falconry and the hunting of antelopes and deer of all kinds, generally with hounds, formed the principal pastime of the rich, whilst the riverside *fellaheen* often engaged in the pursuit of the hippopotami.

The administration was conducted on lines similar to those of the Abbassides, although some of the offices bore different names.[3] The most important difference between the two systems of government was the preponderating influence possessed in Egypt by the military commander, the *Ameer ul-Juyûsh*, who combined in his person the office of vizier as well as of commander-in-chief of the forces, and who, under the weaker monarchs

[1] Called *Mash-had*, or Meshed. In India these buildings are called *Imâmbaras*. Under the Fatimides all the cities on the Syrian coast had *Mash-hads*. A *Hussainièh* still exists in Cairo.

[2] The following are some of the most famous gates of Cairo: (1) *Bâb un-Nasr* (the Gate of Succour), opening in the direction of the Nile; (2) *Bâb ul-Futûh* (the Gate of Victories); (3) *Bâb ul-Kantara* (the Gate of the Bridge); (4) *Bâb uz-Zawîlah* (the Gate of Zawilah, a city in Barbary); (5) *Bâb ul-Khalîj* (the Gate of the Canal), opening in the direction of Ghizèh.

[3] See Appendix.

785—1171 A.C. of the Fatimide dynasty, effaced the personality of the sovereign. Under the first ten Caliphs, however, they fulfilled the ordinary functions of their office. The decline of the Fatimides began in the reign of Mustansir. *Quem Deus vult perdere prius dementat.* From his time intrigue took the place of statesmanship. Character and moral worth were regarded of little moment; "political services" opened the door to honour and preferment; the scholar made room for the spy and the pander; the honest, independent and loyal for the sycophant and parasite. The rulers tried to govern by disintegrating the people and creating factions; their attempts only recoiled on themselves with deadly effect.

The early Fatimides, like their ancient prototypes the first Ptolemies, were grand supporters of learning and science. They established colleges, public libraries, and scientific institutes (*Dâr ul-hikmat*), richly supplied with books and mathematical instruments, and a large professorial staff. Access to and the use of these literary treasures were free to all, and writing materials were afforded gratis. The Caliphs frequently held learned disputations, at which the professors of these academies appeared, divided according to their different faculties, logicians, mathematicians, jurists, and physicians, dressed in their *Khalaa*, or doctoral mantles.[1] Two hundred and fifty-seven thousand ducats, raised by a carefully regulated taxation, constituted the annual revenue of the colleges, and was employed for paying the salaries of the professors and officials, and providing the requisites for teaching, and other objects of public scientific instruction. In these institutes they taught every branch

The *Dâr ul-hikmat.*

[1] The gowns of the English universities still retain the original form of the Arabic *Khalaa.*

of human knowledge. Observatories for the cultivation of astronomy were erected in various places; and litterateurs and scientists were invited from Asia and Spain to give lustre to the reigns of these Moslem Pharaohs. 169—567 A.H.

No history of the Fatimides can be complete without some mention of the extraordinary propaganda established by them, for in their desire to promote the diffusion of knowledge among their subjects, they did not ignore the political advantages of obtaining proselytes to their sect. To the central *Dâr ul-hikmat*, "House of Science" was attached a Grand Lodge, where the candidates for initiation into the esoteric doctrines of Ismâilism were instructed in the articles of the faith. Twice a week, every Monday and Wednesday, the *Dâï ud-Daawât*, the Grand Prior of the Lodge,[1] convened meetings, which were frequented by both men and women, dressed in white, occupying separate seats. These assemblages were named *Majâlis ul-hikmat*, or "philosophical conferences." Before the initiation the *Dâï ud-Daawât* waited on the Imâm (the Caliph), the Grand Master, and read to him the discourse he proposed to deliver to the neophytes, and received his sign-manual on the cover of the manuscript. After the lecture the pupils kissed the hands of the Grand Prior, and reverently touched the signature of the Master with their foreheads. Makrîsi's account of the different degrees of initiation adopted in this Lodge forms an invaluable record of freemasonry. In fact, the Lodge at Cairo became the model of all the Lodges created afterwards in Christendom.

As a political factor, the Fatimide *Dâr ul-Hikmat* came to an end with the dynasty to which it owed its origin; but its love of learning and science illumined

[1] The Vizier, or the Chief Kâzi, generally held this important post.

785–1171 A.C. the cities of Egypt until it died away under the anarchy of the later Mamelukes, whilst its esoteric spirit has survived the lapse of ages, and finds expression in countries and among communities widely differing from each other in instinct and genius.

APPENDIX

Page 108.—The episode relating to Florinda and the King of the Visigoths, Roderick, is thus told by Ibn ul-Athîr (vol. iv. p. 443): "Ghîtisha (Witiza) died leaving two sons; and the people of Spain accepted neither [for their king]; and they elected Ruzrîk, who was a brave man but did not belong to the royal family. And it was a custom among the princes of Spain to send their sons and daughters to Toledo, where they remained in the service of the king. And they alone waited on him. Thus they were trained and educated. And when they grew up they were married one to the other. And the king was their guardian in everything. When Ruzrîk became king, Zuliân (Julian), who was governor of Algeciras and Ceuta etc., sent his daughter to the Court. And Ruzrîk liked her and wished for her. And the girl wrote an account of it to her father, who was greatly angered thereby." Ibn Khaldûn has the same (vol. iv. p. 117). He calls Roderick, Luzrîk.

Page 108.—"Crossing the sea they [Târick and his soldiers] proceeded towards the mountain of Manîf which is right on the sea. And here they landed; *and that is the reason why it bears until this day* the name of Jabl(u) Târick. When Abdul Momin became the master of this country, he ordered a city to be built on this rock which he called *Jabl ul-Fatah* ('the rock of victory'); but this name did not continue. On the tongues [of people] the former name [*Jabl(u) Târick*] remained current;" Ibn ul-Athîr, vol. iv. p. 444. "And he (Tarîck) landed near the Jabl ul-Fatah, and hence it is called Jabl(u) Târick;" Ibn Khaldûn, vol. iv. p. 117. See also Makkarî (Nafhut-tîb), vol. i. p. 142. "Then Ruzrîk came with his army to oppose them, and met them on the banks of Nahr(u) Lakkèh appertaining to [the District of] Shizona (Sidonia) on the remaining two nights of Ramazân of 92. And the fight lasted for eight continuous days;" Ibn ul-Athîr, vol. iv. p. 445.

Page 231.—Khaizurân means a willow-wand.

Page 272.—Leo the Wise relates with visible satisfaction how, on the re-conquest of Crete by the Byzantines, the Saracen colonists in the island "were flayed alive or plunged into cauldrons of burning oil."

Page 315.—Zubaida, the daughter of Nizâm ul-Mulk the vizier of Malik Shah, appears to have been a remarkably cultured woman. She was married to the vizier Ibn Jâhir. The sister of Malik Shah, named Zulaikha, was equally celebrated for beauty, wit and learning.

Page 319.—On the assassination of Nizâm ul-Mulk, Tâj ul-Mulk Abu'l Gharâim al-Kummi, secretary and privy-councillor to Turkhân Khâtûn, the queen of Malik Shah, succeeded to the vacant office.

Page 336.—The Arabic name of the plain situated between Lebanon and Anti-Lebanon, called by the ancients Cœle-Syria or "Hollow Syria," is *Sahl ul-Bakâa;* of the Plain of Antioch, *Sahl Antâkièh*, and of the Plain of Mount Tabor or Esdraelon, *Sahl ul-Kabîr*, whilst the country around Damascus is called *Ghôtatu Damishk*. That also was the name of the Vega of Granada.

Page 344.—Joscelin II. died whilst a prisoner in the hands of Nûr ud-dîn Mahmûd.

Page 363.—The modern Turkish name of the river Calycadnus is Ghiûksu.

Page 366.—The brutality and coarseness of the Crusaders can scarcely be wondered at when we bear in mind the manners and habits in their original homes. After a feast in the hall, the baron and his knights lay scattered about helpless from the extent of their potations and reclining on the laps of their women; "in the midst stood a jongleur or minstrel, alternately singing and exciting their mirth with coarse and brutal jests." In the reign of Stephen of England, "the amusements of the hall were varied with the torture of captured enemies." William of Malmesbury, writing in 1130, says, "The Saxon nobility passed entire nights and days in drinking, and consumed their whole substance in mean and despicable houses; they had their hair cropped, their beards shaven, their arms laden with golden bracelets, and their skins adorned with punctured designs; they were accustomed to eat till they became surfeited, and to drink till they were sick. And these latter qualities they imparted to their conquerors." Among the Normans the dinner was partaken of early in the forenoon. After the hands were washed the company adjourned into another apartment, where commenced the usual carousal interspersed with story-telling and performances by jongleurs, which were often very obscene even in the presence of ladies. "We need not be surprised that the performances of the jongleurs before ladies were indecent, for the ladies themselves were by no means refined." Manners were worse in Germany. The student of comparative history will find some curious facts in Wright's *Homes of Other Days*, Fosbrooke's *British Monachism*, and Samuelson's *History of Drink.*

Page 369.—According to the *Mujam-ul-Buldân*, "al-Kharrûba is a fortress on the *Bahr ush-Shâm* (the Mediterranean) near Acre (*Mushrife aala Akka*"); vol. ii. p. 428.

(Note on p. 362 is according to the *Recueil des Historiens des Croisades*, where it is stated in another place, "Kharrûba is a strong fortress on Mount Carmel ten miles to the south-east of Acre.")

Whilst Saladin was encamped at Natrûn, "Malik Inkiltâr," says Ibn ul-Athîr, "sent a message demanding a truce (Muhâdanèh). The ambassadors came to and fro (several times) to al-Malik al-Aâdil Abî Bakr bin Ayûb, brother of Salâh-ud-dîn. Then it was settled that the Malik Inkiltâr should give his sister in marriage to al-Aâdil, that al-Kuds (Jerusalem) and all that was in the hands of the Moslems on the littoral (*Bilâd us-Sâhil*) should belong to al-Aâdil; that Acre and all that was in the hands of the Franks should be given to the sister of Inkiltâr over and above what she possessed beyond the seas, and which she had inherited from her [deceased] husband; that the Templars (ad-Dâwièh) should give their assent to all that had been agreed upon. Al-Aâdil placed these [conventions] before Salâh-ud-dîn, who accepted the same. When the news [of this] spread, the priests and bishops (*al-Asakifèh*) and monks assembled before the sister of Inkiltâr, and protested to her on the subject, and she thereupon refused to consent [to the marriage"].

Ibn Khaldûn says as follows:—"And messengers went backwards and forwards between Malik Inkilterrah (Richard) and Aâdil on this subject, that Malik Inkilterrah should give his sister in marriage to Aâdil, and that Kuds (Jerusalem) and all the Moslem territories on the coast should belong to Aâdil, and that Acre and the French possessions on the littoral should be the Queen's on condition of the assent of the Templars. And Salâh-ud-dîn accepted [the same];

but the priests and monks prevented the sister of the King of England and she refused it; and therefore it was not completed."

Ibn Shaddâd's account of these negotiations is as follows:—"On the 29th of Ramazân (587 A.H.), al-Malik al-Aâdil sent for me; and Ibn ud-dîn Sulaimân bin Jundar, Sâlik ud-dîn, Lord of Shaizar, Izz ud-dîn bin al-Mukaddam, and Hisâm ud-dîn Bashâra were (also) called. And he mentioned to us the proposal brought to him by the messenger from Inkiltâr, that al-Malik al-Aâdil should marry Inkiltâr's sister, whom he (Inkiltâr) had brought with him from Sicily after the death of her husband, its king; that she would be established at al-Kuds (Jerusalem), and her brother should give her all the littoral in his hands, viz. Acre, Jaffa, Ascalon, and all their dependencies; that the Sultan should bestow on al-Malik al-Aâdil all that was held by him on the littoral, and make him the king of the Maritime country (*Malik us-Sâhil*); and that he should keep in addition all the countries and fiefs (*Aktâa*) he was already in possession of; that the Cross of the Crosses [the Cross of the Crucifixion] should be restored to them (the Franks), that the villages of the Templars and Hospitallers and the fortresses should appertain to them both (al-Aâdil and his wife); that the Moslem and Frank prisoners should be set at liberty; and Inkiltâr should return to his country by the sea; thus the whole affair be settled. The envoy of al-Aâdil having brought this message from Inkiltâr, he believing that it would be carried into effect, sent for us, to take the latter to the Sultan. I was to be the spokesman whilst the rest of the assembly listened. I was to submit that if the Sultan approved of the arrangement and considered it would be to the benefit of the Muslimîn, we would bear witness to his sanction of the same and his approval; and if he rejected it, we would bear witness that the negotiations had reached thus far, and that he had considered it advisable to reject it. When we came into the presence of the Sultan, I submitted all this to His Majesty; and then read the letter before all the persons afore-mentioned. He (the Sultan) at once gave his assent to the proposal, (although) he knew that Inkiltâr would never keep his word and that it was a trick and a joke on his part. Then I requested him thus three times [to say if he assented to the proposal], and as often he replied in the affirmative and he swore upon it by his soul [to signify the sincerity of his approval]. When we ascertained his assent, we returned to al-Malik al-Aâdil, and acquainted him with all that had taken place. My colleagues also mentioned to him that I had several times asked the

Sultan [if he approved of the proposal], so as to bear witness to the fact and that he had persisted in his approval. It was thus the proposal was settled.

"On the 2nd of Shawwâl, Ibn un-Nahâl went as envoy from the Sultan and al-Malik al-Aâdil, and when he reached the camp of the enemy, and Inkiltâr learnt of his arrival, he sent information to him (the envoy) that the king (Richard) had placed before the queen (his sister) the proposal of marriage, and that she was greatly displeased and angered thereby, and that she refused obstinately, and had sworn by her faith she would never marry nor accept a Moslem for her husband. Then Inkiltâr said, 'al-Malik al-Aâdil will become a Christian, and I shall have the marriage completed.' And the door for negotiations was thus left open. When the envoy returned with this news, the Sultan was informed of it by letter." To my mind, there is nothing in this statement to suggest that beyond a natural suspicion of bad faith on the part of Richard, who was not noted among the Moslems for keeping his pledged word, the negotiations on either side were other than *bonâ fide*.

Page 373.—I forgot to mention that the great Hebrew philosopher Maimonides, of whom Munk speaks so highly in his *Mélanges de Philosophie Juive et Arabe*, was a contemporary of Saladin, by whom he was held in great esteem. Abdul Latîf mentions meeting him at Cairo.

Page 381.—In the year 659 A.H. [1260–61 A.C.] al-Malik uz-Zâhir, Sultan Baibars, Sultan of Egypt and Syria, sent Kâzi Jamâl ud-dîn bin Sâlim bin Wâsil, chief Shâfeïte Kazi of the principality of Hamâh, as an ambassador to the Emperor Manfred or Mainfroy, called *Anberâtûr* or *Anberûr* Manfrîd by the Arabs. "The word *Anberâtûr*," says Abu'l Fedâ, "signifies in the language of the Franks, *King of the Ameers*, and his realm comprises Sicily, Lombardy, and other countries on the mainland." Of Manfred Jamâl ud-dîn speaks thus :—"The father of the prince to whom I was sent was named Ferderîk [Frederick II.]. He was on terms of amity with al-Malik ul-Kâmil, Sultan of Egypt [see p. 381]. He was succeeded in the year 648 A.H. [1250–51 A.C.] by his son Kôra [Conrad]. Kôra was succeeded by his brother Manfrîd [Manfred]. All these sovereigns bore the title of *Anberûr*. Manfrîd was distinguished among all the Frankish prisoners for his friendship towards the Moslems and his love for the sciences. When I arrived at his Court he received me with great honour, and established me in a city of Apulia. . . . I had several interviews with him, and found him possessed of high talents. He knew by heart the ten books of Euclid. Near the town where I had my quarters was a city called Lujèra [Lucera], which was inhabited entirely by Mussulmans from Sicily. They performed the Friday services and openly practised the religious duties of Islâm. I observed that the principal officers of the Anberûr were Moslems; and in his camp they gave the *azân*, and publicly offered their prayers. The city where I resided was five days' journey from Rome. At the moment of my departure from the Court of the *Anberûr*, the Pope, who is the Caliph of the Franks, and the *Rîdafrans* [King of France] formed a league to attack Manfrîd, the Pope having already excommunicated him for his sympathy with the Mussulmans. His brother Kôra and his father Ferderîk had been similarly excommunicated for their leaning towards Islâm. . . . In the battle that ensued the *Anberûr* was defeated and taken prisoner. The Pope ordered his throat to be cut, which was done; and his realm fell into the hands of the brother of *Rîdafrans*." "This occurred, I believe," says Abu'l Fedâ, "in 663 A.H. [1264–65 A.C.]."

Jamâl ud-dîn wrote a treatise on logic for the emperor, which was called the *Anberûrièh* (*The Imperial*). He died on August 28, 1298 A.C.

Page 386.—The title of *tashtdar* is still borne by the Khans of Khiva, who call themselves the *tashtdars* of the Sultan of Turkey.

Page 400.—Sultan Baibars received the surname of *Bundûkdâr* from the regiment of arquebusiers organised by him.

Page 408.—The Abbasside sovereigns frequently employed a special envoy to transact confidential business with neighbouring potentates. This officer was called the *Nizâm ul-Hazratain*.

Page 415.—The literal meaning of the word *zimâm* (spelt with a *zay*) is the bridle or reins. In a secondary sense, it means control or the act of checking; when spelt with a *zâl* it means protection. Ibn ul-Athîr (vol. vi. p. 39, Tornberg's ed.) under the year 162 A.H. says: "In this year Mahdi established the *diwân ul-azzimah*;" Masûdi in the *Tanbîh* states, "he confirmed Rabii in the charge of the offices of *al-azzimmah*," and again, "he placed Mûsa at the head of the office of *al-azzimah*." The *Kâtib uz-zimâm* (spelt with a *zâl*) in Spain was entrusted with the duty of protecting and safeguarding the interests of the non-Moslem subjects (the *ahl-uz-zimmah* or *zimmis*).

Page 417.—Some of the official designations in vogue among the Fatimides were different from those in use under their rivals of Bagdad. I shall give here a few of the Egyptian names and the Arabic equivalents for English words frequently occurring in European histories. The Commandant of the Postal Couriers, or the head of the post office, was called in Egypt, *Mukaddam ul-barîdièh ;* the Cabinet Secretary, *Kâtib ud-darj ;* the Secretaries of the Chancery Office, *Kuttâb* (pl. of *Kâtib*) *ul-inshâ ;* the Chancery Office, the *diwân ul-inshâ ;* the Treasurer, *Khâzindâr ;* the Inspector, *Mushid ;* the Master of Robes, *Jamdâr* (this word was also in use under the Abbassides) ; the Head of the Armoury Office, *Silâh-dâr ;* Departmental Ministers, *Sâhib ;* Governor, *nâib ;* the Viceroy, *nâib ul-hazrat ;* Administrator of the Empire, *Kâfil ul-Mumâlik ;* Secretary to the Secret Chancellery, *Kâtib us-Sirr ;* Inspector-General, *nâzir un-Nuzzâr ;* War Office, *diwân ul-juyûsh ;* Paymaster-General's office, *Diwân ur-rawâtib* (in Bagdad it was called *Diwân ut-tartîb*) ; Pension Office, *Sandûk un-nafakât ;* Inspector-General of the colours and bands of regiments, *Ameer Alam ;* military inspectors, *nâzir ul-Jaîsh ;* Public Demands Recovery Office, *Diwân ul-murtaja ;* the Head of the Jews, *râs ul-Yahûd ;* general of cavalry, *sâhib ul-khail ;* store-house, *hawâij khanèh* (same under the Abbassides) ; minister in attendance, *Vizier us-Suhbat* (ditto) ; cellar, *sharâb khanèh ;* commander, *Kamandore ;* vessels of war, *butâs* (pl. of *batsèh*), also *Shawânî ul-Bahrièh ;* barques, *harârik* (pl. of *harakèh*) ; armada [Spanish *almadia*], fleet of ships, *al-Mâadi* (pl. of *al-Maadièh*) ; corvettes, *ghurâb ;* transport vessels, *tarrârid* (pl. of *tarîda*, Greek ταριδεος) ; fleet, *astûl ;* Capital of the Cæsars, *Kursî ul-Kyâsira ;* ministerial officers, *dawâwîn ;* surgeons, *jarâriheyèh* (pl. of *jarâhi*) ; stables, *jashîr ;* escort, *khafîr ;* cross-bow, *kazzâf ;* Chief of Police in Cairo, *Mutwalli ul-Kâhira ;* scavenger, *al-mashâali ;* cohort, *Kardûs ;* battalions, *tullâb* (pl. of *tulb*) ; chandeliers, *atwâr ;* port or harbour, *Mîna ;* the cataracts of the Nile, *al-Janâdîl ;* Tyre, *Sûr ;* Nubia, *ad-Diâr un-nûba ;* Memphis, *Mimf ;* Chalus (the river of Aleppo), *Kawîk ;* Belgrade, *Kalât Bair ul-Aghrâz ;* Coimbra, *Kulumbria ;* Grand Master of the Order of Templars, *Mukaddam Bait ud-dâwièh ;* Grand Master of the Order of Hospitallers, *Mukaddam Bait ul-Isbitâr ;* Minorca, *Minurka ;* Ivica, *Iâbisa ;* Majorca, *Mâyurka ;* Orontes, *al-Aâsi* (Yâkûb calls it *Aurantas*) ; Antioch, *Antâkièh ;* Seleucus, *Silukûs ;* Antiochus, *Antikhûs ;* Antigonus, *Antighunûs ;* the Strand, *ad-Dakka ;* the Volga, *Atîl ;* Odessa, *Daksîta ;* Red Sea, *Bahr Kulzum* (Sea of Clusium) ; Caspian Sea,

Bahr ul-Khazar ; Sea of Aral, *Buhairat Khwârism ;* Heraclius, *Harkal* or *Harkles ;* England, *Inkilterah,* " a large and wide island, containing many cities and forming a powerful kingdom ; " Arbela, *Irbîl ;* Hyrcania, *Jurjân ;* Jericho, *Arîka ;* Hebron, *Khalîl ;* Seleucia, *Salukièh ;* the Fortunate Isles, *Jazîrat ul-Khâlidât ;* Atlas, *Jabl(u) Daran ;* Peloponnesus (*Belobûnès*) ; Adriatic Sea, *Khalîj ul-Bunâdika ;* Xeres, *Shirish ;* Tagus, *Tâja ;* Sierra, *Sharat ;* Carcassonne, *Karkashûna ;* Burgos, *Barghasta ;* France, *Bilâd Afransièh ;* Gascony, *Ghaskunièh ;* Gironnes, *Jironda ;* Lombardy, *Ankabardièh* or *Anbardièh ;* Russia, *Bilâd ur-Rusièh ;* Bayonne, *Baiûna ;* the Taurus, *Jabl us-Silsilla ;* Toulouse, *Tulûsha ;* the Alps, *Jabl(u) Jûn ;* Burgundy, *Burghûnièh ;* Pisa, *Bîsh* or *Bîsha ;* Aquilia, *Aukillâèh ;* Germany, *Jarmânièh* or *Bilâd ul-Almânîn ;* Bohemia, *Marâtièh* or *Buwâmièh ;* Croatia, *Jerâshièh ;* Normandy, *Narmândièh ;* Flanders, *Bilâd Aflades* or *Aflandes ;* Saxony, *Shasûnièh* or *Belâd Sakes* (*Saxes*) ; Lorraine, *Luhrunka ;* Brittany, *Britânièh ;* Frisland, *Arz Afrîsa ;* Poland, *Bulûnièh* or *Fulûnièh ;* Hungary, *Unkurieh ;* Carpathians, *Jabl(u) Balwât ;* Servia, *Jasûlièh* (with a :) ; Norway, *Jazîrat ul-Barghâfa* or *Narbâgha ;* Scotland, *Askûsièh ;* Ireland, *Ghirlandèh ;* Denmark, *Arrundi* or *Darmûshèh ;* Iceland, *Rislândèh.*

Page 445.—In the *Mujam ul-Buldân* there is an excellent and full description of the famous palace of the Abbassides called the *Tâj* or Crown. Yâkût says it was originally a villa of the unfortunate Jaafar Barmeki, vizier of Rashîd. On the fall of the Barmekides, it came into the possession of Mâmûn, who converted it into a palatial mansion, laid out a race-course, a polo and hockey ground, and created a menagerie, etc. The palace was called after him *Kasr ul-Mâmûn,* and gave the name to the Mâmûnièh quarter, which was soon filled with beautiful palaces and mansions. At the *Kasr ul-Mâmûn* resided Bûrân until her death in 883 A.C., when the vast palace and grounds with all its beautiful art treasures reverted to the State. Mutazid pulled down the mansion and built it up afresh, but the new structure was not completed until the time of Muktafi. Mustazii further embellished it. It was a magnificent building of variegated marble, the ceilings resplendent with gold, and the walls covered with delicate floral tracery of inlaid precious stones. The central dome was called the *Kubbat ut-Tâj.*

Page 445.—The *Mâmûnièh,* says Yâkût, was a rich, big, populous quarter of Bagdad, which stretched from the *Nahr ul-Muallâ* to the

Bab ul-Azaj. At the end of the *Mahallah ul-Mâmûnièh*, in the middle of the *Sûk* (the public square), was situated the *Manzarat ul-Halbah*, "where now the Caliph sits on festive occasions (*Ayyâm ul-Iyâd*) and reviews the troops." Yâkût mentions several gates at Bagdad besides those enumerated in the text, such as the *Bâb ul-Hujrah*, the *Bâb ul-Khâssèh*, the *Bâb ul-Muhawwal*, the *Bâb ush-Shîïr*, etc. Several of the *mahallas* (quarters) were named after the gates, such as the *Bâb ush-Shîïr*, which lay above the *Medînat ul-Mansûr; Bâb ut-Tâk*, a large *mahalla* to the east of the city; the *Bâb ush-Shâm*, situated to the west. The *Harbièh* was another celebrated large *mahalla* near the *Bâb ul-Harb.* The *Nahr ul-Muallâ*, named after the aqueduct or canal of that name, was in Yâkût's time the most celebrated and the biggest quarter of the city.

Page 457.—Among the musical instruments chiefly in use in those days were varieties of flute (called *mizmar* and *shabâba*), the *rabâb* (a kind of guitar), the *barbat*, the *kânûn* (dulcimer), the *ûd* or lute, the *tambûr* (a kind of pandore), the *mizief* or harp, the zithern, the mandolin and hautboy (*zamûr*). The custom of giving musical soirées (*noubat khatûn*) was followed by the princesses and ladies of high rank under the Fatimide Caliphs and Mamluke sovereigns of Egypt.

Page 463.—The distinguished geographer Ibn Haukal flourished under the great Fatimide Caliph al-Muiz li-dîn Illâh. He travelled for some time in Spain, and submitted a report to his patron concerning the Peninsula so much coveted by the Fatimides. Muiz was also the patron and friend of the celebrated poet Ibn Hâni.

Page 532.—The modern Tuaregs are the direct descendants of the *Mulassamîn.*

Page 545.—Ibn Khaldûn does not properly belong to Spain. Although his family was long settled in Seville, the capture of that city by Ibn Adfûnsh (Ferdinand II.) in 1248 A.C. compelled them to remove to Tunis. Here was born in the year 723 A.H. (1332 A.C.) the great historian (*Abû Zaid* Abdur Rahmân, son of *Abû Bakr* Mohammed), whose career was one of the most remarkable recorded in history. At the age of twenty he became secretary to the Hafside Sultan (of Tunis) Abû Ishâk II. In 1356 A.C. we find him filling the same office to the Marînide Sultan Abû Aïnân, and his successor Abû Sâlim at Fez. In 1362 A.C. he went to Granada and for a time was ambassador to the Court of the Castilian king, Peter the Cruel

(Betruh son of Alhunsa, son of Adfunsh). From 1365 to 1382 we find him either engaged in important services to various princes or writing his great work. In 1382 he settled in Cairo; two years later he was made the Chief Mâliki Kâzi of that city, which office he held until his death. In 1400 A.C. we find him in the camp of Tamerlane (Timûr). Ibn Arab Shah describes in his usual stilted language the Western historian's interview with the great conqueror of Asia. He died at Cairo on March 15, 1406, at the grand age of eighty-four. His universal history was designed for his friend and patron the Hafside Sultan, Abu'l Abbâs, in whose service he was from 1378 to 1382. The patronymic Ibn Khaldûn is derived from his tenth progenitor. The family was of Yemenite descent from Hazramaut (Hadhramaut).

Page 552.—Polygamy was in vogue among the Merovingian kings of France. Gontran, Segibert, and Chilperic had several wives at one time. Gontran had within his palace acknowledged as his legitimate wives, Mercritrude, Ostregilde and Veneranda. Caribert had Merflida, Marconesa and Theodogilda. Dagobert I. had three wives. Theodobert married Dentary during the lifetime of his wife Visigelde. Clotaire, Æribartus, Hypercius and his sons all had several wives. Pepin, Charlemagne, Lothaire and his son, as also Arnulf VII., Frederick Barbarossa, and Philip Theodatus king of France, took advantage of similar privileges. Charlemagne is said to have had nine wives at one time.

Page 560.—Of all the Christian sovereigns of the Middle Ages, Alfonso VII., Ferdinand II. and Manfred of Germany alone rose to the height of equal justice and toleration to both Christians and Moslems. After the surrender of Toledo, Alfonso VII. assumed the title of "the Ruler of the two Religions" (Christianity and Islâm), and guaranteed to the Moslems security of person and property. This, however, did not last long, as the ecclesiastics proved too strong for him.

Page 569.—A European writer says that the Spanish Saracens "taught us the use of the pendulum in the measurement of time; and also of the telegraph, though not with all the speed and effect of modern improvement;" and adds, "it is unquestionable that a great number of the inventions which at the present day add to the comforts of life, and without which literature and the arts could never have flourished, are due to the Arabs."

Page 569.—There were two kinds of educational institutions among the Spanish Saracens. One was composed of primary schools, where children, chiefly of the lower orders, were instructed in the elements of reading, writing and religion ; whilst in the academies were taught all the higher branches of learning. The academies of the Saracens " were the shrines at which the barbarised nations of the West rekindled the torch of science and philosophy." To the Colleges of Cordova, Seville, Toledo, Jaen and Malaga flocked the seekers for knowledge from Italy, France, Germany and England. Here came Abelard, Morley the famous monk of Bath, and the celebrated Michael Scott. The kingdom of Granada alone contained seventy public libraries, seventeen colleges, and two hundred schools for primary education.

Page 569.—Casiri has given to the Western world the names of 170 eminent Saracen scholars and savants born in Cordova, the birthplace of Lucan and Seneca ; and of 120 authors, theologians, civilians, historians, philosophers and scientists whose talents conferred dignity and fame on the University of Granada.

Page 574.—The kings of Granada always kept on foot a regular frontier guard composed of veteran soldiers, whose duty it was to repel the sudden and murderous forays of the Castilians. The captain of these troops was called the *Shaikh ul-Ghuzzât*—" the chief of the warriors."

Page 613.—In Cairo and many other places in Egypt, " the Feast of the Gourd," which fell about the beginning of spring, and was probably a survival from pre-Grecian times, was observed as a carnival. Is not the modern carnival of the cities of Southern Europe the same as the *Floralia* or *Liberalia* which the Romans celebrated with such reckless disregard of decency ?

Page 614.—Benjamin of Tudela mentions in his Itinerary that under the Fatimides in Alexandria alone he found more than twenty academies for the cultivation of philosophy. Cairo possessed an immense number of colleges : and the Imperial library consisted of 100,000 manuscripts, elegantly transcribed and splendidly bound, which were freely lent out to the students. Similarly Kairowân, Fez and the large cities of Northern Africa contained magnificent establishments for the support of learning and the education of the people, and their rich libraries preserved many valuable works which would otherwise have been lost to posterity. To show that the Arabs could not have been unacquainted with the writings of Greek or Roman authors, it is enough to mention that the great library of Fez possessed a complete copy of Livy in Arabic.

Page 201.—Zu'r-Rumma died 127 A.H. There are some beautiful lines referring to Kharka in the poems of Al-Kahaif-al-'Ukaili.

BIBLIOGRAPHICAL INDEX

(Authorities consulted)

IBN UL-ATHÎR [d. 1233 A.C.] (*al-Kâmil*—Comprehensive Hist.); (*Târîkh ud-dowlat il-Atâbekia*—History of the Atâbeks of Mosul); Masûdi [d. 957 A.C.] (*Murûj uz-Zahab*); Ibn Khaldûn [d. 1406 A.C.] (*Kitâb ul-Ibr*, etc.—Universal History of the Arabs, Persians, Berbers, etc.); Suyûti [d. 1505 A.C.] (*Târîkh ul-Khulafâ*); Balâzuri [9th century] (*Futûh ul-Buldân*); Az-Zahabi [d. 1348 A.C.] (*Târikh ul-Islâm*); Jamâl ud-Dîn Abu'l Mahâsin Ibn Tughrâbardi [d. 1470 A.C.] (*An-Najûm uz-Zahira*, etc.); (*Maurid ul-Latâfat*); Fakhr ud-dîn Râzi [13th century] (*Târîkh ud-Dawal*, etc.); Abu'l Fedâ [d. 1331 A.C.] (*Akhbâr ul-Bashar*, etc.—Hist. of Mankind); Takî ud-Dîn Makrîsi [d. 1442 A.C.] (*Kitâb ul-Khittat*, etc.); (*Kitâb us-Sulûk*); Suyûti (*Husn ul-Mahâzira*); Wâkidi [d. 822 A.C.] (*Futûh ush-Shâm*); *Umdat ut-Tâ ib*, etc.; Al-Makrî or Makkarî [d. 1631 A.C.] (*Nafhut-Tîb*, etc.—History of Spain); Kamâl ud-Dîn [d. 1262 A.C.] (*Zubdat ut-Tawârîkh*); Osâma [d. 1188 A.C.] (*Kitâb ul-Itibâr*); Rashîd ud-Dîn [d. 1318 A.C.] (*Jâmaa ut-Tawârîkh*); *Târîkh Wassâf* [14th century]; *Muntakhib ut-Tawârîkh* [16th century]; Mirkhond [16th century] *Rouzat us-Safâ; Minhâj us-Sirâj;* Ferishta [17th century] *Târikh-i-Ferishta;* Ibn Shaddâd [d. 1235 A.C.] (*Mahâsin ul-Yusufia*—Life of Saladin); Ibn Khallikân [d. 1282 A.C.] (*Kitâb Wafiât ul-Ayyân*); Yâkût [d. 1229 A.C.] (*Mujam ul-Buldân*); Mukkadassi al-Bashâri [d. 998 A.C.] (*Ahsan ut-Takâsim fi-Maarfat ul-Akâlîm*—geographical work); Abu'l Faraj Isphahâni [d. 967 A.C.] (*Kitâb ul-Aghâni*); *Marâsid ul-Ittilâ; Safarnâmèh* of Nâsiri Khusrû [d. 1178 A.C.]; *Ilâm un-Nâs; Nahj ul-Balâghat; Rasâil Ikhwân us-Safâ; Nawâdir ul-Akhbâr; Jannât ul-Khulûd; Târîkh ul-Andalus;* Otbi [d. 1358 A.C.] (*Târîkh Yemîni*—History of Mahmûd the Ghaznevide); Ibn Arab Shah [d. 1476] (*Ajâib ul-Makdûr*, etc.); Abu'l Faraj [d. 1281 A.C.] (*Târikh Mukhtasar ud-Dawal*); Al-Beirûni [d. 1038] (*al-Âsâr ul-Bâkièh*, etc., the Vestiges of the Past); Ditto (*Fi't Tahkîk mâ l'il Hind*, etc., Book on India); Lutf Ali *Azar*

(*Atesh Kadèh*—Lives of the Poets); *Siâsatnâmèh* of Nizâm ul-Mulk; Harîri (*Makâmât*); Hâji Khalîfa [d. 1657] (*Kashf uz-zunûn*); Ibn Haukal [d. 976 A.C.] (*Kitâb ul-Mumâlik wa'l Masalik*—geographical work); *Muntaha ul-Arab*—Dictionary, etc.; C. de Perceval (*Hist. des Arabes*); Sédillot (*Hist. des Arabes*); Gibbon (*Decline and Fall of the Roman Empire*); Bury (*The Later Roman Empire*); Lebeau (*Hist. de Bas Empire*); Ockley (*History of the Saracens*); Von Kremer (*Culturgeschichte des Orients unter den Caliphen*); *Historiens Occidentaux des Croisades;* Von Hammer-Purgstall (*Literatur-Geschichte der Arabes*); Von Hammer (*Landerver-waltung unter den Chalifate*); (*History of the Assassins*); Howorth (*History of the Mongols*); De Guignes (*Hist. des Huns*); Amari (*Storia dei musulmani di Sicilia*); Reinaud (*Extraits des Historiens Arabes relatifs aux Croisades*); *Invasions des Sarrazins;* Dozy (*Hist. des Musulmans d'Espagne*); Dozy (*Hist. des Noms des Vêtements chez les Arabes*); Michaud (*Hist. des Croisades*); Mills (*Hist. of the Crusades*); Sismondi (*History of the Italian Republics*); Archer and Kingsford (*Hist. of the Crusades*); Watt (*Hist. of Spain*); Gayangos (*History of the Mohammedan Dynasties in Spain*); Murphy (*Arabian Antiquities in Spain*); Ditto (*Mahometan Empire in Spain*); Lane Poole (*Hist. of the Moors in Spain*); Muir (*Hist. of the Caliphate*); De Slane (*Translation of Ibn Khallikan's Biographical Dictionary*); Prescott (*Ferdinand and Isabella*); Condé (*Domination des Arabes en Espagne*); Vambery (*Hist. of Bokhara*); Malleson (*Hist. of the Afghans*); *Hist. of Ghazni;* Quatremere (*Hist. des Sultans Mamlukes*); Van Lennep (*Bible Lands*); D'Ohsson (*Tableaux Générale de l'Empire Ottomane*); D'Herbelot (*Bibliothèque Orientale*); Burckhardt (*Travels in Arabia*); Palgrave (*Travels in Central Arabia*); Blunt (*Pilgrimage to Nejd*); Fraser (*Travels in Persia*); *Travels of Ibn Batutah;* Rey (*Etude sur le Monuments*, etc.); Viardot (*Scènes des mœurs Arabes en Espagne au dixième Siècle*); *Recueil des Historiens de France;* Vaissette (*Hist. Générale du Languedoc*); Sismondi (*Hist. de la Chute de l'Empire Roman*); Noel des Vergers (*l'Histoire de l'Afrique et de la Sicile*); Reinaud (*Relation des Voyages des Arabes*); Abdul Latîf (*Relation de l'Egypte*, etc., trad. de Sacy); Berchem (*la Propriété Territoriale et l'impôt Foncier sous les premiers Califes*); Mohammed ibn Jubair (*Voyage en Sicile*); De Sacy (*Chrestomathie Arabe*); Ranke (*Hist. of the Popes*); Hallam (*Middle Ages*); Munk (*Mélanges de Philosophie Juive et Arabe*); Shahrastâni, *Millal wa'n-Nihal; Tajârib-ul-Umam*, etc.

INDEX

THE END

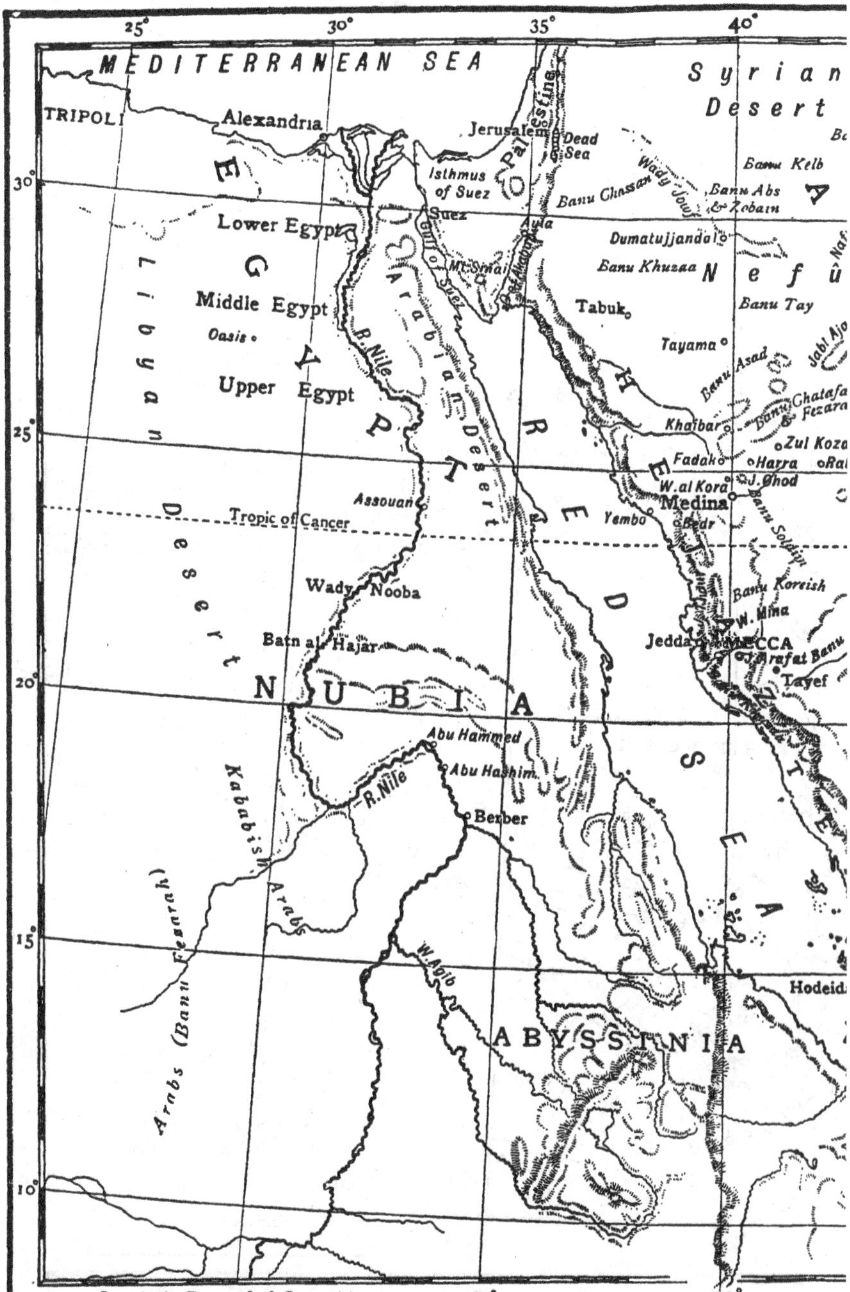
MEDITERRANEAN SEA
Syrian Desert
TRIPOLI
Alexandria
Jerusalem
Dead Sea
Palestine
Isthmus of Suez
Suez
Gulf of Suez
Ayla
Mt. Sinai
Banu Kelb
Banu Ghassan
Wady Jouf
Banu Abs & Zobain
Dumatujjandal
Banu Khuzaa
Nefûd
Banu Tay
Tabuk
Tayama
Banu Asad
Banu Ghatafan & Fezara
Khaibar
Fadak
Zul Koza
Harra
W. al Kora
J. Ohod
Medina
Yembo
Bedr
Banu Solaim
Banu Koreish
W. Mina
Jedda
MECCA
J. Arafat
Tayef
EGYPT
Lower Egypt
Middle Egypt
Oasis
Upper Egypt
Libyan Desert
Arabian Desert
R. Nile
Assouan
Tropic of Cancer
Wady Nooba
Batn al Hajar
NUBIA
Abu Hammed
Abu Hashim
Berber
Kababish Arabs
Arabs (Banu Fezarah)
W. Agib
ABYSSINIA
Hodeida
RED SEA
HEJAZ
Longitude East 30° of Greenwich
25°
30°
35°
40°
10°
15°
20°

ARABIA
in the time of The Prophet

Walker & Boutall sc

BLACK SEA
Constantinople
Str. of Bosphorus
SEA OF MARMORA
Gallipoli
Dardanelles
C. Baba
Nicaea
BITHYNIA
Marsiwan
Amasia
GALATIA
Siwas
MYSIA
Ancyra
PHRYGIA
Mytilene or Lesbos
ASIA MINOR
Amorium
LYDIA
Ephesus
Konieh (Iconium)
CAPPADOCIA
Malatia
Chios or Khio
Tyana
Marash
CILICIA
Tarsus
Adana
Rhodes
ARCHIPELAGO
Membij
Antioch
Aleppo
Kinniserin
Orontes
SYRIA
Saffin
Laodicea
Apamea
CYPRUS
Hama (Epiphania)
Hems (Emesa)
Tripolis
Laodicea
Tadmor (Palmyra)
MEDITERRANEAN SEA
Berytus (Beyrout)
Cariatein
Baalbec
Sidon
Damascus
Tyre
Mt. Hermon
Acre (Ptolemais)
Tiberias
Mt. Carmel
R. Yarmuk
Caesarea
Fihl (Pella)
Jebel Hauran
Bozra (Bostra)
Nablus
Jerash
Joppa (Jaffa)
Ramleh
Jerusalem
Ascalon
Bethlehem
Gaza
Maab
Hebron
Dead Sea
Alexandria
Arish
Muta
PALESTINE
Ain Shems (Heliopolis)
Ghizeh
Suez
Buzzir
Fostat (Cairo)
Memphis
Ayla
EGYPT
R. Nile
English Miles
0 50 100 150 200 250
30°
35°
40°
Longitude E
AR

Walker & Boutall sc.

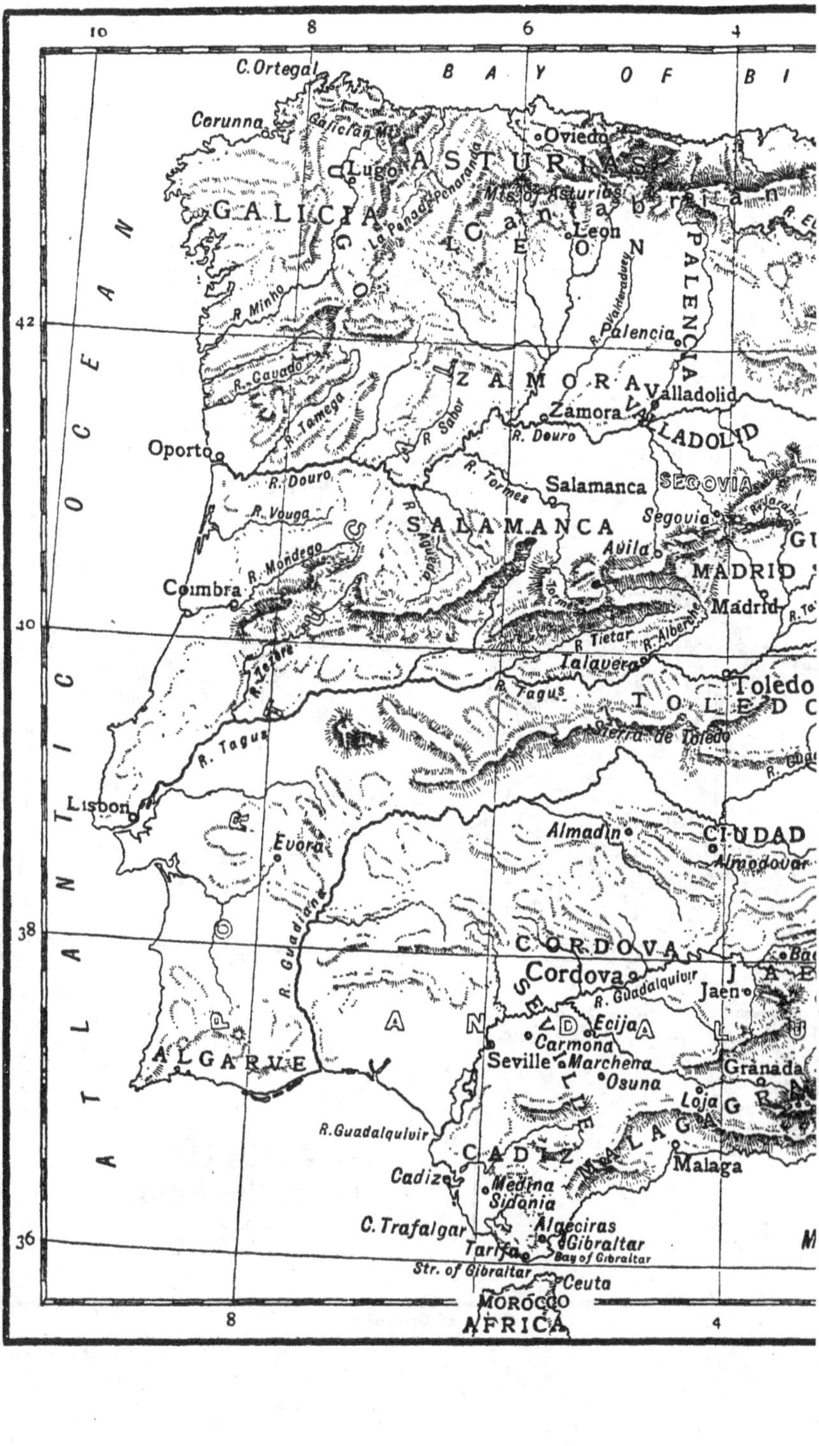

BAY OF BI
ATLANTIC OCEAN
C. Ortegal
Corunna
Galician Mts.
Oviedo
Lugo
ASTURIAS
Mts. of Asturias
Cantabrian
GALICIA
La Pena de Penaranda
LEON
Leon
PALENCIA
R. Valderaduey
R. Minho
Palencia
R. Cavado
ZAMORA
Valladolid
R. Tamega
R. Sabor
Zamora
VALLADOLID
R. Douro
Oporto
R. Douro
R. Tormes
Salamanca
SEGOVIA
R. Vouga
Segovia
R. Jarama
SALAMANCA
R. Agueda
R. Mondego
Avila
MADRID
Coimbra
Madrid
R. Tormes
R. Alberche
R. Tietar
R. Zezere
Talavera
Toledo
R. Tagus
TOLEDO
Sierra de Toledo
R. Tagus
Lisbon
Almadin
CIUDAD
Evora
Almodovar
R. Guadiana
CORDOVA
Cordova
R. Guadalquivir
Jaen
Ecija
Carmona
Seville
Marchena
Osuna
ALGARVE
Granada
Loja
R. Guadalquivir
CADIZ
MALAGA
Malaga
Cadiz
Medina Sidonia
C. Trafalgar
Algeciras
Gibraltar
Tarifa
Bay of Gibraltar
Str. of Gibraltar
Ceuta
MOROCCO
AFRICA
10
8
6
4
42
40
38
36

SPAIN
under the Arabs.

Walker & Boutall sc.

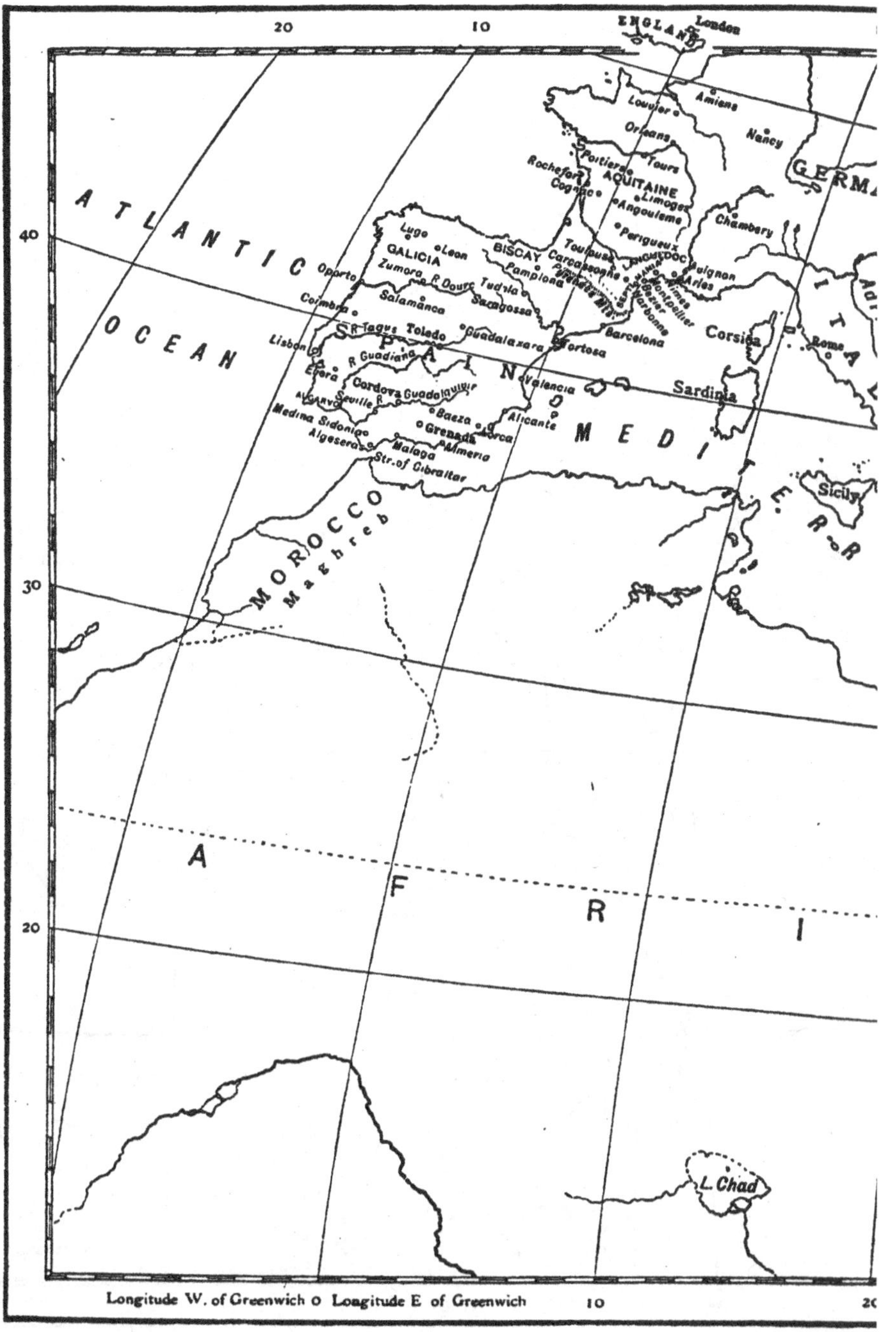
ENGLAND
London
Amiens
Louvier
Orleans
Nancy
GERM
Poitiers
Tours
Rochefort
AQUITAINE
Cognac
Limoges
Angouleme
Chambery
Perigueux
ATLANTIC
OCEAN
Lugo
Leon
GALICIA
BISCAY
Carcassonne
Toulouse
Pamplona
Avignon
Arles
Oporto
Zumora
R. Dourc
Tudela
Salamanca
Saragossa
Coimbra
Montpelier
Narbonne
Barcelona
Lisbon
R. Tagus
Toledo
Guadalaxara
Tortosa
SPAIN
Corsica
Rome
ITALY
R. Guadiana
Evora
Cordova
Guadalquivir
Valencia
Sardinia
Seville
Baeza
Alicante
Medina Sidonia
Grenada
Algesera
Malaga
Almeria
Str. of Gibraltar
MEDITERRANEAN
Sicily
MOROCCO
Maghreb
AFRICA
L. Chad
20
10
40
30
20
10
Longitude W. of Greenwich 0 Longitude E of Greenwich

10
20
30
40
50
60
R U S S I
ANY
iatic Sea
Sea of Azof
Crimea
Goths
BLACK SEA
CONSTANTINOPLE
Archipelago
Candia
Cyprus
ANEAN SEA
SYRIA
Damascus
Jerusalem
Dead Sea
Alexandria
Cairo
Fostat
Suez
Ailah
EGYPT
RED SEA
NUBIA
ABYSSINIA
ARABIA
Medina
MECCA
GEORGIA
Azerbijan
ARMENIA
CASPIAN SEA
Aral
KHORASAN
BAGDAD
Madain
Ispahan
Yezd
PER
Bassora
Bahrein
Oman
HADRAMAUT
Mareb
YEMEN
Mokha
Aden
Str. of Bab el Mandeb
Socotra
C A

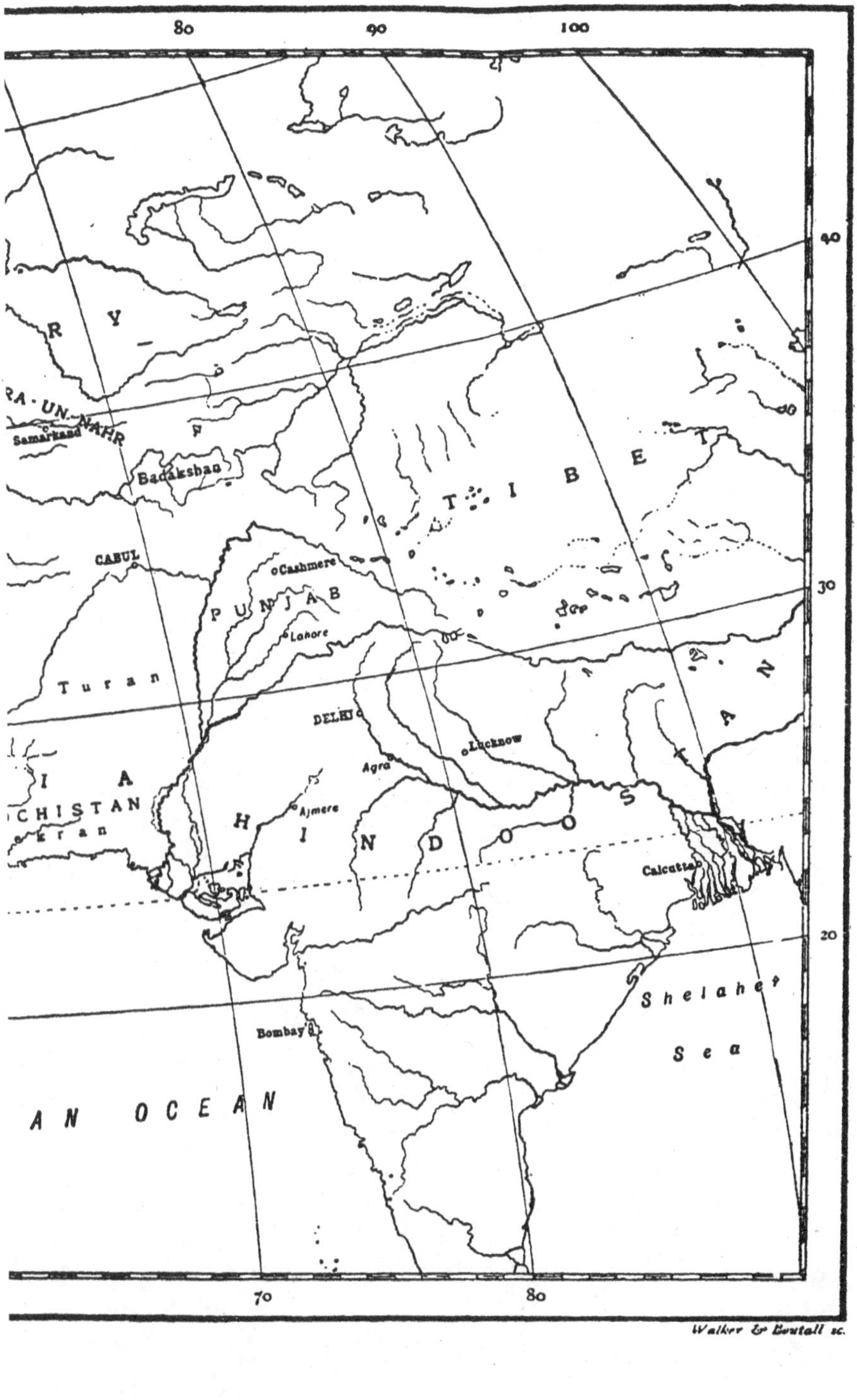

Walker & Boutall sc.

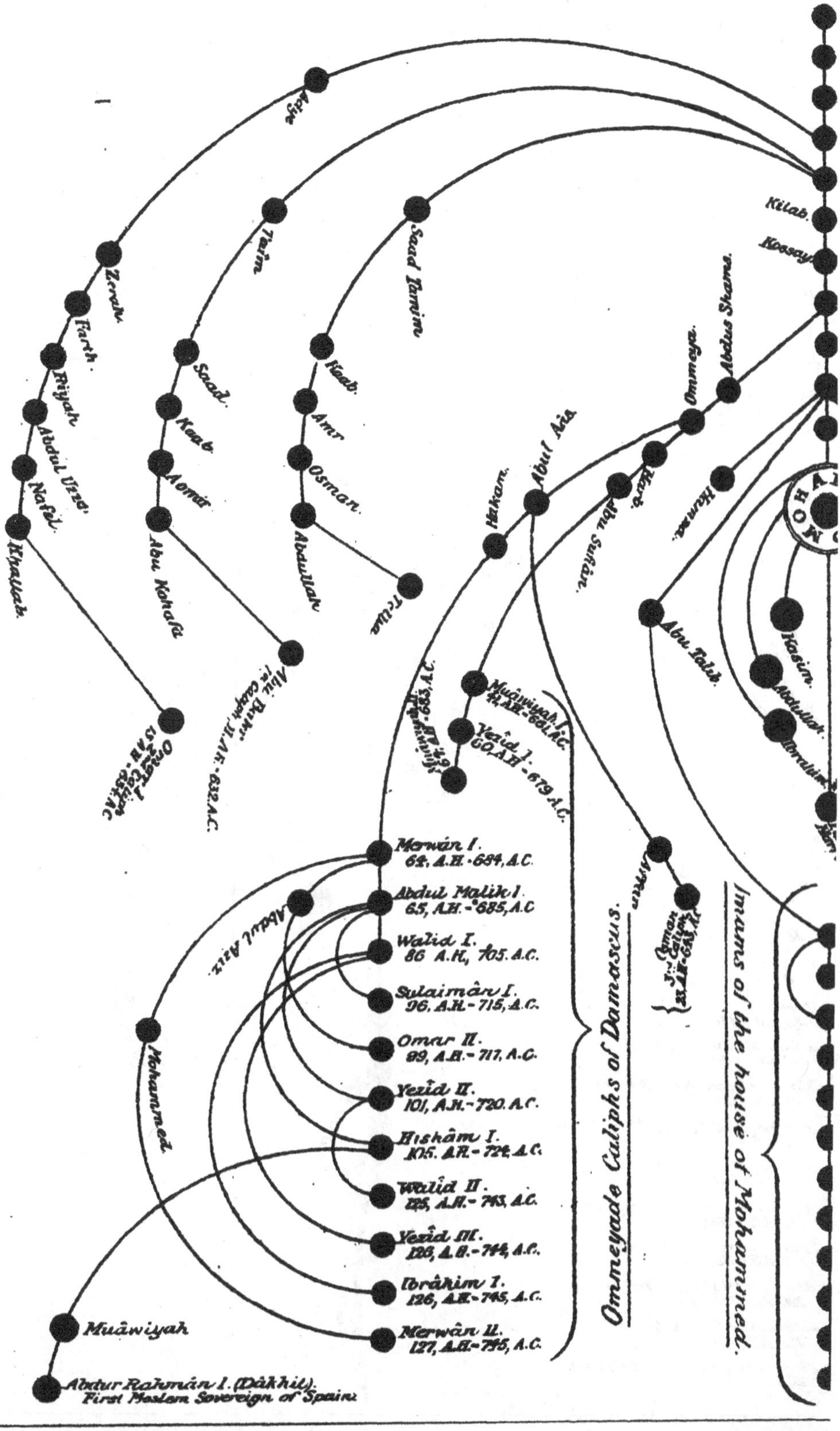

Kilab.
Kossay.
Abdus Shams.
Ommeya.
Abul Aās.
Hakam.
Harb.
Abu Sufiān.
Hamza.
Abu Talib.
Kasim.
Abdullah.
Adiye
Zerah.
Farth.
Fiyah.
Abdul Uzza.
Nafil.
Khattab.
Omar I.
Taim
Saad.
Kaab.
Aomir
Abu Kohafa
Abu Bakr
Saad Tamim
Kaab.
Amr
Osman.
Abdullah
Muāwiyah I.
Yezīd I.
60, A.H. - 679 A.C.
Merwān I.
64, A.H. - 684, A.C.
Abdul Malik I.
65, A.H. - 685, A.C
Walid I.
86 A.H., 705. A.C.
Sulaimān I.
96, A.H. - 715, A.C.
Omar II.
99, A.H. - 717, A.C.
Yezīd II.
101, A.H. - 720. A.C.
Hishām I.
105. A.H. - 724, A.C.
Walid II.
125, A.H. - 743, A.C.
Yezīd III.
126, A.H. - 744, A.C.
Ibrāhim I.
126, A.H. - 745, A.C.
Merwān II.
127, A.H. - 745, A.C.
Abdul Aziz
Mohammed.
Muāwiyah
Abdur Rahmān I. (Dākhil).
First Moslem Sovereign of Spain.
Ommeyade Caliphs of Damascus.
Imams of the house of Mohammed.

Genealogical Chart of the Hashimides and Ommeyades

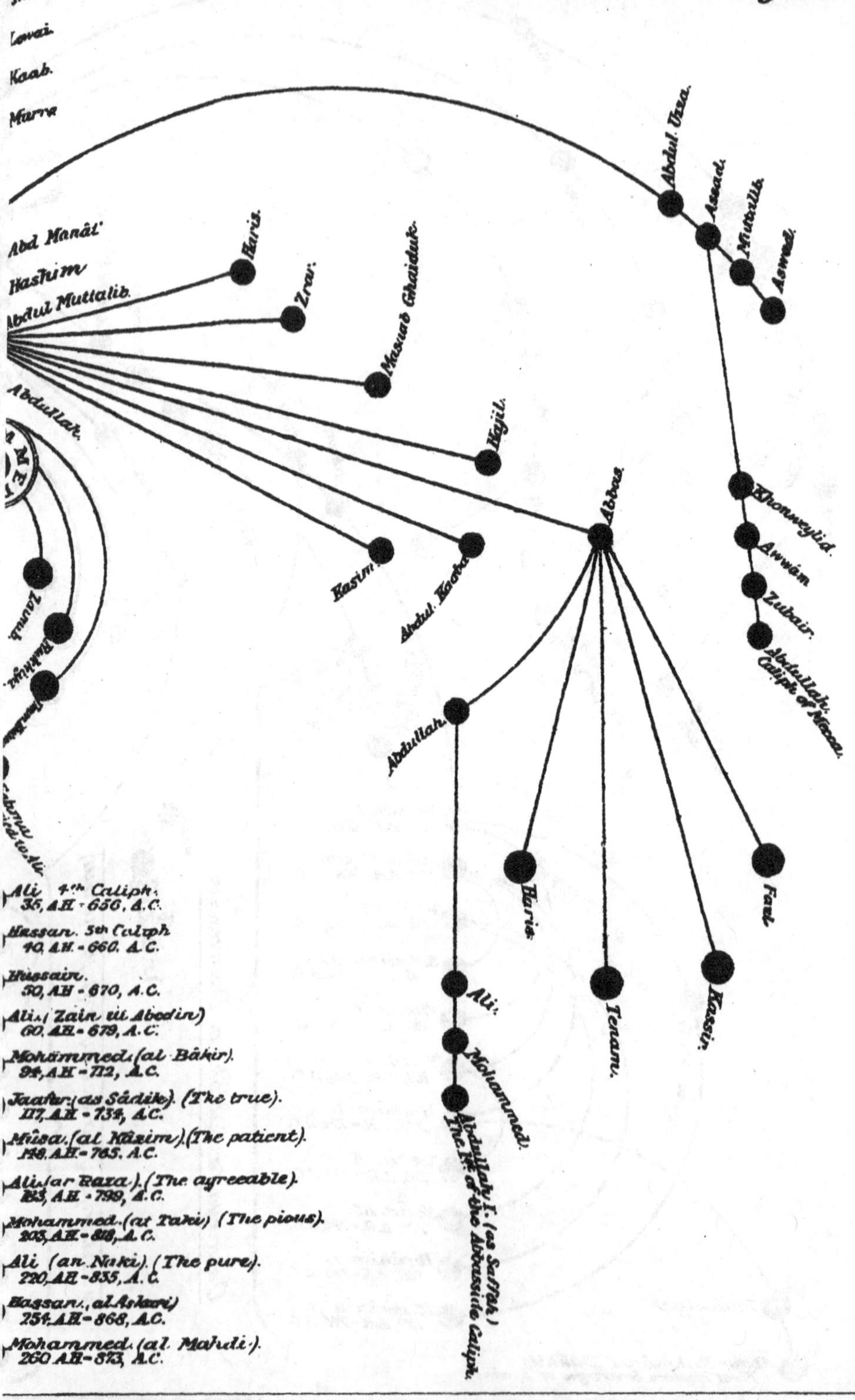

The Abbas

Calip

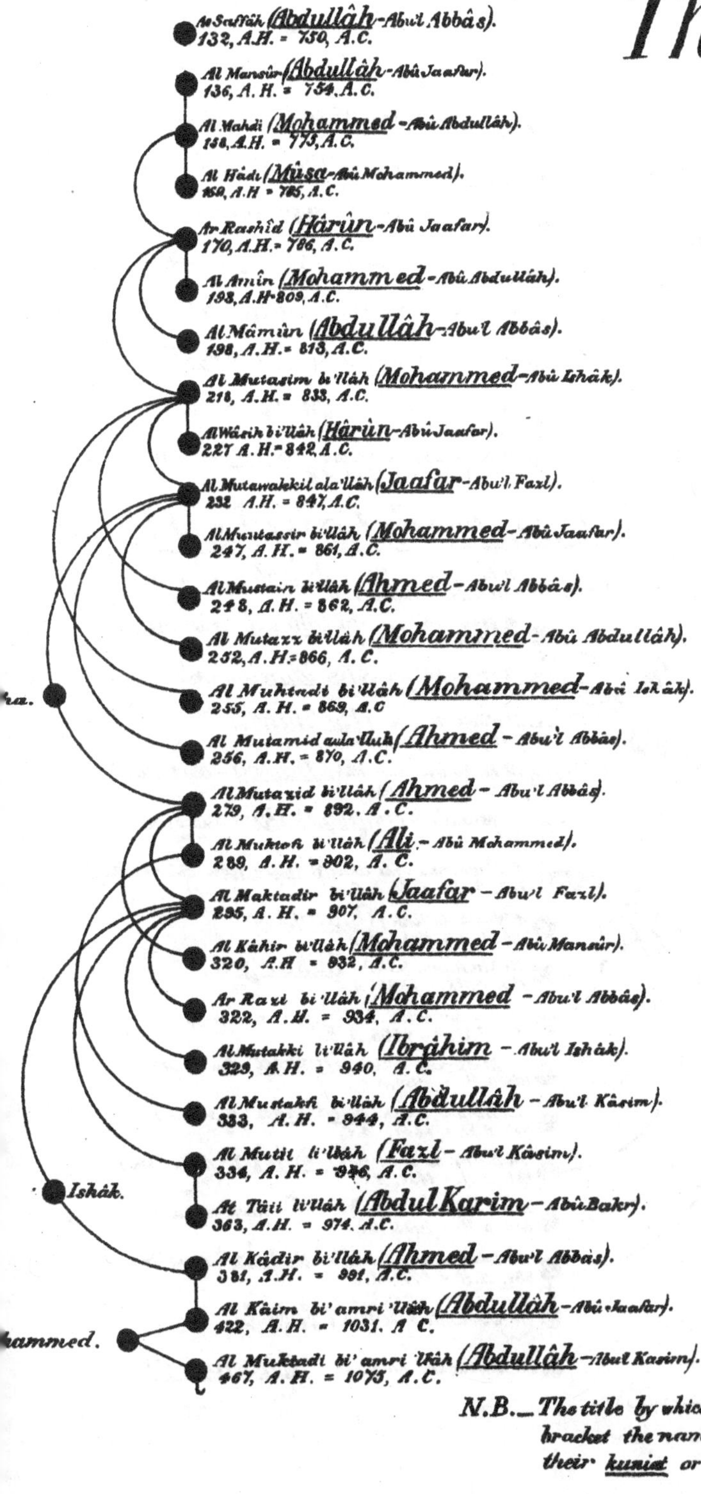

N.B.—The title by which these Caliphs are known ... bracket the names underlined are their re... their kuniat or surnames by which they ...

…sside

…hs

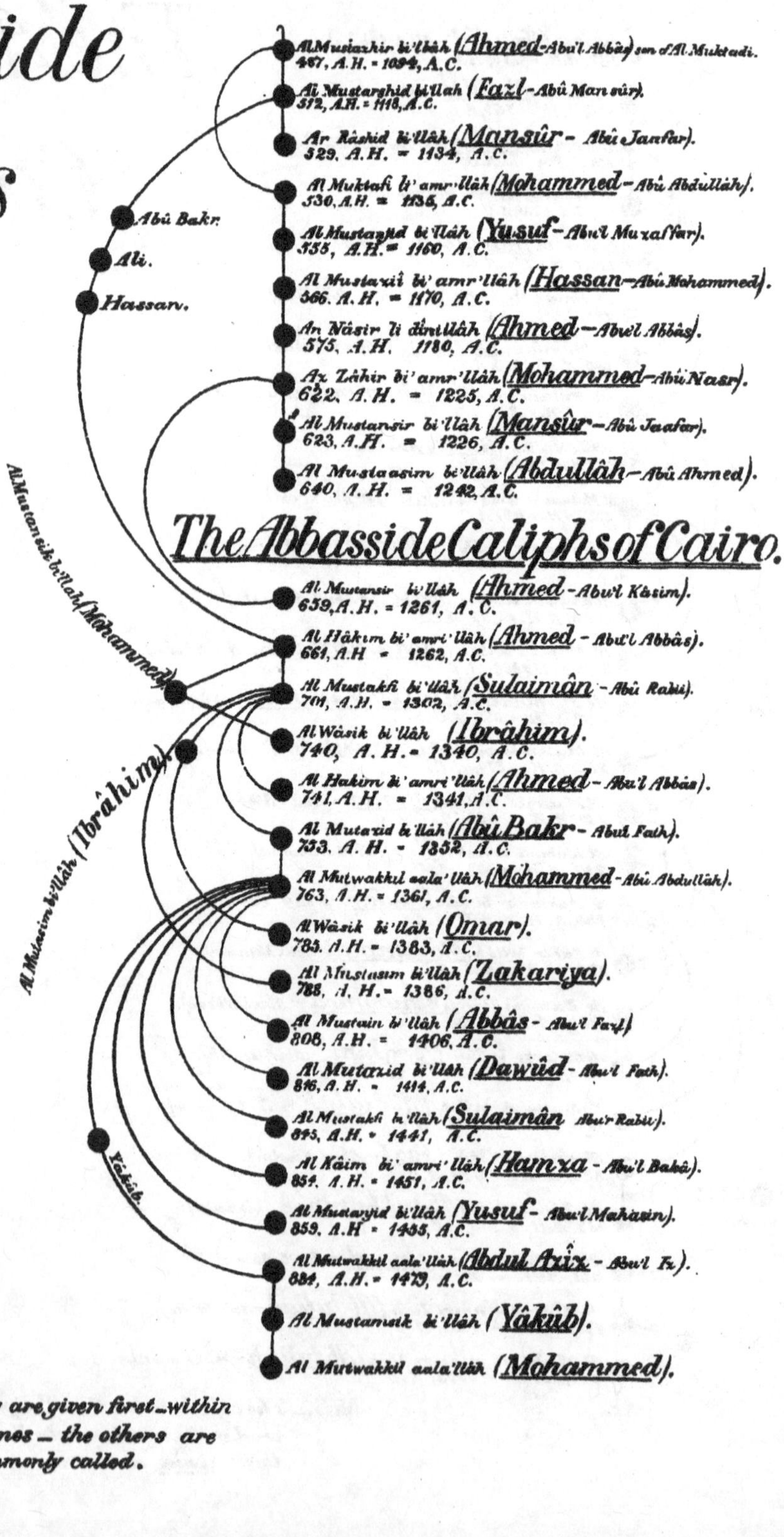

…history are given first – within …al names – the others are …ere commonly called.

The Ommeyade Caliphs of Cordova and the Banû Hamûd Usurpers.

138-422 A.H., 756-1031 A.C.

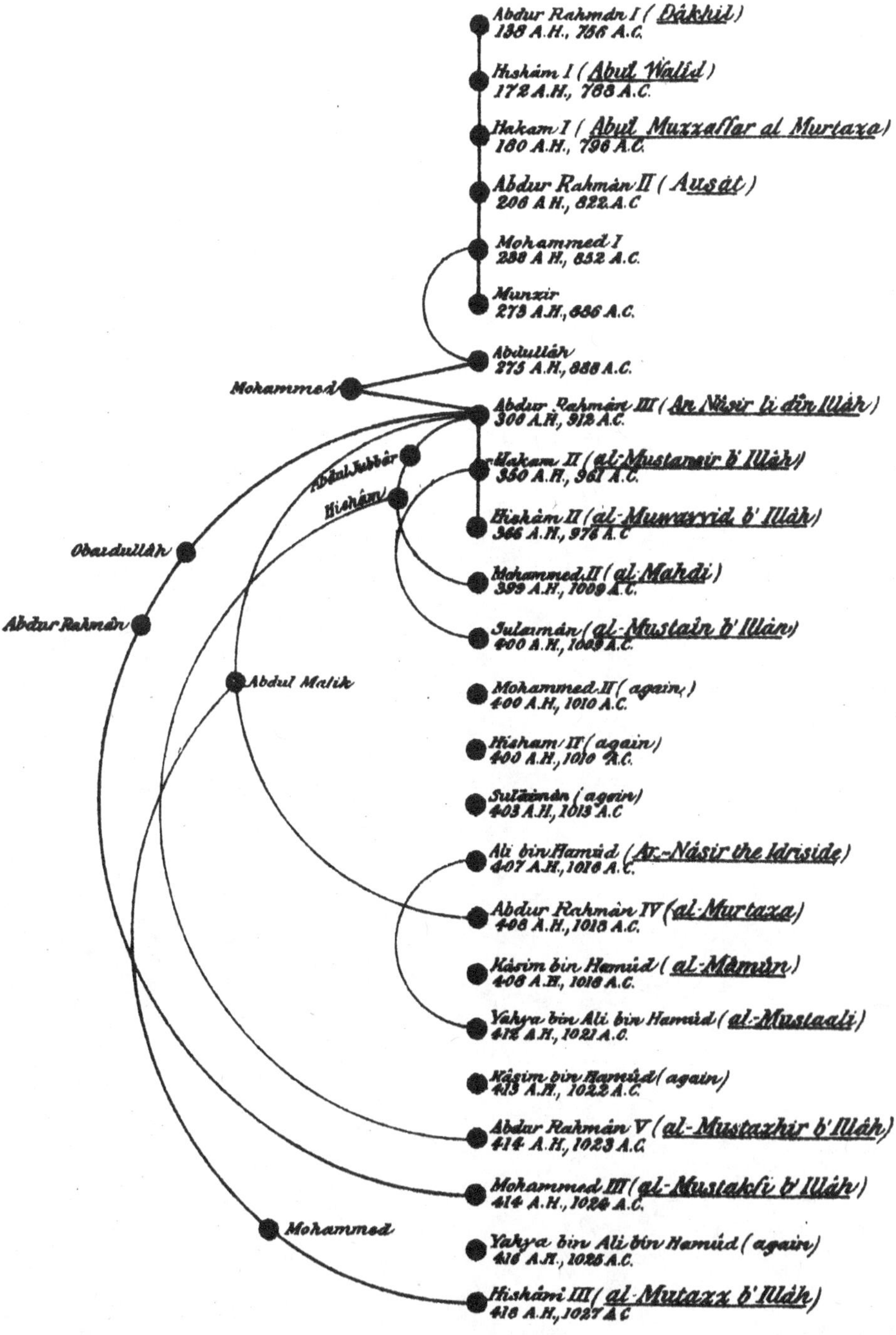

The Fatimide Caliphs of Africa.

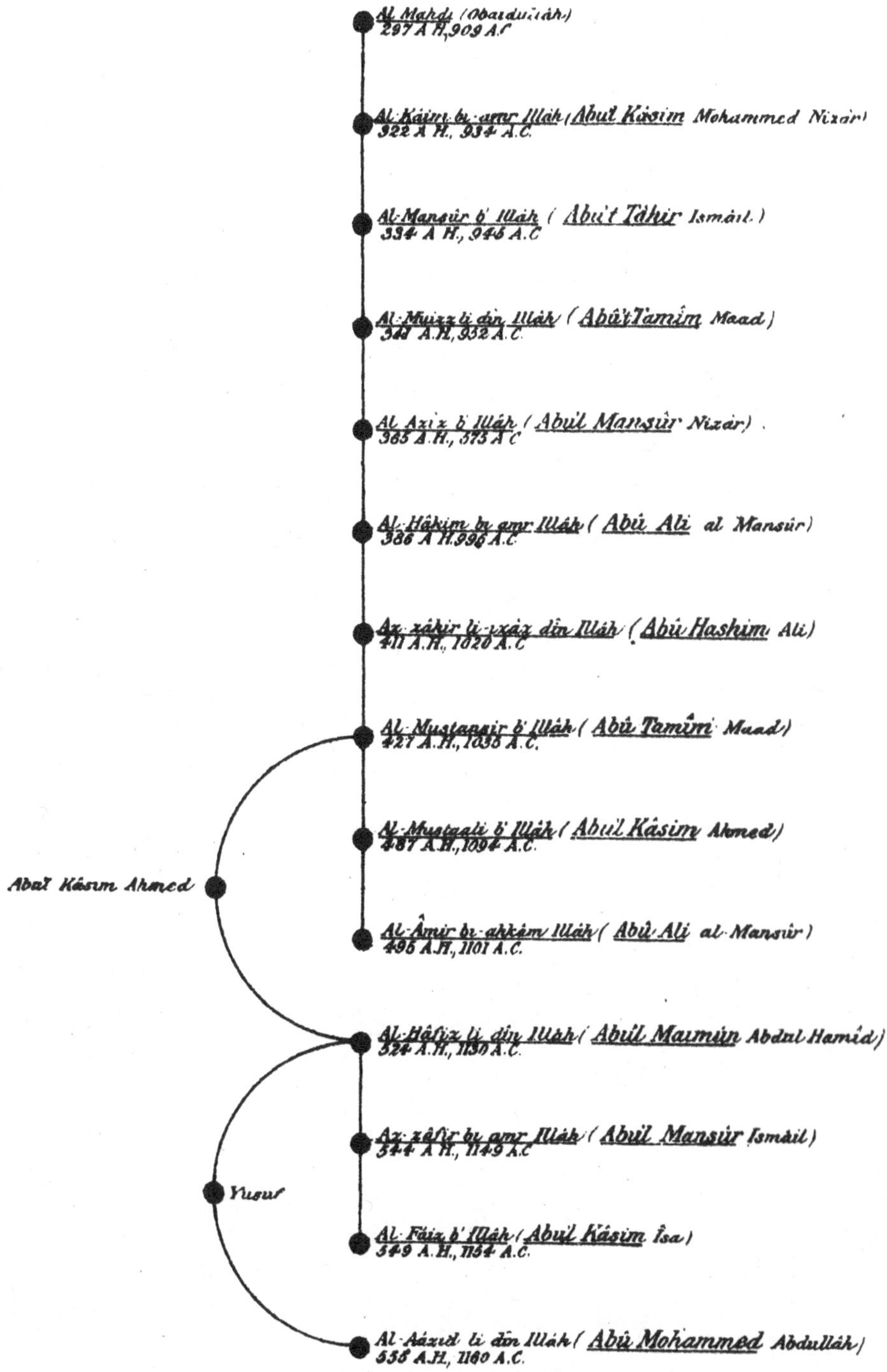

The Samanides.

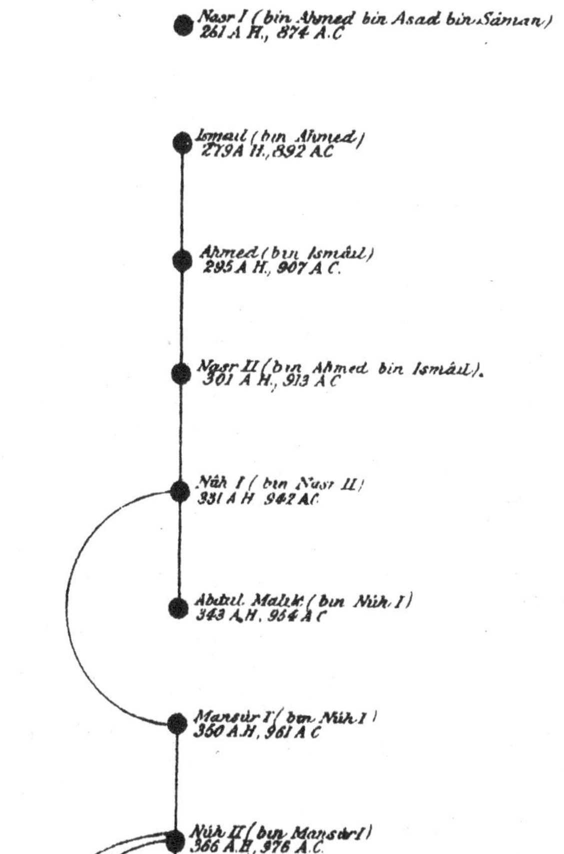

The Ghaznavides.

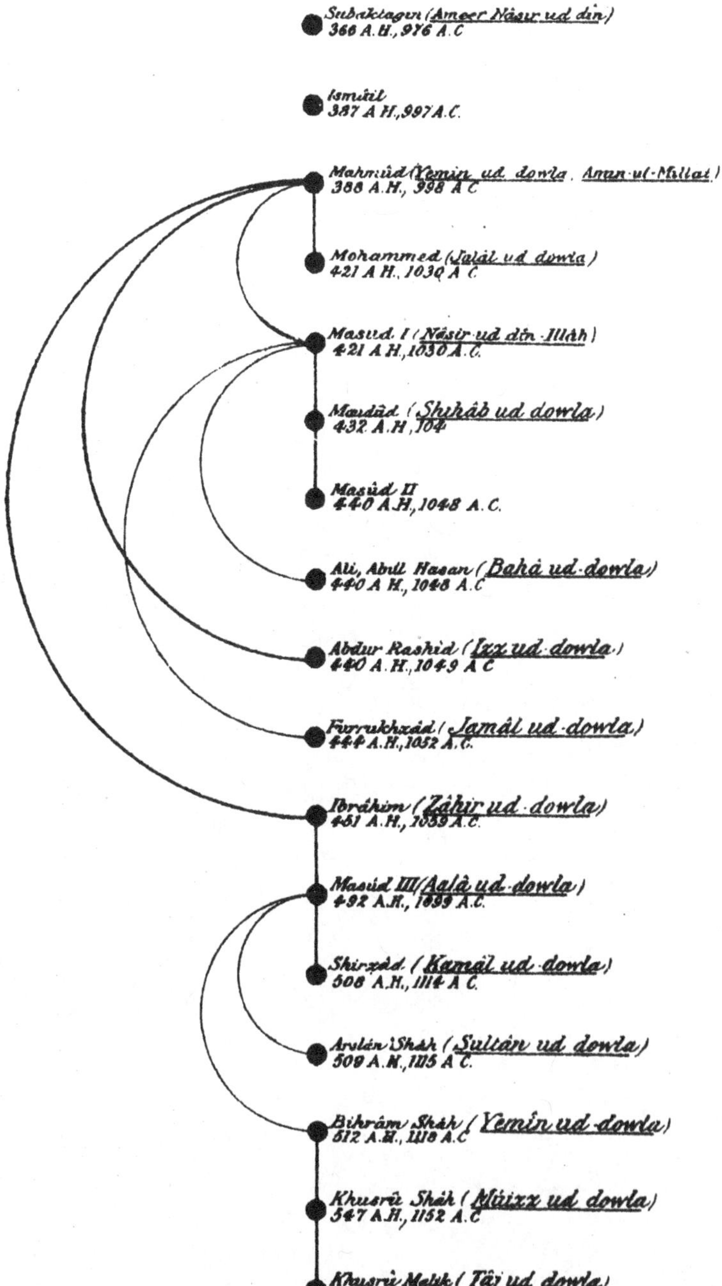

The Sultans of Iconium (Rūm)

470 - 700 A.H., 1077 - 1300 A.C.

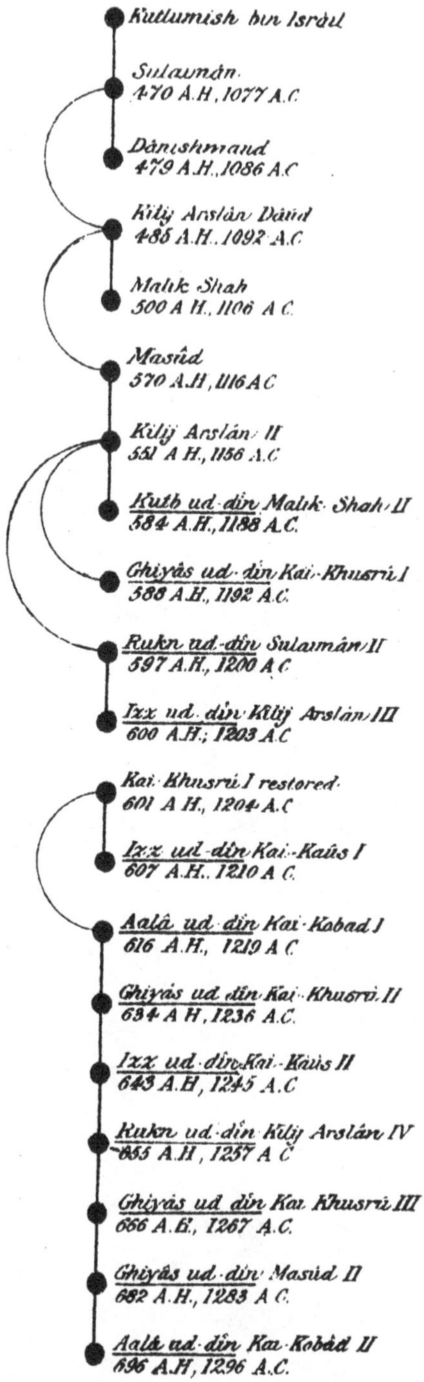